LANGUAGE IN KENYA

EDITED BY W.H. WHITELEY

LANGUAGE IN
ETHIOPIA
KENYA
TANZANIA
UGANDA
ZAMBIA

This study was partly subsidized by funds from the Ford Foundation who also financed the Survey of Language Use and Language Teaching in Eastern Africa. The present volume is co-sponsored by the Institute of African Studies, University of Nairobi.

NAIROBI ● 1974
OXFORD UNIVERSITY PRESS
DAR ES SALAAM ● LUSAKA ● ADDIS ABABA

Oxford University Press, Ely House, London W.1.

GLASGOW NEW YORK TORONTO MELBOURNE WELLINGTON
CAPE TOWN IBADAN NAIROBI DAR ES SALAAM LUSAKA ADDIS ABABA
DELHI BOMBAY CALCUTTA MADRAS KARACHI LAHORE DACCA
KUALA LUMPUR SINGAPORE HONG KONG TOKYO

Oxford University Press, P.O. Box 72532, Nairobi, Kenya

Made and Printed in East Africa

Dedication

Only Wilfred Whiteley, by his brilliant work as chief of the team of scholars that produced *Language in Kenya*, really earned the right to dedicate this book. Since he never exercised that right, those who were responsible for the Survey can have the consolation of dedicating the volume to him.

Clifford H. Prator

FORMER FIELD DIRECTOR
SURVEY OF LANGUAGE USE AND LANGUAGE
TEACHING IN EASTERN AFRICA

Professor Wilfred H. Whiteley

Professor Wilfred H. Whiteley, the editor of this volume, died suddenly some months before its publication. I have been asked by the publishers to write this note of tribute to him on their behalf and that of the other contributors.

In one sense *Language in Kenya* might be considered as a literary monument to Professor Whiteley, and no memorial could be more fitting for a number of reasons. This work represents the culmination of the years of scholarly activity and endeavour that he devoted to the study of languages in East Africa; it serves, also, to illustrate the range of his interests in the fields of language use and description; and it manifests his concern that such knowledge as he had should be communicated to and applied by those who could make best use of it. He made this concern explicit in an address I heard him give at the University of Georgetown shortly before his death, in asserting that 'if what has been achieved so far is not to remain of purely academic interest to a scholarly universe remote from that from which it derives, it must be integrated into local institutions and used as a basis for further locally-based research.'

I do not think it is to be questioned that more than any other scholar in his field Wilfred Whiteley has helped establish the academic setting in East Africa in which the research that he thought was necessary can be undertaken; nor has any one person contributed more to the training of those who can undertake it. His influence derived not primarily from his international reputation as a linguist but from his qualities as a teacher in whom authority was tempered by kindness, and learning by wit. It was, in part, these qualities that led so many people in Kenya to co-operate with him in this particular project without direct recompense. *Language in Kenya* is a testimony to his ability to affect others and often to inspire them with his own understanding of the areas in which research was needed in East Africa and of the responsibilities of those involved.

Thomas P. Gorman

UNIVERSITY OF CALIFORNIA, LOS ANGELES

Contents

Foreword

As a multilingual country, Kenya is bound to face the usual problems associated with multilingual situations all over the world. What are the social situations of the different languages? Is there a need for an official language? What educational policies and practices should be adopted? In short, such multilingual situations need a language policy.

But before a meaningful language policy can be evolved, it is necessary to know the actual linguistic situation in a country. And although various attempts have been made in Kenya during the last seventy years to evolve a language policy, as Dr Gorman shows in Chapter 14, no systematic and comprehensive investigation has up to now been carried out to discover what the linguistic situation in Kenya is. It is for this reason, therefore, that I welcome this volume which for the first time deals with the problems of multilingualism and language choice in Kenya.

Linguistic diversity is an inescapable fact in most African countries. This poses difficult political and educational problems for these young nations. Can we afford and is it necessary to develop all the vernacular languages? What should be the role of non-vernacular languages in nation-building and in education? Which of the vernaculars should be adopted as the official language in a country? What should be the place of the vernaculars in the educational system? When should we introduce a second language? Can we understand the nature of African cultures without knowing the contribution of African languages to those cultures? For example, is the kind of historical-linguistic study discussed by Dr Sharman in Chapter 4 possible without a thorough knowledge of the African languages?

All these are fundamental questions which African countries, including Kenya, cannot afford to gloss over. Language in Kenya has raised most of these questions and suggested answers to some of them. It is my sincere hope that others in Kenya will continue to seek answers to these basic questions; for the establishment of a viable and culturally meaningful Kenya nation depends, to a large extent, on how soon we can answer them. It is for this reason that I agreed to serve on the Council of the Language Survey for Eastern Africa, and it is for the same reason that the Institute of African Studies agreed to co-sponsor the publication of this book with the OUP.

Bethwell A. Ogot

DIRECTOR, INSTITUTE OF AFRICAN STUDIES
UNIVERSITY OF NAIROBI

Introduction

W. H. WHITELEY

Some people may be hoping that this volume will indicate the lines along which a solution to some of Kenya's language problems might be sought. Such a hope would, I consider, be to misconceive the objectives of the Survey;[1] yet if such a hope does exist then it must at least be recognized and responded to, even if it cannot be fulfilled. To do so, and to open a dialogue between the university and the community is an obligation whose importance has recently been stressed by Dr M. Hyder.[2] He rightly emphasizes the need for research that is oriented towards development but recognizes that in the humanities it is not always easy to demonstrate the relevance of particular pieces of research to development. In such circumstances it is particularly important for those planning and carrying out projects to explain their purpose, especially if, as basic research, their relevance to practical or developmental issues is neither close nor immediate. On the other hand no useful purpose is served by popular accounts of research projects which, as a concession to lay readers, make generalizations which their data cannot support or for which the necessary interpretation is not provided. A dialogue thus based is likely only to confuse and mislead, especially if qualifications are subsequently introduced.

Many people treat language as one of the facts of life, like breathing, and it is true that social life as we know it does not exist independently of language. In those countries which lack important linguistic minorities, language problems may assume importance only infrequently, but in multilingual countries like Kenya the situation is quite different. Here a number of factors have contributed to a situation in which the use of a particular language comes to be characteristic of a particular social domain, in much the same way that domains are characterized in England by varieties of English. In time the languages themselves take on the complex of emotions, prestige, etc. that are associated with the domains themselves. Thus, local languages[3] like Kamba or Kipsigis may be linked with the rural homestead or with traditional values; Swahili may be linked with town life, trade, certain kinds of jobs; and English with government

1

service, the professions, and high status jobs. At a still later stage the languages acquire symbolic status[4] and may then serve political ends. Thus one may condemn the use of local languages as encouraging tribalism or praise them as expressing the true spirit of African-ness; one may condemn Swahili as divorced from local culture or praise it as transcending tribalism; one may condemn English as a colonialist language or praise it as making for the efficient operation of government services. One does not commonly find language as an overt symbol of political action: for many years it may lie dormant and be activated along with or independently of other factors by issues of local or national importance apparently unconnected with language. Far more commonly one finds it functioning as one of a number of variables signalling socio-economic status in the community in various subtle and pervasive ways. To some extent a government may control language use: through the educational system, by passing edicts, or by setting examples, but there are limits to the extent to which this can be done, and it is clear, on the evidence of history, that if the choice of language runs counter to prevailing patterns of language use then the language will only be used in those contexts where some degree of enforcement can be assured. This is likely to be an expensive and difficult undertaking, and one not likely to enhance the prestige of the language being enforced.

The use of language in a community, therefore, is likely to be surrounded with many and conflicting emotions, and to serve as an expression of tensions in social life for which no alternative outlet is available. It is thus a matter of some importance to know what the patterns of language use are, in what ways they operate, and for what sections of the community they hold good, if only as a prerequisite to the formulation of any policy. It is also important that men and women should understand something of the role of language in society, so that irrational fears and beliefs may be reduced. Anyone who has worked on a local language committee knows how tenaciously people cling to unworkable, impracticable orthographies because they feel somehow that to tamper with the spelling is to tamper with the language. How much more material in local languages would be available now, if agreement could have been reached on orthographic questions—though one is bound to add that to create the conditions for an event is not to create the event itself. Finally, any educational system requires to be underpinned by continuing research into methods, content and objectives. If the system is dealing with two or more languages it is surely pointless to restrict one's research efforts to one of the languages and pernicious to assume that what goes for one will go for the other. The amount of work done on Swahili and the local languages in this field is negligible, and is itself an important contributory factor to current attitudes to these languages.

The Survey's first task was to establish facts. In some cases this has been relatively easy; in others it is much more difficult. If you want to know what language a person uses in a particular context and how he uses it, it is not enough simply to ask him. He may tell you what he thinks you want to hear, or what he thinks he ought to say, or what he thinks he does say, or what he would like others to think he says, and so on. As Labov has neatly put it, we are faced with the 'Observer's Paradox', '. . . the aim of linguistic research in the community must be to find out how people talk when they are not being systematically observed; yet we can only obtain this data by systematic observation'.[5] In this situation the methods to establish the facts have also got to be worked out, and in this sense some of the chapters are essays in methodology. Finally, the Survey disposed of only three full-time members, who were in the field for a little over a year from July 1968. Those engaged on part-time research—who contributed Chapters 3, 4, 9, 10, 13, 14, 15, and 16 —usually had to fit their research into already overcrowded timetables. The result is necessarily only a partial picture; many readers will be aware, as we ourselves are aware, of areas that have not been covered. Yet a start has been made, and it is hoped that bodies like the newly formed Language Association of Eastern Africa will be able to follow up some of the questions that emerge from this initial project.

The material is presented in three parts: dealing with the language situation, language use and language in education. In Chapter 1 I deal with the present language situation, and the distribution and classification of Kenya's African languages. These are the languages through which much of Kenya's regional and national culture is transmitted. Many still have no standard orthography, few books or newspapers are printed in them and most have no adequate grammar or dictionary. Where printed materials do exist they are mainly religious in character or suitable only for small children. These languages are essentially to be spoken, not to be written or read. In many there is a rich oral literature, and for many Kenyans their use symbolizes not merely continuity with the past but, more important than this, the reassurance of something that is known and understood in a world of shifting and often alien values. Some of these languages, Luo, Kikuyu, Kamba, 'Luyia',[6] Gusii, 'Kalenjin', whose speakers number between half and one and a half million, are grouped on the whole in rather densely populated homogeneous units and are likely to remain important factors in the language situation for a long time. At the same time their speakers are likely to add both Swahili and English formally through the educational system, to an extent

3

determined by such factors as access to education, high social mobility, quality of communications, relative prosperity, and so on. The extent to which Swahili will continue to be added will depend on the extent to which its use complements rather than duplicates that of English. The extent to which either of these languages supplants the use of other local languages in border areas (see Chapter 12) will depend on a number of factors including, for example, the importance of language as such within the total network of relationships in a particular setting.

During the course of the Survey many people asked us how many people in Kenya 'knew' Swahili, a deceptively simple question to which there is no correspondingly simple answer. As is discussed more fully in Chapter 1 there are at least three main factors to be taken into account:

    1. The difficulty of deciding what constitutes 'knowing' Swahili.

    2. The variation in the competence that people claim in the language from area to area. This may be associated with variations in linguistic homogeneity across the country, or with differential access to education. There are also differences between the generations and between the sexes.

    3. The fact that the language may be 'known' for different purposes, e.g. trade, casual encounters, ploughing, football matches, etc., which may occupy quite a small part of a person's waking life.

Nevertheless from the sample surveys we carried out in various parts of the country we can say that fewer non-Bantu speakers claim a high degree of competence in Swahili than Bantu speakers;[7] that more people claim to speak Swahili in towns than in the country; and that more people in lower-income jobs claim a competence in the language than do those in, say, 'white collar' jobs. These are not original conclusions, but they do have important implications for educational policy. In assessing the present position of the language there are probably more variables to be taken into account than when considering that of English where competence is directly and closely correlated with educational attainment, and where people appear to use the language more often than one might expect in terms of their claimed competence (see Chapter 12). Overall the incentives to acquire English are probably greater at the present time than those to acquire Swahili: even in neighbouring Tanzania where Swahili has been the national language for the past ten years, it is still possible for the Second Vice-President to say:

. . . a very large percentage of the masses, especially those who had acquired some education, despised Swahili and preferred to speak foreign languages like English and French to speaking Swahili . . . it is a pity to note that after ten years of independence there are people who are still inhibited by this colonial hangover.[8]

Chapter 2 discusses Asian languages: it is not certain what the actual size of the Asian minority will be in the future, but they share two languages with other Kenyans, Swahili and English, and it is of importance to see how their use is distributed if one wishes to know something of the total language situation. Chapter 3 is devoted to the Luyia 'experiment' in which an attempt was made to devise a common orthography and grammar for the sixteen or seventeen closely related 'dialects' spoken in the western part of the country. The problems it raised are typical of those which are provoked by language 'engineering' generally; in East Africa one need look no further than the history of Standard Swahili.[9] Firstly there is the discussion on whether engineering should take place or not; secondly, there are the purely linguistic problems of how to select the basis for the orthography and grammar, which of the dialects to select, which features to give particular emphasis to, how to establish a standard lexicon. Understandably it was amongst speakers of the dialects most divergent from those selected, e.g. Logoli and Bukusu, that reaction to 'standard' Luyia was most marked, and in the recently produced series of primary school readers their objections are upheld by according them separate status. Thirdly, there is the question of the relationship of the written to the spoken language: it is sometimes held that the experiment failed because people do not speak in it. One should not be surprised at this; people in England do not, by and large, speak standard written English, but a wide range of social and geographical dialects. Acceptance of a common written form of Luyia does not imply that one is abandoning one's spoken varieties, but simply that one is providing a form of the language that is more viable economically. It is easier and cheaper to print books for a reading public of several hundred thousand than for one of only a few thousand. The history of educational policy in Kenya (see Chapter 14) has been punctuated by pronouncements about the importance of 'the vernacular', but educational practice has always found obstacles to justify inaction—lack of finance, shortage of trained personnel, conflicts over orthographies, etc. It may well prove easier to introduce these languages at university than at primary school level! In many respects the history of Luluyia is a microcosm of the problems that educators face in the country as a whole in respect to local languages.

Finally, in Part One, is a chapter on the comparative study of the Bantu languages; not, I hasten to add, because the comparative study of Nilotic or Cushitic languages is any less important, but because it is on the Bantu languages that most work has been done. The linguistic techniques involved are not easily acquired, though the implications of such work have been quickly seized upon by historians anxious to push back the screen of ignorance which divides what we know of Kenya's history with some certainty, from what can only be guessed at in the most tentative way. A great deal remains to be done before the screen of ignorance can be pushed back with any confidence, but there are exciting possibilities for co-operation not only with historians and archaeologists, but also with plant geneticists, palaeobotanists, geographers, ecologists and others.

Part Two is devoted to a number of detailed studies of language use. Seven chapters deal wholly or in part with Nairobi. This may seem to be a disproportionate amount of space to devote to the capital, but in view of the high rate of urban migration, it is of some urgency that documentation of language use be available for those concerned with educational and housing policies in the city and in such heterogeneous rural areas as settlement schemes. What emerges from Parkin's detailed analysis of material from Kaloleni and Bahati is the persistence of Swahili as an important, growing medium of communication at all status and educational levels, apparently regardless of whether it has been taught at school or not. It would seem that when people move to urban areas which are ethnically—and linguistically—heterogeneous, then they are virtually obliged to learn Swahili—if they do not already know it—or to improve their knowledge. To fail to do so would result in obvious disadvantages in social and economic activities. An extreme case is provided by Janet Bujra from her work in Pumwani, where to a characteristic urban heterogeneity is added the dominance of Islam and a tradition of association with things coastal. Here not only is Swahili the language of social life but the variety of Swahili is more coastal, and serves as a standard against which other suburbs view their own varieties with diffidence. What happens to these skills when people move back to a rural, homogeneous area is not yet clear. There is some evidence from our survey that they may be under-utilized, but more work needs to be done. In these rural areas the position is not so straightforward (see Chapter 12): Swahili has to compete with local languages, which are securely entrenched as the language of the homestead and of domestic affairs generally. Here, Swahili's place is in the market, at the 'duka', in bars and offices, etc., where the level of homogeneity falls. However, it is then in competition with English and it is noticeable that as the educational level of informal groups rises English is increasingly characteristic of them. If the primary schools continue to turn out pupils with competence in English and the expectation that it will be of benefit to them when they leave school, one would expect it to oust Swahili from certain domains, not only in the country but also in towns. On the other hand, as has been stressed throughout this volume, it is difficult to make predictions where so many variables are involved.

David Aoko's brief chapter affords an illuminating insight into an area where language use is highly symbolic, and where a detailed study would be of great value in helping us to understand the social role of language. This is an aspect of the wider study of religious life in Kenya which has been very much neglected, and I hope that some redress of the balance will now follow.

Part Three is devoted to language in education and Chapter 14 provides a historical documentation of language policy in Kenya with particular reference to the educational system. One is particularly struck by the extent to which successive generations of educators have advocated the use of the vernacular at the outset of education, only to discover that for one reason or another their recommendations were diluted, even vitiated altogether, by the difficulty of putting them into practice. One possible reason for this, it seems to me, was a preoccupation on the part of educators with the outset, rather than the outcome, of education. The question does not seem to have been asked—or not asked insistently enough—whether a man or woman who could only read and/or speak the vernacular, when he/she finished formal education at the end of primary school, would thereby be able and content to live a full life within these limits, or whether he would regard himself and be regarded by others as one who had failed to achieve higher things, e.g. competence in other languages, notably English. One of the difficulties in an educational system of running languages 'in harness'—if one can use such a metaphor of language—is that unless very great care is taken to see that their use is complementary, the languages will pull differently. One language will tend to acquire greater prestige than the others, and a series of imbalances will result throughout the system. This is well illustrated in the conclusions to Chapter 15, where Dr Gorman discusses the difficulties encountered in the teaching of Swahili in the secondary schools. Pupils come up from the primary schools with widely differing abilities and attitudes, having suffered not only from a lack of trained teachers in the primary schools but also from a shortage of suitable textbooks. This situation is perpetuated in the secondary schools where the disparity between Swahili and English in terms of resources, personnel and time allocated are strikingly obvious to the pupils. Efforts are now being made to remedy this situation but a great deal needs to be done. If the importance of developing oral skills is not questioned, one of the difficulties for the teacher of Swahili is the question of the models available to his pupils outside the class-room, and the incentives and opportunities for their using them. In rural Kenya the home language will almost certainly be the local language, and the pupils' most accessible contact with Swahili may be listening to the Voice of Kenya, reading newspapers, or listening to people talking at the 'duka'—though by the same token if the first two are available

7

then English is also likely to be accessible. At all events three different models of Swahili may well be available with little incentive to talk in the language (see also R. Hemphill's comments on this in Chapter 15). The situation in the towns is strikingly different: though pupils have the opportunity and incentive for speaking Swahili outside the class, their models of spoken Swahili vary widely from those of the classroom. The teacher of English in South London who complains of the unreality of teaching standard English to boys and girls whose outside lives will be spent in using dialect, has a close counterpart in Nairobi.

In conclusion I would like to comment that it would not have been possible to achieve as much as we did without the generous co-operation of many Kenyans too numerous to mention by name. On behalf of all the team I would, however, like to express our gratitude to the Government of Kenya for granting us permission to carry out the Survey: also to the University College, Nairobi, for generously providing us with office space and according us visiting status; and to the staff of the Survey Office, especially Dr D. Bowen and Mr C. Lutton, for their constant help and support. Finally, our gratitude to the Ford Foundation, who not only financed the whole project but who, through its office in Nairobi, contributed in innumerable ways to our well-being.

To all the above I hope this volume serves as a small recompense for the efforts expended.

NOTES

[1] In his Introduction to the first volume in this series, *Language in Uganda* (Oxford University Press, Nairobi, 1971), Professor Clifford Prator, the first Field Director of the Survey of Language Use and Language Teaching in Eastern Africa, summarized the aims of the Survey as follows:

1. To gather and disseminate basic information on the use and teaching of languages in Ethiopia, Kenya, Tanzania, Uganda and Zambia.
2. To stimulate research and development in linguistics and language pedagogy in the region.
3. To assist in strengthening the resources of Eastern African institutions concerned with the language arts and sciences.
4. To foster closer, productive, intraregional and international relations among specialists in linguistics and related disciplines.

[2] Mohamed Hyder, 'The University, the Government and National Development in Kenya', *East Africa Journal*, April 1970, pp. 7–12.

[3] I distinguish here between 'local' languages, e.g. Kamba, Luo, Samburu, etc., also known as 'vernacular' or 'tribal' languages; and 'common' languages like Swahili, English and French, also known in some contexts as 'lingua franca' languages. The first of this latter group might be classed as a 'national' common language, while the other two might be classed as 'international' common languages.

[4] Good examples of this can be found in the press, following the recent statement by the acting Secretary General of KANU, relating to the implementation of KANU's Governing Council's resolution that Swahili '. . . as our national language, shall be

encouraged . . . '; a resolution made in September 1969. Correspondence continued for over a month from 5 April 1970, and the fires are maintained by articles like that of Dr Bernd Heine, 'Swahili is Closest to the "National Soul"' (*Sunday Nation*, 9 August 1970).

[5] W. Labov, 'The Study of Language in its Social Context', *Studium Generale*, vol. 23, part 1, 1970, p. 47.

[6] For the sake of consistency certain spellings have been adopted throughout this book which may not always be those most familiar to the reader. The spelling 'Luyia' is that recognized by the Luyia Language Committee, although the alternative form 'Luhya' is often preferred. Similarly, although the spelling 'Maasai' is used here, the form 'Masai' still generally predominates. Finally, throughout the volume the form 'Logoli' has been adopted in preference to 'Maragoli', although it is recognized that the latter is much more familiar. The 'note on spelling' accompanying 'Kenya: A Language Map' at the end of this book discusses orthographic problems in more detail.

[7] In this we differ from Dr B. Heine in his articles in the press (*Sunday Nation*, 2 and 9 August 1970) and 'On the Distribution of Swahili in Western Kenya', *Journal of the Language Association of Eastern Africa*, 1, 1970. In seeking an answer to the question, how many people 'know' Swahili, Heine does not distinguish between degrees of 'knowing' and includes, therefore, both those who know only a few greetings and those who speak the language 'fluently' and on a wide range of topics.

[8] Reported in the *Nationalist*, Dar es Salaam, 8 June 1970.

[9] See my *Swahili: the Rise of a National Language*, Methuen, London 1969, ch. V.

9

The Language Situation

The Language Situation

I

The Classification and Distribution of Kenya's African Languages

W. H. WHITELEY

A. LANGUAGE CLASSIFICATION

INTRODUCTION

The African languages of Kenya have traditionally been regarded as belonging to four major groups, of which Kamba, Nandi, Luo and Somali may be taken as typical examples. As readers of the literature will know, however, there has, in recent years, been a good deal of controversy over the methods and terminology used in African language classification, and the groups to which Nandi and Somali, for example, belong have figured largely in this. The present position may be summarized as follows. The Bantu languages, of which Kamba is one, had until recently been regarded as one of the great autonomous language families of Africa. In the classification of Greenberg, however,[1] they were relegated to one of four subdivisions of the Bantu-Congo group, one of the six sub-families of the Niger-Congo family. In this genetic classification the Bantu languages are thus firmly linked to languages on the western side of the continent and lose their former autonomy. This is not the place to discuss the merits or otherwise of this classification: what is of greater local interest is the possible relationship of Kenya's Bantu languages one with another. Languages of the Nandi type were previously called Nilo-Hamitic,[2] but Tucker and Bryan have now renamed them Para-Nilotic, in deference both to their Nilotic affinities and the need to dispense with the misleading term Hamitic.[3] Greenberg had earlier reclassified them as belonging to the Nilotic branch—one of ten—of his Eastern Sudanic division of the Chari-Nile branch of Nilo-Saharan languages. Within this branch they are listed among the 'Southern' group. A modified version of this classification has been adopted by some historians, where 'Plains' and 'Highland' Nilotes are distinguished.[4]

13

The Luo languages have traditionally been known as Nilotic, and recent controversy has not affected them, Greenberg simply including them among his 'Western' group of Nilotic languages. Somali was formerly classified as Hamitic, but the many non-linguistic overtones of this term have given it a pejorative connotation and it has been generally discarded by all except those unaware of recent discussion. Greenberg includes Somali among the Eastern Cushitic branch of one of the five co-ordinate divisions of his Afroasiatic family of languages. Tucker and Bryan too use the term Cushitic. For the purposes of the present volume I shall refer to the languages of Kenya under the following headings: Bantu, Para-Nilotic, Nilotic and Cushitic as providing relatively straightforward mnemonics for the general reader.

THE BANTU LANGUAGES

All Kenya's Bantu languages, with the exception of Taveta and Swahili, are placed by Guthrie in his Zone E,[5] along with most of Uganda's Bantu languages and many of the Lacustrine languages of Tanzania. What can one infer from such a classification? Before answering the question, one needs to return to the problems faced by Guthrie when making his classification. Granted that we can decide what constitutes a Bantu language—at least in the central part of the field—how shall we subdivide the several hundred languages thus classified, into smaller and more manageable units within which the languages might be presumed to be more closely related to one another than to those outside the unit? The question is important both from a linguistic and a historical point of view. It is reasonable to assume that over the course of time the Bantu languages have neither all changed in the same way, nor to the same extent, nor at the same rate, so that one might hope from a demonstration of present patterns of relatedness to be able to set up some intermediate grouping between the hypothesized 'Common' Bantu and present day languages. For example, if one accepts Guthrie's view of a central African dispersal point for the Bantu languages, is the relatedness of Kenya's Bantu languages such that one might suppose that the original speakers of these languages participated in a single migration movement across the country, or can we postulate one or more intermediate dispersal points? One might, like the dialect geographers, have attempted to solve the problem empirically by plotting isoglosses of various differentiating features, and demarcating language areas where the isoglosses coincide. In practice, however, Guthrie found it impossible to apply the method consistently, since none of the differentia could be applied over the whole

Bantu field. The solution he adopted was to modify the empirical approach by recognizing an element of arbitrariness as an essential ingredient of the method. Starting from an individual language he moved outwards, grouping with his initial language all those adjacent languages which displayed similar characteristics. At a certain point he recognized that 'we have moved into another group' and the process starts again from another centre. The arbitrariness occurs both in making the cut-off from one group to another and in selecting the 'similar characteristics', since in practice it seems likely that the inequality of the data available circumscribed, to some extent at any rate, the choice of characteristics. However, by following this procedure he was able to isolate some eighty groups of languages, which for convenience he placed in sixteen Zones. At this point it is important to stress that the procedure of starting from one individual language and working outwards is not necessarily reflected in the actual numbering of the groups. In other words one cannot infer that the head language of Group E40, i.e. Logoli, was the one that Guthrie started with, nor that E42, i.e. Gusii, is more closely related to it than is Kuria, E43. In fact, the actual numeration seems to have been based on geographical, rather than on linguistic features,[6] i.e. Logoli is the most northerly of the group. The sixteen Zones were established on criteria that were partly geographical and partly linguistic, each showing in general a set of differentiating features arbitrarily selected. In this way it was possible for him to bring order to the field, though he was at pains to stress that in many cases the grouping was purely experimental and should not be taken as authoritative in any way. However, as often happens, what is advanced tentatively comes to be maintained authoritatively, and a new look at the problem is overdue. From the classification it could be inferred that languages within a group were more closely related generally to one another than to those outside it, though the linguistic evidence for this was not presented. The same could be inferred for languages within a Zone, *but only* in terms of the differentia selected. If different features had been selected then a different grouping might well have resulted. The difficulties can be seen clearly by examining the differentia for Zone E—which *were* presented—as set out in Table 1.1.

If one compares the incidence of the features between the groups of the Zone, E40 and E50 have the highest score while E70 has the lowest. But if one compares the features common to E70 and G40, then E70 shares 9 out of 14, and would share a tenth, feature 2, on the evidence of Giriama.[7] Of the six features of Zone E not occurring in Zone G, four do not occur in E70 anyway, so that their non-occurrence in Zone

TABLE 1.1 *Characteristic features of Zone E*

In the final column comparison is made with a G40 language, Swahili, where the features listed occur for the Zone.

	E30	E40	E50	E70	G40
	Masaba' (Luyia)	'Logoli'	'Kikuyu'	'Pokomo'	'Swahili'
1. Standard vocabularies contain a large percentage of items common to other Zones, e.g. Kikuyu c.20 per cent	+	+	+	+	+
2. Genders indicating smallness or bigness	+	+	+	−	+
3. Double-prefix in independent nominals	+	+	−	−	−
4. Nomino-verbal prefix **ku-/uku-**	+	+	+	+	+
5. Extra-independent prefixes (e.g. E72c)	+	+	−	−	+
6. Nominals used as sentences	+	+	+	+	+
7. Suffix **-e** characteristic of dependent tenses	+	+	+	+	+
8. Suffix **-ile**	+	+	+	— (largely) —	
9. Almost unparalleled wealth of tenses	+	+	+	+	
10. True negative tenses	−	−	+	+	+
11. Copula **-li** little used	+	+	+	+	
12. Unusual consonant alternances	+	+	+	+	−
13. Seven-vowel system	−	+	+	−	−
14. Two quantities of radical vowel	+	+	+	−	−
15. Alternance voiced/voiceless stops masked in junction with nasal consonant	+	+	+	−	
16. If C₂ of radical is nC, no distinction between a voiced stop and its corresponding nasal, in junction with a nasal consonant in first position	+	+	+	−	
17. Dahl's Law operates	−	+	+	−	
18. Lexical tone present	+	+	+	+	−
19. Complicated tonal system	+	+	+	+	−
20. Extra dependent prefixes of Classes 1, 4, 9 exhibit tonally distinct behaviour	−	−	+	−	

G might imply affinity rather than otherwise. Of the two plus features in E70 not occurring in Zone G (features 11 and 19), one at least (feature 19) seems, on the evidence from Giriama and Pokomo,[8] to be less characteristic of E70 than of the other E groups. In short, in terms of adding up features, the E70 group might appear to be closer to G40 than to, say, E50, unless the common features are in some sense held to be more important than the minus features.[9] Lexical material from Giriama and Pokomo was collected during 1968/9 using Guthrie's list of general starred forms. It will be recalled that by examining groups of cognates, marked by regular sound shifts, Guthrie was able to construct (see *Comparative Bantu*, vol. I, 1968) more than 2,000 sets from some 200 Bantu languages. The member of a set can be inferred to occur by virtue of the existence of some item in a proto-language. This is termed a root and the members of the set are termed reflexes of that root. Those 500 or so roots which occur over the whole or a very large part of the Bantu field are termed general roots. Those languages which appear to have the highest percentage of such roots include Bemba (54 per cent) and Luba-Katanga (50 per cent) which seem to form a nucleus in central Africa. Both Kongo, on the western, and Swahili on the eastern coast have high scores, 44 per cent. From this evidence Guthrie suggests that proto-Bantu was spoken somewhere in the centre of the nucleus, and attributes the progressive diminution from the nucleus to the dispersal of ancestor groups outwards. The only two Kenya groups for which Guthrie provides percentages are Kikuyu (32 per cent) and Kamba (30 per cent). Now, although it is not stated which variety of Swahili was chosen as the basis for computing the 44 per cent, if we assume that a comparable figure obtains for the whole of the Swahili-speaking area, we have a tongue running up the coast, bordering Zone E, and reaching right to the boundary with the Cushitic languages, a tongue which manifests a sharp discontinuity with the percentages of the Zone E groups. Data from Giriama and Pokomo is, therefore, of particular interest. While it will be some time before all the data is analysed, and while it must be recognized that Guthrie might well reject reflexes which I have accepted, initially Giriama scores rather more than Swahili (*c.* 55 per cent) while the two dialects of Pokomo (Ngataana and Zubaki/Gwano) score rather similarly to Swahili (*c.* 43–48 per cent). Furthermore if one compares the number of reflexes that Giriama and Pokomo share with Swahili, as opposed to those which they share with Kamba, the figures are *c.* 140 as against *c.* 109. This would tend to confirm the suggestion made above with reference to specific features, that these two languages of E70, at any rate, seem to fall in with Swahili. Aside from the relevance of this data in arguing for an expansion of the nucleus, or even for setting up a second-stage nucleus, it is particularly interesting when viewed in conjunction with Lambert's comment (see below, and references to note 4, for a historical discussion) that Meru have an oral tradition which he interprets to mean that they came from the sea. All this is highly speculative, but it would seem to be worth pursuing the lexical links of Giriama/Pokomo with Meru and/or Tharaka, as against those with Meru/Kikuyu/Kamba, and Giriama/Pokomo/Kikuyu/Kamba.

Material of this kind underlines an important problem: though great progress has been made in our knowledge of the Bantu languages in the twenty years or so since Guthrie's classification appeared, rather little progress has been made in the field of typological classification. While we are in no doubt that the selection of different features would yield a different grouping, we are not at all clear about how to select particular features. Are, for example, the number of vowel phonemes of equal, greater or less significance than the shape of nominal prefixes? The problem becomes acute at the intra-group level when deciding whether to regard X as a different language from Y, or as a dialect of it or whether both should have equal status within a dialect cluster Z. Should the criteria for making such decisions be quantitative, qualitative or both, or should they be essentially non-linguistic? In their recent survey of Uganda's languages the team used a word list of some 94 items as the basis for establishing the closeness of relationship among the Bantu languages of Uganda. Languages which share 75 per cent or more of this list were treated as dialects, those which shared less as distinct languages. They also make the point that, from their own material, it seemed generally true that those languages which are at present geographically closest are likely also to be linguistically most closely related. Guthrie had also recognized this problem, treating it in a more flexible manner. He admitted that linguistically Sukuma and Nyamwezi might be regarded as members of a dialect cluster, while sociologically they should be regarded as two distinct entities. Examples of this kind, and also of the reverse situation, are to be found in Kenya, especially with reference to the Kikuyu, Luyia, 'Mijikenda' and Pokomo groups.

In Group E50, Guthrie lists Kikuyu (E51), Embu (E52), Meru (E53) and Tharaka (E54), along with Kamba and Dhaiso (Tanzania). Lambert speaks of four main tribal groups 'speaking closely related languages', Kikuyu, Embu, Meru and Chuka, which is a simplification of the situation as he described it in his 1950 study and which is worth quoting in full here:

... the languages ... divide themselves into two main groups. One includes Kikuyu, Ndia, Gichugu, Embu and Mbere, and is closely related to Kamba, the principal difference being the dislike of a voiced plosive and of slurring between two vowels

18

Map of the Kikuyu Land Unit Showing Approximate Distribution of Tribes

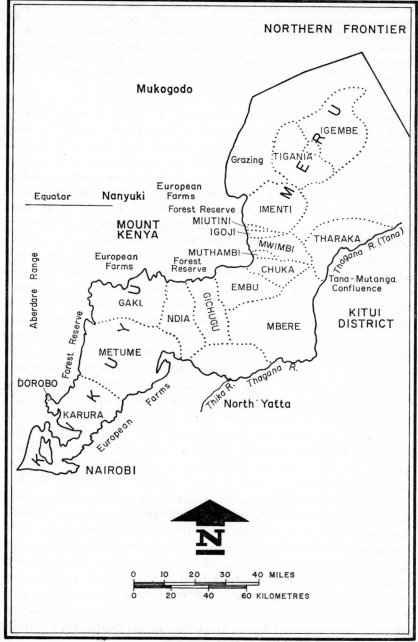

G.deS.

in the latter, though there are also noticeable differences in vocabulary. The other group includes Meru, Muthambi and Mwimbi, and shows closer affinity with the coast languages (Pokomo, Nyika) than does the first; a knowledge of Swahili, in fact, would help a Kikuyu to understand Meru. Chuka perhaps comes somewhere between the two groups, and Tharaka is generally regarded as a conglomerate of similar dialects which are scarcely yet merged into uniformity: its present leanings are towards the Meru group, but the similarities with Kikuyu are marked. There has been some borrowing from Kamba.[10]

It is on this evidence that Bryan (op. cit. pp. 115 and 125) places Tharaka and Chuka in her Taita group, though I do not think that her reading of the passage leads strictly to this conclusion. A further classification is provided by the 1962 census where we find Kikuyu, Embu, Meru, Tharaka and Mbere separated, Mbere having been previously mentioned by Lambert as one of the two main divisions of the Embu (a possible contrast to the Sukuma/Nyamwezi example?).[11] Finally, in a recent article on the Kikuyu group, Patrick Bennett lists Mwimbi as an apparently isolable dialect along with Southern Kikuyu and Embu, and remarks parenthetically that linguistically Meru is not '. . . as much of a unit as one might be led to believe'.[12] As pointed out above, any grouping will be a reflection of the criteria used in setting it up: what one must keep clearly distinct are assertions of affinity from demonstrations of coincident features. Not, it must be stressed, that one is necessarily more valid than the other; if Mbere assert that their language is different from Meru, this will not be disproved by any set of features common to both; two kinds of relationship are involved. Sentiments or assertions of affinity are certainly more accessible than the data required for a systematic typological comparison—even assuming there was agreement about what was to be compared. Many people are prepared to make judgements about the degree to which they can understand other languages, and to rate such languages on the basis of their own and other people's opinions, though it may take some time to discover the basis for such opinions. Discussing the matter with Gusii, in reference to Kikuyu, I found quite a number of people who claimed it was possible, indeed rather easy, to understand Kikuyu—certainly easier than Kamba. On the other hand some of those who made this claim had never even heard Kikuyu so far as I could ascertain, so that they were talking from 'group' rather than 'personal' experience. Others, who had lived among Kikuyu, averred that intelligibility depended on the subject of conversation, and others agreed that, in the case of a fairly simple transaction in a shop or market, intelligibility was easier than if one were trying to discuss more serious or more extended topics. The Uganda team established a correlation between given percentages of shared lexical items between two languages, and ability to understand material in these languages. This is clearly a useful step forward as a measurement of potential ratings of high intelligibility.

The problems raised for the Kikuyu group are also present for other Kenya Bantu groups: Peter Itebete discusses the Luyia situation in Chapter 3, but for the Mijikenda there is virtually no documentation, apart from Miss Deed's work on Giriama and my own inadequate field-notes for Giriama and Digo. The same is true for Pokomo, whose thirteen sub-groups stretch along the Tana River until at the northern end it is claimed that they do not speak a Bantu language at all. I was able to do some field-work among the southern groups in 1968/9 and hope to be able to continue this.

TABLE 1.2 *The Bantu languages of Kenya*

The grouping in general follows that of Bryan (op. cit.) but Guthrie's numeration is added where relevant. The languages are cited in the forms used by members of the group themselves, but in a broad transcription for the general reader, thus E51 is cited as Kikuyu, and not Gĩkũyũ, as would be required in the current orthography. Finally the languages are cited without the prefix characteristic among Bantu languages, thus Kamba, and not Kĩ-Kamba. (See the note on spelling appended to 'Kenya: a Language Map.')

'Kikuyu' Group	'Gusii' Group	'Taita' Group	'Luyia' Group	'Swahili' Group
Kikuyu (E51)	Gusii (E42)	Dabida (E74a)	Bukusu (E31c)	Swahili (G42)
Embu (E52)	Kuria (E43)	Mbololo	Tachoni	Mvita (G42b)
Mbere	Logoli (E41)	Werugha	Wanga (E32a)	⎰ Jomvu
Meru (E53)		Mbale	Shisa	⎹ Ngare
Mwimbi		Chawia	Nyore (E33)	⎱ Chifundi
Chuka		Bura	Marama	⎰ Vumba
Tharaka (E54)		Mwanda	Isukha	⎰ Amu (G42a)
Kamba (E55)		Kasigau	Marach(i)	⎹ Bajuni (G41a)
		Saghala (E74b)	Idakho	⎰ (Tikuu)
		Dambi	Tsotso (E32b)	⎹ Pate
		Mugange	Kabras	⎱ Siu
		Teri	Nyala (North)	
		Kishamba	(Kakelelwa)	
		Gimba	Khayo	
	'Shambaa' Group	(Information	Tiriki	'Mijikenda'
		supplied by	Samia (E34)	
		Miss M.	Nyala (Lake)	Giriama (E72a)
	Taveta (G21)	Slavikova)	(Gwe? MAB,	Duruma (72d)
			p. 112)	Kauma (E72b)
				Chonyi (E72c)
				Ribe
				Rabai (E72e)
				Jibana
				Kambe
				Digo (E73)
				Pokomo (E71)

In the list of Kenya's Bantu languages presented in Table 1.2, I have included all those which seem isolable from one another on present evidence by some set of characteristic features, but I am leaving aside for the moment the question of whether any of these can be considered as dialects of any other. The list is given in the hope of exposing our present state of ignorance and attracting more research: work is already in progress among the Luyia and Taita groups, and I hope myself to be able to continue my work among Kamba and Pokomo. What has already been done will be found in the Bibliography. Where a rather close relationship between languages has been asserted, I have inset the second and subsequent languages; where the evidence for a closer relationship is substantial I have placed the languages within brackets.

THE NILOTIC LANGUAGES

There is only one Nilotic language in Kenya, Luo, so that problems of classification do not arise. Tucker and Bryan have listed the following features as characteristic of the Southern Nilotic languages, amongst which Luo is grouped:[13]

Characteristics of Luo

1. Five open ('hard') and five close ('hollow') vowels.

2. As with other Nilotic languages there is a contrast between dental and alveolar consonants, thus, t/ṭ, d/ḍ. Two pitch levels are recognized, with 'down-step' as a significant feature.

3. The most common word shape is CVCV, in which the final V is invariably a suffix.

4. No morphological classes in verbs. Derivative verbs associated with internal change. Noun formatives are mostly associated with internal change but in some cases with vowel suffixation.

5. A change of final consonant is characteristic of the noun plural. Many adjectives have a distinct plural form but others are invariable.

6. No grammatical gender.

7. Nouns are not generally marked for case.

8. A suffixed element is characteristic of the possessive.

9. Verb. Tenses: there are two series of tenses which distinguish 'complete' as opposed to 'incomplete' action. These are, in many cases, distinguished only by the tone-pattern. In comparison with Bantu languages these are not numerous. Negation is expressed by particles all of which precede the verb.

10. Characteristic word order is S-V-O. Adjectives and numerals follow the noun.

PARA-NILOTIC LANGUAGES

The languages of Kenya which have been classified as Para-Nilotic, may be divided into three groups:

'Teso' Group	'Maasai' Group	'Kalenjin' Group
Teso	Maasai	Nandi
Turkana	Samburu (Sampur)	Keyo
	Njemps (Ntiamus)	*Kony
		Kipsigis
		Tugen
		*Terik (Nyang'ori)
		*Sapiny ⎱
		Sabaot ⎰
		Bung'omek
		Okiek, etc. (Ndorobo)
		Päkot (Pokot)
		Marakwet
		*Endo

Asterisked items do not appear in the census, but Sabaot—which does—has been noted as a dialect of Sapiny by Tucker and Bryan (1956).

Problems of classification are well illustrated here by Maasai/Samburu, which in linguistic terms share a very large number of features, are mutually intelligible to a very high degree, and are recognized by speakers to be in some sense 'the same' language. Nevertheless they have traditionally been separated on sociological grounds.

Some of the smaller groups which are surrounded by, or have inter-penetrated with groups speaking a language of a different type, e.g. Mukogodo (see Cushitic below), may number some, possibly of different generations, who speak both languages, thereby confusing research workers who only hear one. Dr A. Jacobs of Nairobi comments that at the present time all Mukogodo appear to speak Maasai, and that those under 35 speak only Maasai. A similar situation obtains among the Waata (see Cushitic below) who are commonly encountered speaking a Bantu language.

Characteristics of Para-Nilotic Languages

1. There are five open ('hard') and five close ('hollow') vowels in these languages with two degrees of vowel length. Päkot is distinguished by having three of its vowels centralized. The Teso group is characterized by 'shadow' vowels. (See footnote 14.)

2. Consonantal features include the implosion of voiced stops in Maasai, while in Kalenjin the voiced series occurs only allophonically. Two level tones are recognized, with 'down-step' as a significant feature. Final glottal-closure is characteristic in the Teso group.

3. The most common word-stem shape is CVC, usually with affixes.

4. Morphological classes of verbs may be established with distinctive grammatical and tonal behaviour. Verbal derivation by suffix is common; the underlying ideas of these, e.g. motion towards, away, etc., being similar to those of Nilotic languages. Nominal derivation is by suffix and prefix. In Kalenjin, nouns have a Primary ('indefinite') and Secondary ('definite') form.

5. Number is marked in nouns by a wide variety of suffixes and also by internal change. There is a T/K dichotomy in nouns; an N/K dichotomy in pronouns.

6. Sex-linked gender is a feature of Teso and Maasai, but not of Kalenjin, which does, however, have sex-determining prefixes in a few nouns.

7. Nouns are marked for case in all the languages, usually by tone alone.

8. In Maasai the possessive is self-standing and marked for both gender and number, in contrast to Teso where it is invariable. In Kalenjin the possessive is suffixed to the Secondary form of the noun and marked for number.

9. Verbal system: in Maasai there is a distinction between indicative/subjunctive but no distinction for aspect. Teso distinguishes between indicative/dependent and momentary/continuous aspects. In Kalenjin the indicative is additionally divided into an actual/subsequent and single/repeated implications for each of the two aspects. Time-linked tenses are few in number.

10. Word order is characteristically V-S-O.

THE CUSHITIC LANGUAGES

There are two main Cushitic languages spoken in Kenya, each with a number of linguistically identifiable variants:

'Somali' Group	'Galla' Group	
Common Somali	Galla	?
Central Somali	Sakuye	Mukogodo
Rendille	Boran(a)[14]	
Boni (Bon, Aweera)	Orma	
	Gabra	
	Waat (a)[14] (Sanye, Langulo, Ariangulu)	

Dahalo

Somalis of Kenya speak two dialect types, which are also spoken in Somalia and Ethiopia: 'Common Somali' and 'Central Somali'.[15] Common Somali is a dialect type spoken all over the Somali-speaking territories with the exception of the Upper Juba Province and the Benadir

Province of Somalia where Central and Coastal Somali are spoken respectively. Outside the Benadir Province Coastal Somali is spoken mainly in riverine agricultural settlements. In Kenya, roughly speaking, all pastoralists and townsmen speak Common Somali, while Central Somali is restricted to a small minority who are riverine agriculturists and usually also know Common Somali which they use as a lingua franca in contact with other Somalis. The Voice of Kenya in their Somali programmes use Common Somali. There is no direct correlation between tribes and dialect type and consequently the division made by the census into Ogaden, Hawiya, Ajuran, Garre and Gosha has little linguistic value. It may be pointed out however that almost all the Ogaden and the Dagodia and Ajuran tribes of the Hawiya group are mainly pastoralists and almost all Gosha people are agriculturists. The Garre are mainly pastoralists and some of them are agriculturists. Andrzejewski further notes that many Ajuran are bilingual, speaking also a Boran-type Galla: similarly some Garre speak a Gabra-type Galla as well as Rahanweyntype Somali.

Mukogodo is tentatively placed here following Hobley's evidence re-presented by Greenberg, and more recently corroborated by Heine.

Waata is placed with Galla on the evidence of Tucker and Andrzejewski, but it may well be that more than one language is involved. Groups of (elephant)-hunters known variously as Sanye, Langulo, Ariangulu seem to have been attached to Duruma, Giriama, Pokomo and Orma communities for a longish period, and to have become bilingual in the host language. Until we know a great deal more about these scattered communities our conclusions must remain extremely tentative. The Boni, at least among the Pokomo, have a reputation for being good cultivators, and they seem largely to be restricted to the area north of the Tana River. Dahalo seem to live mainly between the Tana River and Lamu, and while Tucker's evidence points indubitably to Eastern Cushitic it is hoped that research into all these languages by Derek Elderkin of Nairobi[16] will provide much more substantial grounds for classification.

Characteristics of Cushitic Languages

1. Galla has a six-vowel system with two degrees of length; Somali has a double five-vowel system consisting of both a 'normal' and a 'fronted' series, for both of which two degrees of length occur. Galla is characterized by 'shadow' vowels.

2. In Somali post-velar consonants are characteristic, while in Galla consonants include ejective stops and one implosive stop. Three level

tones are recognized in both languages but tone is '. . . more grammatical than lexical'.

3. Most verb stems have the shape CVC, CVCC, CVCVC, while nouns have additionally CV, CVCV, CVCVCV stem shapes.

4. Morphological classes for verbs can be set up for Somali. Nouns in both languages can be divided up into those which end in glottal closure and those which do not.

5. In Galla, categories of number and gender are parallel, whereas in Somali polarity of gender is characteristic.

6. Grammatical gender occurs in both languages.

7. Nouns are marked for case in both languages.

8. Possessives in both languages are marked for case and also for the gender of the possessed noun.

9. Verbal system: a distinction between Perfect (Past)/Imperfect (Present), each with its own affix series, is characteristic. Other series, e.g. Optative, Dependent, Relative, etc., also occur. Verbal root extension classes are a common feature of all Cushitic languages.

10. Most common word order is S-O-V.

B. SIZE, DISTRIBUTION AND HOMOGENEITY OF THE LINGUISTIC GROUPS

One of the major problems here is the fact that the periodic censuses of the population have used ethnic rather than linguistic affiliation as a means of identifying people. To the extent, therefore, that ethnic and linguistic units are not comparable, we lack precise information. We have figures for Mbere and Tharaka, but not for Chuka; figures are available for Mijikenda and Luyia but not for their constituents; we know how many Bajun and Swahili/Shirazi there are but not how many Vumba, Chifundi or Pate. Furthermore a number of ethnic sub-groups are listed for what, in the case of Somali and Galla, are linguistically little differentiated. The figures for 1962 and 1969 must, therefore, be read with these facts in mind (Table 1.3).

A second question to be considered is the distribution of speakers over the country. While each ethnic/linguistic group has what might be termed as a 'homeland', there are a number of forces which serve to attract people away from their own areas into those of other groups (see Table 1.4), either as temporary or more permanent residents. These include employment in towns, settlement areas and large estates, government service, and pressure on the land. Government service has been an important heterogenizing factor for many years; from colonial times it has been

TABLE 1.3   *The Kenya Population Census 1962 and 1969*[17]
(Original spelling retained)

		1962	1969
Bantu:			
	Kikuyu	1,642,065	2,201,632
	Luhya	1,086,409	1,453,302
	Kamba	933,219	1,197,712
	Gusii	538,343	701,679
	Meru	439,921	554,256
	Mijikenda	414,887	520,520
	Embu	95,647	117,969
	Kuria	41,885	59,875
	Tharaka	38,474	51,883
	Taita	83,613	108,494
	Mbere	38,172	49,247
	Pokomo	30,350	35,181
	Bajun	11,280	24,387
	Swahili (Shi.)	8,657	9,971
	Taveta	4,855	6,324
	TOTAL:	5,407,777	7,092,432
Nilotic:			
	Luo	1,148,335	1,521,595
Para-Nilotic:			
	Kipsigis	341,771	471,459
	Turkana	181,387	203,177
	Nandi	170,085	261,969
	Masai	154,079	154,906
	Tugen	109,691	130,249
	Elgeyo	100,871	110,908
	Pokot	76,537	93,437
	Teso	72,357	85,800
	Samburu	48,750	54,796
	Marakwet	66,965	79,713
	Sabaot	28,012	42,468
	Ndorobo	14,378	21,034
	Njemps	4,861	6,526
	Kelenjin (thus)	4,312	—
	TOTAL:	1,373,876	1,716,442
Cushitic:			
	Somali	275,241	249,731
	Rendille	13,724	18,729
	Galla	83,151	70,869
	Boni/Sanye	4,797	3,972
	TOTAL:	376,913	343,301
Others:		59,041	—

customary to send civil servants anywhere in the country, so that district headquarters have long presented sharp contrasts with the surrounding homogeneous rural areas. Some groups, too, have become associated with particular branches of government; thus Kalenjin and Kamba with the police and army; Kamba and to a lesser extent Kalenjin with the Game

TABLE 1.4 *Distribution of each tribe inside and outside 'home districts'*[18]
(Original spelling retained)

Tribe	Total		Home Districts		Outside Home Districts		Home Districts
	Number	Percentage	Number	Percentage	Number	Percentage	
Kikuyu	1,642,065	100.0	1,140,164	69.4	501,901	30.6	Kiambu, Fort Hall, Nyeri Embu.
Embu	95,647	100.0	89,334	93.4	6,313	6.6	Embu.
Meru	439,921	100.0	431,489	98.1	8,432	1.9	Meru.
Mbere	38,172	100.0	36,870	96.6	1,302	3.4	Embu.
Kamba	933,219	100.0	817,361	87.6	115,858	12.4	Machakos, Kitui.
Tharaka	38,474	100.0	37,298	96.9	1,176	3.1	Meru, Kitui.
Luhya	1,086,409	100.0	899,541	82.8	186,868	17.2	North, Elgon and Central Nyanza.
Kisii	538,343	100.0	511,688	95.0	26,655	5.0	Kisii.
Kuria	41,885	100.0	38,471	91.8	3,414	8.2	South Nyanza.
Mijikenda	414,887	100.0	370,354	89.3	44,533	10.7	Kilifi-Malindi, Kwale, Lamu.
Pokomo/Riverine	30,350	100.0	28,288	93.2	2,062	6.8	Tana River, Garissa.
Taveta	4,855	100.0	4,658	95.9	197	4.1	Taita.
Taita	83,613	100.0	71,631	85.7	11,982	14.3	Taita.
Swahili/Shirazi	8,657	100.0	6,775	78.3	1,882	21.7	Kilifi-Malindi, Kwale, Mombasa, Lamu.
Bajun	11,280	100.0	9,041	80.2	2,239	19.8	Lamu, Kilifi-Malindi, Lamu.
Boni/Sanye	4,797	100.0	4,274	89.1	523	10.9	Tana River, Garissa.
Luo	1,148,335	100.0	1,025,039	89.3	123,296	10.7	Central, South, North and Elgon Nyanza.
Nandi	170,085	100.0	129,537	76.2	40,548	23.8	Nandi, North Nyanza, Kericho.

Tribe	Total		Home Districts		Outside Home Districts		Home Districts
	Number	Percentage	Number	Percentage	Number	Percentage	
Kipsigis	341,771	100.0	285,364	83.5	56,407	16.5	Kericho.
Elgeyo	100,871	100.0	90,966	90.2	9,905	9.8	Elgeyo-Marakwet.
Marakwet	66,965	100.0	65,052	97.1	1,913	2.9	Elgeyo-Marakwet.
Pokot	76,537	100.0	73,474	96.0	3,063	4.0	West Pokot, Baringo.
Sabaot	28,012	100.0	22,553	80.5	5,459	19.5	Elgon Nyanza.
Tugen	109,691	100.0	103,190	94.1	6,501	5.9	Baringo.
Masai	154,079	100.0	139,691	90.7	14,388	9.3	Kajiado, Narok.
Samburu	48,750	100.0	47,055	96.5	1,695	3.5	Samburu.
Turkana	181,387	100.0	167,498	92.3	13,889	7.7	Turkana, Samburu.
Iteso	72,357	100.0	62,686	86.6	9,671	13.4	Elgon Nyanza.
Nderobo	14,378	100.0	12,255	85.2	2,123	14.8	Nanyuki, Nakuru.
Njemps	4,681	100.0	4,192	89.6	489	10.4	Baringo.
Rendille	13,724	100.0	13,638	99.4	86	0.6	Marsabit.
Boran	58,346	100.0	56,822	97.4	1,524	2.6	Marsabit, Isiolo, Moyale.
Gabbra	11,478	100.0	10,734	93.5	744	6.5	Marsabit.
Sakuye	1,681	100.0	1,404	83.5	277	16.5	Moyale.
Orma	11,646	100.0	10,767	92.5	879	7.5	Tana River, Garissa.
Gosha	7,257	100.0	7,251	99.9	6	0.1	Mandera.
Hawiyah	84,371	100.0	84,091	99.7	280	0.3	Mandera, Wajir.
Ogaden	121,645	100.0	121,211	99.6	434	0.4	Garissa, Wajir.
Ajuran	19,919	100.0	19,678	98.8	241	1.2	Wajir, Moyale.
Gurreh	34,603	100.0	34,365	99.3	238	0.7	Mandera.

Department; Luo on the railway and in Mombasa port; Kikuyu in the settlement areas, in the navy,[19] and in what was formerly the 'White Highlands'; and Luyia in the tea estates and in domestic service. All this has provided incentives and opportunities for people to acquire skills in several languages, but it seems to be true that such personal mobility has been associated with the acquisition of skills in the two 'common' languages, Swahili and English—especially the former—rather than in other 'local' languages. These latter skills seem to be associated with more stable situations, such as the border areas between groups, but there appears to be a very wide range of variation. The situation in the towns is discussed in detail in Chapters 5–9 while the rural areas are treated at greater length later in the present chapter. The towns, understandably, have provided the most powerful attraction: in Nairobi City, for example, Kikuyu form 42 per cent of the population, Kamba 15 per cent, Luyia 17 per cent, and Luo 16 per cent (1962; by 1969 the percentages were 47, 15, 16 and 15). Unfortunately, however, comparable figures are not available for the 34 towns listed as having a population of more than 2,000 people in 1962. This lack of information on the towns is particularly serious: while, on the basis of the 1962 census it was calculated that no more than 7.8 per cent of the population lived in towns,[20] yet the average increase for the preceding 14 years was over 6 per cent, and there is no evidence that the rate has slackened since then, indeed it may even have increased through such factors as the exodus of Asian traders. Pressure on the land is greatest in Western, Nyanza and Central Provinces, so that it is no surprise to find a large number of Luyia, Luo and Kikuyu living outside their home areas (see Table 1.5). While we cannot be sure exactly where they have moved to, the figures in Table 1.5 are, nevertheless, rather revealing. They show large numbers of Kikuyu in and along the Rift Valley and spreading out into Kericho on the one hand and into Uasin Gishu and Trans-Nzoia on the other. On the evidence of my own visits to West Pokot during 1968/9 it is clear that numbers of Kikuyu farmers and traders are increasing markedly. Luyia are numerous in Kericho, South Nyanza and Nakuru, but their presence in Trans-Nzoia and Uasin Gishu should occasion no surprise since the 'homeland' of one of the Luyia groups, Bukusu, is in this area. Luo are strong in Kericho, adjoining their own home area, and on the coast.

Viewed as a whole, however, as from Table 1.6, the rural areas are homogeneous to a high degree, though it must be remembered that the census figures only present the situation for administrative areas—themselves now out of date—so that one cannot be sure just where such heterogeneity as does obtain, is located. On the basis of impressions gained during extensive travelling during 1968/9 and from long residence

TABLE 1.5   *Groups with large numbers living outside the home area*[21]

Kikuyu			Luo		
126,864	(169,363)	Nakuru	33,144	(26,864)	Kericho
57,598		Naivasha	16,975	(20,606)	Nakuru
46,185		Laikipia	10,875	(22,058)	Mombasa
31,412	(41,530)	Uasin Gishu	5,133		Thika
17,014	(26,477)	Kericho	4,987		Elgon-Nyanza
11,830	(17,625)	Trans-Nzoia	3,469	(4,014)	Trans-Nzoia
8,094	(14,919)	Mombasa	3,438	(5,252)	Kisii
6,233	(16,258)	Kajiado	3,263	(5,310)	Uasin Gishu
3,345	(7,751)	Machakos	2,567	(3,581)	Taita
1,762	(9,350)	Nandi	2,091	(1,707)	Kilifi
1,751	(2,902)	Elgeyo-Marakwet	2,085	(3,667)	Kwale
1,268		C. Nyanza	1,985	(4,643)	Kiambu
1,169	(1,600)	Taita	1,677		Naivasha
1,016	(12,122)	Baringo	1,664	(2,263)	Machakos
987		Elgon-Nyanza	1,023	(1,612)	Kajiado
316,528			94,276		

1969 only:			1969 only:		
	6,042	Bungoma		1,347	Bungoma
	4,578	Narok		1,143	Murang'a
	3,043	Kisumu			
	2,153	Kisii			
	1,375	W. Pokot			

	Luyia	
47,773	(58,601)	Trans-Nzoia
20,712	(24,154)	Nakuru
23,686	(28,742)	Uasin Gishu
14,166	(7,608)	Kericho
10,663	(11,412)	S. Nyanza
8,419	(23,715)	Nandi
7,272	(15,160)	Mombasa
4,897		Thika
3,467	(4,833)	Kiambu
2,955		Naivasha
2,572	(2,392)	Taita
1,560		Laikipia
1,269	(1,166)	Kajiado
149,411		

1969 only:	1,372	Murang'a
	1,320	W. Pokot

Note: It must be appreciated that the districts referred to here were reorganized subsequent to the 1962 census, so that comparison with later censuses will not be possible in all cases. Nevertheless, the bracketed figures for 1969 suggest a scale of dispersion for Kikuyu which is not being matched by the other two groups.

in certain rural areas, I would say that heterogenizing influences are most marked along the lines of communication, between and in the towns, in the many much smaller trading posts, and in such places as schools, health centres, missions, etc., which are themselves often attached to other focal points, such as local courts, 'dukas', post office, 'baraza', etc. Even in a completely homogeneous group like the Turkana, the few stores in

TABLE 1.6 *Percentage of ethnic homogeneity by district* (*1962*)

Figures in brackets indicate overall density of population per sq. mile.

Dominant unit constituted 90 per cent of the population or above:

Fort Hall (491)	*Kikuyu*	*99*	*per cent*
Kiambu (557)	*Kikuyu*	*98*	*per cent*
Meru (125)	*Meru*	*92*	*per cent*
	Tharaka	7	per cent
Nyeri (428)	*Kikuyu*	*99*	*per cent*
Kilifi/Malindi (52)	*Mijikenda*	*95*	*per cent*
	Kamba	1	per cent
	Luo	1	per cent
Kwale (49)	*Mijikenda*	*91*	*per cent*
	Kamba	5	per cent
	Luo	1	per cent
Kisii (691)	*Gusii*	*99*	*per cent*
N. Nyanza (507)	*Luyia*	*92*	*per cent*
	Luo	5	per cent
Nandi (167)	*Nandi*	*90*	*per cent*
	Luyia	7	per cent
W. Pokot (30)	*Pokot*	*90*	*per cent*
	Nandi, Sabaot	5	per cent
Kitui (24)	*Kamba*	*97*	*per cent*
Machakos (95)	*Kamba*	*99*	*per cent*
Isiolo (5)	*Boran*	*91*	*per cent*
	Somali	4	per cent
Mandera (7)	*Somali*	*99*	*per cent*
Turkana (7)	*Turkana*	*100*	*per cent*
Wajir (6)	*Somali*	*100*	*per cent*

Dominant unit constituted 80 per cent of the population or more:

Taita (16)	*Taita*	*80*	*per cent*
	Taveta	5	per cent
	Luyia	3	per cent
	Luo	3	per cent
	Kamba	3	per cent
Tana (3)	*Pokomo*	*80*	*per cent*
	Orma (Galla)	20	per cent
C. Nyanza (366)	*Luo*	*86*	*per cent*
	Luyia	13	per cent
S. Nyanza (218)	*Luo*	*89*	*per cent*
	Kuria	8	per cent
Naivasha (54)	*Kikuyu*	*83*	*per cent*
	Luyia	4	per cent
	Kipsigis	2.5	per cent
	Maasai	2.5	per cent
	Luo	2	per cent
	Kamba	2	per cent
Garissa (4)	*Somali (Ogaden)*	*85*	*per cent*
	Orma (Galla)	5	per cent
	Pokomo	8.5	per cent
Samburu (7)	*Samburu*	*83*	*per cent*
	Turkana	16	per cent

Dominant unit constituted 70 per cent of the population or more:

Nanyuki (20)	*Kikuyu*	*74*	*per cent*
	Ndorobo	9	per cent
	Meru	4	per cent
E. Nyanza (232)	*Luyia*	*73*	*per cent*
	Teso	18	per cent
	Sabaot	6	per cent

Dominant unit constituted 70 per cent of the population or more: (Cont'd.)

Kericho (183)	Kipsigis	74	per cent
	Luo	9	per cent
	Gusii	4.5	per cent
	Kikuyu	4	per cent
	Luyia	4	per cent
Baringo (33)	Tugen	79	per cent
	Pokot	16	per cent
	Njemps	3	per cent
Kajiado (8)	Maasai	79	per cent
	Kikuyu	9	per cent
	Kamba	6	per cent
Narok (15)	Maasai	79	per cent
	Kipsigis	15	per cent

In eight districts the dominant unit constituted between 50–69 per cent of the population, and only in three did it fall below 50 per cent:

Marsabit (1)	Rendille	47	per cent
	Somali	37	per cent
	Boran	11	per cent
Mombasa (2,217)	Mijikenda	38	per cent
	Kamba	15	per cent
	Luo	10	per cent
	Taita	8	per cent
	Kikuyu	7	per cent
	Luyia	7	per cent
Uasin Gishu (61)	Kikuyu	33	per cent
	Luyia	25	per cent
	Nandi	18	per cent
	Kipsigis, Elgeyo, Kalenjin (so stated)	11	per cent

Lodwar are owned by Meru, Kikuyu and Luyia, and a similar diversity characterizes the civil servants stationed there. Whether the resettlement schemes in the former White Highlands will develop as heterogeneous or homogeneous rural communities it is too early to tell, nor is it easy to assess the extent to which a group like the Kikuyu, for example, are moving in as a farming community to the foothills of the Cherangani Hills.

C. THE CONCEPT OF MULTILINGUALISM

In a community that was completely homogeneous linguistically, there would be no need for anyone to speak any other language, so far as internal communication was concerned. On the other hand no group at the present time, nor indeed at any recent historical period, has completely insulated itself from contact with other groups, and to the extent that contact was maintained and encouraged, even to the extent of group inter-penetration as in western Kenya, then some form of multilingualism could be expected at some level of society. Where, by contrast, whole communities or sections of communities have remained relatively homogeneous and isolated, as, for example, in northern Kenya one would expect to find a high incidence of monolingualism persisting at all levels of society. Yet the fact that all Kenya's linguistic units have been subsumed under a single political authority for the best part of seventy years has resulted, among other things, in the need for some common language, through which government's aims, policy, etc., can be presented to people as a whole, and, indeed, through which the business of government can be carried on. During the colonial period this meant in practice a good deal of translation, from English into Swahili and from Swahili into the local languages (see Chapter 14). It also meant the adoption of one or other of the available common languages in those branches of government where personnel might be required to serve anywhere in the country, e.g. the administration, agricultural, veterinary and health services, the army, police, railways and harbours, and so on. Men and women who spent their working lives in government service would be likely to live their lives in linguistically heterogeneous surroundings, perhaps even marrying outside their own linguistic group and bringing up a family whose first language would be English or Swahili, but who might very well acquire some competence in each of their parents' languages against the time when kinship ties might need to be invoked.

Monolingualism and multilingualism, therefore, represent two rather extreme forms of language competence, this being seen as one form of adaptation to particular patterns of social life. One might expect to find a high incidence of monolingualism under the following conditions:

(a) where the community is linguistically homogeneous;

(b) where access to education is limited and of short duration;

(c) where communications are poor and/or where incentive to use them is lacking;

(d) where personal mobility is low;

(e) where there are strong constraints against other languages being used, e.g. some separatist churches.

In some cases it may be possible to point to whole communities to whom such conditions apply, such as the pastoral nomads of northern Kenya, but in many cases the conditions operate differentially within a society, being themselves conditioned by such factors as geography, sex and occupation. It may happen, for example, that one section of a group occupies a quite different habitat from that of the rest of the group and follows a quite different way of life in consequence. Thus, the Päkot living below the Escarpment in West Pokot are nomadic pastoralists thinly scattered over the country, while their fellows living above the Escarpment around Kapenguria are more settled agriculturalists. School attendance figures for the two areas leave no doubt as to whose competence in Swahili and English will be the greater.

Again, it may be that in some communities women have fewer opportunities for meeting women of other groups, or for moving about generally or for acquiring education. Under these circumstances one would expect to find a higher incidence of monolingualism among them (see Table 1.8). Or the reverse may occur, where perhaps women are responsible for a particular craft or trade, as pot-making and selling among the Luo (see Table 1.20).

Finally, it may happen that some jobs will require a wider range of language skills than others: representatives of tobacco companies have assured me that the use of a local language is an excellent device for establishing rapport with potential customers. On the other hand tea or coffee farming can be carried on quite successfully without extra language skills; it may be useful to be able to read instructions for the application of fungicide, but not essential, since there is usually someone around who can assist in the matter.

One might expect to find a high incidence of multilingualism under the following conditions:

(a) where the community is linguistically heterogeneous;

(b) where access to education is unlimited and protracted;

(c) where communications are good and there are incentives to use them;

(d) where personal mobility is high;

(e) where strong attempts are made to encourage people to speak a particular language, e.g. recent (April 1970) asseverations that Swahili will be the official language of KANU.

The settled agricultural groups living in the fertile highlands east and west of the Rift are good examples of whole communities where the above conditions apply. The towns, of course, represent special and extreme cases of areas where such conditions apply, but these are dealt with separately in Chapters 5–9; I am concerned here only with the rural areas.

The above remarks are intended merely as illustrations of the kind of problems that have to be faced if one wishes to make any useful comment about the state and/or degree of rural multilingualism. It is particularly important to specify the unit within which one's remarks about multilingualism are to be held to apply, and to find out what are the incentives which, in Kenya today, impel men and women to learn, and speak, other languages than their first language. Like other skills it is acquired in order to be able to deploy it to one's own advantage in the game that is everyday living.

To obtain this kind of information it is necessary to carry out a large number of intensive studies of small groups and to supplement these with surveys based on interviews. This we had neither the time nor the resources to do for the rural areas. Instead it was decided to acquire some basic data through the use of interviews. There are, as is well attested from the growing literature on the subject, many problems in trying to establish not only what people claim to be their competence in specific languages, but also in what situations they claim to use their languages. It may be that one learns more about attitudes than about aptitudes, but it seemed worth making the attempt, and the availability of students during vacations provided an invaluable source of interviewing personnel.[22] An initial test was made during December 1968, and further samples were collected during June–August 1969. Interviewers were asked to make 100 per cent samples of households within a 2–5 mile radius of their own homes, the precise area covered being dependent on the density of settlement. All members of the household over the age of 15 were to be interviewed. The use of interviewers known to householders and thoroughly familiar with the local languages, would, it was hoped, lower resistance to the questions asked, and raise the value of the responses. Even then many problems arose: some women students felt shy about interviewing men, especially older men; some men had similar misgivings about women, while others were denied access to women members of the households.[23] In some cases it is evident that the samples were skewed in various ways: by interviewers failing to return to a household one or more of whose members were absent at the time of interview; by many adult males being absent from their homes at work, either in the towns or on estates; by the presence of numbers of young people who were temporarily—one hopes—unemployed. In some cases only small samples were obtained and the interviewers were not able to add to them in subsequent vacations; in other cases, where this was possible, substantial samples were obtained. In all, 20 samples were collected from what might be called 'core' areas, and 3 from 'border' areas. All the major Bantu groups were sampled, plus the Nilotic Luo and the Para-Nilotic Kipsigis. No other Para-Nilotic group was sampled, nor was any sample obtained from the Cushitic groups so that Dr Andrzejewski's note in Appendix B is particularly valuable. Of the border areas, one sample was taken from the Luo/Luyia border near Maseno; one from the Luo/Gusii/Kipsigis border near Sondu; and one from the Luo/Gusii border near Oyugis. The fact that there were so few samples from the Para-Nilotic/Cushitic groups means that the level of monolingualism reported is probably lower than would otherwise have been the case, since what impressionistic evidence there is suggests that these groups are characterized by a rather high level of monolingualism.

The interview was divided into two parts. In the first the interviewee was asked to answer a short, straightforward questionnaire. In the second he was asked to describe the events of the preceding twenty-four hours and say what language was used in what situation. He was also asked to recall what he could of the events of the preceding week and the languages associated with them. The questionnaire asked first for basic personal data such as sex, age, education, occupation; moving on to first language, first language of spouse, and language competence generally. A five-point scale was used along which the interviewee was asked to rate his competence in speaking particular languages, thus:

5 Very well, fluently, can talk on any topic
4 Enough for most conversations
3 Quite a lot
2 Enough for simple conversations
1 Very little

A five-point scale was also used for assessing frequency, the interviewee being asked to rate the frequency with which he used each language, thus:

5 Regularly, every day
4 At least once a day
3 Quite often (several times a week)
2 From time to time (once a week)
1 Very little (once a month)

The rest of the questionnaire dealt with skills in writing and the choice of languages for listening to the radio, but these are not dealt with here. Tables 1.8–1.16 tabulate the information relating to claimed competence, in terms of the numbers of languages for which some competence is claimed. Tables 1.18–1.19 present graphically the degrees of competence claimed for Swahili and English.

INTERPRETING THE TABLES

Table 1.7 presents some general features of the samples, so that the tables can be read with the limitations of the samples in mind. It will be evident that where the samples are small to begin with, the samples of particular patterns of language competence are likely to be so small as to be at best suggestive. Where the samples are substantial the results may be seen as throwing some light on existing trends in education and

TABLE 1.7 *Samples of rural communities*

			Men			Women					(Kenya 1962)* Differential		Average Years' Education			
													Men		Women	
	Total in sample	% Homogeneity	% Overall total	15–29	30+	% Overall total	15–29	30+	Total % 15–29	Total % 30+	Age 15–29	% Groups 30+	15–29	30+	15–29	30+
Luo (*Oyugis*) (a)	110	99	55	21	34	45	25	20	46	54		+5.4	7	2	4	nil
(Gusii border) (b)	43	77[1]	79	42	37	21	14	7	56	44		+5.4	7	5	7	3
Gusii (*Manga*)	97	100	74	22	52	26	10	16	32	68		+0.45	6	4	5	1
Kuria (*Kihancha*)	28	93	54	29	25	46	25	21	54	46		+0.45	8	2	4	nil
Luyia (Bukusu) (a)	80	99	67	45	22	33	21	12	66	34		+0.45	7	4	5	2
(Idakho) (b)	131	100[2]	62	40	22	38	22	16	62	38		+0.45	5	2	3	nil
(Logoli) (c)	35	100[3]	60	11	49	40	26	14	37	63		+0.45	7	3	4	3
(Khayo) (d)	78	72[4]	47	3	44	53	9	44	12	88		+1.37	8	nil	1	1
Kipsigis (Lugumek s/1)	197	100	50	18	32	50	25	25	43	57		+2.65	6	3	6	nil
Taita (*Wundanyi*)	36	100	36	22	14	64	31	33	53	47		+2.65	8	4	6	nil
Pokomo (Salama) (a)	88	95	73	16	57	27	16	11	32	68		+2.65	6	3	3	2
(Gwano) (b)	88	98	42	19	23	58	31	27	50	50		+2.65	6	2	1	nil
(Zubaki) (c)	93	100	63	10	53	37	3	34	13	87		+2.65	6	6	10	1
Kikuyu (*Karatina*) (a)	24	100	67	54	13	33	25	8	79	21		+3.67	10	6	9	5
(Kirimukuyu) (b)	26	100	77			23			57	43		+3.67	9	8	9	5
(Kiambaa) (c)	43	91	86	81	5	14	14	nil	95	5		+3.67	10[5]	8	8	—
Embu (*Runyenjes*)	36	95	53	29	24	47	29	18	58	42		+3.67	9	2	4	6
Meru (Katheri s/1) (a)	162	100	47	32	15	53	30	23	62	38		+3.67	6	3	6	nil
(Ntima) (b)	149	98	54	32	22	46	16	30	48	52		+3.67	8	3	10	1
Kamba (Mbitini) (a)	29	100	76	59	17	24	14	10	73	27		+3.67	9	4	4	nil
(Kambai) (b)	44	95	61	13	48	39	19	20	32	68		+3.67	7	2	5	4
Kips./Luo/Gusii (*Sondu*)	80 Luo 39 / Kips. 34 / Gusii 26 / Nub. 1)		85	19	66	15	9	6	28	72		+3.67	4	2	5	5
Luo/Luyia (*Maseno*)	51 Luo 53 / Luyia 47		73	24	49	27	18	9	42	58			7	4	7	nil

* Abstraction from figures in table V.4 of *Kenya Population Census* (1962) vol. III, Ministry of Economic Planning and Development, Nairobi, 1966, p. 38. The figures represent the percentage difference between the two age groups.

1 Included 5 Gujarati, 2 Arabs, 1 Kuria, 1 Logoli, 1 Gusii. The sample is anomalous in that it contains no farmers, 86% being semi-skilled, skilled artisans or professionals, including 30% teachers.

2 The sample is 100% homogeneous Luyia but at most only 89% homogeneous Idakho.

3 The sample is 100% homogeneous Luyia but at most only 94% homogeneous Logoli.

4 Includes 28% Teso.

5 Educational figures largely estimated due to failure to answer questions.

Note: Samples are identified by their geographical location, in locational or sub-locational terms. In some cases the nearest settlement has been used to identify the sample e.g. where more than one sub-location is involved. In these cases the reference is italicized.

TABLE 1.8 *Percentage claiming monolingual competence*

	% of sample	% Constituents				Average years' education	
		Men		Women			
		−30	30+	−30	30+	Men	Women
Luo (*Oyugis*)	49	5	43	15	37	1	1
Meru (Katheri)	39	2	17	32	49	nil	nil
Kipsigis (Lugumek s/1)	37	2	7	38	53	nil	nil
Gusii/Kips./Luo border. Luo	23	14	43	29	14	nil	4
Kuria (*Kihancha*)	21	—	33	—	67	nil	nil
Taita (*Wundanyi*)	17	—	15	—	100	—	nil
Meru (Ntima)	17	4	15	4	77	nil	nil
Pokomo (Zubaki)	16	—	40	—	60	nil	nil
Luyia (Idakho)	14	10	25	16	74	2	—
Luyia (Logoli)	11	—	25	—	75	—	1
Kamba (Mbitini)	10	—	—	—	100	—	nil
Gusii	9	—	10	50	90	nil	nil
Luo (Gusii border)	5	—	10	—	50	1	2
Kikuyu (*Karatina*)	4	—	100	—	—	1	—
Luo/Luyia border. Luo	4	—	—	—	100	nil	nil
Embu (*Runyenje's*)	—	—	—	—	—	—	—
Kikuyu (Kiambaa) (Kirimukuyu)	—	—	—	—	—	—	—
Kamba (Kambai s/L)	—	—	—	—	—	—	—
Pokomo (Salama) (Gwano)	—	—	—	—	—	—	—
Luyia (Bukusu) (Khayo)	—	—	—	—	—	—	—
Gusii/Kips./Luo border. Kipsigis Gusii	—	—	—	—	—	—	—
Luo/Luyia border. Luyia	—	—	—	—	—	—	—

TABLE 1.9 *Percentage claiming bilingual (L1+Sw.) competence*

	% of sample	Men −30	Men 30+	Women −30	Women 30+	Average years' education Men	Average years' education Women
Pokomo (Gwano)	52	7	13	37	43	1	nil
Gusii	51	12	66	6	16	2	1
Pokomo (Salama)	45	—	55	18	27	2	2
(Zubaki)	38	9	34	6	51	1	nil
Kuria (*Kihancha*)	36	—	40	40	20	2	1.5
Luyia (Idakho)	34	48	18	20	14	1	1
(Bukusu)	34	26	22	19	33	3	1
(Logoli)	29	—	50	40	10	—	1
Taita (*Wundanyi*)	28	—	20	30	50	2	3
Kipsigis (Lugumek s/1)	26	—	56	21	13	nil	nil
Luo (Gusii border)	23	20	70	—	10	2	3
Gusii/Kips./Luo border. Luo	19	33	67	—	—	2	—
Luyia (Khayo)	18	—	21	8	71	4	3
Kamba (Kambai)	16	—	14	57	29	nil	1
Luo (*Oyugis*)	12	8	31	46	15	5	—
Meru (Ntima)	11	6	59	23	12	1	—
(Katheri)	8	38	54	—	8	—	—
Gusii/Kips./Luo border. Gusii	5	—	100	—	—	4	—
Kikuyu (Kirimukuyu)	4	—	100	—	—	nil	—
(Kiambaa)	2	—	100	—	—	8	—
Embu (*Runyenje's*)	—	—	—	—	—	—	—
Kikuyu (*Karatina*)	—	—	100	—	—	3	—
Kamba (Mbitini)	10	—	—	—	—	—	—
Gusii/Kips./Luo border. Kipsigis	—	—	—	—	—	—	—
Luo/Luyia border. Luo	—	—	—	—	—	—	—
Luyia	—	—	—	—	—	—	—

TABLE 1.10. *Percentage claiming bilingual (L1 + Eng.) competence*

	% of sample	Men		Women		Average years' education	
		−30	30+	−30	30+	Men	Women
Gusii/Kips./Luo border. Gusii	30	50	16	17	17	7	7
Luo (*Oyugis*)	18	45	5	50	—	8	7
Luo/Luyia border. Luo	7	100	—	—	—	7	—
Gusii/Kips./Luo border. Luo	6	50	50	80	—	8	5
Meru (Katheri)	6	20	—	50	—	8	8
Luo (Gusii border)	5	50	—	86	—	8	6
Meru (Ntima)	5	14	—	—	—	7	—
Gusii/Kips./Luo border. Kipsigis	4	100	—	100	—	—	10
Kikuyu (*Karatina*)	4	—	—	—	—	3	—
Kuria (*Kihancha*)	4	100	—	—	—	—	8
Embu (*Runyenje's*)	3	—	—	50	—	7	6
Kipsigis (Lugumek s/1)	1	50	—	50	100	7	—
Taita (*Wundanyi*)	—	—	—	—	—	—	—
Kikuyu (Kiambaa)	—	—	—	—	—	—	—
(Kirimukuyu)	—	—	—	—	—	—	—
Kamba (Mbitini)	—	—	—	—	—	—	—
(Kambai)	—	—	—	—	—	—	—
Pokomo (Salama)	—	—	—	—	—	—	—
(Gwano)	—	—	—	—	—	—	—
(Zubaki)	—	—	—	—	—	—	—
Gusii							
Luyia (Bukusu)	—	—	—	—	—	—	—
(Logoli)	—	—	—	—	—	—	—
(Khayo)	—	—	—	—	—	—	—
(Idakho)	—	—	—	—	—	—	—
Luo/Luyia border. Luyia	—	—	—	—	—	—	—

TABLE 1.11 *Percentage claiming bilingual (L1+L2) competence*

	% of sample	Men −30	Men 30+	Women −30	Women 30+	Avg yrs educ. Men	Avg yrs educ. Women	L2
Gusii/Kips./Luo border. **Kipsigis**	41	27	73	—	37	nil	—	Luo (10)
Luo/Luyia border. **Luo**	30	—	63	17	17	1	nil	Luyia
Luyia	25	25	66	25	25	1.5	nil	Luo
Gusii/Kips./Luo border. **Gusii**	20	25	50	—	20	nil	3	Luo (2)
Luo	13	—	50	20	50	1	4	Gusii (3); Kipsigis (2)
Kamba (Kambai)	11	—	60	—	50	nil	1	5 Kikuyu, i.e. all
Luyia (Khayo)	6	—	50	—	100	—	—	
Embu (*Runyenje's*)	3	—	100	—	—	nil	3	
Pokomo (Salama)	1	—	—	—	100	—	nil	
(Gwano)	1	—	—	—	100	nil	nil	
Meru (Ntima)	1	—	100	—	100	—	nil	
(Katheri)	0.5	—	100	—	100	nil	nil	
Kipsigis (Lugumek s/1)	—	—	—	—	—	nil	nil	
Luo (*Oyugis*)	—	—	—	—	—	—	—	
Taita (*Wundanyi*)	—	—	—	—	—	—	—	
Kuria (*Kihancha*)	—	—	—	—	—	—	—	
Kikuyu (Karatina)	—	—	—	—	—	—	—	
(Kiambaa)	—	—	—	—	—	—	—	
(Kirimukuyu)	—	—	—	—	—	—	—	
Kamba (Mbitini)	—	—	—	—	—	—	—	
Pokomo (Zubaki)	—	—	—	—	—	—	—	
Gusii	—	—	—	—	—	—	—	
Luyia (Bukusu)	—	—	—	—	—	—	—	
(Logoli)	—	—	—	—	—	—	—	
(Idakho)	—	—	—	—	—	—	—	
Luo (Gusii border)	—	—	—	—	—	—	—	

TABLE 1.12 *Percentage claiming trilingual (L1+L2+Sw.) competence*

	% of sample	Men -30	Men 30+	Women -30	Women 30+	Avg. years' ed. Men	Avg. years' ed. Women	L2
Luyia (Khayo)	37	—	38	4	58	1	—	Teso dominant here
Gusii/Kips./Luo border. **Kipsigis**	26	—	100	—	—	1	4	6 Luo
Luo/Luyia border. **Luyia**	25	—	83	17	—	1	1	Galla as L2
Pokomo (Zubaki).	23	5	71	25	24	1	2	4 Luo
Gusii/Kips./Luo border. **Gusii**	20	—	75	—	—	2	—	3 Gusii; 2 Kipsigis
Luo	16	—	100	—	—	2	—	8 Sanye; 2 Galla
Pokomo (Gwano)	16	—	57	—	22	nil	—	Maasai (10); Kikuyu (6); Kamba (1)
Kipsigis (Lugumek s/1)	14	21	81	8	11	—	nil	Galla as L2
Pokomo (Salama)	7	—	100	—	—	nil	5	9 Kikuyu
Meru (Ntima)	6	23	11	33	33	2	1	5 Kikuyu; 3 Nandi
Luyia (Idakho)	6	13	50	25	12	2	—	
Gusii	5	—	100	—	—	nil	—	
Luo/Luyia border. **Luo**	4	—	100	—	50	nil	1	
Kamba (Kambai)	4	—	50	—	50	4	—	
(Mbitini)	3	100	—	—	—	nil	—	
Taita (*Wundanyi*)	3	—	100	—	—	nil	—	
Luo (Gusii border)	2	—	100	—	—	5	—	
(*Oyugis*)	2	—	50	50	—	nil	nil	Gusii (1)
Kikuyu (Kiambaa)	2	—	100	—	—	8	—	
Kuria (*Kihancha*)	—	—	—	—	—	—	—	
Embu (*Runyenje's*)	—	—	—	—	—	—	—	
Kikuyu (*Karatina*)	—	—	—	—	—	—	—	
(*Kirimukuyu*)	—	—	—	—	—	—	—	
Meru (*Katheri*)	—	—	—	—	—	—	—	
Luyia (*Bukusu*)	—	—	—	—	—	—	—	
(*Logoli*)	—	—	—	—	—	—	—	

TABLE 1.13 *Percentage claiming trilingual (L1+L2+L3) competence*

	% of sample	Men		Women		Average years' education		L2
		−30	30+	−30	30+	Men	Women	
Luyia (Logoli)	6	—	—	50	50	nil	3	2 Tiriki; 2 Luo
Gusii/Kips./Luo border. **Kipsigis**	4	—	100	—	—	nil	—	Luo/Nandi
Meru (Ntima)	1	—	100	—	—	nil	—	Embu/Kikuyu
Luo (*Oyugis*)	—	—	—	—	—	—	—	
(Gusii border)	—	—	—	—	—	—	—	
Taita (*Wundanyi*)	—	—	—	—	—	—	—	
Kuria (*Kihancha*)	—	—	—	—	—	—	—	
Embu (*Runyenje's*)	—	—	—	—	—	—	—	
Kipsigis (Lugumek s/1)	—	—	—	—	—	—	—	
Kikuyu (*Karatina*)	—	—	—	—	—	—	—	
(Kiambaa)	—	—	—	—	—	—	—	
(Kirimukuyu)	—	—	—	—	—	—	—	
Kamba (Mbitini)	—	—	—	—	—	—	—	
(Kambai)	—	—	—	—	—	—	—	
Meru (Katheri)	—	—	—	—	—	—	—	
Pokomo (Salama)	—	—	—	—	—	—	—	
(Gwano)	—	—	—	—	—	—	—	
(Zubaki)	—	—	—	—	—	—	—	
Gusii	—	—	—	—	—	—	—	
Luyia (Bukusu)	—	—	—	—	—	—	—	
(Idakho)	—	—	—	—	—	—	—	
Gusii/Kips./Luo border. **Luo**	—	—	—	—	—	—	—	
Gusii	—	—	—	—	—	—	—	
Luo/Luyia border. **Luo**	—	—	—	—	—	—	—	
Luyia	—	—	—	—	—	—	—	

TABLE 1.14 *Percentage claiming trilingual (L1+L2+Eng.) competence*

	% of sample	Men		Women		Average years' education		
		−30	30+	−30	30+	Men	Women	
Luo/Luyia border. Luo	33	44	23	33	—	6	9	
Gusii/Kips./Luo border. Gusii	10	—	—	50	50	—	7	Kikuyu as L2
Kamba (Kambai)	4	100	—	100	—	7	—	
Gusii/Kips./Luo border. Kipsigis	3	—	—	—	—	—	5	
Meru (Katheri)	1	—	—	100	—	—	—	
Luo (Oyugis)	—	—	—	—	—	—	—	
(Gusii border)	—	—	—	—	—	—	—	
Taita (Wundanyi)	—	—	—	—	—	—	—	
Kuria (Kihancha)	—	—	—	—	—	—	—	
Embu (Runyenje's)	—	—	—	—	—	—	—	
Kipsigis (Lugumek s/1)	—	—	—	—	—	—	—	
Kikuyu (Karatina)	—	—	—	—	—	—	—	
(Kiambaa)	—	—	—	—	—	—	—	
(Kirimukuyu)	—	—	—	—	—	—	—	
Kamba (Mbitini)	—	—	—	—	—	—	—	
Meru (Ntima)	—	—	—	—	—	—	—	
Pokomo (Salama)	—	—	—	—	—	—	—	
(Gwano)	—	—	—	—	—	—	—	
(Zubaki)	—	—	—	—	—	—	—	
Gusii	—	—	—	—	—	—	—	
Luyia (Bukusu)	—	—	—	—	—	—	—	
(Logoli)	—	—	—	—	—	—	—	
(Khayo)	—	—	—	—	—	—	—	
(Idakho)	—	—	—	—	—	—	—	
Gusii/Kips./Luo border. Luo	—	—	—	—	—	—	—	
Luo/Luyia border. Luyia	—	—	—	—	—	—	—	

TABLE 1.15 *Percentage claiming trilingual (LI+Sw.+Eng.) competence*

	% of sample	Men		Women		Average years' education	
		−30	30+	−30	30+	Men	Women
Kikuyu (Kirimukuyu)	92	46	29	17	8	8	8
(Kiambaa)	84	83	—	17	—	10	9
(*Karatina*)	83	60	10	25	5	10	10
Kamba (Mbitini)	72	76	5	19	—	9	10
Luyia (Bukusu)	64	57	23	20	—	8	6
Taita (*Wundanyi*)	50	44	6	44	6	7	7
Meru (Ntima)	47	51	14	30	5	8	8
(Katheri)	37	52	10	38	—	6	7
Luyia (Idakho)	36	61	7	32	—	7	7
Gusii	31	47	33	17	3	8	7
Luo (Gusii border)	28	67	8	25	—	7	7
Kuria (*Kihancha*)	25	86	—	14	—	8	6
Pokomo (Gwano)	22	37	10	53	—	8	6
(Salama)	20	55	12	33	—	9	7
Embu (*Runyenje's*)	17	67	17	16	—	9	8
Kipsigis (Lugumek s/1)	16	77	4	19	—	9	5
Luo (*Oyugis*)	15	50	38	12	—	8	6.5
Luyia (Khayo)	15	25	50	8	17	8	7
Gusii/Kips./Luo border. Gusii	15	34	66	—	—	7	
Luo	13	—	100	—	—	5	
Kamba (Kambai)	11	40	20	20	20	6	5
Luyia (Logoli)	6	50	—	50	—	7	5
Pokomo (Zubaki)	6	34	66	—	—	7	
Gusii/Kips./Luo border. Kipsigis	4	100	—	—	—	7	
Luo/Luyia border. Luo	—	—	—	—	—	—	
Luyia	—	—	—	—	—	—	

46

TABLE 1.16 *Percentage claiming quadrilingual competence (commonly L1+Eng.+Sw.+L3)*

	% of sample	Men		Women		Average years' education		Most common 4th language
		−30	30+	−30	30+	Men	Women	
Embu (*Runyenje's*)	78	14	36	39	11	8	7	Kikuyu (26)
Kamba (*Kambai*)	52	17	65	—	17	5	4	Kikuyu (19) Luo (5)
Luo/Luyia border. Luyia	50	33	42	25	—	7	8	Luo (12)
Luyia (*Logoli*)	49	17	65	18	—	4	6	Kik. (9); Nandi (6) Luo (5)*
Luo (*Gusii border*)	37	44	44	6	6	7	8	Gusii (16); Kamba (4); Kikuyu (4); Kipsigis (2)
Pokomo (*Salama*)	31	14	78	8	—	5	8	Gir. (18); Galla (11); Digo(6)
Luyia (*Khayo*)	23	—	67	17	16	4	6	Teso dominant
Luo/Luyia border. Luo	22	33	50	17	—	8	12	Luyia (5)
Gusii/Kips./Luo border. Kipsigis	18	—	100	—	—	4	—	Luo (5)
Pokomo (*Zubaki*)	17	25	75	—	—	4	—	Galla
Kuria (*Kihancha*)	14	25	25	50	—	6	7	Luo (2)
Kikuyu (*Kiambaa*)	12	100	—	—	—	9	—	Kamba (2); Gusii, Kal. Luo
Luyia (*Idakho*)	12	12	81	7	—	3	3	Kik. (10); Luo (8); Nandi (6); Kamba (5); Ganda (4)
Meru (*Ntima*)	12	39	33	22	6	7	7	
Pokomo (*Gwano*)	9	50	50	—	—	6	—	Galla (2); Sanye (3); Digo (1); Gir. (1)
Gusii/Kips./Luo border. Luo	10	—	33	33	33	8	5	Gusii (2); Kips. (1); Luyia (1)
Meru (*Katheri*)	8	62	23	15	—	9	9	Kikuyu (9)
Kikuyu (*Karatina*)	8	50	—	—	50	13	4	Kamba (2)
Kipsigis (*Lugumek s/l*)	6	36	64	—	—	2	—	Kik. (7); Maasai (2); Gusii (2); Luo (2)
Kikuyu (*Kirimukuyu*)	4	—	100	—	—	8	—	1 Luo; 1 Kamba
Luo (*Oyugis*)	4	40	60	—	—	7.5	—	Gusii (3); Sukuma (1)
Taita (*Wundanyi*)	3	—	100	—	—	10	—	Kikuyu (1)
Kamba (*Mbitini*)	3	—	100	100	—	4	—	Kikuyu (1)
Luyia (*Bakusu*)	2	33	—	—	—	—	4	Tachoni (2)
Gusii/Kips./Luo border. Gusii	—	—	67	—	—	7	—	Luo (2)

*Figure affected by nine respondents listing other Luyia languages.

Note: For the purpose of this table a competence in French or other European languages was *not* regarded as contributing to quadrilingualism.

possible lines for future development. If some readers feel that they only confirm what common sense could have predicted, they can at least have the satisfaction of some corroboration for intuition. What must be stressed, however, is that the figures by themselves do not *prove* anything: they merely point to areas for further and more detailed study.

MONOLINGUAL COMPETENCE (Table 1.8)

This is generally a feature of the older generation and of women rather than men. It is also a function of lack of access to education, and it is certainly true that the samples of groups with scores of 14 per cent or more (Luo, Meru (a), Kipsigis, Luo (Sondu), Kuria, Taita, Meru (b), Pokomo (Zubaki) and Idakho), were taken, with the possible exception of the last, from somewhat less developed areas. All these samples were highly homogeneous, with the exception of Luo (Sondu), where the figure is markedly lower than for the 'core' Luo of Oyugis and might be interpreted as a concession to the increased heterogeneity of the area (cf. figures for L1+L2).

Areas marked by a low incidence of monolingualism or a complete absence, include Kikuyu, Kamba, Embu, Pokomo (the two southern samples), Bukusu and Khayo. While it is true that in two of the Kikuyu samples the 30+ group are markedly under-represented, it seems at least possible that other factors are responsible for this fact: in the case of Kikuyu, Kamba and Embu, the average education of the 30+ group is high enough for them to have had at least some schooling in Swahili and/or English, indeed in Kikuyu (Kirimukuyu) 37 per cent of those claiming competence in L1+Sw.+Eng. were over 30. In Embu there appears to be a strong incentive to learn Kikuyu, and 78 per cent of the admittedly small sample claim competence in four languages. Forty-seven per cent of this group was over 30. The southern locations of Pokomo are so close to the coast that ability to speak Swahili seems wholly understandable. While the Bukusu sample was homogeneous, the area generally seems to be one of markedly lower homogeneity (see Table 1.6), where Swahili has a wider application than in neighbouring areas. The general level of education is also fairly high. This is also true for Khayo where the sample was only 72 per cent homogeneous and where the use of Teso and Swahili appears to be widespread.

BILINGUAL COMPETENCE, L1+SW. (TABLE 1.9)

In those areas where the general level of homogeneity is lower, or where there are strong ties with the coast, the over-30 group with minimal education tends to claim competence in Swahili as well as in the Ll. These factors alone, however, do not account for the pattern that emerges from the sample. Why do more than half the total sample of Gusii claim to speak Swahili? The sample as such, and Gusii generally, are highly homogeneous; there is little tradition of urban migration, and Gusii, as a whole, are in my experience, rather nationalistic about their language. There are at least two possible explanations for this: since over 80 per cent of those claiming this competence are over 30 (average age 40) their competence might go back to the period when the district administered both Gusii and Luo. Returning to the district in 1968 after an absence of ten years it was certainly my impression that Swahili had yielded ground to English in government offices. A second possible explanation is that, since Gusii has never had a stable orthography nor any tradition of primary school materials, Swahili was taught from the outset of education. This would need to be so in this case, since the average years' education is only 2 for the men and 1 year for the women.

The figures for Kipsigis and Kuria are less problematical: both have a long tradition of service with the police and the army where Swahili was usual; but it is interesting to note that for both these groups more than 50 per cent of those claiming competence in Swahili claim it at the lower end of the scale as is also the case with frequency. As again it is the older age group that claims such competence it seems reasonable to suggest that their Swahili competence represents a skill no longer needed as frequently as formerly.

There is an overall lower level of homogeneity among the Luyia but it is noticeable that of the 34 per cent reported from the Idakho sample, 68 per cent are from the *under*-30 age group, with a rather low educational level. Could this be interpreted as indicating poor educational facilities, with youngsters acquiring their skills in Swahili informally?

BILINGUAL L1 + ENG. (TABLE 1.10)

With two exceptions the recorded percentages are very low; in general people with a competence in English acquired at school have also acquired some competence in Swahili. In the case of Luo (a), 95 per cent are under 30 and have an average educational attainment which elsewhere would have involved a competence in Swahili. It seems reasonable to infer that either the language is not taught in schools locally or there is an antipathy to the language such that people will not admit to knowing it.

How one is to interpret the Gusii figure from Sondu is more difficult but it is a very small sample and too much importance should not be given to it. The sample is again mainly under 30, and if Swahili were not

49

being taught in Luo schools then this might well be true of border schools. If this were so, however, one would have expected Luo and Kipsigis in the sample to have been affected.

BILINGUAL L1+L2 (TABLE 1.11)

Again the recorded percentages are very low, with three exceptions, all of which are really border areas. The Kamba sample is close to the southern border with Kikuyu and the figure is remarkable only in its smallness. In the two border areas in western Kenya it is mainly the over-30s with minimal education, and particularly the men, who acquire the extra skills. Kipsigis, Luyia and Gusii seem somewhat readier to learn Luo than do Luo to return the compliment, but this requires to be supported by more detailed sociological evidence. On the Luo/Luyia border, however, it is the Luyia who seem reluctant to learn Luo.

These remarks should be read as applying to this pattern of competence only. If the total sample were considered then 100 per cent of the Luyia claim some competence in Luo—irrespective of what other language they may speak—while only 88 per cent of Luo claim competence in Luyia. In Sondu the percentage of those who claim competence in other languages is as under:

Group claiming competence	Language of claimed competence		
	Kipsigis	Luo	Gusii
Kipsigis	100	88	4
Luo	13	100	19
Gusii	10	45	100

TRILINGUAL L1+L2+SW. (TABLE 1.12)

This is really an extension of the previous pattern, with the high scores occurring in those samples which border on or are near other groups. Thus Kipsigis report 14 per cent, of whom the largest number claim competence in Maasai, reasonable enough for this southern group of Kipsigis bordering on the Mara River and Maasai country. Similarly, the most northerly of the Pokomo samples, report 23 per cent, with the largest number claiming competence in Galla. Khayo, with the highest incidence of this pattern, 37 per cent, is also the sample characterized by the lowest degree of homogeneity—24 per cent of the sample being Teso. The differential competence in Luyia/Teso is well illustrated from the following figures:

Interviewee	Spouse	Number	% claiming competence in	
			Luyia	Teso
Teso man	Teso	4	100	
Teso man	Luyia	3	100	
Teso woman	Teso	4	100	
Teso woman	Luyia	8	100	
Luyia man	Teso	10		60
Luyia man	Luyia	20		37
Luyia woman	Teso	5		60
Luyia woman	Luyia	21		20

Note: The numbers involved contain discrepancies because some spouses were not available for interview.

It seems to be the case that Teso are an intrusive minority in this area, which would provide an adequate incentive for them to acquire skills in Luyia, but further work is necessary before such a suggestion merits serious consideration.

As one would expect, the Luo/Gusii/Kipsigis and Luo/Luyia border samples report a high score for this pattern, but again, Luo resistance to Swahili shows up in a score lower than those of the other groups.

TRILINGUAL L1+L2+L3 (TABLE 1.13)

This is a rare pattern and in no case was a substantial percentage reported: the two highest being 6 and 4 per cent respectively. In both these cases, Logoli and Kipsigis (*Sondu*), high percentages are reported for L1+L2 (Kipsigis) or for quadrilingual competence (Logoli), and both these may be seen as functions of the heterogeneity of the areas concerned.

TRILINGUAL L1+L2+ENG. (TABLE 1.14)

Again a rare pattern, but a high percentage is reported from Luo (*Sondu*), recalling the high figure from Oyugis for the L1+Eng. pattern with its characteristic lack of competence in Swahili. The second highest figure from Gusii (*Sondu*) recalls the high L1+Eng. score for that group. Here, however, the lack of competence in Swahili is more difficult to account for and certainly quite different from the Manga situation.

TRILINGUAL L1+SW.+ENG. (TABLE 1.15)

Six groups report percentages of 50 per cent or above, with the three Kikuyu samples reporting over 80 per cent. Five more groups would fall into this category if cognizance were taken of quadrilingual competence. In the Kikuyu samples the under-30 group tends to be very much over-represented, due to the presence in homesteads of numbers of young

TABLE 1.17 *Some characteristics of those claiming quadrilingual competence*

	Men					Women			
		Average					Average		
	%	Age	Years' education	% earning	% lived away	%	Age	Years' education	% earning	% lived away
Embu	50	35	7	79	—	50	26	7	71	—
Kamba (Kambai)	83	41	5	63	95	17	45	4	nil	75
Luyia (L/Luy. border)	82	33	8	89	—	18	19	6	100	—
Luyia (Logoli)	82	48	4	43	—	18	20	6	nil	—
Luo (b)	87	30	7	85	70	13	26	8	100	100
Pokomo (Salama)	90	40	5	38	75?	10	25	8	33	75?
Luyia (Khayo)	71	43	4	42	75	29	30	6	20	40
Luo (L/Luy. border)	71	45	8	40	—	29	24	12	100	—
Kipsigis (L/G/K border)	100	36	4	100	60					
Pokomo (Zubaki)	100	38	5	14	64					
Kuria	50	36	6	100	—	50	21	7	50	—
Luyia (Idakho)	94	43	3	73	53	6	25	3	nil	nil
Meru (Ntima)	72	31	7	54	70	28	22	6	100	40
Meru (Katheri)	85	29	8	91	82	15	20	9	nil	nil
Some particularly small samples:										
Kikuyu (Kiambaa)	100	20	9	40	—					
Luo (L/G/K border)	33	51	8	nil	100	67	40	5	50	100
Kikuyu (Karatina)	50	21	13	nil	nil	50	40	4	100	100
Areas reporting lower percentages:										
Pokomo (Gwano)	100	37	6	33	100					
Kipsigis	100	36	2	64	100					
Luo (Oyugis)	100	32	7	80	80					

Note: (a) Column 4 gives the percentage of those claiming to be wage-earners, whether or not they also report being peasant farmers.
(b) Column 5 gives the percentage of those who report having lived away from their home area for more than a year.

people who are at present unemployed. This pattern is treated in greater detail below.

QUADRILINGUAL COMPETENCE (TABLE 1.16)

If one were to meet a Kenyan who claimed quadrilingual competence, the chances are that he would be a man in his middle thirties or rather older (unless he were a Meru), with 5/6 years' education. He would probably be a wage-earner, and have spent some time out of his home area. Should the Kenyan turn out to be a woman, she would be likely to be several years younger, perhaps in her mid-twenties, and to be slightly better educated. She might well be a wage-earner, but, though the evidence is scrappy and the sample small, she would probably be rather less likely to have spent time away from home (Table 1.17).

Some groups show a far greater propensity for quadrilingual competence than others. As will be seen from Table 1.16, Embu, Kamba (Kambai), Luyia (L/Luy. border) and Logoli show the highest incidence—half the sample or more. In the first two cases the commonest fourth language is Kikuyu, and since the samples are not far from the Kikuyu border this fact is not difficult to account for, though it would be interesting to have much further data to account for the high percentages. In the case of the Luo/Luyia border, the commonest fourth language reported by Luyia is Luo, a compliment not returned, it may be remarked, by their Luo neighbours. Logoli are near neighbours of both Luo and Nandi and both these languages figure in the reports, but both are less frequently reported than is Kikuyu. In this connection it is worth noting that taking all the samples Kikuyu is reported as a fourth (fifth, sixth, etc.) language more than twice as often as any other language. Luo is next most frequent, and then Kamba, Luyia, Giriama, Gusii and Galla (cf. census figures in Table 1.3). Of other groups reporting a high degree of quadrilingualism, mention should be made of the Luo sample from the Gusii border, where Gusii is the most frequently reported fourth language, and where the incidence of quadrilingualism is in marked contrast to the other sample, taken from some miles to the south-west. Pokomo (Salama) should also be noted, with a high incidence of competence in Giriama and Galla; as one moves north the competence in Giriama diminishes, while that of Galla, in the north, increases.

Of the areas reporting low scores, Luo and Kipsigis are conspicuous examples (cf. their monolingualism scores in Table 1.8), though the most frequently cited fourth language is Kikuyu and not Maasai, as one might be led to expect from the location of this sample. We need here to know much more about the character of inter-group relations across borders.

SUMMARY

It is probably easiest to summarize the information contained in the tables by a diagram which indicates very roughly the patterns which appear to characterize the various groups, and thus provide some initial hypotheses for further research in this field.

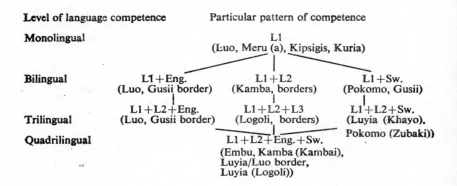

Level of language competence	Particular pattern of competence		
Monolingual		L1 (Luo, Meru (a), Kipsigis, Kuria)	
Bilingual	L1+Eng. (Luo, Gusii border)	L1+L2 (Kamba, borders)	L1+Sw. (Pokomo, Gusii)
Trilingual	L1+L2+Eng. (Luo, Gusii border)	L1+L2+L3 (Logoli, borders)	L1+L2+Sw. (Luyia (Khayo),
Quadrilingual		L1+L2+Eng.+Sw. (Embu, Kamba (Kambai), Luyia/Luo border, Luyia (Logoli))	Pokomo (Zubaki))

D. SWAHILI IN RURAL KENYA

Kenya is rich in myths about the competence in Swahili of her rural populations. They vary from travellers' tales to the dogmatic assertions of the European settler: 'It was perhaps a relief to the waiter to encounter our clumsy, basic version of the language, which at least he understood. The words were Swahili, but by ignoring all the grammar everything was greatly simplified, provided that no profound, complex or subtle thoughts had to be conveyed.'[24] There are also myths held by one group of another, thus, 'Luo don't speak good Swahili, they don't like it', 'Luyia speak the best up-country Swahili, much better than the Kikuyu', and so on. We know very little about the varieties of Swahili current in rural Kenya,[25] and equally little about the models available to people either for formal or informal acquisition. The books used in schools may reflect 'Standard' Swahili as described by such texts as Ashton or Perrott, but what is the model of the recently published *Masomo ya Kiswahili*?[26] Is it the speech of the author; current speech in Dar es Salaam, or Nairobi; or is it the Swahili of existing written descriptions that is being used?

Similarly, the programmes put out by the Voice of Kenya offer no particular model but a choice, exemplified by different programmes. Advertisements appear to belong to a special language of advertisement; the news owes much to English; 'Mzee Pembe' presents a 'coastal' type

54

of Swahili characteristic—or at least commonly held to be characteristic—of the Nairobi suburb of Pumwani where several of the participants live (1968/9). On the other hand 'Cheka na Kipanga' draws its laughs from parodying the different varieties of Swahili which are held to be recognizable, e.g. Luo, Kikuyu, Kamba, Kipsigis, etc.

The Press Directory for 1968/9 listed thirteen papers which appear either wholly or partly in Swahili; some of these are published by religious bodies, e.g. *Sauti ya Vita, Mapenzi ya Mungu;* others by commercial organizations, e.g. *Sikio, Uchumi wa Kahawa,* and yet others are published by government ministries, e.g. *Kenya Yetu.* All these are directed towards specific audiences and probably have a rather small reading public. The two nationals, the daily *Taifa Leo* and the weekly *Baraza,* have a much wider impact: about half of *Taifa Leo's* daily sale in Kenya (September 1968) was in Nairobi and Mombasa, while *Baraza's* main sales appear to be in the Rift Valley and Central Provinces (November 1968). One cannot make any useful generalizations about the Swahili of these papers without a protracted and detailed analysis, and one must in any case recognize that editorial policy, even with respect to language, can change. At the time of the Survey, I was told on many occasions that the Swahili of *Baraza* was much more 'coastal' than it had been, that it was clearly aiming at a 'Tanzanian-type' Swahili, but it was not clear by what features such trends could be discerned. Certainly there is a noticeable absence of Arabic-derived words such as are common on the coast; equally there is much use made of English loans, and many constructions that seem to derive from English. This is no more than an impression, but it would be worth following up.

In addition to the newspapers there are the periodic broadsheets put out by the Ministry of Information and to be found hanging up outside government offices along with a mixture of other notices in local languages and English.

Finally, there are the exclusively spoken varieties of Swahili that have developed as a result of contact between Kenya Africans and Europeans. Barbara Neale discusses some of the characteristics of Asian Swahili in Chapter 2, and the characteristics of 'Kisettla' were amusingly described some years ago in the *Kenya Weekly News.*[27]

I draw attention to these points merely to illustrate that apparently simple questions about the incidence of Swahili in rural Kenya may have complicated answers, if indeed they can be answered at all. The questions need to be set in terms of competing incentives to achieve particular objectives. Will a farmer, for example, anxious to know more about improved methods of coffee cultivation, find it easier, more profitable or more satisfying to do this through English or Swahili, and, what is more, which of these factors is likely to take precedence? It might be easier to increase one's skills in Swahili but more profitable in the long run to increase them in English. Opportunities to acquire or to improve one's skills in Swahili are not easy to come by; he who has a radio may listen to the Voice of Kenya but the time given, for example, to Swahili in its service for schools was running at less than half an hour per week in 1968/9. The range of Swahili books is substantially narrower than that of books in English and a good Swahili dictionary costs more than one in English. If on balance English is favoured for this semi-technical field, there are certainly others in which Swahili is preferred, but in attempting to find answers to the question of incentive, answers to a further set of questions will need to be found, amongst which the following seem to me among the most important:

(a) Will the language be used in the spoken or written mode?

(b) Will the language be used for personal or impersonal reasons, i.e. for entertaining friends or acquiring information on a topic?

(c) Will the language be used as an optimal choice, as *faute de mieux* or for other reasons?

(d) Is it believed that, ideally, skills in both languages should be developed to cover the range of settings for which each language is held to be an optimal choice?

(e) Is there any recognition that different varieties of Swahili may operate in different settings?

Such questions cannot be answered on the basis of interviews alone, but they provide a base on which further work can be carried out. Consideration of aspects relating to language use will be deferred until Chapter 13; here we shall be concerned with the degrees of competence reported by the samples.

In Table 1.18 is listed the claimed competence in Swahili of the rural samples. With the exception of Meru (Katheri) and Kuria, the Bantu groups all reported a high percentage with *some* competence in the language, and the Kikuyu figures seem particularly worthy of note. The non-Bantu groups report a predictably low figure, with those Luo claiming a knowledge of 'quite a lot' of Swahili or more comprising only 6 per cent. Either the non-Bantu groups were unrepresentative, or they concealed their knowledge, or they are antagonistic to the language, or do not require it, or have fewer educational opportunities. There is some evidence that the latter may be, or may have been, a contributory factor since claimed competence in English and/or Swahili (column 1 of Table 1.18) is also low, and the educational levels of the over-30s especially are markedly low. On the other hand, there is also some evidence to suggest that rural Luo, at any rate, show some aversion or lack of incentive, only 15 per cent of the sample claiming a knowledge of Swahili without English, as opposed to 44 per cent for Kipsigis and 39 per cent for Kuria. Even this figure for Kipsigis in substantially below that reported by Heine, but in either case their long tradition of service with army and police is probably a contributory factor to their high figure in comparison with Luo. By contrast 18 per cent of the Luo claim a knowledge of English without Swahili, as opposed to 1 per cent for Kipsigis and 4 per cent for Kuria.

TABLE 1.18 *Claimed competence in English and/or Swahili* (expressed as a percentage of the total sample)

	English/ Swahili	English+ Swahili	English — Swahili	Swahili — English
Luyia (Bukusu)	100	66	nil	34
Kikuyu (Kiambaa)	100	95	nil	5
Pokomo (Salama)	99	38	nil	61
Luyia (Khayo)	92	30	1	61
Gusii (*Manga*)	91	33	1	57
Kamba (Kambai)	89	55	2	32
Luyia (Idakho)	85	39	1	45
Pokomo (Zubaki)	84	10	nil	74
L/K/G border. **Gusii**	80	15	40	25
Kuria (*Kihancha*)	79	36	4	39
L/Luy. border. **Luyia**	75	50	nil	25
L/K/G border. **Luo**	65	19	7	39
L/Luy. border. **Luo**	63	22	37	4
Kipsigis (Lugumek)	62	17	1	44
Meru (Katheri)	60	44	7	9
L/K/G border. **Kipsigis**	56	15	8	33
Luo (*Oyugis*)	51	18	18	15

In Appendix A is presented the details of competence in Swahili and/or English claimed by the samples according to the five-point scale mentioned above. The percentage of the total sample claiming this competence is placed in brackets following the name of the language group. The diagrams thus provide the details for column 1 of Table 1.18. Some of the small samples have been omitted from this tabulation.

While there is a number of straightforward right-ward increasing (Meru) and decreasing (Pokomo (S)), curves, many appear to have two peaks (Kipsigis, Luyia, Pokomo (Z)), at a greater and lesser competence. How can one account for this? One might imagine the higher peak to be associated with a lower age group who had had the benefits of some Swahili at school, but the average age of those claiming competence 4 among Kipsigis and Luyia (Khayo) men, for example, is over 40 in both cases, while that for competence 2 is 39 for Kipsigis, and 38 for Luyia (Khayo) at competence 1 (the number claiming competence 2 is too small to provide a useful basis for comparison). One might suggest from this that older Kipsigis, with less education, for example, required a higher competence in Swahili for their work, while younger people would aim at greater competence in English. Certainly it is among the lower age groups that competence in English is most marked. A more significant factor, however, is the distribution of the sexes. In the Luyia (Khayo) sample mentioned above, all are women, and in the Kipsigis and Luyia (Bukusu) cases also it is the lower age of the women who bring the average age of the sample down to 39 and 33 respectively. In other words it looks as if women not only get less education, but have got it more recently than men; thus if a man of 45 were claiming a competence of 4 in Swahili, then a woman of that age was probably monolingual (see Table 1.8); where a woman of 30 claims competence in Swahili, it is likely that her menfolk will also have competence in English. A further illustration is provided from the Luyia (Idakho) diagram, which shows an overall peak of 3 if men and women are taken jointly, but of only 1 if women are selected.

T A B L E 1.19 *Percentage of males/females in the sample of those claiming competence in Swahili but not English, contrasted with the ratio in the total sample*

	Males		Females	
	Total sample	Swahili sample	Total sample	Swahili sample
L/G/K border	85	(Luo) 92	15	(Luo) 8
		(Kips.) 100		(Kips.) nil
		(Gusii) 80		(Gusii) 20
Gusii (57)	74	80	26	20
Pokomo (S) (61)	73	74	27	26
Luyia (Bukusu) (34)	67	48	33	52
Pokomo (Zubaki) (74)	63	64	37	36
Luyia (Idakho) (45)	62	80	38	20
Kamba (Kambai) (32)	61	36	39	64
Luo (15)	55	44	45	56
Kuria (39)	54	45	46	55
Kipsigis (44)	50	74	50	26
Luyia (Khayo) (62)	47	42	53	58

Note: (a) Figures in brackets indicate the percentage of the total sample who claim this competence.

(b) Those groups for which information is not here included reported very small samples for this pattern of competence.

Further information on the distribution of the sexes is provided by Table 1.19, which relates the overall ratio between the sexes in the sample, to the ratio in the sub-samples claiming L1+ Swahili competence. In most cases men are more numerous overall, and their numerical superiority tends to increase in the sub-sample. In some cases, though, the proportions are reversed, or, in one case, the women simply increase their numerical superiority. This certainly tends to occur where the numerical disparity between the sexes is least great, but not exclusively so. Why, for example, is the ratio in Luyia (Idakho) increased while that of Luyia (Bukusu) reversed? At least part of the answer lies in the fact that in Idakho women constitute 27 per cent of those, who, additionally, claim competence in English, while in Bukusu the figure is only 23 per cent. Again, in Kamba where the reversal of numerical ratios is more striking, women constitute only 17 per cent of those claiming additional competence in English. In other words, one might say that an increase in the number of women in this pattern of bilingualism is suggestive of a situation where women achieve a certain level of education only—enough to give them some competence in Swahili but not enough to take them into competence in English.

TABLE 1.20 *Swahili competence in rural Kenya*

	Percentage of total sample claiming some competence in Swahili	Percentage claiming 1/2 competence, i.e. adequate for simple conversation or less	Percentage claiming 3/5 competence, i.e. 'quite a lot' or more	Heine's figure*
Luyia (Bukusu)	100	53	47	58
Kikuyu (Kiambaa)	100	26	74	49
Pokomo (Salama)	99	6	93	
Kikiuyu (Kirimukuyu)	96	35	61	49
Luya (Khayo)	91	33	58	58
Gusii (*Manga*)	90	31	59	53
Kamba (Kambai)	86	20	66	61
Embu	86	42	44	53
Luyia (Idakho)	84	23	61	58
Pokomo (Zubaki)	84	15	69	
Taita	83	5	78	
Kuria	75	39	36	
L/Luy. border. Luyia	75	54	21	
Kipsigis (Lugumek)	61	42	19	76
L/K/G. border. Luo	58	52	6	
Meru (Katheri)	53	48	5	
L/K/G. Kipsigis	48	48	nil	
L/K/G. Gusii	40	25	15	
Luo (*Oyugis*)	33 (32.7)	26(26.4)	6(6.3)	57
L/Luy. Luo	26	19	7	

* Dr B. Heine, of the University of Cologne, carried out a sociolinguistic survey of western Kenya during 1968. These figures are from his preliminary report, and relate to those who claimed to 'know' Swahili. More precise information on the meaning of this term will doubtless be presented in his final report.

A summing up can be provided through Table 1.20. With the exception of Kuria and Meru (Katheri), 75 per cent or more in the samples from Bantu groups claim some competence in Swahili. If, however, we ask what percentage claim to know 'quite a lot' of Swahili or more, then, apart from Pokomo and Taita, the average falls to 60 per cent. Even so, if this is substantiated by further and more delicate tests, the fact that more than half of the samples claim such competence is highly suggestive for those who wish to see the language established as some form of 'national' language. When it comes to the non-Bantu groups and the border areas, however, the picture is quite otherwise; at this level of competence the average reported is only a little over 10 per cent. Any generalization from these figures would be dangerous, but if one recalls that the non-Bantu groups in Kenya's population constitute something under 30 per cent of the total population, it is clear that if this picture of competence were found to be accurate for these groups, then rather intensive efforts would need to be made to raise the level.

NOTES

[1] J. B. Greenberg, 'The Languages of Africa', *International Journal of American Linguistics*, 29, 1, 1963.

[2] M. A. Bryan and A. N. Tucker, *Distribution of the Nilotic and Nilo-Hamitic Languages of Africa*, Oxford University Press, London, 1948, and retained in their *The Non-Bantu Languages of North-Eastern Africa*, OUP, 1956.

[3] A. N. Tucker and M. A. Bryan, *Linguistic Analyses: the Non-Bantu Languages of North-Eastern Africa*, Oxford University Press, London, 1966. It is surprising that such recent studies as the census (see note 19) and Ominde (see note 18) still retain the use of these terms.

[4] See, for example, ch. 4 by J. E. G. Sutton in B. A. Ogot and J. A. Kieran (eds.), *Zamani: a Survey of East African History*, Longman and East African Publishing House, Nairobi, 1968. See also chs. 7–10 for a more general discussion of the early history of Bantu, Para-Nilotic and Cushitic groups.

[5] M. Guthrie, *The Classification of the Bantu Languages*, Oxford University Press, London, 1948.

[6] Personal communication.

[7] F. I. Deed, *Giryama Exercises*, n.d. and personal notes.

[8] On the evidence of Würtz and personal field-notes.

[9] M. A. Bryan in her compilation *The Bantu Languages of Africa* includes the Pokomo, along with the Nyika languages, in her 'Taita' group.

[10] H. E. Lambert, *The Systems of Land Tenure in the Kikuyu Land Unit*, Communications from the School of African Studies, no. 22, University of Cape Town, 1950, p. 5. H. E. Lambert, *Kikuyu Social and Political Institutions*, Oxford University Press, London, 1956, p. 1.

[11] op. cit.

[12] P. R. Bennett, 'Dahl's Law in Thagicǔ', *African Language Studies*, VIII, 1967. His division of the 'Kikuyu' group is essentially the same as Lambert's.

[13] Tucker and Bryan (1966), op. cit., pp. 402–42. This indispensable mine of information is also my source for the characteristics of Para-Nilotic and Cushitic languages, though I am also indebted to Dr B. W. Andrzejewski for his help. It should be noted that Greenberg lists Luo among his 'Western' Nilotic group.

[14] The bracketed item represents a semi-mute or 'shadow' vowel, the latter term having been introduced for the Para-Nilotic language, Teso, by J. H. Hilders and J. C. D. Lawrance in their *An Introduction to the Ateso Language*, East African Literature Bureau, Nairobi, 1956.

[15] I am grateful to my colleague, Dr B. W. Andrzejewski for the following paragraph. The terms Common, Central and Coastal Somali were introduced by him and I. M. Lewis in their *Somali Poetry: an Introduction*, The Clarendon Press, Oxford, 1964. The term Central corresponds to Moreno's Dighil, and Coastal to his Benadir.

[16] A project which is also being financed through the Survey as a 'Type B' project.

[17] Figures taken from *Kenya Population Census (1962)*; advance report of volumes I and II, Ministry of Finance and Economic Planning, Nairobi, 1964, and (1969), volume I, Ministry of Finance and Economic Planning, Nairobi, 1970.

[18] Reproduced from table V/2 of *Kenya Population Census (1962)*, vol. III, Ministry of Economic Planning and Development, Nairobi, 1966, p. 36.

[19] Dr J. Knappert (personal communication).

[20] S. H. Ominde, *Land and Population Movements in Kenya*, Heinemann, London, 1968, pp. 63–4. Ominde discusses problems of migration in great detail in his chs. 7–8.

[21] Figures taken from *Kenya Population Census (1962)*, tables; advance report of vols. I and II, Ministry of Finance and Economic Planning, Nairobi, 1964.

[22] I should like to express my gratitude to the following students of University College, Nairobi, for their help in carrying out the Survey: Messrs Gacheche, Kimoli, Lang'at, Muriungi, Muchena, Mulwa, Ombogo-Ndong'a, Otula, Radoli, Ruchoya, Sagia, and Tunu; as also to the Misses Macharia, Mjomba, Ngaira and Khasiani.

I should also like to express my gratitude to Mr Onyango-Omuodo of the University College, Dar es Salaam; to Messrs Darigu and Odo of Kwale Secondary School; to Mr Abuga of Manga, Kisii; to Mr Munyinyi of Ndendero, Kiambu; and to Mr Bayles and his assistants from Kangundo.

[23] The following comment from an interviewer is worth quoting: '. . . With the younger, educated élite it was possible to explain and make understand the nature, purpose and importance of this work. But the older generation who are always suspicious of anything on paper, especially when this involves them, proved to be quite an obstacle to the smooth running of the undertaking. Cracking down their suspicion, and attaining their co-operation was like demanding water from a stone, and unless you were a second Moses, the best you could do was to step over them and try more promising fields.'

[24] Elspeth Huxley, *The Mottled Lizard*, Chatto & Windus, London, 1962, p. 11.

[25] Though a substantial collection of taped material on urban varieties of Swahili has now been collected by members of the team.

[26] D. N. Michuki, *Masomo ya Kiswahili* (Teacher's Book I), Jomo Kenyatta Foundation, Nairobi, 1967.

[27] J. W., 'Kisettla', *Kenya Weekly News*, 23 December 1955.

APPENDIX A

Degrees of Competence Claimed in Swahili and English

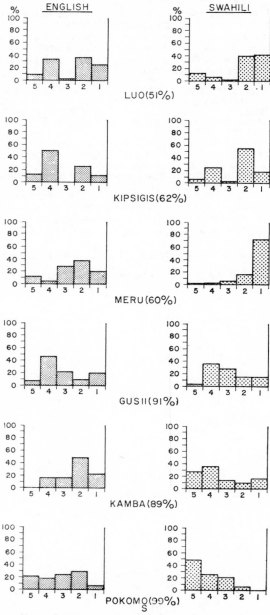

Note: Competence decreases from left to right.
Figures in brackets represent percentage of the total sample claiming competence in Swahili and/or English.

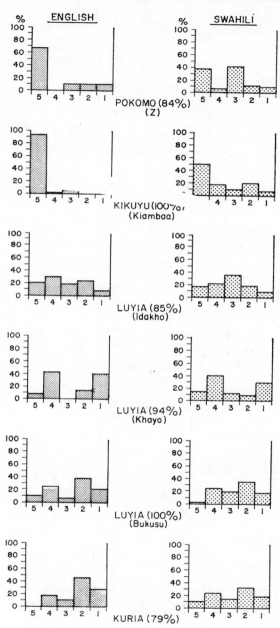

POKOMO (84%)
(Z)

KIKUYU (100%)
(Kiambaa)

LUYIA (85%)
(Idakho)

LUYIA (94%)
(Khayo)

LUYIA (100%)
(Bukusu)

KURIA (79%)

Note: Competence decreases from left to right.
Figures in brackets represent percentage of the
total sample claiming competence in Swahili
and/or English.

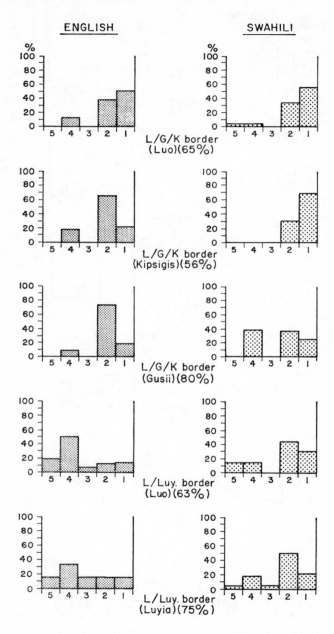

ENGLISH   SWAHILI

L/G/K border
(Luo)(65%)

L/G/K border
(Kipsigis)(56%)

L/G/K border
(Gusii)(80%)

L/Luy. border
(Luo)(63%)

L/Luy. border
(Luyia)(75%)

Note : Competence decreases from left to right.
Figures in brackets represent percentage of the
total sample claiming competence in Swahili
and/or English.

64

APPENDIX B

Note on the Linguistic Situation of the Somali and the Galla in Kenya

B. W. ANDRZEJEWSKI

INTRODUCTORY NOTE

The statements presented here are based on observations made during my linguistic research tours in Kenya in 1957–8 and 1969. As my researches were mainly concerned with the study of the structure, vocabulary and oral literature of Somali and Galla, I have no statistical data at my disposal.

GEOGRAPHICAL DISTRIBUTION AND NOMENCLATURE

The present geographical distribution of the Galla and Somali in Kenya is approximately the same as shown in the *Atlas of Kenya** (p. 22).

The nomenclature referring to tribes that is used by the *Atlas of Kenya* needs some clarification. The Borans, Sakuye, Gabra and Orma are all branches of the Galla. None of these four groups are subdivisions of each other and none of them are Somali.

The designations of Somali tribes in the Atlas are correct but it is necessary to mention certain important points about the Gurreh (pronounced *gárri* in Galla and *gárre* in Somali), and the Ajuran. The former spread into Somalia and Ethiopia, the latter into Somalia.

On the grounds of their historical traditions and their genealogies all the Gurreh and all the Ajuran claim to be Somali; yet the Gurreh in Kenya and Ethiopia predominantly use Galla as their mother tongue, even though the Gurreh living in Somalia use Somali and seldom know any Galla at all.

The case of the Ajuran in Kenya is more complex. They use Galla like the Gurreh, but many of them are bilingual in Galla and Somali. The Ajuran in Somalia normally speak Somali as their mother tongue.

In addition to the Somalis who inhabit the areas indicated in the *Atlas of Kenya*, there are Somali communities in many Kenyan towns.

There are Galla communities in Isiolo and Nairobi.

THE SOMALI

THE MOTHER TONGUE

All Somalis except the Gurreh and the Ajuran speak Somali exclusively as their mother tongue. The Ajuran are very often bilingual in Somali and Galla to an extent which makes it difficult to assess, without very elaborate investigation, which is their dominant language.

The Somali spoken in Kenya is divided into two dialect types:† Common Somali and Central Somali. 'Common Somali' is a dialect type spoken all over the Somali-

---

* Published by the Survey of Kenya. under the direction of R. J. Butler, Nairobi, 1959.

† For further information, see the section 'The Somali Language' in *Somali Poetry: an Introduction* by I. M. Lewis and myself, Oxford Library of African Literature, The Clarendon Press, 1964.

inhabited territories in the Horn of Africa, with the main exception of the Upper Juba Province of Somalia, where the 'Central' (or Rahanweyn) dialect type is spoken, and the Benadir Province of Somalia where Coastal Somali is spoken. Note that Common Somali is used as the standard spoken language of public life in Somalia (including broadcasting) and is used as a lingua franca by many speakers of Central and Coastal Somali.

In Kenya Common Somali is used by all Somalis except in the agricultural riverine settlements in the Mandera district, where Coastal Somali is spoken; however, most of the speakers of Coastal Somali there also speak Common Somali as their second dialect.

It should be noted that the Voice of Kenya also uses the Common Somali dialect type in all their broadcasts in Somali.*

MONOLINGUALISM

The vast majority of the rural Somali population, both pastoral and agricultural, speak only Somali. This statement needs, however, a slight modification which is explained under the headings *Classical Arabic* and *Colloquial Arabic* below.

GALLA

See the statement relating to the Gurreh and the Ajuran tribes in the section on *Geographical distribution*. See also the section *Other languages*.

CLASSICAL ARABIC

Somali men of religion, both in rural areas and in towns, usually have a good reading and writing knowledge of Classical Arabic. Those who have studied in Arab countries speak it well, but those who have not, have a very limited fluency in speaking. Some men of religion have reached such a standard of knowledge that they compose religious poetry and treatises in Classical Arabic, and in fact Wajir is one of the most important centres of Muslim learning in the Horn of Africa, along with Harar, Bardera and Mogadishu.

All Somalis are Muslims, and the vast majority of the ordinary population have some knowledge of Classical Arabic which they use only in private and public prayer. The degree of their knowledge varies, and is usually higher in men than in women. It is quite normal for ordinary people to recite prayers with a very low degree of comprehension of the meaning of individual words.

COLLOQUIAL ARABIC

Colloquial Arabic of the Yemen and Hadramaut dialect type is known by many Somali traders and is used in their contacts with Arab traders in Kenya, and sometimes also when trading with Ethiopia.

SWAHILI

Most urban Somalis know some Swahili, and some are proficient in it, but in the rural areas knowledge of Swahili is limited to government employees and traders.

* For the role of this dialect type in broadcasting see my 'The Role of Broadcasting in the Adaptation of the Somali Language to Modern Needs' in *Language Use and Social Change*, ed W. H. Whiteley, Oxford University Press, 1971.

ENGLISH

An increasing number of Somalis in urban areas know English. This is to a large extent a result of the emphasis given to English in Kenyan education programmes.

OTHER LANGUAGES

Somali traders usually have some knowledge of the languages of the areas where they trade. In the predominantly Galla-inhabited areas all Somali town-dwellers speak Galla as their second language, usually without a trace of foreign accent.

THE GALLA

THE MOTHER TONGUE

All the Galla people speak the Galla language as their mother tongue.

There are three dialect types of Galla spoken in Kenya:

(a) The Galla spoken by the Boran and the Sakuye (and the Ajuran Somali);

(b) The Galla spoken by the Gabra (and the Gurreh Somali);

(c) The Galla spoken by the Orma (Wardai).

It should be noted that the first two dialects extend to southern Ethiopia, while Orma is spoken also in Somalia.

The Galla spoken in Kenya forms the southernmost part of the vast Galla-speaking territory covering almost half of Ethiopia.

MONOLINGUALISM

The vast majority of the Galla people in the rural areas of Kenya are monolingual. For slight modification of this statement see the sections *Classical Arabic* and *Colloquial Arabic* below.

SOMALI

Among the Galla, knowledge of Somali is rare and mainly occurs among the Muslims (who form possibly half of the Galla population in Kenya), especially men of religion who are in close contact with the Somali centres of Muslim learning.

For the Ajuran Somalis who speak both Galla and Somali see the section *Geographical distribution.*

CLASSICAL ARABIC

Like their Somali counterparts, Galla Muslim men of religion usually have a good reading and writing knowledge of Classical Arabic, but very few of them speak it.

Many ordinary Muslim Galla, like Somalis, have some knowledge of Arabic which they use in prayers, but it seems that this is less widely spread than among Somalis. This may be due to the fact that many Galla Muslims are recent converts.

It is to be noted that all Sakuye and Orma are Muslims, while among Borana and Gabra both Muslims and pagans are found, and there is a tiny Christian minority.

SWAHILI

The Galla who follow urban occupations or are in government employment usually have some knowledge of Swahili.

LANGUAGE IN KENYA

ENGLISH

Among the urban Galla population and those in government employment there is an increasing number of people who have a knowledge of English acquired in government schools.

A NOTE ON THE NON-CUSHITIC PEOPLE LIVING AMONG SOMALI AND GALLA

The Asians and Arabs, who are traders, usually know the local languages of the area reasonably well, but have a foreign accent. They also know Swahili, as well as their own languages which they use at home.

In the Marsabit district there is an increasing number of agricultural settlers who are speakers of African languages of Kenya from outside the Cushitic linguistic area. These settlers speak their own languages and some Swahili, which they use in contact with the original local population and government officials. In this and other districts there is a sizeable number of government employees, soldiers and policemen who also come from outside the Cushitic linguistic area. They speak their own languages and Swahili. Many of them, especially teachers and government officials in the higher grades, also speak good English and use it among themselves both in speech and writing.

2

Kenya's Asian Languages

BARBARA NEALE

Monolingualism is almost unknown among the Kenya Asians, who have added the languages of Kenya to the languages of India and reached a synthesis which has no parallel in either society. Multilingualism is one aspect of the Asian population and linguistic diversity is another; four languages are the norm, but no one can list a typical set of languages for this complex minority.

Some Kenya Asians are recent arrivals from India and Pakistan, but most are descendants of the immigrants who came to Kenya in the early years of this century; traders from Gujarat, railway workers and troops from Punjab, clerks and artisans from Goa. Nationalities have been obscured by the partition of India and the annexation of Goa, and Kenya Asians are best described as they describe themselves—as North Indians with three major sub-groups: Gujaratis (about 70 per cent), Punjabis (about 20 per cent), and Goans (about 10 per cent), with some very small minorities from other regions (Sindhis, Marathis, Bengalis, etc.).

Two generations have been born in Kenya now, and the immigrants are outnumbered by their children and grandchildren; 70.4 per cent were under 30 and 61.7 per cent were Kenya-born in 1962, when Kenya had a total population of 8,636,263, including 8,365,942 Africans, 176,613 Asians, 55,759 Europeans, 34,048 Arabs, and 3,901 others. Asians were a small minority in the country as a whole, but almost all were urbanized and proportions were very different in the towns and cities where Asians were often a tenth and sometimes as much as a third of the local population: 75 per cent were concentrated in the two large cities of Nairobi and Mombasa, and the rest were located in other towns and settlements along the main trade routes.

None of these figures are current, and proportions will be different in the next census report but they give a fair picture of the Asian population in the recent past before established patterns were disturbed by the Kenyanization of Asian occupations. Asians lived in every part of Kenya then, and all were middle class in local terms: i.e. the middle rank of a plural society which provided separate facilities—schools, residential areas, etc.—for Africans (poor), Asians (fair), and Europeans (good). Incomes were ranked in the same way and occupations were non-competitive; Europeans were large farmers and government officials, Africans were small farmers and unskilled workers; and Asians were in the middle: 40.2 per cent were in commerce, 28 per cent in services (largely government service), 12.3 per cent in manufacturing, and the rest were variously employed as professional people, artisans, contractors and clerks.

Asians were isolated from Africans by residence and occupation and many were still further isolated by religion: 55.4 per cent were Hindus and Jains, and the rest were Muslims (22.7 per cent), Sikhs (12 per cent), Christians (9.3 per cent), and others (0.6 per cent). Asians make a further subdivision of Hindus and Jains and five religions are recognized in their major social divisions: the Gujarati Hindus, Jains, and Muslims; the Punjabi Hindus, Sikhs and Muslims; and the Christian Goans. Goans are Catholics by sect with some vestiges of the Indian caste system, and other communities are further subdivided by Hindu and Sikh castes and sects, and Muslim sects.

All major sub-groups are still represented in Kenya, but Asians are now transitional in the literal sense and statistics are changing rapidly. Europeans and Asians were satisfied with the plural society, but Africans were not, and steps were taken to redress the balance when power was transferred to Africans in 1963. Facilities are integrated now, and expatriate occupations are being Kenyanized: European farmers were affected in the first phase, European and Asian civil servants in the second, and Asian traders in the third, and current, phase. Asians are less restricted now in some ways (schools and residential areas) but more restricted in others (occupation and locality) and their future is uncertain at best. Fourteen per cent have emigrated in the last two years as their work permits and trading licences expired, and others are expected to leave shortly. Estimates range from 50–70 per cent of the Asian population but these are largely guesswork: some are citizens (about 45,000) who may stay on, but most of these are children who cannot stay alone.

Much has happened in the last decade and social change is reflected in the patterns of language use, but no languages have been added or lost by Kenya Asians. Languages of British India and Goa are still used as community languages and three lingua francas—Hindustani, Swahili and English—are still used as links with other communities, Asian, African and European.

Immigrants used one European language in India (English) and two in Goa (Portuguese and Latin) and their other languages were regional vernaculars (Gujarati, Bengali, Cutchi and Konkani), classical languages (Sanskrit, Ardhamagadhi Prakrit, and Arabic) and the lingua franca of India (Hindustani). Swahili was added as a link with Africans in Kenya, and English was used with Europeans. Other African languages, like Luo and Kikuyu, are additional lingua francas for some rural traders, and other vernaculars (Sindhi, Marathi, Parsee Gujarati, etc.) and classical languages (Avestan) are used by Asian minorities, but these are the main divisions. African languages are lingua francas, Hindustani and English are lingua francas and community languages, and other languages are community languages.

Kenya Asians use their community languages as home languages, languages of religion, and standards (i.e. literary idioms), and each major sub-group has its own set. Some languages have two roles, or three, Portuguese has none, but patterns are clear: regional languages are used at home and other languages, if any, are used as religious languages (classical) and standards. Regions are shared by some Asians and religions by others, but the Goans are isolated by both and their isolation is reflected in their languages.

Two deviations are noted and both are associated with sects: the Arya Samajists (Punjabi Hindus) use Vedic for religion and the Swami Narayans (Gujarati Hindus) use Gujarati. Both are modern sects but the Arya Samaj has chosen a classical language for prayer with religious explanations in their standard (Hindi). Other communities with classical languages make the same division between 'unintelligible' languages of prayer and standard languages of religious explanation, and all use their standards in other contexts as languages of secular explanation, i.e. as literary languages for adults and school languages for children.

Hindi and Urdu are listed below as separate languages, but both are varieties of Hindustani: Punjabi Hindus use a sanskritized version (Hindi in the Devanagari script) as their standard, and Punjabi Muslims use a persianized version (Urdu in a perso-arabic script) as theirs. Differences in script and vocabulary are neutralized in the spoken language which is called Hindustani in Kenya, but literary idioms are still known as Hindi and Urdu. Both have been adopted as official languages of India (Hindi) and Pakistan (Urdu), and both were mediums of instruction for Punjabi Hindus (Hindi) and Muslims (Urdu) in Kenya before the recent shift to English. Gujaratis used Gujarati in their schools, and the Punjabi Sikhs used Punjabi in their religious script (Gurumukhi, 'from the mouth of the Guru'). English was also taught, as a subject, and the Goans used English alone.

Kenya-born Goans are literate in English, other Asians are biliterate

71

TABLE 2.1   *Community languages*

	Home	Religion	Standard	Other
Gujaratis				
Hindus	Gujarati, Cutchi	Sanskrit	Gujarati	
Jains	Gujarati	Prakrit	Gujarati	
Muslims	Gujarati, Cutchi	Arabic	Gujarati	
Punjabis				
Hindus	Punjabi	Sanskrit	Hindi	
Sikhs	Punjabi	Punjabi	Punjabi	
Muslims	Punjabi	Arabic	Urdu	
Goans				
Christians	Konkani, English	Latin, English	English	Portuguese

in their standards and English, and literacy rates are high: Asian men, aged 20–29, had an average of 8½ years of education in 1962 and Asian women an average of 6. Fifty-three per cent of the men had 9–12 years and 30 per cent of the women. Kenya-born Asians have more education than immigrants and these figures drop quite sharply as age increases, but Asian men aged 50–59 still had an average of 5.7 years, and Asian women an average of 2.1.

Cutchi and Konkani were excluded from the schools as non-standard languages, and Portuguese was excluded for other reasons. Some Goans had learned it in Goa as English is learned in India, i.e. as a language of administration and élite education, others had been to Bombay for higher education in English, and some were illiterate in both. Goans who expected to become civil servants in Goa were educated in Portuguese while those who expected to work in English contexts (British India or East Africa) were educated in English. As Goa is now part of India, Portuguese has been displaced by the official languages of India—Hindi and English; some immigrants in Kenya remember Portuguese, and sometimes use it with affection, but others have rejected it as a colonial language. None have passed it on to their children, and Portuguese survives, where it survives at all, as a language of friendly greetings and a link with the past.

Other standards were passed on to the Kenya-born Asians as school languages, and all are heavily reinforced by communications from India and Pakistan. Hindustani is the language of Indian films, and its literary idioms are used in national publications, religious materials and broadcasts from India (in Hindi) and Pakistan (in Urdu). English is also used as an Indian standard in newspapers and periodicals and, sometimes, in 1eligious materials. Gujarati and Punjabi are regional standards with a minor role in commercial publications, but Gujaratis are numerous in Kenya and they get most of the available materials—a few films each year, and many paperback books and periodicals. Punjabi is used only by Sikhs who get a few newspapers, and both languages are used extensively in religious publications.

Standard languages are also used when Asians publish for themselves and other Asians in Tanzania and Uganda. Gujarati is the language of the local Asian press[1] and other publications (community newsletters, announcements, pamphlets, etc.) are produced in all standard languages. Broadcasts on the Asian service of the Voice of Kenya were another context in the recent past, but hours have been reduced from about 63 a week in four languages (including Konkani) to ten a week in Hindustani alone, and no increase is foreseen. Emigration has reduced the circulation of Gujarati newspapers from two to one, and other publications are shrinking. Standard languages are still needed as languages of religious explanation and all are still taught as subjects in the Asian schools, with private tuition in some cases for children who are attending former European and African schools. Punjabi Hindus and Muslims also encourage the use of Hindustani in their homes, and some claim the literary idioms as first languages, but there is no evidence as yet of community shift: Punjabi is still their mother tongue in the usual sense and Hindustani is spoken in some homes, as an auxiliary language, to encourage children who are now learning it as a subject when they learn it at all.

African languages have not, so far, been adopted as community languages by any section of the Asian population, but a mixture of Cutchi and Swahili is the first language of some Gujarati Muslims (Ismailis and Ithnasheris) who have come from Zanzibar, and Swahili is also used, with other African languages, when Kenya Asians publish for Africans. None were taught in Asian schools and Asians who can use them as literary languages are predictably scarce. Gujarati materials have been translated into Swahili by Mr B. V. Trivedi of Mombasa and Mr Ramesh Patel of Nairobi, while Punjabi materials have been translated by Africans, working directly from Arabic and indirectly from Punjabi, via English. Religious explanations and translations are the central theme in these publications, and Swahili the leading language, but biographies of Indian leaders have also been published and other African languages are also used.[2]

LINGUA FRANCAS

Standard Swahili is rare among Asians, but a spoken variety of the language has been added by a very large majority, who use it with Africans and, sometimes, with Asians and Europeans. Hindustani is the lingua franca of the Asian population but some Asians have never learned it and others communicate with them as best they can—in English, if both know it, and in Swahili if they do not. Non-English-speaking Asians also use Swahili with Europeans, and all Asians use Swahili with non-English-speaking Africans.

English-speaking Asians have more choice and most adhere to another division: Hindustani is used with Asians, Swahili with Africans, and English with Europeans and, sometimes, with Asians and Africans. Many are aware of the linguistic chasm between their varieties of Swahili (Asian Swahili) and the standard language and English is, therefore, preferred in formal contacts with English-speaking Africans, but Swahili is used when Africans request it: television forums are the most striking example at present.

Informal contacts are less stylized and decisions more complex. English-speaking Africans were scarce when Asians first came to Kenya and Asians had no choice: Swahili was added by all in order to communicate with African servants in their homes and African employees and customers in their shops. Kenya-born children learned Swahili at home, where first languages were spoken with the family and Swahili with servants, and all learned Asian versions which are characterized by a great deal of interference from first languages. African servants also learned this idiom and used it with their employers, thereby supporting the popular belief that grammatical Swahili is only used by coastal Africans. Kenya-born Asians added English in school and later used it in offices and other European contexts, but Kenya Asians had few contacts with English-speaking Africans and none employed them.

Relationships were altered by the emergence of an English-speaking African élite, and Asian traders now use Swahili with employees and Swahili and English with African customers, where their fathers used Swahili alone with both. Other Asians meet English-speaking Africans as colleagues in government offices where English is used as an office lingua franca, but Swahili is still spoken at home with African servants.

Another generation of Kenya Asians is growing up now and relations are still changing. Asian children are involved in the recent shift to English as the medium of instruction in the newly-integrated schools, and English is their peer group lingua franca; first languages are used with other children from the same region, in informal contacts, and English is used with everyone else—Asian, African and European. Hindustani has become redundant for Gujaratis and Goans who know it largely as a language of the Indian film song, but Punjabis still need it as a language of religious explanation.

Asian children are also learning Swahili as a subject in some schools and these are faced with the difficult task of shifting from 'pidginized' varieties to the standard language. Parents have tried to help by studying with their children, but English texts are used in the schools and many mothers are immigrants with no English. One Swahili grammar was translated into Gujarati in Zanzibar and another was published with dictionaries in Kenya,[3] but nothing of the kind has been attempted for Punjabi and the Gujarati materials have been out of print for many years. English-speaking Asians have access to Swahili grammars, but barriers to learning are still large, and progress is slow. Excerpts from tape recordings of Asian Swahili give some indication of their problems.

1. *Asian Swahili*

Kama nafika Mombasa sei ilikuwa, likwa saa senashara labda jioni, nakwenda kwa rafiki yetu na hawa likwo najua ndiyo sisi natoka safari kubwa sana. Likwo machi moto kabisa 'ready' kwetu.

Standard Swahili model

Nilipofika Mombasa ilikuwa—labda saa kumi na moja jioni. Nikaenda kwa rafiki yetu naye alijua kwamba tumetoka katika safari ndefu sana. Maji moto yaliwekwa tayari.

2. *Asian Swahili*

Mimi nasarewa apa Nairobi mwaka elfu moja mia tisa salasini na tisa. Mimi nakwisha soma apa dani ya Kenya skuli ni itwa 'Duke of Gloucester'.

Standard Swahili model

Mimi nilizaliwa hapa Nairobi, mwaka elfu moja mia tisa thelathini na tisa. Nilimaliza masomo hapa katika shule iliyoitwa 'Duke of Gloucester'.

3. *Asian Swahili*

Mimi naondoka subui saa nishara nakwenda oga. Narudi kuoga naondoa mutoto ote, namwita jina kila mwitu. Nasema ondoka ile mutoto nataka kwenda skulu. Nasema saa nakusha, ondoka, kuleni chai, kuleni mukati, ile mikwisha piga naveka natiari juu a meza. Bas avana doka . . .
. . . Basi nakwisha ukwa saa tatu, basi naona 'television' kidogo, paka saa inne, paka saa tano television namliza. Sisi nakwenda laleni basi. I dio kazi ya kila siku.

Standard Swahili model

Mimi naondoka asubuhi saa kumi na mbili niende kuoga. Baada ya kurudi naondoa watoto wote na kuwaita kwa majina yao. Nawaa-

75

mbia, 'Ondokeni, watoto nyote lazima mwende shule, saa imepita, ondokeni, kuleni chai na mkate, nimekwisha pika na kuweka tayari mezani, basi si bora kutoka?' . . .
. . . Basi ilikuwa saa tatu, halafu tukaona televisheni kidogo mpaka saa nne hata mpaka saa tano ilipokwisha. Halafu tukaenda kulala. Basi, hii ndiyo kazi ya kila siku.

4. *Asian Swahili*

Lakini apana wesa jua watu ingine iko msuri watu ingine kama apana iko msuri.

Standard Swahili model

Lakini huwezi kujua kama watu wengine ni wazuri au watu wengine si wazuri.

Standard Swahili forms are cited for comparison, but their status as models is doubtful. Coastal Asians are in contact with Africans who use Swahili as a first language, but many have learned it from other Asians who do not. Up-country Asians are in contact with Africans and Asians who speak it as a second language and many have had no other models. Standard Swahili was available in newspapers and radio programmes for Africans but Asians had their own versions of both, and household conversations were their primary models. New immigrants and little children learned by listening to the conversations between Asian house-wives and African servants, and their choices were further restricted when all concerned used Asian Swahili grammar for greater intelligibility. Phonological contrasts were still available, between servants with some interference, and Asians with a great deal, but children imitated their parents.

Television is a new medium for Standard Swahili and an important one for Kenya Asians who have a choice of programmes in English or Swahili. English-speaking Asians prefer English programmes and non-English speakers prefer Swahili ones, but most watch both with transla-tions, if necessary, by Asian children (English to Asian languages) and African servants (Standard to Asian Swahili). Television is recent, and restricted still in range, but Nairobi Asians hear Standard Swahili in their homes now, and other Asians expect to hear it in the future. None have so far shifted to the standard language, and predictions would be rash at this stage: Swahili programmes are a useful reinforcement for Asian children who are learning Swahili in school and adults also benefit from having a wider choice of models. Asian Swahili still prevails, but contrasts with the standard language are available.

Conflicts are extensive on all linguistic levels and several different varieties of Asian Swahili are involved: grammar varies, to some extent, with the exposure to Standard Swahili and phonology varies markedly with the first language of the speaker and his education. Some general characteristics of Asian Swahili are outlined below, but one would need a volume to do justice to the subject.

1. PHONOLOGY

Asian Swahili has 21 consonants /p b t d k g č j f v h s z š m ny ŋ l r w y/ and five vowels /i e a o u /.

Voiced stops are realized explosively, and not implosively as occurs for /b d g/ in coastal dialects, and / č j / are realized as affricates. Three Swahili fricatives / th dh gh / are lacking and / ŋ / does not occur initially.

/ z h y / are unstable in all positions (i.e. lacking in some idiolects and occurring sporadically in others) and / w / is unstable following a consonant. Initial vowels and nasals are also unstable before consonants, and / p t d j ny f v š l r / have further interference in some idiolects, leaving a basic core of the three phonemes / k č s / with no interference at all.

Swahili			
	th → s	e.g.	**thenashara→senashara**
	z → s, j	e.g.	**mzuri→msuri**
			pumzika→pumsika
			weza→wesa
			anza→wanja
			zamani→jamani
	h, y → 0	e.g.	**hapana→apana**
			huko→uko
			asubuhi→subui
			yetu→etu
			yote→ote
	ŋ → g	e.g.	**ngombe→gombe**
	Cw → C	e.g.	**bwana→bana**
			mwaka→maka
			kwisha→kusha
	VC → C	e.g.	**asubuhi→subuhi, subui**
			isharini→shirini
			ilikuwa→likwa

Homorganic nasals are lost in some forms and expanded with anaptyctic vowels (ə in unstressed position, u elsewhere) in others:

	mC → C	e.g.	**mbili→bili**
	məC		**mchanga→machanga**

	muC		**mtu→mutu**
			amka→muka
	nC → C	e.g.	**ndani→dani**
	nC → nəC	e.g.	**Ngara→Nagara**

Also in some idiolects—

p → b, v	e.g.	**mpaka → baka**
		hapana→avana
t → ch	e.g.	**kitu→kichu**
		Mtito→Machicho
j → ch, jh	e.g.	**maji→machi**
		jaza→chasa
		jioni→chioni, jhioni
f → p	e.g.	**fanya→panya**
v → β	e.g.	**Voi→Boi**
š → s	e.g.	**isharini→sirini**
f → f,p	e.g.	**fanya→faiya, paiya**
n → l	e.g.	**tengeneza→tengelesa**
ny→ ~y	e.g.	**fanya→faỹa**
l → r, l	e.g.	**skulu→skuru**
		zaliwa→sarewa, saliwa
w → v	e.g.	**wewe→veve**

The last correspondence, **w → v**, is common in Punjabi speech where /t d/ also occur as retroflex stops [ṭḍ] and /r/ as a retroflex flap, [ṛ].

2. GRAMMAR

Sentences have a characteristic pattern of NP+VP (+NP), with a negative transformation, NP+**hapana**+VP (+NP), and adverbial additions, e.g. **kama** 'when' in initial position, and **huko** 'there' in final position.

Other constructions (passive, relative, etc.) are lacking and concord is also lacking.

Verbs occur with three prefixes: the infinitive, **ku-**, and two tenses, **na-** present, past, **ta-** future, which are omitted in negative sentences.

e.g. **kuona** 'to see'   **kwenda** 'to go'
naona 'see, saw'   **nakwenda** 'go, went'
taona 'will see'   **takwenda** 'will go'
sisi hapana kwenda 'we did not go'
mimi hapana jua 'I don't know'

Swahili **si-** negative and **hu-** survive in a few fixed forms (**sijui** 'I don't know', **hujua** 'don't you know'), and **li-** past survives in one, **ilikuwa** 'be-past'. **Ilikuwa** also occurs with verbs in some idiolects with a further contrast between present (na-) and past (ilikuwa+na-), e.g. **hawa ilikuwa najua** . . . 'they knew . . .'.

Other prefixes and suffixes are lacking, and functions are expressed, where feasible, by other forms, i.e. pronominal subjects and objects, the negative (**hapana**) and adverbial expressions of time (**kama**) and place (**huko**).

e.g. **sisi naona hawa**   'we saw them'
     sisi hapana simama 'we didn't stop'
     kama nafika Mombasa 'when we reached Mombasa'
     mimi nakwenda huko   'I am going there'

Nouns occur with four prefixes, **ki-, m-, wa-, Ø** and adjectives with three, **ki-, m-, Ø.**

Qualifiers are invariable, thus **yetu, yote,** etc., and **hii, ile,** with Swahili word order, but **ile** also occurs before noun (e.g. **Lakini ile watu likwa namuka upesi sana subui**). Concord is lacking and semantic contrasts are also lacking: **wa-** has plural reference, and other prefixes may be singular or plural.

e.g. **watu . . . msuri**   'men . . . good'
     mutoto ote   'all of the children'
     kifaru bili   'two rhinos'
     kichu yote   'everything'
     kichwa msuri   'good thoughts'

Nouns also occur with locative, **-ni,** and other locatives are reduced to two forms, **-pa and -ko.**

e.g. **barabarani**   'on the road'
     hapa   'here'
     huko   'there'

-ni is also redundant in some forms, e.g. **ndani ya barabarani** 'on the road', and innovational in others, e.g. **nakwenda laleni** 'we went to sleep'. Meaning is extended in **jikoni** 'charcoal stove' (contrasting with electric stove), and word order is reversed, on English models, in **kidogo breakfast** 'a little breakfast'.

Other affixes occur in forms which may be regarded as fixed forms:

e.g. **siku hizi**   'these days'
     pale moja   'one place'

Asian Swahili is limited in grammar and vocabulary, but Asians speak it fluently and almost universally. English is their standard lingua franca, but some have never learned it, and Hindustani is in the middle in both respects: more standardized than Asian Swahili, but less widely known; less standardized than English and more widespread. Gujarati has a wider base than English, in terms of speakers, and Hindustani has a wider range, and these relationships were recognized when Gujarati was chosen as the language of the local Asian press, a commercial venture, and Hindustani as the language of the non-commercial radio.

Distributions are illustrated in our survey of Asian languages in a section of Ngara, a middle class neighbourhood in Nairobi with a population which is still largely Asian. All Asian households were visited, and all Asian adults (over 15 and currently in residence) were included in the survey population of 402, consisting of 305 Gujaratis (201 Hindus, 75 Jains and 29 Muslims), 90 Punjabis (36 Hindus, 11 Sikhs and 43 Muslims) and 7 Goans (all Christians).

All major sub-groups were represented in the Ngara survey, but Sikhs and Goans were scarcer than one would expect when proportions are compared with unofficial estimates of regional proportions in the Asian population as a whole, and 1962 census statistics for religious divisions.

TABLE 2.2   *Regions of origin*

	Ngara Asian population	Kenya Asian population
Gujaratis	75.9%	70%
Punjabis	22.4%	20%
Goans	1.7%	10%

TABLE 2.3   *Religious affiliation*

	Ngara Asian population		Kenya Asian population	
	Number	Percentage	Number	Percentage
Hindus	237	59.0 ⎫	97,841	55.4
Jains	75	18.7 ⎬		
Muslims	72	17.9	40,057	22.7
Sikhs	11	2.7	21,169	12.0
Christians	7	1.7	16,524	9.3
Others			1,022	0.6
Total	402	100.0	176,613	100.0

Discrepancies are partly a result of clustering since Punjabi Hindus and Muslims have nearby schools and Sikhs do not, but neighbourhood profiles have also changed since 1962. Middle class Goans and Sikhs were largely civil servants in Nairobi then, and many left Kenya in the exodus of 1968. Gujaratis were largely traders who were first affected by the trade licensing laws of January 1969, and Punjabi Hindus were largely professional people (doctors, lawyers, teachers) who have not, so far, been Kenyanized. Proportions in the Ngara survey may be taken as representative of most of the larger towns, but statistics for Goans would be higher in Mombasa where many are employed in the Customs service which was still unaffected in 1969. Traders have also been leaving Kenya since the survey, and Gujaratis are therefore scarcer now.

Occupations were fairly homogeneous in the survey population which had 151 professional and managerial people including 48 who listed their occupation in more specific terms as 'trader'. Others were employed as clerks (24) and artisans (5), and the rest were unemployed students (53), housewives (144) and retired men (25).

Ngara Asians are fairly prosperous and many send their sons abroad for higher studies, creating an imbalance in the proportions for men and women under 30. Estimates for East Africans (born in Kenya, Tanzania and Uganda) were roughly the same (65 per cent) as those in the 1962 census for Kenya-born Asians (61.7 per cent), but both would be higher if more younger men were represented.

TABLE 2.4 *Birthplace, age, sex*

	Men		Women		Total
	Under 30	Over 30	Under 30	Over 30	
East Africans (incl. Tanzania) and Uganda)	47	63	88	62	260
India-born (incl. Pakistan)	9	56	18	59	142

One hundred and thirty-three households were surveyed and all, except two with European wives, were characterized by a single region and religion. Three communities reported a single first language (Gujarati Hindus and Jains, and Punjabi Sikhs), and others were diverse: Punjabi Hindus and Muslims claimed Punjabi and both versions of Hindustani, and the Goans claimed English and Konkani.

TABLE 2.5 *First languages*

	Hindus	Jains	Muslims	Sikhs	Christians
Gujaratis					
Gujarati	201	75	11		
Cutchi			18		
Punjabis					
Punjabi	14		10	11	
Hindi	21		1		
Urdu	1		32		
Goans					
Konkani					3
English					4

Religious languages were lacking for a small minority (10) with 'no religion' and the rest claimed classical languages or standards. Classical languages are heard, and sometimes recited and read, in transcription, but they are not spoken languages in the usual sense and this distinction is reflected in the figures for 'languages of prayer': Sanskrit was reported by 55 Hindus, Arabic by 67 Muslims, Prakrit ('Magdhi') by 2 Jains, Latin by 2 Goans, and the rest simply listed their standards.

Multilinguals were a large majority (89 per cent) and some Asians reported 8 languages with totals rising to a dozen or more when classical languages and occasional languages (African languages of greeting) were included. Both are omitted here but figures are still impressive; 61 per cent have 4–5 languages and 13 per cent have 6–8.

Asians from East Africa have more languages than the India-born and differences are most striking among those with 5 languages or more.

TABLE 2.6 *Total language competence*

	East African	India-born
1–3 languages	45	49
4 languages	104	65
5 languages	65	22
6–8 languages	47	6

Six East Africans were bilingual and the rest had three languages or more, with a norm of 5 for men under 30 and a norm of 4 for others. Men had more languages than women and differences are marked among those with 3 languages or less:

TABLE 2.6a *Total language competence—East Africans*

	Men		Women	
	Under 30	Over 30	Under 30	Over 30
1 language	0	0	0	0
2 languages	0	1	2	3
3 ,,	1	3	20	15
4 ,,	14	25	41	24
5 ,,	20	14	16	15
6 ,,	9	17	9	3
7 ,,	2	3	0	1
8 ,,	1	0	0	1

One India-born Asian was monolingual and 19 were bilinguals. Others had 3–7 languages, with a norm of 3 for women over 30 and a norm of 4 for the rest. Five languages were the maximum for men and women under 30, and older men had more languages than older women.

TABLE 2.6b *Total language competence—India-born*

	Men		Women	
	Under 30	Over 30	Under 30	Over 30
1 language	0	0	0	1
2 languages	0	0	2	17
3 ,,	1	3	2	23
4 ,,	5	34	11	15
5 ,,	3	14	3	2
6 ,,	0	3	0	1
7 ,,	0	2	0	0
8 ,,	0	0	0	0

Young men from East Africa are at one end of the spectrum when these two tables are compared, and older women from India are at the other. Asians with 1–2 languages are India born, and others with 6–8 languages are largely East Africans. Men have more languages than women, and younger women have more than older women.

LINGUA FRANCAS

Swahili was universal among bilinguals, and Swahili, Hindi and English were spoken by a large majority of those with 3 languages or more. Language combinations varied with origin, to some extent, and this difference is best illustrated by Asians with 3 languages: Swahili+ Hindustani was the dominant pattern for the India-born, and Swahili+ English the dominant pattern for East Africans.

TABLE 2.7 *Pattern of second/third language competence*

Additional languages	East Africans	India-born
Swahili alone	6	19
„ +English	23	1
„ +Hindustani	14	24
„ +Punjabi	1	3
English +Hindustani	1	1

Asians with 4 languages or more had 3 dominant patterns:

TABLE 2.8 *Patterns of competence for speakers with 4 languages or more*

	East Africans	India-born
Swahili + English + 1 Asian language	97	62
„ + „ + 2 „ languages	52	18
„ + „ + 3 „ „	25	4
Other	41	7

One hundred and seventy-five men and 127 women were included in the sample, and Swahili was clearly the dominant language for both. Three lingua francas were spoken by about 95 per cent of the men, and a majority of women, and Hindustani had more speakers than English in both groups. Differences are negligible among men, and marked among women.

TABLE 2.9 *Distribution of lingua francas*

	Men		Women	
	Number	%	Number	%
With Swahili	175	100.0	223	98.2
With Hindustani	168	96.0	181	79.7
With English	165	94.3	120	57.3

Second languages were typically Swahili, Hindustani and English but one-third reported two Asian languages or more and a few reported additional African and European languages:

TABLE 2.10 *Distribution of all second languages*

	African	Asian	European
% with no language	1.0	13.4	22.1
% with 1 language	94.0	51.2	71.6
% with 2 languages	3.9	25.9	5.7
% with 3 languages	1.1	9.5	0.6

Language distributions in Ngara give a fair picture of Asian languages at present, but major social changes are taking place and Asian languages may be very different in the future. Patterns which have been stable for half a century or more are in the balance, and some are already changing. Standards are affected by the shift to English as a school medium, and English and Swahili are competitive in a wider arena. Tribal languages of Africa will not be passed on to the next generation of Kenya Asians, and Portuguese will be lost. Other languages should survive as home languages, and languages of religion, but proportions will change if some communities remain in Kenya and others leave. Asians cannot, themselves, predict but none expect to live, as they have lived, as an isolated minority in a plural society which tended to foster multilingualism on the one hand and linguistic diversity on the other.

NOTES

[1] Gujarati was the language of the Asian press (*Navyug* and *Africa Samachar*) in the Survey year, but other languages have also been used: English in the *Indian Times, East African Chronicle, Tribune,* and *Forward;* Gujarati and English in the *Kenya Daily Mail, Daily Chronicle, National Chronicle, Democrat, Guardian* and *Colonial Times;* Urdu and English in the *Observer;* Konkani and English in the *Goan Voice;* Punjabi in one or two periodicals. The *National Guardian* later became *Navyug* in Gujarati alone, and the *Colonial Times* later produced separate editions in Gujarati, English and Swahili. Swahili articles by Harry Thuku also appeared in the *East African Chronicle.*

[2] Sponsored by the Indo-Africa Literary Society, Mombasa, 1948–53

B. V. Trivedi and R. V. Trivedi,	*Swahili-Gujarati--Shabda Pothi* (Dictionary).
	Gujarati-SwahiliShabda Pothi (Dictionary).
	Shabda Bhandar (Combined dictionary).
B. V. Trivedi and R. B. Patel,	*Swahili Bhasha Pravesh* (Grammar).
R. V. Trivedi,	*Khutha za Gandhiji* (*Sayings of Gandhi*).
R. V. Trivedi and N. S. Malik,	*Jawaharlal Nehru: Hadithi ya Maisha yake aliandika Mwenyewe* (Abridged autobiography of Nehru). Also in Chinyanja, Bemba, Tonga, Lozi and English.
	Daima Gandhiji (Abridged biography of Gandhi). Also in Chinyanja, Bemba, Tonga, Lozi, Luganda and English.
Mulk Raj Anand,	*Kisa cha Bara Hindi* (*Story of India*).

Sponsored by Punjabi organizations:

Kurani Tukufu (Qur'an), E.A. Ahmadiyya Muslim Mission, Nairobi, 1953.
Dini ya Sikh (*Sikh Religion*), The Sikh Students Federation, Nairobi, 1968. Also in Gujarati and English.

Unpublished Swahili manuscripts
  Biography of Mme. Pandit.
  Biography of Swami Narayan by R. B. Patel
Published Elsewhere and Circulated in Kenya
  Uislama na Dini Nyingine, Ahmadiyya Muslim Foreign Mission, Rabwah, 1967.
  Mafundisho ya Bwana, The Theosophical Society in East Africa, Dar es Salaam.
  T. P. Khetani (Zanzibar C.S.D.),   *Swahili bhasha na svayam shikshak* (Gujarati translation of Bishop Steere's *Swahili Exercises*), Rajkot, 1947.
                                                  The Song of God or the Bhagavadgita, Rajkot (for the Indo-African Literary Society, Mombasa).

[3] B. V. Trivedi, op. cit., T. P. Khetani, op. cit.

3

Language Standardization in Western Kenya: the Luluyia Experiment

P. A. N. ITEBETE

INTRODUCTION[1]

In this study I intend to examine briefly how the various Luyia[2] groups came to be where they are, and the historical background to the exercise of unifying and standardizing the orthography of their dialects. In the course of so doing it will be necessary to examine firstly why it was important, at that particular time, to have a common orthography, and, secondly, the work of standardization itself, bearing in mind the background studies that had to be undertaken before the exercise could be carried out. A variety of objections were raised to the proposed standardization, leading to total and open rejection by at least two of the dialects concerned. These objections will be examined both from a linguistic and non-linguistic point of view. A period of ten to twenty years is hardly long enough to establish whether a standardized orthography has taken root, to the point where every literate person of the group both can and does use it. This is especially so when there are important factors militating against its acceptance: these include financial shortages; some internal disagreements; and, especially, the introduction of English, which was thought to be of greater practical use lower down the primary schools. Nevertheless Luluyia *was* written and used, and I shall examine its use during the past two decades. Finally, an attempt must be made to determine the present extent of its use and perhaps its prospects for the future.

BACKGROUND TO THE PROBLEM

Writing about 'Linguistic Commonality' Punya Sloka Ray[3] refers to two ways in which 'commonality' or conformity may be sought for a language. He continues,

Map of Luyia Dialects

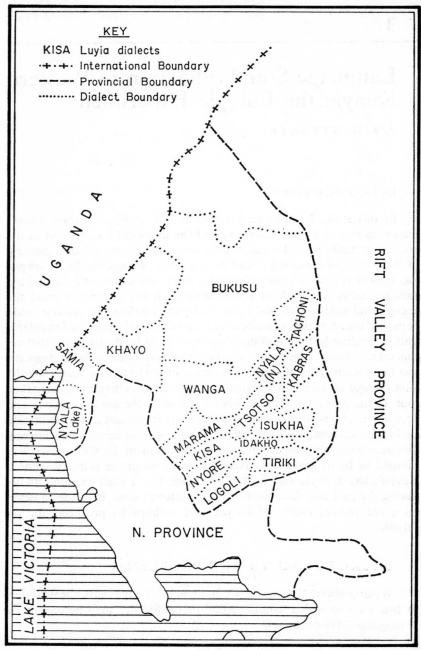

KEY

KISA Luyia dialects
·+·+· International Boundary
--- Provincial Boundary
········ Dialect Boundary

UGANDA

RIFT VALLEY PROVINCE

BUKUSU

TACHONI

SAMIA

KHAYO

NYALA (N)

KABRAS

WANGA

NYALA (Lake)

TSOTSO

ISUKHA

MARAMA

IDAKHO

KISA

NYORE

TIRIKI

LOGOLI

LAKE VICTORIA

N. PROVINCE

G. deS.

. . . firstly, we may have a set of people who identify themselves as the group of the users of the language, and yet who do not use the same forms for the same meanings. This situation is usually described as existence of dialects. All languages are fragmented into dialects, but not to an equal degree.

He comments that German is more fragmented than French. Whereas the Germans and the French are not usually thought of as tribes, in Africa tribes are usually thought of as having a common language.

The points quoted above fit the Luluyia situation rather neatly. The Baluyia of western Kenya are a group of Bantu-speaking peoples on the Kenya-Uganda border, whose northern limit is Mount Elgon, and who border the Kalenjin and Luo to the east and south respectively. Within a few miles of the southern border is Lake Victoria. However, Ray's definition covers a larger number of people than those calling themselves Abaluyia. Their language is also spoken by groups of people—numbering about one-third of the total Abaluyia in Kenya—who live on the Uganda side of the border, this border not having been drawn on a tribal basis by the colonial governments. The Abaluyia form the third largest single tribe in Kenya. Their population of 1,086,409 (1962 census) compares well with other major tribes in Kenya and East Africa, all but one of which are Bantu.[4] Two points need to be made here: firstly, the number of dialects within Buluyia. There are 16 or 17 of these, depending on how they are counted, within an area of something over 3,000 square miles.[5] Secondly, there is the difficulty of deciding on the dialect boundaries; how is one to decide when one has crossed from dialect A into the area of dialect B? It may well be that people began feeling the 'commonality' of dialect as a result of the 'locations' into which Buluyia was divided for administrative convenience.[6] It may also be that some people within an area thought they stood to gain by claiming a unity for the location in which they lived and hence for the dialect which they spoke, a unity which was essentially not language-based but kinship-based. The fluctuating boundaries of locations like Isukha and Idakho might seem to corroborate this point. Linguistically it would be difficult to prove that Lwisukha and Lwidakho are separate dialects, unless one took as criteria small differences in vowel quality and quantity and some tonal variations. By most other criteria the two constitute one dialect. This serves merely to illustrate that the dialects might easily be reclassified into a smaller number, and that it is only in a few areas that the transition from one to another is at all sharp. The two areas where this is so are Bulogoli and Bubukusu. There seem to be very few differences between the four central dialects which were chosen to form the basis of the standardized orthography and one might wonder, indeed, whether they might not be regarded even as a single dialect.

When Miss (now Deaconess) Appleby[7] started her work of standardizing the orthography of Luluyia, the first full Secretary of the Luyia Orthography Committee (later renamed the Luyia Language Committee) made the following estimates of the numbers of speakers in each dialect:[8]

Maragoli	49,000
Batiriki	17,000
Bedakho	7,000
Besukha (Bakakamega)	33,000
Kabras	11,000
Bakakalelwa	5,000
Bakitosh (Babugusu)	56,000
Banyore	32,000
Bakisa	13,000
Batsotso	10,000
Marama	18,000
Bawanga	30,000
Bakhayo	18,000
Bamarachi	14,000
Basamia and Banyala	22,000

These figures give a total of 335,000 which is clearly an underestimate in view of the census figures twenty years later. It should be noted that Besukha (Bisukha) and Bedakho (Bidakho) are sometimes referred to as Bakakamega. The name Kitosh is no longer used, the people calling themselves Babukusu. Bakakalelwa are now known as Banyala, and to differentiate them from the Banyala who live near Lake Victoria I shall refer to them as Banyala (North), the others being referred to as Banyala (Lake). There was some debate earlier as to whether Bakabras were also to be called Banyala, but this has not occurred and the former name is currently retained.

THE FORMATION OF THE DIALECTS: A HISTORICAL SKETCH

Most commentators on the history of the Abaluyia, and especially Were[9] and Osogo,[10] stress that it is unrealistic to study the settlement of Buluyia without taking into account the movements of the constituent clans. Osogo estimates that there are an average of 30 clans to each sub-tribe or dialect area.[11] The number is staggeringly large, though it is evident that clans joined together at times of crisis, e.g. wars, even though there were also bitter internal quarrels. What one can infer linguistically from these temporary unions is questionable.

Of the two major tribes in western Kenya, the Abaluyia settled into their present habitat slightly earlier than the Luo. Were[12] concludes from various sources that '. . . the earliest immigrants arrived between about twelve and seventeen generations ago, therefore c.1463–1625. It is further apparent that the original settlers came from different countries.' Between 1490–1706, western Kenya and eastern Uganda were being occupied simultaneously by Bantu, Kalenjin and Luo settlers, while the Teso expanded later (1760–1868) from around Mbale and Tororo in eastern Uganda to their present habitat in Kenya. Were concludes that all these movements contributed to the formation of the Abaluyia, though they were not at that time known as such. They were simply Bantu-speaking groups. He ends, '. . . the early history of the Abaluyia can only be examined by analysing their various clans and sub-tribes within the wider context of inter-tribal movements in eastern Uganda and western Kenya.'[13] Such movements contributed to the formation of the dialect areas and I would, therefore, differ from Sapir, in his assertion that:

Under primitive conditions the political groups are small, the tendency to localism exceedingly strong. It is natural, therefore, that the languages of primitive folk or of non-urban populations in general are differentiated into a greater number of dialects.[14]

While there have probably been additional factors in the dialect formation in Buluyia it seems likely that what was happening in the period 1760–1868 was a levelling out of dialectal differences among those dialects which had been brought into contact during the period of early settlement.

It is difficult to point to a single dispersal area from which the Abaluyia came, but it can be argued that they came from the general direction of eastern Uganda. From this one may except many of the Isukha and Idakho clans who migrated from Kalenjin areas and abandoned their language in favour of Luluyia. Following Were and Osogo one can distinguish four major groups and their associated dialects. The most northern, the Babukusu, claim to have come from Ethiopia, Sudan or even Misri (Egypt), and to have moved both northwards and southwards on both sides of the Kenya-Uganda border, coming into contact with the Basoga, Bagishu, Kalenjin (Maasai) and finally the Teso, who seem to have been responsible for their settling in their present habitat. There are claims and counter-claims that they are the 'same' people as the Bagishu, but amidst a great deal that is confused and conjectural there does seem to have been long contact with the Bantu-speaking tribes of eastern Uganda. Some clans claim to have migrated into such areas as Isukha in eastern Buluyia, but because oral tradition on both sides of the border speaks of ancestors having come from Ethiopia or even Sudan, passage through Uganda is not too unlikely.

The next two groups both claim to have their ancestry in eastern Uganda (see Were, p. 65). The first might be labelled the central and western Abaluyia, who migrated from Busoga into Bukhayo (Abaguri), Bumarachi (Abafofoyo), Buwanga (Abashitsetse) and a few into Busamia. There is a high degree of inter-intelligibility between these dialects. Both Batsotso and Bakabras (Were, pp. 71–2) moved into their present location from eastern Uganda, as did the Banyore who moved from Bunyole (Uganda) through the present Luo areas to their present location (Were, p. 73). It seems, however, that many clans in Bunyore hived off from Bidakho (Bashimuli), Babukusu (Babayi) and some from the Luo areas. The second group, comprising the Balogoli and Batiriki (Were, pp. 73–5), also came from eastern Uganda. The Balogoli followed a similar route to the Banyore but appear to have stayed long enough around Lake Victoria for them to have developed a rather different dialect to that of the other Baluyia. Some commentators have noted its similarity to Gusii, and suggest that the two groups might have split while in the vicinity of the Lake, the Logoli going north and the Gusii south. Little movement has taken place subsequently. While the Batiriki are held to have come from Wanga (Osogo, p. 56), they also seem to have travelled through Central Nyanza (Were, p. 74) and to have gathered a number of Kalenjin clans on the way. Their dialect is more like that of the Kakamega group, to be discussed below, than that of the Balogoli.

The fourth group is that which Osogo (p. 58) calls the Kakamega sub-tribes, and which Were (p. 73) lists among the south-eastern locations of Buluyia. It is uncertain where the Bisukha and Bidakho came from, but they appear to have reached Idakho first from the direction of the Lake, and Were (p. 73) suggests that they might represent a very early offshoot of the lacustrine Bantu who settled in this area before 1598. All these groups (including the Batiriki) include some clans of Kalenjin origin, particularly of Maasai (see Osogo, pp. 59, 63 on the Abashimuli and Abamilonje). While the Nandi escarpment and the Kakamega forest may have prevented incursions by Kalenjin/Maasai, neither their customs nor their vocabulary were so easily kept out (see Osogo, p. 58, on the origin of the name Kakamega as Nandi *Lumek*). These south-eastern groups are linguistically so similar, yet sufficiently distinct from those around them, to warrant setting them up as a single unit, eastern Baluyia.

Some mention must also be made of the Banyala (Lake), who may be grouped with the Basamia and Bakhayo mentioned above, and with whom the Banyala (North) may be presumed to have some relationship. They also came from eastern Uganda but travelled via the Lake and fought numerous wars with the Luo (Osogo, p. 109). They share a number of linguistic features with Basamia and Bakhayo.

The groups may now be summarized as follows:

Northern: (i) Babukusu
            (ii) Batachoni (those speaking Lubukusu)
Central: (i) Bawanga, Bamarama, Batsotso, Bashisa, Bamarachi
            (ii) Basamia, Bakhayo, Banyala (Lake)
            (iii) Banyala (North), Bakabras, Batachoni (those speaking Lukabras)
            (iv) Banyole (?)
Eastern: (i) Bisukha, Bidakho, Batiriki
Southern: (i) Balogoli

THE BACKGROUND TO STANDARDIZATION

(a) MISSIONS AND LANGUAGE POLICY

Though the linguist may recognize a cluster of dialects as having an overall close relationship to one another, such that they may be served by a single orthography, the early missionaries who came to western Kenya did not have such an overall view, and consequently committed to writing the speech of the area in which they started their missionary work.[15] Yet from an early date there were those who viewed the situation of linguistic diversity with concern. Thus the Executive Committee of the Church Missionary Society sent a memorandum on the language question in Uganda to its missionaries there in 1902, with a copy to Bishop Tucker. In it they expressed the view that

... there will be many advantages gained in the future for a united church, if, without undue pressure, one language may come to prevail and become the language of educated people throughout at least that part of the area covered by the Church in which Bantu languages are used, and they hope that no avoidable step will be taken to hinder such development on natural lines ... [16]

Just what kind of practical policy is envisaged in such a statement is not clear, but if it is a question of raising the status of one dialect or language at the expense of others then a wide range of problems are involved. Writing half a century later R. F. Amonoo comments,

Unifying dialects is a fairly tricky problem. Historically a strong dialect imposes itself over a passage of time, through its greater cultural richness, its numerical superiority and so on. Whether in modern times, given the improvement in methods of propagation, it is feasible to impose a uniform script, or grammar, arrived at by compromise, is debatable.[17]

This may be true, and certainly the 'unifiers' were to encounter many problems in the course of their campaign which was not to come to fruition until almost half way through the century. The question of unification is next raised in a most interesting letter from the Rev. W. Chadwick on the political and religious importance of standardizing the Wanga dialect, written in 1914:

I fear that I am taking a great liberty in bringing the subject of the Bantu languages before your notice again, and I do so with diffidence, knowing as I do that Mr Rees' experience in this country for so many years makes the rest of us appear like children; yet we have had similar experience in Uganda, and elsewhere, and I am emboldened by two things:

First. I am told that your mission hesitated for a considerable time before deciding to work in the Maragoli dialect.

Secondly. The importance of our all working in the same dialect, seems to me to be extremely great.

Our protestant missions are now working in 6 different districts of Bantu Kavirondo: Maragoli, Kaimosi, Kakumega, Bunyori, Mumia's and Kitosh. Now I understand Mr Rees to be of the opinion that all these dialects are so much alike, that, if we all agree to work in any one of them, we would succeed in ousting the rest, and he argues that the language of the Maragoli is more beautiful, and their population greater than that of any other single tribe.

As to the beauty of the dialect I cannot speak, but as to its importance, I feel very strongly, though I speak my opinion under correction after my short knowledge of the country, that it is very much LESS GENERALLY REPRESENTATIVE than either Kakumega or Mumia's; Maragoli may be the largest single tribe, but I believe that the Mumia's and Bunyori together are larger and they are most similar to each other and I think I am right in saying that both Kitosh and Kakamega would learn Mumia's more easily than Maragoli, and both Kitosh and Mumia's would learn Kakamega more easily than Maragoli. Thinking merely of the dialects, my opinion is, that Kitosh and Maragoli are as it were, the furthest apart, and therefore either of the central dialects would be much better.

Of course this is only a loose way of describing them; it would scarcely even be true to say that they are all branches of one original language, for some have drawn quite considerably from different roots altogether.

However, if this were all we had to consider, I should be inclined to agree with Mr Rees in thinking that it would be possible to force any one dialect on the people, though I think even so, Maragoli would take longer than any other probably.

But we have other forces to consider. The POLITICAL SITUATION of the Maragoli is such that neither the R.C. Mission nor the British Government have found it advisable to make it a centre. I am told that they have few chiefs of much authority, and that of them the most powerful speaks Kakumega. The main road is not near it nor is the railway likely to be so. The three outstanding chiefs in the country are without doubt Mumia, Mulama and Murunga: these all speak Mumia's and their power is, so far as one can see, likely to increase more than any other Bantu chiefs'. At present also, the position of the Government Station undoubtedly has been helping to familiarise all the tribes with Mumia's dialect, as so many come in there more constantly.

These are my main reasons for preferring the Mumia's dialect. And next to it I would prefer the Kakamega's dialect. If we all tried to press forward, we should have the cooperation of the R.C. Mission, whose main work is in it, and who would undoubtedly be a great power in advancing its spread, while I feel certain that the general adoption by us of the Maragoli dialect would play into their hands. The people as a whole have not yet any very strong preference either for R. Catholicism or Protestantism and if the bulk of them found it easier to read in the Kakumega dialect than in the Maragoli, they would most certainly follow them. I therefore feel it is quite impossible for us to adopt the Maragoli dialect, but while I still feel that Mumia's is really the best, I am so much impressed by the desirability of our all working with the same books that if you would consent to adopt Kakumega, I should do my best to try and spread it, and I believe that we should probably succeed.

Of course, when I speak of adopting any one dialect I mean that that dialect should be the criterion in *all the main points of grammar* (italics mine). If we all worked with the same books it would naturally be found that the language would become enriched in vocabulary from all the dialects, and we should have to consider each other in all cases where a similar word exists in another dialect with a different meaning, especially when as occasionally happens the meaning is an objectionable one.

May I again acknowledge my consciousness of the superiority of Mr Rees' work; but at the same time I cannot forget his saying that even three years ago he would have welcomed this suggestion. I know how strenuously he has been working, and I am asking a great sacrifice but if it is for the general good of the country as I believe, even three years' work is worth sacrificing for the sake of the people whose welfare we all have at heart.

I remain, Sir, etc.[18]

The compromise solution advocated by the Rev. Chadwick was not adopted and a few years later the matter was raised again by the Rev. W. E. Owen who argued strongly against the use of three separate written forms of the language (those of the CMS, the Church of God, and the Friends' African Mission).[19] In the meantime each mission went its own way: at a meeting of missionaries from the Friends' African Mission at Lirhanda in 1921, it was stated that henceforth

. . . all new missionaries shall come under the supervision of the Language Committee, whose business it shall be to require from each one four or five hours language study daily for a period of one year or until such time as the Language Committee shall decide they are capable for definite service. Until such a time, they shall not be placed in charge of any station or Department.[20]

It can be safely stated that each missionary society in Buluyia demanded similar requirements from its missionaries, in the local dialect in which the first mission station had been established or in which the headquarters of that society was located. One further attempt at unification was made in 1924 at the instigation of the Rev. Owen, when the three Protestant groups met to try and grapple with the problems which unification of dialects would entail. Their conclusion was that the time was not yet ripe for such a step, and nothing further was done until 1940.[21]

At this point it is worthwhile summarizing the spheres of influence of the four main missionary societies in the region. First to arrive was the Friends' African Mission (Friends' Industrial Mission initially) who settled at Kaimosi in 1902, in Butiriki. However, their early linguistic

95

work was carried on from Vihiga in Logoli country, by Emrys Rees, to whom reference has been made above. By 1907 a First Reader had been printed, soon to be followed by other readers, history and geography books, and a number of religious translations. Rees also prepared a grammar of the language for fellow missionaries.[22] It is greatly to be regretted that this early impetus was not maintained beyond the twenties, but it depended—like so much else—on the abilities and dedication of individuals; when such were not available the work languished. From their headquarters at Kaimosi the FAM spread through eastern and south-eastern Buluyia and up into Bukabras, Bunyala (North) and Bubukusu.

The linguistic work of the CMS started with the arrival of the Rev. W. Chadwick in 1912, who began work in Bumarama and Buwanga, but it was his colleague Canon A. J. Leech who made the greater contribution. Rather than work with one dialect only, he worked with the four central dialects, Luwanga, Lumarama, Lushisa and Lutsotso, also drawing vocabulary from Lusamia, Lukhayo and Lumarachi. The resultant form he called Luhanga. Like his colleagues in the FAM Canon Leech translated the New Testament but, unlike them, nothing else.[23] From their main stations at Butere and Maseno the CMS spread mainly through the central and western areas of Buluyia into Busamia, Bukhayo, Bumarachi and Bunyala (North), but also to some extent into the north and east.

The Roman Catholics came into the area from Buganda and their first religious materials were in Luganda, but they soon started work in Luwanga from their station at Mumias, and later from Kakamega (Mukumu). Unlike the Protestant missions who, as they expanded, took with them materials written in the language spoken at their first or main station, the Catholics wrote in the dialect of the people of each area into which they penetrated so that they produced materials not only in Luwanga but also in, e.g. Lwisukha and Lubukusu. Their influence was greatest in the central and western areas (see Chadwick's letter above) but they also established stations in the north and east of Buluyia.

The Church of God was established at 'Kima' in Bunyore in 1905,[24] and the early missionaries soon produced an orthography of Lunyore in which religious and secular materials were produced. The New Testament was translated by 1929. Their main influence was in central Buluyia, in Bunyore, Butsotso and Bushisa.

Two points need to be stressed here: firstly, the written language in most of the dialect areas was that of the dialect in which the first religious or secular materials had been written by the mission which was operating in that area—and not necessarily that of the area itself. Secondly, in a dialect area which was under the influence of two or more missions, then two or more written forms of the language co-existed. The sort of problems that this might entail is exemplified from Bwisukha, where both Catholics and FAM operated:

1. FAM/Logoli form.
   Mwana wa Nyasaye yavugula muvili gu mundu
   The Son of God took on a human body

2. Catholic/Isukha form.
   Mwana wa Nasayi yabukula mubili ku mundu

In some areas of Bwisukha the Church of God operated so that a third version might occur:

3. Church of God/Nyore form.
   Omwana wa Nyasaye yabukula omubili kw'omundu

If any unification were going to be effected it is clear from a consideration of the above spheres of influence that the CMS and Catholics would stand to gain the most, while the FAM would see a great deal of their efforts wasted.

The discussions which were ultimately to lead to standardization began in the late thirties and early forties following the formation of a working committee to act as a Kenya Advisory Committee of the British and Foreign Bible Society. The American Bible Society was also interested in discussions that might lead to the production of cheaper Old and New Testaments but the Church of God seems to have withheld its support for a 'Union' Testament for some time on doctrinal grounds.[25] In opposition to the arguments for unification and standardization were those which stressed that the Word of God should be understood by the local people[26] and assumed that any unified written form would be unintelligible to a large number. There was also, prior to 1942, a certain amount of opposition to any form of experimental translation of the Scriptures.[27] Finally, reactions among Abaluyia themselves were now becoming heard. One such opinion was that expressed in a letter dated 20 August 1942 to the Rev. L. J. Beecher from the Friends' Mission at Broderick Falls (presumably from Mr Ford) who commented that after a recent meeting at Maseno at which the problems of a common orthography had been discussed, he was asked by Africans present, 'What are the White people trying to do?' and although he had tried to explain to them what was hoped, one had remarked, 'Bwana, whose language is it?' and yet another, more thoughtful, said, 'Bwana, go very, very slowly about that kind of thing'. Nevertheless, in spite of these doubts and a certain amount of opposition, the experiment to standardize and unify went ahead, largely under the leadership of the CMS.

(b) EDUCATION AND THE GOVERNMENT

While missionaries had been responsible for virtually all of the early educational work, this passed increasingly under government control, though many missionaries continued to play a prominent role in education and as members of government committees relating to educational policy. Archdeacon Owen of the Anglican Church in Nyanza (Kavirondo) will be remembered in the history of Kenya as one who supported Africans in their political wilderness during the time when the white settler community felt the need to rule the country. He was a tireless opponent of linguistic diversity and campaigned ceaselessly for some form of unification. After his death in the forties a number of people felt that his biography should be written; prominent among these were members of the Luyia Language Committee in the mid-forties. In a draft headed 'This dangerous Archdeacon Owen of Kenya' written by 'a fellow missionary', it is stated,

In a 1917–9 Report on Butere district he (presumably Owen—PANI) states that 'the Sunday congregations have steadily increased in numbers, so that where a year ago one building sufficed, two are now well filled . . . A beginning was made with the training of teachers, and in February 1919 eleven Catechists commenced a year's special instruction'.

Amongst these and also amongst the ordinary teachers Owen speaks of

. . . the difficulties caused by the presence in schools and Council meetings of people speaking different dialects of Luyia and of the intention of overcoming this by the use of another Bantu language with a rich vocabulary and in which there was already a literature, including the Bible, Prayer Book and some educational works. This great language, Swahili, has been stated to be one of the seven most important languages of the world.

The attempt to unify people through the use of Swahili failed '. . . because of the natural desire of the people, and of the Missionaries who had learned them, to use the local languages'. The author continues,

The progress of development of East African Literature has not been helped thereby, for most of the languages are spoken by less than a million people, numbers which can never support more than the minimum of literature. Owen may yet be considered by Africans to have been wiser than his contemporaries thought him in this abortive attempt to convey to Africans the benefits of a common African tongue, in the interim stage when the acquiring of the more desired medium—English—was virtually an impossibility.[28]

Owen became a member of the Central Advisory Committee on Native Education in Kenya, and in 1924 we find him still pursuing his earlier line in criticism of Dr J. W. Arthur:

Dr J. W. Arthur was (not) in a good position to judge the relative language values, as he was working among the Akikuyu people only, who had one language. In Kavirondo it was different, there were numerous Bantu tribes, each with its own dialect, if not language, genetically classed as Bantu Kavirondo, that the Kiswahili should be the medium of instruction. It was impossible to avoid the use of Kiswahili as it was the mode of inter-tribal communication.[29]

His agitation came to nothing and he seems to have reconciled himself to a second-best objective, that of unifying the 'Orthography for Bantu Dialects of North Kavirondo', as is shown by a letter written in 1942 to the Chairman of the District Education Board. In it he reiterates how a Mr W. J. W. Roome, the then Secretary of the Bible Society in Central Africa, had come to Kavirondo and failed to convince the Protestant missions either to adopt a common system of orthography or any language of the North Kavirondo group. Owen continues,

. . . With the development of education and the need for common textbooks in the schools becoming more and more evident I took up the matter with the Inspector of Schools, Mr G. E. Webb, from 1933 onwards. A Committee had been working on the orthography of the Luo language during 1933–5 in which latter year it made its Report. During the Meetings of this Committee it was inevitable that some of us should desire to see a similar Committee make an attempt to get uniformity of orthography for the Bantu tongues in North Kavirondo.[30]

It could be said that by 1926 some policy towards the teaching of vernaculars had been formulated, and it is clear that the vernacular was being taken as an examination subject, presumably at the end of primary schooling, to judge from the following minute of the Central Committee on African Education.

(a) Mr Barlow raised the question of the difficulties which are encountered in setting and marking vernacular reading, writing and dictation examinations. It was agreed that for the Vernacular Examination 1927 in Kikuyu, the Board of Examiners should be asked to select passages for dictation from readers used by:—

      (i) The Catholic Mission, Nyeri
      (ii) The French Mission, Nairobi; and
      (iii) The Protestant Alliance, and to give instructions for the marking.

(b) It was further agreed that local committees should be formed to deal with the establishment of authorized *spelling* conventions for Luo, Kikuyu, Swahili and *certain* Bantu Kavirondo dialects respectively. The Committee should, in case of failure to secure agreement *state the issue clearly* and put up a case to Government for decision. The following names were suggested:—

      (i) Luo . . .
      (ii) Kikuyu . . .
      (iii) Swahili . . .
      (iv) *Bantu Kavirondo*: the advice of the School area committees concerned should be as to the personnel of a committee to consider the possibility of obtaining any standard spelling.[31]

During 1934 certain rules were drawn up governing the award of grants-in-aid of African education. Part IV of these rules dealt specifically with grants-in-aid of vernacular textbooks and is of relevance here:

Grants-in-aid of the preparation and publication of approved textbooks and reading books in vernacular languages to be used in elementary or sub-elementary schools may be made.

The Grants described in the previous paragraph shall be payable only in respect of books being prepared in a language which is:—

(a) approved by the Director as being used by large groups of pupils, or is

(b) standardized in regard to orthography with the approval of Government.

The grants-in-aid shall be devoted to expenses connected with the preparation and publication of approved books provided that a grant may also be made to enable the price of the book to be reduced and shall be limited to an amount not exceeding £100.

These rules shall come into operation on 1st. January 1935 . . . By command of His Excellency the Governor in Council.[32]

While it is clear that the government was in favour of standardization, the main result of such rules was to exclude those working in the Luyia languages from such grants, though they probably did something to undermine the resistance of those opposing standardization.

By the early 1940s the situation was ripe for the experiment to take place, and it is appropriate that one should include here the comments of a Muluyia on the position. He wrote what might be termed an open letter

. . . to Missionaries, Educationists and to Administrators; to all those men and women to whose charge the people of North Kavirondo have been committed and who are interested in the well-being and progress of the *Abaluhya*, in the name of my fellow countrymen, I beg to present to you our greatest and most urgent problem, namely the linguistic situation of North Kavirondo.

To a casual observer, North Kavirondo has an infinity of languages, and no doubt from location to location dialectical divergences in pronunciation, speech melody, and vocabulary are apparent. However, the so called languages have such a strong affinity that the whole district falls into one broad linguistic category. This fact hardly deserves further elaboration, suffice it to say that, go where a *Muluhya* may in North Kavirondo, he is understood, and is at home, and speaks to his fellow Abaluhya in no other medium than his own peculiar dialect.

Hitherto, *Lunyore*, *Luragoli* and *Luwanga*, have been REDUCED to writing and are employed as media of instruction in our schools. Take *Lunyore* for instance. As a rule it is the language of the *Banyore* of *Bunyore*, but its use now goes far beyond its natural locality. Besides Bunyore, it is used in *Kisa*, *Kakamega*, *Butsotso* and wherever a Church of God Mission Station has been established in North Kavirondo. *Luwanga* of *Buwanga* is used in *Buk'ayo*, *Buwanga*, *Bumarachi*, *Samia*, *Kitosh*, *Kisa*, *Marama* and *Bunyole* in the African Anglican Church. Similarly *Luragoli* is used in *Maragoli*, *Kakamega*, *Kabras*, *Kitosh* and throughout the Friends Africa Mission. What a confusion worse confounded![33]

(c) LOCAL ASSOCIATIONS

So far we have been dealing with religious and educational arguments in favour of standardization, but during the period under discussion there was also a slowly developing sense of political unity in the area, which made some contribution to acceptance of linguistic unification when it was finally proposed. The history of Kenya during the thirties has sometimes been referred to as the history of Associations. They sprang up everywhere and Abaluyia did not lag behind. The North Kavirondo Central Association was modelled on the Associations of Central Province and others elsewhere, and its immediate effect in Buluyia was to unite all Baluyia together, not only in terms of its welfare activities but in respect of many other things as well, e.g. the gold rush at Kakamega in 1931. There was also substantial agitation for a Paramount Chief. When Mumia, the Paramount Chief of Abaluyia, relinquished his duties in 1927, his Paramountcy went with him. Mulama, whom most Baluyia thought should succeed him, was dismissed in 1935, presumably for indulging in politics when he himself was a civil servant. In June 1935 there was a protest memorandum entitled 'Abaluhyia Ba North Kavirondo Central Association (N.K.C.A.), Protest at Administration Treatment of the Paramount Chief'. They claimed that Mulama had been chosen by 'all Baluhyia'.[34] Although it was subsequently claimed that the term Abaluhyia was used for the first time in the early forties,[35] it appears that this was the first time when the term was used to cover all the Baluyia, and forms like Buluyia, Muluyia, Luluyia, etc. were clearly in general use at that time. In 1939 the Provincial Commissioner reported,

The N. Abaluyia C.A. is the new name for what we used to know as the N.K.C.A., which was a conscious imitation of the K(ikuyu). C.A. It (the N.K.C.A.) is intensely tribal in character and perhaps its only constructive achievement so far is to devise the name Abaluyia for the Bantu Kavirondo ... in the Southern locations ... Lumadede and his assistants are Moses Muhanga and John Adala.[36]

In the period 1935–9 both District and Provincial Reports speak of 'Abaluhyia'. It seems likely that any suggestion during this time of bringing the Abaluyia together in any way was welcome to the government: the local Native Council at Kakamega, which later gave approval to and financed the orthography standardization exercise, was perhaps designed as a device to channel political grievances in a constructive way. Certainly it served as a unifying factor and provides part of the explanation for the wholehearted acceptance of the proposals for linguistic unification when these were put forward in the early forties. That dissenting voices were subsequently raised will be discussed later.

(d) OTHER FACTORS

An additional factor which needs to be mentioned, though its importance is difficult to assess, is the existence of a sizeable and growing body of educated men and women who, through their contact with English and

Swahili, were aware of the advantages accruing to a language with a standardized orthography. They could, therefore, be relied upon to support such an exercise in principle, though they might well have reservations about the precise form it should take.[37] One reason for this was an awareness that those dialects which were most divergent from the majority of the Luyia dialects would be likely to suffer most, and in some important sense lose their identity.

THE PROBLEM STATED

The four separate orthographies in use prior to 1942 catered for four dialect areas and four areas of mission influence, thus:

1. Luhanga. Used by the CMS. This was, to some extent at least, a standardization of some central dialects.
2. Lunyore. Used by the Church of God.
3. Luragoli. Used by the FAM.
4. Luwanga. Used by the Catholics, who also used other dialects.

As has been noted above, where an area was exposed to the activities of two or more missions, several orthographies were liable to co-exist in a very small area. The first question to consider is the extent to which the dialects actually differed from one another; the second, the extent to which the orthographies represented different solutions to essentially similar problems. The main differences are in the field of vocabulary and phonology. Not only do we find similar meanings with different forms, e.g.

Lubukusu	ekhafu	'cow'
Luwanga	eng'ombe	
Lulogoli	lidigolo	'crow'
Luwanga	likhokho	
Lubukusu	kumurongoro	'tree'
Lulogoli	musaala	

But there are also similar forms with different meanings, e.g.

Luwanga	khulaama	'to pray'
Lubukusu	khulaama	'to curse'
Luwanga	likhanda	'knife'
Lubukusu	likhanda	'skin'

Finally, as one might expect, there are a very large number of items with similar forms and meanings but differing phonological realizations, e.g.

Lusamia	chidatu	'three'
Luhanga	tsitaru	
Lulogoli	maguta	'oil'
Lubukusu	kamafura	

102

There are also important tonal differences, differences in the number of vowel phonemes (Lulogoli, Lwisukha, Lutiriki and Lwidakho having seven, while the rest have only five), differences in the shape of nominal prefixes (e.g. Cl. 3 Lubukusu **kumu-**, Lunyore **omu-**, Lulogoli, **mu-**), and so on. All the orthographies had to solve the problem of word division which was essentially the same for all of them, and the following example illustrates their differing solutions:

Luhanga:	**Mana**	yacaka	ok'wegesya	k'ulukuku
Lulogoli:	**Kandi**	ya tanga	kwegidza	ku luginga
Lunyore:	**Olundi**	yachieka	okhwibala	khuluginga

Given this kind of difference, the question before the standardizers was, which dialect or dialects should constitute the basis for a standard form of Luluyia, and what kind of standardization should be aimed at.[38]

THE PROBLEM TACKLED

The obvious candidate to act as co-ordinator of the exercise was Archdeacon Owen, but the choice lay to some extent with the different missions and, especially, with the Local Native Council which, after all, was going to finance the operation.[39] The first meeting of the Orthography Committee took place on 4 April 1941, and learned that the CMS had seconded Miss Appleby to be at the disposal of the committee. The meeting could apparently not agree on the issues before it and sent in its resignation to the District Education Board, which was itself chosen by the Local Native Council.[40] It seems that the disagreements sprang either from a belief that the time was not yet ripe for the experiment, or from dissatisfaction over the choice of co-ordinator. However, a substantial part of the committee decided to go ahead with the exercise, with or without the support of the remainder, and a second set of First Minutes appear for 12 December 1942, one item of which reads, 'The Committee regretted that the F.A.M. had not appointed a representative'. At this later meeting certain guide lines were laid down to assist Miss Appleby, thus:

1. That Miss Appleby is requested to formulate a Standardized Luluhya alphabet and to submit it to the Committee for consideration. The Secretary be requested to ask Miss Appleby to submit the alphabet by the middle of February 1943, and to append a short comparative passage in Ragoli, Hanga and Nyore, in the suggested alphabet.
2. In formulating the alphabet Miss Appleby was requested to bear in mind the following principles:—
   (a) to relate the Luluhya alphabet to the alphabets of the surrounding main Bantu languages, viz. Ganda and Swahili.
   (b) to avoid diacritical marks as far as possible.
   (c) to make the alphabet as simple as possible.

(d) to suggest symbols not at present employed in the English alphabet if the English alphabet is inadequate for this purpose.

(e) to consider 'Some general principles of Luluhya orthography' by Mr W. Akatsa.

Miss Appleby, a trained linguist with considerable knowledge of Comparative Bantu took Dr Wagner's suggestions (see footnote 38) into account, and applied herself to the task. She made a thorough study of the problems involved, with particular reference to problems of sound change, vocabulary, etc., and in due course the committee made the following recommendations:

1. **Spelling** was to be based on the pronunciation of the majority of the Luyia people.

2. **Grammar** was to be that of the central dialects, i.e. Lumarama, Lushisa, Luwanga and Lutsotso which give least difficulty to those in outlying areas.

3. **Vocabulary**: any word in a Luyia dialect was good enough to be used. In preparing books for use over the whole area care had to be taken to use the most widely known words, and where necessary to give dialectal equivalents in a footnote. The four dialects mentioned above would again, on the whole, serve as the basis for the choice of the 'most widely known' words.

As a result of these general recommendations detailed proposals were put forward.

SPELLING

Five vowels only, **i, e, a, o, u,** were recommended as being sufficient to represent the sounds used. Vowel length was to be indicated by doubling the vowel 'only where semantic length differentiates words, or where there is grammatical lengthening, i.e. where two adjacent vowels coalesce to form a long vowel, but not where one is elided.'

(a) A long vowel in the stem of a word.

    amabeele   'milk'   cf. **amabele**   'millet'
    okhukaana   'deny'   cf. **okhukana**   'tell (a story)'

(b) (i) Where the vowel of a noun class prefix is the same as the initial vowel of the stem following, both are written.

    eshi + ilima   eshiilima[41]

(ii) Where the vowel of a subject or object concord or of a tense marker is the same as the initial vowel of the stem immediately following, both are written.

    ba   **+ ahula**   **baahula** (subject prefix)
    khu+ba + ahula   **khubaahula** (object prefix)

(iii) An **a** in any prefix coalesces with the initial vowel of the stem to form a long vowel.

    a + e = ee aba + eka abeeka

    a + i = ee khu+a+injila khweenjila (vowels before nasal compounds are long and do not need therefore to be marked)

    a + o = oo   ba + ora boora

    a + u = oo   ya + ula yoola

(iv) In combined forms with **ifwe** (we) and **inywe** (you pl.) the resulting vowel is doubled and the whole written as one word.

    wa ifwe   weefwe

    nina inywe   nineenywe

(v) In polysyllabic verbs, the vowel of the penultimate syllable is lengthened in forming the near and intermediate past.

    abukuule 'he took'   cf. **abukule**   'that he may take'

(vi) When a possessive particle is joined to a demonstrative beginning with a vowel, the **a** of the possessive particle is not lost. Infrequent.

    omwana waabo the child of those (people)

    cf. **omwana wabo** his/her brother

SEMI-VOWELS

There had been some confusion as to where **y** and **w** should be used. Some authors had used them in words like **bakasiye** and **likhuwa**, others did not. It was decided to use **y** in the following cases:

(a) Initially in a word or stem: **yeyaka, ayera;**

(b) Intervocalically: **bakasiye;**

(c) In combination with **n** to represent the palatal nasal: **inyama, okhunyala,** cf. **okhuniala.**

Following any other consonant, **i** is to be used.

A **u** occurring penultimately before **w** is not realized in the orthography. It is to be noted that **w** sometimes corresponds to **b** in other dialects, thus:

    likhuwa to /lixuba/

CONSONANTS

At least three dialects have voiced as well as unvoiced obstruents. However, because they were a minority, the consonants of the majority were taken. The following were therefore recommended:

p, b	**t**	**k**	
	ts, ch		
f	**s, sh**	**kh**	**h**

together with the nasals

m   n, ny   ng'

The difficulty over l and r was noted. It was suggested that r should represent the rolled sound, while l should represent the other sounds. The following homorganic nasals were recognized for use in Luluyia: **mb, nd, ng, nz, nj.**

No account in the orthography was taken of stress, pitch or intonation, all of which are significant in the dialects.

WORD DIVISION

The following principles were recommended:

(a) The verb should be fully conjunctive: all pronominal, negative, locative, tense and other formative affixes should be joined to the word:

nabamunyoolela 'and they got for him'

Auxiliary verbs with separate concords would be written separately:

ndalinji nikholanga 'I used to be doing'

The **ta** negative particle should be written separately:

shikhulitsiakhwoyo ta 'we shall not go there at all'

(b) The possessive particle should be joined to the following noun:

wa + omwana   womwana 'of the child'

(c) Of possessive adjectives, the second and third person singular personal class should be joined to their preceding noun; all others should be written as separate words.

omukhaanawo 'your daughter'

likondilie 'his sheep'

cf. **inzu yefwe** 'our house'

(d) Locative prefixes, **ha, khu, mu, ena, ewa** should be joined to the noun. These had often been treated as separate words.

mu + inzu   munzu 'in the house'

khu + injira   khunjira 'on the road'

(e) **Ni** copula should be joined to the following word

ni + wina   niwina? 'who is it?'

(f) **Na** 'and' should also be joined to the following word

omukhasi na + omwanawe   omukhasi nomwanawe 'the woman and her child'

(g) **Ne** 'but' should be written separately. In speech it is usually followed by a slight pause:

Yamboolela, ne shindasuubila ta 'She told me but I didn't believe her'

It was recommended that sections (b) to (f) should not apply before proper nouns: in such cases the preceding particle is then to be written in full, and the initial letter of the noun should be capitalized.

omwana wa Sara   'Sara's child'

GRAMMAR

As there were not held to be any basic differences in language structure among the various dialects, it was simply recommended that the grammar of the central dialects should be the grammar of written Luluyia (see the bibliography of Kenya languages at the end of the volume).

VOCABULARY

Some of the lexical problems facing the committee have already been pointed out above, THE PROBLEM STATED, and they were to occupy Miss Appleby for many years, although she produced a stencilled Luluhya-English Vocabulary in 1943 (see bibliography). In building up her collection of words she started from a Lumarama translation of an English item, and added the equivalent in other dialects as she moved about the country. Where a particular term was not used she added 'NU' after the entry. Finally, the full entry would have the number of dialects in which the item occurred, the number in which it did not, and a recommendation as to which should be used, thus

Entry No. 60. 'Praise'

Itsomia	10	NU	2
Fumia	12		
Paaka	5	NU	7
Ikhwasia	1	NU	10
Koha	3	NU	2
Laha	12		

Suggest: Use **itsomia** and **fumia**. **Laha** may be used when praise names are used.

It is not immediately clear, however, why **itsomia** should be used here: there are two dialects in which it does not occur and only ten in which it does, while both the other terms have a wider distribution.

Such an outline can give at best only an extremely sketchy picture of the work involved in this exceedingly laborious task, which in essence can probably not be completed in one lifetime. This is not the place to discuss the difficulties in the field of eliciting information on the meaning of words, but it is, nevertheless, a very real area of difficulty and controversy, and one which could well be treated more fully on another occasion.

AFTER STANDARDIZATION

When some of the preliminary work had been done, Miss Appleby circulated the proposed rules to those whom she thought were sufficiently knowledgeable and interested to make comments: the responses varied from approval with some reservations to complete rejection. It is fair, I think, to say that those comments coming from the FAM were generally hostile, one writer commenting that the proposed forms were based on Luhanga,[42] while a Catholic Father who had been recruited on to the committee stated,

Far from discouraging you I am sure you do not mind me criticising some of your ways in spelling and also in the selection of words which you want to adopt in order to be able to use one common language in publications. I am afraid that in the spelling of words you have been confined only to the pronunciation of words of the very local districts in your surroundings. I can easily understand this because I suppose you have never been stationed in the big districts of Bukhayo and Samia . . . A few examples:

Instead of	*eshindu*	why not	*esindu*
	okhuchinga		*okhukinga*
	okhuleshera		*okhulekhera*[43]

Granted that this particular clergyman had not served with the committee from its outset and therefore did not know what had previously been decided, nevertheless this tone of criticism was very common. It appeared that the opposition had not weakened in the course of thirty years! In the end it was only the FAM who decided not to support the proposals: they decided to write their primers and readers in their own dialect. Later, however, they decided to consult the committee over the technical devices adopted for standardizing, and in this they were later joined by the Bukusu, when in the mid-fifties they too pulled out of the standardization exercise.[44]

From the fifties onwards support for Standard Luluyia appeared to be on the wane. At first money had been forthcoming from the Local Native Council; as support dwindled, they withdrew their backing, but recommended that those locations under their jurisdiction who were willing to help should do so directly to Miss Appleby—her own salary and that of her assistant were provided by the CMS and the British and Foreign Bible Society. The size of the contributions received after 1957 speaks for itself:

	1957	1958	1959	1960	1961	1962	1963	1964[45]
Tsotso	200/-		50/-					
Kisa	200/-	200/-	100/-					
Nyore	100/-							
Marama	250/-			100/-				
Wanga				200/-	50/-			
Samia				250/-				
Marachi				60/-	100/-	60/-		60/-
Chairman: Elgon-Ny.					50/-		50/-	
	750/-	200/-	150/-	610/-	200/-	60/-	50/-	60/-

The fall-off in support provoked the following appeal:

Our special needs at present, for which I ask your interest, are as follows:

1. That the Abaluyia themselves should take an interest in promoting the correct spelling and writing of the standard written form of the language. They should note that nobody wants to change the way any person or tribe speaks; but while for example, some people write AMAFURA, some AMAFUTA, some AMAKURA and some KAMAFURA, or while some say and write TSING'OMBE TSITARU and others ENG'OMBE JIDATU, we cannot say we have a common written form. The rules are clearly set out in the little booklet *Obukatulusii bwoluLuyia;* but very few even among the teachers will take the trouble to learn them. Could you, please, use your influence to help people to see that an educated man should write his language correctly, and not according to his own ideas? You may even be able to sow these seeds in the Education Department; unfortunately they don't seem interested in teaching children to write their own language correctly, or indeed to read it.

2. This work does cost money. From time to time I write to the Chairmen of the Location Councils, but with very little effect, as you have seen from the above list. Would you be so kind as to suggest to these gentlemen that this matter is their concern, and that they should bear some at least of the financial responsibility.

While sympathizing with the deep disappointment felt by the standardizers, and especially by Miss Appleby, it must be recognized that the two dialects which broke away had from the earliest times been recognized as the two most divergent from the rest of the cluster. In a questionnaire to a group of Baluyia women and Baluyia chiefs in seminars at Musaa and Bukura it was clear that speakers from these two areas find it most difficult to understand each other, though not so difficult to understand what is said in one of the other dialects. There was, for a time, some doubt about the support of the Bunyore,[46] but the difficulties were ironed out and a number of booklets were written in Lunyore, after scrutiny by the Luyia Language Committee.[47]

The comment cited above that teachers were not interested in teaching children to write their own language correctly or indeed to read it, must be understood in the context of a surge of enthusiasm for the teaching of English right from the first classes of the primary school. One cannot be too hard on the teacher who pays little attention to the vernacular for he knows that its only importance is as an educational device to hasten the pupils' progress towards the time when they learn through English—the language of all serious education. If few pupils at the time went on to secondary school, most believed that they would, and were willing accomplices of the teachers who preferred the English medium approach. Nevertheless, a number of primary school books were published and a list is given in Appendix A. Similarly both Balogoli and Babukusu produced reading materials. The Luyia Language Committee served as a filter through which books to be printed by the East African Literature Bureau were sent, and the Secretary was required to give the imprimatur.

In exercises like this a great deal depends on the extent to which it can be publicized, and to which key members of the community—in this case teachers—can be persuaded to give their full support. Because most of the teacher training colleges for training primary school teachers were run by missionaries, a great deal depended on which mission controlled the college: generally speaking CMS and RC colleges supported the exercise, so that trainees who were sent back to areas within these spheres of influence stood a good chance of being able to pass on their knowledge to the next generation. Those whose home areas were in Bubukusu, for example, were in a more difficult position. Even here, however, a great deal depended on the enthusiasm of the individual teacher.

Miss Appleby has always emphasized that she did not want to change people's speech habits, but to give them a common written language. It is true today that most people continue to speak their local dialect as they have always done, reserving the use of Standard Luyia for religious services, primary schools and for some other written contexts.[48] It may be that if there is a renewal of interest in the vernaculars Luluyia may again become a focus of interest and of written materials. What is somewhat ironical, however, is that the whole point of the standardization exercise was to reduce the number of written orthographies from three Protestant varieties and one Catholic: what has resulted is still a plurality of orthographies—where there were four there are now three. Yet, I suppose, even this could be called progress.

NOTES

[1] This study could not have been done without the help and generosity of many people. I should like to thank members of the District Administration at Kakamega, Bungoma and Busia for granting me permission to work in their districts. I should also like to express my appreciation to the Principals of the Kenya Institute of Administration for making it possible for me to visit the area of my research as often as possible.

In Buluyia itself I would like to thank Deaconess Appleby of Butere, Mr T.G. Lung'aho, Secretary of the Friends' Yearly Meeting, Kaimosi, Mr F. Ingutia of Butere, and Sister Karoli of the Mukumu Ursuline Convent. To Dr John Lonsdale of Trinity College, Cambridge, I would also like to express my thanks.

[2] I use, throughout, the terminology and spelling adopted by John Osogo, *A History of the Baluyia*, Oxford University Press, Nairobi, 1966, pp. 2–3, thus:

Country	People		Language
	Singular	Plural	
Buluyia	Muluyia	Baluyia	Luluyia
Bubukusu	Mubukusu	Babukusu	Lubukusu
Bulogoli	Mulogoli	Balogoli	Lulogoli

This terminology is not always consistent with the Standard Luyia orthography, but is the most commonly used at the present time. Were also uses this terminology but where he mentions locations (administrative units corresponding to dialect areas) he does not use a prefix, thus, Samia, Idakho, Kabras, etc.

The forms Buluhya, Muluhya, Luluhya, etc. are still very widespread but are not accepted by the Luyia Language Committee which refers to the language as Luyia, and not Luluyia as I do here. Other spellings also occur, see for example letter CD/17/5 of 9 July 1951 from Commissioner for Community Development at Lower Kabete to District Commissioner, North Nyanza, Kakamega.

[3] P. S. Ray, *Language Standardization*, Mouton, The Hague, 1963, p. 54.

[4] See *Language Problems in Africa*, EARIC Information Circular no. 2, 1969.

[5] *Statistical Abstracts, 1964*, Ministry of Economic Planning, Nairobi.

[6] In Kenya a location is an administrative unit with a chief at its head. In Buluyia the boundaries of locations coincided fairly accurately with groups that formed, or thought they formed, a distinct dialect area.

[7] Deaconess Appleby herself mentions elsewhere that she had been appointed to undertake the task of creating a common orthography, e.g. in her memorandum to the President of the Western Region on 8 March 1964. But see Owen's letter of 4 October 1942, paras. 5 and 6 to the Chairman of the District Education Board, North Nyanza, Kakamega.

[8] L. L. Appleby, survey and suggestions file.

[9] G. Were, *A History of the Abaluyia of Western Kenya*, East African Publishing House, Nairobi, 1967, p. 60.

[10] Were, op. cit., p. 7.

[11] Were, op. cit., p. 7.

[12] Were, op. cit., p. 61.

[13] Were, op. cit., p. 60.

[14] E. Sapir, *Language*, Harcourt, Brace, New York, 1921.

[15] Western Kenya was no special case: indeed in other parts of the country the various missions adopted different solutions for essentially the same orthographic problems, without the excuse of the dialectal variation which occurred in western Kenya in Buluyia.

[16] CMS, *Memorandum on Language Question in Uganda*, 1902. From J. Lonsdale (unpublished notes).

[17] 'Problems of Ghanaian *Lingue Franche*' in J. Spencer (ed.), *Language in Africa*, Cambridge University Press, 1963, p. 83.

[18] Walter Chadwick to Kaimosi Mission Secretary, file IR.1/Maseno. Packet X, Early Records and Reports, in Kaimosi mission records.

[19] N. Grace Donohew, 'The Development and Evaluation of a Course of Study in the Grammar of the Luyia Language for Use in the Teacher Training Colleges for the Baluyia', M. A. Thesis, University of Washington, 1963, p. 36. In ch. II of her thesis Mrs Donohew gives a rather detailed account of the background to standardization, and I am indebted to her for permission to quote from this chapter.

[20] Taken from the minutes of this meeting, 13 October 1921, presumably held at Lirhanda.

[21] Donohew, op. cit., p. 36.

[22] Donohew, op. cit., p. 26.

[23] Donohew, op. cit., p. 34.

[24] Though originally the Bunyore Mission operated under the South African Compounds Mission, and was not transferred to the Missionary Board of the Church of God until 1922.

[25] This appears to be the implication of a letter written by L. J. Beecher to the General Secretary of the American Bible Society of 3 December 1941. See file 'Luyia Orthography Committee—Correspondence to 1947' of Deaconess Appleby, Butere. See also F. J. Ainsworth's letter of 10 November 1941 to Mr Ford, unclassified papers, Kaimosi.

[26] See above.

[27] See above and also the letter of J. W. Ford to Dr Eric North, Bible House, New York, of 22 October 1941, unclassified papers, Kaimosi.

[28] See file minutes, memoranda and notes. Unclassified loose papers, Butere.

[29] See discussion of minute 5 of the fourth committee meeting, 21 December 1924. Loose notes from Kaimosi.

[30] See letter by W. E. Owen of 4 October 1942 to Chairman, District Education Board, North Kavirondo, Kakamega. File, 'Luyia Orthography Committee, Correspondence to 1947', Butere.

[31] See minute 5, the Report of the Vernacular Examination, 1926; the Committee of African Education, 23 November 1926. File, 'Education Department Correspondence, 1924–38', Kaimosi.

[32] See, Grant-in-Aid of African Education Rules, 1934, Colony and Protectorate of Kenya Education Department. File, 'Education Department Correspondence, 1924–38', Kaimosi.

[33] W. B. Akatsa, 'An Appeal for Linguistic Unity among the Abaluhyia', as appended to L. J. Beecher's note on what happened on Friday, 10 October 1941. See file, 'Luyia Orthography Committee, Correspondence to 1947', Butere.

[34] Provincial Archives, Nyanza Province Annual Report, C. Tomkinson, 1935, Kakamega. Andrew Jumba (President) and John Adala (Secretary) to D.C., ADM 1/13/B, 7/6/35. J. Lonsdale, unpublished notes.

[35] L. L. Appleby, Memorandum to the President of the Western Region, 8 March 1964.

[36] Provincial Archives, Nyanza Province Annual Report, S. H. Fazan, 1939.

[37] See for example the following letters:
  1. Stanley Godia of 13 August 1943 in file, 'Luyia Orthography Committee, Correspondence to 1947', Butere.
  2. Benjamin S. Ngaira of 28 July 1943 to Mr Chapman, copies to Miss Appleby. File as above.
  3. Solomon Adagala of 28 July 1943 to the Secretary, N.K., DEB. File as above.

[38] In a memorandum on 'Bantu Orthography' Dr G. Wagner (file as above) made the following suggestions:
  '1. *General*: a unified orthography of the different Bantu Kavirondo dialects, should, in my opinion take into consideration the following principles:—
     (a) *Drift* i.e. the tendency towards changes in the manner and place of articulation of sounds, is a natural, inevitable and generally speaking non-reversible process. A common orthography should, therefore, be based on present day usage and not on any former stages of the dialect in question, even if such a former stage can be regarded as the common source from which the present sub-dialects have developed.
     (b) In so far as the present vernaculars present different stages in the process of phonetic drift, the more "advanced" stages should be given preference to the more "conservative" ones. By analogy with the history of sound changes in European languages, I would assume that the tendency of drift in the Bantu Kavirondo dialects is from plosives (or stops) to fricatives and rolled rather than vice versa. If this is a true criterion, then it is more likely that e.g. Luragoli *t*, *ng*, *k* will gradually become *r* (or *f*), *ndj* and *x* than that Luhanga *r*, *ndj* and *x* will become *t*, *ng*, and *k* respectively.
     (c) In determining which sound should be chosen out of a number of corresponding sounds in different dialects, the sound represented in the dialect (or dialects) spoken by the largest number of people should be given preference. Where

112

(b) and (c) do not coincide a compromise between the two principles should be reached.'

[39] At the first few meetings both government and missions were represented. It is not easy to tell whether the government representatives were from the Local Native Council, from schools or from particular areas. The Principal of Kakamega Government African School was Secretary for the first five meetings.

[40] See Chapman's letter of 13 April 1942 to the Chairman, North Kavirondo, DEB (on Government African School headed paper), copied to all members of the committee, ref. 27a/52(?), unclassified papers, Kaimosi.

[41] For greater exemplification see my 'The Standardization of the Orthography of Luluyia', *Journal of the Language Association of Eastern Africa*, 1, 1970.

[42] For example, Mr S. Adagala (see note 37) commented, 'The pamphlet is written in Luhanga and should therefore not bear the name of Luluhya . . . It appears as if the Committee is trying to force the whole of N.K. to abandon their orthography entirely and turn to Luhanga . . . . Old Luhanga is the worst written dialect in N.K. and the New Luhanga (in which the pamphlet in question is written) can now and will be taken into account when the proper "Luluhya Committee" will consider: Luhanga (New), Lunyore, and Luragoli, and the outcome will be "Luluhya".' Mr Ngaira, more favourably disposed towards the new orthography, commented (see note 37), 'All the dialects in North Kavirondo should be represented, and the orthography and vocabulary be selected on the majority basis. Basing these on already printed matter only is not enough and will only cause discontentment among the tribes left out. (2) No one dialect should serve as the standard. It is because of this point that many have felt that whoever heads the committee should be one without the denominational bias.' Finally, a practical comment from Mr Stanley Godia (same file): 'We are to teach the children that "ka" means "ga" and "kha" means "ka" from sub- Stds. A onwards and when they get up to Std. I, they will be learning Swahili. Will boys make mistakes when they read "katika": "gatiga"?' Even such a disinterested observer as Dr Malcolm Guthrie expressed the view that what was happening was less a unification of dialects than a promotion of Luhanga.

[43] See the Rev. Fr. P. Coenen's letter of 5 May 1945 to Miss Appleby. File as above.

[44] The separatist movement at that time seemed likely to spread further. W. H. Whiteley mentioned to me that around 1957 he was asked to participate in an orthographic exercise among the Batachoni, some of whom were anxious to differentiate themselves not only from Standard Luluyia, but also from Lubukusu.

[45] See Memorandum to the President of the Western Region by Deaconess Appleby, 8 March 1964.

[46] See J. S. Ludwig's letter 21 November 1941 to the Rev. L. J. Beecher. File as note 37 above.

[47] The authors of most of these were Mrs N. G. Donohew and Kaleb Olala.

[48] Standard Luluyia appeared in a number of publications:
 (a) *Mwangaza wa North Nyanza*. A newspaper edited by a Muluyia and published in Nairobi. Discontinued.
 (b) Adult literacy materials.
 (c) News bulletins put out by the Department of Information.

APPENDIX A

Luyia Publications prior to 1957

The standards for which they are suitable as school readers are noted in brackets.

Khweche Okhusoma (I) (Reader).
Ochole nende Tsingano Tsindi (II) (Reader).
Khusome Oluluyia (II) (Supplementary reader).
Omukhasi Omubooli (III/IV) (Reader on hygiene).
Mundaalo Tsiamanani (III/IV) (Folk tales).
Tsingano tsia Olwisukha (III/IV) (Isukha folk tales).
Amatala amasangafu (V/VI) (Village hygiene).
Aggrey owe Achimota (V/VI) (Life of Aggrey).
Abasungu abaranjirira okhwitsa mu Kavirondo (*The First Europeans in Kavirondo,* a history reader).
Obulamu bwabaana (Baby welfare manual).
Emilimo chiabakhasi mungo (*Women's Work in the House*).
Akobusanjirisani (*Co-operatives*).
Abaluyia bemumbo (*The Western Abaluyia*).
Okhuchaka (Genesis, Old Testament).
Tsinjero (Proverbs, Old Testament).
A First Luyia Grammar.

4

Some Uses of Common Bantu

J. C. SHARMAN

One field of investigation which might seem non-practical or over-academic concerns the study of Common Bantu. Various languages of Uganda, Kenya, Tanzania and Zambia were selected for an apparently highly specialized kind of investigation, which was confined, initially, to the collection of 'reflexes of starred forms' in a list of some 500 items. Stated thus baldly this sounds very much like an 'ivory tower' project, but it does have some much more practical implications. To justify this, we had better first define what we mean by a starred form, as far as this study is concerned. There are three or four quite different varieties, only one of which we used in this study. The first does not really concern us, but it might be as well to list the main varieties.

1. This is a theoretical word or even sentence that *might* exist in a given language but does not, and which is marked by a star.

2. This older variety is the better known and probably the easier to explain. By studying a large number of languages belonging to a recognized family, we can reconstruct an ancestral language to which all present day descendants can be rigorously related (that is, by a rigorous application of sound-shifts). The 'words' in this ancestral language are starred forms: they are more or less accurate reconstructions of how the ancestral words were actually pronounced. Thus— *βantu, people: a Meinhof-type reconstruction of what a word in Ur-Bantu may actually have sounded like. All such reconstructions are attempts to approximate the pronunciation of a 'real' (if putative) ancestral language.

3. We may best begin with two examples:

     (a) *-jàdà, 'hunger'   cf. **insala, njaa**
   This is a synchronic reconstruction. The *d is likely to be 'realized' as /l/, as a 'flapped' l, as /r/ or even as /zero/ rather than as /d/, but for the *abstract* consonantal system *d is the logical choice.

115

(b) * **mití midaị íbidí gíaguịdé mudubánjá dúáịtú**
trees tall two have fallen in courtyard our

This is a sentence reconstruction in the same way as (a). It follows the rules of Common Bantu 'morphology and syntax', and is composed entirely of well attested items (both morphemic and lexical). What this means is that if you knew how to make the necessary sound-shifts, and uttered this sentence to any randomly selected speaker of any Bantu language, you would stand a good chance of being (at least partly) understood. Of course the language you are trying to 'deduce' (from the Common Bantu reconstruction) may well have introduced some idiosyncrasies, and it may well not even have some of these Common Bantu lexical terms. But if you tried this experiment all over the Bantu area, Common Bantu would guarantee you a gambler's degree of success—probably better than evens (see Appendix B).

This third major variety (whether 'words' or 'sentences') is the one we are constantly talking about and the one we are using in our comparative studies today. To reconstruct this kind, we again study a large number of languages in one family, but this time we evolve forms that are a sort of common denominator. That is, we invent the simplest (vowel, consonant and tone) system to which all the sounds actually heard can rigorously be reduced. Not by a diachronic system of sound-shifts as before, but by an equally rigorous synchronic pattern of sound relationships. The starred forms do *not* tell us just exactly how anything was or is pronounced—but they do give us the simplest abstract 'common denominators' for all presently existing 'common words' (that is, words held in common between pairs or larger numbers of languages as spoken *today*). Thus, in synchronic Comparative Bantu, the starred form for a whole group of interrelated consonants normally heard in front of certain vowels as something like 'l' or 'r' is called *d. This is simply because the neatest consonant system in the abstract synchronic language has a pattern:

	lab.	alv.	pal.	vel.	
unvoiced plosives	*p	*t	*c	*k	
voiced plosives	*b	*d	*j	*g	*∅ (zero)
nasals	*m	*n	*ny	*ng'	

From this very simple consonant pattern, allied to an equally simple vowel pattern (*ị *i *e *a *o *u *ụ, which is comparable with the phonetic /i e ɛ a ɔ o u/), and to a two-tone system, all synchronic relationships between spoken forms may be naturally and absolutely rigorously established, in all three respects. Apparent anomalies in tone normally arise from rules of manifestation, representation or 'realization', themselves ultimately susceptible of rigorous analysis. To give an example from Guthrie (1967)[1] (tones are not given, but would reconstruct as H):

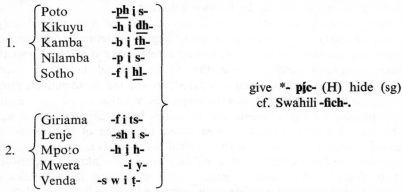

1.
Poto	-ph̲ i̱ s-
Kikuyu	-h i̱ dh̲-
Kamba	-b i̱ th̲-
Nilamba	-p i s-
Sotho	-f i̱ hl̲-

give *- pj̱c- (H) hide (sg)
cf. Swahili -fich-.

2.
Giriama	-f i ts-
Lenje	-sh i s-
Mpoto	-h i̱ h-
Mwera	-i y-
Venda	-s w i ṯ-

In (1): *p is (ph̲, h, b, p, f) whatever the following vowel, but -i̱- is what follows in these cases.

In (2): *p cannot be pinned down as in (1), but consistently turns up as (f, sh, h, 0, sw) if the following vowel is *-i̱-. From the two groups we can reconstruct *-pi̱-. Similarly from the following consonant one gets *c. Result $*-C_1V_1C_2- = *-pj̱c-$.

In this north-eastern study, we have always been dealing with this last type, 3. We have been looking at a pre-selected list of some 500 such, and trying to find 'reflexes' in certain languages. The 'reflex' must be rigorously relatable to the starred form: the sound-shifts must not be in doubt. There are of course always some marginal cases, which may lead us to doubt either the reconstructed starred form and/or the 'meaning in English' given in the list, and also more subtle cases about which the linguist-technicians might be disposed to argue among themselves. But in two important ways these do not much matter. If we consider 'any' few hundred items, it is obvious that it will be very likely to contain most of the items found in another 'good' list at the same numerical level. Thus, in about 100 items, the selection differences might perhaps amount to nothing at all. At the level of 500, the differences might become some-what significant (for example, I might have a list of 500, and you might have another of 500 but we overlap only in 475—so our original 'selection list' is in 'only' a 95 per cent agreement). Because of such difficulties, we decided to use only one list: this is the list circulated in cyclostyle by Guthrie from 1949/50 onward. Neither he nor we are saying that this list necessarily equals '*the* most common' 500 reflexes over the whole Bantu area. Nor do we say that this list simply equals 'the most solidly attested 500'. The criteria according to which items are selected naturally vary from one observer to another, and the list represents an individual collection of forms plus 'individually' attested meanings of the 500 most 'general' items as assessed by its own collector.

But—or so the reasoning ran—if we use one list and one list only, and if we always try to apply its author's degree of rigour to both sound-shifts and meaning ambience, we should surely arrive at a set of properly inter-comparable results within the whole field of languages being examined; these results, when compared, should tell us something more about the relationships between the languages, whether we all agree about the absolute validity of items and meanings in the original list or not. The lists of reflexes provide a measurable indication of the degrees of lexical overlap (at the level of the original list) and also, as an automatic but none the less welcome bonus, an easy means of making comparisons of phonologies. We are thus greatly aided in the task of classification, and hence in the setting up of probable more and less close genetic relation-ships. Furthermore, if we accept that the original list represents a fair sample of the more widespread starred forms, the new individual 'recovery rates' should tell us more about how closely each language is related to a common foundation, even if we reconstruct this synchronically. From this, it may be possible to deduce something concrete about the overall history.

Starred forms may be used in yet another way. Obviously, if a given form is widespread, it must reflect something that was familiar to the ancestral people, something in the proto-language. This does not necessa-rily mean that a starred form with a restricted distribution was *not* in the proto-language; in such a case, there is no certainty either way. From the widespread items, however, we can tentatively deduce at least something of the ancestral culture. To give a very generalized example of what may be done in this field, Roland Oliver,[2] supporting Malcolm Guthrie, suggests that the pre-Bantu immigrants left the sunny uplands of the northern savannah strip and plunged into the gloom and never-ending rain of the Great Forest, camping on river banks, at an altitude 4,000 feet below their own country, following the Ubangi (very hurriedly) down-stream via swampland-forest till they met the main Congo, continuing downstream for a further 200 miles, ignoring all tributaries to left or right, then inexplicably turning sharper than right angles upstream along the Kasai (or other), somehow unerringly avoiding (or else exploring and rejecting?) various fruitless branches, finally to emerge once more into the old familiar savannah or mosaic in Katanga—where they promptly reverted to their former, still unforgotten, way of life; and thereafter for hundreds of years (and for once unsurprisingly) did not venture back into the forest.

But, if we start from the Cameroon Highlands, near the home of the so-called semi-Bantu languages, and march along the open watersheds to the east, we pass Guthrie's area of origin near the Bongo Massif, and eastward we arrive at the Lake Albert gateway. Once across the one river[3]—the Semliki—to the south of the lake, and carrying on thereafter along watersheds, we are automatically led to the Rukwa—another gateway, this time straight into Guthrie's central nuclear area. We have seldom moved out of savannah or the mosaic, we have travelled almost all the way in relatively cool and for us healthy uplands, and have not needed to change our way of life in any respect.

If the watershed theory is correct, we should expect to find 'very early' carbon datings along the northern part of the hypothesized 'Bantu Trail.' In some places it might well be that the same sites could have been used twice—first by southbound 'early Bantu' (pre? proto?) and then perhaps again by a later reverse flow from Bembaland—then we would perhaps expect to get the same site datings up to or even more than a millennium apart. In any case, we must surely find fairly early datings (c. first half of first millennium A.D.) in what is now Bemba-Hemba country. For the Bantu Trail, I would recommend a deliberate exploration from around 8°N, 25°E, with special attention given to such places as Murchison, S. Kivu, Malagarasi River source and potential crossings— the mountains above the Rukwa Lake/Swamp (western watershed to Lake Tanganyika), and above Mbala, always looking for plausible seasonal movement. Aerial photo-survey at key points (gates) might help.

A very important to-me-imponderable: how long did the journey take? For instance, at an average 10 miles per season (this could obviously include zero movement to a hundred miles or so within 'a few years') it would have taken about 400 years. But if they were all really seized with an urge to press on quickly, they might have pushed on 100 miles at a time—a 40-year journey, or two or three generations overall. What would be the comparable time scale through the forest? How long ago would either hypothetical group have arrived in the Katanga-Bemba area? How long did they stay after arrival?

According to a map published by the Centre de Recherches Historiques de l'Ecole Pratique des Hautes Etudes, sorghum appears to have spread from around Lake Albert quite suddenly during the latter half of the last millennium B.C. and on into the first century A.D., into the whole of the area south of the rain-forest and north of the Zambezi, perhaps 2,000 miles. During the next 300 years it got as far as the Save River, about

119

600 miles. It took a further 600 years to cover the next 'straight' 400 miles southward, and perhaps another 200 to reach the southern coastline. It is especially noteworthy that sorghum did *not* appear in an expanding area from the south of the rain-forest, which it certainly would have done if it had been brought by the conjectured boatmen. (How they would have kept it and propagated it in the rain-forest would still be something of a mystery: I would have thought it would all have germinated or gone mouldy in the first few weeks.) The fact that it spread relatively fast from the northern lake area could indicate that it was carried by my hypothetical watershed travellers. (Even if the map has its dates wrong, I assume its contour shapes could not be wrong.)

Sorghum was perhaps already in the Meroë area in the second half of the second millennium B.C., so the sorghum and the iron could have moved away and even on to the Bantu Trail together, later. We should get 'recent' (i.e. the last 2,500 years) datings for sorghum reassessed with very much greater accuracy.

To revert to the rain-forest and some direct linguistic evidence. If there could have been *one* animal that would have impressed that Ubangi-Kasai expedition team, it would have been the crocodile. Yet we have **-gùèna** (east) and **-gàndú** (west): which clearly indicates that they did not bring one word for 'crocodile' with them out of the rain-forest. The very near-complementary west-east distribution tells us that the later proto-Bantu must have developed two dialect forms, *after they had split up*. (This actually adds more support to the watershed Bantu Trail—you are not so likely to be impressed by crocodiles if you are moving along head-waters.)

Our major sources for starred forms are (a) Guthrie's main list (containing some 2,200 lexical items), and (b) Meeussen's compilation (with about the same number, themselves collected from some 16 different publications). Nowhere do we find reconstructions for 'swamp', 'to drown', 'mudbank', 'other side of the river', 'rapids', or 'downstream'. (There exist very localized forms for 'upstream', which more normally means 'hill, top, up'; 'waterfall', and 'river-bank'.[4])

It seems almost inconceivable that the proto-language would not have had these as general forms if the proto-speakers had indeed come through the rain-forest. That is to say, 'common' versions of these words should be geographically everywhere in the Bantu area. Not only are they not everywhere, they are not even anywhere, within the 'common' series, or even in Guthrie's 'partial series'.

On the other hand, there is a widespread general form for 'well' or 'spring'—an unlikely feature in the forest basin, but very likely on the watershed. (Also an item for 'cross-river-by-fording': not so unlikely perhaps, but still somewhat improbable for canoeists.) There are also widespread general forms for 'cattle', 'goat', 'pig' and 'cattle-tick': together with these, 'guinea-fowl', 'kite', 'eagle' and 'impala' must presumably have developed after the putative forest trip, because the first group certainly could not have come through successfully by canoe (or even if driven?) and the second would not have been seen. The general 'thirst', 'dew' and 'forest-*patch*' seem unlikely—indeed they would be impossible *within* the forest. 'Rubbish-heap' seems to argue fairly long-term settlements. Then there are items we would certainly expect for the forest, but with the wrong kind of meanings: 'continuous rain' is normally more the drizzly kind (this could be mutation, of course); 'float' seems to be more 'on air' than 'on water'; and 'sink' means to be basically 'into ground' rather than 'into water'.

There are several other items which are subject to argument (e.g. 'buffalo', 'pangolin' and 'puff-adder' (what species?); also somewhat questionable are: 'moonlight', 'bright-day', 'great-lake'—and even 'paddle (liquid food v. canoe)' has an east-west distribution). And incidentally, there is absolutely no word for 'the great forest' itself.

Guthrie and Oliver are surely inconsistent with all ecological and linguistic probability. And, what is more, the watershed theory turns out to give us more reasonable reasons for existing language distribution patterns, both inside and outside the Bantu area.[5]

For example: very interesting is the distribution of the forms for 'iron'. There are at least four of these (six, if we follow Guthrie). Ironically, the form suggested as the most 'proto' by Guthrie is found in extreme western A, in the enclave round Mount Kenya, and in a great swathe reaching from D into M. The geographical implications will be apparent. The form *-tádè for 'stone' is far-west-coastal A, northern C, D and F. In E it means 'iron-ore'. In R, K, L, southern M and northern S, it means 'iron' (and in a very near-similar distribution it means 'pig-iron'). The full distribution is very complex, but may it not be significant that *-tádè means at least 'stone' in non-Bantu languages ranging from Temne in Sierra Leone to Kam and Mumuye on the upland border between Nigeria and Cameroon, across into languages of the Ubangi-Chari watershed? So in northern Bantu and bordering non-Bantu languages it means 'stone', but in southern Bantu it means 'iron'. On the other hand, in Bantu languages around Lake Victoria it means 'iron-ore'. Not one scrap of any of this can be made reasonably to fit with a people bringing iron with them via the Ubangi-Congo-Kasai route. But it could fit very well with one proto-word for 'stone' or 'ironstone'—*the* stone—being spread all across the peoples to the north of the forest and another word (this time for 'iron') penetrating (a) widely from around the north-eastern corner and (b) just a little from the far western (Cameroon) area; (c) perhaps subsequently re-linking with 'iron' while in our north-eastern area -*tádè stayed on as 'iron-ore' (in contrast to both *-gèdà 'iron' (hoe) and the very widespread *-úmà 'iron'. Incidentally, although *-úmà *is* widely 'iron', its most basic meaning is really more likely to be the more general 'thing' (hence, perhaps, its other meanings, 'things' or 'belongings' (*Siebensachen*), 'iron' (*the* 'Thing') and 'beads'). In some places, especially in the north-west, it carries a similar connotation to (and behaves very like) *-ntu, 'some (thing/body)'. It is in the far north-east that it means 'iron'.

The problem should be easy enough to resolve, by looking north of the Bantu border, and the answer would add one more piece of evidence to the Bantu 'iron story'. While on the subject of 'iron', let us note that *-tụ́d- 'forge' covers all but a small fraction of the Bantu area, and does not just stop dead along the northern Bantu line: this sort of evidence does not yet point either way, but e.g. Didinga -tur- is interesting.

To become more 'general' again, the relatively high percentage overall recovery rate in most of the north-eastern languages might further suggest that some of the people in this area branched off the main Bantu Trail early in the proto-period, and formed a nucleus of their own; the main stream carried on, mostly to settle for a time in what is now Bemba-Luba country. Some of this latter group may subsequently have retraced their steps, and overlaid the Bantu Trail and neighbouring areas to the east and north-east. ('Retracing' has often been noted in oral traditions: so has the 'leaving behind' phenomenon.) As an example of both, one might cite the Kamba or Kikuyu-like people who seem to have moved from the vicinity of Mount Kenya to the south of Kilimanjaro, even to the coast and back again, leaving behind them the Segeju/Dhaiso.

The lexical evidence will have to be sifted with very great care: can we sort out just what items might be associated with the hypothetical earlier wave? In this regard, it is especially noteworthy that Guthrie's own topogram analysis shows a very pronounced high 'ridge' along the presently hypothesized Bantu Trail (although his overall per cent recoveries in the north-eastern area seem to be lower than ours—and ratios are not regular—we can nevertheless assume that a *proportionally* similar high ridge will emerge when all results from further investigations have been collated). Whether the ridge has to do with the possible original southerly migration, or a later northerly, or both, it is there, and its languages should be subjected to very much more delicate inter-comparison. We must try to get more of a diachronic view if we possibly can: is there any detectable 'layering' or not? We now realize that so far our investigations have been relatively superficial—we must probe more deeply.

The chain along the eastern watershed could be examined fairly easily, consisting as it mostly does of languages which have been quite well or very well documented already, viz. Nyankole/Kiga—Ruanda/Rundi—Ha—(Holoholo)—Fipa/Lungu/Mambwe. Holoholo is bracketed because it is presumably an 'invader' from the western side of the Lake. At this point we do have a weak link: the Tongwe-Bende alternative would (as far as I know) have to be worked over from scratch, but the task is not all that daunting. The western watershed, on the other hand, would be a very tough proposition indeed; the chain has perhaps more than a score of languages, most of them small, many difficult to get at, and not previously investigated in any depth—or not at all.

For comparison with the eastern watershed chain, we could take languages to the east and south of Lake Victoria, viz. Gisu: 'Luyia': Logoli/Gusii—Jita—Sukuma—Nyamwezi—Kimbu.

The eastern watershed chain alone would give rise to the 'high ridge' in Guthrie's topograms, and Bemba-Luba form the yet higher 'plateau'. If, from closer study, we can establish direction for the arrow(s) on the map, and if the archaeologists can produce confirmatory chains of carbon dates (both 'early' and 'late') we may even be able to put a realistic number for 'r' into the presently near-meaningless formula for Bantu glottochronometry. Once we have this, the patterns of dispersion should become both clear and dateable. Two kinds of decay rate, one physical and one linguistic, may thus be used to help two social sciences to solve each other's problems.

The steady decay rates in radioactive elements are by now familiar (and also very accurately determined). Lexical decay rates are perhaps not so widely known about, and certainly not so well determined—except for languages that became 'written' a long time ago; for these, we do have a pretty good idea of the rate at which they lost words, replacing them with others.

There is, or once was, an elegant formula for this which reads: $t = \dfrac{\log C}{2 \log r}$ where t is the minimum length of time ago in thousands of years, C is the percentage of words left in common in a specially constructed list, and r is the 'standard' rate of retention per thousand years. This looks beautifully simple, but there are one or two snags. We are still not really sure about the value of r anywhere, and not at all for Bantu. It seems likely that it lies between about 75 and 85 per cent—provided that (and this is a very big proviso indeed) there has been no interference from mass conquest, mass migration or large scale natural

123

disasters. Since these events may themselves be part of the very history we are trying to find out about, the method is far from reliable. If we do not actually know r beforehand, then log r can vary between limits that give results as vague as somewhere between 4 and 7 thousand (or 4/7 anything) years ago.[6]

A small difference in decay rate will make a difference of several hundred years to our answer. There are some serious implications when we come to consider the 'fine structure' of r. In the basic vocabulary that we use, the words must have been selected by processes of elimination—there is no other way: we have no external or *a priori* criteria that would say, 'This item must be in the list—you have only to look at it to see'! Now, there are several different classes of word in the list: in the English list we find pronouns, nouns, adjectives, demonstratives, interrogatives, verbs. If we consider these semantically, we find words relating to natural phenomena, parts of the body, colours, animals, people, qualities, kinship terms, verbs of motion, verbs of action. We can also divide them into phonetic shapes such as CV, CVC, CVCV—and we can refine this kind of classification into 'what sort of C or V, followed by what?' Firstly, we know that different categories decay at different rates within one given language; secondly, we know that the same meaning categories decay differently in different languages; thirdly, a given grammatical or phonetic category may not even occur at all in a given language, or an item may occupy different classes in different languages.

In Bantu languages, it is very likely that r is much more stable and (potentially) accurately determinable than any of the foregoing might suggest, if only because of the overall appearance of homogeneity within so many hundreds of languages. The only trouble is, we have as yet no value for it at all. The C percentage should be very accurately determinable indeed, though I do most strongly feel we shall have to agree beforehand on a modified basic vocabulary. Just to take three or four very simple examples: in the 100-item list, we find the word 'not', which is not a word at all in Bantu; 'cut', which can mean so many different things in Bantu that it is quite unusable without further definition; 'red' and 'yellow' which are indistinguishable, and the word 'green' which does not even exist.

Outside of such obvious drop-outs, the five or six hundred general Bantu list only covers about two-thirds of the one hundred Swadesh list, so we clearly need to do some work (from and in Common Bantu) on new glottochronological basic lists. Finally, if we call the formula t=log C/j log r we need to establish a Bantu j: the Swadesh j equalled 2: overall, Hattori suggests j should be refined to 1.4 (11!). So much possible variation may well imply that the Bantu value is yet something else;

perhaps our comparative Bantu studies may help us to find both a more accurate Bantu *j*, and also a 'good' Bantu retention rate.

SUMMING UP

1. We are already on the way to a new assessment of the relationships between various north-eastern languages. Those so far tackled (at the 500 starred form level) include Gisu, Kiga, Kikuyu, Logoli, Ribe, Swahili: and from material supplied, Giriama, Gusii, Kamba, Pokomo (all W. H. Whiteley) and Nyamwezi (J. D. Collinson). In general, percentages of reflexes so far observed seem to be somewhat higher than comparable percentages quoted by M. Guthrie; but perhaps yet more important results will be found as a kind of 'side effect'—as the relationships between the sub-families of these languages become clearer, we shall be able to offer more help to historians
    (a) of comparatively recent times (~ 500 years);
    (b) conceivably, further back still (cf. Greenberg's much wider kind of study)—e.g. see my very elementary remarks on 'stone' and 'iron'.
2. We have arrived at an alternative to the Guthrie hypothesis which might suggest a 'secondary' role for the 'nucleus'. Earlier branchings and later retracing of steps could be considered—we can try to test the new hypothesis by making definite suggestions to archaeologists about where to look, and even what to expect.
3. We are also on the way to further comparison between the north-eastern languages in general, and the Guthrie nuclear languages. This already seems to show that the nucleus is fairly recent (consequently high but 'flat', rather than bumpily diversified).
4. We may be able to establish the value of r; if we do, we shall be able to give the historians some fairly accurate datings.
5. Quite apart from 'historical' results, we are obtaining an insight into comparative phonotonologies, and (on the side) even into comparative morphologies, which will enable us to give 'deep' advice on the structuring of primary school course books, in several different ways, viz.
    (a) Orthographies (vitally important to ease of learning, but difficult to change as we know, because of vested interests—but if we can show that 'our' orthographies could create better readers/writers quicker, we should surely be given the chance to conduct some controlled experiments).

(b) Order of 'presentation' in a given language.

(c) Advisability of using a given 'sub-structure' for a given course (languages may or may not be compatible for one sub-structure). Could one, for instance, employ one basic text for two or more languages? Personally, I doubt it.

6. We might be in a position to advise on possible wider and less 'tribal' configurations which would help in both primary education and in administration. This is rather long-term, because people give up even local dialect forms only under internal pressure—rarely from external requirements, however rational these may be.

NOTES

[1] *Comparative Bantu*, vol. I, Gregg International Press, 1967.

[2] Roland Oliver, 'The Problem of the Bantu Expansion', *Journal of African History*, VII, 3, 1966.

[3] One could also stay on the western side, and get as far as the Mitwanzi Gorge, without crossing any rivers, or stay on the western side of the lakes until the gap between Lake Kivu and the volcanoes (Mufumbiro and others), but I think the watershed would have been very much more difficult to negotiate.

[4] Meeussen cites Homburger (1925) *-cinja, river-bank, and *-pupa, waterfall, *-pup-fall drop by drop, in languages of the S.W.

[5] Later lexico-statistical work by Henrici (1971) (on Guthrie's 28 test languages) and especially by Heine (1973) (on his much wider selection of 137 languages) shows that virtually the whole Bantu domain is now occupied by one giant sub-section of the family, and that there must have been some relatively slow (and limited?) penetrations of the forest along the Atlantic coast from the Benue-Cameroon area, and also from the north-central and north-eastern forest fringes (I believe probably somewhat prior to the vastly wider occupation we have at present). This means that almost all vocabulary examined belongs to the giant sub-section; but this need not invalidate the theory of an expansion or migration along the watershed—indeed, it can be construed as offering very considerable support. Ehret (1972) postulates a slow expansion south-eastwards through the forest generally; this is perhaps superseded by the present suggested modifications. But in all our more recent work, there is a general agreement on a much greater 'Eastern' area than that put forward by Guthrie. Ehret divides Zones ABC/D-S, while Henrici's results would cut off Zone A from the rest, and Heine cuts some of A, B and D out from B-S.

[6] Since this was written (1969) the author has realized that the earlier formula was in any case much too crude. Instead, summation formulae must be used, to allow for changes in r through time, different r's between languages, and different hardnesses of lexical items. Then with computer aid, and fixes from oral history, it should be possible to construct realistic distance-diagrams with reasonably accurate time-metrics (at least for Bantu).

Appendix A

Suggestions for Further Research

Investigate (non-linguistic):
(a) sorghum-spread over last 2,500 years: can anything yet be done on pollens?
(b) archaeological evidence on watersheds and at certain river crossing places, especially:
    (1) Bongo Massif and east/west watersheds, to
    (2) (a) Cameroon Highlands, and (b) Volta;
    (3) (a) Murchison, and (b) south of Lake Albert; (c) south of Kivu;
    (4) Malagarasi crossings; and perhaps opposite side of Lake at
    (5) Mitwanzi Gorge;
    (6) above Rukwa, on range above south of Lake Tanganyika;
    (7) dispersal watershed point, south of this;
    (8) dispersal watershed point in central area;
    (9) other dispersal watershed points.
Investigate (linguistic):
(a) 'phonological' cross-correspondences between languages in detail:
    (1) at 500 level;
    (2) at 2,000 level;
(b) 'meaning' cross-correspondences in detail (not necessarily in either list; but also looking for items reasonably expected);
(c) 'shape + meaning' cross-correspondences in the 2,000 starred form list, and in my own 3,500 item service list. To lead to publication of 'basic Bantu' vocabularies, and comparative lists at any convenient levels between, say, 800 and 3,500;
(d) place names: (i) meanings;
                  (ii) stratigraphy;
(e) last but obviously not least: there is an urgent need to do a similar study on Cushitic, Nilotic, Para-Nilotic and 'unclassified' languages in this area. For this purpose, the 'area' should be regarded as at least Uganda-Sudan-Ethiopia-Somalia-Tanzania,as well Kenya.

PART TWO

Language Use

5

Nairobi: Problems and Methods

D. J. PARKIN

While problems of multilingualism and language choice are clearly most conveniently studied in densely populated 'hetero-lingual' communities such as occur in towns (see Whiteley, 1969, p. 106), there is not yet agreement as to what constitutes the sociolinguistic approach to these problems. This chapter suggests a particular approach which is both deliberately restricted and exploratory.[1]

Nairobi, the capital of Kenya, has many of the characteristics of African towns of relatively recent creation: it has a strong historical association with European colonialism; and a large African labour force which has only recently, since independence, become fully represented in the administration of the city. A low proportion of this African population was born in the city; most of the African population expect to retire to their rural homes after a career of urban employment. Men are more numerous than women in the city, and rural homes remain important for members of the various ethnic groups, many of whom continue to choose a wife from home, hold land there, and send their children to school there.

Nevertheless, there is an increasing commitment to Nairobi by many of its residents, and it is incorrect to view the city's African population as little more than transitory migrants.

Nairobi is the largest town in East Africa, with a population at the 1969 census of 509,286. Its growth rate is about 6 per cent per annum, twice that of the rural areas and thrice that of Kenya as a whole. Africans constitute about 82 per cent of Nairobi's population, Asians about 14 per cent and Europeans 4 per cent.

In such a large African population, it might at first sight seem meaningless to talk in terms of constituent group relations. But, as Mitchell showed (1956), ethnic categories emerge as convenient units of interaction and reduce the plethora of urban social relations to more manageable proportions. More than this, there is mounting evidence to suggest that in a number of African towns ethnic interest *groups* may be said to exist

(Cohen 1969a, Parkin 1969). That is to say, many economic, political and social relationships seem to be clustered among people who call themselves 'fellow tribesmen' and who are thereby distinguishable as such by more than simple differences of esoteric custom.

Nairobi is no exception. While there are important internal divisions which cut across ethnic ties, it is legitimate to talk in terms of the main ethnic units in Nairobi as constituting interest groups, provided that the concept of interest group is regarded as a matter of degree.

The four main ethnic groups in Nairobi are, in the order of their size in the city, Kikuyu, Luyia, Luo and Kamba. Together these four make up 90 per cent of Nairobi's African population. Kikuyu are by far the most numerous at over 45 per cent, Luyia are just over 15 per cent, Luo nearly 15 per cent, and Kamba just over 14 per cent.

As well as being divided into ethnic groups, the city is physically divided into distinct residential zones. The most significant are the ones labelled 'Asian' and 'European' areas, which no longer are exclusively so (see Neale *infra*), and the African housing areas, mostly located in the eastern part of the city. In this eastern part, some of which is actually called Eastlands, are many housing estates, few of which can be said to be true 'communities', but which nevertheless are often associated in the minds of many people with certain ethnic and status groups.

As well as looking at Pumwani, the predominantly Muslim area which most closely approaches a definition of 'community' (see Bujra *infra*), we looked at public and private housing areas. For statistical and demographic purposes which are discussed in Chapters 6 and 7, I have concentrated here on two city council housing estates, but in Chapter 8, where I analyse conversational and local-level speech patterns, I draw my examples more widely.

But before I present concrete data, I believe it is important to discuss the problem of what we should be looking for in a sociolinguistic analysis and what methods we should use in that analysis. This, then, is my immediate task.

THE SOCIAL ANTHROPOLOGICAL VIEW

Many social and cultural anthropologists are concerned with the study of language as a cultural phenomenon in its own right rather than as simply an indispensable tool of field-work. Some are definitely linguistically oriented and incorporate assumptions and methods from linguistics in their intensive analyses of small scale societies (Bright 1966, Burling 1962, Colby 1966, Conklin 1955 and 1962, Coult 1966, Faris 1968, Goodenough 1956, 1965, Lounsbury 1965, Metzger and Williams 1963, and Whiteley 1966).

Certain other social anthropologists fall into two broad categories which are relevant for the present analysis. First, there are those who analyse language use and verbal categories as distinguishing symbols in relations within and between groups or whole societies (Epstein 1959, Finnegan 1969, Fox 1968, Leach 1954, 1958, Tambiah 1969, and others). Members of this category do not start on the basis of linguistic assumptions and methods but from those which are central to that brand of social anthropology which studies 'customs' (i.e. customary modes of behaviour) in social relations (see Cohen 1969b). An early good example of this is Leach (1954). Leach was able to provide a systematic account of how a people shift their language affiliations in order to denote an impending shift in political affiliations. As indicated above, a few studies have recently appeared which are of this tradition, and it is clear that this view will continue to command the attention of some social anthropologists.

A second category, who have yet to make their presence felt in sociolinguistics, appear to be influenced by or show similarities with the work of Frederick Barth (1966). Barth is concerned with transactional analysis, or the way in which dyadic relations are conducted on the basis of a series of 'prestations' and 'counter-prestations' between persons who have different kinds and quantities of resources of 'power' at their command and are at the same time subject to normative constraints. This is a microscopic view of the individual in personal interaction.

Cohen (1969b) has suggested that these group-focused and individual-focused anthropological approaches tend to lead away from each other in different directions: the more you focus on the individual the less you focus on the group. Bailey (1969 and London University Lectures 1970) appears to have successfully ridden both horses and it remains to be seen how far the straddling can go.

I use certain of Bailey's theoretical constructs in the analysis of conversations in Chapter 8. But I am here less concerned with the attempt to straddle than with using these two approaches as means of ordering the data. That is to say, I shall show how language shift may occur as a result of the state of power relations between groups, some ethnic and some socio-economic; but I shall also show how individuals in dyadic relations use language in order to compete with each other in an apparent attempt to maximize personal interests.

This two-fold ordering of the data is put very simply here and can be expressed more sophisticatedly later. It represents a basic social anthropological standpoint. But there are those sociolinguists who have drawn on anthropological and sociological assumptions and methods but who have not made explicit use of this two-fold distinction. Bernstein, Fishman, Gumperz and Hymes are four of those who may be regarded as having considerable influence at the present time, though this is inevitably a somewhat personal limited choice and excludes consideration of many other important scholars.

Their views can be discussed very briefly in an attempt to link them up with the social anthropological approach adopted in this section.

SOCIOLINGUISTIC VIEWPOINT

Fishman's concept of situational domains is defined initially by sociological rather than by formal linguistic criteria. Simplifying somewhat, his 'domains of language behaviour' are based on spheres of activities. These are organized into specific sets of role-relations which are culturally designated as belonging to a particular sphere of activities. In his study of Puerto Ricans in their New York *barrio* (lit: neighbourhood), he sees six domains: home, school, church, work sphere, neighbourhood, and public places outside the neighbourhood. The number, type and relative importance of such domains will of course vary from one area of study to another, though certain consistent associations may be expected depending on the particular structure of, say, the family or the neighbourhood (Fishman 1968b).

Fishman wants to reconcile the macro- and the micro-sociolinguistic factors in a single analysis. For him, the concept of domain links (1) the minutiae of detail involved in the intensive analysis of language use in face-to-face role-relations, with (2) the broader, more generalized characteristics of numerically large linguistic communities, such as ethnic groups and nations.

Fishman's concern with the macro- can be seen in two facets of his work: his use of extensive quantitative data, which are *statistically* analysed and not used simply to illustrate empirical impression; and his interest in the role of language in national and international integration and in classifying types of integration (in Whiteley 1971). These interests are always likely to draw the investigator away from intensive analysis of individual speech events (i.e. 'instances of parole'), a problem which Fishman seems to recognize. For instance, he reproduces a diagram from R. L. Cooper (1968) as an illustration of the 'several levels and approaches to sociolinguistic description . . . ', choice of which 'depends on the particular problem at hand' (Fishman 1968a). The diagram is excellent in its comprehensiveness and provides a blueprint for research and analysis. Because it is comprehensive, it inevitably embraces a wide range of phenomena relating to speech activities. At the macro-level there are the community 'value clusters', which surmount 'domains' and 'network types', within which respectively, there are individual 'social situations' and 'role-relationships', which are micro-level phenomena. Fishman recognizes the difficulties of studying all these facets of speech development and activity in a single analysis but does applaud the blueprint as such. In applauding it, he applauds also the approach proposed by Gumperz, which is incorporated in Cooper's diagram.

Gumperz is not concerned like Fishman with domains but wishes to isolate 'only those roles or role clusters which correlate with significant speech differences' (in Fishman (ed.) 1968c). In other words he sees language, dialect, or code-switching as likely to result from the properties of particular role-relations which may or may not be tied to a particular domain. This focus on role-relationships suggests that Gumperz is more interested in analysing *intensively* a limited number of 'speech events', and the 'transactional' elements governing interactions. He thus contrasts with Fishman who appears to be more interested in analysing more *extensively* the problem of identifying domains and their constituent social situations.

At first sight this appears to be a contrast of *tendencies* rather than theoretical orientation. Both Gumperz and Fishman see value in reconciling the macro- and micro-sociolinguistic approaches and would probably see themselves as differing only in (a) analytical starting point, and (b) emphasis. This may be so. But it is worthwhile to note that there is here a problem similar to that expressed by Cohen for social anthropology within the scope of a single analysis, in which it is difficult to focus in great detail on both group relations and on essentially dyadic transactional relations. Thus, in sociolinguistics too, we should at least be aware of the possible difficulties in attempting to straddle two divergent tendencies.

The concern in Gumperz's work with 'transactional' elements in individual interactions is reflected in some of the analytical concepts used by both him and Hymes. These include 'speech economy' as an aspect of a 'speech community', which may be understood by plotting an 'ethnography of speaking' (see Hymes' article in *Readings in the Sociology of Language*, Fishman (ed.), 1968c). More specifically, Hymes suggests that '. . . a comparative ethnography of speaking is but one kind of comparative study of the *utilization of cultural resources*' (my italics). This view of language as a resource is surely bound to lead to analysis of the transactional elements in speech interactions.

Bernstein's approach can be seen as an attempt to describe the various ways in which differently structured or ranked groups make use of their particular language resources either to achieve efficient intra-group communication or to communicate with other groups. Key concepts in Bernstein's analysis are elaborated as against restricted codes, and now-codes (formed on the spot in a verbal interaction) as against high-codes (ready-made codes). These depend essentially on the operation of two variables: the degree of lexical and syntactic predictability in a verbal interaction. The concepts are well known and will continue to stimulate much thought and discussion, as they have already. What is important for the social anthropologist is Bernstein's attempt to see these codes as, among other things, 'properties', 'tools', and symbols of variously defined groups. Individuals make use of these codes by virtue of their membership of such groups. Though Bernstein has yet to present ethnographic detail illustrating the operation of these codes, it is possible that this general scheme is one which will help social anthropologists in straddling the problem of transactional and group analysis. That is to say, we can agree with Bernstein's suggestion that a speaker is, on the one hand *constrained* by the language resources which his group's status, situationally defined, allows him. Yet, as an individual he is sometimes offered the possibility of moving into different groups and so into possession, sometimes privileged, of different language resources (Bernstein 1965 and 1966).

There is in all this material, and in additional studies correlating language styles with social status and mobility (see Labov, Levine and Crockett, and Hunt in Lieberson 1966), an important implicit distinction. On the one hand, we can discern empirically the *immediate* 'on the spot' switching of codes, dialects or languages made by an individual within a single verbal interaction or conversation. On the other hand, we can discern the more *enduring* differences of code, dialect or language use which distinguish different groups. An individual may be a member of a number of groups, but he is excluded from membership of other groups because he lacks the appropriate ascribed or achieved qualifications. Some of these he may achieve or inherit and so be able to move into the groups. An interesting problem then posed is not only to observe how he adopts the appropriate code/dialect/language after entering the new group, but also, beforehand, how his *anticipation* of entry into the group affects his linguistic behaviour.

All this begins to fit in well with much 'conventional' social anthropological analysis. We are thus able to move from (a) an investigation of the groups whose memberships frequently overlap and are bound variously by networks of ties and obligations based on selected spheres of activities, to (b) an investigation of how an individual makes use of existing language resources by virtue of his group membership and how he increases, or even decreases, his resources by anticipating movement into other groups.

Two questions must be answered before we can claim that this is truly a social anthropological standpoint. First, how do we define and evaluate the groups? Are some quasi-groups or simply close-knit or loose-knit groups? Are they corporate? Most importantly, which groups may be said to be most significant as regards the dominant social organizational principle articulating the activities under study? In other words, who controls the operation of the activities and how is their control maintained? A second, related question is to ask the nature of the particular 'problem'. It may be methodologically less useful for a social anthropologist as such, to go straight to an investigation of sociolinguistic phenomena. His problem should be broader to begin with and gradually focus on the particular role of language as a cultural phenomenon. Our problem here is ethnicity, or more particularly, the role of cultural differences in the formation of political interest groups. Language is one of these cultural differences, which has its own special qualities.

I have tried to outline similarities in the approaches of some sociolinguists, and of much 'functionalist' social anthropology. This is a deliberately restricted approach, since I wish here to concentrate initially on a few variables.

Let me now present my own scheme for analysing material collected on language shift and language choice in selected areas of Nairobi. This methodological approach can be given in the form of stages:

SCHEME FOR ANALYSIS

1. The 'problem' has been defined as that of 'ethnicity', or more specifically the role of language in the political relations of ethnic or 'tribal' groups. No prior assumption is made that such groups are necessarily in political competition. This is a conclusion reached after observation.

2. We must distinguish language shift and language switching. A 'shift' refers to language changes that are associated with whole groups, for instance, ethnic groups. A 'switch' refers to a change in code/dialect/language within a single conversation or between different 'situations'. The 'shift' and the 'switch' do not necessarily represent a change from one 'pure' form to another. There may be so much lexical, syntactic or phonological 'mixture' of two or more forms that it may sometimes be difficult to distinguish what constitutes a 'switch' or 'shift' from supposedly different forms. This latter is more obviously a socio-*linguistic* problem. Though I touch on examples of this, I am here interested in the more easily observable (though not necessarily more frequent or common) changes between regularly distinguishable forms. This is a matter of ease

and convenience. It is also methodologically in line with the initial emphasis in the analysis on group relations and dyadic relations with respect to group membership.

3. The problem of language shift as against language switching is part of the problem of macro- as against, or, more accurately, as a complement to, micro-sociolinguistic analysis as discussed above. Let me at least attempt to tackle this problem by making use of and extending Fishman's concept of language maintenance and language shift (Fishman 1968c). I believe that, technical difficulties apart, and provided that one controls for lexical, phonological and syntactic factors, it is theoretically possible to trace and measure within a speech community the extent to which there is (a) language stability (maintenance); (b) language adding; and (c) language substitution. By *language stability* is meant the absence of any 'significant' change in the respective language repertoires of interacting and linguistically different groups. 'Significant' is only meaningful in relation to the phenomena compared, and language stability, like the other concepts, is quite obviously relative. By *language adding* is meant the adoption by, say, group A of the language of group B. In other words group A has increased its repertoire of languages. Relevant questions to ask are: under what social and political conditions does this adoption occur; and is the added language used for 'new' situations which have recently emerged (as, for example, in a swiftly industrializing environment), or does it operate in conjunction with an existing language in either 'new' or 'old' situations? By *language substitution* is meant the absolute replacement of one language by another (the added one) either in all situations relevant to the group or in no more than one or a limited number of situations. The same questions may be asked as for language adding. Language substitution is, of course, preceded by language adding and so reflects a radical change in the nature of group relations.

Using these measures, we can construct a single 'model'. The model assumes that language adding and substitution can occur at different levels of scale within a system of interacting groups. In other words, a group can be 'adding' simultaneously a number of languages, some of groups with which it interacts, others which are lingua francas. More than this, the rates of 'adding' or increased usage may vary with different languages for any one group. Finally, language 'substitution' may occur when, even while one language is being 'added' for certain purposes by all or some of the population, a more embracing language is being added at an even greater rate for a wider range of purposes and thus may ultimately replace not only the languages recently added for limited purposes but also the group's 'mother tongue'.

I have the image of wider and more comprehensive circles around any one group, each circle denoting a language being used or added. As a simple hypothetical example, 'tribe' A, our ego, is adding the language (denoted by the innermost circle) of its neighbour, tribe B, who are the local traders. Meanwhile, both are adding the language (the intermediary circle) of a numerically larger and politically more powerful group, tribe C. At the same time, for the increasing proportion of educated within each of these groups, a prestigious lingua franca, say English (the outermost circle), is being used a great deal in certain workplace and political activities and is even ousting the vernaculars in these important social areas. Or, 'filling in' between the wider, more 'official' uses of English and the domestic and local uses of the vernaculars may be another lingua franca like Swahili, which in Kenya has a highly practical value in border and mixed areas, though its prestige may be less.

If we make tribe B or C our ego, then we have a different pattern of concentric circles corresponding with varying degrees of language adding or substitution, each pattern resting on variable situational uses to which the languages (and, of course, I include here codes and dialects also) are put. The distance from the centrally placed ego to a circle can represent at any given time the language denoted as a proportion of a people's total language repertoire as based on self-reports and checked as far as is possible by systematic observations. By making simple statistical measures over time, actual rates of language adding and substitution can be diagrammed using this scheme.

The approach suggested by this scheme would in itself require a separate study and I do no more than present the scheme here. Border areas or other ethnically mixed areas, such as towns, and rural markets and trading centres, are the best loci. For example, in the Gusii/Kipsigis/Luo rural border area for which we have data (see Whiteley *infra*, p. 321) and in Nairobi (*infra*, p. 169) each ethnic group shows widely varying patterns of language adding. Further investigation could reveal the situations in which specific languages are used, the rates of language adding, and the substitution in particular situations of one language by another.

Actual processes of language adding and substitution are, of course, highly complicated and it is the work of the model to depict only the most salient characteristics. The process described is thus (a) measurable, and (b) essentially a political process, if we accept that language shift is a form of cultural shift and that cultural shifts occur in conjunction with changes in the economic and power relations of 'groups' (ethnic, national, local, regional, occupational, etc.).

Most individual conversations are not directly determined by the prevailing political situation. But some are (see Parkin 1971) and, few though they may be, they do at least constitute data which link the problems of language shift and language switching. Other conversations involving switching may be compared with them so that contrasting sociological governing factors, if any, may be isolated for analysis. These concerns are distinct from those of that brand of sociolinguistics which seek to demonstrate how essentially linguistic changes, rather than simply conversational switching, are influenced or determined by social factors (e.g. P. Friedrich, and L. Levine and H. J. Crockett, in Lieberson 1966).

I think, therefore, that the subject matter of sociolinguistics can be summarized as falling into the following categories:

1. language *shift*: (a) language adding
   (b) language substitution
   } converse: language stability.
2. language/dialect/code *switches*: i.e. small group/dyadic transactional speech patterns seen in *paroles*.
3. socially determined *linguistic changes*: i.e. specific lexical, syntactic, and phonological alterations in *langue*.

I am concerned with the first two categories but not with the third, which must be analysed at a level of detail which cannot be attempted in the present study. I now discuss two major organizing principles in the social lives of Nairobi's residents. One stems from ethnic affiliation; people claim that they have obligations and duties by virtue of their membership of an ethnic group. A second derives from membership of what Weber called status-groups; people tend to choose friends and neighbours with similar life styles to their own and so become involved in a web of mutually reinforcing expectations, some of which conflict with the alleged duties to fellow members of ethnic groups and sub-groups. Language use in Nairobi can be seen against these two principles, whose precise operation is governed very much by the degree of ethnicity in the prevailing political situation: the greater the degree of ethnicity, the stronger the sanctions against personal commitment in relationships which cut across ethnic groups. Personal commitment of this kind, such as mixed marriages, friendships, or joint economic enterprises, may involve learning and using the vernacular of an ethnic group other than one's own. In conditions of considerable ethnicity, this *may* invoke the disapproval of fellow members of one's ethnic group who see this social and linguistic integration as tantamount to 'treachery' or desertion. But sometimes, it does not. It is interesting, therefore, to understand which vernaculars may be learned and used with impunity and which not, and in which situations. In contrast to the vernaculars are the lingua francas, which are associated less with a particular ethnic group but more with affiliations of a national or, particularly, socio-economic kind.

ETHNIC INTEREST GROUPS IN NAIROBI

I have not the space to detail the present conditions of ethnicity in Nairobi. There is the impressionistic view and there is also the view conveyed by extensive systematic surveying. For anyone familiar with Kenya politics, it is almost a truism to state that the popularly expressed cleavage is between Kikuyu, on the one hand, and Luo on the other, the two numerically largest ethnic groups. The two other important and also large ethnic groups represented in Nairobi are the Luyia and Kamba.

It is not my task here to justify or question this popular view of the current dominant cleavage, nor to ask whether this is really an idiom for expressing another more 'concrete' underlying cleavage. It would of course be foolish to suggest that 'all' Kikuyu or 'all' Luo felt the same way about each other, or that they were all locked in a state of mutual hostility. At the interpersonal level, as anywhere else in the world, people of different tongues and cultural backgrounds interact with each other without reference to their respective origins: there are the tasks of workplace, the chores of domestic life in a mixed neighbourhood, the friendliness of dance and drink in city bars and clubs, all conducted according to the expectations of the situation at hand, and not according to whether, say, a workmate is a Luo or Kikuyu.

It is likely that divisions along 'class' lines are occurring within and also across ethnic groups. Yet, at the same time, ethnic groups are continuing to maintain their distinctiveness. There is very little intermarriage between the four major groups, and when it occurs, it is more likely to do so under the unifying rubric of Islam (see Bujra *infra*). Close friends are still likely to be chosen from within one's own ethnic group. It is to such friends and to one's own close kin that a man turns for help. Most of Nairobi's African population are born in 'tribal' districts to which many of them plan to return. They invest savings from urban incomes in farms and build 'permanent' houses on their farms. None of this is to suggest that a man indiscriminately asks any fellow tribesman for help. He is likely to get short shrift if he does. But appeal to common ethnic group membership does at least provide an established relationship with a morally approved idiom or enable a new relationship to be established through it. Relationships are established and continued when there is short-term or long-term mutual advantage, which may be of an affective as well as material kind. Common ethnic group membership provides not only an approved idiom with which to justify the relationship, it also provides the participants with a common knowledge of the customs and language which is at least initially useful.

If this is obvious, it has at least to be stated as an alternative to the

141

simplistic view that emerging socio-economic divisions preclude the usefulness of ethnic ties. Socio-economic ties and ethnic ties may, of course,
converge. But, even where they do not, they each may be used separately
according to situation. Both are reinforced by ideal norms and distinct
symbolism, but socio-economic ties tend to have a more pragmatic
utilitarian content while ethnic ties are couched in an idiom of high
'moral' content.

It is especially since independence that the cleavage, as it is seen,
between Kikuyu and Luo has developed. Before independence and for
some time afterwards, these two groups were in a political party alliance,
the Kenya African National Union. This party became the ruling party
in the independent Kenya and was opposed by the Kenya African Democratic Party, which included a majority of the Luyia and possibly half
of the Kamba.

Under the colonial regime, the Kenya Emergency from 1952 to 1959
was especially aimed at restricting the activities of the Kikuyu. In Nairobi,
the proportion of Kikuyu in the labour force and in the city's resident
population declined considerably. Since the ending of the Emergency
in 1959 the proportion of Kikuyu has swung back to the pre-Emergency
situation. In the context of a rising rate of unemployment proportionate
to the growing Nairobi population, it is inevitable that this sharp reversal
of the ethnic proportions should constitute a major cause of the current,
popularly expressed ethnic cleavage. The founding of the Kenya People's
Union in 1965 with its apparently core Luo membership, such issues as
the disqualification of KPU candidates at the Nairobi City Council
elections in 1968, the banning of KPU prior to the general elections in
1969, and allegations of Kikuyu oath-taking at about the same time,
seemed to confirm the popular expression of the cleavage and, on the
strength of this, actually caused a hardening of ethnic lines. Let me repeat
that I do not intend to discuss the 'true' nature of the cleavage. I simply
accept that the majority of ordinary people in Nairobi were made especially
conscious of the cleavage by issues of the kind mentioned. This is part
of the Nairobi town dweller's 'world view' and it is this which I find
relevant in my analysis of language use.

Our figures from a number of housing areas confirm that, in recent
years, the proportion of Kikuyu residents has increased. Housing is in
direly short supply in Nairobi and is a major grievance underlying much
friction and political activity. Similarly, in a number of city council markets,
the proportion of Kikuyu stall-holders has increased. Again, these increased
proportions may simply reflect a reversion to the pre-Emergency situation.
But it is town dwellers' personal experience of such visibly obvious, local
changes that feed the popular impression of a growing ethnic cleavage.

Yet, jobs *are* increasing even if the rate of increase is not high enough to keep pace with the demand stimulated by growing numbers of school-leavers and urban migrants. Significant numbers of men and women are developing life styles and aspirations which variously mark them off as members of distinct status-groups. Use of language, say English as against Swahili or a vernacular in certain situations, is one obvious indicator of such life styles and aspirations.

Now that I have introduced briefly the two organizing principles: one deriving from ethnic group membership, and the other from status-group membership, I can concentrate on describing the salient characteristics of each of them with regard to language use. I begin first in the next chapter with status-group membership and its effect on language adding, (defined on page 147). One area in Nairobi lends itself particularly well to an initial experiment to measure this effect. This is Bahati housing estate, which is 97 per cent Kikuyu and which has a large proportion of long established residents who have lived in Nairobi since before the Emergency. Most of the residents are low-income earners and there is little heterogeneity of socio-economic status (i.e. of educational, income, and occupational levels). Because it is predominantly Kikuyu, with low-income workers showing a limited range of educational and occupational levels, it enables us to focus in detail on the more subtle sociological factors underlying language adding. In other words, to put it simply, we can control for the ethnic variable and can more easily concentrate on slight differences within one or two status-groups rather than broad differences between a number of status-groups. As I shall show, this facilitates the 'intensive analysis of extensive data',[2] yet produces conclusions of almost universal application in the study of language use in Nairobi. I shall later apply these conclusions in a more extended analysis of a housing estate, called Kaloleni, which contrasts with Bahati in being ethnically and socio-economically highly diverse.

As well as providing these conclusions, the following chapter on language adding among the Kikuyu of Bahati is also an exercise in methodology. I explain in some detail each stage in the analysis, but give now a simple shorthand statement of the conclusions reached:

1. Swahili and English are both lingua francas.
2. There is an inverse correlation between (a) educational level, and (b) the usage and growth in usage of Swahili in Nairobi, i.e. Swahili is spreading from the lower socio-economic categories upwards.
3. English is consistently used at the level of the clerical and above occupational grades. (However, with increased education in English at the expense of Swahili in Kenya, one can speculate that English might percolate down and oust Swahili. But this *is* speculative,

and depends very much on (a) the provision of employment opportunities, and (b) education policies with regard to the use of English).

4. The ethnic groups of Kikuyu and Kamba may each be said to stand on a threshold of knowing each other's vernacular. It seems to be the Nairobi workplace environment which constitutes the biggest 'push' from ignorance to competence in the vernacular.

5. It is urban rather than rural conditions of socio-economic status, summarized in the concept called the 'age syndrome', which prompt the informal acquisition of either Swahili or Kamba among the group of Kikuyu studied.

NOTES

[1] I have been greatly helped in this by an unpublished manuscript, *Notes on Current Developments in the Study of Language and Culture*, by J. B. Pride.

[2] A phrase suggested to me by H. C. A. Somerset.

REFERENCES

BAILEY, F. G. *Stratagems and Spoils*, Blackwell, Oxford, 1969.

BARTH, F. *Models of Social Organization*, Occasional Paper 23, Royal Anthropological Institute, London, 1966.

BERNSTEIN, B. 'A Socio-Linguistic Approach to Social Learning' in *Penguin Survey of the Social Sciences*, London, 1965.

—— 'Elaborated and Restricted Codes: an Outline' in S. Lieberson (ed.), 1966.

BRIGHT, W. 'Language, Social Stratification, and Cognitive Orientation' in S. Lieberson (ed.), 1966.

BURLING, R. 'A Structural Re-statement of Njamal Kinship Terminology', *Man*, 62, 1962, pp. 122–4.

COHEN, A. (a) *Custom and Politics in Urban Africa*, Routledge and Kegan Paul, London, 1969.

—— (b) 'Political Anthropology: the Analysis of the Symbolism of Power Relations', *Man* (N.S.), 4, 1969, p. 2.

COLBY, B. 'Ethnographic Semantics', *Current Anthropology*, 7, 1966, pp. 3–32.

CONKLIN, H. 'Hanunoo Color Categories,' *Southwestern Journal of Anthropology*, 11, 1955, pp. 339–44.

COOPER, R. L. 'How can we Measure the Roles which a Bilingual's Languages Play in his Everyday Behaviour?' in W. Mackey (ed.), *Measurement and Description of Bilingualism*, Canadian Commission for UNESCO, Ottawa, 1968.

COULT, A. 'A Simplified Method for the Transformational Analysis of Kinship Terms', *American Anthropologist*, 68, 1966, pp. 1476–83.

EPSTEIN, A. L. 'Linguistic Innovation and Culture on the Copperbelt, Northern Rhodesia', *Southwestern Journal of Anthropology*, 15, 3, 1959, pp. 235–53.

FARIS, J. C. 'Validation in Ethnographical Description: the Lexicon of "Occasions" in Cat Harbour', *Man* (N.S.), 3, 1968, pp. 112–24.

FINNEGAN, R. 'How to Do Things with Words: Performative Utterances among the Limba of Sierra Leone', *Man* (N.S.), 4, 1969, pp. 537–52.

FISHMAN, J. (a) Article in D. H. Hymes and J. J. Gumperz (eds.), *Directions in Socio-Linguistics: the Ethnography of Communication*, Holt, Rinehart & Winston, New York, 1968.

—— (b) *Bilingualism in the Barrio*, United States Department of Health, Education and Welfare, 1968.

—— (c) *Readings in the Sociology of Language*, Mouton, The Hague, 1968.

—— (d) 'National Languages of Wider Communication in the Developing Nations' in W.H. Whiteley (ed.), 1971.

FOX, R. 'Multilingualism in Two Communities,' *Man* (N.S.), 3, 1968. pp. 456–64,

FRIEDRICH, P. 'The Linguistic Reflex of Social Change: from Tsarist to Soviet Russian Kinship' in S. Lieberson (ed.), 1966.

GOODENOUGH, W. H. 'Componential Analysis and the Study of Meaning', *Language*, 32, 1956, pp. 195–216.

—— 'Yankee Kinship Terminology: a Problem in Componential Analysis' in E.A. Hammel (ed.), 1965.

GULLIVER, P. H. (ed.), *Tradition and Transition in East Africa*, Routledge and Kegan Paul, London, 1969.

GUMPERZ, J. J. 'Linguistic and Social Interaction in Two Communities,' *American Anthropology*, 66, 1964, p. 2.

—— 'Language' in B. J. Siegel (ed.), *Biennial Review of Anthropology*, Stanford University Press, 1965.

—— 'On the Ethnology of Linguistic Change ' in W. Bright (ed.), *Sociolinguistics*, Mouton, The Hague, 1966, pp. 27–49.

HAMMEL, E. A. (ed.), *Formal Semantic Analysis*, American Anthropologist Special Publications, 4, American Anthropological Association, Menasha, 1965.

HUNT, C. L. 'Language Choice in a Multilingual Society' in S. Lieberson (ed.), 1966.

HYMES, D. H. 'The Ethnography of Speaking' in T. Gladwin and W. C. Sturtevant (eds.), *Anthropology and Human Behaviour*, Anthropological Society of Washington, Washington D.C., 1962.

—— (a) 'Toward Ethnographies of Communication', *American Anthropologist*, 66, 6, 1964, pp. 1–34.

—— (b) 'Directions in (Ethno-) Linguistic Theory', *American Anthropologist*, 66, 3, 1964, pp. 6–56.

—— (c) (ed.), *Language in Culture and Society: a Reader in Linguistics and Anthropology*, Harper & Row, New York, 1964.

LABOV, W. 'The Effect of Social Mobility on Linguistic Behaviour' in S. Lieberson (ed.), 1966.

LEACH, E. *Political Systems of Highland Burma*, Bell, London, 1954.

—— 'Concerning the Trobriand Clans and the Kinship Category *Tabu*' in J. Goody (ed.), *The Developmental Cycle in Domestic Groups*, Cambridge Papers in Social Anthropology, 1, Cambridge University Press, 1958.

LEVINE, L. AND CROCKETT, H. J. 'Speech Variation in a Piedmont Community: Postvocalic r' in S. Lieberson (ed.), 1966.

LIEBERSON, S. (ed.), *Explorations in Socio-Linguistics*, University of Indiana, Bloomington, Mouton, the Hague, 1966.

LOUNSBURY, F. G. 'Another View of Trobriand Kinship Categories' in E. A. Hammel (ed.), 1965.

METZGER, D. AND WILLIAMS, G. 'A Formal Ethnographic Analysis of Tenejapa Ladino Weddings', *American Anthropologist*, 65, 1963, pp. 1076–101.

MITCHELL, J. C. *The Kalela Dance*, Rhodes-Livingstone Paper 27, Manchester University Press, 1956.

PARKIN, D. J. 'Language Choice in Two Kampala Housing Estates' in W. H. Whiteley (ed.), 1971.

PRIDE, J. B. *Current Developments in the Study of Language in Culture and Society*, unpublished manuscript.

TAMBIAH, S. J. 'The Magical Power of Words', *Man* (N.S.), 3, 1968, pp. 175–208.

WHITELEY, W. H. 'Social Anthropology, Meaning and Linguistics', *Man* (N.S.), 1, 1966, p. 2.

—— 'Language Choice and Language Planning in East Africa' in P. H. Gulliver (ed),. 1969.

—— (ed.), *Language Use and Social Change*, International African Institute, Oxford University Press, London, 1971. (Introduction thereto.)

6

Status Factors in Language Adding: Bahati Housing Estate in Nairobi

D. J. PARKIN

AIMS OF THE CHAPTER

I can perhaps begin this chapter by distinguishing a little arbitrarily between formal and informal language learning. If you ask a university student how, when, where and with whom he came to know, say English, French and Swahili, he may answer your questions quickly, confidently and with precision and probably also in detail. If you ask a semi-educated or uneducated man in Nairobi, who just happens to be, say, Kikuyu, the same questions with regard to his remarkably fluent command of Swahili, Kamba and perhaps English, none of which he necessarily writes, he will probably express greater difficulty in specifying the sources of his knowledge. Informal language acquisition is, by definition, a process dependent on factors other than those of conventional education and is not normally perceived in quantitative temporal-spatial terms. I have not received satisfactorily consistent answers to such direct questions relating to informal language acquisition and would not now expect them. I have found it more profitable to tackle the problem indirectly by trying to adduce what social, economic and political conditions appear consistently to complement claims of informal language acquisition. Apparently consistent associations between linguistic and non-linguistic factors are not necessarily causal relationships but may suggest hypotheses.

The problem involves many variables and I shall confine myself to a 20 per cent systematic list sample of Bahati.

The city council housing estate of Bahati in Eastlands, Nairobi, was built in 1950 for low-income earners. It soon achieved notoriety when, from 1952 until 1954, it became the largest residential detention area for Kikuyu rounded up and arrested in Nairobi during the Kenya Emergency. They were taken forcibly from homes in Pumwani, Shauri Moyo, Kaloleni and Old Kariokor. Even today (1969), Bahati is 97 per cent Kikuyu and those original detainees constitute about a half of its population of 1,890 household heads. Bahati is still an area for low-income workers, but there is some heterogeneity of education, occupational skills and age. The old are committed urban workers, while the young are unlikely to leave Nairobi, if at all, until they reach retiring age.

Kaloleni housing estate across the Jogoo Road and a little to the west of Bahati contrasts in being tribally mixed, with Luo and Luyia predominating, in having slightly higher-income earners, and in being a principal area from which Kikuyu were evicted during the Emergency. The popular associations of Bahati with Kikuyu and Kaloleni with Luo and Luyia are confirmed by census data and by the fact that many public activities run along the lines of these tribes.

Among the Kikuyu of Bahati, statistically significant proportions of them claim to have added Swahili and Kamba to their vernaculars for use in particular situations. It is fairly easy to suggest by means of extensive survey data that Swahili has, for the vast majority, been acquired or enriched through urban residence and urban role involvement. It is less easy to show convincingly by this means that Kamba has been acquired in this way rather than through an introduction to it in rural Kikuyu areas which border Kamba, and though the extensive data suggest strongly the predominance of urban factors, more intensive investigation was required to confirm the suggestion beyond reasonable doubt.

I hope to demonstrate that common factors operate in the adding of both Swahili and Kamba among Bahati Kikuyu. I start with Swahili.[1]

SWAHILI AMONG NEIGHBOURS, FRIENDS AND WORKMATES

In my 20 per cent systematic list sample of Bahati, which consisted of 378 household heads of whom 349 were Kikuyu, only one Kikuyu claimed an ignorance of both Swahili and English. None claimed to know English but not Swahili. Thus, all but one of the 349 Kikuyu household heads professed to know Swahili, some 42 per cent of them knowing English as well.

Household heads were asked to state the order of frequency in which they used English, Swahili, their mother tongue (in the case of the present sample, Kikuyu), and any other identified vernacular, first with neighbours, second with friends (and here it should be noted that care was exercised in interviewing to establish a meaningful conceptual difference between neighbours and friends), and thirdly with workmates or workplace colleagues.

As with children, neighbourhood relationships in a single ethnic estate like Bahati are conducted principally in the vernacular. A couple of younger men occasionally use English as a secondary language, while 13 per cent of all respondents use Swahili, five of them originally resident in Swahili-speaking areas like Pumwani and actually using it as a first language in Bahati. Otherwise the vast majority of Kikuyu, 93 per cent, use their mother tongue most with neighbours. As is shown in the following chapter, the situation in Kaloleni estate is much more varied, with Swahili the most frequently cited language among neighbours, and with different vernaculars and English being used much more than in Bahati.

Friendships for most people operate outside as well as within an urban housing estate and it is not surprising that, in answer to questions about friends, respondents in Bahati show signs of being less hemmed in linguistically by ethnocentric factors. A number of them clearly have friends from other tribes, even if these are a small minority. This fact is reflected in their professed usage among friends of English, Swahili and, frequently, vernaculars other than Kikuyu. In the case of English the users are generally below the average age for the estate. This is significant because, as other figures show, younger people are more educated and more likely to have had formal instruction in English and, also, in Swahili. English, once taught, is unlikely to be forgotten in the urban context and is likely to be improved on. This may by no means always be the case with Swahili, in Nairobi at least, a suggestion to which I shall return.

Over 30 per cent use English with friends, of whom over a third cite it as the most frequent choice. They are among the youngest and most educated in the sample and monopolize the few clerical and similar jobs. Eight per cent talk to friends in vernaculars other than Kikuyu, a couple of men using them most frequently, a figure which is small but in obvious contrast to complete non-use of other vernaculars among neighbours in Bahati. As usual it is for Swahili that we have the most interesting responses. Nearly 70 per cent of the sample use Swahili with friends, usually as the language second most frequently used after Kikuyu, though somewhat remarkably, the percentage who use Swahili most frequently is only four. This means that there are more respondents, 11 per cent, claiming to speak English most frequently with friends than those claiming Swahili as the first language, even though, otherwise, Swahili is by far the most extensively known and used.

We could attempt to explain this contrast by differences in the perceptions of the linguistic situation by respondents. The English speakers tend to be young, 'modern' in their outlook, educated, and work in offices as clerks. It could be argued that their perception of their statuses obliges them to over-rate their use of English to conform with the common stereotype held of persons in their position. Alternatively it could be argued that such persons of middle or high socio-economic status suffer most the onerous demands of kinship and fellow tribal obligations, and so actually go out of their way to seek at least casual friendships with persons of other tribes to whom they are not so bound by custom and common home area, and with whom, as status equals, they speak English. From observation, I suggest that both factors operate. The second is the more interesting from the viewpoint of this study, since it touches on the moral dilemma confronting bilinguals, a problem dealt with in Chapter 8.

This second of the two arguments seems most likely to explain the very high estimation of Swahili as the second most frequently used language with friends and its very low estimated use as the main language. There is an inverse correlation between claimed use of Swahili and English which, as other figures show, partly reflects a divergence of socio-economic categories. The interpretation may be that the lower status, more Swahili-speaking respondents have many friends of different tribes with whom they use Swahili, but that their closest friends tend to be fellow Kikuyu, since, for persons of restricted income and occupational opportunities such as themselves, fellow tribesmen and, in particular, kinsmen, provide essential or at least useful sources of aid and comfort. They are therefore chosen as primary friends who are spoken to in the common vernacular while secondary friends of other tribes are spoken to in Swahili.

The extent or absence of ethnic heterogeneity in a residential area clearly influences language use among neighbours, while the formation of the potentially more widely dispersed and more expressive relationships of friendship is influenced very much by socio-economic equality, which in turn influences the frequency with which English, Swahili and the vernaculars are used. For men, the norms of relationships based on differences or similarities of socio-economic status are surely most obviously advertised on the factory floor, in the office, or in the workshop, in short at workplace. Contractual relationships are the essence of modern industrial life and notions of rank and authority receive their clearest expression at workplace. Such intrinsic urban factors as length of residence in the town, and the degree of urban role commitment and involvement, are governed by the way in which jobs are allocated and distributed among and between ethnic groups.

The question on language use among workmates did provide answers which seemed to point to the crucial significance among adult men of workplace in determining the spread of Swahili, or, in certain cases, its curtailment. In this question, I decided not to probe for a distinction between professional and social conversations at workplaces. Very likely, language switching according to these two situations does occur, but the complexity and frequently unconscious part played by persons in this process suggest that the phenomenon could best be observed rather than elicited by questioning alone. My question therefore simply asked in which order of frequency, if at all, respondents used English, Swahili, Kikuyu, and any other vernaculars, with workmates actually at workplaces.[2]

Only 8 per cent of the sample claimed to speak their mother tongue, Kikuyu, with workmates, though virtually all said that they used it if not as a first then as a second language. This low figure may represent as much persons' awareness of the stigma attaching to tribal in-group talking, as their perception of the actual situation. But again, from observation, it seems clear that, in small, multi-tribal workplace groups, the stigma does have some effect in deterring persistent use by cliques of their vernacular, though much depends on the particular ethnic composition of the groups, and on the particular speech situation.

As in other contexts, those claiming to speak English most at workplace tend to be the younger, more educated men in clerical positions. Clearly, the general level of knowledge of English at Bahati is very low, since only about a fifth (22 per cent) of the sample said that they used it at all at workplace. This is no more than the proportion who claimed to use a vernacular other than Kikuyu, which, incidentally, was in almost all cases Kamba.

The predominant position enjoyed by Swahili at workplace seems confirmed by the following two responses: less than 4 per cent claimed *never* to use Swahili at work; while over three-quarters, or 76 per cent, said they used it as their *main* language with workmates. Now, it has to be admitted that the Bahati sample consists of a large majority of men of low socio-economic status in jobs where English is not required, and for which men of limited education and skills, and therefore with little formal training in English, apply. A cross-checking question asked respondents to state whether or not they thought the use of English was essential in their jobs. Only a seventh of the sample thought it was, while the rest thought not. Given, then, that most Bahati men neither know much English nor need it in their jobs, should we not expect them to speak Swahili most, in view of the stigma and impracticalities attaching to persistent use of the vernaculars? Indeed, this is a popular expectation and appraisal of the situation. But how, then, do they acquire this proficiency in Swahili? Is it from an initial knowledge taught at school and improved on, or from having to participate in situations where the language is the only wholly acceptable common medium?

I shall answer these questions in the following section. As a preliminary to the explanation, let me examine the comments made so far. They are conveniently summarized in the following two tables, in which it is clear that (1) only people in non-white collar jobs claim to use Swahili most in their work, and (2) a general rise in education is highly inversely correlated with claimed use of Swahili at workplace.

TABLE 6.1 *Swahili usage with workmates: by occupational category*

Claimed frequency of Swahili usage	White collar mostly clerical, also professional, highly technical and supervisory (45)	Blue collar artisans, drivers, m/c operators, & semi-skilled (124)	Unskilled messengers, labourers, cleaners, watchmen (93)	Self-employed traders, shopkeepers, artisans, craftsmen (81)	Proportions of total sample (343)*
Not at all	2.2	1.6		6.2	2.4
First	13.3	81.4	95.7	82.5	76.6
Second	64.4	12.0	3.2	9.9	16.0
Third	20.0	4.8	1.0	1.2	4.9
Total %	99.9%	99.8%	99.9%	99.8%	99.9%

*6 of the total sample of 349 household heads were unemployed.

TABLE 6.2 *Swahili usage with workmates: by general educational level*

Claimed frequency of Swahili usage	No education (88)	Primary 1–3 years (56)	Primary 4–8 years (165)	Secondary 9–14 years (34)
Not at all		3.6	2.4	6.0
First	94.3	89.3	74.5	21.2
Second	5.7	7.1	15.8	57.6
Third			7.3	15.2
Total %	100%	100%	100%	100%

By a X^2 test of significance (with $D = 20.6$), $X^2 = \dfrac{D^2}{E} = 26.9$, therefore $P < 0.005$.

In the third table, given below, there is also a very high inverse correlation between number of years' instruction in Swahili as a subject and the frequency of Swahili usage at workplace. The factors explaining the inverse correlation cited for this and the second table are the same and are simply that the higher educated are also likely to have received more formal education in Swahili but do not need it, or need it less, in their jobs.

THE UNINSTRUCTED SWAHILI SPEAKERS

We can best tackle our problem of accounting for factors in the spread of Swahili by isolating for analysis the 126 respondents who, in Table 6.3, claimed to speak Swahili more than any other language at workplace but who had never received any formal instruction in it. Since they are over a third of the total sample of Bahati Kikuyu, they may be regarded as an important representative element of the Bahati population, and, more generally, of other Kikuyu in Nairobi. It is at this point that personal knowledge of the local situation is helpful. It will be remembered that about half of the population of Bahati consists of original detainees of the Kenya Emergency period of the early fifties. A very large proportion of these are men who were removed from such long established areas of residence as Pumwani, Old Kariokor (now demolished), Shauri Moyo, and Makadara. With the exception of Makadara which has for a long time been predominantly Kikuyu, all the other areas cited have retained a cultural continuity from their beginnings as original sites of early Nairobi workers, porters, and army personnel who emanated from the coast, who were Muslim and who often spoke Swahili either as their first language or very proficiently.

TABLE 6.3 *Swahili usage with workmates: by number of years' instruction in Swahili*

Claimed frequency of Swahili usage	No years' instruction	1 year	2 years	3 years	4 years	5 years and over
	(135)	(28)	(47)	(41)	(85)	(7)
Not at all	1.5		2.1	7.3	1.2	
First	93.3	78.6	85.2	75.5	51.8	14.3
Second	5.2	21.4	10.6	14.6	31.7	57.1
Third			2.1	2.6	15.3	28.6
Total %	100%	100%	100%	100%	100%	100%

With $D = 20.2$
$X^2 = 25.4$, therefore $P < 0.005$.

The Bahati sub-sample of 126, whom for convenience I call the uninstructed Swahili speakers, has a significantly larger proportionate number who had previously lived since childhood in these Swahili areas, 56 per cent as against 26 per cent for others in the total sample, 90 per cent of whom have received formal instruction at school in Swahili. Those who have not lived in Swahili-speaking areas have nevertheless lived in different parts of Nairobi. Again, proportionately few have resided only in Bahati, 15 per cent as against 40 per cent. Thus, previous residence in Swahili-speaking areas and shifting urban residence generally may well be factors affecting their acquisition of Swahili.

While a proportionate number of the uninstructed Swahili speakers are self-employed and have semi-skilled jobs, rather more of them are unskilled. None of them are in clerical or white collar positions, while only two of them are artisans. In terms of occupational prestige, therefore, they are lowly ranked. They are also below the median income. But

153

they are well above the median in age and length of residence, both in Bahati and Nairobi, but have been to fewer other towns (see Table 6.4).

TABLE 6.4

	Uninstructed Swahili speakers	Rest of sample (including 90% who have received formal school instruction in Swahili)
	(126)	(223)
Median age	46.4 years.	36.2 yrs.
Median education	−0.75 (i.e. 0 yrs.)	7.3 yrs.
Median income	sh. 164	sh. 227
Median length of residence in Nairobi	19.6 yrs.	14.8 yrs.
Median length of residence in Bahati	15.2 yrs.	10.9 yrs.
Percentage proportions in:		
white collar	1.6%	19.3%
blue collar/manual	32.5%	37.2%
unskilled	41.3%	18.4%
self-employed	23.8%	22.9%
unemployed	0.8%	2.2%

We can attempt to construct a model on the acquisition of Swahili by persons such as those represented in the sub-sample, by presenting the above conclusions in the form of interrelated facts:

Fact 1: For the last twenty years, long residence in Nairobi as a high proportion of an individual's life span is likely to have provided him with knowledge of a form of Swahili which is acceptable for workplace and other activities, even though he may not have received formal instruction in Swahili.

Fact 2: Indeed, in relative terms, the uninstructed are likely to learn proportionately more Swahili in Nairobi, because they tend also to have no or limited education and so to be debarred from jobs requiring the use of English, the only other acceptable common medium to Swahili. Workplace, then, has the effect, *either* of encouraging them to enrich their knowledge of Swahili, *or* of obliging them to learn it virtually from scratch.

Fact 3: Those persons in the sample who have acquired a knowledge of Swahili from sources other than, or in addition to, workplace, are likely to have lived in Swahili-speaking areas like Pumwani, Shauri Moyo or Old Kariokor.

Fact 4: An ethnic variable is introduced by the circumstances of Nairobi's place as the centre of administration during the Kenya Emergency, so that older, lower status Kikuyu in Bahati have a particular type of urban linguistic experience of living in a housing estate in which neighbourhood relationships are conducted almost wholly in the vernacular while those of workplace are almost wholly in Swahili. Kampala-Mengo in Uganda had more examples than Nairobi of this alternating linguistic experience produced by urban mono-ethnic 'villages' and poly-ethnic workplaces (cf. Parkin, in Gulliver 1969).

This model progresses from higher to lower level facts. At any point one may try to demonstrate how alternatives develop. Thus, a possible corollary of Fact 2 is that those who are the most educated have come to town with a formal knowledge of Swahili acquired at school. In spite of this early start, their higher education has qualified them for jobs in which English is required and the use of Swahili inevitably suppressed. It may be that their fluency in or knowledge of Standard Swahili actually decreases as they stay in Nairobi, without being matched by a corresponding replacement with Nairobi Swahili. Two variables must interfere with this corollary: one is the increasing rise in the ratio of educational levels to urban manpower requirements; and the second the possible removal or demotion of Swahili as a subject in school curricula. Both would have the effect of turning out able English speakers, of whom the few who obtain jobs may be forced to take on work where their English is not required but nevertheless becomes the most common medium of communication among co-workers similarly placed. If and when this point were reached, Swahili in Kenya would have a limited future. It has to be admitted that, even given these factors, this development must be many years hence, until which time the growing numbers of undereducated may actually extend the use of Swahili.

An extension from Fact 4 in the model might be to find, in microscopic detail, how children brought up in Bahati differ in their linguistic experience and responses from children brought up in an estate of intermediate Swahili extent like Kaloleni, or in one of much greater Swahili extent such as Pumwani and perhaps Shauri Moyo. (See Bujra *infra*.)

THE KAMBA SPEAKERS

By focusing on Kikuyu I have controlled for the tribal or ethnic variable. I can see at least two relevant components, therefore, which are omitted from the model. One is the way in which a vernacular becomes a symbol or token of, and perhaps even a mechanism for, political solidarity. I deal with this aspect in Chapter 8. The second is simply the degree to which linguistic affinity influences whether and to what extent a language is 'added'. I do not believe that the Bantu affinities of Kikuyu and Swahili constitute a significant factor in the analysis I have presented. Luo and Kalenjin may, under similar socio-economic circumstances, undergo the same process of 'adding' Swahili, even if phonological and lexical variations exist.

One can hardly say the same of the relationship between Kikuyu and Kamba. These two are clearly sufficiently close to enable mutual acquisition, as well as mutual comprehension, under specific, long-term circumstances, with an ease which would surely not be the case with Luo and Kamba. Again, we control for the tribal or ethnic variable, and concentrate on those Kikuyu at Bahati who claim to speak, as well as hear, Kamba. More, I should point out that when Bahati informants refer to their knowledge of Kamba, they state, after being prompted, that they know only the Machakos and not the Kitui dialect. They claim, and Kamba support their claims, that the Kitui dialect is the least like Kikuyu.[3] There seem to be, incidentally, relatively few Kamba from Kitui district in Nairobi. It is popularly said that Kitui Kamba tend to migrate to Mombasa for work. Even the Kikuyu and Machakos Kamba vernaculars are by no means mutually intelligible after simply a short number of interactions. There must be other, non-linguistic factors affecting the acquisition of competence in the additional vernacular.

We can ask two broad questions: what are the sociological factors leading only some but not all Kikuyu into the interactions which bring about a competence in Kamba; and are these interactions set more in the home rural area or more in Nairobi?

Of the Bahati sample of 349 Kikuyu, 98 claimed to speak Kamba. This claim was cross-checked by questions located further on in the schedule asking respondents to state languages used with neighbours, friends and workmates. The same sub-sample of 98 all claimed to use Kamba at some time with workmates, and almost a third (27 out of 98) of them claimed to use it with friends.

Unlike the uninstructed Swahili speakers, whose distribution according to home district is proportionate to the total sample, the 98 Kamba speakers include an inordinate proportion from Murang'a district (previously Fort Hall). They number 61 and are over-represented by 16 per cent from the total sample (61 out of 98, or 62 per cent as against 160 out of 349 or 46 per cent).

There are a number of interesting general features of the Murang'a people. Theirs is said to be the least economically developed of the four Kikuyu districts (Kiambu, Murang'a, Nyeri and Kirinyaga), with a tradition of considerable labour migration to Nairobi. My data from a number of housing areas in Nairobi support the popular conviction among Kikuyu that Murang'a people are the most numerous in the city. The Murang'a people of the Bahati total sample are also significantly distinguished in terms of the usual socio-economic criteria from other Kikuyu in the estate. They are older, are of lower educational and socio-economic status, and have lived in Nairobi longer, differences which will be seen to be of relevance in the Kamba 'adding' processes.

Apart from asking directly all Kamba speakers how, when and where they learned Kamba, an exercise which was attempted, I have to try to show by what measurable criteria they differ from other Kikuyu in Bahati who do not speak Kamba. I have attempted this comparison on two levels: by comparing the 98 household heads who claim to speak Kamba with the 251 who do not; and by comparing the partial sub-sample of 61 household heads from Murang'a with the 160 Murang'a of the total Bahati sample.

It is tempting to assume, right from the beginning, that we have a partial answer to the second of my two questions posed earlier, asking whether rural home factors are responsible for competence in Kamba. The assumption is that the many Murang'a in the sub-sample know Kamba because they share a border with Kamba along a couple of their administrative locations. This assumption has to be tested.

In fact, and somewhat surprisingly, most of the Murang'a Kamba speakers live in locations which are furthest from the common border, thirty or a half of them in the most distant Kangema division. Not a single Murang'a is from any of the immediate border locations, in which, it is said, there is indeed intermarriage and other relations of a mixed nature. This seems to be a reversal, then, of the initial assumption. I investigated the history of relationships in Murang'a further and discovered that Kamba used to go to the district to buy or barter for food during times of famine, but that the most recent intrusion of any scale occurred during the forties. This seems to be too distant chronologically to be an overriding explanatory factor, though it may be a contributory one, since the locations from which most Kamba speakers in the sample come are among the most productive agriculturally in Murang'a.

I then tried a more direct line of approach and, without any set pattern, asked Kamba speakers in the sample from Murang'a *and* other districts when, where and how and with whom they learned Kamba. As expected, this direct line of questioning did not elicit satisfactorily the data asked for. Very few persons could specify the period during which they learned Kamba, though most thought they learned it in Nairobi. A typical response was that 'every Kikuyu can hear Kamba and it is just a matter of getting to know Kamba before you can speak it'. On being prompted, a few suggested workplace or 'hotels' as likely domains encouraging speaking ability in Kamba. Those stating that they thought they had picked it up in early years at home did not tend to come from Murang'a more than other districts.

The data suggested that it was not rural factors which are especially important in fostering competence in Kamba, and that the inordinate representation of Murang'a people in the sub-sample was probably due to other than rural factors. I then had to compare urban life experiences on the two levels I have mentioned.

I deal first with the 98 Kamba speakers. I shall not reproduce the relevant tables but will simply state some general comparisons. The Kamba speakers are of significantly higher median age (42.2 years) than the non-Kamba speakers (38.8 years). Fifty-eight per cent of them are over forty, while the corresponding proportion for the non-Kamba speakers is 46 per cent. More significantly, 5 per cent of the Kamba speakers are in their twenties, as against 19 per cent of the non-Kamba speakers. (Applying a X^2 test of significance, X^2 came out as 4.4 which is a significant age difference and gives a $P < 0.05 > 0.025$.)

As shown in the data presented for Swahili speakers, age tends to be a controlling variable with regard to such criteria of socio-economic status as education, income, and occupation, and also with regard to length of urban residence. Thus, the Kamba speakers are significantly differentiated in age from other Kikuyu and deviate slightly from the medians for the other characteristics, with differences which individually do not satisfy the X^2 test of significance but which, taken together, may be regarded as significant.

TABLE 6.5

	Kamba speakers (98)	Non-Kamba speakers (251)	All Kikuyu (349)
Median age	42.2 yrs.	38.8 yrs.	39.8 yrs.
Median education	3.1 yrs.	4.2 yrs.	3.75 yrs.
Median income	sh. 290	sh. 298	sh. 295
Median length of residence Nairobi	20.3 yrs.	18.5 yrs.	19 yrs.
Median length of residence Bahati	14 yrs.	12.4 yrs.	13 yrs.
Percentage proportions in:			
white collar	7%	15.5%	14.5%
blue collar/manual	38%	34.1%	35.5%
unskilled	30%	25.1%	27%
self-employed	24%	22.7%	23%
	99%	98%*	100%

*2 % unemployed not included.

That is to say, these differences are slight but, because they are consistently so in one direction, constitute a suggested syndrome of factors: that the Kamba speakers tend to be a little older and so to have had less education, and to occupy fewer white collar jobs, though their incomes are only a little below the median, probably due to the fact that they have stayed in town and therefore in employment slightly longer. The syndrome is no more than a general explanation for the fact that these and not other Kikuyu speak Kamba. It is important in that it parallels the statistically highly significant difference between uninstructed and instructed Swahili speakers discussed earlier. I call this the age syndrome. It suggests a dominant model tendency towards and away from which lesser tendencies may be discovered.

Another parallel with the earlier data is that only 8 per cent of the Kamba speakers regard English as essential at their workplace, as against 19 per cent for non-Kamba speakers. This is statistically quite significant, and may suggest workplace environment as partially encouraging and giving rise to competence in Kamba. I have investigated all the occupations, past and present, undertaken by the 98 respondents. They do not appear to differ significantly in general type from those of non-Kamba speakers. So it may be that there are subtle features to do with actual workplace interaction and the inclusion of inordinate numbers of Kamba co-workers which constitute the partial explanatory factor. For instance, from other surveys, it seems clear that Kamba occupy proportionally more lower status and fewer white collar jobs than the other major ethnic groups, so that, for Kikuyu similarly placed, the chances of interacting with Kamba are greater than for Kikuyu in higher status employment.

A further less marked parallel with the Swahili data is that proportionally more of the Kamba speakers (52 per cent as against 41 per cent) came to Bahati as detainees in the early fifties. This, however, simply replicates the factors of above average age and urban residence which have already been discussed, and is not a factor of singular significance.

Nor is there variation between the Kamba and non-Kamba speakers regarding residence in other towns. Seventy-five per cent and 77 per cent respectively have never lived in any other town than Nairobi. Of the few Kamba speakers, however, who have lived in other towns, a small but proportionally large number have lived in Mombasa and Nakuru (13 per cent as against 5.5 per cent), to whom I shall return later, whereas only one person as against eight among the non-Kamba speakers, has lived in Thika. We might have expected more than simply one Kamba speaker to have lived in Thika, which is in many ways one of the most obvious mixed Kikuyu/Kamba towns. The fact that this is not so, and that residence in towns other than Nairobi does not appear generally to have encouraged use and knowledge of Kamba, throws us back again on the earlier suggestion that the major preconditions are indeed set in Nairobi.

From the possible effects of residence in towns other than Nairobi, then, we may move to the possible influences of residence in different areas within Nairobi. It will be remembered that a significantly large proportion of the uninstructed Swahili speakers have lived in such Swahili areas as Pumwani and Shauri Moyo. Interestingly, among the Kamba speakers, too, larger proportions have lived in these two areas, 47 per cent as against 30 per cent for non-Kamba speakers.

This difference in proportions is surely not to be accounted for solely in terms of the greater median age of the Kamba speakers and their tendency to have lived in more areas of Nairobi. The difference in age median in the two samples is, after all, only 3.4 years. Do the Kamba speakers, then, include a number whose knowledge of Kamba was fostered, partly or completely, through residence in either Pumwani or Shauri Moyo, where there is a long tradition of mixed marriages and relationships involving Kikuyu and Kamba, among others? This, at least, may be yet another contributory factor.

The parallels with the data on uninstructed Swahili speakers need not be laboured. The Kamba speakers show above median characteristics of age, length of residence in Nairobi, lower socio-economic status, and residence in longer established areas of Nairobi. For them, too, factors of workplace interaction appear to encourage and perhaps originally to have been primarily responsible for initiating their claimed competence in Kamba. Rural factors do not seem to be significant in this process.

One can go further and suggest that the fact that the Kamba speakers are for the most part only slightly differentiated by the above characteristics from non-Kamba speakers is in itself significant. I would suggest that this slight differentiation in status characteristics parallels the slight differentiation in inter-intelligibility between Kamba and Kikuyu. It would seem, and respondents' informal comments support this, that it requires only a slight 'push' from one source or another for a Kikuyu to move to a comprehension and then speaking knowledge of Kamba. If this is so, then we would not expect Kikuyu who claim to know Kamba to be any more than slightly differentiated from their fellows who do not claim competence in the vernacular. One could conclude that, for reasons of general linguistic affinity, all Kikuyu in Bahati stand on a threshold of adding Kamba to their vernacular repertoire, but that, as a social category, older men in lower status employment are more likely to do so the longer they stay in town. This conclusion invites a hypothesis: that younger men who enter lower status employment now, but who may be more educated than their parents, will include fewer who undergo the same 'adding' process as they get older, if, as stated earlier, the increasing glut of educated underemployed forces young men into jobs where English is not specifically required but which nevertheless becomes a more extensively used common medium among workmates.

These are suggestions generalized out from the total sub-sample of 98 Kamba speakers. I now consider briefly the 61 members of the sub-sample who are from Murang'a district. Since they are over-represented in the total sub-sample, we may ask whether they differ significantly in their social attributes from all 160 Murang'a people in the total sample of 349 Kikuyu. It will be remembered that I excluded specifically rural factors as giving rise among the Murang'a people to their knowledge of Kamba.

Some of the same factors distinguishing the sub-sample from the total sample of Kamba speakers appear also to distinguish Murang'a within the sub-sample from those in the total sample. That is to say, compared with the 160 Murang'a in the sample, the 61 Kamba speakers from Murang'a are older, less educated, do not need English in their jobs, have lived in both Bahati and Nairobi longer, have smaller incomes, and include a proportionally larger number who have lived in either Pumwani or Shauri Moyo. Their only difference is in occupational distribution, however, where the Kamba speakers include proportionally about a quarter more in self-employment. Most of these self-employed are from Kangema division in Murang'a district. The Kangema people are well known throughout Nairobi for their business activities. They own shops, butcheries, stalls, bars, barbers' shops, night clubs, and taxi services, and are found in River Road, Eastleigh, Makadara and, of course, the city council housing estates, invariably prefixing the names of their businesses with their own name for themselves, Rwathia.

There is little doubt that the Rwathia have encouraged their own sense of collective identity. They are the only division in Murang'a district to have established very large numbers of commercial enterprises in Nairobi and, in proportion to their total population, probably own the greatest number of Kikuyu and therefore African concerns in the city. My impression is that they are among the most, if not the most, close-knit of Kikuyu small sub-groups. On the basis of impression again, I would suggest that their rural physical isolation, relative to most other Kikuyu groups, and their considerable business acumen in Nairobi combine to necessitate effective communication networks between town and country in order to safeguard the economic interests they have built up in the city and even at home in Kangema, where they have also emerged as probably the most productive agriculturally.

While there are a few Kamba small businesses in Nairobi, many Kamba appear also to frequent those owned or run by Kikuyu. Informal comments refer frequently to the presence of Kamba in Kikuyu hotels, bars and shops. Undoubtedly, they are likely to pick up more Kikuyu than disseminate the use of Kamba among Kikuyu. But something of the latter surely occurs and, indeed, is supported by occasional informal statements.

Thus, while not all Rwathia are engaged in private enterprise in Nairobi, many have important positions in the businesses of their fellow Rwathia, especially in view of their likely involvement in the communication network

161

mentioned earlier. Given this fact, and the fact that such businesses are also likely to be frequented by numbers of Kamba, we might expect the Rwathia to be in greater contact with Kamba and to be over-represented among Kamba speakers.

Small scale business activity in Nairobi, then, suggests a second syndrome of factors affecting the slight 'push' as I called it, from the threshold of ignorance of Kamba to claimed competence in it. In other words, small scale business activity consolidates ethnic and home local ties but at the same time invites the clientele of groups like the Kamba, who are in many ways culturally and economically marginal in Nairobi and who, in default of other likely alternatives, patronize Kikuyu concerns. We can call this the business syndrome.

Let us move for a moment to the 160 Murang'a people in the Bahati total sample. They are clearly differentiated from other Kikuyu by the age syndrome previously mentioned; that is to say, they are older, less educated, have smaller incomes, have been in Bahati and Nairobi longer, have lived in more areas of the city, in particular Pumwani and Shauri Moyo, and have lower status jobs. On the basis of the evidence presented earlier, we would expect them, therefore, to be over-represented in the sub-sample of Kamba speakers.

Returning again to the 61 Kamba speakers from Murang'a district, we are able to summarize their position thus: (1) they most probably owe much of their competence in Kamba to the operation of factors constituting the age syndrome. (2) Those of them who are Rwathia, that is from Kangema division, probably also owe it to their direct or indirect involvement in the sub-group's Nairobi business activity, that is, to the business syndrome.

What then of the 37 non-Murang'a Kamba speakers? The most striking fact about them is that they are by far the oldest of all Kikuyu in the sample. They are also well below the median level of education. But their incomes are not below the median and they are proportionally represented in all forms of employment. The age syndrome then does not fully operate in their case. But, while they have not lived longer than the median in Nairobi, they have lived in a proportionally larger number of other towns. Thus, while the Murang'a Kamba speakers have shifted residence frequently in Nairobi but have rarely lived outside the city, the non-Murang'a Kamba speakers have shifted less within Nairobi itself but more between towns, most often Mombasa and Nakuru. Is this, then, another independent factor encouraging competence in Kamba? I have to speculate rather wildly here and suggest that, because a consequence of the Kenya Emergency was to withdraw nearly all Kikuyu from all East African towns other than Nairobi, those few Kikuyu who remained in, say,

Mombasa or Nakuru, were more likely to establish relationships with Kamba than they might otherwise have done, since they were linguistically and culturally close to them, and then to move from the threshold to competence in Kamba. A few comments by some of these informants do suggest this.

SUMMARY AND CONCLUSIONS

I can summarize very briefly the data on both Swahili and Kamba 'adding' by suggesting that the age syndrome is the constant and crucial set of factors. For Kamba 'adding' alone, the business syndrome may operate additionally under certain conditions of consolidated ethnic or sub-ethnic enterprises, while direct historical consequences of the Emergency resulting in a reduced distribution of Kikuyu in East African towns and their likely closer involvement with Kamba may also have accounted for Kamba 'adding' among a few of them.

Another suggested finding was that, except for those born and/or reared in Nairobi, workplace seemed likely to comprise the most common sphere of activities encouraging learning of and competence in Swahili and Kamba among those in jobs where English was not required.

If one wanted to make predictions on the basis of these findings, the most important controlling variable would seem to be the apparently inevitable widening of the education-employment ratio, ignoring such possible developments as major change in the relationship of English to Swahili as media of instruction in Kenya schools. The use of English would be seen to percolate down to jobs in which Swahili and vernaculars are at present almost exclusively used, as younger, more educated men are forced into such employment. This process would undoubtedly be complicated by the increasing number of young, relatively educated men and women who have been born or reared in Nairobi and who clearly have fluent command over a developing form of Nairobi Swahili as well as English. A cultural distinction and perhaps even cleavage between 'townies' and 'home folk' might well be expressed in such differences of language use according to situation. It would be ironic if in the capital of a country not officially encouraging the use of Swahili the in-group language of the 'townies' was Swahili, with English used for outside relationships and workplace, while the vernaculars and English had the same functions among immigrant 'home folk'. One could then predict that the extent to which 'home folk' learned Swahili would now depend on the position occupied by 'townies' in the city's employment and commercial structure. Their dominance might encourage the extension of Swahili while their subordination might have the opposite effects.

In conclusion, the method outlined in this chapter is an attempt to deduce factors encouraging language 'adding' by means other than, or as a complement to, direct questioning, since it is clear that, in the case of Kamba in particular, and to a lesser extent, Swahili, persons are generally unable to specify the factors. Language 'adding' of this kind and in the conditions I have been describing, is essentially an untimed, unconscious process, and it is hardly to be expected that people will report accurately and consistently, how they added a language to their repertoire, or, if I may give a parallel, in the case of the linguist's data, how they incorporated modifications in their speech.

In the following chapter I consider in quantitative terms language adding among people of the ethnically mixed housing estate of Kaloleni. The focus in the present chapter has been on socio-economic status factors in language adding, with little regard for the ethnic variable. But in the next chapter I try to analyse the interplay of the ethnic and status variables. In particular I move more positively to the problem of language use between people as members of ethnic groups, which are regarded as variously divided or allied.

NOTES

[1] *Note on survey techniques used*

Survey methods have been criticized by those who dislike them as laboriously proving the obvious only at the cost of great effort and time, and sometimes even of missing the truth which the participant observer, with his intensive techniques, captures. Both criticisms can sometimes be justified, though the first fails to give credit to the precision obtained which is surely essential for certain forms of comparative work, while the second simply exhorts us to ensure that, where possible, the participant observer's systematically acquired data are used to check the quantitative and not ignored. Not all things are possible even in the best of worlds, so that extensive surveys cannot always be carried out in conjunction with participant observation and so have to have many built-in checks, while intensive analysis of situations where extensive data are unobtainable has to confine itself to generalizations based on extended case studies, recounted as well as observed. I have used both techniques in my work, and here merely justify my method of collecting extensive data.

For Bahati, I used only one assistant, himself a Kikuyu, over a period of time, rather than a number over a shorter period. Ideally one might do the surveying oneself, after becoming thoroughly known and accepted in the community. But the size of the sample can make this impracticable, as can the problems created by the field-worker, now well integrated as a 'friend' into the community, suddenly turning to the role of formal interviewer, and acting as if he were an outsider. A single assistant operating in a single community with and on behalf of the researcher seems to me to be in a position of getting over such problems. Unlike a short-term team of assistants, he can establish a close relationship with the field-worker over the months and, among other tasks, can administer survey schedules with an understanding related to the wider context of the work. Time, patience and, I trust, understanding went into the administration of our schedules. The questions in the schedules were tested in preliminary surveys and modified if necessary, and, very important, were cross-checked often more than once, by other questions located in sometimes widely separated parts of the schedule. I am pleased to say that responses were constant with each other and with prior expectations, where these were possible. Even so, consistent discrepancies between observed and stated facts, had they existed, might have been meaningful.

[2] Like others of its kind, the question caused no problems of comprehension and respondents did not suggest awareness of switching between professional and non-professional contexts. In fact, objectively it would be difficult to state when a verbal interaction at workplaces was not connected with the tasks of workplaces: 'friendships' are often simulated and articulated in the interests of getting a task done and may bring about a specific verbal exchange; and, in the face-to-face group of an office or workshop, commands are rarely passed down to a subordinate without some gesture of appeasement, commonly verbal, if only of a patronizing kind.

[3] W. H. Whiteley doubts whether, in linguistic terms, there are substantial differences between Machakos and Kitui Kamba, but, as has been pointed out in Chapter 1, such differences are really irrelevant to what speakers themselves regard as difference or affinity. It is possible that the perceived contrast here parallels others of a historical and sociological nature for which there is some evidence.

7

Language Shift and Ethnicity in Nairobi: the Speech Community of Kaloleni

D. J. PARKIN

On the basis of the Bahati data, a number of suggestions have been made:

1. Competence in Swahili and in vernaculars other than the mother tongue may be acquired through long urban residence.
2. This competence may arise from a number of situational networks, but the most important for working men, i.e. the majority of household heads, appears to be workplace.
3. This emphasis on the importance of workplace is particularly marked in the case of Bahati. This is because nearly all its population were Kikuyu, who therefore use the mother tongue exclusively in neighbourhood contexts. Household heads thus operate within what is for them the strikingly contrasting sphere of workplace, in which Swahili is by far the most frequently used language.

We now turn to the more complex situation of Kaloleni housing estate. It is more complex because Kaloleni is (a) ethnically mixed; (b) more socio-economically heterogeneous, and (c) as a result of these two factors, does not provide residents with the sharply distinguished linguistic experience of neighbourhood relationships conducted in the mother tongue as against workplace ones in Swahili and other languages than the mother tongue.

I think it can be shown fairly easily that, for employed adult males in Kaloleni also, competence in Swahili and other languages is encouraged through workplace. But the intervening factors of greater socio-economic and ethnic variation in the estate's population must affect the rate and extent to which this occurs. For housewives, unemployed adult women and children not at school who have spent some time in Kaloleni or similar estates, we may expect neighbourhood to be an important factor in the acquisition of new languages. In fact, the vast majority of children of school age in Kaloleni do attend schools and inevitably add languages informally in this context. But from systematic observation of their play groups which tend to be physically confined to Kaloleni and indeed to their immediate neighbourhood units which use Swahili as the major common medium, it seems that school and neighbourhood relationships provide something of a mutual feedback process in the dissemination of Swahili and the main vernaculars.

But I shall concentrate here on household heads of Kaloleni, all adults and nearly all male, and try to confirm as briefly as possible some of the suggestions arising from the Bahati data. Instead of comparing ethnic sub-groups as in Chapter 5, I shall compare the four main ethnic groups of Luo, Luyia, Kikuyu and Kamba.

For the Kikuyu of Bahati the acquisition and range of Swahili and Kamba were seen to rest on age and such socio-economic criteria as education, occupation, income and length of residence in Nairobi and the housing estate. Let me first, then, compare household heads of the four main ethnic groups of Kaloleni by these criteria.

TABLE 7.1   *Numerical profile of the household heads of Kaloleni*

	Luo (333)	Luyia (222)	Kikuyu (122)	Kamba (133)	Others (42)
Percentage of household head population	39.0	26.0	14.3	15.6	4.9
Median age	37.3	36.4	37.1	37.0	38.7
Median education (in yrs.)	8.2	6.6	7.1	6.2	6.0
Median formal instruction in Swahili (yrs.)	1.4	1.1	1.3	1.2	—
Median income (sh.)	539	475	549	450	542
Median length of residence in Nairobi (yrs.)	17.6	15.2	16.7	14.2	16.9
Median length of residence in Kaloleni (yrs.)	11.3	9.1	6.7	8.3	7.6
Percentage proportions in:					
(a) white collar employment	36.3(121)	30.2(67)	39.3(48)	27.1(36)	30.9(13)
(b) blue collar/ manual employment	38.1(127)	39.2(87)	23.8(29)	43.6(58)	40.5(17)
(c) unskilled	10.2(34)	24.3(54)	21.3(26)	23.3(31)	19.0(8)
(d) self-employed	13.2(44)	4.5(10)	15.6(19)	5.3(7)	4.8(2)
(e) unemployed	2.1(7)	1.8(4)	— (0)	0.7(1)	4.8(2)

There is clearly very little difference in median ages between the ethnic groups. Luo are among the oldest yet are also by far the most educated. On the basis of the Bahati data this is a reversal of what one might expect of older men. Their age together with their long residence both in Nairobi and Kaloleni, suggest that the Luo at Kaloleni comprise a proportion of their ethnic group in Nairobi who are established, older workers of some skills and education. Compared with other groups in Kaloleni, they include by far the lowest proportion of unskilled workers and predominate in the white collar and skilled and semi-skilled blue collar and artisan occupational categories. Since the time in the early fifties during the Emergency when Kikuyu were forcibly removed from Kaloleni, the Luo have been the largest ethnic group living on the estate, which was and still is a focus for Luo commercial activities and meetings. It is the close ethnic association which helps explain this large proportion of established, older yet reasonably well educated Luo workers. The same reason probably explains the high proportion of Luo in self-employment, a proportion almost equalling that of Kikuyu who are reputed to be otherwise dominant in all forms of African self-employment in Nairobi. The Luo are the principal group in the estate and influence very much the estate's sociolinguistic structure.

NEIGHBOURS

It is appropriate to begin again with perceived frequency of use of language with neighbours. The tribally mixed nature of Kaloleni is reflected in the extensive use by all ethnic groups of Swahili as the main language of communication in neighbourhood relations.

TABLE 7.2(a) *Main[1] language used with neighbours*

% of household head population	English	Swahili	Mother tongue	Any other vernacular	Total %
Luo (333) 39.0%	0.9	71.5	27.6	0.3	100
Luyia (222) 26%	—	90.0	6.8	2.2	99
Kikuyu (122) 14.3%	0.8	91.8	7.4	—	100
Kamba (133) 15.6 %	—	83.5	16.5	0.7	100
Others (42) 4.9%	2.4	90.5	4.8	2.4	100
Total (852) 100%					

[1] i.e. Cited as the most frequently used.

TABLE 7.2(b) *All languages used with neighbours (expressed as percentage values)[2]*

	English	Swahili	Mother tongue	Any other vernacular
Luo	18.5	90.4	70.0	0.7
Luyia	14.4	96.4	52.7	6.3
Kikuyu	18.4	97.3	43.4	2.2
Kamba	12.0	93.6	50.6	3.8
Others	15.5	97.6	25.0	3.6

[2] i.e. On a four-point scale the highest value is given to a language cited most frequently, and a lower value is given to that cited least frequently, progressing through the possible maximum of four language categories. The total is then converted into a single percentage of the highest possible frequency for each language or language category.

169

If the level of formal school education instruction in Swahili largely determined Swahili usage in the neighbourhood, then we should expect Luo to use it most (see Table 7.1). In fact, they give the lowest claimed frequency, and there is no such correlation among the other groups. It would seem, therefore, that it is the neighbourhood structure itself rather than influences of school education which govern the use of Swahili in this sphere.

All except Luo and Kamba have very similar high proportions using Swahili as a main and general language. The lower proportion of Luo using Swahili and the correspondingly larger proportion using their mother tongue is in line with what one would expect of this dominantly Luo housing estate. Luo were more numerous at Kaloleni a few years ago than now. Other figures dealing with arrival and length of residence in the estate demonstrate that at about the time of independence in late 1963, the proportion of Luo tenants was very much higher. It is possible, indeed probable, that they once constituted a plural majority rather than, as now, a simple majority. In spite of the proportional decline of Luo Kaloleni remains the 'headquarters' (as it is often called) of Luo communal, recreational and political activities. Luo residents in other parts of Nairobi congregate for meetings at the estate, while, adjacent to it, is the City Stadium, at which soccer is a principal activity involving almost exclusively Luo and Luyia.

The traditional association of Kaloleni with Luo has thus continued even though the proportion of Luo actually resident in the estate is on the decline. The most recently arrived residents are Kikuyu and 'Others'. Luyia approximate more to the longer Luo length of residence, while Kamba are somewhat intermediary between the longer established Luo and Luyia, both from western Kenya, and the more recently arrived Kikuyu and 'Others'.

The relatively high proportion of Kamba using their mother tongue with neighbours as a main language (Table 7.2(a)), i.e. with other Kamba on the estate, is related not so much to their length of residence on the estate as to the fact that a large majority of them are residentially congregated in the cheaper one-roomed flats on the west side of the estate. These flats are intended to cater for lower-income workers, and it may be seen from Table 7.2 (b) that Kamba do indeed have the lowest median income. A large minority of their neighbours are thus likely to be fellow Kamba also. They tend not to have moved frequently to other parts of the estate and so, in their years of residence there, have come to constitute if not a regularly interacting ethnic community then at least a close-knit network of some durability.

The Kikuyu and 'Others' are both small minorities and recent arrivals.

170

Both groups are residentially dispersed in Kaloleni. Their high frequency of Swahili usage and reduced usage of their mother tongue suggest that, primarily due to these factors, they have been slotted into an established framework of neighbourhood relationships and so have encountered and accepted an existing tradition of Swahili among neighbours. Those grouped under 'Others' are representative of over thirty tribes from all over East Africa and their obvious individual and collective linguistic isolation is reflected in a very low usage of their mother tongues.

The Luyia constitute a puzzle at first sight. They use Swahili with neighbours almost as much as do Kikuyu and 'Others' and use their mother tongue as a main language even less than Kikuyu. This goes against expectations since, as the second largest group, we would expect them to use their mother tongue rather more at the cost of a reduced usage of Swahili. But if we consider in Tables 7.2(a) and 7.2(b) their relatively high usage of a vernacular other than their mother tongue both as a main and general language, we move towards a solution. Thus, Luyia claim to know and use the vernacular Luo more than any other vernacular apart from their own (see Table 7.5, p. 176), a fact deriving partly though not wholly from rural-based patterns of linguistic interaction between Luo and Luyia. Since Luo are so numerous in Kaloleni and since Luyia are not residentially concentrated (as are the Kamba, for instance), the Luyia frequently find themselves sandwiched between Luo neighbours. It follows therefore that the Luo vernacular is likely to detract from the use by Luyia of their own dialects in neighbourhood relationships. A second possible reason may be the tendency among some Luyia to regard some of the Luyia dialects as quite distinct from their own. To the linguist observer, the dialects may well be mutually intelligible, but if some Luyia do not, for whatever reason, perceive this to be the case, then they may well use a little Swahili in conversation on occasional meetings with Luyia whose dialects differ from their own.

I may now suggest some simple conclusions regarding language use among adult, mostly male, neighbours in Kaloleni.

1. Tribal heterogeneity in a low- and middle-income residential area in Nairobi is, as expected, likely to foster the use of Swahili as a main language among neighbours.
2. Nevertheless, a single ethnic group may emerge as numerically and culturally predominant in the tribally mixed area. This ethnic group is then likely to use its own vernacular in neighbourhood relationships more extensively than other groups to the detraction of its use of Swahili, e.g. Luo.
3. Or a group, though small, may be residentially concentrated in a section of the estate catering for lower-income workers. The

171

Kamba in Kaloleni predominate in lower-income employment and are also mostly resident in the area of the cheaper one-roomed flats, originally built to cater for unskilled male urban migrants without families. Proportionally more of their immediate neighbours are fellow tribesmen, so that, for them, the Kamba vernacular is used at the cost of a reduced usage of Swahili among neighbours.

4. But minority groups who are neither residentially concentrated nor long established residents are likely to make very little use of their vernaculars among neighbours, e.g. Kikuyu and those classified as 'Others'.

5. On the other hand, a numerically large ethnic group does not necessarily make correspondingly high use of its vernacular among neighbours. A rural-based pattern of linguistic interaction may be a partial determining factor giving rise to a sociolinguistic relationship with another well represented group in the urban area. Use of this other group's vernacular may then reduce slightly the use of its own vernacular, e.g. Luyia in relation to Luo (dealt with in more detail in Chapter 13). A second possible reason reducing the rate of vernacular usage may be the presence of marked dialectal variation within an ethnic group, as among Luyia. Faced with dialectal variation they can 'fill in' with Swahili, which they claim to speak well, a claim which is mirrored incidentally in the Luyia rural samples (see Whiteley, p. 321).

These suggestions are based on the perceptions about themselves of household heads alone, almost all of whom are adult males fully employed in jobs requiring them to spend most of their day out of Kaloleni. Though it would be inaccurate to suggest that neighbourhood relationships play little part in these men's lives, it is certainly true that their wives and children (i.e. up to and including the age of sixteen) do have more of their relationships set in and around Kaloleni. I will not present the findings relating to women and children here, except to say that, in general, the same conclusions given above apply. Let me, however, move from men's linguistic perception of neighbourhood to that of workplace. We may test whether workplace is seen to be the strong governing factor of language adding as it was in the case of Bahati.

WORKPLACE

The conclusions drawn from Bahati Kikuyu respondents with regard to workplace language use do indeed apply also to Kaloleni household heads. Use of English is roughly correlated with a larger proportion of a group in white collar employment (compare with Table 7.1); the individual vernaculars are in all groups strongly suppressed as a main language but flourish as secondary, tertiary or fourth languages (i.e. non-main languages); while Swahili is by far the most extensively used (see Tables 7.3(a) and 7.3(b) below). I shall now extend the analysis beyond these simple conclusions.

TABLE 7.3(a) *Main languages used with workmates*

% of all household heads	Swahili	English	Mother tongue	Any other vernacular	%
Luo (333) 39.0	62.8	34.5	1.5	—	98.8
Luyia (222) 26.0	71.6	25.2	1.8	0.4	99.0
Kikuyu (122) 14.3	68.8	29.5	—	—	98.3
Kamba (133) 15.6	77.4	18.8	0.8	—	97.0
Others (42) 4.9	76.2	19.0	—	2.4	97.6
Mean	71.6	25.4	0.8	0.6	

TABLE 7.3(b) *All languages used with workmates (expressed as percentage values[1])*

	Swahili	English	Mother tongue	Any other vernacular
Luo	89.4	54.1	38.8	0.5
Luyia	91.8	42.8	33.9	3.3
Kikuyu	90.3	45.0	37.9	0.8
Kamba	92.6	34.4	36.2	6.2
Others	90.4	35.0	27.3	5.4
Mean	90.9	42.3	34.8	3.2

[1] For method used in conversion, see footnote to Table 7.2(b), p. 169.

By subtracting the percentage in Table 7.3(a) from the percentage in the corresponding cell in Table 7.3(b), we have the proportion of the language known by an ethnic group and used by it as a non-main language at workplace. Thus, the value for Luo of Swahili as both a main and non-main language is 89.4. If we deduct 62.8 from this, we have a value of 26.6 for Swahili as a non-main language among Luo. We can convert this difference into a figure which can be used comparatively to measure the relative use which other groups make of languages as main and non-main media of workplace communication. To do this we establish the difference as a percentage proportion of the total value of the language in the particular group. In our Luo example, this would be:

$$\frac{26.6}{89.4} \times \frac{100}{1} = 29.7$$

By the same process the figure for Luyia is : 22.0.

This means that Luo report that they are more inclined to use Swahili as a non-main language at workplace than are Luyia.

If these comparative figures are deducted from 100.0, then of course we have a comparative statement on their proportionate use of Swahili as a main language, i.e. with Luo it is 60.3 as against Luyia 68.0, which means that Luyia report that they are more inclined than Luo to use

Swahili as a main language at workplace, while both claim to make much more use of Swahili at workplace as a main than as a non-main language.

These proportions can be expressed in tables for all ethnic groups and for all languages. With the present data, however, it is unnecessary to reproduce the proportions for mother tongues and other vernaculars (columns 3 and 4 of Tables 7.3(a) and 7.3(b)) since it is only too clear that—

1. the mother tongue is claimed to be reserved almost exclusively as a non-main language at workplace;
2. the use of other vernaculars is too low to warrant further investigation at this level.

We may focus on Swahili and English alone.

TABLE 7.4 *Proportionate main and non-main use of languages at workplace as between ethnic groups*

| | Swahili | | English | |
	Main	Non-Main	Main	Non-Main
Luo	70.3	29.7	63.8	36.2
Luyia	78.0	22.0	58.9	41.1
Kikuyu	76.2	23.8	65.6	34.4
Kamba	83.6	16.4	54.6	45.4
Others	85.4	14.6	54.3	45.7
Mean	78.8	21.2	60.1	39.9

Table 7.4 expresses in a conveniently clear form that both Luo and Kikuyu are less inclined than Luyia and Kamba to use Swahili as a main language at workplace. The difference between the Kikuyu and Luyia percentages is admittedly slight. But the same basic contrast is reaffirmed with regard to English. Both Luo and Kikuyu are more inclined than Luyia and Kamba to use English at workplace. If we look again at Table 7.1 and consider the three standard criteria of socio-economic status, namely education, income and occupation, we see that Luo and Kikuyu are in all cases ranked more highly than Luyia and Kamba, i.e. they are of higher socio-economic status. Of the Luyia and Kamba, the Kamba are of lower socio-economic status and, accordingly, use Swahili a great deal more as a main than non-main language but, when they use English, use it almost as much as a non-main than a main language. This suggests that, even when they know English, there is little compulsion on them to use it as a primary means of communication in performing workplace tasks.

Those grouped under 'Others' are at first sight anomalous. In Table 7.2 (a) their percentage use of Swahili is almost the same as that for Kamba, the lowest status group. But 'Others' are relatively low status only in education and occupation. They are high in terms of income. The implication, therefore, is that, like the Kamba, they tend to operate

174

in low status jobs in which English is not required as a means of communication. Cross-checking information confirms that this is indeed the case (see Table 7.1). The 'Others' have high incomes, it is true, but this can be explained by their above average age and correspondingly long period of urban residence: which implies again that, though in lower status jobs, they have been employed long enough to warrant higher than average increments for their skills.

Summarizing the results drawn from Tables 7.3(a), 7.3(b) and 7.4, we can confirm the strong association, first shown for the Bahati data, between socio-economic status and proportionate use of English and Swahili. The higher status ethnic groups, instanced by Luo and Kikuyu, use proportionately more English and less Swahili both in absolute quantitative terms and as a main language at workplace. The lower status groups, Kamba and Luyia, use proportionally less English and more Swahili, both absolutely and as a main language. 'Others' have lower status jobs and a lower level of education, and in this respect parallel the Kamba. Their workplace language use also parallels that of Kamba. Their incomes are high, a fact probably due to their older age and longer period in employment but not of relevance to their use of language at workplace.

Age, education, length of urban residence, and type of job thus emerge again, as in the Bahati data, as the crucial factors in any statistical approach to the study of workplace language use. In neighbourhood relations the residential area's ethnic composition and degree of ethnic dispersal or concentration are additional equally important factors. The method outlined could, if space allowed, be applied to show how individual occupational categories vary in their use of English, Swahili, the mother tongue and other vernaculars, both within and between ethnic groups. All that has been attempted here is a demonstration of the possibilities of the method.

OTHER PEOPLE'S LANGUAGES

I do not compare the formally 'uninstructed' Swahili speakers of Kaloleni (i.e. those who were never taught Swahili at school) with those of Bahati, since the same highly marked distinguishing factors making up the age syndrome apply. Let me proceed instead to the interesting question at Kaloleni of people's claimed knowledge of vernaculars other than their own.

Table 7.5 below gives a breakdown of claimed knowledge of vernaculars other than the mother tongue among Kaloleni's household heads.

TABLE 7.5 *Claimed knowledge of vernacular other than the mother tongue*

Ethnic group	None	VERNACULARS Luo	Luyia	Kikuyu	Kamba	Others	Total claims
Luo (333)	80.8	—	6.9	9.9	3.0	6.6	(357)
Luyia (222)	64.4	25.7	—	12.6	4.9	2.7	(245)
Kikuyu (122)	70.5	4.9	2.5	—	27.0	4.9	(134)
Kamba (133)	52.6	2.2	3.0	45.9	—	6.0	(146)
Others (42)	59.5	9.5	11.9	21.4	9.5	—	(47)
Total (852)[1]							(929)[1]

[1] Since some respondents claim a knowledge of more than one non-mother tongue vernacular, the total number of respondents' claims cited (929) does, of course, exceed the number of respondents (852).

It seems to me that in defining a 'speech ethnography', it is necessary to depict clearly the kind of pattern that is expressed in the figures in Table 7.5. A point of departure is to consider possible reciprocal socio-linguistic relations of pairs of ethnic groups. Three indices may be suggested:

Index 1 is the combined incidence, within any one pair, of claimed competence in the other (i.e. alter's) vernacular as a proportion of all vernaculars known by the pair. For example, in the pair Luo-Luyia, Luo state that Luyia accounts for 6.9 per cent of their knowledge of all non-native vernaculars, while for Luyia the corresponding proportionate knowledge of Luo is 25.7 per cent. Their *combined mutual knowledge of each other's vernaculars* is therefore $\dfrac{25.7 + 6.9}{2} = 16.3$.

Index 2 is the relative difference between members of the ethnic pair with regard to claimed knowledge of each other's vernacular. For example it is quite clear that Luo speak proportionally less Luyia (6.9 per cent) than Luyia speak Luo (25.7 per cent).

As with the use of main and non-main languages at workplace (see pp. 172–5), these differences must be converted into values which may be used in comparison with other ethnic pairs. In the sense that Luyia 'add' much more Luo than vice versa, they have a high *reciprocal value*, which can be represented as 25.7 as a proportion of $25.7 + 6.9 = \dfrac{25.7 \times 100}{32.6 \times 1} = 78.8$.

The lower Luo reciprocal value is 6.9 as a proportion of $25.7 + 6.9 = 21.2$.

Index 3 is the difference between the two scores for each member of the ethnic pair as a measure of the *degree of vernacular reciprocity*.

Thus, in the Luo-Luyia pair being discussed, the difference is high, namely 57.6. This represents a low degree of vernacular reciprocity (i.e. that Luyia receive the Luo vernacular much more than Luo receive the Luyia vernacular).

176

The usefulness of these three indices is as follows:

Index 1 tells us how much mutual vernacular competence there is within an ethnic pair, but does not tell us which member of the pair knows most and in what proportion.

Index 2 supplies this information and shows how different ethnic pairs may be compared with each other.

Index 3 shows the degree of vernacular reciprocity within a pair and can also be used for comparing pairs.

Excluding the category of small ethnic groups listed under 'Others' in Table 7.5, there are six ethnic pairs, alongside which scores for each of the three indices may be ranged as in Table 7.6 below.

In Table 7.6 the ethnic pairs are listed in order of scores for Index 1. The italicized members of each pair are those which receive proportionally more of alter's vernacular, the precise values for which are given for Index 2.

TABLE 7.6 *Vernacular adding by ethnic group*

	INDEX 1 Combined mutual vernacular knowledge	INDEX 2 Proportionate knowledge of ethnic pair-members	INDEX 3 Difference between proportionate knowledge of ethnic pair-members
Kamba-Kikuyu	36.5	63.0/37.0	26.0
Luyia-Luo	16.3	78.8/21.2	57.6
Luyia-Kikuyu	7.5	83.3/16.7	66.6
Luo-Kikuyu	7.4	67.0/33.0	34.0
Luyia-Kamba	4.0	62.3/37.7	24.6
Luo-Kamba	2.6	57.7/42.3	15.4

It is immediately apparent from the scores under Index 1 that the two ethnic pairs, Kamba-Kikuyu, and Luyia-Luo, represent by far the strongest instances of combined mutual vernacular knowledge. The score for Kamba-Kikuyu is very high, with 36.5 per cent of all Kamba and Kikuyu in the sample claiming to be able to switch into the other's vernacular. The score for Luyia-Luo is less than half this, but still over twice that for any other pair. Clearly, these two pairs will require special attention.

Moving to the scores under Index 2, it is interesting to note that in no pair do Kikuyu figure as a group who have received more of their partner's vernacular than has the partner received of theirs. That is to say, Kikuyu do not learn other groups' vernaculars as much as other groups learn theirs. I will suggest that this is a direct function of Kikuyu national and Nairobi numerical dominance and, as an extension, of their dominance also in the African employment and commercial structure. They are the 'host' group in Nairobi and the dominant group both in the city and in the nation as a whole. Even the Luo in the Kaloleni sample have learned more Kikuyu than they have Luyia (see Table 7.5), in spite of their special relationship with Luyia, a phenomenon to which I return.

The groups listed under 'Others' are not included in Table 7.6 since they do not constitute a single, homogeneous ethnic group, but a quick glance at Table 7.5 gives us information confirming that there is a tendency for the Kikuyu vernacular to be 'added' by non-Kikuyu in Nairobi; over a fifth of the 'Others' claim to speak Kikuyu, nearly doubling their next nearest claim.

Similarly, Kamba, though not the 'host' group in Nairobi and in fact numerically less in Nairobi than the two western Kenya peoples, Luo and Luyia, learn less of the vernacular of these two peoples than they learn Kikuyu. Admittedly, the combined mutual vernacular knowledge of Luyia-Kamba and Luo-Kamba is so low in each case that not too much can be made of this Kamba vernacular 'dominance'. But, ignoring the relative significance of proportions, we can construct a hierarchy of vernacular transmission on the basis of positions determined by scores under Index 2.

TABLE 7.7

The hierarchy	Prop. of Kaloleni's population (1969)	Prop. of Nairobi African population (1969)	Prop. of Kenya African population (1969)
Kikuyu	14.3	45.5	20.1
Kamba	15.6	14.4	10.9
Luo	39.0	14.8	13.9
Luyia	26.0	15.5	13.2
Others	4.9	not comparable	not comparable

Alternatively, the directions of vernacular 'dominance' among the four main ethnic groups can be diagrammed thus:

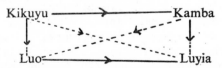

We have in fact constructed a crude 'model' of the sort I suggested could be made in Chapter 5, though there I spoke in terms of ego-centred concentric circles depicting language adding. In the model presented here, we can pick out four (or, if 'Others' are included, five) simultaneous processes of language 'adding'; (1) Kikuyu are extending the use of their vernacular to all ethnic groups; (2) Kamba are 'adding' Kikuyu to their vernacular repertoire but are not providing Kikuyu with as extensive a knowledge of their Kamba vernacular; (3) Kamba is being learned by Luo at a rate exceeding the learning of Luo by Kamba; (4) Luyia are learning Luo at a rate exceeding the reverse; while (5) the languages of

'Others' are not being extended significantly among any major ethnic group. Obviously, for this model to mirror reality with any precision, proportions both of population and of non-native vernaculars learned by any one ethnic group must not be inordinately low. As it is, the model does seem to correspond well with the situation as it is conveyed impressionistically to the observer on the ground. It thus depicts a general process of vernacular transmission among predominantly adult males of the housing estate of Kaloleni.

This does not mean, of course, that it is the neighbourhoods making up the locality of Kaloleni which are responsible for the particular directions this process takes. Kaloleni merely provides the sample of adult males, whose language adding is stimulated very much more by factors of workplace and by the economic and political situation of Nairobi as a whole and, possibly, by that of Kenya at a less significant remove. The earlier results showed the crucial importance of workplace and of socio-economic status generally as governing factors in language adding, especially Swahili. The process of vernacular transmission described here is thus characteristic of much of Nairobi's African adult working population, a claim borne out by studies in such different areas of Nairobi as Eastleigh, which has private and not public housing. It is quite true that since housing estates and localities do differ in their ethnic and socio-economic composition, some variation will occur. But these are, I believe, variants on a process which is determined by wider political and economic forces associated with Nairobi and to some extent the nation as a whole.

To put the point simply, men may indeed have occasional neighbourhood relationships which oblige them to deploy their language repertoires in particular ways according to the situation, but most of their time is spent outside the neighbourhood. The hard economic and political facts of life in the city seem to place a much greater premium on learning languages informally for a number of purposes: for successful, efficient or simply friendly workplace interaction; for establishing tolerable and mutually beneficial cross-ethnic short-term relationships; and even, in very rare cases, for establishing more committed cross-ethnic relationships of a patron-client nature or as in marriage. The usefulness of focusing on employed, adult men is that we get a picture of these more general influences which are not bounded by a small local area or housing estate. Language adding among women and young children tends, as explained, to be affected much more by the type of local area which by necessity circumscribes many of their day-to-day activities.

We can continue along the lines of this explanation by turning again to Table 7.6 and considering the scores for Index 3. We find that by far the highest score (and therefore the lowest degree of equivalence in vernacular reciprocity among an ethnic pair) occur for the Luyia-Kikuyu and Luyia-Luo pairs. They are followed by the pairs, Luo-Kikuyu and Kamba-Kikuyu. Finally the Luyia-Kamba and Luo-Kamba show the highest degree of equivalence. Alternatively, we can divide the six ethnic pairs into two halves, 'high-scoring' and 'low-scoring'. In the high-scoring half we have Luyia-Kikuyu, Luyia-Luo and Luo-Kikuyu who are thus instances of pairs in which there is great discrepancy between the respective pair-members' knowledge of each other's vernacular. In the low-scoring half, we have Kamba-Kikuyu, Luyia-Kamba and Luo-Kamba, who thus more closely approach equivalence in the knowledge by pair-members of each other's vernacular.

Against this distribution of scores, it must be remembered that a high combined mutual vernacular knowledge (as under Index 1) increases the significance of scores under Index 3. Thus, though the score under Index 3 for Kamba-Kikuyu is ranked fourth, it clearly has much more significance than that for, say, Luyia-Kamba, which is a pair consisting of only a small proportion of speakers. Indeed, this is a point which we may return to consider on the special relations of the two ethnic pairs, Kamba-Kikuyu and Luyia-Luo, who each include many speakers.

The discrepancy in mutual vernacular knowledge is greatest in the Luyia-Luo pair, but is still considerable in that of Kamba-Kikuyu. That is to say, in each pair there is a sociolinguistically 'dominant' partner: Luo in the first pair, and Kikuyu in the second. The task now is to compare the factors underlying sociolinguistic relations in each pair. Four main overlapping factors appear to be relevant:

1. The interplay of rural and urban influences.
2. The socio-economic status of the ethnic pair-members relative to each other and to other groups; and, as an aspect of this, the degree to which each fulfils the criteria of the 'age syndrome' (as discussed in the preceding chapter).
3. The cultural and geographical proximity of ethnic pair-members.
4. The degree of linguistic affinity of ethnic pair-members.

It is more convenient to deal with the factors together rather than singly.

In the Bahati data analysed in the last chapter, rural influences were not especially important in providing Kikuyu with competence in Kamba. Likewise in the Kaloleni sample, neither Kamba nor Kikuyu appear especially to owe their competence in each other's vernaculars to rural factors. There is not a disproportionate number of them living in rural Kikuyu/Kamba border areas, but there is a disproportionate number of them who are older, of long urban residence, lower status, less educated, and who in general show the characteristics of the 'age syndrome'.

180

Thus, though they appear to have some effect, rural-based influences are not paramount.

By contrast, nearly all Luyia and Luo knowing each other's vernacular are (a) from border areas, and/or (b) have been to schools at or near borders, and/or (c) show some incidence of intermarriage, either of themselves or of their parents. (The offspring of legitimized mixed marriages take their father's 'tribe'.) They do, nevertheless, show characteristics of the 'age syndrome'. There is the strong suggestion, therefore, that rural factors are here a definite *instigator* of a sociolinguistic relationship but that specifically urban factors *emphasize* it considerably and even mould some of the forms it takes.

Focusing on the 'age syndrome', it is interesting to note that the two linguistically 'dominant' pair-members, the Luo and Kikuyu, each have much higher socio-economic status than their pair-partners. That is to say, Luo outrank Luyia, and Kikuyu outrank Kamba (see Table 7.1). Moreover, the particular Luyia and Kamba included in the ethnic pairs exhibit strong features of the 'age syndrome'. To repeat, urban factors are, therefore, crucially important in both cases, with, in the case of Luo-Luyia, a basic rural pattern raised to a level of even greater significance in Nairobi.

The idiom of Luyia-Luo sociolinguistic relations may indeed be rural in origin. But the pattern of close interaction among members of these two groups in Nairobi suggests that special features of the urban environment bring them even closer and that this is reflected in greater knowledge of their respective vernaculars. The pattern of close interaction is as follows.

The Luo and Luyia have strong recreational ties, evidenced particularly by their intense and latently political soccer competitions in which they emerge as perennial rivals. The soccer competitions mobilize in a very effective pyramidal manner urban sub-tribal, clan, and sometimes even lineage groupings in a common organization. Luo and Luyia tend to live in the same housing area in Nairobi. They not infrequently trace affinal and matrilateral links to each other. During political crises, as when a foremost Luo politician, Tom Mboya, was assassinated, they express common interests. To a man, they claim that they are culturally and socially closer to each other than to either the Kikuyu or Kamba. Luo and Luyia intermarry, though usually only across certain common border areas. It is interesting and relevant to note here that, according to my sample, there are slightly more Luyia men who marry Luo women than Luo men who marry Luyia women.

These contexts of close interaction explain why Luo and Luyia learn each other's vernacular. But how are we to explain the marked discrepancy between Luo and Luyia in the knowledge of each other's vernacular? It will be remembered that while over a quarter of the Luyia in the Kaloleni sample claim to be able to speak Luo, less than 7 per cent of the Luo claim to know Luyia. Since the same one-sided relationship is reported in surveys for residents in other areas of Nairobi in which Luo are not predominant, the basic cause cannot be put down to Luo cultural dominance of Kaloleni.

There is an important general rural explanation, such as the tendency of certain Luyia sub-tribes which border Luoland to have a high proportion of men claiming to know the vernacular Luo in addition to their mother tongue. The following table shows which Luyia sub-tribes are over-represented among Luo speakers (column 1) in the total Kaloleni sample of Luyia (column 2).

TABLE 7.8 *Luyia claiming to know the Luo vernacular in addition to their mother tongue: by sub-tribe.*

	COLUMN 1 Distribution of Kaloleni Luyia sample by sub-tribe (222)	COLUMN 2 Distribution of Luo- speaking Luyia by sub-tribe (57)
Logoli (Maragoli)	35.0	8.8
Tiriki	3.6	3.5
Puoyo	0.4	—
Bukusu	2.3	—
Shisa	8.6	17.5
Nyore	13.0	21.0
Marama	7.2	7.0
Marachi	2.7	7.0
Wanga	2.7	—
Nyala	2.3	1.8
Samia	5.4	10.5
Kabras	0.9	—
Idakho	2.3	—
Isukha	4.5	1.8
Khayo	3.2	3.5
Tsotso	1.4	—
Other areas	4.5	17.5
Total	100.0%	99.9%

The Luyia sub-tribes which border Luoland are, in the order of the table, Logoli (Maragoli), Tiriki (marginal), Puoyo, Shisa, Nyore, Marama, Marachi, Wanga, Nyala, Samia, Khayo (marginal). Those which do not have common borders with Luoland are Bukusu, Kabras, Idakho, Isukha and Tsotso.

As expected, men of these latter few Luyia sub-tribes which do not share borders with Luo areas include none or inordinately few among them in the Kaloleni sample who claim to speak Luo. Conversely, there is a tendency for those sharing borders to claim some competence in Luo. This, as I say, fits in with a general common-sense expectation. But there are certain of the bordering sub-tribes which are definitely over-represented among Luo speakers, i.e. Shisa, Nyore, Marachi and Samia. Conversely, there is one, Logoli, which is remarkably under-represented among Luo speakers.

There is, as I have suggested above, a partial explanation for this and other similar discrepancies in terms of rural patterns of relations. This originally rural pattern is then seemingly 'exploited' and exaggerated in the urban environment *according to need*. I shall explain what I mean by this.

First, let us consider the rural pattern of relations with specific reference to the bordering Luyia sub-tribes, just mentioned, which are over-represented among the Luyia claiming to speak Luo.

To begin with, there are at least three main reasons suggested by data given by respondents themselves: (a) more Luyia seem to emigrate for work to Luo towns and townships in Nyanza Province than vice versa (Kisumu being perhaps the biggest draw); (b) in border area primary and secondary schools, with most of the latter apparently located on the Luo side of the border, Luyia tend to be in a minority; (c) Luo maintain, and Luyia do not generally disagree, that when Luo women are married to Luyia men, the women insist on their children learning Luo as well as Luyia. This latter claim sounds typically idealized. But the consistency with which Luo report it, and the absence of an equivalent claim by Luyia, suggest that it may have some truth.

The relative rural spread of Luo may also be explained by a complex of historical and cultural factors. For instance, the south-eastward movement by Luo many generations ago from what is now Uganda into Kenya and their present locale traversed the country of Bantu speakers, the possible ancestors of the people we now call Luyia. There are reasonably concrete and recent examples of predominantly Luo-speaking areas having once been Bantu-speaking. Therefore, it is possible that less recent Luo-ization occurred as the Luo moved south-eastward. Whether these occurred more through simply vernacular than population sub-stitution is difficult to say, though obviously both factors would have operated.

In addition to all this, one cannot resist recording the strong impression that Luyia do not conceive of themselves as being as close-knit culturally as do the Luo. The term Luyia is, of course, itself of recent origin. Bukusu and Logoli, when asked in our interview which 'tribe' they belonged to, very frequently referred to themselves as 'Bukusu' or 'Maragoli' rather than as Luyia. Bukusu often deny that they are Luyia. They are extra-ordinarily few in Kaloleni and, I believe, in Nairobi, in spite of numbering some half a million in their rural home area. They need no longer be considered here. The Logoli, by contrast, are very numerous among Luyia in Nairobi, yet are greatly under-represented among the Luo speakers.

Many of these Logoli in Kaloleni may, of course, stem from parts of Logoli country which are fairly distant from Luo border areas, and this might partly explain their low proportion of Luo speakers. But the same part-explanation does not apply, apparently, in other cases, since there is, as mentioned, some over-representation among Shisa, Nyore, Marachi and Samia.

A more satisfactory explanation may rest in the relative sizes of the Luyia sub-tribes in Nairobi.

It is legitimate to talk in terms of these sub-tribes as distinct units, since the rate of sub-tribal endogamy remains high. Endogamy maintains the corporateness of groupings and ensures that they interact each as distinct units. Now, since the Logoli are by far the largest of the Luyia sub-tribes in Kaloleni and, apparently, in Nairobi (see Table 7.8), it is not surprising that we find them organizing themselves almost separately from non-Logoli Luyia sub-tribes. Thus, they have their own Maragoli Association and football team in Nairobi, which frequently plays against the Abaluhya Association team, consisting of players, officials and supporters from non-Logoli Luyia sub-tribes. In other contexts and in conversation, also, Logoli emphasize their separateness and individual identity while other Luyia sub-tribes are more prepared to interact with each other and regard themselves as 'Luyia'. It follows, therefore, that Logoli are less likely than non-Logoli in Nairobi to learn or claim to have learned Luo.

I suggest, therefore, a general hypothesis relating this contrast to the process of vernacular 'adding': when an ethno-linguistic collectivity (like the Luyia) has pronounced internal divisions separating large sections from smaller ones, then the latter are more likely to 'add' foreign vernaculars than are the larger ones. That is to say, large groups can develop the common interests and power to expect to be accepted more on their own terms with 'foreigners' with whom they interact in a single system of relations. By contrast, small groups are more likely to develop relations of clientship or dependence and to assume rather more readily the languages of larger and/or more powerful 'patrons' as a means of communication with them and possibly of expressing deference to them. Thus, again, as for urban Kamba-Kikuyu relations, we see the potential relevance of patron-clientship or of dominance-subordination as a means of spreading language.

This hypothesis is more likely to apply to those groups who already have an established, rural-based pattern of sociolinguistic relations with each other. It thus applies to some, though apparently not all, Luyia sub-tribes who share borders with Luo.

Kamba-Kikuyu relations in Nairobi contrast in being not only urban-encouraged but also predominantly urban-established. As suggested for the Bahati data, Kikuyu and Kamba seem more likely to interact in economic and commercial contexts rather than, as with Luo and Luyia, in recreational and political contexts. For example, our surveys suggest that in the many Nairobi market stalls and shops run or owned by Kikuyu, virtually the only non-Kikuyu employed there are Kamba. Affinal and matrilateral links between the two ethnic groups are not important, since the rate of intermarriage among Kamba and Kikuyu is, on the basis of our figures, even lower than that for Luyia and Luo. It seems, therefore, that because Kikuyu are so predominant in Nairobi, they provide the most obvious, numerous and culturally and linguistically convenient source of 'patronage' for Kamba, whose generally low socio-economic status tends to foster their dependence.

A further contrasting variable is the fairly obvious one of degree of linguistic affinity in an ethnic pair. As I showed in the last chapter on Bahati, we can talk in terms of Kamba and Kikuyu as each standing on a 'threshold' of learning each other's language. By all common-sense measures, their vernaculars are very 'close'. The Luyia and Luo vernaculars are of quite different linguistic families. As I stated in the preceding chapter, I do not regard linguistic affinity as a significant variable in itself in language 'adding'. It becomes significant only in such cases as that of Kamba and Kikuyu, where urban economic interests and considerable language 'closeness' reinforce each other.

We can now summarize the differences and similarities between the two ethnic pairs with regard to the four sets of factors introduced on page 180.

The Factors	Luyia-Luo	Kamba-Kikuyu
1(a) High degree of rural influence which is 'exploited' under urban conditions for specific needs.	+	−
1(b) Low degree of rural influence which is not particularly relevant to the urban conditions and needs, giving rise to language 'adding'.	−	+
2 Significant difference between pair-members in socio-economic status and in age syndrome.	+	+
3 Close cultural and geographical proximity of pair-members.	+	+
4(a) No formal linguistic affinity of pair-members.	+	−
4(b) Close formal linguistic affinity of pair-members	−	+

In short, the two ethnic pairs are similar in the second and third factors but differ in the first and fourth. If there were sufficient vernacular reciprocity, other ethnic pairs in Nairobi might usefully be compared on the basis of such factors. The purpose of an analytical scheme of this kind is to reduce to a few simple variables the apparently complex process of language adding among groups of people obliged to interact with each other.

SUMMARY AND CONCLUSIONS

I have discussed language 'adding' in the uni-ethnic housing area of Bahati (preceding chapter) and in the polyethnic area of Kaloleni with regard to workplace and neighbourhood and, as a check in the case of Bahati, friendship. Though the conclusions drawn for neighbourhood were, as expected, different for each area, those for workplace were similar; language adding of Swahili and the vernaculars tends to be urban-based or urban-encouraged; rural influences may initiate competence in one or two vernaculars and sometimes Swahili, but urban influence strengthens it, especially when the speakers have lower status employment in which the use of English is neither required nor encouraged.

An ethnically mixed 'speech community' exhibits quantifiable patterns of sociolinguistic relations among its constituent ethnic groups. The ebb and flow of vernacular interchange among specific pairs of ethnic groups is a function of their positions of 'dominance' relative to each other. 'Dominance' is seen as resting singly on or on a combination of socio-economic status, and political and numerical factors.

In Nairobi, those groups which are significantly sociolinguistically 'dominant' (i.e. are extending their vernacular to another group) tend also to be of higher socio-economic status, and/or to be politically superordinate, and/or simply to be larger in numbers.

Language 'adding' is the logical precursor of language 'substitution'. The latter has not yet occurred on any wide scale. There are a few exceptions such as the Kikuyu and Kamba Muslims born and bred in the distinctive area of Pumwani, who speak Swahili as a first language (see Bujra *infra*), or certain élite families (some Kikuyu cases have been documented) in which children speak English as a first and their parents' vernacular as a second language. But it is much too early to be able to make even such tentative predictions for the rest of the population as those attempted at the end of the previous chapter.

The general pattern of relations in the 'speech community' is defined on the basis of the quantitative data so far presented. Ordinary conversations may be affected by this overall pattern of relations. As a simple instance, our figures suggest that Luo and Luyia who speak to each other are most likely to use Swahili, but that in a smaller but still reasonably large number of conversations they may use the Luo vernacular or English. These simple conclusions may not seem worth the welter of quantitative data on which they are based. All that one can say in answer is that the ordinary impressions of day-to-day observation have been given a precision which enables them to be viewed comparatively on a more 'scientific' basis.

But it is to the analysis of ordinary conversations that I now turn. I want to see how the two basic variables, socio-economic status and ethnic group membership, affect language choice and switching.

8

Language Switching in Nairobi

D. J. PARKIN

SOCIAL DISTANCE

Some interesting work on perceptions of 'social distance' among townsmen in the Zambian Copperbelt (Mitchell 1956) shows how ethnic labels denote group membership and are useful in providing a blueprint of relationships. The blueprint is a cognitive 'map' enabling a townsman to 'place' other people in the town in a category of closeness or distance according to their ethnic groups. 'Placing' according to the ethnic map is necessary when the only information a person has is the 'tribe' of the person he encounters. It may still be necessary even when the person has other information, such as the occupation, income, education, and area of residence of the other person. In other words, we can use more than simply one referent for deciding how we should behave towards a person.

The work from the Copperbelt illustrated the importance of the two variables with which I have been concerned in this section: ethnic group affiliation and socio-economic status. Mitchell's study of the Kalela dance (1956) demonstrated the interplay of these two in a single activity. It should be pointed out that ethnic closeness or distance was, for Mitchell, based on cultural (including linguistic) factors. Putting the situation simply, I might act towards a person in a specific way because he is of a 'tribe' which is culturally close to my own. We understand each other's customs. But, additionally, I might also act in a specific way towards that man because I recognize that he is of the same socio-economic status as myself. I may behave in a quite different way when I recognize that the man is neither of a 'tribe' like my own nor my socio-economic equal. There is in both cases a compounding of cues for 'placing' each other. Or there may be a divergence of cues. The cues for ethnic placing are the stereotypes we have of 'other tribes'. The cues for socio-economic status are the stereotypes we have of poorer or richer men, men with less or more education, or men who have menial or prestigious occupations compared with our own. The almost constant competition for prestige, or honour, or esteem, and the desire to avoid shame, seem pronounced in many East and Central African towns of colonial creation (see Epstein 1959, and Parkin 1969). A concern with notions of prestige seems to be strongly associated with a 'constantly changing skyline of status' (Douglas 1962) such as typifies the rapidly changing social situations characteristic of such towns. The claims and counter-claims for prestige underlie much behaviour centring round differences of socio-economic status.

The situation in Nairobi is in one respect more complicated than that reported for the Copperbelt of Zambia. In Nairobi, ethnic closeness has also to be seen in conjunction with the political processes at work. It is quite clear, for instance, that it is possible to talk in terms of at least putative political alliances between ethnic groups which do not always coincide with cultural closeness. Shortly before and after independence, Kikuyu and Luo provided most of the membership of the Kenya African National Union, the party which came to power at Kenya's independence. The Luo and most Luyia were sharply divided between KANU and the Kenya African Democratic Union, the opposition party, while Kamba were mostly KADU but with an apparently substantial minority in KANU. In more recent years, as I have explained briefly in Chapter 5, there has been a complete reversal of these alliances, with Kikuyu and Luo now opposed and Luo and Luyia now in alliance, and with Kamba possibly somewhat neutral. It is obvious that these are the kinds of folk definitions one would get from people in Nairobi and necessarily are not more than abstractions from the reality. They are additional stereotypes: the political stereotypes of ethnic groups. These are different from the cultural stereotypes dealt with by Mitchell for the Copperbelt, which were based on affinity of custom.

Our original ethnic variable should, therefore, be regarded as having two aspects, a cultural as well as a political one. In actual analysis it may not always be possible to demonstrate which aspect governs language or code switching in a conversation, but the possibility of an analytical distinction of this kind has to be noted (see Parkin 1970). The socio-economic status variable is much easier to pick out in analysis.

When people interact they try to judge, consciously or unconsciously, what mode of behaviour best suits the interaction. In any role-relationship, even one occupying no more than a few minutes, there is a constant process of adjustment and counter-adjustment to each other's expectations by the role-players. The values, stereotypes, and symbols, of ethnic and socio-economic status are just two of many basic contours on the general cognitive 'map' within which these adjustments are made. In a total population of people who interact fairly frequently, there is inevitably something of a feed-back process between the basic values and individually replicated, interpersonal adjustments.

Following the lines of Barth's analysis (1966), we can say that the inter-personal adjustments take the form of 'transactions' or 'prestations' between the role-partners. That is to say, the role-partners recognize certain basic postulates of the relationship (i.e. that a man is of X tribe and of A, B, C, education, job and income), yet make concessions, or challenges and counter-challenges to each other on the basis of qualities and skills which fall through the net of the necessarily loose definition of the role-relationship as made by the over-arching values or stereotypes.

There do seem to be certain conversations which include this transac-tional element. In them we can see clearly the influence of socio-economic status, particularly in the use of English and Swahili, and of ethnic status, particularly in the use of the vernaculars. But we can also perceive the speaker making use of a limited number of choices: how should he respond to the use of a particular language; is the use intended to connote 'solidarity' or assertiveness; at what stage in the conversation is it strategic-ally sound for him to reveal a wider repertoire of languages known by him; what response may he expect in revealing a 'new' language? I emphasize now that these are not necessarily conscious choices nor are they randomly made. They represent a limited range of alternative ways of speaking which arise logically from a particular recurring situation.

In confining myself to the two variables, ethnic and socio-economic status, I see three ideal types of transactional conversation. One can be regarded as a type of language game, since an element of gamesmanship seems to be present. The 'game' is to use language to resolve a logical contradiction between personal interests (here socio-economic) and ethnic group loyalties. The second type of transactional conversation is dis-tinguishable by the way in which putative relationships of alliance or opposition between ethnic groups affect language use. In the third type of conversation notions of socio-economic status affect language use or affect the interpretation of language choice. In practice these ideal types may partly overlap, and I have selected conversations in which the values of one type appear to predominate. In all types, paralinguistic features such as tone, gesture and, possibly, physical stance, are important, perhaps crucially so in the first type.

I regard these transactional conversations as *critical* 'speech events' (Hymes 1962). That is to say, they reveal certain fundamental ethnic and socio-economic status values attaching to the use of languages in Nairobi. The language game is undoubtedly the most significant in this respect.

From repeated transactional conversations flow the continually modified values, or non-verbal messages, of particular languages. In the much more common, non-transactional conversations of everyday life, these values or messages are assumed and incorporated frequently in the form of idiomatic usage and clichés. This modification of values has to be seen, or is most easily seen, in transactional conversations between persons of different ethnic groups, which thus constitute nearly all my examples.

TRANSACTIONAL CONVERSATIONS 1: JOKING AND GAMESMANSHIP: THE LANGUAGE GAME

One of the most interesting aspects of conversations concerning ethnic and status relationships is that they are frequently jocular and accompanied by banter. This was the case in Kampala and the Copperbelt (Epstein 1959) and is so in Nairobi. In other words, though people compete for prestige and status and may express their ethnic stereotypes in conversation and behaviour, they may refrain from doing so in a manner which is visibly hostile. It is hardly surprising that this is so. One does not normally score points over a rival by crude abuse or violence if public approval is one's aim. Approval has to be sought by manipulating subtly and skilfully norms of the existing social order, but not by breaking them. If abuse is used, it has to be witty but not crude and unsophisticated. In what I have elsewhere (1970) called a 'conversational arena of prestige competition', the game breaks down when a competitor runs out of witty abuse and resorts to violence.

In this example, men competed with each other in a taunting but jocular manner for the prestige of being regarded as the most articulate speaker of English. Each competitor acted here on the basis of personally achieved socio-economic status. The break-up of the game occurred when the honour of a man's nation (a Kenyan) was impugned and he rose to defend it. From other cases it might well have been the honour of his ethnic group that he sought to defend. In other words, one of the two variables of interaction, that of ethnic or national status (group membership), intervenes and conflicts with the second variable, personal socio-economic status.

This is, of course, a universal phenomenon. We may at one level seem to compete for prestige as individuals regardless of ethnic affiliation. In Nairobi, a dire scarcity of jobs and housing is at the basis of much competition. Yet, at another level, we may be drawn to those who are closest to us ethnically and culturally. As members of a common group we may then blame the scarcity of jobs and housing on other ethnic groups who appear to us to have a monopoly. Personal status and ethnic group each has its own set of stereotypes, symbols and conventions of behaviour. For much of social life these are either kept apart or are mutually reinforcing. But sometimes, as in the example of a conversation I have just mentioned, they conflict.

This occasional conflict of expectations arises from what is ultimately a logical contradiction between the two variables of ethnic group member-ship and achieved personal status. There is a contradiction here because a man cannot maximize personal interests at all times without flouting the rules of group membership. Alternatively, he cannot fulfil the group's norms at all times without sacrificing at least some self-interest. In practice, men reach compromises. But, as an intellectual puzzle played out in the minds of men, a solution seems possible through a reversal of logic. For example, a Luo who initiates a conversation with a Kikuyu in the friendly atmosphere of a bar, may recognize that there is a stereotyped opposition between Luo and Kikuyu over certain issues. He may denote his recognition of this basic blueprint for behaviour by pointed jokes. Having expressed the putative state of hostility between them in the most friendly manner possible, i.e. having reversed the logic, he can then get on with the main task for which the particular relationship was established, namely the satisfaction of personal interests. This is stated simply here, but constitutes a basic strategy in many conversations which I have recorded between persons who are of different 'tribes'. As will become clear from my illustrations, language use and switching are convenient methods of succeeding in this strategy and of tempering conflict-ing role-expectations arising from this fundamental contradiction.

Following Bailey (1968, 1969), I have introduced such notions as 'strategy', 'game', 'scoring points', and 'competition', since I believe that these may be useful concepts in analysing certain day-to-day speech transactions or conversations of people who try to maximize personal interests yet are each members of groups which are putatively opposed in some contexts.

I have found it necessary to be selective and have concentrated on part-conversations heard and afterwards written down[1] to the best of our memories by my assistant and myself in the market place of Shauri Moyo, or 'Bama' as it is called locally, which is across the Jogoo Road from Kaloleni. Its stall-holders and customers are ethnically mixed and it is a good area for hearing language switching and 'mixing'. Market place transactions are additionally useful from the analytical viewpoint simply because they *are* transactional or contractual. That is to say, the transactional aspects of speech are thrown more clearly into relief because language is an important tool and symbol in the haggling which accompanies the economic transaction. I should emphasize that nearly all my examples in this chapter are of very short, casual encounters with very few words exchanged. The simplicity and brevity of these encounters makes them manageable for the limited analytical aims which I have set myself. I do not yet feel equipped to analyse an extended conversation of 'normal' dimensions.

In the following case of a Luo and Kikuyu speaking to each other the aim of my analysis will be to see the apparent effect on language use when individuals successfully joke off the contradiction between (a) what they want personally from the transaction and their use of numerous and novel techniques to satisfy this want, and (b) how they ought to behave on the basis of the limited information they have on each other as members of groups and categories laid out according to a blueprint.

Case 1: Kikuyu female stall-holder and Luo male customer. Parts of actual conversation as heard, with dashes denoting language switch.

1. KIKUYU STALL-HOLDER: Omera, nadi!
2. LUO CUSTOMER: Maber.
3. KIKUYU: Ati—nini?
4. LUO: Ya nini kusema lugha ambao huelewi mama?
5. KIKUYU: I know—kijaluo—very well!
6. LUO: Wapi!—You do not know it at all.—Wacha haya, nipe mayai mbili.
7. KIKUYU: Unataka mayai—ariyo, omera,—haya ni—tongolo—tatu.

Languages used:
1. Luo
2. Luo
3. Kikuyu—Swahili
4. Swahili
5. English—Swahilized form—English
6. Swahili—English—Swahili
7. Swahili—Luo—Swahili—Luo—Swahili

Rough translation:
1. How are you, brother!
2. Fine.
3. What—what?
4. Why (try) to speak a language you don't know, Mum?
5. I know Luo very well!
6. Go on! You don't know it at all. Anyway, let's leave the matter, and give me a couple of eggs.
7. Two eggs, brother? O.K., that will be thirty cents.

We cannot be too adventurous about an analysis of this limited conversation. Even in so few words, switching is considerable. The paralinguistic data are important also, as I now show.

194

1. The Kikuyu stall-holder opens up with a breezy, friendly and jocular Luo greeting, having recognized the customer to be a Luo. (In this case the two did not know each other and the Luo was recognized as such by certain distinctive features.) Here the Kikuyu stall-holder concedes to the Luo a claimed knowledge of the Luo vernacular, a customary way of attracting and holding the custom of Luo who are reputedly proud of their language. In making this language concession, we may speculate that the stall-holder hopes to profit from the economic transaction. Should she elicit a Luo response from the Luo, she may have pleased him. In terms of a language game, she will have scored a point.

2. The Luo does answer the greeting in Luo and so awards her a point, but he answers her in an uncharacteristically (for Luo) brief and curt manner. We possibly see why in 3 and 4 below.

3. The Kikuyu does not appear to have understood or to have heard even this simple Luo reply, thus seeming to betray immediately her very limited knowledge of the Luo vernacular. Thus, her gamble did not come off and she loses her point. The score is now even.

4. With what is clearly a jocular mock indignation, the Luo lets the Kikuyu woman know that he realizes that she has virtually no knowledge of his vernacular. To put it simply, he exposes her as having been using *his* language for her personal economic gain.

Significantly, the Luo here uses Swahili. It is pointless continuing to use Luo anyway, but the use of Swahili puts them back on neutral ground and denies the mock 'friendship' which the woman tried to create. The score is surely now in the Luo's favour.

5. The Kikuyu tacitly admits that she does not really know the Luo vernacular by replying in English in even more jocular vein. Her switch to English after the Luo's previous use of Swahili may be regarded as a challenge to the Luo. Can he match her English and save his point?

6. He successfully staves off the challenge and replies in English, now openly returning the banter. Having settled the challenge, he turns to the matter-of-fact business at hand and switches back to the neutral language of Swahili in order to purchase some eggs, which is for him the pragmatic purpose of the transaction.

He has won the language tussle, but the Kikuyu stall-holder has won her custom. She seems to accept this and offers, as a final friendly gesture, some more words of Luo, including the word, 'omera', 'my brother'.

While there may be alternatives to this analysis, we at least have here an explanation for language switching which is consistent. Language use here is viewed as part of a contest. Admittedly, winning the language contest did not help the Luo buy his eggs more cheaply, which was not, anyway, his intention. But, at least, his 'honour' was maintained. More than this the 'honour' of his own vernacular, an undisputed source of pride, was maintained also. It could be argued fairly that it is in the interests of the stall-holders to stimulate and then lose such language contests, provided that they win their custom. And this, of course, is perfectly true. Indeed it is precisely by manipulating such systems of honour, and not just those concerning language, that such economic and thereby political interests are created and strengthened.

In this particular conversation, the use of English set up a challenge of a socio-economic nature. Because it is a prestigious lingua franca, English has normally to be used with caution. So, in some contexts, must Swahili. But English seems to have much less of the neutral emotional 'colour' that may sometimes characterize Swahili. If used incautiously with a man who is known by the speaker to know no English, the use of English is likely to cause offence. Sometimes, of course, it can be used in this situation as a deliberate snub.

It is important to observe how the vernacular, Luo, stimulates a different response from English and Swahili. Use of 'my' vernacular or mother tongue constitutes a form of borrowing and can please my sense of language loyalty or can offend it depending on the particular use to which the vernacular is put. This response is illustrated clearly in the Luo's reply (no. 4) in the case above. Here the Kikuyu's use of the Luo vernacular is too obviously out of enlightened self-interest. It 'offends', ostensibly at least, and requires a riposte. In contrasting situations, in a beer bar for instance, a Kikuyu, say, may greet and carry on a limited conversation with, say, a Luo across the table from him in the Luo vernacular for no other apparent reason than to express friendliness. This use of the vernacular is here more likely to please the Luo's sense of language loyalty and may elicit a concession, though not necessarily of a language or vernacular kind.

In general the different responses to, on the one hand English and Swahili, the lingua francas, and on the other hand the vernacular, Luo, can be explained by the contradiction discussed above. That is to say, the response prompted by use of the vernacular derives from wider scale expectations of inter-ethnic group relations, which have their cultural and political aspects. By contrast, the response set up by use of English and Swahili has more to do with socio-economic status relations of an interpersonal nature. The most obvious form of this contradiction in the case was the fact that, though both stall-holder and customer competed in the same language game, the stall-holder clearly had economic profit as her primary 'prize' (personal interest), while the customer saw the maintenance of ethnic honour as his 'prize' (the group interest). It is a contradiction for opposing sides in a game to compete for different prizes. The contradiction is resolved by being phrased in jocular terms. As Douglas says, following Freud, 'the essence of wit is neatly to span gulfs between different ideas' (Douglas 1968, p. 363). Regulated joking is a form of ritual behaviour, and like ritual it may reconcile, if only temporarily, conflicting and contradictory principles of social organization and intellectual classification.

To repeat, language games phrased in a jocular idiom represent one way of resolving the contradiction of ethnic group loyalties and personal status considerations. In resolving the contradiction the language game throws into relief the basic behavioural stereotypes which use of each language conveys. In the next case, we see something of what may occur when the language game ceases to be phrased in a jocular idiom: the contradiction is openly expressed and language use may become an issue over which genuine hostility is voiced.

Case 2: Kamba stall-holder, neighbouring Kikuyu stall-holder, and Luo customer.

Parts of the conversation as heard:

1. LUO CUSTOMER: Bwana sikuweza kukulipa pesa zako za mwezi jana kwa sababu nilikuwa na haja zingine za haraka sana. Nisamehe, nitakulipa mwisho wa mwezi huu.

2. KAMBA STALL-HOLDER: And why did you not report this at the end of the month? Nyakati nyingine ninyi wanunuzi na hasa wale—employed—mnatuletea taabu nyingi sana katika biashara.

3. NEIGHBOURING KIKUYU STALL-HOLDER: Makiria aya—Jaluo—niandu acenji muno.

4. LUO CUSTOMER: Sasa ukisema—ati—sisi—joluo—tu washenzi, unafikiri sisikii lugha yako ya Kikuyu. Na ninyi wakikuyu si mwashenzi zaidi?—You nigger!

5. NEIGHBOURING KIKUYU STALL-HOLDER: Nenda zako mjinga wee!

6. KAMBA STALL-HOLDER: Go away and remember to bring this money at the end. And I am not supplying you with food this month until you pay the amount due.

Languages used:

1. Swahili
2. English—Swahili—English—Swahili
3. Kikuyu
4. Swahili—English
5. Swahili
6. English

Rough translation:

1. Mister, I wasn't able to pay my last month's account because of some other urgent expenses. I'm sorry but I'll pay at the end of this month.
2. Why didn't you let me know at the end of last month? You customers, especially those of you who have jobs, are always giving us businessmen trouble.
3. Sometimes these Luo have no sense.
4. So, by speaking in 'ati' (i.e. refers to the Kikuyu language) and calling us Luo barbarians, you think I can't understand your Kikuyu language. Well, aren't you Kikuyu even greater barbarians? You nigger! (a not uncommon form of abuse).
5. Go home, you fool.
6. (As the original.)

1. The Luo opens up the conversation in the spirit of a frank request. He is not jocular about the debt. He uses the 'neutral' language of Swahili, chosen presumably because it is here the most efficient medium of communication in this business matter. He does not therefore initiate a language game. Note his 'standard' style of Swahili.

2. But the Kamba does, it seems, initiate a language game by replying in English. He does so in a tone of mock haughtiness. His haughtiness is necessarily mock rather than real, since the Luo, for all his indebtedness, is a regular customer. If he genuinely offends the Luo, he may lose not only regular custom but also the debt. Retaining custom and eventually having his debt repaid may be regarded as the Kamba's primary 'prize' (compare the Kikuyu stall-holder in Case 1).

By using English in what amounts to a jocular if taunting tone of voice, the Kamba has scored a point and has set up a challenge which the Luo may accept.

Having established his challenge the Kamba then switches to Swahili. In switching to Swahili he sheds the mock haughtiness and adopts a more ostensibly relaxed and friendly tone. He awaits the Luo's riposte.

We may note that in his switch from English to Swahili and from a mock haughtiness to a more openly friendly tone, he moves from a *specific* condemnation of the customer to a general condemnation of debtors. There is the suggestion here that not only is friction reduced by moving from use of the second person singular to the second person plural, but that this movement is best achieved by switching from English to Swahili. Swahili, it should be noted, frequently connotes equality or irrelevance of status and even connotes 'brotherhood' (see Parkin 1970), a point to which I return.

In parenthesis, we should note also that the Kamba uses the English word, 'employed', instead of, say, the Swahili 'wenye kazi' or 'wafanya-kazi'. From other contexts, it seems that the English term tends to refer to office workers who, by definition, know English, while the Swahili terms refer to workers of all status levels in a more general context. The significance of the inclusion of the English term in an otherwise Swahili sentence seems to reinforce the general condemnation, i.e. they may be office workers, speak English, and wear suits, but they still don't pay their bills.

3. At this juncture, the nearby Kikuyu stall-holder enters the arena. His entry was presumably not anticipated by the Kamba when he made his challenge to the Luo by replying in English. And now the Luo's acceptance of the challenge is forestalled. But, before seeing the effect the Kikuyu's entry has upon the game, let us ask what might have been the Luo's response to the challenge.

There might have been four possible alternatives open to the Luo.

(a) He could have continued to use Swahili. But he would not thereby have met the Kamba's challenge and so would have ceded the point.

(b) He could have used his own vernacular, Luo, but since the aim of the game is to exceed your opponent's expectations by disclosing an increasingly large repertoire of languages, this would hardly have achieved that aim and he would have ceded the point. Also, since few Kamba appear to know Luo, as we saw in the last chapter, this would have been tantamount to closing the lines of communication. It would have been literally pointless.

(c) He could have used English. This would have at least met the challenge and put the score at even.

(d) Finally he could have used his opponent's own vernacular, Kamba. As we saw from the last chapter it is extremely rare for a Luo to know even a little of the Kamba vernacular. For the Luo customer to have done this, therefore, would probably have been completely against the Kamba stall-holder's expectations and would have either cancelled out the Kamba's point and given the Luo one, or been seen by the Kamba as a new and very powerful counter-challenge (compare the initial use by the Kikuyu stall-holder of her Luo customer's vernacular in Case 1).

Let us now return to the effect that the Kikuyu's entry into the arena has on the game. The Kamba had previously switched from English to Swahili and from mock haughtiness to open friendliness. This might well have been an invitation to bring more jocularity into the game.

The Kikuyu nearby stall-holder does intervene in a jocular tone but does so in his own vernacular, in effect addressing himself to the Kamba.

199

He seems to have broken some rule of the game by throwing his own vernacular uninvited into the arena. By speaking in Kikuyu to the Kamba, he quite clearly closes the lines of communication with the Luo and creates a relationship of confidence with the Kamba which excludes the Luo.

4. Even if the Luo could understand Kikuyu, this esoteric use of the vernacular is almost bound to offend him. Indeed, he claims to have understood the Kikuyu but takes the remark more as an insult than a joke and returns the insult. His final insult is traded in English, presumably as a final riposte. There is now little chance of bringing more jocularity into the game. As a result the game seems abandoned.

5. The Kikuyu replies to the insults in the language of most efficient communication, Swahili. He seems also to regard the game as abandoned.

6. The Kamba stall-holder, presumably still anxious to retain the Luo's custom and/or to have his debt settled, reminds the Luo of this. He uses English. Is this a last attempt to restart the game and so reduce friction, or is it simply a means of asserting his demands in the language of highest authority? Either interpretation seems possible.

Again, as in Case 1, ethnic and status factors bring about conflicting expectations: competitors can make use of Swahili and English and the status associations that go with them; they might even have made use of each other's vernaculars; but when the esoteric use of a mother tongue is brought into the arena, ethnic stereotypes are connoted and ethnic loyalties are hurt. The language game and jocularity are then likely to be abandoned and hostility to be openly expressed in ethnic terms.

I do not wish to appear defensive about this approach to the analysis of conversations. But I cannot pretend that it is a panacea. There are many different ways of looking at the same data. I suggest that this is one of them. The problem before us is to discover factors prompting language switching. In everyday life, differences of status and of 'tribe' are frequently joked about and there is often a certain gamesmanship in competitions for prestige and status and in relations between people of different ethnic groups. This, as I have said, is a fact which has already been well demonstrated.

Given that the lingua francas, English and Swahili, invoke status stereotypes, and that the vernaculars, by definition, invoke ethnic stereotypes, it seems reasonable to assume that in conversations involving switching between these languages, we should sometimes find evidence of jocular gamesmanship.

I think I should emphasize again that people are not necessarily conscious that they are playing these language games. Sometimes they are (see

Parkin 1970). Usually they are not. Whether or not the games are consciously played seems to me irrelevant, provided the same basic aims, rules and techniques are employed.

The irrelevance of consciousness leads to another remark I would like to make about this mode of analysis. This is that it is not a psychological analysis. It is true that it makes use of such notions as 'stereotypes', which are essentially mental associations stimulated by symbols of a material or non-material nature, including words and languages. It is true, too, that it depends on observation of such paralinguistic phenomena as mood, stress, and even gesture (though I have not included the latter here). But the analysis is not concerned with how neuro-sensory processes give rise to, say, moods, or with how these processes are stimulated by stereotypes. The stereotypes and moods are deliberately loosely defined, are based on empirical observation, and are no more than descriptive labels. The essence of analysis is the limited number of language choices which a speaker has: he is limited by his personal repertoire as well as by that of his role-partner. The aim of the game is to expose the limits of his partner's repertoire before exposing the limits of his own. A game of this kind can be analysed without reference to psychology, though possibly psychology might be helpful.

Finally one definitely has to be selective about the cases which may be analysed. The sort of conversations I have in mind are those in which there is a progressive unravelling of fresh languages by those conversing with each other. The simplest conversational set is between two people. The simplest unravelling is of the two lingua francas, Swahili and English, and each of the competitor's mother tongues. Each language is shown to have its own symbolic or communicative value in the conversation. These values seem highlighted when language use itself becomes a topic of conversation. It seems legitimate, therefore, to begin an analysis of language switching by selecting 'natural' examples of people actually talking about language, a topic which, except perhaps under the conditions of a simulated or controlled discussion, seems likely to invoke jocularity.

TRANSACTIONAL CONVERSATIONS 2: ETHNIC RELATIONS

Even in some cases of language switching in which jocularity and gamesmanship are less easily discernible or absent altogether, it is possible to preserve the view that switching involves the granting of concessions as the following cases show.

The concessions in these cases are made on the basis of certain assumptions about the nature of ethnic group relations.

As shown in the first two cases, Luo-Kikuyu relations appear to be potentially sensitive over even a matter such as language. But it is possible for Kikuyu and Kamba in conversation, and for Luo and Luyia in conversation, to make certain assumptions about each other's likely language repertoire and not risk offence. These are assumptions which directly reflect the special sociolinguistic relations of these ethnic pairs, as based on self-reports and described in the previous chapter.

(a) Kikuyu-Kamba

Case 3: Kikuyu stall-holder and Kamba customer.
1. KIKUYU: Hullo bwana—ukwenda kugura ki? (What do you want to buy?)
2. KAMBA: Ndienda maigu. (I want some bananas.)
3. KIKUYU: Ya pesa ngapi? (For how much?)
4. KAMBA: Ya—fifty cents.
5. KIKUYU: Unataka kitu gani kingine? (Anything else?)
6. KAMBA: Hakuna. Huwezi kunipatia—commission? (Nothing. Can you put it on account for me?)
7. KIKUYU: Kwa—commission—kuja kesho. (Come tomorrow for anything on account.)

Languages used:
1. Swahili—Kikuyu
2. Kikuyu
3. Swahili
4. Swahili—English
5. Swahili
6. Swahili—English
7. Swahili—English—Swahili

1. Here, the Kikuyu stall-holder operates on the reasonable assumption that the customer (whom, he later told us, he knew to be either Kikuyu or Kamba but was not sure which) would understand and would not visibly resent being addressed in Kikuyu, even though he might happen to be Kamba (or Meru or Embu).

2. The assumption was correct. The Kamba customer seems to accept the legitimacy of the assumption and replies in Kikuyu. It would seem that, somehow, the Kamba's reply indicates that he is not Kikuyu and the stall-holder switches to Swahili in 3. Thereafter, in 4–7 both stall-holder and customer talk in Swahili, incorporating the English 'fifty cents' and 'commission'.

In the following interesting case, there is a similar indirect statement of Kikuyu-Kamba linguistic and cultural affinity. But here the Kikuyu stall-holder actually knows the Kamba customer and makes the appropriate initial concession by speaking in her vernacular.

Case 4: Kikuyu stall-holder and female Kamba customer.
1. KIKUYU: Nata yu. (Now how are things then.)
2. KAMBA: Ni nesa kabisa. (I'm fine.)
3. KIKUYU: Ukwenda kungurira kii riu? (Now what do you want to buy?)
4. KAMBA: Nataka mandizi ya shimoni. Ni ngapi? (I want fifty cents' worth of bananas. How much are they?)
5. KIKUYU: Nauza moja kwa peni. (I'm selling one for ten cents.)
6. KAMBA: Nipatie basi na uniongezee moja. (O.K. but give me one extra.)
7. KIKUYU: Hapana siongezi ni—hathara. (No extras. I can't afford it.)
8. KAMBA: Asi! Naku mwikuyu uu.—Leta tu. (Ah! You Kikuyu (singular)—O.K. give me some.)

Languages used:
1. Kamba
2. Kamba
3. Kikuyu
4. Swahili
5. Swahili
6. Swahili
7. Swahili—Kikuyu
8. Kamba—Swahili

1. The stall-holder makes the concession of addressing the customer in her language.

2. The customer accepts the concession by replying in her mother tongue. It should be noted here, however, that a greeting is likely to be continued in the language in which it is started since it most obviously constitutes a single linguistic set. Choice of language in a greeting is thus a very potent factor in establishing the 'tone' of a conversation.

3. Here, the Kikuyu, having made his concession, reverts to Kikuyu.

4–8. From here on, the conversation is most conveniently conducted in Swahili, with a possibly significant temporary reversion to her mother tongue by the Kamba as she jokingly condemns the Kikuyu stall-holder.

(b) Luo-Luyia

As I showed in the last chapter, many more Luyia claim to know the Luo vernacular than do Luo make the reverse claim. From observation this claim is certainly borne out. In the following case, the Luo stall-owner not only uses his mother tongue with a Luyia customer but actually elicits from her an agreement to incorporate Luo words in her Swahili. In other words, the Luyia concedes the frequent use of the Luo vernacular by her ethnic group and so confirms indirectly their special, what I have earlier called, alliance relationship.

Case 5: Luo stall-holder and Luyia female customer.
1. LUO: Nadi mama. (How are you, Mum.)
2. LUYIA: Maber ahinya. Adwaro—nunua—mana—unga. (Very fine. I want to buy some flour.)
3. LUO: Haya, unga—nitie.—Unataka ratili ngapi? (Yes, we have some flour. How much do you want?)
4. LUYIA: Adwar—ratili kumi. Ah! Unga hiyo haonekani kama nzuri. Endelea tu. (I want ten pounds. Ah! This flour doesn't look right. Never mind.)
5. LUO: Magi agolo mana e KFA—hiyo ni—first class—inashinda unga yote hapa Kaloleni. (I bought this from the KFA—it's first class and is the best flour in Kaloleni.)
6. LUYIA: Haya, nzuri, nitaona.—Oriti. (Well, we'll see.—Goodbye.)

Languages used:
1. Luo
2. Luo—Swahili—Luo—Swahili
3. Swahili—Luo—Swahili
4. Luo—Swahili
5. Luo—Swahili—English—Swahili
6. Swahili—Luo

Moving now from conversations between Luo and Luyia in the market place to those occurring in and around Kaloleni itself, we see the same mutual realization of their alliance relationship reflected in the unquestioning way in which Luyia incorporate the Luo vernacular in their Swahili or respond positively to the Luo vernacular. Kaloleni housing estate is, of course, numerically and culturally predominantly Luo and so, in neighbourhood women's gossip sets and in children's play-groups, these factors are perhaps even more evident.

Case 6: A group of three women sitting together in Kaloleni (one Luo and two Luyia).
1. 1ST LUYIA: Nitajaribu kumaliza yako sababu mpaka niende Uhuru. (I'll try and finish your (hair) because I have to go to Uhuru market.)
2. LUO: Kuleta nini? (To get what?)
3. 1ST LUYIA: Si chakula. (Food, of course.)
4. LUO: Jabwana olosi. (Your husband keeps you well.)

5. 2ND LUYIA: Ongere—sababu yeye bado mpya. (It's a well known thing—it's because she is still a new wife.)
   (The 2nd Luyia and the Luo here laugh.) Mpaka abembereze bwana. (And she has to please her husband in return.)
6. LUO: Siku hizi sisi wazee tunaweza kufanya wewe wote. (We older women have been through it all and can tell you young wives all about it.)
7. 2ND LUYIA: Bwana siku hizi hatembei sababu wewe bado mpya. (Your husband isn't on the loose because you're still a new wife.)
8. 1ST LUYIA: Alikuwa akitembea. (He *was* on the loose.)
9. LUO: Si ndiyo. (Of course.)
10. 1ST LUYIA: Kama mimi iko hawezi. (But if I'm around he can't be.)
11. LUO: Manindo! (You really think that!) (Literally 'a sleeping matter', i.e. you are in a dream world.)

Languages used:
1. Swahili
2. Swahili
3. Swahili
4. Luo
5. Luo—Swahili
6. Swahili
7. Swahili
8. Swahili
9. Swahili
10. Swahili
11. Luo

These jocular teasing sessions at the expense of a newly married wife are very common, both in Nairobi and, as I have documented elsewhere (1969), in Kampala. The Luo woman and the 2nd Luyia woman are longer married and, one may assume, have spent more time in Nairobi in contexts such as this. They each use a word or two of Luo in their Swahili. The usage of Luo is very little but perhaps represents a recognition of the alliance relationship.

The following case illustrates this more strongly.

Case 7: A group of three Luyia women and two Luyia adolescent girls and a passing Luo male neighbour and his Luyia male friend (who does not figure in the conversation).

1. LUO: Habari ya wasichana akina bibi. (How are you, women and girls.)
2. LUYIA GIRL: Salama wote labda—in. (We're all well, and what about you.)

205

3. LUO: An—salama tu. (I'm just fine.)
4. LUYIA WOMAN: Ingima. (You are well.)
5. LUO: Angima. (O.K.)
6. LUYIA WOMAN: Maber ahinya (all laugh). (Very good.)
7. LUO: Mzuri tu. (Good enough.)
8. LUYIA WOMAN: Umepotea—kanye? (Where have you been?)
9. LUO: Niko tu. (I am just around.)
10. LUYIA WOMAN: Tinde—unataka kuwa mkora sana. (Nowadays you like to act the playboy/rascal.)
11. LUO: Kama ni mkora sasa—then—nilikuwa mkora zamani— If not I am not (a sentence here missed). (If I am a playboy now, then I have been so for a long time.)
12. LUO: Haya, asante. (O.K. thanks.)
13. LUYIA WOMAN: Udhi kanye—sasa? (Where are you going now?)
14. LUO: Bayo. (For a stroll.)
15. LUYIA WOMAN: Wapi? (Where?)
16. LUO: Twende na sisi utaona. (Come with me and you'll see.)
17. LUYIA WOMAN: Ilikuwa yenu, ungeniambia kitambo ninge— prepare—tunge—accompany—nyinyi, sasa ni yenu. (This is your stroll. You should have let us know in good time and we would have got ourselves ready to accompany you, but now it's your stroll alone.)
18. LUO: Haya, kwa heri. (O.K. Goodbye.)
19. LUYIA WOMAN: Oriti—uniletee vitu ya uko. (Goodbye—bring me something from where you're going.)

Languages used:
1. Swahili
2. Swahili—Luo
3. Luo—Swahili
4. Luo
5. Luo
6. Luo
7. Swahili
8. Swahili—Luo
9. Swahili
10. Luo—Swahili
11. Swahili—English—Swahili—English
12. Swahili
13. Luo—Swahili
14. Luo

15. Swahili
16. Swahili
17. Swahili with English verb roots
18. Swahili
19. Luo—Swahili

In this jokingly flirtatious encounter, there is something of a language game in the progressive unravelling of languages by the Luo man and the Luyia woman. The Luyia woman first greets in the Luo vernacular and gets a reply in the same vernacular. There is a general switch to Swahili but both Luo and, latterly, English are incorporated. Almost as if to challenge the pleasantly provocative Luyia woman, the Luo man introduces the few English words. The Luyia woman belatedly meets the challenge if only partly by incorporating English verb roots but preserving Swahili affixes. In parenthesis it should be noted that forms involving English roots and Swahili affixes occur commonly. I have no cases of the reverse.

TRANSACTIONAL CONVERSATIONS 3:
SOCIO-ECONOMIC RELATIONS

When I say, with reference to Case 7, that the use of English here constitutes a challenge, I do not mean that only English can be used for this purpose. All languages can, depending on the person being spoken to and the situation in which the conversation is held and its topic. These are details which cannot be discussed here. I am simply referring to the socio-economically prestigious stereotypes with which English is frequently associated. At other times, this stereotyping of English as socially exclusive is used as a weapon against the language. Swahili is then held up as the 'true' national language, freed of colonial implications and of the status divisions brought about by an urban, industrial and monetary complex, and alone likely to express the 'fraternity' of all ethnic groups in the nation and the dignity of their political independence. This powerfully emotive argument underlies many of the interesting debates in parliament and press regarding possible national language policy. Nevertheless, at the personal level in Kenya, the prestigious and socially exclusive stereotype of English remains the dominant one.

As well as Case 7, other cases in this chapter provide instances of English and Swahili possessing certain values which derive directly and indirectly from differences between people of socio-economic status. Having analytically isolated the use of vernaculars between people in 'special' ethnic relations of putative alliance or opposition, I can now outline very briefly the more general socio-economic factors prompting switching into English and Swahili. I shall not need to illustrate my comments with actual conversations.

207

In Chapters 6 and 7 I showed that while the household heads who know English are likely to be younger and better educated than average, there is evidence that Swahili is used at all status levels, but most frequently used at the lowest rung of the occupational ladder. I showed further that Swahili may be learned informally in Nairobi, particularly through interaction at workplace. I then suggested that the relation to each other of Swahili and English is a dynamic one about which predictions may be attempted, arising from projections of an increasing imbalance in the ratio of 'educated' to employed.

Both English and Swahili are lingua francas in the sense that each provides an alternative to the use of vernaculars. Neither is associated with any particular cultural grouping as a mother tongue, with the special exception of the Muslim and possibly certain other residents of Pumwani (see Bujra *infra*, p. 218). Swahili may be said to bridge both ethnic and status differences: it is a common medium of communication between ethnic groups as well as between men of different socio-economic status. Swahili thus stands in some contrast to English, which, though it can be said to bridge ethnic differences, nevertheless carries by its use an additional message defining the statuses of the persons talking to each other in it. These statements refer to 'normal' situations and constitute further stereotypes or symbols denoting modes of behaviour between status peers or unequals. In actual situations, people make use of these symbols in conversation.

Thus, in encountering someone for the first time, I may not know his ethnic group nor be able to guess it. I am not therefore likely to use a vernacular. The choice now is between English and Swahili. Do I want to establish a 'formal' relationship or an 'informal' one? If I am a government officer, use of English may affirm my authority and set a tone of formality. But if the man knows no English then, clearly, I must switch to Swahili. Alternatively, I may start on the assumption that the man knows no English and address him in Swahili. If the man does not know English then he is likely to welcome this 'fraternal' gesture, which is less humiliating to him than the step-down in status implied by the switch from English to Swahili. But he may resent it if he does know English, since he has thereby been classed as a non-speaker of English and therefore, according to the stereotype, as 'uneducated'. The whole course of the conversation may be affected by such initial choices. Tone and gesture do not always mitigate the effects of wrong choices, since they are themselves frequently ambiguous.

In most first-time encounters, the status of the speaker and his respondent cannot be demonstrated or guessed and, from an investigation of many such encounters, I suggest that Swahili is likely to be the initial choice, with adjustments being made to English or a vernacular as information about the role-partners becomes available in conversation. It is for this reason that I referred earlier to the sometimes 'neutral' standing of Swahili.

In encounters between people of different ethnic groups it is much more difficult to account for variation in the initial choice of language, and I would not attempt to do so here, though, as explained earlier, some choices can be seen as concessions or challenges sometimes giving rise to a language game.

A NON-TRANSACTIONAL CASE

Because my interest has been focused on ethnicity, I have dealt only with selected speech transactions between persons of different 'tribes'. I have not the space to illustrate the many examples of language switching occurring between speakers who are of the same ethnic and language group.

Why should such cases occur? Sometimes, of course, they occur as language games to the accompaniment of a variable degree of banter or jocularity. At other times, a specific topic of conversation or even physical or organizational setting may seem to prompt switching. Sometimes, switches may be marked by specific parts of speech, for example conjunctions. But perhaps more frequently, we can only speculate as to whether topic, context, the particular role-relationship, a particular part of speech, or a combination of all four variables, prompt switching.

These cases of switching between members of the same ethnic group who share a common mother tongue necessarily characterize studies of 'bilingualism' or 'multilingualism' focused on a single ethnic group (Fishman *et al.* 1968b). Though it is presumably a matter of degree and definition, many of Nairobi's African population can be said to be multilingual, and it would certainly be possible and profitable to concentrate analysis on one ethnic group. But I suggest that even if this were done, there would have to be a preliminary survey of language use between ethnic groups. They are, after all, involved together in a single urban system of relations and, as I have tried to show, need to forge relations across ethnic boundaries, sometimes at the cost of a conflict of personal and group interests. In this process of common interaction, common problems are coped with and similar solutions reached. Thus, even in relations between members of the same ethnic group language evaluations and choices are made on the basis of information received from a wide range of social interactions not confined to any one ethnic group.

As an illustration of this 'feed-back' process and for the sake of completeness, I present a final case in which two men, of the same ethnic group,

incorporate the use of Swahili and a little English in their speech, seemingly in response to a conversational topic involving speech forms likely
to occur in all groups represented in Nairobi. The two men are Luo tailors
who work together in the market already referred to.

Case 8:

1. 1ST LUO: Onego ikendi. (You ought to marry.)
2. 2ND LUO: Kinyalo miya dhok. (If you can give me the cattle.)
3. 1ST LUO: Dhi penj wuoru. (Go and ask your father.)
4. 2ND LUO: Baba bado anasema mimi niko—young. (My father still
   says I am too young.)
5. 1ST LUO: In—young—nadi? Itiyo—umetosa kuwa na mtoto— and
   everything. (How are you young? You are working. You've left
   being a child and (childish) things.)
6. 2ND LUO: Nyaka ayud nyako maber. (I have yet to get a good girl
   as a bride.)
7. 1ST LUO: Karango, masani to ichiegni bedo—mzee—ni. (But when?
   You are now swiftly becoming an old man.)

Languages used:

1. Luo
2. Luo
3. Luo
4. Swahili—English
5. Luo—English—Luo—Swahili—English
6. Luo
7. Luo—Swahili—Luo

In 4 there is a switch to Swahili and a word of English when the 2nd
Luo has to confess that he is considered too young by his father to be
given bridewealth for marriage. This switch *may* be caused by embarrassment. But it is interesting to note that in 4, 5 and 7 all references to
youthfulness, age and to seniority (e.g. 'baba' for 'father') are in either
English or Swahili.

More generally, certain basic kinship terms of reference and terms
referring to seniority and juniority are indeed frequently in either Swahili
or English among all ethnic groups in Nairobi. There are a number of
explanations for this. An important general one is the need to place a
possibly wide range of associates in categories denoting some degree
of personal intimacy. To call a man 'baba' ('father' in Swahili) when he is
not a relative and perhaps not even of your ethnic group, may indicate
actual, potential or anticipated intimacy or friendliness. The use of Swahili
or, as in some cases, English (e.g. 'brother') rather than the vernacular

may carry the additional information that this is an achieved, transferable and perhaps even negotiable rather than ascribed relationship.

This convention of sometimes using Swahili or English primary kin terms for non-ascribed relationships appears to 'feed-back' into conversations between long settled townsmen of the same ethnic group even when they are referring to 'real' kin or to age or youth, for which they could use their own vernacular terms. This might explain the switch in Case 8, which may thus be said to be prompted by a specific element in the topic of conversation and not by any discernible transactions of speech between the two men.

The conventionalized use of these Swahili and English terms is made possible only by the 'value' constantly placed on each of the lingua francas in ordinary daily conversations: English is constantly emphasized as a language of high status persons; Swahili is a common medium language, sometimes of 'neutrality' or 'fraternity', but sometimes connoting 'low' or 'ordinary' status. It is surely in the important if numerically limited cases in which these languages are used to make challenges or award concessions that these values are given their most poignant expression. Thus, the few cases of language switching which appear to be transactional may well have an inordinate influence on the vast majority of cases in which language does not set up challenges, counter-challenges, and concessions. This is at least an hypothesis worth testing.

SUMMARY AND CONCLUSIONS

I have suggested that we distinguish initially between transactional and non-transactional conversations. Transactional conversations are those in which there seems to be a progressive unravelling of a repertoire of different languages (or codes) by each of the two speakers. The two processes of unravelling are seen to be triggered off by each other in a to-and-fro fashion. This reciprocal stimulus-response mechanism may take the form of challenges, counter-challenges, and concessions.

In the particular ethnographic situation which I have described, these challenges and concessions are made on the basis of claims and assumptions concerned with two variables: ethnic group membership and personal socio-economic status. Each of these involves a defence of or struggle for symbols of honour and esteem in all spheres of social life in Nairobi, not just in transactional conversations. In transactional conversations the competition can be played in two ways. One way involves defence of one's own mother tongue, concessionary or provocative use of one's opponent's, or 'neutral' usage of a vernacular which is not native to either speaker.[2] Or it may involve competitive use of either Swahili or English. English will tend to have high status connotations but must be used strategically to achieve this effect. Swahili can carry connotations which play down ethnic and status differences. It can thus connote 'humility', 'solidarity', or 'brotherhood', or simply 'neutrality'. But, because it is associated in much of Kenya with situations of socio-economic disadvantage or deprivation, it can also mark off from each other persons of 'higher' and 'lower' status. All these connotations are dominant, in that they recur frequently in many situations.

These two ways of using language in prestige competitions are logically contradictory in that vernacular usage is likely to symbolize group interests and loyalties while usage of the lingua francas, English and Swahili, is more likely to symbolize individual interests. In actual conversations, people may 'joke off' the contradiction. Joking about ethnic and status differences is, indeed, a crucially important technique by which people of different 'tribes' and of different levels of education, income, and occupation cope with the sensitivity of these evaluated differences. This fact of everyday life is sometimes carried into a conversation with the result that the conversation becomes a language game, in which speakers of different 'tribes' and/or of different statuses display their knowledge of and skills in different languages.

The language game is one type of transactional conversation because it includes challenges and concessions which assume knowledge of the two major but logically contradictory principles of social organization: ethnic group affiliation, and personal socio-economic status ties.

Two other types of transactional conversation are each based on assumptions deriving from one rather than both principles. Thus, a conversation may consist predominantly of challenges and concessions made in vernaculars which assume knowledge of putative ethnic relations of alliance and opposition in Nairobi. Or, it may include challenges and concessions which turn on the socio-economic status connotations of English and Swahili. In practice, transactional conversations are likely to include elements of all three types.

This said, it must be emphasized that transactional conversations as defined here are a minute proportion of all conversations. What, then, is their significance if any? Their significance is two-fold.

First, they highlight the normative value attaching to use of a particular vernacular or lingua franca in a particular situation. Thus, in a particular conversation English is seen to express, say, social exclusiveness, as against Swahili which may express social inclusiveness. In another conversation, this set of values may be reversed. Since English and Swahili may express other values, the number of value sets is numerous. When vernaculars are also included in the conversations, then the span and number of sets increases even more. Yet it is very likely that the number of different possible sets is logically limited even if, in practice, many elude our attention. Nevertheless, some sets seem to recur in more situations than others, e.g. English expressing social exclusiveness and Swahili expressing social inclusiveness. Frequency of occurrence is at least one criterion of dominance and so it should be possible eventually to construct a hierarchy of sets combining the same languages and, conversely, to isolate those contextual situations or 'domains' showing the greatest variation of sets.

The second significant aspect of transactional conversations is that they may well play an important part in generating new styles of language use. We know for a fact that there are many English and Swahili clichés, idioms and other recurrent forms in use among people of all ethnic groups in Nairobi. They do not appear overnight. What then is the process by which such forms are generated and diffused in the population? Common experience suggests that people do not sit down and rationally calculate the need for new forms and then create them. It is more likely that the forms arise in response to needs through the many separate but parallel experiences of persons in a single social system. The adoption of Swahili and English kinship terms in Nairobi is, I believe, an example of this process, which I have only touched on in this chapter. But there are probably many less obvious examples. Since transactional conversations require verbal inventiveness against a template of specific language values, it seems reasonable to hypothesize that they are important generators of the new forms.

Let me now summarize the role of the preceding three chapters in reaching these conclusions. I noted in the first chapter the apparent dilemma confronting students of language use as to how they can bring together in a single, coherent analysis the investigation both of large scale language shift among groups and of language switching between individuals in a single conversation. My own approach to this problem was to start from a consideration of the believed state of power relations among Nairobi's four major ethnic groups. I started from the fact that language is a cultural phenomenon and as such may be regarded as either demarcating ethnic boundaries, as with vernaculars, or transcending them, as with lingua francas. This use of lingua francas to transcend ethnic differences usually occurs when socio-economic differences need to be expressed.

Language shift can therefore be regarded as reflecting the relations between ethnic groups in their adoption of each other's vernaculars. Or language shift can occur in response to an emerging but constantly changing division of the society into socio-economic status categories. Thus, in Chapter 6 I showed how Swahili is increasingly fulfilling the main criteria of a lingua franca but is still associated with low status groups, yet English is potentially a long-term threat to Swahili because of the flood into Nairobi from rural districts of young, educated and English-speaking but unemployable migrants.

Extensive surveying of self-reports of competence in different languages provides a picture (in Chapter 7) of the differential rates of vernacular adoption between pairs of ethnic groups. The types and rates of adoption correspond with putative political relations of alliance and opposition between Nairobi's four ethnic groups. Both simultaneously and over time it is clear that language shift tells us much about political and power relations between groups. This is perhaps an obvious fact but is nonetheless a crucially important background against which ordinary day-to-day relations and conversations occur.

It is facts of such magnitude which constitute the broad, even crude, stereotypes with which people in any system of relations deal. These stereotypes are among the most important in Nairobi of what Barth might call the 'over-arching, more general principles of evaluation' (1966, p. 14). A very few individual conversations, or, more likely, parts of conversations, appear to be conducted broadly on the basis of these principles. But people do not adhere rigidly to the stereotyped evaluations. They use the manifold behavioural connotations of different languages to compete with each other or to make concessions. I have called these transactional conversations. 'Bits' of different languages are transacted. This has two related effects. One is that the various 'values' attaching to any one language are publicized in distinct and regularly recurring situations. A second is that, because inventiveness is required in selecting and discerning the various values and in devising new ways to surprise an 'opponent', new contextual sets of 'meaning' are generated and also publicized. Common needs in similar situations produce similar sets which may eventually catch on in the population at large and may even affect the expression of group relations. Thus, the example touched on in this chapter of the development of a code of non-vernacular kinship and seniority terms could well constitute a 'bridge' between personal relations which might otherwise be more brittle in a society made increasingly more heterogeneous by socio-economic and ethnic distinctions. This approach is, as yet, at a beginning, but I believe it may continue to be fruitful because it is based on a consistent and comprehensive and yet manageable methodology, which I find lacking in other sociological approaches to the study of language use.[3]

NOTES

[1] We have not tried to 'standardize' what we heard in order to make it conform to grammatically 'correct' forms. On the other hand we cannot claim to have recorded conversations as accurately as a tape recorder, which, for various reasons, could not be used in this context. I have no evidence either way to determine whether my presence in the market place and elsewhere influenced the tone and course of conversations, but I should point out that I had become a regular and accepted figure in the area and believe that the cases I present are 'natural' instances of language use. They do not appear to differ significantly from those acquired independently by assistants.

[2] Luganda in Kampala is used in this way by some non-Ganda conversing with each other (see Case 2 in Parkin, 1970). Nairobi does not seem to have a vernacular which is used in this way.

[3] I would like to acknowledge my gratitude to W. H. Whiteley for originally suggesting to me the usefulness of applying 'transactional analysis' to the study of language switching.

REFERENCES

BAILEY, F. G. 'Parapolitical Systems' in Marc Swartz (ed.), *Local Level Politics*, Aldine Publishing Co., Chicago, 1968.
—— *Stratagems and Spoils*, Blackwell, Oxford, 1969.
BARTH, F. *Models of Social Organization*, Occasional Paper 23, Royal Anthropological Institute, London, 1966.
DOUGLAS, M. 'Lele Economy Compared with Bushong' in P. Bohannan and G. Dalton (eds.), *Markets in Africa*, Northwestern University Press, Chicago, 1962.
—— 'The Social Control of Cognition: some Factors in Joke Perception', *Man* (N.S.), 3, 3, 1968, pp. 361–76.
EPSTEIN, A. L. 'Linguistic Innovation and Culture on the Copperbelt, Northern Rhodesia', *Southwestern Journal of Anthropology*, 3, 3, 1959, pp. 235–53.
FISHMAN, J. *Bilingualism in the Barrio*, United States Department of Health, Education and Welfare, 1968.
HYMES, D. H. 'The Ethnography of Speaking' in T. Gladwin and W. C. Sturtevant (eds.), *Anthropology and Human Behaviour*, Anthropological Society of Washington, Washington D. C., 1962.
MITCHELL, J. C. *The Kalela Dance*, Rhodes-Livingstone Paper 27, Manchester University Press, 1956.
PARKIN, D. J. *Neighbours and Nationals in an African City Ward*, Routledge & Kegan Paul, London, 1969.
—— 'Language Choice in Two Kampala Housing Estates' in W. H. Whiteley (ed.), *Language Use and Social Change*, International African Institute, Oxford University Press, London, 1971.

Pumwani: Language Usage in an Urban Muslim Community

JANET BUJRA

Pumwani is an African, and predominantly Muslim estate situated in Kenya's capital city, Nairobi. As a long-established multi-tribal area, and with an active community life, it is unique within the city. Although there are other areas in the city where Muslims live, none is so tribally heterogeneous as Pumwani, and there are few other estates in Nairobi which can boast of so much locally organized community activity. Pumwani is also a slum, and at the present time is under the threat of demolition.

Kenya is a nation in which a multitude of languages are spoken by a multitude of tribes, and most of these tribes are represented in Pumwani. The medium of communication between the various tribes has long been Swahili, a language which originated on the Islamicized coast of East Africa. But Kenya's official national language is English,[1] a language spoken only by the élite and by those who have been to school for several years. The people of Pumwani are poor for the most part, and few of the older people have been to school.

My intention in making a study of the language situation in Pumwani was two-fold. In the first place I wished to discover the patterns of language usage in a multi-tribal setting. In this context it was important to know which languages were being used for social interaction within the area, and for economic and political relations with the wider society. If some form of lingua franca was being used for these functions, as seemed likely, then it was the intention to discover what role, if any, was still being played by tribal vernaculars.

Secondly, in view of the fact that a long established Muslim community existed in Pumwani, I wished to assess the influence on language loyalties of adherence to the Muslim faith. Muslims living on the coast of Kenya speak Swahili as a first language, and one of my interests in studying Pumwani was to see how far this would apply to the Muslims there too.

217

I also wanted to study the extent to which Swahili was replacing tribal languages not only as a medium of communication between members of different tribes, but also as a medium of communication between members of the same tribe. Finally I was interested in knowledge of Arabic, the holy language of the Muslims. I wanted to estimate the extent to which Arabic might act as a focal language for the African Muslims of Pumwani, serving perhaps to differentiate them from non-Muslims.

This chapter attempts to show that although there are several languages in daily use in Pumwani, each has its context of relevance. I shall argue here that Swahili functions in Pumwani as a language of community, an integrative mechanism for many diverse elements. I shall also show that Swahili is not only a language enabling people of different ethnic groups to communicate, but that it is also the first language of many African Muslims in Pumwani. Pumwani Swahili thus has a richness and vitality of its own, deriving from its use as a primary language by the Muslim community in the location. Secondly, I shall show that for Pumwani Muslims Arabic is thought of, not so much as a spoken language of everyday life, but rather as a tool imbued with supernatural power.

I shall argue thirdly that English functions as a language of political brokerage between the inhabitants of Pumwani and the political and administrative authorities. Finally, I shall suggest that tribal vernaculars play a double role in Pumwani. Firstly they are the languages of secrets and intimacy between members of the same ethnic group—an assertion to some extent of their difference from others. On the other hand I shall show that people in Pumwani often have at least a superficial knowledge of vernaculars other than their own, and that they consider such knowledge to be a way of indicating camaraderie across ethnic lines. This may be socially significant in an area where the population is so ethnically diverse.

The way these different languages are used may thus indicate social convergence or social disjunction, and in so doing they reflect the complexity of cross-cutting ties in Pumwani. In what follows I shall first describe the patterns of social interaction in Pumwani and then show how these are related to language usage. The material in this account is based on field-work carried out during 1968–9 and on a questionnaire administered in May 1969.[2]

PUMWANI: SOCIAL CONTRASTS

Pumwani is the oldest existing African estate in Nairobi, having been built during the period 1921–3. It is bordered on one side by Nairobi

River with Shauri Moyo City Council Estate beyond it, and by other city council estates on two of its other sides. On the fourth side are built the concrete and glass blocks of flats making up 'New' Pumwani, an estate built by the city council to rehouse the Pumwani people when their present homes are demolished.[3] 'Old' Pumwani stands out incongruously from its surroundings, looking more like a coastal village than a city housing area. It consists of 343 single-storey houses huddled close together and built of mud and wattle with corrugated iron roofs. The plots on which the houses are built are owned by the city council, but the houses are privately owned by individual landlords. Each landlord pays sh.42.50 a month as rent for his plot, the lease of which may be withdrawn at a month's notice. Each house is divided into ten or so rooms, one of which is usually occupied by the landlord and his family, while each of the others houses tenants. Women cook in their rooms or, more often, in the central passage of the house.

Pumwani was Nairobi's first 'site-and-service' scheme.[4] Public latrines and water points were built at strategic points amongst the houses and streets laid out (only the two main roads passing through Pumwani are surfaced with tarmac however). Some of the houses are better built and cared for than others, and such houses may have their own pit latrines, taps and electricity. The majority of houses in Pumwani, however, have none of these things.

The streets are always busy and crowded. Every street has several little shops selling food, tobacco and many other items, and there is a small vegetable market in the centre of the area. There are several bars and small hotels,[5] and there are two social halls. In the centre is situated the mosque, a small white building built in 1935, and nearby there are administrative buildings, a children's clinic and a dispensary. Women are always to be seen sitting outside their houses, cooking, sewing, washing, plaiting each other's hair or selling vegetables or cooked food. Other women pass to and fro, visiting friends and relatives and buying food. Children play in the streets. Men wend their way to the mosque or the bars whilst others sit at machines sewing clothes or making shoes for customers. During the day many huge petrol lorries park in the narrow roads as their drivers eat at one of Pumwani's hotels, and in the evening the district attracts many people from the surrounding area who come to visit friends, to drink or chew *miraa*,[6] to attend the cinema shows put on in one of the social halls, or to visit prostitutes.

The population of Pumwani is almost impossible to estimate. Some people have put it as low as 9,000, others as high as 11,000.[7] There are various problems in attempting any estimate. First is the suspicion of the people themselves against any such attempt; Pumwani harbours a host of people who would prefer to remain hidden from the eyes of officialdom. Secondly, however, there is a large floating population, consisting of people who either have no proper accommodation and sleep outside, in the mosque, in passages or with one friend after another, or who reside only temporarily in Pumwani, spending most of the year in one of the rural areas. Thus whilst it seems likely that at any one time there may be ten or eleven thousand people staying in Pumwani, the permanent population of the locality is probably much smaller.

Pumwani contrasts with other African estates in Nairobi in several respects. Because of its long history, two or three generations have grown up within its social milieu. Fourteen per cent of the people who answered my language questionnaire had actually been born there and a further 6.9 per cent had been born in other parts of Nairobi. Some of Pumwani's oldest inhabitants in fact come from even earlier African settlements in Nairobi, now long since demolished, such as Mji wa Mombasa and Pangani. The median length of residence in the city of those people who had been born outside Nairobi was 13 years,[8] and 18.6 per cent of the sample had lived for more than 25 years in Pumwani itself. It is partly for these reasons that Pumwani is a more balanced community, demographically speaking, than other estates. Its population is almost equally divided between men, women and children, instead of men preponderating, as they seem to do in other estates.[9] Pumwani too, however, has many adult men living alone, recent immigrants who have come to look for work and who have either not yet married or who leave their wives and children behind in the rural areas, but the numbers of these men are more than balanced by the large number of single, divorced and widowed women. The fact that Pumwani has a long established core of older residents means that there is a partial network of kinship and affinal ties linking them together.

The second factor of considerable sociological importance concerning Pumwani is its multi-ethnicity.[10] Practically every ethnic group in Kenya is represented there, as well as people from Uganda and Tanzania. Only the Kikuyu and Kamba are represented in any large numbers however, and together they account for perhaps one-third of the inhabitants. The rest of the population is made up of people from many different tribes. There is practically no clustering together of members of the same tribe; people live in houses which are almost without exception ethnically mixed. Not only is there great ethnic diversity in Pumwani, but there is also a remarkable degree of tribal intermarriage. It would seem that about one-third of Pumwani's population are children of mixed marriages.[11]

If we divide the population of Pumwani into people who were born there, people who have lived there most of their lives, and more recent immigrants, we find that there are members of every ethnic group in all these categories, so that tribal membership and length of residence cut across each other as sociological factors.

Pumwani's population is also diverse from an economic point of view. One of the most striking features of the locality is the extent to which local initiative and business acumen have given it a thriving economic life of its own. Many people, both men and women, make their living within Pumwani itself, either by engaging in petty trade or by providing local services. Of the employed people in my sample, 39.2 per cent were self-employed and these were engaged in occupations as diverse as selling vegetables, plaiting hair, teaching in a Qur'an school, driving a taxi and prostitution. In addition there were other people working in the area for local employers, as shop and hotel assistants or as dhobis or servants. Almost half the working population was employed within Pumwani itself. Thus, unlike some Nairobi estates, Pumwani is not simply a dormitory for industrial labourers, deserted during the daytime except for women and young children. Instead it supports an active economic existence of its own. Of those people who work outside Pumwani, most seem to be occupied in service industries in the town centre rather than in jobs in Nairobi's Industrial Area. On the whole they are not working in well-paid occupations. Of my sample, 27.5 per cent were employed as manual or semi-skilled workers and would not be earning much above sh.250 or sh.300 a month. Another 21.6 per cent were in skilled jobs and many have been earning up to about sh.600 a month. 11.8 per cent were working in clerical or professional jobs, and some of these undoubtedly enjoyed higher wages. The income of the self-employed is more difficult to estimate. Some of them are probably barely scraping a living, whilst others are relatively prosperous traders. The point is that few people in Pumwani achieve their jobs by having adequate educational qualifications. Most have to live by their physical strength or by their initiative. 40.7 per cent of my sample had never been to school and 80.4 per cent of the rest had received only a few years of primary education.

In any sociological description of Pumwani one of the most significant factors to be taken into account is that the people are divided on religious grounds, and that religious loyalties cross-cut ethnic loyalties. The largest religious group in Pumwani are the Muslims. In addition there are Christians of various denominations, and a small category of people who either have no religion or who follow their tribal religion. Muslims from almost every ethnic group are to be found in Pumwani—Kikuyu Muslims, Kamba Muslims, Maasai Muslims, and so on. Christianity also claims adherents from many different ethnic groups. The category of people following no religion or following a tribal religion is not a self-confessed one—nobody will say openly that he has no religion. But generally Muslims and Christians have religious names as well as, or instead of, tribal names. People without any religious name usually claim to be Christians, though other people will say of them that they have 'no religion'.

No count has ever been made, so far as I know, of the number of Muslims in Pumwani as opposed to followers of other religions. My own survey was by no means complete, but in thirty-one houses surveyed there were 510 people, of whom 58.8 per cent were Muslims, 28.1 per cent Christians, and 13.1 per cent doubtful cases.

I consider the Muslims to be the most important religious category in Pumwani for three reasons. Firstly, it was Muslims who were the original settlers in the area. They came mainly from the older African Muslim settlements called Mji wa Mombasa and Pangani. These settlements in their turn are supposed to have originated when 'Swahili' (that is, coastal) and Sudanese soldiers settled down there and intermarried with the local population of Africans. This means that the longest settled people in Pumwani are Muslims rather than Christians. In my sample of 86 adults, ten had spent more than thirty years in Pumwani, and only one of these was a Christian.[12] A further twelve had been born in Pumwani, and all but two of these were Muslims. Six others had been born elsewhere in Nairobi and all these people were Muslims. This means that it is the Muslims who are the permanently settled people in Pumwani, either having been born there or having lived there for a long period of time. Many of the Christians, however, as well as the doubtfuls, are really labour migrants, who will spend some years in the town and then return to their rural homes. They go home to marry, and often leave their wives and children in the rural areas. Muslims, however, tend to marry in the town and to bring up their families there. This means that it is Muslims rather than Christians who are town born. Muslims thus tend to have both feet firmly planted in town, whilst others have one foot in town and one foot in their rural homes.[13]

It is because of their long residence in Pumwani that the Muslims have a more balanced population in almost every respect than the Christians. The ratio of men to women in my sample was 1 : 1.27 for the Muslims, as compared with 1 : 0.7 for the Christians. Of the Muslims 12 per cent were over sixty, as compared with 4.8 per cent of the Christians. The Muslim population contrasts most strongly with the Catholics amongst the Christians, 73.3 per cent of whom were under thirty, and none of whom were over sixty. Thus the Muslim population is more demographically balanced in terms of age and sex than the Christian population. It is this demographic balance and stability which enables Muslims to marry in Pumwani and to live there until their old age or until they die. Old Muslims often have their children or other relatives living nearby within the locality and can thus be supported when they are too old to work. Of those Muslims in my sample whose fathers were still alive, 34.7 per cent had fathers living in Pumwani. None of the Christians were similarly placed. Of those Muslims whose mothers were still living, 36.9 per cent had mothers living in Pumwani, as compared with only 2.7 per cent of the Christians.

Many Christians would appear to settle only temporarily in Pumwani, moving out to better areas when they have made good in town. Those who are more educated and who can get well-paid jobs are unlikely to settle there in the first place. For the Muslims however—and especially for those born in the location—Pumwani means more than cheap housing[14] and temporary accommodation. It means also a community life and a network of friends and relatives, to whom one can turn for support in times of difficulty. I shall return to this point later. Thus, although some of the successful and educated Muslims may leave, enough stay behind to ensure that the Muslim community does not embrace a single economic category. Thus although 54 per cent of the Muslims in my sample had never been to school, compared with 28.6 per cent of the Protestants and 13.3 per cent of the Catholics, more Muslims had been to secondary school (12 per cent) than Christians (8.3 per cent), and the only university-educated man in my sample was a Muslim. This range of educational qualifications which the Muslims possess is reflected in the fact that slightly more Muslims are unemployed than Christians, whilst all the professional and clerical workers in my sample were Muslim.

The main reason why I consider Muslims to be the most important religious category in Pumwani, however, is that they are aware of them-selves as a religious *group*, rather than as a mere collection of individuals, and that they are organized on this basis. This is true both in a narrow religious sense, and in a wider social sense. They have built their own mosque and *madrasa* (a religious school), and it is they, not outsiders, who organize and finance the running of these institutions. They hold religious ceremonies on important Islamic occasions such as the end of Ramadhan (the 'Id festival), and the birthday of the Prophet (the *maulidi*), and on such occasions a large majority of the total Muslim population of Pumwani is involved, as well as many Muslims from outside. In addition there are many Muslim welfare organizations in Pumwani which collect money for burials and for helping Muslims in need. Interest-ingly enough, each of these welfare organizations is organized around a particular ethnic group. Thus the Baladia Association is an almost entirely Kikuyu Muslim affair, whilst the Kamba Muslims have their association, and Nyanza and Uganda Muslims theirs, and so on. The mosque and *madrasa* committees are ethnically mixed, but there are frequent accusations of 'tribalism' and domination by one ethnic group. Tribal loyalties are never entirely divisive, however, for various reasons.

First, the Muslims of any one ethnic group are not always united amongst themselves—the Kikuyu, for example, have two Muslim welfare societies. Second, within any tribal Muslim association there are many people who were either born in Pumwani or who have lived there most of their lives. These people no longer think of the tribal area as their home, and they may not even speak the tribal language adequately any more. Often it is such people who hold important positions in the association. Third, there is some movement towards the unity of all Muslims in Pumwani, irrespective of ethnic group. The two Kikuyu associations combined in 1969 to organize a *maulidi* celebration for the whole location, and several other tribal associations co-operate together on some occasions, when they describe themselves as *Mungano*—i.e. the co-operative association. It was *Mungano* which built the *madrasa*, for example. Finally, and most important, is the fact that many Muslims in Pumwani are the products of inter-ethnic marriages such that internal division on ethnic lines can never be really disjunctive.

In addition to these primarily religious activities, the Muslims in Pumwani have established a social life which is focused within the locality, and which does not look to the rural areas. Muslims are born, get married, die and are buried within the confines of an urban Muslim community.[15] They interact frequently and help each other when in difficulties. They are bound together by a web of kinship and affinal ties. They are set off, culturally speaking, from non-Muslims by their beliefs and values, their food habits and their dress, their manners and their customs.

If we contrast the Muslims of Pumwani with the Christians we find many differences. The Christians are divided amongst themselves in terms of religious denominations, though most of them describe themselves as either 'CMS' (Church Missionary Society—Protestants, that is) or Catholics. The Catholics have to go as far as Racecourse Road (about one and a half miles away) if they wish to attend church. Protestants may attend St John's Church which adjoins Pumwani. But neither of these churches were built by local Christians, and their religious leaders are rarely local men. There are no specifically Christian societies in Pumwani, and there is no tribal society whose members are all Christians. It would be true to say then that Christians are not organized in Pumwani. Nor do they have their own social life. They are generally shorter-term migrants whose long-term interests more often lie in the rural areas. They do not appear to interact socially as Christians. They seem to consider themselves first as members of their own ethnic group, and only second-arily as Christians. This is indicated, I think, by two things. First, the many inter-ethnic marriages that exist in Pumwani are nearly all of Mus-lims, not of Christians. Out of my sample of 86 adults, twenty-nine were the children of mixed marriages, and only two of these were Christians. More-over, of those in my sample who were married (48), half were married to a person of a different ethnic group to their own, and again only three of these were Christians. The second factor is that of burial. Christians prefer, if they can afford it, to send the bodies of their dead to be buried in the rural area from which they came. Muslims, however, are almost without exception buried in the Muslim burial ground near Pumwani, and this kind of burial is sanctioned by Islam itself.

I would argue from all this that Pumwani is a community largely to the extent that the Muslims make it so. A conceptual model of Pumwani would perhaps be made up of three concentric circles. The innermost circle is the core community of Pumwani. This is essentially a Muslim community, led and organized (though not united) by long established residents. It has its own traditions and way of life. It is sufficiently similar to other Muslim communities in East Africa for any Muslim who comes from outside to feel immediately at home, and to be very easily absorbed into the network of social rights and obligations which characterize the community. Non-Muslims are nearly always peripheral to this core community. The outermost circle is the most peripheral to Pumwani as a community. It includes all those who live in Pumwani on a short-term basis, whose long-term interests lie outside, and who have only chosen Pumwani as a place to live because it is cheap. Although there are Muslims to whom this description would also apply, Muslims are in an essentially different position to Christians and others who settle in Pumwani. They are looked upon as potential recruits to Muslim welfare societies, and they will be expected to contribute to collections for funerals, feasts and other Islamic ceremonies. They may also be looked upon as potential spouses for Muslims born in Pumwani itself. Christians are generally outside all this.

The middle circle, however, acts as a kind of bridge between these very peripheral individuals and the central core community. It consists of Christians and other non-Muslims who have lived in Pumwani for long periods. Such people have lived in the same houses with Muslims, bought at the same shops as Muslims, worked with them perhaps, and may have established friendships with them. Such people are gradually being absorbed into the Muslim community, though as non-Muslims they never really become members of it. There are also some elements in Pumwani which are organized outside the essentially Muslim core but which have some links with it.

One such element is the Ziba or Haya people living in Pumwani who are organized around the Bukoba Union. The vast majority of Ziba living in Pumwani are women, most of whom make a living as prostitutes. There are also a few Ziba men living in Pumwani who have come to work in Nairobi, and also a few Ziba women who are married. The leaders of the Bukoba Union are men, but the society is essentially a welfare society for Ziba women. The relevant fact about the Bukoba Union here, however, is that its members are from every religious persuasion. There are Muslims, Catholics and Protestants amongst them, though Muslims appear to be in the minority. Although most Ziba stay only a few years in Pumwani, and then go back to Bukoba with their savings, the Muslims amongst them act as links between the core community and the outsiders. Recently an old Muslim Ganda man died in Pumwani. He had lived for many years with a Muslim Ziba woman, and had children by her. The Ziba women of the Bukoba Union collected money to bury the man.

Another category of some interest in Pumwani are the people from Uganda who live in Pumwani, and who are also to some extent organized, under the umbrella of the Uganda Union. In theory the Uganda Union is composed of about ten ethnic societies representing many of the tribes of Uganda—though I doubt that many of these have more than a formal existence. The Uganda Union used to have about 200 members in Pumwani, it is said, as well as branches throughout Kenya. As might be expected, it was controlled by Ganda. Recent political events in Uganda, however, have led to serious internal dissensions within the Union, and to its gradual decline. It is said that it now has only fifty members in Pumwani. However, it does still act as a 'burial society', collecting money to bury Ugandans who die here. Again its membership includes Muslims and Christians and tribes like the Ganda are also divided along religious lines. It is the Christian organizing secretary of the Uganda Union who collects money to bury Muslim Ugandans. This society too, then, acts as a bridge between Muslims and non-Muslims.

There are no firm dividing lines between the three concentric circles of which I have spoken, and in practice the divisions are by no means fixed; Pumwani is changing from year to year and nothing is static. People say that non-Muslims are moving into the locality in ever-increasing numbers, whilst at the same time the whole area is under threat of demolition, and the scattering of the Muslim community seems very probable. It may be partly because of these threats to its existence that the

Muslim core community of Pumwani is so actively organized. At the present time one gets the impression that the social forces within the area are, to continue with my analogy, centripetal, and that the Muslim core acts almost like a vortex, pulling in towards the centre all the peripheral elements. Absorption into the community may occur on any of several levels.

Non-Muslims who stay in Pumwani only for very brief periods, and who work outside the locality are unlikely to be absorbed into the community to any extent at all. There are many non-Muslims, however, who actually live and work within Pumwani. Some are house servants in Muslim households, others are shopkeepers or shop assistants. Such people are absorbed into a Muslim household, or they soon have a network of Muslim acquaintances. Even non-Muslims who work outside Pumwani may make friends amongst their Muslim fellow tenants if they stay long enough. The outsider may also be absorbed to some extent through common recreational activities. Pumwani provides, within its boundaries, for a full range of recreational activities. There are Indian and English films put on occasionally by the Muslim Welfare Society in Ukumbusho Hall, which all may attend. There are dances and concerts put on by local Muslim dance societies—the Black Golden Star Society for example, or the Arabian-Congo Night Star Society. Young men play draughts; others are members of a boxing club. There are numerous small bars, legal and illegal. There are rooms kept by the *miraa* sellers where people go to sit and chew *miraa* all night. By taking part in some or all of these recreational activities a man may build up a network of friends, who will draw him into the community. Women are more often drawn into the community through friendships with neighbours and fellow tenants.

As more and more Christians settle into the area, there is an increasing percentage who bring their wives with them, and whose children are born and brought up there. Such children play with Muslim children and go to school with them, and in many respects they are more like them than they are like their parents. This is particularly noticeable in the quality of their Swahili—a point I shall return to later.

One way in which a person may become absorbed into the Muslim community of Pumwani is by marriage. Generally this is accompanied by conversion—but there are also a few instances in Pumwani of Muslims and Christians just living together.

Ultimately, however, one is only absorbed into the Islamic community by becoming a Muslim. At certain times in the past conversion to Islam was politically advantageous—many Kikuyus were 'converted' during the time of the Emergency,[16] for example. In this way they were no longer suspected by the authorities of being Mau Mau, and at the same time they were less likely to be sent back to the rural areas, as many Kikuyu were during this period. Also it seems that the British favoured and trusted the Muslims, and gave them positions such as judges of the African courts, headmen, chiefs and so on. Nowadays it is probably politically disadvantageous to be a Muslim,[17] but still Islam makes its converts. Twenty-four per cent of the Muslims in my sample were converts to Islam. Several of these were women who were converted when they married Muslim men. Sometimes there are more material reasons for conversion. One old man told me that he was converted when he worked with some Muslim hunters as a gun-bearer. One youth who works as a domestic servant in a Muslim household was converted during this last year. Non-Muslim children who grow up in Pumwani are sometimes converted too. A Nandi boy I know was originally a Catholic. But his best friends in Pumwani were two Muslim boys, with whom he went to school. When he was about fourteen he was converted to Islam and took a Muslim name. I doubt whether most conversions arise as a result of any deep spiritual conviction—it is more the attraction of an active and ordered social life, and the security of being accepted into an on-going network of friends and acquaintances.

In the second half of this chapter I shall show to what extent the existence of this Muslim core community in Pumwani affects language usage there. I shall also describe how the Pumwani people, faced with a diversity of languages and ethnic groups, are able effectively to communicate with each other.

LANGUAGE USAGE WITHIN THE PUMWANI AREA

1. RELIGION AND LANGUAGE

There is no simple and direct relation between language usage and religious adherence in Pumwani. The relationship is an indirect one and stems more from the social relations of Muslims in Pumwani than from purely religious factors. We may look first, however, at the influence on language of these purely religious factors.

There are very few people in Pumwani who speak Arabic, the language of the Muslims' Holy Book. Out of the eighty-six people interviewed, only four claimed to speak 'a little Arabic'. It is significant that one of these was the assistant to a *mganga*, a practitioner of beneficial magic— a point to which I shall return later. One of the others was a Qur'an school teacher who had taught himself to speak some Arabic with help from courses broadcast from Cairo Radio. Another was a coastal man who had been taught Arabic on the coast by a learned Muslim teacher. The fourth was the son of an Arab from Hadhramaut, of whom there are a small minority in Pumwani. For the Hadhramis, of course, Arabic is a language of everyday life, spoken amongst themselves, and in this respect is equivalent to the tribal languages that are similarly used in Pumwani. For other Muslims in Pumwani, however, Arabic is not thought of as a language of communication with one's fellow man. It is, rather, a sacred language, used in set formulae, to bring the pious into communication with God. The comment of one devout Pumwani Muslim, when asked to speak with some visiting Egyptians, is indicative. He said, 'I do not know how to speak Arabic. I can only read the Qur'an.'

Arabic is the language of all the prayers used by Muslims—and if they are pious they pray five times every day. Arabic is also the language used in the Friday sermons. There are certain set sermons written out which the Imam or religious leader can use. Whereas the Imams of the two big mosques in the town centre are said to translate the sermon into Swahili as they go along, there is no such translation in the Pumwani mosque. Does all this mean then that the Muslims in Pumwani spend their religious lives using a language of which they do not know the meaning?

In my questionnaire I included three questions asking Muslims about their ability to read the Qur'an, their understanding of its meaning, and their ability to read and write Swahili in Arabic script. I also asked about attendance at Qur'an schools, since it is only by attending such schools that one achieves the above knowledge. Of the fifty Muslims in my sample, 38 (76 per cent) had attended a Qur'an school, and of these 33 claimed to be able to read the Qur'an. Several of these qualified their answer by saying, 'but only a little'. Twenty-three of the 33 said they could read and write Swahili in Arabic script, though again some of them qualified this to 'a little'. Only twenty said they could understand the Qur'an, and all but five of these said they could only understand a word here and there. For the reasons for these answers we have to look at the system of Islamic education in Pumwani and at the attitudes and beliefs surrounding the language of the Qur'an.

Most Muslim children in Pumwani—both boys and girls—attend a Qur'an school for some period of time, however short. Even the very smallest children can be sent, so it is sometimes a way for a woman to get a bit of peace from her children. There are two Qur'an schools in Pumwani, one built at the back of the mosque (the *madrasa*), and one held in Ukumbusho Hall. (This hall was built by a rich African Muslim.) There are other such schools in Eastleigh (a nearby and, until recently, a predominantly Asian area) which some Pumwani children also attend. In general the standard of teaching at these schools is not very high. The teachers are mainly self-appointed and are often not very well educated (in the Islamic sense, that is). Typically the children are first taught the Arabic letters, and then they begin to learn to recite the Qur'an. Each section must be learnt off by heart before going on to the next section. When a child has completed this process—and it may take years—he can be said to be able to 'read' the Qur'an, that is to say he can recognize the section which he is asked to read and can then recite off by heart. At this stage he may not know the meaning of one single word, but his pronunciation of Arabic words will be quite good. This is in itself quite significant, because there seems to be a carry-over into Swahili of Arabic sounds—a distinction between two kinds of s (ﺱand ﺹ), and two kinds of t (ﻁ and ﺕ) for example. Thus when the secretary of the *madrasa* committee wrote inviting people to attend a *maulidi* being performed by the children of the *madrasa* he used the word **swala** for prayer, instead of **sala** which would be the 'Standard' Swahili form.

Very few Muslim children in Pumwani ever actually complete the Qur'an because the Qur'an schools have to compete with secular schools, and with many other ways in which children may prefer to spend their time. And even fewer children go any further with their Muslim education, simply because the facilities are not available. Only the Qur'an school adjoining the mosque has such facilities. One of its teachers is a Hadhrami Arab, who, though said not to be particularly well educated, does translate passages from the Qur'an and accounts of the life of the Prophet into Swahili, for the children to learn off by heart. There is also a young teacher from Mambrui (a small town on the Kenya coast) who can speak Arabic. In addition the school has a Pakistani teacher (paid for by the Saudi Arabian government) who speaks excellent Arabic. He does not however speak Swahili. He translates the Arabic into English and then the few boys in the class who have been to school translate this into Swahili for the benefit of the others. This teacher teaches the highest class in the Qur'an school.

A person who wishes to learn more must in theory go to a Sheikh and become his pupil. The relationship is more like that of a disciple and his follower. If the teacher is satisfied with his pupil's progress he will eventually give him his blessing to go out into the world and teach others. Essentially what the Sheikh has to teach is how to understand the meaning of the Qur'an. The word used is **kutafsiri** (to translate), but it must be emphasized that what is meant is not a simple mechanical process, but a religious experience of revelation. The language in which the Qur'an is written is not simply a means of communication—it is something sacred and set apart, and one has to be blessed by God before one is enabled to see its meaning. Ordinary people are therefore a little afraid of it, and it is considered slightly blasphemous to 'translate' what can only be 'revealed'. Although there are a few men in Pumwani who are learned enough to teach others in the way described above, none of them in fact does so. In the past the religious leaders of Pumwani tended to be people from the coast (Bajuni in particular). This is no longer wholly true; it is a Kikuyu Muslim who now acts as Imam of Pumwani's mosque, with a Bajuni as his deputy. Both these men studied under Sheikhs from outside Pumwani however, as did the few other learned men of Pumwani. They were taught either by men from the coast, or in one case by an Indian Muslim Sheikh who had lived in the old location of Pangani. Some Pumwani Muslims—generally people of coastal origin—say that the present religious leaders of Pumwani are not as learned as they should be, and that they do not really know how to 'translate' the Qur'an. Whether or not this is true I am not competent to say; the point here however is rather that there is rarely any translation of the Qur'an attempted in the Pumwani mosque.

Although Arabic is not used as a spoken language by any but the Hadhramis in Pumwani, it nevertheless links the African Muslims living there with the wider Muslim, and mainly Arabic-speaking world. This role was activated on three occasions during the period in which I studied Pumwani. The first occasion was when an Egyptian delegation visited the mosque and donated money, records and books to the *madrasa*. The second was when two Saudi Arabian Sheikhs visited the mosque and donated money, and the third was the *maulidi* celebration at the *madrasa* when the audience was addressed by the secretary of the Kuwaiti Embassy in Kenya. On all these occasions the visitors made speeches in Arabic to the Pumwani Muslims. These speeches were translated into Swahili by the Hadhrami *madrasa* teacher.

One interesting reflection of the link between Arabic and religion which showed up in the answers to my questionnaire was the discrepancy between the answers of men and women. Forty-four per cent of the women said they could not read the Qur'an at all compared with only 18.2 per cent of the men, and, as indicated above, none of those who claimed some knowledge of spoken Arabic were women. Although there were more girls than boys attending the Qur'an schools in Pumwani in 1968–9,[18] there were few girls in the top class. And fewer girls than boys seem to have attended Qur'an schools in the past. 67.9 per cent of the Muslim women in my sample had attended a Qur'an school, compared with 86.4 per cent of the Muslim men. This is a reflection of the fact that there are no specifically religious offices which can be held by women in Pumwani,[19] and there is no place for them in the mosque to attend prayers.[20] On Fridays a few elderly women may sit in the *madrasa* building at the back of the mosque whilst the Friday prayers are being held, but generally women (if they are religious at all) pray at home. Thus, for women, there is neither the incentive of positions to be achieved nor the spur of communal prayer to encourage them to excel in religious learning. This difference between men and women did not appear so markedly in the context of any other language except Arabic.

For most people in Pumwani, Arabic seems to carry with it a range of implications, from the religious to the magical. People who can read the Qur'an well are assumed by implication to be pious as well. At the other end of the spectrum, Arabic comes to have a magical significance—words written in it have a power which words in other languages do not have. In Pumwani there are many *waganga*—which we might perhaps translate as doctors of magic. There are two types of these. The first type are the *waganga wa kidini* who are Muslims and who use Arabic books of medicine, write Arabic charms utilizing verses of the Qur'an (*hirizi*) and so on. For most *waganga* this is a specialized and full-time occupation, but in some cases the pious and the learned may write *hirizi* in order to make a little money. Thus a man who taught for a time at one of Pumwani's Qur'an schools also assisted a *mganga* by writing *hirizi*. The other type of *waganga* are the *waganga wa kienyeji*, who are not generally Muslims, and who use medicines and incantations which do not involve the use of Arabic. The interesting thing is that it is the former who seem to be the most popular, even amongst non-Muslims. Ziba prostitutes for example are said often to attend Muslim *waganga* if their business is not going well, and one occasionally sees Muslim *hirizi* hung in the houses of non-Muslims. In fact I suspect that some *waganga* do not read Arabic at all, but only pretend to do so because this helps their business.

To sum up then, it seems that Arabic has a significance in Pumwani, not because it is understood, but simply because it has an aura of religious power and prestige. And to some extent this aura of religion extends to the language of communication of the Muslim community in Pumwani—Swahili. It is the role of Swahili therefore which I would like to discuss next.

2. SWAHILI IN PUMWANI

In general it can be said that Pumwani Swahili resembles coastal Swahili more than do other varieties spoken in Nairobi. It is spoken with greater 'fluency', makes more use of complex sentence constructions through such devices as conjunctions and relative clauses, and it makes greater use of the concord system. This is not, of course, to deny the existence of varieties of Swahili within Pumwani;[21] there are newly arrived immigrants who speak very little Swahili, and there are people who came a long time ago but still speak Swahili with marked interference from their first language. There are also people who were born in Pumwani and speak Swahili as their first language, as well as people from the Kenya coast who speak a dialect of Swahili as their first language. Two different varieties of the language are suggested by the following passages: the first spoken by a Ganda man of forty who had spent fifteen years in Pumwani;[22] and the second by a younger man born and brought up in Pumwani. The contrast between the short, juxtaposed phrases of the first, and the longer, complex sentences of the second is most marked: '**Nkiamka asubuhi, nilioga uso, nikapiga mswaki, nkala chakula cha asubuhi. Nkitoka hapo nkatembea kidogo kuamkua jamaa mjini. Nkitoka uku nkarudi nyumbani kwangu, nkapumzika. Chakula cha mchana chikafika nkala chakula cha mkyana . . .** ' (I woke in the morning, I washed my face and I brushed my teeth and I ate breakfast. I went out for a short walk to greet my friends in the location. After this—or more literally 'when I left there'—I returned to my house and I rested. The midday meal arrived and I ate the midday meal.)

'**Leo asubuhi nilipoamka, mwanzo niliingia baathroom nikaoga. Baada ya kutoka kuoga nlikwenda mpaka nyumbani kwetu kuangalia wazazi. Nalipotoka hapo nkaja moja kwa moja mpaka hapa dukani na kukaa kama nusu saa hivi, nkiuza duka.**' (This morning when I awoke, the first thing I did was to enter the bathroom and bathe. After finishing bathing I went as far as my family's home to see my parents. After coming from there I came straight to the shop here, and I stayed about half an hour, serving in the shop.)

People who come to Pumwani when they are young quickly pick up the characteristic features of the local variety of Swahili, but those who come when they are already mature may retain features characteristic of their first language—especially at the phonological level. Thus the oldest man in my sample was a Kamba man of about ninety, who had spent more than sixty years in Nairobi, and had lived in Pumwani since it was built. Nevertheless, as can be seen from the following passage, certain features of his Swahili suggest that two phonological systems—one of Swahili, one of Kamba—are overlapping:

' **. . . tukawacha nzia ya Mombasa tukasika ile ndia ya Kibwezi. Tukaya zetu mpaka Kibwezi. Kufika Kibwezi tukawa tukisikia gari ya mosi ikija, tukakimbia zhote mwituni. Aa! Hio ni nyama inakuja kutuua. Dzamani hapana kujua gari.**' (We left the Mombasa road and we took the road to Kibwezi. On reaching Kibwezi we heard a steam train coming, and we all ran away into the forest. Aa! This is a wild animal coming to kill us. In the past trains were not known.)[23]

If we recognize, however, that the younger one is, the more easily one picks up a new language, I think it would still be true to say that the longer one stays in Pumwani the 'better' one speaks Swahili, and that the quality of one's Swahili may be taken in many cases as an index of one's absorption into the community. Out of my sample of 86 persons, no one said they could speak no Swahili at all. Sixty-four per cent said they could speak Swahili fluently, 34.8 per cent said they spoke it moderately well, and 1.2 per cent said they spoke 'only a little'.

There are various reasons why Swahili is the medium of communication in Pumwani, and why the Swahili which is spoken there is such as it is. The first reason is that Pumwani is so ethnically heterogeneous that only Swahili, which is known to some extent all over East Africa, would serve as a lingua franca. This statement applies, of course, not only to Pumwani but to Nairobi as a whole and to other towns in Kenya as well. In fact Swahili seems to be associated in the minds of many people with towns and urban living. When asked why they speak such good Swahili people will often reply proudly, 'Sisi ni watu wa towni' (We are townspeople) when they may mean Nyeri or Machakos or some such place, and not necessarily Nairobi.

The second reason why Swahili is used as the language of communication in Pumwani, and why it is such 'good' Swahili, is that the original founders of the Muslim settlements in Nairobi were people from the coast, for whom Swahili was a first language. These people were often referred to as 'Waswahili', though they may have belonged to any one of a number of small coastal tribes or clans. When they intermarried with local Africans whom they had converted to Islam, their children were also called Waswahili, so that here in Nairobi the term has come to mean an African Muslim, and for the Muslims themselves at least has none of the pejorative implications it may have on the coast.[24] For a considerable length of time it was people originally from the coast who were the people of prestige in Pumwani and who held the positions of religious and political leadership. The first five Imams of the Pumwani mosque (built in 1935) were all coastal men, and it was only in 1963 that a Kikuyu Muslim took this position. Coastal people were revered for their knowledge of religion and for their role as Muslim missionaries. Their language—Swahili—full of Arabic vocabulary, was no doubt also given some of the same prestige. For some older people at least the religious aura of Arabic extended also to Swahili. In answer to one question in my questionnaire concerning the language a person would most like to see as Kenya's national language the old man mentioned above (a Kamba convert to Islam) said he would prefer Swahili because it was 'like Arabic, a language of religion and learning'.

One would expect therefore—and this is confirmed by the results of my questionnaire—that Muslims would speak Swahili better than most Christians, and that they would use it more frequently. Thus 88 per cent of the Muslims claimed to be able to speak Swahili fluently compared with only 30.5 per cent of the Christians. Twenty-seven (54 per cent) of the Muslims claimed moreover that they spoke Swahili better than any other language, whereas only three of the Christians made a similar claim. Two of these Christians were girls born in Pumwani, one a Kikuyu, the other a Nandi, whilst the third was a Chagga man from Tanzania. (In Tanzania Swahili is more widely spoken than in Kenya, and generally better spoken.) These figures could be said to indicate language preferences rather than language proficiency, and indeed it is true that there is a distinct element of preference for Swahili amongst Muslims as opposed to Christians. But I think that the figures reflect more than preference—many Muslims do actually seem to speak Swahili more fluently than Christians. The reason for this is not simply that they are Muslims of course. It is a reflection of four social factors. Firstly the Muslims, by and large, have lived in Pumwani longer than the Christians. Secondly, many of the Muslims were born in Nairobi, and of those who were born outside, a sizeable proportion come from areas such as the coast, or from other towns in Kenya, where Swahili is the primary language. The third reason is the high degree of ethnic intermarriage amongst the Pumwani Muslims. This has the effect of making Swahili a language of communication between spouses, and a first language for the offspring of such marriages. The last reason is that Muslims belong to a social community which uses Swahili for all purposes of communication, except communication with God. I shall deal with each of these points in turn.

I have shown in the first half of this account that most of those born in Pumwani are Muslims rather than Christians. For these people Swahili is nearly always a first language since it is the language of everyday life in the community in which they were born. But Swahili is also a first language for some of those Muslims who were born outside Nairobi. Thus of those 29 Muslims who said they spoke Swahili as their first language, fifteen were born outside Nairobi. Three of these were born on the coast where Swahili is equivalent to a local vernacular, but the rest were born in places such as Machakos, Nyeri or Murang'a (Fort Hall). Often these are people who have come from so-called 'Swahili' (i.e. Muslim) settlements in these places. Such settlements deserve further study, as some of them seem to have been in existence for fifty or sixty years. Like Pumwani they were created by coastal people—Arab, Co-morian or sometimes Nyamwezi traders—and they often contain people from several different tribes. Most importantly here, they all seem to use Swahili as a language of community.

Looking at this in a slightly different way one can point out the fact that 66 per cent of the Muslims in my sample were born in towns rather than in rural areas, and it is in multi-ethnic urban areas where Swahili is used as a lingua franca. By contrast most of the Christians (66.6 per cent) came from villages, where the need of a lingua franca such as Swahili is rare.

Possibly the most pressing reason why Swahili is important for Pumwani Muslims, however, is that it enables Muslims of different ethnic groups to communicate, in associations, in social transactions of various types, and in marriage. As I have already shown few Christians are the children of mixed marriages, and equally, few contract such marriages for themselves. The Muslims in Pumwani have, however, intermarried to a large extent. Seventy-five per cent of the married Muslims in my sample were married to a person of a different tribe to their own, compared with only 8.3 per cent of the married Christians. The medium of communication in such 'mixed' marriages is almost invariably Swahili, and for the children of such marriages Swahili is a first language. Even where the husband and wife are of the same tribe, however, they may use Swahili to communicate both with each other and with their children. An example of this is a Muslim Kikuyu born in Nairobi, but who married a Kikuyu girl from Kapsabet and converted her to Islam. The man's Kikuyu is not very fluent, and I heard the woman say one day that she too was forgetting her mother tongue since she now spoke Swahili all the time. Thus we find that 71.4 per cent of the married Muslims use only Swahili in talking with their spouses, whilst a further 17.9 per cent use Swahili together with another language. This is to be contrasted with the situation amongst the Christians, where only 30 per cent use any Swahili at all with their spouses, and only 4 per cent use Swahili all the time. This is reflected in the languages used with children, where it is Muslims rather than Christians who use Swahili. Seventy-three per cent of the Muslims in my sample spoke Swahili with their children, compared with only 15 per cent of the Christians.

Thus we have a situation in which, due to a long history of intermarriage between Muslims of various ethnic groups, Swahili is now used extensively in Muslim homes. Swahili is thus a tongue passed on from generation to generation, a language with an on-going tradition. It would thus seem that it is Pumwani's core community of Muslims which acts as a linguistic reference group for all those who migrate into the area from outside. A migrant who settles in Pumwani will hear almost nothing but Swahili spoken around him. Although at first he may mix only with other people of his own ethnic group he gradually develops a wider set of friends and acquaintances with whom he converses in Swahili. In this way he soon develops a fluency in the language. Thus out of my sample there were a few people who said they spoke only tribal vernaculars with their friends, who were all people of the same ethnic group as themselves. Most of these people had lived in Pumwani for less than a year, and only one of the others had lived for more than four years in Pumwani. People who had lived in Pumwani for longer periods all had friends of various ethnic backgrounds with whom they were forced to speak Swahili.

The greater use of Swahili by Muslims is reflected in almost every sphere of their lives. Thus if Swahili is the language of the home, it is also the language of communication between fellow tenants in the same house. It is probably in this sphere that many Christians are first forced to use the language, since practically every house in Pumwani is both ethnically and religiously mixed and Swahili is almost always the language of communication within the house and between landlord and tenant. At the same time the landlord does have a choice as to which tenants he will have in his house and which he will not. Almost every landlord has a few members of his own ethnic and religious group as tenants, and with these he may converse in their local language rather than in Swahili. It is noticeable, however, that a few houses which have been bought by non-Muslims in recent years have gradually been filled up with people all of the same ethnic group and religion.[25] There is one house, for example, that has twenty tenants, sixteen of whom are Christians, four apparently of no religion, and all except three of whom are Kikuyu. It is Kikuyu rather than Swahili which is the language of communication in this house.

The other important context of Swahili usage in Pumwani is that of the various clubs and societies which flourish in the area. As I explained earlier, nearly all of these societies are organized by and for Muslims. Exceptions are the Bukoba Union—the Ziba organization, and the Uganda Union, both of which include Muslim members. There is also another organization in Pumwani which is neither ethnic nor religious in its aim— this is the Landlords' Association. Of the 343 Pumwani landlords, 38 per cent are claimed to be members of this association. It is difficult to tell from the list of members what their religious affiliations are because many simply have tribal names, and could be either Muslims, Christians or neither. Forty-six per cent of the members are obviously Muslims, 16 per cent obviously Christians, and the other 38 per cent are indeterminate. The committee of fourteen members has eight Muslims, of whom one is the Chairman, five Christians, and two others. Other than these three societies, all others operating in Pumwani are exclusively for Muslims.

I asked in my questionnaire about membership of societies, and out of eighty-six respondents, twenty-five said that they were members of associations operating in Pumwani itself, whilst six more (all except one Christian) were members of societies operating either in other parts of Nairobi, or outside Nairobi in the rural areas from which the respondents had come.[26] Of those people who were members of Pumwani societies, four Ziba women (all Christians) were members of the Bukoba Union. Two more Christians were members of the Uganda Union. The other nineteen persons were all Muslims, and were members of various societies ranging from a religious movement to a dance society, to tribal Muslim welfare associations. All these Muslim societies use Swahili as a medium of communication, even where their membership is drawn almost solely from one tribe. The reason for this seems to be that there are always members who, though belonging to that particular tribe, were born in Pumwani, sometimes of mixed parentage, and who speak Swahili better than they speak their tribal language. There may, however, also be an element of language preference in the use of Swahili in such societies. Two of the non-Muslim associations—the Landlords' Association and the Uganda Union—also use Swahili as a medium of communication because there is no other language which all would understand. It is only the Bukoba Union which uses a tribal language—Ziba— as a means of communication, and even they claim to use Swahili as well. Most Ziba say they speak Swahili as their second language.

What I am trying to argue is that any associational activity in Pumwani is usually either multi-ethnic, or it involves the association together of people with different backgrounds, such that Swahili *has* to be used as a medium of communication. In so far as Christians take part in associational activities they too are involved in this usage, but as we have seen, it is Muslims rather than Christians who belong to associations in Pumwani, although some of the Christians also belong to societies outside Pumwani.

In Nairobi, Swahili is, as one respondent put it, 'the language of work' for all except the élite. Those who know it better are therefore at an advantage, and are not restricted in their choice of work to places where their employer and fellow employees are of the same ethnic group as themselves. Problems of communication do not arise when Swahili can be used as a lingua franca. As we have seen, most people in Pumwani speak Swahili well and are not faced with this kind of problem. Nearly all those who answered my questionnaire used Swahili in their dealings with workmates. The three exceptional cases where the respondent used a tribal language in the context of his work were of some interest, however. All three were men involved in small local businesses; two were assistants in different butchers' shops owned by Kikuyu, and the third was a trader involved in the lucrative *miraa* trade. Both of the butchers' assistants were Kikuyu relatives of the shop-owners. The Kikuyu are well known in Nairobi for their business acumen, and perhaps part of their success can be attributed to the way in which they stick together. The *miraa* trade is monopolized by Meru people and involves a complex chain of business relationships from the actual growers through a series of middlemen to the petty traders in places like Pumwani. It is hardly surprising then that in each of these three cases the tribal language was the language of work. Its use only symbolizes the exclusiveness of the business relations involved. It may mean very little that each of the men involved is a Christian, for Muslims too may be engaged in ethnically exclusive business ventures, though this does not seem to be very common.

Every businessman in Pumwani knows the value of Swahili however, whatever his tribe or religious affiliation. Although one occasionally hears shopkeepers and shop assistants greeting customers in their own language, and although each shopkeeper usually has a small and loyal core clientele of his or her own ethnic group with whom they may deal in their common language, most business in Pumwani is transacted in Swahili.

Swahili in Pumwani thus plays two roles. As in other parts of Nairobi it acts as a necessary lingua franca to facilitate the interaction of people speaking diverse languages. But more than this, Swahili in Pumwani is the cultural symbol of an Islamic community, itself extremely diverse in ethnic make-up. Swahili is often valued by Muslims above tribal languages, and it is rare for anyone but a Muslim to say 'Swahili is the language I understand best'. To some extent one can also speak of Swahili as a language of Swahili culture in Pumwani, since the style of dances and songs performed by Muslim dance societies owes more to the *taarabu* recitals of the coast than to Nairobi influence, and the songs are almost exclusively in Swahili. It is said that in the past, when there were more of these dance societies, their leaders used to compose Swahili verses insulting the members of other societies, and there was keen competition to see which society would deal the most witty and sarcastic insults. Swahili poetry of another kind was recited last year during a *maulidi* celebration organized by one of the Kikuyu Muslim associations, and attended by hundreds of Muslims of all tribes. The Imam of the mosque—an old and respected Kikuyu—had died a few weeks before, and a poem of praise in Swahili had been written by a local Muslim in his honour. Some

Pumwani people have been able to capitalize on their fluent knowledge of Swahili in a wider cultural context. Thus two people in my sample occasionally appeared on the Voice of Kenya in radio programmes of light entertainment. The star of the best known locally produced television show ('Mzee Pembe') was also originally a Pumwani man. This man— a pious Kikuyu Muslim—is the more remarkable for his excellent knowledge of Arabic. Two Swahili films recently made by Asians (*Mlevi* and *Mrembo*) both used several actors from Pumwani, including a girl singer— again a Kikuyu Muslim, and Omar Suleiman, the star of 'Mzee Pembe'. If Swahili were no more than a lingua franca it would be inadequate to play such cultural roles.

3. ENGLISH: POLITICAL BROKERAGE AND THE 'ELITE-IN-TRAINING'

The contrast between the role which Swahili plays in Pumwani, and that played by English, could not be greater. Thus, whereas Swahili is known by the vast majority of Pumwani's population, knowledge of English is reserved to the few. Whereas Swahili is (as one respondent put it) 'the language of the people' (*lugha ya wananchi*), English is a language of the élite in Kenya. In Pumwani it is spoken by men rather than women, and by younger people rather than the old. Again this is in contrast to knowledge of Swahili where no such distinctions arise.

If the knowledge and use of English in Pumwani contrasts on almost every point with that of Swahili, there are interesting parallels between the use of English and the use of Arabic. Like Arabic, English is spoken by the few rather than the many, and knowledge of it derives from a formal educational process—in the one case Islamic, and in the other largely Western and to some extent Christian. Both languages are used for communication with outside worlds—in the case of Arabic with the world of the supernatural, and in the case of English with the encompassing worlds of government and politics. Both languages are known by men rather than women (though English not exclusively so), and this is not surprising since the worlds of religion and politics are largely men's worlds.

The results of my questionnaire indicated very clearly that knowledge of English in Pumwani was linked with both age and sex. 47.7 per cent of the sample said they could speak no English at all, 27.9 per cent said they could speak 'a few words', 18.6 per cent said they could speak it moderately well, and only 5.8 per cent said they could speak it fluently. Of those who spoke English either fluently or moderately well, the majority were under thirty, and none were over fifty. 59.1 per cent of the women

said they could speak no English at all, compared with 35.7 per cent of
the men. Of those who could speak English either moderately or very
well, seventeen were men, and only four were women. Let us then look
at the way in which English is used in Pumwani.

The most important use of English in Pumwani is in the context of
administration and politics. Pumwani forms one of the smallest units in
the political and administrative structure of Nairobi. As a location it
is administered by a chief, who has an office in the location, and who
is responsible to a District Officer working from Makadara location.
The job of the chief is multi-faceted, but basically he acts as an agent
of the central government in regard to the Pumwani people. Most of his
time is spent in hearing cases, since he acts as an informal court of first
hearing. It is he who decides whether or not such cases should proceed
to a higher and more formally constituted court. The present chief was
chosen by the Pumwani people themselves in an election held in 1968 and
is a local man, a Samia Christian. He began to work in late 1969. The
previous chief, a Luo, was promoted after having held the post for many
years. Both these men could speak good English (a knowledge of English
was in fact a prerequisite for their appointment) and they used their
English in dealings with fellow officers in the administration and especially
if these men were their superiors. Hearing cases in Pumwani was however
a different matter, and here Swahili was used almost invariably. It is
noticeable however that many 'technical' English terms referring to
administrative structures are being absorbed into Swahili in this field,
and these are not always understood by the people with whom the chief
is dealing. On one occasion I heard the chief arbitrating in a dispute
concerning a committee which had been set up in a shanty settlement
adjoining Pumwani. He asked the people: '**Munatumia system gani,
kuchagua komitii**? (What system do you use to choose the committee?)'
They did not understand, so he rephrased the question: '**Mwachagua
komitii kwa njia gani—munapiga kura, au munawaappoint**? (In what way
do you choose the committee—do you vote, or do you appoint them?)'
This *was* understood and the answer given: '**Tunawaappoint**'. Whereas
the word 'committee' has been assimilated into Swahili, the words 'system'
and 'appoint' have not.

If the chief gives his approval the case may be taken to a higher court.
In one such instance which I observed, a case was sent to the Rent Tribunal.
Here it was conducted formally, and in English. The plaintiff—a Muslim
woman house-owner—spoke only Swahili however, and she was assisted
in her case by the secretary of Pumwani's Landlords' Association. This
is interesting in several ways because the Landlords' Association may act
as an even more informal 'court' than that of the chief, and sift out the

more serious cases to be sent to the chief. They settle disputes only about houses, however—quarrels about rent unpaid, noisy tenants and the like. The secretary is a complete outsider and was hired by the association to type letters and so on. He speaks English well, however, in contrast to the elderly chairman and most of the other officials of the association who are Pumwani landlords. He has been able to capitalize on this in some cases by acting as a link-man between Pumwani landlords and the chief, the courts, and the city council. When he speaks for someone in a case he is given a 'present'.

It is in the context of housing that the Pumwani people are most in need of political brokers. This is in view of the impending demolition of the area. In this context Pumwani people are dealing primarily with the Nairobi City Council (NCC). The lines of communication between the people and the NCC are rarely direct, and are usually mediated through brokers. One of the reasons for this is that all the council's work is conducted in English. Most of Pumwani comprises one ward which has an elected councillor. The present incumbent is a Nyamwezi Muslim woman. The smaller part of Pumwani (called Mashimoni) is included in another ward, the councillor for which is a Kikuyu man. Both these are local people, and both had to be able to speak English before they could seek election. Their role as intermediaries was hardly an easy one in a period when the area was under constant threat of demolition. It was difficult for people to appreciate the reasons prompting the city council to plan the destruction of their homes. Nor did the building of modern housing meet with their approval as the latter were of unfamiliar design and a good deal more expensive than their present accommodation. Likewise the city council did not altogether sympathize with or even understand the plight of the people, whose constant cry was 'Where shall we go?' Communication was not made easier by the fact that the NCC's circulars, letters and pamphlets to the landlords explaining the new scheme were mostly written in English. (This was however being remedied to some extent before I left the field.) It is difficult to say how effective the councillors were in mediating between the two sides, though they certainly tried. The woman councillor was the more hard-pressed since it was her side of Pumwani which was due to be pulled down first. She often went around trying to explain to the people the letters and pamphlets which they had been sent. It was strange that the city council did not see the need for the use of Swahili in these pamphlets—they seemed to be under the misapprehension that many people in Pumwani could understand English. But even school children found it hard to make sense of the technical language used in some of these missives.[27] The NCC's direct agent in the area was the Pumwani Estate Officer, but his job seemed to be simply to deliver the council's statements rather than to explain their meaning.

Pumwani people are often in difficulties when they have to deal with bureaucracy, since the language required to obtain even ordinary rights such as birth certificates or passports is English. It is sad to relate that although most of the personnel involved in government and administration are well able to speak Swahili, they are often unwilling to do so, since they feel this would imply that they are not educated people. It is not perhaps surprising that in a situation where education is so important in achieving élite status, those who have it are over-eager to distinguish themselves from those who have not. It is English which is widely recognized as the symbol of this status. In order to deal with the élite the people of Pumwani are therefore forced to rely on brokers—their Members of Parliament, the chief, the councillors, or any man who has been to school and who is ready to make use of his ability to speak English.[28]

Although knowledge of English is directly related to formal secular education, not everyone who has been to school can speak it. This is especially true of those who have had not more than a primary education. It has to be remembered that in Pumwani we are dealing with a great diversity of people of all ages, from all over East Africa, and that educational practice has never been uniform. 40.7 per cent of my sample had in any case never attended school, and it is rare for anyone to have learned more than a few words of English in any other way. Of the rest, 37.3 per cent had been taught partly in English, and only 3.9 per cent wholly in English. This can usefully be compared with the use of other languages as school media. 25.5 per cent had been taught wholly in Swahili and 35.3 per cent partly in Swahili. 23.6 per cent had been taught solely in a tribal vernacular, and 27.5 per cent in both a tribal vernacular and English or Swahili. (These figures of course overlap.) Thus we can say that 41.2 per cent of those in my sample who had attended school were taught some English. It is men rather than women who have been to school (52.3 per cent of the women in my sample had never been to school compared with 28.6 per cent of the men). It is for this reason that more men than women speak English.

There is also an interesting contrast between Muslims and Christians in this respect. Although fewer Muslims than Christians had been to school (46 per cent compared with 77.7 per cent), the most highly educated people in my sample, and the only ones who said they could speak English fluently, were Muslims. This may be accidental, since it is after all a very small sample. On the other hand it may lend force to a suggestion I made earlier—that is that educated Muslims do not necessarily move out of Pumwani when they have made good (as most Christians would), since Pumwani offers a rich community life which cannot be found in more élite areas of Nairobi. It is also the case that more of the Muslims have been educated in Nairobi or other towns, where English is more likely to be used in schools.

As I have shown, it is younger people in Pumwani who know English, not old people, and this is of course a reflection of the fact that educational opportunities have widened over the years. Other than the political brokers, it is adolescents who are most often to be heard using English in Pumwani. I would suggest that the use of English has two meanings for such people. Firstly, and perhaps most importantly, it acts as a secret language in which to discuss the affairs of adolescence. Even when using Swahili, such young people will often switch to English when they talk of activities which might be frowned upon by their elders—parties, dancing, sex, girl and boy friends, imported drinks such as whisky, and so on. These words and phrases in many cases have no exact Swahili equivalent. Often they are part of a semi-universal language of youth deriving from popular songs. It would also seem to be the case that the use of English allows such adolescents to express themselves in a way that would not be appropriate in either Swahili or local languages. It is an indication of rebellion against the older generation and against established norms. Thus one Muslim girl, when speaking of the black *buibui* which most Muslim women in East Africa wear outside the home, and which is considered the sign of a modest and respectable woman by Muslims, said she did not wear one in Nairobi at all,[29] but was forced to wear one when visiting relatives in Mombasa (where the whole cultural milieu is pervaded by Islam). But she added in English, and very vehemently, 'Oh boy, you die from the heat!'

For these young people English plays a second role, since it establishes them as educated people, heirs to future high status, power and good jobs. Their use of English can be said to be, in fact, the mark of the élite-in-training.

For the majority of people in Pumwani, however, English is an alien language. Their feelings about it were perhaps best expressed when Pumwani's new Maternity Hospital was opened, with great pomp and circumstance, by President Kenyatta and many other dignitaries. The first few speeches were all in English and the great crowd present began to stir restlessly. Then President Kenyatta himself rose to speak, and commenting that most people present could not understand English, he announced that he would give his speech in Swahili. The crowd showed its appreciation by much cheering and clapping.

4. TRIBAL VERNACULARS: SECRETS AND FRIENDSHIPS

Tribal languages play many roles in Pumwani. In two senses they are very important, whilst in a third sense they seem to be becoming less and less important. Thus, firstly, they are used as symbols of differentiation between different ethnic groups. Secondly, the degree to which people in Pumwani are at least superficially conversant with each other's languages is quite high. Thirdly, they could in some respects be said to be dying out since people of mixed parentage speak Swahili as their first language rather than a tribal language.

Monolingualism is almost unknown in Pumwani. Only two people in my sample could speak only one language, and in each case the language was Swahili. One of these people was a youth who had come fairly recently from Lamu, where Swahili is the first language of almost the entire population. The other was a girl from Tanzania whose father was a Zigua and whose mother was a Sambaa. People who speak only Swahili are not of course in any way inconvenienced in Pumwani, since Swahili is spoken in every sphere.

The rest of my sample were all multilingual, though for some of these this consisted of knowing their own tribal language and speaking Swahili and/or English as a second language. But sixty people (69.7 per cent) out of my sample of 86 claimed a knowledge of one or more local languages other than their own. Thirty-three said they could speak one other such language, eighteen claimed a knowledge of two, five a knowledge of four, and four a knowledge of more than four. In many cases this did not of course mean that the respondents were fluent in these languages. In many cases they knew only a few words. A constantly recurring phrase was 'Najua kuomba maji (I know how to beg for water).' I have also heard people on many occasions greeting people in their own language, even if they would not be able to say any more. But there were also quite a few people who claimed to be able to speak one or more other tribal languages quite well. Perhaps the largest claim was made by the Soga who worked as a *mganga's* assistant. In addition to his own Soga, he could speak Swahili and some Arabic. But in addition he claimed to be able to speak Ganda fluently (this being the language in which he was taught at school) and to speak Kikuyu, Kamba and Gusii moderately well. If this is any more than a claim, such wide language knowledge must be very useful to this man in his work.

The two most popular tribal languages for people to learn seem to be Kikuyu (mentioned in 60 per cent of the cases) and Kamba (mentioned in 40 per cent). This is understandable since it is members of these two ethnic groups who are most numerous in Pumwani. Many other languages were mentioned, however, ranging from Luo, Luyia and Ganda to Nandi and Nubi. When asked where they had learned these languages many said that they had learned them right there in Pumwani, from friends and neighbours of different ethnic groups. When asked in what contexts they used these languages they nearly all replied, 'To please people of other tribes'. This was stated so often that one can only think that people are aware of the importance of ethnic harmony in a multi-ethnic situation such as Pumwani. In view of the arguments which I have been presenting in this paper, it is of some interest that more Muslims than Christians learn other tribal languages than their own. Eighty-two per cent of the Muslims claimed to know one or more other tribal languages, compared with 52.8 per cent of the Christians. This is partly because the Christians are, by and large, more recent immigrants into Pumwani than the Muslims, but it also reflects the relatively greater degree of ethnic exclusiveness amongst the Christians. Muslims of many different tribes mix freely, and in so doing they learn a smattering of each others' languages.

Tribal languages may be used in Pumwani, however, to exclude others, and to symbolize the difference between one ethnic group and another. Thus one sometimes passes little groups of women working together out-side their houses and conversing in their common language. When visiting members of one's own ethnic group, it is usual for the tribal language to be used, unless there are people present who do not understand it (either people of another tribe, or people born in Pumwani), in which case only greetings will be exchanged and then there will be a switch back into Swahili. If matters are to be discussed which are private, again the tribal language may be used. In one rather exceptional case I found two women using the languages of their mothers to achieve the same end. Both of them had 'Swahili' fathers, and their first language was therefore Swahili. Both their mothers were Maasai, however, and both spoke Maasai. One of them told me that they used a mixture of Swahili and Maasai when they talked, 'but if we have secrets of course we use Maasai'. For some people their local language is very important and they fear that their children, born in Pumwani, may never speak it properly. Thus one man, a Ganda whose wife is also a Ganda, has a small son born and brought up in Pumwani. The boy speaks Swahili as his most fluent language, but his father and mother always address him in Ganda, and he replies similarly.

Even if tribal languages are used to symbolize ethnic exclusiveness, such loyalties are never completely divisive in Pumwani, simply because there are too many cross-cutting ties. Religion brings together people who are divided ethnically. People of the same group are not clustered

246

together in one house or street, but scattered. Relations between neighbours, between shopkeepers and customers, between friends and acquaintances, all these often cut across ethnic lines. Most important are the many marriages in Pumwani which unite people of different ethnic groups and create a network of relations of affinity across ethnic lines. It is interesting to see what happens to tribal languages in this event.

One woman remarked to me that children these days are forgetting their tribal language. This would not however seem to be true except in cases where the children are the offspring of a 'mixed' marriage, and here it is very marked. Thus 15.1 per cent of my sample could not speak a word of their father's language although they claimed to belong to his ethnic group. All these people were the children of ethnically mixed marriages, as were the few who said they could only speak a few words of their tribal languages. This is not to say that these people do not learn other tribal languages. More than half could speak their mother's language and many knew other languages too.[30] Thus tribal languages can only be said to be declining in the sense that a person cannot always speak his own. The reasons why a person does not learn his father's language may of course be many. In one case a young woman did not speak her father's language (Somali) simply because he divorced her mother and went away when she was very young. In some cases the interest of the children themselves may affect the process. Thus there are two sisters in Pumwani whose father is a Ganda and whose mother was a Kikuyu. One of the sisters speaks Ganda quite well, mainly because she has often gone to visit her father's relatives in Uganda. She also speaks Kikuyu. The other sister speaks neither language very well. On one occasion I was with her when she met a Kikuyu man whose Swahili was not very fluent, but with whom she nevertheless spoke in Swahili. When I asked her why she had not used Kikuyu she said that the man would have laughed at her if she had tried to use her 'bad' Kikuyu.

CONCLUSION

In this paper I have emphasized that the language of communication in Pumwani, and indeed of social life itself, is Swahili. Although other languages may play specialized roles, it is Swahili which a person most needs in order to live without difficulty in Pumwani. This came out very clearly in the answer to the last question in my schedule which concerned the language which the respondent would prefer to see as the national language of Kenya.

The answers to this question suggest two points. First, they indicate the language preferences of the respondents, and secondly they are a summing up of the logic of the language situation as it seems to the respondents themselves. Out of 86 respondents all but four said that Swahili should be the national language. The reasons they gave throw some light on the role which the people themselves ascribe to Swahili. At one extreme the answers were purely personal: 'If Swahili were the national language, then I should understand it'. At the other they were general statements such as 'Everyone knows Swahili'. In between these two extremes there was a range of interesting comments. Many people said that Swahili should be the national language because it was the language of towns, thus making it clear, I think, that they are aware of the role of Swahili as a lingua franca of urban life. There were several answers pointing out the fact that Swahili can be understood by those who have not gone to school: I think this answer expresses some of the resentment which ordinary people feel when they are confronted with officialdom and the élitist use of English.

A big group of answers—perhaps the most important of all in view of the arguments I have been putting forward in this paper—point out the role of Swahili in bringing together people of different ethnic groups, countries and races. 'Inasikizanisha watu (It causes people to hear one another).' 'Inaunganisha makabila yote katika Kenya (It brings together the people of all the Kenya tribes).' 'Swahili does not belong to any particular tribe' . . . 'Swahili belongs to everyone' . . . 'People from Tanzania and Uganda can understand it' . . . 'Even Europeans and Indians speak it' . . . and so on. I think that many people are aware of the important integrative role which Swahili plays—and especially in such a place as Pumwani. It is of some relevance to my argument that this answer was given far more by Muslims than by Christians. We also have to remember, however, that most people in Pumwani, unless they are very recent arrivals, speak adequate Swahili. Not one of the 86 respondents said they could speak no Swahili at all. In other words there is rarely a negative feeling about Swahili—attitudes are generally either positive or neutral.

The four people who said they would prefer a different language to Swahili as the national language of Kenya were certainly atypical. Three said they thought Kikuyu should be the national language. Two were Kikuyu women whose Swahili was not very good, and who argued plaintively that if the national language were Kikuyu they would be able to understand it better. The other person who suggested Kikuyu— a Soga—was probably being facetious. She said that Kikuyu should be the national language because the leader of Kenya was a Kikuyu. Finally there was one man who supported the present use of English as the national language, since this, he argued, made for 'clarity in industrial and national life'. This man was the best educated of all my respondents and had studied medicine abroad for several years. He returned home before completing his degree and now works as a trainee manager for East African Industries. He lives in Pumwani because this is where he was brought up and where all his family are. He belongs however to the élite, rather than to the working class of Pumwani.

In view of the overwhelming proportion of my respondents who favour Swahili as the national language it is gratifying to know that government policy concerning the use of English is now changing. After I left the field it was announced that Swahili would eventually be made the official national language of Kenya. A report in *The Guardian* of England (4 April 1970) quoted Mr Robert Matano, the Kenya African National Union's Acting Secretary General as saying that, 'Swahili should be spoken by all people at all times both officially and socially. Any Kenyan professing a knowledge of English or any other language and denying a knowledge of Swahili should be known as a Quisling'. Mr Matano said that the government should establish centres to teach Swahili. After 1974 anyone unable to join in discussion should be told, ' "It's just too bad", and conversation should continue in Swahili'.

If this policy is indeed to be implemented there could be no better study ground than Pumwani for the successful use of Swahili as a bond between people of different ethnic groups. Pumwani also offers a further lesson, and that concerns the important role which a group speaking Swahili as its first language can play in setting a linguistic standard for others to follow.

NOTES

[1] In August 1969, after I had left the field, the National Governing Council of Kenya's ruling party (KANU), under the chairmanship of President Kenyatta, resolved that Swahili be eventually adopted as the official national language of Kenya. In April 1970 this was reiterated by the Acting Secretary General of KANU (Mr Robert Matano), who announced that Swahili would become the national language of Kenya by 1974. A bill to initiate the necessary changes was promised in the near future. Meanwhile considerable public interest in the subject is manifested through debates in parliament, letters to the newspapers, discussions on radio and television and in the trade unions.

[2] The results of this questionnaire are intended to be suggestive rather than definitive since it was administered to only a very small sample. Owing to lack of time and the nature of Pumwani's population, I was unable to carry out a complete census survey on which to base a random sample. It would have been difficult for me to carry out any survey at all by direct questioning and to be assured of the validity of the results. Instead I worked indirectly through local assistants and surveyed altogether 31 houses before beginning the questionnaire. The largest number of these houses (21) was in the area designated as Phase I of the Housing Redevelopment Scheme (see below), whilst the other ten were scattered throughout Pumwani. I have no reason to think these houses were atypical in any way. They were chosen simply because either I or one of my assistants (who came from different ethnic groups and were of differen

religious affiliations) had personal links there. In these 31 houses lived 510 people (an average of 16.4 persons per house). 170 were men, 174 were women and 166 were children. To carry out my questionnaire I took a 25 per cent random sample of the 344 adults (people over 15 years) in these houses—a total of 86 persons, 42 men and 44 women. The interviews were carried out either by myself or by a local assistant, using Swahili as the medium of communication. All the figures given in this chapter were taken either from the 100 per cent sample of 31 houses or the questionnaire sample.

[3] Phase I of the rehousing scheme, involving one-fifth of Pumwani's people, began towards the end of 1969, after I had left the field. The landlords of one section of houses have been moved into the new flats, but their tenants still (mid-1970) remain behind in the old houses, now as tenants of the Nairobi City Council. It is not yet clear what will happen to these people. The entire scheme is designed to take five years, and should be completed by 1975. I shall here describe Pumwani as it was in 1968–9 and shall only deal with the Housing Redevelopment Scheme in so far as it had affected social relations in Pumwani at that time.

[4] The history of the founding and development of Pumwani has been written up in a Berkeley Ph.D. thesis (K. J. McVicar, *Pumwani: The Twilight of an African Slum*, 1968).

[5] The word 'hotel' (Swahili *hoteli*) means here a cafe or eating house rather than a place where people put up for the night.

[6] *Miraa* is a plant grown in Meru country. The stalks of it are chewed and have a stimulating effect. Lorry drivers often use it to keep awake on long journeys. One street in Pumwani is devoted almost entirely to *miraa* stalls.

[7] Thus McVicar in 1965 estimated the population of Pumwani to be about 11,000. A survey carried out by the Department of Social Services and Housing (Nairobi City Council) in 1964 came up with the figure of 9,347 (see J. P. Mbogua, *Pumwani Estate Social Survey*, unpublished manuscript, Nairobi, September 1965).

[8] This should be compared with figures given by Marc Ross (1968) for Shauri Moyo and Kariakor Estates, in each of which he conducted a sample survey. The average length of residence in Nairobi of those in the Shauri Moyo sample was 12.3 years, whilst those in the Kariakor sample had lived in Nairobi on average 6.2 years.

[9] Compare the percentages of men, women and children in the 31 Pumwani houses surveyed (33.3 per cent, 34.1 per cent and 32.6 per cent respectively) with the percentages for Kaloleni Estate, which has 32.9 per cent men, only 17.9 per cent women and 49.2 per cent children (D. Parkin, personal communication). Not all the children, in this case, belong to the adults involved, many are simply being brought up by them—often they are relatives' children. In Shauri Moyo there were 2.1 men for every woman, and in Kariakor 1.8 (Ross 1968).

[10] For the purposes of this paper I use the terms 'tribe' and 'ethnic group' (or category) interchangeably. They are simply shorthand terms to denote a category of people, all of whom are called by one name. I have taken a person's 'tribe' to be the same as that of his father since that is the usual usage in Pumwani. Such categories are recognized by the people themselves as of significance in certain contexts and they use the Swahili word *kabila* or occasionally the English word 'tribe' to denote them.

[11] Out of my sample of 86 persons, 35.4 per cent were the children of a tribally mixed marriage. Again this can usefully be compared with Kaloleni where only 4.23 per cent of all the marriages of household heads are ethnically mixed (D. Parkin, personal communication).

[12] In the sample 50 out of the 86 people were Muslims (58.2 per cent) and 36 were Christians (41.9 per cent). Of the latter 24.4 per cent were Protestants, and 17.4 per cent Catholics.

[13] Very often the Muslims have no rural home, since many of those who were born outside Nairobi were not born in rural areas but in towns, such as Nyeri, Murang'a or Machakos. Of the Muslims in my sample, 32 per cent were born in Nairobi, 34 per cent in other towns, and 34 per cent in rural areas. This should be compared with the Christians in the sample, 5.5 per cent of whom were born in Nairobi, 27.7 per cent of whom were born in other towns, and 66.6 per cent of whom were born in rural areas.

[14] A room in Pumwani costs generally between sh.20 and sh.40 a month to rent. This is in contrast to the somewhat higher rents elsewhere in the city. In Eastleigh, for example, a room may cost as much as sh.150 a month. Rents in city council estates are cheaper than this, but it is not so easy to get a house there.

[15] In using the term 'community' to apply to Pumwani's Muslims I am well aware of the extent to which the unit I describe differs from an isolated village. Pumwani Muslims are not physically isolated from the Christians in Pumwani, and although most of their social links are within Pumwani itself, they also interact with people outside Pumwani, with employers in the town centre and the Industrial Area, and with other Muslims living in other Nairobi estates such as Eastleigh or Kibera. Nevertheless the character of Pumwani is so distinctly different from other Nairobi estates such as Ofafa or Makadara that one is tempted to describe it as an 'urban village'—a term employed by Gans to describe an Italian community in Boston (H. Gans, *The Urban Villagers*, The Free Press, New York, 1962).

[16] In 1952–9 the British were engaged in fighting against a group of Kikuyu (the so-called Mau Mau) who challenged their right to Kikuyu land.

[17] Since the present rulers of Kenya are Christians.

[18] In November 1968 there were 55 boys and 67 girls on the register of the *madrasa*, and in March 1969 there were 81 girls and 58 boys on the register of the other Qur'an school in Pumwani (136 girls and 125 boys altogether).

[19] There are a few elderly women on the *madrasa* committee, but no women on the mosque committee. Moreover, the role of the *madrasa* committee is mainly to raise money for the *madrasa*, not to carry out religious tasks.

[20] There are mosques in East Africa—though they are rare—which are partitioned, so that women may attend prayers without being seen by men. There is one of this kind for example at Machakos.

[21] A considerable body of taped material on the varieties of Swahili in Nairobi including Pumwani Swahili has been collected by the Survey and awaits detailed analysis.

[22] Compare this example with those discussed by C. M. M. Scotton in her 'A Look at the Swahili of Two Groups of Up-country Speakers', *Swahili*, 39, 1 and 2, 1969, pp. 101–10.

[23] These examples were taken from tape recordings which I made of Pumwani Swahili in May 1969.

[24] On some parts of the coast, to call someone a 'Swahili' used to imply that he had slave rather than freeborn ancestry. Freeborn people had specific clan names whereas slaves had none.

[25] About one-third of the houses in Pumwani are owned by people with Muslim names, slightly more than one-sixth by people with Christian names. Others have tribal names from which one cannot tell their religious affiliations. Thirty-five per cent of the landlords are Kikuyu; Kamba own 10 per cent of the houses, Nandi another 10 per cent and the rest are owned by people from many different tribes.

[26] Thus two men were members of the Luo Union which has its headquarters in Kaloleni, one was a member of a body-building club in Eastleigh, another a member of the YMCA in Shauri Moyo, and two were members of rural associations.

[27] Thus one pamphlet for example spoke of, 'Flats in a vertical section'.

[28] The importance of English in the political sphere is indicated by the fact that in the Kenya General Election of December 1969 two Pumwani Muslims were unable to stand for Kamukunji constituency because they failed to pass the compulsory English test.

[29] Most Muslim women in Pumwani wear these *buibui*. It is only a few young and generally well educated women who have abandoned the practice.

[30] In some cases where the respondent was of mixed tribal parentage he might claim to speak the tribal vernacular of his mother as well as, or instead of, that of his father. There were fifteen cases like this amongst the sixty people who claimed to know more than one tribal vernacular. But many of these people could speak more than just their mother's tribal tongue.

REFERENCES

GANS, H. *The Urban Villagers*, The Free Press, New York, 1962.

MBOGUA, J. P. *Pumwani Estate Social Survey*, unpublished manuscript, Nairobi (NCC), 1965.

McVICAR, K. B. *Pumwani: the Twilight of an African Slum*, Ph.D. thesis, Berkeley, California, 1968.

ROSS, MARC H. *Politics and Urbanisation—Two Communities in Nairobi*, Ph.D. thesis, Northwestern University, 1968.

SCOTTON, C. M. M. 'A Look at the Swahili of Two Groups of Up-Country Speakers', *Swahili*, 39, 1 and 2, 1969, pp. 101–10.

10

Language Use within the African Independent Churches of Nairobi

DAVID AOKO

INTRODUCTION

Many different religions flourish in Nairobi, and among the most colourful are those of the African 'separatist' churches. These were formed by African Christians breaking away from the established mother churches or Western Christian churches. Most of them are found in the locations where the members hold meetings in the open air, though some use public halls or private houses.

The services normally start in the morning and go on till late in the afternoon. Most of them are held on Sundays, though some take place on Saturdays and Fridays. There are many of these sects in the city but the best known are listed in Table 10.1, together with their areas of concentration (Table 10.2).

Some of these churches have a well arranged liturgy of worship, as does for example the Maria Legio of Africa. Their services could be mistaken for Roman Catholic ones since they even go as far as to read the liturgy in Latin, though they normally conduct services in Luo or Swahili. English is rarely used—only when there is someone who cannot understand either of the other languages. Swahili is rapidly becoming a common language as other members of this sect are now joining from other tribes. However, Maria Legio draws many of its followers from among Luo.

When the 'padre' is giving a sermon he speaks in more than one language: Luo, Swahili and a bit of English (only when a visitor is there or when there is a large congregation in which other tribes cannot be specified).

The African Israel Church Ninevah has a particularly dramatic type of service. Its adherents use drums, bells and tambourines which produce music of a high pitch and colossal noise. While the instruments are being played, all the members dance vigorously to the music. Some jump in the air like tribal dancers and finally some start to speak in tongues; this is when they say the Holy Spirit is with them.

Most of these sects take off their shoes when they meet to pray. They say that God said to Moses the first time He spoke to him that wherever one stood to speak to God was a holy place.

The separatists usually do not wear ordinary clothes, except for a few like the Church of Christ in Africa. Some wear turbans like the Sikhs.

'SPEAKING IN TONGUES'

Most of the independent church members whom I have heard 'speaking in tongues' seem to mix words from languages of different tribes in Kenya. It is sometimes difficult to understand what a possessed person talks about. If one is fortunate enough to be able to understand every word from each language, especially when a possessed person 'speaks in tongues', one may then be able to build the words into a complete sentence and bring some meaning to it. For example, the words may come from Kamba, Luo, Kikuyu, Luyia and Swahili. Consider the following example: **Ngai ciana ka hano penda,** which translated word by word yields, 'God children here loves'. The first two words are from Kamba/Kikuyu, the third from Luo, the fourth from Luyia and the final word is from Swahili. No attempt is made to bring them into grammatical relation with one another; they are simply strung together.

HEALING SERVICES

Healing services are held when prayers are offered for the sick with the hope of curing their diseases. If, for example, the sick people want prayers to be offered for them, they must first pray in their own languages. If they find it helpful, however, they may use any language, either Swahili or English as the patient prefers.

Healing is not guaranteed but each person is convinced that God will help. Healing services are marked by the laying on of hands or offering special prayers which are said only by the leader in his local language. Each church uses a different way of healing; some, as has already been mentioned, lay on hands; others say general prayers in different languages, that of the sick and that belonging to the founder of the sect. For example the African Israel Church Ninevah use Luyia and the Nomiya Luo Church use Luo for periods of up to thirty minutes.

BAPTISM

Baptism is by water, just as in some 'historical' or the European churches.

254

On one occasion I observed a group from one of these sects which did not take care where it held baptism ceremonies. Instead of going to a clean swimming pool or a river with fresh water, it decided to go to the Gitathuru River at its outlet from the city, near Kariobangi Estate.

At the river two men were brought forward and waded into the uninviting orange-coloured water of the river up to their waists. They stood together, as they were told to in Kikuyu, for some time and prayers were later said in Swahili both by the leaders on the bank and the audience. The leader who was to baptize the men held his arms high above his head with the New Testament in Kikuyu in his hands and in Swahili called the man to be baptized to come along.

Eventually, the man to be baptized waded further out, up to his chin, and finally was submerged. As he submerged the leader spoke to him in Kikuyu and asked him to keep the Christian faith as a real Christian. As he surfaced and began to wade ashore, the congregation on the bank shouted 'Halleluyah' and clapped their hands, singing hymns in Kikuyu and Swahili.

This continued while the two sodden members of the congregation attempted to squeeze the water out of their clothes. The people who watched the event wondered why such dirty water was used.

People who have not accepted independent churches as real churches do not believe they can celebrate Holy Communion. Not all the independent churches celebrate the communion service. Some say that they already have the Holy Spirit representing the Body of Christ within them, so what they wait for is the second coming of Christ in the world.

MARIA LEGIO AT COMMUNION SERVICE

On several occasions I have attended communion services of Maria Legio, the Church of Christ in Africa and the African Brotherhood Church. Most of these groups do almost the same things as the churches from which they broke away. Maria Legio of Africa is a breakaway from the Roman Catholic church, the Church of Christ in Africa from the Anglican church, and the African Brotherhood Church broke away from the African Inland Mission (now the African Inland Church).

For example, a celebrant of the Maria Legio of Africa wears white, with a green cotton chasuble and stole and purple manuple (vestment) and no shoes. He reads at a great speed from the Roman Catholic missal in Latin, translating it into Luo several times.

There are always four candles on the altar. The host is covered in a white cloth with a red cross on it, and the congregation sings in Luo while the celebrant is receiving the Body of Christ.

Incense smokes from a tin can placed on the ground near the altar. Bells ring at appropriate parts in the service while the singing continues in Luo very smoothly and quietly.

Communicants are from the age of 14. They must dress in white and those who are not in white borrow from others before going up to the altar. The whole service is conducted in Luo. The reason why the Maria Legio say they want to use the vernacular is because Luo is the language of the holy father. The holy father is said to have founded the sect in 1962, but the story of Maria Legio goes back as far as 1952, when the prophetesses Mariam Ragot and Gaudencia Aoko were both said to have founded the sect. The two women were Luo of Nyanza Province.

CHOOSING A LEADER

Normally an executive committee sits with the chairman, secretary and treasurer. No other leader can replace the holy father (the prophet), Simeon Ondeto, but other junior officers can be replaced by vote. The group speaks in the vernacular, which is Luo, at every committee meeting.

AFRICAN ISRAEL CHURCH NINEVAH

(a) A TYPICAL SERVICE

The prayers start at normal speed, everybody kneeling down. The leader, speaking sometimes in the founder's language—Luyia—or Luo, says one or two prayers in either language then asks others in the congregation who may be willing to pray to do so. Normally he would pray in Luyia but sometimes in Swahili if others from different tribes are present. After prayer all sit down.

The drum beat then starts; the drummers are allowed to lead a hymn with the rhythm, and continue for some time while the leader finds out from new people whether they come from tribes other than his own (Luyia). If these are numerous, he will start the service again in Swahili. This will last for about forty-five minutes.

After the Swahili service the whole congregation, comprising perhaps Luo, Luyia, Kikuyu and Kamba, will state where they come from in Swahili, whether they had been to the group before or not. During the course of the service everyone tries to recall any sins he might have committed during the past week. During this time no one is allowed to talk or make any kind of sign. Then one by one people start going to tell the leader what problems they have so that they can be prayed for. This

256

is done in any language which the leader can understand. When everyone has repented of their sins, they sing a hymn or two in Swahili. Later there is another prayer for the closing, which is always in Swahili, and finally a hymn in Swahili.

When they pray for their own sins, sometimes they pray in their own language while standing gazing upwards. The sick people are called to the front and state their sicknesses. They are asked, if they do not know what to call the disease, just to mention it in their own languages. Again, every sick person is asked in Swahili to come out or stand up while they are being finally prayed for in Swahili. Everybody in the service will pray for the sick, saying prayers in Swahili. People do not pretend that they are sick, they must be really sick, feeling physically unwell. They believe that with the power of the Holy Spirit they always get cured immediately.

This practice illustrates that the sect does not stick to one language during the service; it keeps shifting from one language to another— Luo, Luyia, Swahili—and sometimes would even go as far as using English if there were someone who could not understand any of the languages used.

During the middle of the service a raucous yelling and howling in both Luo and Luyia languages begins. That means the whole house is busy; the windows are all shut and curtains are drawn.

Some of the people in the congregation who are very much affected by the divine power fall down unconscious. This is when they believe they are possessed by the Holy Spirit and must be left alone, not to be disturbed or touched. The language they use then is not understood; it is said they 'speak in tongues'. After they have regained their strength they all pray in one language—Swahili—then leave for their homes quietly.

(b) A VISIT TO THE PROPHET'S HOME

The Rt. Rev. M. P. D. Zakayo Kivuli, who is the leader and founder of the African Israel Ninevah, lives eleven miles from Kisumu towards Kakamega. His home is five miles from the main Kakamega road. To get there you have either to hire a truck or go on foot as public vehicles rarely go there, if at all.

As is typical of the leaders of the African-founded denominations, the Rt. Rev. Zakayo Kivuli wore a white robe with red bands from the shoulders running the whole length of the robe. The name African Israel Ninevah is clearly printed across his chest.

He sat, with a woman whom I thought wrongly to be his wife, by the door of what I should call 'Church House' for that is where he lives. He is a Muluyia but speaks Luo so fluently that you might mistake him for a Luo. Someone who had shown us the way there told us, in Swahili, to stop for a little while and went to announce our presence and our desire to speak to him. When he came back he said to us, in Swahili again, that we could see him and took us to the reception room.

The Rev. Kivuli welcomed us very warmly. 'You are most welcome here, please sit down. What can I do for you?' He spoke in Swahili because he had already been told we did not speak Luyia.

'We are in Nyanza from Nairobi, and have come to know something about the African Israel Church Ninevah. We shall be particularly interested in how it was started, where the other branches are and which tribes are members of the sect.'

He sent for his secretary and meanwhile asked where our homes were and whether we could speak Luo. When he had learned we could, he began to speak to us in that language. The secretary came and they (Kivuli and the secretary) spoke in Luyia for some time. Then the secretary spoke to us in fluent English:

'The Bishop says', the secretary told us, 'you can direct all questions to him and since you can understand Luo he prefers to speak in that language to Swahili.'

The Rev. Zakayo Kivuli spoke in Luyia to the secretary again, who then disappeared into some room and presently came back with large files. Rev. Kivuli gave us the papers he thought were relevant to read. All were written in English. It was a brief history of the church. Then he began to tell us in Luo how he had thought of starting African Israel Church Ninevah.

'When I was a young boy I attended a school run by Pentecostal Assemblies of East Africa (PAEA). Later I was baptized in this denomination. As a young man I went to Kabete Jeanes' School (now Kabete Technical School) to be trained as an agricultural instructor. I worked for three years as an instructor, before I left to work with the church.

'I continued preaching with the white missionaries until 1939, when some African church leaders began to envy my position. I did not mind this but went on with my good work until their envy had turned into hatred. I could not bear this. How could I be expected to work among people who did not like me? So I asked permission from the Rev. O. C. Keller who was PAEA missionary then, to let me start my own denomination. He agreed and said should I fail he would welcome me back again.

'I had been thinking of this for many years. I thought, for example, of building a gigantic house without the help of a white man and writing my name in very big letters by the door so that when any white man wanted to enter I should tell him "Ah ha! That's not your house, can't you read the name on the door?"

'I went on preaching. I used only one language, sometimes two— Luyia and Luo—until 1941. Then I had enough followers to ask for registration. In 1942 my denomination was then very well known. I later registered it with the name "African Israel Church Ninevah", previously known by people as "Uhuru Israel Church". As you might have realized all members of the African Israel dress in white garments and men wear white turbans whereas women put on their heads white handkerchiefs. This is because in heaven there is no distinction between men and women. We do this to keep reminding ourselves of this fact.'

He went on to tell us in Luo that polygamy was not allowed but anybody who had already married more than one wife at the time of conversion could be accepted. An existing member wishing to be a polygamist is excommunicated.

THE NOMIYA LUO CHURCH

This sect has many kinds of different services; one for Sunday and others for special occasions, such as the circumcision of boys, planting and harvesting. All these are in Luo.

THE SUNDAY SERVICE

The Sunday service is open to all and lasts for two hours. In Nairobi the congregation gathers in private buildings. Sometimes they hold the meeting in a hall. Each Sunday all the members sing along the streets of Nairobi in their vernacular which is Luo. The whole service is conducted by one person with several others who are his helpers. The Bible is read either by the priest or a member of the congregation who stands up in the middle of the congregation to read. There are hymns in both traditional and Western tunes. For traditional tunes African musical instruments are played, such as the African drum, home-made trumpet and bells. The Nomiya Luo Church followers believe that the founder of the sect is a messiah because they say that he has made them see the way of salvation.

There is no translation of their prayers into any other language; the writings are all in Luo, if it is a Christian prayer. I say this because the Nomiya Luo do also use Islamic prayer books and even the Qur'an translated into Swahili. So basically the Nomiya Luo sect use two languages, Luo and Swahili.

APPENDIX A

Details of some African Independent Churches in Nairobi

Church	Founder	Secession from
1. Maria Legio Church of Africa	The holy father Simeon Ondeto	Roman Catholic, Kisii
2. Church of Christ in Africa	The Archbishop Matthew Ajuoga	Anglican, Maseno
3. Nomiya Luo Church	Prophet Johana Owalo	CMS, Butere
4. Musanda Holy Ghost Church	Alfayo Odongo	CMS, Butere
5. African Greek Orthodox Church	Not completely independent	Greek Orthodox
6. African Israel Church Ninevah	Rt. Rev. Zakayo Kivuli	Pentecostal Assemblies of East Africa and Friends' African Mission
7. Divine Christian Church	Jacob Buluku	African Divine Church
8. African Divine Church	Daniel Sande	FAM
9. African Brotherhood Church	Simeon Molande	African Inland Church
10. Red Cross African Church		PAEA
11. Christian Holy Ghost Church	Joshua Mburu	PAEA
12. Holy Trinity Church in Africa	Bishop Meshak Owira	Anglican
13. African Independent Pentecostal Church	J. Kinyua	PAEA
14. Holy Spirit Church of East Africa	Saulo Chabuga	PAEA
15. God's Word & Holy Ghost		FAM
16. Kenya Foundation of the Prophets	Not known	
17. Sinai Church of E.A.		Holy Spirit

TABLE 10.1 *The independent churches of Nairobi*

Tribal group	Church	Congregations Known	Located	Number of adherents
Luyia	African Church of the Holy Spirit	7	5	142
	African Divine Church	1	1	23
	Divine Christian Church of East Africa	2	2	70
	Red Cross African Church	2	2	4
	Sinai Church of East Africa	1	1	11
	African Israel Church (Wakorino)	5	3	327
	African Greek Orthodox Church	1	1	220
Kikuyu	Servants of Christ	3	2	58
	African Independent Pentecostal Church of Kenya	1	1	69
	Christian Holy Ghost Church of East Africa	1	1	32
	God's Word and Holy Ghost Church; Kenya Foundation of the Prophets	1	1	15
	Holy Ghost Church of Kenya Murengeti	1	1	340
Mainly Luo	Church of Christ in Africa	2	1	138
	Maria Legio of Africa	4	3	166
	Nomiya Luo Church	1	1	169
	Musanda Holy Ghost Church	1	1	24
	Holy Trinity Church in Africa	1	1	100
	Power of Jesus Around the World	1	1	24
Mainly Kamba	African Brotherhood Church	2	2	250
Mainly Luo and Luyia	African Israel Church Ninevah	2	2	133
	Holy Spirit Church of East Africa	4	1	30
		44	34	2,345

261

TABLE 10.2 *Areas of concentration of independent churches in Nairobi*

Languages spoken	Number of different churches known to meet in the area	Not located during the survey
A. Kamba, Luo, Luyia, Kikuyu (Areas of concentration: Makadara, Ofafa, Jericho, Maringo, Mbotela, Bahati, Jogoo Rd.)	12	3
B. Luyia, Luo, Kikuyu (Areas of concentration: Shauri Moyo, Kamukunji, Muthurwa, Pumwani, Gorofani, Bondeni, Landhies Market.)	13	3
C. Luo and Swahili (Areas of concentration: Kaloleni, Makongeni.)	3	—
D. Luo and Kikuyu (Areas of concentration: Kariakor, Starehe, Eastleigh.)	4	3
E. Luo and Luyia (Areas of concentration: Kariobangi, Ruaraka.)	4	2
F. Luo, Kikuyu and Luyia (Areas of concentration: Westlands, Dagoretti Corner, Kibera.)	4	3
G. Kikuyu (Area of concentration: Rironi.)	1	—
	41	14

11

Language Use among the Asian Communities

BARBARA NEALE

INTRODUCTION

Kenya Asians are a highly urbanized minority of overseas Indians with a current population of 174,000 largely located in the two main centres of Nairobi (about 50 per cent) and Mombasa (about 25 per cent). Others are settled in all of the towns, with a small, rapidly decreasing minority in the rural areas. Statistics from the 1962 census are included in the appendix, for reference, but settlement figures for all towns have been outdated by a population shift to Nairobi and emigration from Kenya. All sections of the Asian population are heavily involved in the Kenyanization of government service and trade, and all statistics relating to their current distribution are subject to rapid change: current estimates of the impact of Kenyanization are discussed in Part 2 of this chapter, and the 1962 census provides comparable data on their settlement patterns in the recent past. The total population has decreased by some 2,000 since 1962, with the emigration of approximately 18,000 Asians in 1968-9. Two-thirds of the Asians are Kenya-born, but citizens are a small minority of 45,000 and further reductions in the Asian population are expected in the near future.

Asians have been in Kenya for 70 years or more, and their occupations have been diversified over the years (see Chapter 2), but traders have always been the dominant section of the Asian population and they have controlled much of the retail and wholesale trade in Kenya. Asians in other occupations are often associated with the trading section, by descent, and the population as a whole has a strong vested interest in maintaining the Kenya Asian communities, the institutions which have enabled the traders to rise from fairly humble beginnings to their present position as prosperous traders and industrialists. All are divisions of the Asian population, and their existence is a mixed blessing to the Asians

263

who also see their communities as a threat to the political solidarity which was their main defence against the European settlers and the colonial government in the long struggle to establish the Asian right to trade in the White Highlands of Kenya. McGregor Ross provides a lively account of the conflict in his report on *Kenya from Within* (1927), and a sober discussion of the relationships of Asians and Europeans in his chapter 'The Issue'.

Kenya Asians have modernized their social patterns over the years and their current standard of living, for example, far exceeds the picture presented by Ross of the small unsanitary accommodation in the congested Indian bazaar; earnings are well below those of Europeans but significantly higher than Africans. 1.1 per cent of the Africans and 22.2 per cent of the Asians employed in private business and commerce earned more than £900 in 1966 when 28.3 per cent of the Europeans were earning more than £2,400, and 2.2 per cent of the Africans in public service earned more than £900 when 37.1 per cent of the Asians earned more than £720 and 32.6 per cent of the Europeans more than £2,400.[1] Seven Asian industrialists, all non-citizens, are among the top 50 directors listed in *Who Controls Industry in Kenya?*, and three other Asians are members of the management board of the Federation of Kenya Employers.

Asian communities provide a wide and useful set of connections for the trader, with branches in other countries of East Africa and abroad, and sanction the taking of risks which would give another man pause; all are endogamous in Kenya, as in India, and the members of a community are, therefore, relatives or prospective relatives with a commitment to the family and the family firm. Other groups of Asians are also described as communities, and my use of the term is not restricted to these caste groups; the system of arranged marriage is associated with caste communities and one tends to focus on these, but Asians use the term 'community' for any reference group which provides some sort of welfare service or facility (school, place of religion, meeting hall, etc.). Kenya Asians were organized by community to meet the challenge of urban segregation in the colonial period, and their leaders regard their extensive facilities with mixed feelings, proud of the capacity of the people to cope with their enforced seclusion but also concerned to reduce their strong identification with these multiple subdivisions of the Asian population. Numerous associations have been formed with an inter-community focus, or an all-Asian focus, and a balance of sorts has been achieved: Asians can find all of their associates within the family-community, but they can also join groups with a more diversified membership, like the Punjabi Poets' Society which takes in any interested Punjabi, and the Orient Art Circle which takes in any interested person, Asian or non-Asian.

Nairobi has a great many of these diverse associations, other towns have less, but this is only to be expected: settlement patterns of Kenya Asians are related to their occupation and not to their community, and all towns have some associations. Individuals have a family, home and a community religion, but their recreations do not always focus on the home or the community, and their tendency to identify with the community is diffused.

Asians are not wholly isolated from other Kenyans in any of these domains and one cannot look at their relationships with other Asians and omit the African servant in the home, the African or European convert (or co-religionist) in the religion, and the African and European members and guests in their recreations. Contacts with non-Asians are more numerous in other domains like work and education, but one finds a few in their recreations and religions, and African servants are employed by a very large majority of Asian households. Some statistics are given in my discussion of language choice in Part 2 of this chapter, but much of my information on personal networks is derived from my own field work and from language diaries by Asian students. Five domains for language use emerged in my study of Asian social patterns in 1968–9, with a fairly clear division between their private (i.e. inter-Asian) domains of home, religion and recreation, and their public domains of work and education. Personal networks are filled with contacts with Asians in all domains, but non-Asians are largely concentrated in the two domains of work and education.

Some Asians are still active in politics, but direct lines to sources of political power are rare today when Asians are not encouraged to participate in politics; this domain is inactive by Asian standards, or, as they say, 'now defunct'. Asians were surprised, and shaken, by the Trade Licensing Act of 1969 and two committees were formed to bring whatever pressure could be brought upon the governments concerned with their citizenship, but both were soon disbanded at the request of the Kenya government. Asians realized then, if they had not already realized, the futility of political action in Kenya by non-citizens and no further efforts were made. Most of their political leaders 'retired' after independence, and are now engaged in other activities, and their current leaders are men who devote much time to Asian associations and to their communities.

Social patterns were clearly disrupted by the shift from a colonial to an African government, but reduced contacts with other Kenyans in politics have been balanced, to some extent, by the integration of the Asian schools. The colonial period was marked for Asians by seclusion in home, religion, recreation and education, and inclusion in work and politics. The present is marked by seclusion in home, religion and recreation,

265

and by inclusion in work and education. Education is thus transferred from seclusion to inclusion, while politics has ceased to be a viable domain.

Current language use of the Kenya Asian population is my primary focus in this chapter and my opening remarks are motivated by a desire to place them in a setting which is available to all Asians, i.e. to show where they can and cannot use their languages and with whom they are likely to be speaking. New social patterns are emerging with the passing of the plural society and my study is largely one of transitional language use in an immigrant society with a long history of seclusion from its host population of Africans and their European government. The social matrix of the Asian population has so far been maintained and their groups are still defined by region of origin in India and religion, with further subdivisions by caste and sect, but the remarkable symmetry of this system has been heavily reinforced by separate religious schools with different mediums of instruction and different subject languages, and one cannot project their current social patterns beyond the present. Asian children are now attending integrated schools with English as a medium of instruction and the Asian social groups may be diffused in the near future. Other immigrants, in other countries, find it difficult to maintain their identity in similar circumstances and some are simply absorbed by the national majority. Kenya Asians were not faced with this situation in the colonial period and each group was able to maintain, and reinforce, its own identity and, to some extent, its own patterns of language use.

Asians are multilingual now with an Asian norm of four languages, including three lingua francas (see Chapter 2) and all have made numerous additions to, and changes in, their social patterns. Contacts with other sections of society in Kenya did not result in any loss in the Asian sense of identity and one cannot describe them as assimilated in the usual sense of the term. Nor can one describe the Asian population as an accommodating minority, living in virtual isolation, learning just enough of the language to get by and avoiding all other forms of social interaction with the host population, thereby escaping the loss of identity which is associated with assimilation. Accommodation is still possible in Britain where most of the Indians are recent immigrants, still isolated from the rest of the population by a formidable language barrier and further isolated by some individuals who act as intermediaries between the two groups making it possible for new immigrants to live in Indian houses, buying their food from Indian grocers, and working under Indian foremen. Accommodation of this kind is virtually unknown in Kenya where the Asian population is older and more diversified and is, furthermore, part of a larger plural society which provides at least two sources of cultural interference—European and African—and sometimes a third in places like Mombasa where Asians are also in contact with an Arab population which has partly assimilated to local African models by adopting Swahili as its first language. Kenya Asians have maintained a distinct Asian sub-culture, not by accommodation but by a kind of adaptation, or selective imitation, borrowing what they needed or wanted from others and making these loans their own, as bilinguals borrow words from other languages and remodel them to conform to their own language. Borrowings from African models are almost exclusively linguistic but European loans are less restricted. The Goans, who have Westernized their surnames, dress, food and language, as they Westernized their religion, have borrowed freely from local models as they borrowed from the Portuguese in Goa. Other Asians have borrowed rather less freely directly from the Europeans in Kenya or indirectly from Westernized Asians in India, Pakistan, England and Canada. Resistance is slight in Kenya where the Asian élite conforms closely to its version of élite norms in cities like Bombay and Delhi, cities where English is the mark of the educated man and other forms of Westernization have become increasingly acceptable, even fashionable since independence.

Each section of the Asian population has adjusted in its own way and one needs some introduction to the cultural differences among Kenya Asians in order to understand their current social patterns and their language use. Both will be further discussed in Part 2 of this chapter, but the Asians are not identified as yet and I shall try to present them briefly in a short impressionistic survey in the next section, relating the social divisions of the current population to some of their more distinctive patterns of language use, with an emphasis upon the present situation and occasional forays into their past. Former Asian languages are seldom reported in secondary sources, and I shall try to fill the gaps. One can get a clear picture of social change in the Asian population from official documents and other studies, and I am largely concerned with the current scene; supplementary materials are listed in the bibliography, and a few are summarized below.

Mangat's recent study, *A History of the Asians in East Africa* (1969), is a comprehensive survey of their past, and readers are referred to other works like Makhan Singh's recent report on the *History of Trade Unionism in Kenya* (1969), and social studies by Ghai, Morris (largely Uganda Asians, but similar), Pocock, Bharati, and others.[2] Asian 'associations' have not attracted much attention, but Shanti Pandit's biographies, *Asians in East and Central Africa* (1963), include a detailed list of their communities and associations together with an extensive review of major trading concerns with histories of management, and Benedict's work on the family firm is a useful addition.

Little is available on the Kenya Asian situation in the post-independence period, but Desai's study of *Indian Immigrants in Britain* (1963) supplies comparative material on Asian counterparts in another urban society, and Srivinas' work on social networks in India supplies comparative material for their present society. Overseas Indians have been studied by many anthropologists in all corners of the former British Empire, and several different patterns of adaptation are noted, ranging from the East African Asian, who has maintained his own identity with no loss at all in most cases, to the Indian in Trinidad who cannot remember his own community. East African Asians are now entering a new phase, and their current patterns of adaptation are thought to vary from one country to the next with some attrition of Desai's picture of the *status quo* immigrants, dedicated to 'transplanting Indian culture and values by forming themselves into voluntarily exclusive communities and retaining contacts with India wherever economic conditions and means of communications permitted'.[3] Kenya Asians have done both, but their communities and their links with India were heavily reinforced by exclusion from European areas, schools and other facilities (hotels, hospitals, clubs, etc.), and social patterns may be very different in the future. Predictions would be premature at this stage and none are attempted, but the Asian population is clearly in transition and the patterns of social interaction and language use reported in this study are subject to rapid change.

Language repertoires of Kenya Asians have been outlined in another chapter, but differences in the Kenya Asian population have not yet been related to their social groups; Punjabis from north India have their own culture and their norms of language use, Gujaratis from the central region have theirs, and Goans from the south have theirs. All speak north Indian languages with a common ancestor in Sanskrit, but they cannot communicate with each other in these languages and they turn to a lingua franca in their inter-regional conversations as they would do in conversations with Africans or with Europeans. One can also find communities from a single region who have no common language, and the Gujaratis for example do not fit the broad regional pattern, but Asians think of themselves as people from Gujarat, Punjab and Goa and I shall describe them in this way.

Several smaller minorities from other regions in India are represented in the Asian population and all maintain a distinct sense of identity which makes it difficult to reduce the Asian population to a manageable number of ethnic groups; one can, however, recognize a large majority of Gujaratis (about 70 per cent), two large minorities of Punjabis (about 20 per cent) and Goans (about 9 per cent), and a number of 'others'. Some have distinctive patterns of language use in one domain like religion, and others do not, but all have something in their language use which sets them off from other Asians and much of my account will be concerned with 'regional' languages.

Each regional group also has one religion which is not shared with other Asians, but two major religions have members from Gujarat and Punjab and the people who belong to these religions call themselves Gujarati Hindus, Punjabi Hindus, Gujarati Muslims and Punjabi Muslims— focusing on their religion but also on their region of origin; others can simplify and state their religion alone since all Asians know where they came from and one finds Gujarati Jains as Jains (or Shahs), Punjabi Sikhs as Sikhs (or Singhs), and Goan Christians as Christians (or Goans). Seven major sub-groups are thus identified by this dimension of region and religion: the Gujaratis (Hindus, Jains, and Muslims), the Punjabis (Hindus, Sikhs, and Muslims) and the Goans (Christians).

Other Kenyans know the Sikhs by their turbans and beards and this group is as distinctive in Kenya as it is in India where the Sikhs, who call themselves the 'Lions of Punjab', adopted Singh (Lion) as a religious surname after they left the Hindu religion and formed their own, some 400 years ago. All have an intense devotion to their religion, which tends to divide them from the Hindus and Muslims from their own region, but the regional spirit survives and Punjabis often meet together simply as Punjabis with a common interest in their culture in general, and Urdu poetry in particular.

One can, therefore, look at their social patterns and think of the language of poetry as the language which binds one Punjabi to another, and the language of religion as the language which divides them; I shall focus on their languages in this way and try to relate them to their social patterns, but groups can also break apart or come together in other ways and one has, also, to consider other factors like their marriage customs, and their housing patterns. Asians have had a great deal of 'autonomy' in Kenya, by virtue of their social seclusion in the colonial period, and their focus on their regions of origin and their religions has been reinforced in a variety of ways.

Punjabis were chosen as my first example because they tend to reinforce their religions in an 'Asian' fashion, with religious schools and meeting halls; others from Gujarat and Goa do the same, but some groups also maintain private housing estates and one well known Gujarati community—the Shia Ismaili Muslims—has 'strengthened' its community by seclusion in its religion and housing and also by linguistic intermarriage, within the community. All are still clearly Gujarati, and the regional focus is maintained, but the Hindus and Jains, from the same region, reinforce their 'closeness' by meeting together for '*garba* dancing' and the Ismailis do the same dances by themselves.

All Kenya Asians use symbols of some kind to express their difference from each other, and patterns of this kind are easily related to cultural emblems like the flat turbans of the Namdharia Sikhs and the pointed turbans of the other Sikhs; examples can be multiplied almost indefinitely describing differences in surnames, dress, dietary habits, and marriage customs. Some, like the Sikh turban and beard, are traditionally Asian; others, like the European dress of the Goan and Ismaili women, are loans from Western models, and others, like the Zanzibari mixture of Cutchi and Swahili, are a combination of traditional and borrowed forms. Each must contrast with something, and the Zanzibar Asian speech might only be meaningful in Kenya where Asians use Swahili as a language of last resort in inter-Asian communication, i.e. as a language which may be used when no other language is shared. This negative approach to Swahili is shared by all Asians, and some sort of norm might be operating for the population as a whole—an otherwise unknown phenomenon, and one which deserves consideration. Asians might say, with a good deal of truth, that they cannot talk to each other in Swahili because they do not know how to express their thoughts; this does not deter them from using other languages (notably second vernaculars), and one cannot speculate about their attitude to Swahili.

Asians have other link languages like Hindustani and English for thought expression; Tanzanian Asians have adopted Swahili as an inter-Asian language, and Kenya Asians might do the same, but Tanzania has used Swahili as a national language for many years and Kenya has not.

Asians have no other norms for language use for the population as a whole, but some patterns can be associated with the primary divisions by region of origin in India. None can be associated with any geographical division in Kenya, and the solidarity of the Asian social groups is clearly related to the lack of division between the men of Mombasa for example, and the men of Nairobi. Many Kenya Asians have never seen India or lived outside an African town and the maintenance of their geographical distance from one another in India is a curious phenomenon. Some 4,000–5,000 of the total population of 174,000 are thought to be citizens of India, and Pakistan claims another 500 or less. The rest had no intention of returning before independence; English-speaking Goans who have lost all contact with their Indian mother tongue have the same focus as the others, and one hesitates to attribute it to language maintenance. Asians have not adopted African languages as first languages, and one cannot judge the effects: those who speak fluent Maasai, with 45 years or more of residence in Maasai country, still use Punjabi as a home language and count themselves as Punjabis. Religions can still be lost or changed, but region of origin has apparently joined caste as an inherited feature for Kenya Asians.

Caste is vigorously denied by some Kenya Asian religions, and their propensity to organize by religion and sect to provide their community facilities is often related to their history as an anti-caste religion in India. Sikhs and Muslims, for example, have no caste schools or caste clubs and the presence of these two religions in Kenya has done much to destroy the caste ranking and ritual pollution which separates one Indian from another in other countries. Goan Christians have maintained caste clubs in Kenya, and the Hindus and Jains have theirs. All prefer to support religious schools, and caste divisions are de-emphasized; people know them, but Asians who would not have been able to eat together in India have abandoned these divisions in Kenya. The 'most conservative' Visa Oshwal Jains are as liberated as the rest: Asians normally abide by the restrictions of their religion and one would not expect to find a Hindu eating beef, for example, or a Sikh smoking. But these restrictions present no problems if the people themselves are prepared to inter-dine and Kenya Asians are: caterers for a recent Lion's Club ball provided hard drinks for men, soft drinks for ladies, vegetarian meals for Hindus and Jains, non-vegetarian meals for Sikhs and Parsees who avoid beef and Muslims who avoid pork, and English puddings for all. Older people who were raised in India do not normally attend such functions but they are remarkably permissive about their children who do; dinners of this sort are generally regarded as harmless amusements, and often considered beneficial since they tend to reinforce the sometimes elusive sense of unity in the Asian population.

Asian unity seems to stop at the regional level in their patterns of language use, if one discounts the more general treatment of Swahili as a non-Asian language, but the relatively low incidence of markers for caste may well be related to their obvious distaste for highly specific divisions. Some patterns do mark castes, and the home language of the Hindu masons is in clear contrast to the home language of other Hindus: Asians think of them by sect, as Swami Narayan Hindus, and the caste marker is diffused. Patterns of this sort are dealt with below in my general survey, but I raise the matter here to point out the coincidence between the low incidence of caste languages in Kenya and the low content of caste (i.e. little ranking, ritual pollution, etc.). Others have remarked upon the ability of the Kenya Asians to modernize their social patterns, and my data on language markers seems to support the general picture of social mobility.

1. THE KENYA ASIAN PEOPLE

Kenya Asians are largely Gujaratis and one might begin with this group and then turn northwards to the Punjabis and southward to the Goans, but the geographical progression is then lost; so I will start with the north Indian minority of Punjabis, and then turn to the Gujarati majority from the central region, and the smaller Goan minority from the south. North Indians have always had a more turbulent history, with wave after wave of invaders pouring through their mountain passes, and the people of the north have a warlike spirit, and a military tradition, which has no parallel in the quieter areas of Gujarat and Goa. All are north Indians, by virtue of their language, but Punjabis keep a wary eye on the ferocious tribes of the mountains to the north, and the Gujarati focus on non-violence is not shared by the Punjabis.

(a) PUNJABIS

Some of the ferocious tribesmen are also present in Kenya, in small numbers, but the Kenya Asian Pathan is a highly Westernized version of his stereotype in India and the same is true of the Punjabi. Both are still quick to respond to any challenge, but they do not take up arms in Kenya and one finds Kenya Asians living together in a curiously archaic society with none of the fierce hostility that now divides the Muslim in Pakistani Punjab from the Sikh and the Hindu in the Indian Punjab.

Asian Punjabis are, moreover, noted for their resilience and their spirit was in no way impaired by their arrival in Kenya as indentured railway workers, with a 'coolie' image: 32,000 came (with some Gujaratis) in this role but most returned to India when their contracts expired, and the 6,000 who stayed on were presently joined by relatives and friends from their area in the Punjab (Amritsar-Jullundur-Ludhiana districts), and also by troops with a long tradition of service in the British Indian Army. Railway workers were largely farmers and artisans, but agriculture was reserved for Europeans and Africans so the Punjabis turned to other occupations; some became traders, like the Gujaratis, and others turned to the civil service and the professions, when they had the necessary education to do so. Some also stayed in immigrant roles as artisans and railway workers and the Punjabi population is characterized by occupational diversity which is not shared by the Gujaratis and the Goans who came as traders from Gujarat and clerks from Goa. Artisans came from both regions, and the Gujaratis and the Goans have also diversified by entering the civil service and the professions, but the Punjabis are found in every Asian occupation and their contacts with other Asians are more extensive.

Punjabis are also relative newcomers to East Africa, and their links with Asians in Tanzania and Uganda are weak, in comparison with the Gujaratis who have a long history of centuries of trade with the East African coast in general and Zanzibar in particular, and with the Goans who first came to Kenya with the Portuguese in the sixteenth century. Kenya Asians today are seldom descendants of these early immigrants and one does not find many adults who automatically became citizens at independence under the law which granted automatic citizenship to anyone with a Kenya-born parent. Gujaratis do, however, have close links with counterpart communities in Tanzania, and their marriages frequently cross international boundaries in East Africa. Punjabis look to other Punjabis in Kenya, by and large, and also to India, and their regional focus is reinforced by both. Religious groups are largely endogamous, in the Kenya Asian fashion, but Sikhs and Hindus do marry occasionally and their Kenya-born children tend to associate themselves with both religions, worshipping as Hindus, for example, but attending Sikh functions. All have smaller subdivisions by caste, and Indian castes do not intermarry freely, but Punjabis tend to focus on religion and their sense of caste is fragile. Anthropologists in India treat some castes as tribes, and the difference is not great: hillsmen to the north are tribes, and other Hindus (and ex-Hindus) are castes, but the Punjabis are geographically in the middle and their regional sub-groups have elements of both.[4] All associate themselves with some religion, and are often seen as religious subdivisions, but Punjabis do not think of them in this way: Africans might do the same by talking about Muslim Kikuyus, for example, and Christian Kikuyus, but the tribes are then swallowed up by the religion and Asians do not describe themselves in this fashion. A Punjabi may be a Sikh by religion, a Punjabi by birth, and a Jat by tribe and his description of himself can focus on all three characteristics or any combination.

(b) GUJARATIS

Punjabis in Kenya tend to focus on region and religion and the Gujaratis do the same if they are Muslims (with subdivisions by sect), but other Gujaratis focus on caste and their sub-regional communities are largely organized by religion and caste, or caste alone. Africans know the Patel Hindus by their caste surname of Patel, but other groups, like the Lohana Hindus with diverse surnames, are also organized by caste, and the Jains (or Shahs) do the same. I will not dwell on these communities

273

here, as one is apt to lose all contact with their larger regional groups when considering the communities; Gujarati Muslims and all Punjabis do, however, have a strong religious focus, and tend to socialize by religion where others tend to socialize by region and caste.

Gujaratis are a large majority in the Indian society as a whole and their contacts with other Asians are likely to be contacts with other Gujaratis, but this is true for other groups as well; everyone meets large numbers of Gujaratis and their 'trader image' has become the Asian stereotype in Kenya, where the Asian 'dukawalla' (shopkeeper) is the dominant theme.

Gujaratis were largely traders in their homes in India, but artisans are also represented in Kenya and both have 'upgraded' their occupations by prosperity or by branching out into the civil service, the professions (medicine, law, etc.), and industry. Many families include some Kenya-born adults who are carrying on the business and others with diverse occupations and their kinship networks are, in this sense, as heterogeneous as those of the Punjabis.

Gujarati families are, however, often led (or headed) by the trading section and they have maintained the principle of the large joint family in trade, with a common household if possible and a circle of nearby households, if not. Family firms also have branches in different towns in Kenya, where management is largely in the hands of Kenya-born adults, and may therefore include several household heads who are also 'managers'. Large joint households are common in Nairobi, and may also include several household heads under a single roof; one family in my survey sample had 18 adults and 11 children, and others achieve the same size with a circle of houses.[5]

Branches in other parts of Kenya were included in some sample genealogies, and Gujaratis emerged as families with 100–150 adults who kept in touch with each other, in Kenya alone. Others had smaller families and one cannot reduce the Kenya Asian population of 174,000 to 1,740 families (or less), but the large extended family is accepted as typical by Asians from Gujarat, Punjab and Goa. The large trading castes (and sects) are particularly prone to follow this model, but one also finds small castes like the Bhatias with a handful of families in Nairobi and two in Mombasa, with 320 members of one family in Mombasa alone.

Regional culture does not need a great deal of inter-caste reinforcement when it can be maintained by such large families, but Gujaratis do, nevertheless, mend some religious divisions by focusing on drama, dance and song. Gujarati Hindus and Jains share these activities and the Muslims dance alone, and their links are therefore weaker than those of the Punjabis who gather together in a common milieu of Urdu poetry. One excerpt from a language diary by a Nairobi student (non-Punjabi) gives a fair picture of the Punjabi pattern, which is in sharp contrast to the Gujarati model; the writer is a Pathan, and his friend Punja is an Ismaili and their inability to 'follow' is associated with their non-Punjabi status:

After dinner, went with Ali, a Muslim Punjabi, and Punja, an Ismaili, to a Mushaira. Mushaira is a gathering during which poetry is recited. This one was attended by all the leading Urdu poets in East Africa. Most of them, incidentally, were Punjabi and they talked in between recitations in Punjabi. Ali, who is very familiar with Urdu undoubtedly appreciated the Mushaira the most. Punja seemed lost and I could follow only in snatches. The Mushaira was organised to commemorate the centenary of the poet Ghalib. Hindus, Muslims, Sikhs all joined in warmly and the yardstick here was only a person's ability to write and recite verse. There was a singular lack of Brahmins, Cutchis and Gujeratis (both Hindu and Muslim). During the refreshments, however, I noted that different castes tended to group together and the talk seemed to change from poetry to almost petty gossip.

This writer uses the term 'caste' for any social group (e.g. 'I met a small cross-section of the various Asiatic castes today and conversed with them in a number of Asian tongues') and the term, as used above, can also be read as 'religions'. Another excerpt, from the same diary, illustrates the militant spirit of the north Indian Pathan (the writer) which is shared by the Punjabi:

During dinner discussed Urdu poetry with Jit, a Sikh who has done Urdu for school cert—later quarrelled with a Hindu Gujerati—verbal battle done in English, but appeals made to friends were in my case in Punjabi, and in his Gujerati. I lost temper and struck him on the nose—whereupon he discontinued use of English and cursed me in Gujerati and explained my brutality also in Gujerati. Gujeratis, by the way, seldom fight back.

Patterns of language use in these encounters will be discussed in the section on 'languages of recreation', but I quote them here to illustrate the role of language in inter-Asian relationships, between Punjabi sub-groups on the one hand and Punjabis and Gujaratis on the other.

Gujaratis do not fight, but they persevere and the hard-working, serious 'dukawalla' has built the economy of Kenya. Foreign companies are now there with large industries (largely British) and financial enterprises, but the Gujarati trader is widely recognized as the man who followed the early explorers (also British) and his Kenya-born sons are also represented among the industrialists.[6]

Perseverance was also among the more notable characteristics of the Gujarati statesman of India, the late Mahatma Gandhi, who devoted much of his life to the principle of removing the British from India by non-violent agitation. Kenya Gujaratis in general, and Hindus in particular, are warm admirers of Gandhi and the Indo-African Cultural Society was formed to impart his views to Africans, who were then engaged in a similar struggle against their colonial government. Relatives and friends in Zanzibar and Central Africa supported the Kenya-based society (largely Patels and Brahmins) and government reacted as might be expected; biographies of Gandhi and Nehru are still extant (in several African languages)[7] but 14,000 copies of Mulk Raj Anand's history of the struggle itself were confiscated and burned on the spot. Gujarati sponsors sought refuge in their religion (with translations of the Bhagavad-Gita in English) and the regional focus was replaced by religion. This is past history now, but I recall it in order to point out the Gujarati emphasis on regional culture, their links with others in Africa, and the role of language as a bridge across social divisions of all kinds. Very few Asians in Kenya are literate in Swahili, but this group included some from Tanzania and Kenya who were, and also went beyond the resources of its own repertoire to include languages of Rhodesia and Uganda.

Punjabis contacted Africans directly, through trade unionism, but their other efforts focused on religion and I will return briefly to their group to clarify the differences in approach. Each religion is now subdivided into a large majority of 'orthodox' members and a splinter sect, but the Sikh sect is a recent addition and can, for the present, be disregarded as its missionary efforts in Kenya are negligible. The parent body in Punjab has been active in Thailand and the leader visited the Kenya converts last year with a retinue of dignitaries from that country, but the larger Sikh religion has done its own missionary work in East Africa. Punjabi Muslims and Hindus also have large groups but their missionary activity is done by one small Muslim sect (the Ahmadiyya) and one Hindu sect (the Arya Samaj). Both have parent bodies abroad and the Ahmadiyya, who are small in Kenya, also do much missionary work in other parts of Africa with notable success. Africans in Kenya do not respond with much enthusiasm to Asian efforts to introduce them to their religions as the Arabs have already converted the would-be Muslims and the British the would-be Christians. But the Asians try, and the singular lack of missionary activity on the part of the British with respect to Asians in Kenya is in sharp contrast to the earnest endeavours of British counterparts in India. Asians were competing with them in Kenya and that may be the explanation, but one also notes the heavy concentration of non-Hindus in Kenya and realizes that a man who has already been converted to a dynamic religion like Islam or Sikhism is hardly likely to become a Christian. The American Protestant groups are active in Nairobi among the Asians and one finds serious American missionaries learning Gujarati and attempting to attract Hindus (who enjoy the film shows and libraries, but do not leave their religion), but the British have done nothing of the kind, and there is no missionary language bridge between the Kenya Asians and their former government.

Punjabi Asians do have missionary languages for use with Africans, but each group has its own and their choices are largely (but not entirely) in accordance with their parent groups abroad. Muslim Ahmadiyyas have adopted the pattern of the British missionaries in India, and their publications are produced in Swahili and other African languages, with a distinct preference for the vernaculars. African priests are also sent to their headquarters in Pakistan for training, if possible, and given 'parishes' in Kenya when they return. This group is, however, only a small pocket in the Ahmadiyya complex in Africa and their share of the funds is small, and shrinking. Manuscripts in African languages are there, awaiting funds for publication, but their major contribution to date has been the Swahili translation (with Ahmadiyya focused footnotes) of the Holy Qur'an, and numerous pamphlets and tracts in English. Other Muslims find their version of Islam somewhat alarming and their doctrine has not spread in the Asian population in Kenya.

Punjabi Sikhs also have very few converts, and their publications are largely pamphlets to introduce their religion to anyone who cares to listen: English and Swahili appear as missionary languages of a sort with non-Asians, but the English version also serves with other Asians and the Punjabi version is inexplicable since other Punjabis already know all about Sikhism. Sikhs do publish heavily for their own community in Punjabi, and one sees these efforts as a symbol of their religious devotion with no particular focus upon missionary work.

Punjabi Hindus of the Arya Samaj sect are also devoted to their version of Hinduism, which involves a return to the ancient worship of the Indo-Aryans who predate the current mainstream of Hinduism by 2,000 years or more. Vedic Sanskrit is used for their services with explanations in Hindi for those who cannot follow, but Arya Samajists do the same in India and this group is here working within the constraints of its religion. Africans are contacted in two languages—English and Swahili—and this pattern is seen as a local missionary set of languages: the Arya Samajists run a children's home in Nairobi and their contact language with these non-English-speaking children is Swahili (with some Hindi), but English is used with adult converts who have services of their own. Numbers are very small again, and the success of this group among Asians is clearly the dominant theme. Arya Samajists in India have focused heavily on 'progress' and stressed the importance of college education for women as well as men, but some think this is excessive and the Kenya sect has a small split between the 'college section' and the others. Professional men and women from other religions (notably the Sikhs) also contribute speeches to the Samaj functions, and help them as they can, and English is widely used in these speeches which are attended by some old people with no English at all, and a large majority of younger Asians who understand both languages (Punjabi and English) but cannot talk about scientific or philosophical subjects in Punjabi. Gujaratis also appear and one could regard the use of English as a bridge with the Gujarati section of the Arya Samaj; both, however, prefer English for philosophy and one tends to think of the Samaj missionary languages as English and Swahili with Africans, and Hindustani (called Hindi) with Asians.

Gujarati Hindus also focus on philosophy but they combine it largely with religion, where the Samaj dwells on education and their patterns are a little different. Members of the large mainstream Gujarati majority focus on English in organizations like the Theosophical Society (not a Hindu-based religion, but popular in India) which might be expected to attract Europeans (but not in Kenya), and their meetings are held in Gujarati one day a week and English on the other. Some talk of Gujarati alone is heard, but they do have occasional visitors, and the publications from India also appear in English, and no simplification has so far occurred. Punjabis have no interest in such religions, and field-workers like myself can be seriously misled into thinking that the Gujaratis and Punjabis in Kenya have a strong aversion to socializing with each other: one is struck by the heavy concentrations of Punjabis at some functions and Gujaratis at others and some time elapses before the poetry-education-religion focus of the Punjabis and the drama-*garba* dance-Gandhi-philosophy focus of the Gujaratis become clear. Bharati says they 'socialise by language' and he is quite right—but the language is associated with two different regional cultures.

Gujarati Hindus have a splinter sect of Swami Narayan Hindus and the religious distance between this group and the large orthodox majority is reinforced by a language split on the one hand and caste distance on the other. Kenya Asian Gujaratis include a majority of Gujarati-speaking Hindus, Jains, and Muslims from the Gujarati-speaking area of Gujarat and a minority of Cutchi-(or Kacchi-)speaking Hindus and Muslims from the Cutchi-speaking area, leading to one language for the Jains (Gujarati) and two for the Hindus and Muslims. The largest Hindu 'caste' of Patels includes both, and other Hindus are associated with Gujarati, leaving the Patels with a Cutchi-speaking minority of Swami Narayans (who are largely masons by traditional occupation) and a Gujarati-speaking majority of 'other Patels' who have a trader occupation (i.e. trade, industry, civil service, and professions). Asians say the Gujarati speakers also attend Swami Narayan services, and they seem to do so, but the Nairobi Asians also think of the Swami Narayan

278

Patels as a distinct group with a residential cluster of their own (but not a community housing estate), an unusual turban which marks them off as masons, by caste, with the current surname ('Patel') of another occupational caste of village headmen. Caste distance in Kenya is highly diffused by occupational overlaps on the one hand, and the presence of so many anti-caste religions (Islam, Sikhism, and Christianity) on the other. One finds, however, a number of artisans still engaged in caste occupations (with and without upgrading), and Asians can, and do, identify them by their occupations as, for example, Swami Narayan masons, Sikh carpenters, Goan tailors, etc.

Swami Narayan Hindus also want to explain their religion to Africans and have prepared a manuscript in Swahili for this purpose, and the absence of English as a missionary language seems here to be related to the fact that many Swami Narayans (like other artisans) have no use for English as a work language and have, therefore, never learned it. Neither can they write Swahili, and the manuscript was prepared by a former supporter of the Indo-African Cultural Society who is, himself, a Gujarati-speaking Patel, and a civil servant. The Cutchi-Gujarati split within the Patels seems to be the primary division between one Hindu and another, and I may be over-emphasizing the artisan/non-artisan division; this pattern reappears among the Goans and one is tempted to draw parallels.

Gujarati Muslims have been largely excluded from the preceding discussion, and the omission is deliberate: Punjabis have a language of poetry which is shared by all religions, and the Gujarati Hindus and Jains have common dances and songs, but the Gujarati Muslims have patterns of their own and deserve separate consideration. This section of the Asian population has a majority of Shia Muslims and a minority of Sunnis, and the distinction is important because the Shias from Gujarat work with a leadership principle which cuts them off from all other Gujaratis with a shared culture, and also from the Punjabi Muslims who are Sunnis by sect, with a completely different religious focus, and no leader. The small splinter sect of Punjabi Sikhs (the Namdharias) does have a 'leader' of a sort, but the man who came from India to convert them was well within the Indian tradition, and the leaders of the Gujarati Shias are not. All non-Muslims are subject to chastisement from time to time from particularly devout religious men, who feel that the flock is straying from the paths of orthodoxy and should be hustled back to the fold. Indians are used to this in India, and the normal pattern is for a religion to divide, with one group still straying, and the others becoming highly devout members of a 'strict' sect. Charismatic men can draw from many different castes, and found a sturdy sect of their own which grows into a religion, but they are apt to be working with a new ideology: Guru Nanak who founded the Sikh religion was a man of this sort, and Mahavir and Buddha, who founded the Jain and Buddhist religions respectively, were his forerunners. Christ and Mohammed also come to mind, but both began religions which came to India and cannot, therefore, be considered Indian. The sect which stays within the fold of the larger religion is normally founded by saintly men who arouse the admiration of their followers, or men of the Calvinist stamp who chastise them. The Namdharia leader was of the latter kind and his followers in Kenya are now led by his son who is a milder man by all reports. These people are small in number but very 'strict', with daily services and the full regalia of the Sikh religion: turban, sword, untrimmed beard, uncut hair, etc. Other Sikhs in Kenya also wear turbans, beards, and long hair, and carry knives but on a more moderate scale, e.g. trimmed beards, short knives instead of swords, stylish pointed turbans, and members can put aside the regalia if they choose to do so and still remain Sikhs. No Asian considers a split of this kind as a serious religious division, and the Sikhs are simply known to others as the 'flat turban' Sikhs (Namdharia sect) and the 'pointed turban' Sikhs (majority).

The Arya Samaj sect of the Punjabi Hindus was founded by a saintly man, Swami Dayananda, with strict ideas, and the Swami Narayan sect of the Gujarati Hindus is also strict, i.e. characterized by frequent services with full attendance. The first has returned to the ancient religion and the second to a later version but both exemplify the Indian sect, and their leaders are long since gone.

The Gujarati Shia Muslims are, on the other hand, Indian converts to a dissident Muslim sect with a long history of persecution in the Middle East and a tradition of preserving their religion by secrecy. Their original sect fled to India for refuge from the non-Shia Muslims (Sunnis) and achieved a measure of safety, but India also has its Sunnis and the Shia people have stayed in religious seclusion for many years. All have the leadership principle with an active leader in one sub-sect (the Ismailis), a representative leader in another (the Bohoras), and an absent leader in the third (the Ithnasheris), i.e. a leader who will one day appear. The Shia Ismailis (called Khojas) are led by H.H. the Aga Khan, who lives in Europe, and their sect in Kenya owes much of its present vitality to the energetic leadership of the present Aga Khan's grandfather, H.H. the late Aga Khan, who met with, and advised, the leaders of the local Kenya councils. He was also in touch with Gandhi and kept a palace in India but travelled widely in Europe, and the links with India were severed after Indian independence. Large groups of Ismailis are found in other parts of Africa and all are now advised to take the citizenship of their country of residence and adapt themselves to the host population.

No citizenship was available to East African Ismailis in the colonial period, and the time was spent in strengthening the Ismaili focus of the group by providing a full set of facilities (schools, mosques, hospital, clubs, insurance companies, community housing estates, etc.) and encouraging the marriage of Cutchi- and Gujarati-speaking Ismailis. The closed mosques and the walled housing estates reflect the secrecy of the group, the break with India is reflected in the inter-linguistic marriage and the change in women's dress (from sari and long hair to dresses and short hair), and the leadership principle in the hierarchical arrangement of the local councils. Morris sees them as pace-setters for other Asians in Uganda and, in a sense, they are, but the secrecy focus has no parallel among other Kenya Asians and the leadership is of a different kind. Nor have the others attempted to bridge any gaps between their groups with marriage across the lines of language, and the deliberate Ismaili bilingualism in Indian vernaculars (Cutchi-Gujarati) is a socio-linguistic parallel for the languages of poetry and song which reduce the social distance between other Asians.

Other Asians are also, sometimes, bilingual in two Indian vernaculars, but theirs is a spontaneous bilingualism which normally derives from the minority status of their own group, and intensive contacts (work or recreational) with members of a larger group with a different language. Interregional marriage also occurs, but here too one finds members of a small minority marrying members of a much larger group (e.g. Mahrashtrian-Punjabi; Pathan-Gujarati). Marriages with Europeans are also found (but not with the Kenya British), and some marriages with Africans and Arabs, but numbers are very small and intermarriage is largely deplored by non-Muslims. No racialist motivation is involved— all Asians except Muslims belong to religions which do not countenance divorce or plural wives, and their strong family systems are maintained by strict adherence to these two ideals of monogamy and life-long marriage. Cross-cultural marriage is seen as a source of potential friction, and also avoided in inter-Asiatic marriages, which are typically arranged by parents or other relatives of the young people involved. Language distance is thereby maintained, and vernacular bilingualism in Gujaratis, Punjabis, and Goans is associated with other domains of language use, notably work and recreation.

Linguistic intermarriage among Ismailis is illustrated below in an Ismaili language diary written by a student whose own household is now, as she says, of the 'nuclear type'. Others are also found with Gujarati alone, or Cutchi alone, but the Cutchi-Gujarati combination is associated with Ismailis, and other Asians who know some of each (e.g. Gujarati speakers with a few words of Cutchi or vice versa), expect the Ismailis to know both:

1. I think in this report it will be noticed that I speak Kutchi and Gujerati sometimes interchangeably and sometimes in very close connection with each other. This is because my father's mother-tongue is Gujerati and my mother's mother-tongue is Kutchi though she had to adapt herself and speak in Gujerati when she moved over to father's household.
2. At home with aunt and cousins. Aunt's mother-tongue is Kutchi though her husband's mother-tongue is Gujerati—so a sort of situation similar to my family's situation exists. Now my mother and aunt converse in Kutchi, naturally. My young cousins speak to my mother in Kutchi, and to my father and me in Gujerati—and this I think is done quite unconsciously. My aunt, too, speaks to my father and me in Gujerati.
3. Visiting grandmother. Her background is Kutchi. Similar situation arises here. Grandmother speaks to my father and me in Gujerati, and to my mother in Kutchi. All my uncles, though, speak to our family in Gujerati alone because since it is the mother-tongue of the man, it predominates in this household.

And, later, in an encounter with a non-Ismaili:

4. At the same time met—an African from S. Africa and another Asian, a Singh from Kenya. The South African conversed only in English while the Sikh boy spoke in English and making attempts to speak in Gujerati. Here another and interesting development takes place because this boy presumably hears Ismailis speaking in Gujerati and Kutchi and so when he attempts to speak to me in Gujerati, there is a lot of Kutchi in it too—thus this mixing of the two is significant since both are simultaneously associated with the community.

The minority-majority intermarriage is illustrated below in another excerpt from the language diary of the Pathan student, whose uncle married a Gujarati (probably Ismaili) Muslim from Tanzania. The wife's Cutchi-Swahili mixing is associated with Gujarati Muslims from Zanzibar and not with Kenyan Asians who borrow household words from Swahili into their home languages, but avoid 'mixing':

1. Went to see my uncle who stays in (Nairobi) and my aunt who had come from Zanzibar. Aunt talked typical Zanzibar Swahili (for an Asian) with words of Cutchi and Gujerati thrown in, e.g. Masidme (Cutchi) nili ha (Swahili) thamble ja pathia (Cutchi) rough translation 'In the mosque I sat behind the pillar.' This type of bastard Swahili is very common among Zanzibar Asians. My aunt is a Gujerati but can speak Cutchi as well. My uncle is Pathan but speaks Pushto very rarely— as his children and wife do not understand the language.

Vernacular bilingualism in recreational languages occurs in another passage by the same writer who is a Pushto speaker with multiple vernaculars:

Met Naseer, a Gujerati Ismaili girl, who insisted on talking in Gujerati with Akram, my friend—a Muslim Punjabi. Akram made valiant attempts to speak in Gujerati but mixed up all the genders and tenses. He always presses me to teach him Gujerati.

282

Vernacular bilingualism in work languages appears in another diary by a Punjabi-speaking receptionist for a Gujarati doctor: both speak English, but Asian languages are considered more comfortable and her employer bridges the Gujarati-Punjabi gap with a mixture of Gujarati, Hindustani and English. The writer is literate in Hindustani and English and says she can 'understand Gujerati language but cannot speak Gujerati fluently':

My doctor is a Gujerati and usually he speaks to me in English but sometimes he starts talking to me in Hindustani and sometimes he uses most of the words in Gujerati. For instance he said in Hindustani 'Yay card bohot juna hay' means this card is very old. The word card he used in English and 'juna' is a Gujerati word for old. So he used three different languages in one sentence. He told me, Koi patient chay? Means is there any patient? The word 'Koi' is a Hindustani word, 'patient' English and 'chay' Gujerati word. He again used three different words in one sentence.

Gujarati Muslims also include (besides the Shia Ismailis) the Shia Bohoras and Ithnasheris and the Sunni Memons. All are involved in trade, and also have connections with the Gujarati Muslims in Tanzania and Zanzibar and the Gujarati Muslims in Kenya are generally considered 'coastal people' by other Asians. Nairobi has a strong Ismaili community however, and the others are represented in smaller numbers. Bohoras are Gujarati speakers with no Cutchi section and the Ithnasheris have a Gujarati-speaking majority with Punjabi-speaking leadership in Nairobi, i.e. an absent leader with no language at all, and local control by an eminent Punjabi-speaking doctor. This community breaks the Kenya Asian focus on a single region but maintains the regional marriage pattern and its households use Gujarati or Punjabi but not both. The Gujarati-speaking majority is associated with the coast and the Punjabi-speaking minority with Nairobi but both are in the Nairobi mosque and their language gap is bridged by using Hindustani (Hindi-Urdu) as a language of religion. I have no reports on their coastal language of religion, but the Nairobi pattern is clearly illustrated in another passage from the diary of the gregarious Pathan:

About 9 p.m. went to Ithanasherie Mosque to listen to 'Majlis', a talk on religion given by a person learned in all aspects of Muslim religion. Majlis was held to commemorate Martyrdom of Imam leader Hussein, about 14 hundred years ago. It ended by people assembled weeping openly and then there was what is called 'Matam' or beating of the chest very vigorously. When this was finished, everybody sat around and were served with food. I talked with many people there: most were Punjabis and there were quite a few Khojas (i.e. Gujarati Muslims) from the coast, mostly from Mombasa. The Majlis was preached in Hindi or to be more exact in a very elementary form of Urdu.

Other religious languages are reviewed at a later stage but I have digressed in order to point out the unique patterns of these Gujarati

Muslims; i.e. the Shia Ismailis, with two languages in their homes, and the Shia Ithnasheris with two home languages in their religion. Other Gujarati Muslims have monolingual homes and the third Shia sect of Bohoras presents no problems: they follow the usual leadership principle of the Shias, have the usual links with counterpart communities on the East African coast, speak Gujarati in their homes, and have a regionally homogeneous religion. The fourth large Gujarati Muslim group of Memons are Sunnis by sect and their links with Gujaratis are partly neutralized by the difference in religious focus. Asians recognize their geographical link with other Gujaratis and their religious link with the Punjabi Muslim Sunnis and find it difficult to place them, but think they are 'somewhere in the middle'. Memons know where they come from and what they believe in but also find it difficult to describe themselves in terms which will not place them in some other group: the Punjabi Muslims are usually called 'Muslims' and the Ismailis are often called 'Cutchis', by virtue of their dominant language on the coast. Memons vary and one finds some describing themselves as Memons, and others combining the language and the religion and calling themselves 'Cutchi Muslims'. No other group in the Asian population has a split focus of this kind, and the Memons are therefore classed as Gujaratis with 'something different' about them.

The Sunni Muslim population includes a number of other minorities who live on the coast but these are small groups with no Gujarati focus and the Sunnis are usually seen as including a large number of Punjabis ('Muslims'), a minority of Gujaratis ('Memons' or 'Cutchi Muslims') and a number of smaller groups from other regions (e.g. Bhadalas from Baluchistan).

(c) GOANS

Kenya Asian Goans come from the third and smallest region of the major groups, and their isolation from other Asians is partly due to their distance in India and partly due to their long history as Portuguese subjects. Each of the large regional groups—Gujarati, Punjabi and Goan—is separated from the next by intermediate regions (with a few representatives in Kenya), but all except the Goans have come from British India and were recognized as Indians by the British government in Kenya, which classified the Asian people as Indians and Goans for many years. The Indian section has, moreover, a notable lack of Christians and the Goan section a notable lack of non-Christians, and the regional and political distance is reinforced by the difference in their religions. India does have many Christians and Goa many Hindus, and the Kenya Asian split

284

is therefore a local phenomenon but this is also true of other divisions; one finds heterogeneous Jains in India, from different regions, but all of the Kenya Asian Jains are Gujaratis.

Kenya Asian Goans are often seen as a homogeneous group, and they identify themselves in this way—as 'Goans'—but this is largely because their region of origin coincides with their religion (Christianity) and sect (Catholic). Castes are represented and known, but Goans do not conform to the normal Indian pattern and their castes are simply thought of as social groups, each with its own club. Brahmins are still at the top rung of their social ladder and low status artisans at the bottom, and here the Goans conform to the Kenya Asian pattern, but their middle castes have lost contact with their traditional occupations and caste names and Goans call them 'the Kshatriya', using a catch-all Indian category (lit. 'warriors') which might include a number of groups, but not Brahmins or traders.

Kenya Goans are not engaged in trade and their name for the middle section seems apt, but neither are they warriors and their use of the term does not carry its Indian rank of being lower than Brahmins but higher than traders. Goans have been heavily involved in occupational shifts in Kenya (with upgrading) and also in a language shift to English as a mother tongue and a work language, and the caste distinctions in the middle group are dimmed by overlaps in current occupation and first language. Some artisans are still engaged in the caste occupations (e.g. tailor) or variations on the same theme with little upgrading (e.g. cook to barman, caterer, etc.), but many now overlap with the current occupations of the higher groups, including Brahmins, and the Goan Institutes in towns like Mombasa are open to all except traditional artisans (largely tailors).

This meteoric social rise of the artisan group of Goans is due to the adoption of English as the medium of instruction in the Goan schools and their school language can therefore be seen as an eraser for the divisions in the two top sections: Brahmins still marry each other, but their sense of endogamy is weaker than that of other Indians and the Goans view themselves as a large loose group with a majority of English-speaking Goans at the top and a minority of Konkani-speaking tailors at the bottom.

The immigrant population also included an English-speaking section with clerical occupations, but the majority (including wives of clerks) was Konkani-speaking and the shift in proportions is attributed to 'education'. Many are known to be bilingual at all levels, but there is 'more English' in the high status homes and the population is divided into 'uneducated' artisans (or tailors) and 'educated' others.

Kenya Goans have, however, remembered their place of origin in Goa and their Kenya-born children were taught to recognize the difference between the 'higher' dialect of the Bardez area of Konkani and the 'lower' dialect of the Salcete area: this distinction still survives as a social marker for Konkani speakers. Both are found among the Kshatriya, but the current artisan group is largely Salcete speakers and the Brahmins are associated with Bardez. All Goan children are now learning English and the current division between the tailors (with Salcete Konkani) and the others (with English) may soon be neutralized by the loss of Konkani but this has not yet happened. Konkani was passed on to Kenya-born Goans in artisan households and one now finds Konkani-speaking men in this group and Konkani-speaking women at all levels. Women also work in 'English-speaking occupations' and Konkani-speaking housewives adapt themselves by shifting to the language of their husbands; this, however, is done in the Ismaili fashion by using Konkani with other women and English with the household head and the children.

Bilingual households of this sort will reappear in the section on home languages but the role of the school language in occupational upgrading and the relationship to language substitution are largely Goan, and therefore stressed here. Ismailis also adopted English as a school language shortly before independence, but much later than the Goans, and their school shift was not intended to upgrade to clerical occupations since most were already engaged in trade and associated work (industry, professions, etc.). Ismaili women do work as secretaries, stenographers, etc., but many also help in the shop and the focus on trade is clear.

Goan culture survives in Konkani folk dances and Portuguese literature, but the link with Portugal was broken by the Indian annexation of Goa and the memory of the village is fading. Annual 'village festivals' are held with village dancing, but the Kenya-born dance once a year in the village fashion, and the rest of the year in Western fashion, and their focus on region seems to be sentimental. Konkani-speaking Goans are now involved in the recent shift from church Latin to the vernacular (i.e. English with a little Konkani in Goan churches), and their children are exposed to English on a massive scale, with English in religion, recreation and education. Asian children do, however, abide by the conventions of their parents in home languages, as in marriage, and the primary language of the Goan household is still the work language of the household head.

Incipient shift to English is illustrated below in a passage from a diary by the Konkani-speaking student, but her shift will not take place until she marries an English-speaking Goan. Her parents might shift in the future, but one cannot—at this stage—predict; English influence is apparent now, but the language of the 'immediate question' is, as the writer says, Konkani.

In the morning I had an oral French exam for two hours, immediately after which I went home for lunch. My father greeted me at the door in English, and then asked about my exam—in Konkani. I greeted back in English and then went on in Konkani to answer his question. We have no equivalent for the English 'hello' so I am always greeted in English, but the immediate question is in Konkanim.

Mother then told me of a 'telephone call' she had from a friend of mine. She switched to English to tell me about the conversation, fumbling a little for words. She turned back to Konkanim. I answered back in Konkanim, with a few English words interspersed, e.g. 'first-class', 'praise', 'grade 1 scale'—all of which have equivalents in Konkanim, but not exactly the same connotations as we know them to have in English. Speaking to the servant, I asked in Swahili for a 'glassi' of water. Telling him how well he had cooked, I used the word 'super'.

The shift to English as a mother tongue in other Goans has obscured the difference between Konkani speakers with the higher Bardez dialect and others with the lower Salcete dialect, but status still derives partly from the use of English and partly from the place of origin and this household can outrank another with bilingual adults. Current occupation and caste occupation of the household head are also factors in status ranking and the Goans have arrived at a three way division: the Konkani-speaking artisan from Salcete is at the bottom of the ladder; the Brahmin from Bardez is at the top; and everyone else is in the middle—in 'the Kshatriya'. Brahmins can speak any language they like, but Goan Brahmin men are educated in Kenya, as in India, in English and have English-speaking occupations. Housewives adapt themselves to the language of the household head and Konkani-speaking monolinguals in high status Goan families are typically widowed grandmothers.

All Goan children speak English now (including the children of tailors) and the present division is unstable, but nevertheless of interest; other Asians also rank, to some extent, by caste but none have participated in the Goan language shift to English and no parallels occur for the Goan caste system.

Portuguese-speaking Goans in Goa may have provided a model for the Goan shift to English in Kenya, and I do not discount the possibility of a counterpart 'Kshatriya' in Goa. The role of English as an eraser for two ranked dialects of Konkani is associated with Kenya, and therefore considered a pattern of adaptation by Kenya Asian Goans. All still have a strong sense of regional identity, but the cultural focus seems to have shifted to Kenya and to English.

Social diversity within the Asian population has not been reduced by any mergers, but patterns of language use have clearly changed as each group made its own adaptation as immigrants. The social matrix now in use is outlined below, and relative proportions in each group are indicated in the next section. These will serve as the framework for the following sections where I relate the social groups to their current language of home, religion, recreation, education and work.

SUMMARY OF THE COMMUNITIES

Kenya Asians are a highly urbanized minority, with middle class occupations, and most of their communities are able to provide some kind of meeting place for their members and some services. Each has its own idea of service and one finds some communities with a full set of schools (nursery, primary, secondary) and their own place of religion; others with more, and some with nothing but a social club. The Nairobi Sikhs, for example, have primary and secondary schools for boys and girls and six religious centres, called *gurdwaras*, and Sikhs in other towns also maintain their own religious centres. Visa Oshwal Jains also maintain schools in Nairobi with hostels for out-of-town students, meeting halls for socio-religious gatherings (weddings, festivals, etc.) and social clubs, and the Ismaili community has schools, places of religion, community housing estates, insurance schemes, a hospital, etc. All three are large communities with 6,000–10,000 members in Nairobi and branches in other towns, but one also finds small communities like the Arya Samaj with a full set of schools, and very large communities like the Patels, with nothing but clubs. Patels do go to school but their schools are shared with other communities, with the same religion, and no one speaks of Patel schools or temples.

All are nevertheless recognized as communities and I shall refer to them in this way, but I also think of 'community' as a set of characteristics (or distinctive features) for the individual Asian and would therefore divide the Sikhs, who organize by religion, into three smaller castes (or tribes) of Ramgharia Sikhs, Tarkhan Sikhs and Jat Sikhs. Some belong to a large orthodox majority (called Sikhs) but others are members of a small 'strict' sect called the Namdharia Sikhs and I would therefore identify an individual by his sect (Namdharia or 'Sikh'), his caste (Ramgharia, etc.), his religion (Sikh) and, finally, by his region of origin in India (Punjab). Some communities cross the lines of region, but most do not and all are associated with a single region: the Arya Samaj, for example, has a Punjabi majority and a Gujarati minority and everyone thinks of it as a Punjabi community.

Asian marriages are normally arranged by matching community characteristics and most households are characterized by a single region, religion, caste, and sect, but corporate groups are often more inclusive and one finds Punjabi Sikhs, for example, organizing by religion and sect and Punjabi Hindus doing the same. Gujarati Muslims organize by sect and Gujarati Hindus by caste, and one caste of Gujarati Hindus then emerges as the social equivalent of the whole Sikh religion, a Gujarati Jain caste and a Gujarati Muslim sect. All are corporate groups, and therefore communities, but the religious focus of the Sikhs is preserved and the others have obscured theirs by divisions.

Asians identified themselves in this way in a survey of Mombasa Asians[8] and the Sikhs emerged as the dominant 'community' in an Asian population of 25,987 which included 2,698 Punjabi Sikhs, 7,595 Gujarati Muslims and 4,539 Gujarati Jains. The Muslims had split themselves into 4 sects (3 Shia and 1 Sunni) and the Jains had split themselves into 2 castes, and the rest of the Asian population variously identified with their region of origin (2,057 Goans, 52 Mahrashtrians, etc.), their caste (2,396 Patels, etc.), their region and caste (647 Rajput Dhobis) and so forth. All were classified as Goans, Mohammedans, or Hindus (including Sikhs and Jains) and some confusion was inevitable, but I mention this survey because it counted the Asians as they count themselves, i.e. on several different levels of specificity.

Government counted them by 4 religions in the 1962 census (Hindu, Sikh, Muslim and Christian) and the Nairobi City Council counted them by 'nationality' in another[9] (Indian, Pakistani, and Goan) and one can piece bits together, but no official statistics are available for most and one has to go to the Asians themselves to find out who is there and who is not. Some keep no community census at all, but they have a fairly clear idea of relative proportions, and small town Asians know how many households each community has and, sometimes, how many members. Nairobi Asians have some representatives of all communities and roughly half of the total Asian population of Kenya, and Asians arrive at their estimates for Mombasa Asians by estimating half as many in numbers, and assuming a higher proportion of Gujarati Muslims and a lower proportion of Punjabis in general. Up-country towns have a higher proportion of Punjabis, but seldom a majority, and the Goans are always outnumbered by Punjabis and Gujaratis.

Current estimates are given below, but several different levels of identification are involved (as in the Mombasa survey) and the figures are meaningless without a componential analysis of the Kenya Asian communities.[10] My own treats the Kenya Asian population as a category of social groups (corporate or not) with two primary divisions by region of origin and religions and further subdivisions by caste and sect. Majority sects are given names if they have one (e.g. Sunni, Sanatan), but Sikhs and Jains had no divisions when they came to Kenya and their majorities

289

are known by the name of the religion. Small splinter sects have a distinct identity, in both religions, and one has to include them, but Asians do not think of these groups as real communities as yet and the majorities in both religions would rather not think about them at all.

Gujaratis are a large majority with 65 per cent of the Asian population or more, but I follow the Kenya Asian fashion of thinking in terms of the geographical arrangement in India and list the Punjabis from the north first, the Gujaratis from the central region second, and the more southerly Goans third. Other regions are also represented but omitted here, as their total membership is less than 2 per cent of the Asian population.

TABLE 11.1 *Kenya Asian communities*

Region of origin	Religion	Sect	Caste
Punjab	Hindu	Sanatan	Brahmins, etc.
		Arya Samaj	
	Sikh	Sikh	Ramgharia, Jat, Tarkhan
		Namdharia	
	Muslim	Sunni	
		Ahmadiyya	
Gujarat	Hindu	Sanatan	Brahmin, Patel, Lohana, Vanza, etc.
		Swami Narayan	
	Jain	Jain	Visa Oshwal, Navnat
		Mumuksh	
	Muslim	Sunni	Memon
		Shia—Ismaili	
		,, Bohora	
		,, Ithnasheri	
Goa	Christian	Catholic	Brahmin, Kshatriya, Tailor, etc.

Muslims deny caste and one would like to omit all, but the Memons have retained a distinct identity by virtue of the sect difference from other Gujaratis and the regional distance from other Sunnis, and their sense of caste is active. Other Muslims can be identified by their ex-Hindu castes, and often are, but the contrast with the isolated Memons is lost if one includes them, citing the Ismailis for example as Lohanas. Other ex-Hindus, like the Goans, maintain some caste facilities also (e.g. Goan tailor clubs) and one must include them; Muslims have none, and their sense of caste is (except for the Memons) inactive, i.e. not forgotten but redundant.

All Asian communities have been affected by the recent Kenyanization programme, which is designed to admit Africans to former Asian occupations, and some have been decimated by Asian emigration to Britain and other Commonwealth countries. Shia Ismaili Muslims are more secure than others because most applied for Kenya citizenship at independence, but small traders and artisans from all communities fled in the

Asian exodus of 1968, when Britain was shifting from an open door policy for Kenya Asian subjects to a more rigid policy which now admits some 6,000 a year (i.e. 1,500 'voucher holders' plus dependants (1970)) from all East African countries. Kenyanized civil servants also left in large numbers and the Kenya Asian population estimates its loss at 18,000 for March 1968-March 1969, with a major exodus in the initial months and a reduction thereafter. Large traders and others are well represented, but new trade licensing restrictions were introduced in January 1969 and many non-citizen traders are now left with no licences to trade in Kenya and no papers to take them out.[11] Current figures are not available on citizenship but official estimates in 1969 placed the number of Kenya citizens at 45,000, and unofficial sources estimated the number of British passport holders at 110,000; the number of Indian citizens was estimated at 4,000–5,000, the number of Pakistani citizens at 450, and the rest were thought to be stateless persons with no papers of any kind.[12] Asians estimated their population at 174,000 by subtracting the emigration figure of 18,000 from the government estimate of 192,000 for 1967.[13]

Nairobi Asians estimated their population at 76,000–80,000 with a loss of 6,000–10,000 since the last city council report in 1967, which listed 86,454 Asians in the total urban population of 266,794. The number of Asians employed in the public service had fallen from 12,000 in 1962 to 7,400 in 1966,[14] to 3,264 in 1968 (1,007 in local government and 2,257 in central government),[15] involving a total loss of nearly 9,000 jobs for the whole Kenya Asian population. Some clearly found work in private industry where the numbers rose from 23,500 in 1962 to 29,000 in 1966,[16] but many had left in the exodus and the working population was in a state of imbalance, by colonial standards, with an unusually low proportion of civil servants and small artisans and petty traders.

Relative proportions of Kenya Asian communities to one another had also changed with Kenyanization, and the occupational focus of the Asian communities is reflected in reduced numbers of Sikhs and Goans. The 1962 census[17] classified the Asian population by religion alone and my own figures have been adjusted to that pattern.

Nairobi Asian religious groups

	1962 census	1969 Asian estimates
Hindus & Jains	46,284	45,000
Muslims	15,752	16,000
Sikhs	14,000	10,000
Christians	9,577	3,000
Total	85,633	74,000

291

Further estimates for Nairobi communities are made below but no comparative material is available.

Nairobi Asian communities in 1969

		Current estimate	Major community	Community estimate
Punjabis	Hindus	10,000	Sanatan	9,000
	Muslims	9,000	Sunnis	8,700
	Sikhs	10,000	Sikhs	9,500
Gujarati	Hindus	25,000	Patels	20,000
			Lohanas	2,000
	Jains	10,000	Visa Oshwal	9,000
	Muslims	7,000	Shia Ismaili	6,000
Goan	Christian	3,000	—	—

All Kenya towns are losing large sections of their Asian population through emigration and population shift to the cities and the loss in Nairobi from approximately 86,000 in 1962 to 74,000 in 1969 is clearly minimal by up-country standards. Asians in Kitale had, for example, 634 children in their local school in 1966 and 325 in 1969. Census figures for 1962 listed 2,057 Kitale Asians, with a 57.2 increase since 1948 and Kitale Asians think they have lost half of their population since 1962.[18]

Eldoret Asians estimate their current population at 2,500 to 3,000 now, representing a loss of 700–1,200 from the 1962 level of 3,758, but not yet reducing them to the 1948 level of 1,845.

Kisii Asians think they have an Asian population of 400–500, again placing them between the 1948 level of 348 and the 1962 level of 673.

Kericho Asians estimate their current population (for the district) at 1,500, representing a loss of about 1,400 from the 1962 level.

Other towns make similar reports,[19] and Kenya Asians are clearly losing contact with the countryside of Kenya. Small town Asians were also expecting another 40–50 per cent cut in their current populations when these estimates were made in 1969 but their present status is not clear since they are no longer able to emigrate as they lose their licences to trade in their own locality.

Asians who left in the exodus of 1968 were typically small scale artisans and petty traders with easily transportable skills and no investments in Kenya, on the one hand, and Kenyanized civil servants (largely Sikhs and Goans) on the other. Those who were applying for vouchers for admission to Britain in 1969 were often large scale traders who were currently involved in the trade licensing restrictions and others who expected to be Kenyanized shortly.[20] Teachers, for example, thought they had two years left if they were English teachers, four if they were science teachers, and only months to go if they were headmasters. Africans were then entering Asian occupations in managerial positions, like that of headmaster, but non-citizen Asians were still relatively secure if their occupations involved some years of special training, and the senior magistrates in the judiciary were expected to remain for several years.[21]

All Gujarati Muslims and Jains are heavily involved in trade and all except the Ismailis think their present position is precarious. Gujarati Hindus also have a large trading section but many are in the professions as well and the impact of Kenyanization is spread out. Punjabi Hindus are also in the professions and often teachers, and the Sikhs are in all of the foregoing and also in a variety of occupations which reflect their former Indian occupation of farmer (forestry, farming) and their interest in mechanics (garages, automobile sales, etc.). This is an oversimplification, but some communities are affected severely by restrictions in one sphere, and others are more heavily involved in another. Asians from all regions and religions were involved in the Kenyanization of the civil service, but the Punjabi Sikhs and the Goans were hardest hit and these two groups left Kenya in large numbers in the 1968 exodus.

Relatively poor artisans and traders also left in large numbers, and 'low-rent Asian neighbourhoods' in Nairobi now house a mixed population of Africans and Asians, with many shared houses. This is a new phenomenon in Kenya and the relationships between African and Asian in areas of this kind are sometimes wary. Asians have, however, found that the people who share their houses now are also 'middle class' and they are relaxing. Goans have a religious overlap with African Christians and the meeting of cultures is thereby reduced by a lack of conflict between the non-vegetarian African and the vegetarian Asian. Hindus and Jains are vegetarians in their homes, but other religions are not and these are now the dominant majority in residential areas, like Eastleigh and Juja Road in Nairobi, which are now being shared with Africans. Gujarati Hindus were also there in large numbers before the exodus of artisans and small traders, but Eastleigh is now associated with the Goan tailor, and Juja Road has always been known as a Sikh colony.

Emigration patterns are still obscured by the lack of community figures for departing Asians, but Asians tend to cluster by region of origin in Nairobi and one finds some residential areas like Parklands with a heavy concentration of Gujaratis and others like Eastleigh with a heavy concentration of Goans. The area between is shared by all, but religious clusters appear and one finds the Pangani area, for example, being associated with Punjabi Muslims, and the Juja Road area with Punjabi Sikhs.

Community facilities are typically located within walking distance of these clusters and one can estimate the dominant community by looking at the focus of the schools and meeting halls. Patterns are diffused in the smaller towns where Asians often had an 'Indian' school, and an Indian

Association, but some communities maintain their own places of religion (e.g. Sikhs and Christians) and clusters appear. Patterns of this kind are also being diffused in Nairobi by a movement of wealthy Asians (and Africans) into 'former European areas', and 'former European schools'. But the strong community focus remains in other areas as a colonial legacy.

2. KENYA ASIAN LANGUAGE USE

(a) HOME LANGUAGES

Diversity in Kenya Asian home languages is due to their steadfast adherence to the system of community marriage, and their resistance to change is largely due to the ability of the trading section to make a distinction between their debits, like caste ranking, and their assets like community marriage. No one says so, in so many words, and one needs to see the connection between the family firm and the community in order to appreciate their point of view. Many Asian youths would like more choice, but they do see the connection and no generation gap divides the trader from his sons. Grown men also sacrifice their ambitions to become doctors or lawyers if their father needs them to take over the business, due to illness, and their younger siblings watch and learn. Asian traders have a real dilemma when they are asked to teach new African traders the secrets of their success and one can see why.

Goans are not involved in trade and their commitment to arranged marriage is weaker, but the sanctions of their church upon divorce tend to keep them within the Asian fold. Traders by caste are largely Gujaratis, and Asians think of Gujaratis when they think of trade. Many Punjabis joined them, in their search for new occupations (i.e. non-agricultural) in Kenya, but their attachment to community marriage is partly dispersed by their traditional pattern of dividing by religion. The Arya Samaj sect of Hindus is willing to provide marriage services for Asians who want to marry out of their community and people accept this, as a Punjabi pattern.

Inter-regional marriages are nevertheless avoided by Gujaratis and Punjabis who come from areas in India with a cultural division: no households with both languages appeared in my sample of 478 adults in two separate areas of Nairobi (Ngara and Nairobi West), none were mentioned in language diaries by university students from all regional-religious divisions, and I did not find any in my field-work. Some no doubt exist. I did find a wide variety of other marriages which broke the pattern of arranged marriage by community, but numbers were very small. Inter-regional marriages and marriages between Asian and non-Asian bring two languages into the same household, and would therefore appear in a survey: inter-community marriages within a region will also appear if they involve Cutchi and Gujarati speakers from Gujarat, but one has to be careful: the Ismaili community has two sections of Cutchi and Gujarati speakers, with intermarriage, and these have to be treated as instances of community marriage. Two sects of Asians draw members from Gujarat and Punjab (the Arya Samaj Hindus and the Shia Ithnasheri Muslims), and one would have to look at instances of Gujarati-Punjabi intermarriage with the same care.

Exceptions to the system of community marriage are largely isolated men (early immigrants, overseas students, members of small communities, etc.), rebels (university professors, etc.), and Ismailis. Asian men normally bring their wives to their fathers' households, but the pattern is reversed when they marry Africans ('unlike India', they say) and bilingual families are not likely to appear in surveys of urban Asian areas. Some have gone off to distant places like the middle of Lake Baringo, others are within shouting distance of their Asian relatives in Maasai country. Ismailis are largely in the coastal areas, and their adjustment to the situation is different; children of Ismaili marriages are automatic Ismailis, and the Indian pattern of the paternal household is maintained in a metaphorical sense. Ismailis are also Gujarati traders and their concern to avoid divisions in their community is apparent: other Gujarati communities are homogeneous with respect to language but the Ismailis have one section from the Cutchi-speaking area of Gujarat and another from the Gujarati-speaking area, and their rise from a loose, disorganized status to the present eminence is due to their decision to merge their sub-regional divisions by linguistic intermarriage within the community. Cutchi and Gujarati are similar, they say, 'like English and Welsh', but mutually unintelligible and, therefore, divisive. Religious persecution has kept the Ismailis together for centuries, but nobody was persecuting them in East Africa and the community focus was weak. H.H. the late Aga Khan provided the necessary leadership to pull them together, and the Ismailis are deeply devoted to his memory. Small boys carry pictures of the current Aga Khan in their school satchels when children of other communities carry slogans of the Texaco Company. This is a frivolous example, but symbolic of their gratitude to his grandfather.

Punjabi and Goan communities tend to focus on their religions and present themselves as people with no communities at all, and their maintenance of the system of community marriage is obscured in their home languages. Residential areas and occupations are often shared by Punjabis and Goans, but four distinct patterns emerge in their home languages and each is associated with a focus upon the former medium of instruction in their religious schools in Kenya: English for Goans, Punjabi for Punjabi Sikhs, and two varieties of Hindustani for the Punjabi Hindus, who claim Hindi, and the Punjabi Muslims, who claim Urdu. Punjabis brought their pattern with them from British India, and their language shift to Hindustani is metaphorical, i.e. widely reported, but unreal. Goans developed theirs in Kenya and one can, in fact, find Goans who cannot speak Konkani at all. Patterns of self-report among the Punjabis are illustrated in my survey of Ngara in Nairobi (see Chapter 2): all Sikhs reported Punjabi as a first language as expected; 14 Hindus and 11 Muslims reported Punjabi, 32 Muslims reported Urdu; 21 Hindus reported Hindi, and 1 person from each religion reported the wrong language, i.e. 1 Muslim with Hindi and 1 Hindu with Urdu. Two different scripts are used and these two people may have attended the wrong schools. Urdu was the official school language in British India, where dissident Hindus set up their own schools in an effort to reduce the impact of the British preference for Urdu. It may be remarked that Hindi is a language of prose and Urdu a language of poetry.

English is lacking in some Goan families, who could not afford to send their children to school in Kenya in the colonial period; one finds these people in low-rent areas like Eastleigh in Nairobi, and none appeared in my two samples of middle class Asians in Ngara and Nairobi West. Most are tailors and others with a low caste ranking in Goa. People can shift to new occupations if they have English, and many tailor families are now doing this with the father working at his traditional occupation and the daughter, for example, working as a hairdresser in the new, elegant, English-speaking, Panafric Hotel. Others send their children on to university, and the Goan language shift is proceeding at a rapid rate.

Punjabi is spoken in all Punjabi households and language diaries of students are filled with references to Punjabi-speaking relatives. Hindi crops up from time to time as a language of greeting and jokes, and Urdu frequently appears as a language of poetry. Middle class Punjabis are heavily exposed to English as a work language, and they use it at home as a formal language but none report it as a first language. Twenty-three households were included in the Nairobi West survey of a Sikh-Goan colony with an adult population of 80. Seventy-six were interviewed by a resident student who knew most of the people involved, and was herself a Punjabi with English as a second language. Four households of 12 Goans reported Konkani as a first language for 2 widowed grandmothers and English as a first language for others. Ten households of Sikhs reported Punjabi as a first language for all, as in the Ngara survey.

Thirty-seven people were employed in the total population of 76 which also included a scattering of other households (4 Gujarati Hindus, 1 Gujarati Memon, 2 Gujarati Jains, etc.); all but one used English as a work language and 12 worked in English alone, with traders using 4 languages or more. Sikhs also reported Punjabi as their language of religion; all Goans reported English, 1 added Konkani, and 1 added Portuguese and Latin. Nairobi has a few Konkani-speaking priests but Portuguese was evidently used for private prayers.

Punjabis normally talk Punjabi with each other in ordinary (i.e. non-joking, non-poetic) conversations, but many begin in Hindustani with strangers as one cannot be sure who knows Punjabi and who does not. This pattern is illustrated below in an excerpt from the Punjabi-speaking receptionist cited earlier.

A Singh lady came in the afternoon and started talking to me in Hindustani instead of talking to me in Punjabi. When I replied her in Punjabi she also started talking in Punjabi.

Some people carry their religious preference around with them in all situations, and this pattern is illustrated in another excerpt from the same diary:

A Punjabi patient came in and started talking to me in Hindustani. She had a child with her to whom she had been talking in Punjabi language. When filling the form I asked her what is her name. She gave me a Punjabi name so then I asked her since she is a Punjabi what was the reason for her talking in Hindustani. She replied me that she doesn't like anyone to know that she is a Punjabi.

The religious preference is associated with Hindustani, but the child is, of course, addressed in Punjabi.

Asian home languages rarely cross the lines of region in India, but two communities draw members from Gujarat and Punjab. The predominantly Punjabi Arya Samajists are included in the Punjabi Hindus, in my table of home languages below, and the predominantly Gujarati Shia Ithnasheris are listed separately since their home language is not shared by other Shias; the Punjabi minority is, however, omitted. Exceptions to this table include a small number of households with two regional languages, or one regional language and one non-Asian language, i.e. Punjabi-Maasai, Gujarati-English, Gujarati-Finnish, Pushto-Cutchi, Punjabi-Mahrashtrian, etc.

Swami Narayan masons are largely masons by occupation and Swami Narayans by sect, Goan 'Others' includes some members of the tailor caste, and Goan 'Tailors' includes some other castes, notably the cooks.

TABLE 11.2 *Asian home languages*

Punjabis

Hindus	Punjabi and Hindi
Sikhs	Punjabi
Muslims	Punjabi and Urdu

Gujaratis

Hindus: Swami Narayan masons	Cutchi
Others	Gujarati
Jains	Gujarati
Muslims: Sunni Memon	Cutchi
Shia Ismaili	Cutchi and Gujarati
,, Bohora	Gujarati
,, Ithnasheri	Gujarati

Goans

Tailors	Konkani
Others	Konkani and English

Home languages are not complete without some mention of the exposure to Swahili. Every household but one in my two neighbourhood surveys in Nairobi reported Swahili with the household servant. The exception had no servant. Three individuals reported no language with the servant, apparently relying upon others to do their talking for them; 478 people were interviewed in the joint surveys.

(b) LANGUAGES OF RELIGION

Asians do merge some of their community divisions in their religions, and I shall return to them in due course. Religious languages have been maintained with little attrition, and the Kenya Asian religions deserve consideration. Most of their sacred languages are wholly unintelligible to users, as in India, but Asians need them if they worship divinities. Many do not, and one has to see the differences in religion in order to appreciate the use of sacred languages in some religions and modern languages in others. Christians are a notable exception to the widespread use of sacred languages with divinities, but they worship a God who speaks the tongues of men as well as of angels and their church has often changed from one language of prayer to another. Asian Christians are also unique in having no religious divisions to stand between the communities and the region; Goans achieve a regional unity when they meet together for religion, but other Asians only manage to submerge some of their communities in a more inclusive religion, leaving the religious divisions (and some community divisions) as a threat to unity.

Two Asian religions cross regional lines in the Kenya Asian population and both use sacred languages for prayer: Islam uses Arabic and Hinduism uses Sanskrit. Orthodox Sunni Muslims follow the Islamic pattern among Kenya Asians, and the Gujarati Shia sects do the same with some modification. Shia Ismailis like to pray in a language they can understand and once used Gujarati, but their present solution is rather different; Arabic is used in the Islamic fashion and their prayer books provide transcriptions and translations in Gujarati for those who cannot read the Arabic prayers. Their focus on divinity remains, but their leader H.H. the late Aga Khan has also acquired an aura of divinity, now passed on to his grandson the present Aga Khan. Ismailis have a long line of leaders of this kind, called Imams, and I do not discount the continuation from one to the next—East African Ismailis have a large debt of gratitude to their late leader—but one hears little about his predecessors. The Cutchi-speaking section of the community does not use its language for religious transcriptions, since it has no grammars, but Arabic is now shared by both. None of the Shias have any overlaps with African Muslims who are Sunnis by sect, but Ismailis have a few African converts and a few children of mixed marriages.

The Sunni Muslim Asians include the Cutchi-speaking caste of Memons from Gujarat and a number of Punjabi castes. All diffuse their caste focus by concentrating on the religion except the Memons, and I have omitted the Punjabi castes in the summary table of religious languages below. Arabic is their language of prayer, with Urdu as a language of religious explanation for those who do not understand Arabic. One dissident Punjabi sect has translated the Holy Qur'an into Swahili, with their own Ahmadiyya footnotes, as part of their missionary work with Africans. Sunni Muslims do have an overlap with African Sunnis, but numbers are relatively small: Asian Sunnis are roughly 6 per cent of the Asian population of 174,000 and African Sunnis were 3 per cent of the African population of 8½ million in the 1962 census. Sunni Asian mosques are open to Africans, but their committee work seems to be done largely in Punjabi. Muslim mosques are a problem for women field-workers like myself, as theirs is a public religion for men and a private religion (largely) for women. Ismaili women take an active part in their religion, breaking the pattern, but their mosques are unfortunately closed to all non-Ismailis and one cannot listen to their languages of religion. My own reports are based on answers to sample surveys, language diaries by Ismaili students, and prayer books loaned to me by Ismailis, but I have not heard their prayers.

Other Asian religions are open to everyone who cares to visit, and women take an active part in all religious activities. Sanskrit is rarely claimed as a religious language by Hindus, but all hear it at their weddings and most other socio-religious activities. The Swami Narayan sect says that they use Gujarati for everything—prayers, explanations, etc.— and they seem to do so. Their worship is, however, diffused by a focus on their founder, Swami Narayan, and their use of Gujarati bears an interesting resemblance to the pattern of the Ismailis.

Other Asian Hindus include Gujaratis and Punjabis of the Bhakti (or orthodox) persuasion who worship the well known pantheon of Hindu gods—selecting those which are associated with their places of origin in India. Punjabi Hindus have a temple devoted to Ram (Ram Mandir), and the Gujaratis focus heavily on Shiva. All attend large gatherings of Hindus, and a recent visit by a revered leader, Shri Sant Guru Shankaracharya, also attracted interested members of the Arya Samaj sect which began about a century ago. Several meetings were held with speeches in Gujarati and in Hindustani.

Arya Samajists further down the road were having their annual festival, and their attention was deflected, but a man of this sort is respected by all. Hindu cult leaders appear from time to time, and work miracles, but this visitor was a philosopher and people came to hear his advice. Miracle workers attract smaller crowds, with no focus on the 'great tradition' of Indian religion. Asians prefer the philosophers, but they do have some illnesses which do not respond to their usual treatment (European and Asian specialists, trained in Western medicine), and people sometimes turn back to the 'little tradition' for help. Counterparts in Indian cities have the same problem, but they have Ayurvedic and homeopathic doctors to stand between the modern Western system on the one hand and the village curer on the other. Kenya Asians have a hard time finding herbal medicines, and they do not search very hard. A Muslim up near Kisumu has some spells (i.e. verses from the Qur'an), which dispel bronchitis in any religion, and witches can be dealt with in various ways. Indian villagers have a multitude of witches on their doorsteps, but men who move to the cities find that they 'are not much troubled'. Nairobi has very few Asian witches. One Goan grandmother of my acquaintance can get rid of them by burning a few chillies and reciting bits of the creed in Latin. She is not troubled by them herself, but others sometimes are. One is not sure how to treat such usage, and it might fall into another domain, but the languages of religion seem to be an appropriate setting.

The visit of Guru Shankaracharya was a momentous occasion for Asian Hindus, but my description of him as a leader is somewhat misleading. Local Hindus have no living leader like the Aga Khan, with a strong father image and a permanent connection with his people; Gandhi is gone and India has no substitute. Their gurus are religious leaders in another tradition; India has some simple Brahmin priests, some educated Brahmin laymen, and some gurus like the Shankaracharya who combine both roles. Kenya Asians have the simple priests and the educated laymen but no gurus, and they welcome men like the Shankaracharya with great enthusiasm.

Arya Samaj Hindus do have an educated Sanskrit-speaking priest who devotes his full time to the community, and occasional visiting Brahmins who help. Other orthodox Hindus have maintained Sanskrit by a division between the Brahmin laymen, who give lectures about Sanskrit, and the priests who use it to some extent at weddings and other services, just 'giving the headlines' as they say, in Sanskrit verses with explanations in modern languages. Arya Samajists taught it in their Nairobi school for fourteen years, but they have no teacher now, and the community maintains the language. Everyone attends their regular religious services, and ladies gather in their weekly *satsangs*, practising hymns with the help of printed materials in Sanskrit and Hindi (the former medium of instruction in their schools). All Hindus have *satsangs*, but the Arya Samaj focuses heavily on Sanskrit and the rest do not. Their sect is recent, but the religion predates orthodox Hinduism by some 2,500 years and their Sanskrit is Vedic, the language of the Indo-Aryan gods of the elements, long since abandoned by other Hindus. Almost all are Punjabi speakers, and their use of Hindi as a language of religious education is associated with their parent body in India, also largely Punjabi. The Nairobi branch has a home for orphan African children, who are being raised as Hindus, and these children also know Sanskrit and Hindi; patterns are illustrated below in an excerpt from a student's language diary, reporting a community function.

The President of our committee (DCC) thanked them for the unexpected reception we had received in English. We met the children of the Dayanand Home who are being brought up as Hindus. They are all Africans. They spoke to us in English. They sang songs for us in Swahili, Hindi and English. Just before we left they said their prayers in Sanskrit. They all spoke with an excellent accent.

Hindus rarely have any Africans in their religion, but the Arya Samajists also have a few adult converts. Sanskrit and Hindi are not, however, used as both take some time to learn.

There is also a Hindu, of the orthodox tradition, who has a following of Africans who can sing (or chant) in Hindi but his version of religion seems a bit 'jungly' to other Asians who have very few travelling Indian holy men, i.e. people who travel about with their disciples, carrying their religion from one village to the next. Africa has no Indian villages at all, in any case, and the appearance of a band of this sort in a town like Machakos is not exactly in the Indian tradition of the wandering holy man.

Other Asian religions are not associated with Islam or Hinduism, and one finds no Hindu gods or Brahmin priests. Goans do have a caste of Brahmins, left over from their previous connection with Hinduism, but their priests are largely Europeans and their religious languages are governed by their parent body, the Roman Catholic church. Portuguese and Latin were used in Goa, English and Latin in the colonial period in Kenya, and English and Swahili in the survey year, with some explanations in Konkani in Nairobi for non-English-speaking Goans. Swahili is for their African services and the number of Africans who share their sect is enormous by Asian standards, i.e. 22.2 per cent of the African population in 1962. 36.7 per cent of Africans are Protestant Christians, with no overlap, but numbers are still impressive. Goans are the smallest of the major regional groups of Asians, with roughly 9 per cent of the Asian population before Kenyanization, and adding their overlap to that of the Sunni Muslims one finds 15 per cent of the Asian population sharing religions with Africans.

Goans rarely attend Swahili services, and their self-reports of languages of religion do not include Swahili. English is the primary religious language for Kenya Goans now, since the church shift to the vernacular as a language of prayer, but High Masses are still said in Latin in some churches and non-English-speaking Goans still use prayer books in Latin, 'following' but not understanding.

Gujarati Jains and Punjabi Sikhs are ex-Hindus with reform religions (i.e. no gods, no Brahmin priests), and roughly 2,000 years between their languages of prayer. Both use the speech of their founder, but the Jains can no longer understand theirs, dating back some 2,500 years; Sikhs can follow the slightly archaic form of Punjabi (about 400 years old) with fair comprehension. But they cannot read their religious script without special training, and this script (Gurumukhi, 'from the mouth of the Guru') is taught in Sikh schools all over the world and regarded as a holy language. Their founder made no claims to divinity himself, and all of his successors are regarded as teachers, but the holy book (the Granth Saheb) has acquired divinity and they treat it with great reverence. A Sikh who cannot read the Gurumukhi script is thought to have lost his religion and cases are extremely rare in Kenya. Jains have no tradition of this kind, and no holy book, but their set prayers in the ancient Ardhamagadhi Prakrit are recited in Kenya as in India, and the language lives on. Their founder has acquired divinity, over the centuries, but is also seen as a teacher in the same tradition as the Buddha who lived in the same period and founded another religion with another local language (Pali).

Minority Asian religions include a handful of Buddhists from Ceylon, with household prayers in Pali and explanatory books in Sinhalese, and a larger minority of Parsees, with household prayers in an ancient Persian language (Avestan) and explanatory books in Gujarati. The Parsees are Zoroastrians, by religion, and their god is a sun god, Ahuramazda. Other minorities are largely Muslims and Hindus, with a handful of Christian Protestants (including Plymouth Brethren). Small regional communities, like the Sindhis, turn up in Sikh temples but none are Sikhs.

Asian languages of prayer are summarized below for the three major sub-groups only:

TABLE 11.3 *Kenya Asian languages of prayer*

Punjabi
Hindus:	Sanatan	Sanskrit
	Arya Samaj	Vedic Sanskrit
Sikhs		Gurumukhi Punjabi
Muslims		Arabic

Gujarati
Hindus	Sanskrit
Jains	Ardhamagadhi Prakrit
Muslims	Arabic

Goan
Christian	English, Latin.

Religious overlaps with Europeans and Arabs also deserve some consideration, but it will be appreciated that Europeans are also involved in the Kenyanization and the 1962 census figures are outdated. Europeans had a total population of 55,759 in that year, roughly three-quarters Christian Protestant (77.1 per cent); 18.6 per cent were Christian Catholics like the Goans, and the rest included 115 Muslims and '66 Hindus or Sikhs'. Arabs had a total population of 34,048 with a large majority of Muslims (99.1 per cent); some overlaps with Asians occurred (66 Catholics, 34 Hindus or Sikhs) but the census report discounts these figures as suspected errors in enumeration or processing. Muslims in both cases would be largely Sunnis, with a few cases of intermarriage with the Shia Ismailis and European Hindus or Sikhs might also be Asian wives. Two were found in my sample surveys of 478 Asians in Nairobi in 1969, but the samples were small and the proportion high by comparison with the census (66 Europeans in an Asian population of 176,613).

(c) RECREATIONAL LANGUAGES

Asian recreations are so numerous that one scarcely knows where to begin. Early immigrants may have worked from dawn to dusk, with no break at weekends, but this pattern has long since gone; Asian communities have functions of all kinds, all year long, finishing up with great religious festivals and beginning again the next day. Indian villagers slot their festivals and weddings into the slack seasons of the agricultural year but Africa has no Indian villages and the patterns are divided now, with religious festivals as in India and other festivities, like weddings, in the school holidays when large parties of Asians are free to travel all over Kenya and East Africa by all available transport; buses, long-range taxis, large Mercedes automobiles, etc. Urbanization has made many changes in their social patterns, and links with village India are weak but much time is still devoted to their festivals and weddings and the songs and dances of village India have been passed on to Kenya-born grandchildren who may never have seen an Indian village or lived outside an African town. The village bridegroom on his white horse has been left behind in India and the rites of Holi are not celebrated by Kenya Asians—but young Asians have a lively interest in the Indian heritage and the festival of Holi was revived last year, by some Mombasa youths who set up their own committee and arranged a proper Asian function with refreshments and speeches by members of the committee and African and Asian guests.

Indian villagers light Holi bonfires on the hillsides, and go out into the local streets to throw indelible powders at all passers-by, but the Mombasa Asians held a 'function' instead and this was only to be expected. Kenya Asians are expected to be orderly, and consider others, and their recreations are adapted to fit their current status as an immigrant minority in a country with a culture of its own. The fireworks and explosions of the festival of Diwali have been silenced; the bells and gongs of India are muffled in East Africa and Kenya Asian recreations are sedate by village standards.

Languages of recreation are also affected by government direction and I raised the matter of Holi to illustrate the Kenya Asian pattern of adaptation in a semi-public domain with a great deal of freedom in some areas and some restrictions. Jungly recreations like Holi and the Punjabi game of *Kabadi* are largely gone, but Indian recreations are flourishing. Many are organized by committees with English as a contact language with government (corporate committee registration, invitations, official guests, etc.), and community languages with their own membership. Hindustani is used largely as an Asian lingua franca, but here one has to be careful because some 'associations' follow the pattern of their parent body abroad, e.g. Hindi for the Gujarati-speaking membership of the Seva Dal, a social service organization. No Indian languages are used by the Lions' Club, and other organizations with an international or 'interracial' focus. Hindustani is also omitted in homogeneous community recreations, but English is often combined with the community language at formal functions, and the membership is sometimes notified in advance; the Detailed Programme of the Sikh Students' Seminar, 1969, included addresses, oratorical contests, and debates in Punjabi (Guru Nanak and the Philosophy of Sikhism, Recognise all Human Race as One, etc.), and English (Sikhs as a Nation of Martyrs, Religion Can Promote World Peace, etc.).

English prevails in informal recreations with an English context (European coffee houses, cinemas, etc.), and regional languages in Asian gatherings with a focus on dance, drama, sport, etc. Cricket is shared by all, leading to what one observer described as 'a babble of tongues' (Punjabi, Gujarati, Hindustani, English, etc.), but other sports divide, the Punjabis focusing on rough sports (notably hockey and the East African Safari) and the Gujaratis on the milder sports (badminton, table tennis, etc.). Goans divide their energies between mild sports and dancing, with great gala dances in the holidays, ordinary dances every weekend, and many dance bands on Western models, i.e. pop groups, hard rock groups, etc. Punjabis and Gujaratis also do some Western dancing, but Punjabis keep the village *bhangra* (rough, but not jungly) and the Gujaratis have their *garba* (vigorous but not rough). Regional languages prevail in these gatherings and the programme of the annual East African *Garba* Dancing Competition, for example, is printed in Gujarati. Attendance would include Hindus and Jains, who practise this dance for the Diwali festival, and not Muslims, who have their own festivals; Punjabi Hindus and Sikhs also share the festival of Dussehra, but not Muslims. Urdu poetry is, however, loved by all Punjabis and no religious divisions appear in the Punjabi Poets' Association. Urdu songs (called *ghazals*) are also popular with Gujaratis, and Hindi film songs belong to all Gujaratis and Punjabis.

Urdu *ghazals* are associated with Pakistan and Hindi film songs with India, but Kenya Asians have long since decided to treat the spoken language as their joint property and their songs are treated like speech. Directors of the Hindustani programme of the Voice of Kenya made a conscious decision when they drew up the still unpublished word lists for broadcasting; Gandhi strongly urged his people to merge religious differences in the lingua franca of Hindustani (or Hindi-Urdu), and the Kenya Asians followed his advice. Politicians in India drew a national boundary instead and separated their religions by physical distance. Massacres followed as the Muslims in India fled to Pakistan and the Sikhs and Hindus in Pakistan to India, and both new nations retreated to their own version of the language, as people are apt to do in times of violence.

Religious materials for Kenya Asians came, thereafter, from two different nations in Hindi and Urdu, but the people in Kenya heard and used their lingua franca. Cultural divisions remain between the Punjabis and Gujaratis, but forms are freely exchanged. No one borrows the religious turbans of the Sikhs, for example, but girls appear in Punjabi trousers one day, Gujarati saris the next, and dresses the next. Culture switching of this kind is 'modernization' or fashion, with 'Westernization' reserved for the permanent shift of the Goans to short hair and European dress. Shia Ismailis from Gujarat are somewhere in between, with a recent shifting to the Westernizing pattern at the suggestion of H.H. the late

Aga Khan, who was concerned that Indian dress might cut his people off from their host government and population.

Surnames have also been changed by Asians, but here most take care to keep within their own community names, borrowing an old sub-caste name of Harkhani, for example, to separate oneself from the other five pages of Shahs in the Kenya phone book. All Jains are named Shah, almost, with a few Chandarias and others (with old surname differences), and new names like Harkhani and Minoo add a little variety. The pages full of Patels, however, include some people who have adopted the Patel name of the Patidar caste, and thereby closed the gap between the higher name of Patel and their own surnames; Patels do not accept this, and no census is taken of their caste. Nor is there any sign of 'assimilation' resulting from this surname shift.

Regional divisions have been bridged with Hindustani, but Asians see the language more as a preventive measure against a split into Pakistanis and Indians. The Goans have long been separated from other Asians by their association with Portugal and Asians want no more national divisions. None seem to have any attachment to the new national traditions of India (flag, classical dancing, classical music, etc.), and the Gujarati Muslims have no loyalty to Urdu as the national language of Pakistan. The Punjabi Muslim pattern is blurred by their long association with Urdu as a language of religion, with Arabic for prayers and Urdu for explanations.

Kenyans are now expected to identify with the nation and Asians do this to some extent with household pictures of President Kenyatta, but few attend large public meetings with a national focus. Shop pictures of the President are obligatory and one can discount these, but the household pictures are not and these may be taken as symbols. Ismailis also have both Aga Khans on their walls and other Asians have their gurus and the gods. Nor can they yet identify with a national language as Kenya is still choosing between English and the spoken and literary idioms of Swahili. Asians maintain the colonial pattern of English with official guests at all community functions and international (or interracial) associations—cf. past use of English in the 'interracial' Frangipani Society and the Kenya Women's Club and present use of English in the 'international' Lions' Club. Recreational overlaps with Africans and Europeans occur in such associations, but numbers are small: Asian members are a large majority, Europeans are decreasing, and Africans are increasing. All focus on social service, but some information about cultural differences is exchanged in the ladies' societies: no one asks the European members to talk about their culture because Kenya is full of it, but Asian ladies do give talks on religion

306

and saris, calling upon non-members if they feel they cannot cope themselves. African members are largely Christians and often wives of government servants, and their major contribution is their resourcefulness in raising funds, a revelation to their Asian and European colleagues who have been relying upon charity bazaars and raffles for many years. Raffling goes on at all Asian functions and impressive sums are raised by some organizations, but they welcome all new ideas.

Sports had little overlap in the colonial period, but new arrivals from Britain brought cricket to Kenya, and Nairobi University has a mixed team; others may have played before, but Asians have no tradition, unlike India. Asians and Africans are also joining the European East African Safari now, and both have taken up the European sport of swimming in school swimming pools and others (e.g. the YMCA pool, Nairobi). Europeans have a few new Asians in their games of golf and tennis, and other sports are as before, i.e. soccer for Africans and others for Asians (hockey, badminton, etc.).

Africans also join the Goan dances in low-rent Asian areas which are now shared by both, and here, one finds some exchange of Swahili as a language of recreation in contrast to the élite use of English in social service associations and sports. Swahili-speaking Africans also watch the *garba* dancing of Asians in these marginal areas but few non-Asians appear at similar functions at Nairobi University and none at the annual competition in the Christmas holidays. The Sikh *bhangra* is also danced at some university functions, but non-Asians are advised to check in advance: they might well find themselves at a gathering devoted to the memory of Guru Nanak, or possibly an evening of *ghazals* and Hindi film songs. Some Africans and Europeans do appear at the Punjabi Hindu-Sikh celebration of their religious festival in a local Asian sports ground in Nairobi, but it is hard to find them in a crowd of several thousand turbaned Sikhs.

African children are, however, included in many Asian recreations connected with such festivals (school plays, etc.) and the gap between the Asians and their host population is shrinking. The Arya Samaj, for example, holds most of its functions in Nairobi in its school facilities and their new African students are able to watch the community worship, ladies' weekly *satsangs*, baby health shows, Gujarati *garba* dancing, Hindi plays, etc. African teachers are rare in 'former European and Asian' schools and both continue to stress their own cultures as in the colonial period, but Swahili songs are also heard as part of their efforts to identify with Kenya. Some 2,000–3,000 Americans (including dependants) are now in various advisory roles but the Peace Corps teachers are not assigned to Asian schools and Asian children have little contact with Americans. The

American Community School prepares its own children to pass American, not Kenyan, examinations and no Africans or Asians were attending in the survey year. Adults of both groups work as clerical staff in offices of American foundations and cultural exchanges are largely between adults, thus tending to perpetuate the colonial period of no family contact between Asian and non-Asian. Office parties are, however, held in the evenings to try and establish some contact with Africans and Asian families and these are similar in intent, but not in format, to the 'bridge' parties in colonial India. The language is predictably English for all concerned: Englishmen in Kenya often speak Swahili but Americans are, by and large, monolingual and Swahili would not, in any case, be considered suitable with the élite Africans who work in offices of this kind.

Asian housewives rarely meet non-Asians and events like office parties have not facilitated further contacts with Europeans in élite Asian areas, now shared with some non-Asians. School contacts are reflected in increased interaction of Asian and African children: patterns in such an area are illustrated below, in another excerpt from a language diary:

(Tues. 25th. March) My house is situated on Blenheim Rd, off Ainsworth Hill, the precinct of the renowned National Museum. Having resided in that locality and, in fact, that very household ever since I can remember, many different people of different races and religions have moved in and out of the neighbourhood; some being the settling-in type have remained in our vicinity for decades.

Immediately to our left and right stay two of our fellow Ismaili families, one of them being that of my uncle. Although we stay in two separate houses, they can be regarded as one unit in that we see a lot of each other and there is a considerable communication between us, invariably in Cutchi.

Directly opposite our little house resides a whole colony of Patels (with a couple of odd Lohanas) most of them occupying two double storeyed blocks of apartments. My mother, especially, has become friendly with several of these Patel womenfolk. A gathering of these gossipy housewives who exchange not only words but ideas (for example my mother often helps some of them with their knitting patterns which happen to be in English) is a familiar sight at home. The medium of communication is a high blend of Gujerati which, apparently, my mother has picked up quite well. I, on the other hand, whenever an opportunity to exchange a few words with some of them arises, find my Gujerati rather inferior in quality and have to invariably fumble for words. Most of these Patel women know not a word of English.

The menfolk rarely come into contact with my family being apparently busy with their businesses; some of them being big-time businessmen. Having apparently had the opportunity of being educated most of them have a considerable knowledge of the English language although it's not likely that it is used as a medium of conversation at home.

During the pre-independence days, there used to be some British army officers occupying a block of flats next to my uncle's residence. Since then several families of different races have come to live there. There is a Goan family, three Hindu, one Sikh and three

African families. Only the Sikh and one of the African families have any connection with my family in some way or the other. My mother is quite friendly with the Sikh woman and whenever they are together, I notice they chat in Hindustani (not Punjabi of which my mother cannot utter a word). My eight-year-old kid brother has made friends with the young Sikh boy and with a couple of African children and they rigidly use English as a medium of conversation . . . though they play more than they talk.

Just around the corner is a European family with whom we have absolutely no communication. Several other European and African families live in the block of flats behind our house but we don't see them and they don't see us.

As for my own family, that is my mother, sister and three other brothers, we belong to the Cutchi speaking sector (there is no dividing line though) of the Ismaili community. Our dialect differs appreciably in style to that of the Tanzanians or the Zanzibaris (who charmingly mix a bit of Swahili with it).

More often than ever there is a tendency, especially amongst the younger generation to either borrow words and phrases from English or switch over entirely to English during the course of conversation (in either Cutchi or Gujarati).

(d) LANGUAGE IN EDUCATION

Kenya Asian languages of education have been adapted to the current restrictions of the domain, but some autonomy remains and the contrast between the community schools in Nairobi and other larger towns and the Indian (inter-community) schools in smaller towns is still reflected in current languages of education. English is the medium of instruction in all 'former Asian schools' and subject languages include Swahili, Indian languages, and French. Goan schools exclude Indian languages as in the colonial period and the Aga Khan schools of the Ismailis maintain their recent exclusion of Gujarati in most schools, in accordance with their spontaneous shift to English shortly before independence. Nairobi Ismailis plan to use Gujarati in one private school (i.e. non-government), but this is clearly exceptional, and their children normally receive no formal instruction in Indian languages. Other 'former Asian schools' in Nairobi use their former school languages as secondary languages and their children in these schools are still learning Indian languages; the full range is represented with Punjabi in Sikh schools, Gujarati in Jain schools, Hindi in Punjabi Hindu (Arya Samaj) schools, and Urdu in Punjabi Muslim schools.

All of these languages are taught in a primary school in the small town of Kericho which has Gujarati for 88 students, Punjabi for 19, Hindi for 3, and Urdu for 7, and this repertoire (with different languages for each religion) is not unusual in towns with diverse Asian communities. The town of Kitale has an Asian population of approximately 1,500 and teaches Gujarati alone in its Asian nursery school, but the lack of other languages is clearly due to the composition of the local Asian population which includes minorities of Goans and Punjabis (Hindus, Sikhs and Muslims) and a large majority of Gujaratis (i.e. 1,000 Gujarati-speaking Patels, Lohanas and Jains, and 350 Cutchi-speaking Patels).

Small town Asians cannot maintain secondary schools, and the inter-Asian focus is lost when their children go to separate religious schools in large towns for further education. Some are also sent to government (i.e. non-Asian) primary schools, with no Indian languages at all, and the Asian focus is dispersed. Nairobi Asians send many children to 'former European schools' and a few to 'former African schools', and similar conditions obtain. Asian children are often illiterate, now, in their religious languages and their parents are concerned; Arya Samaj Hindus have private classes in Hindi, and Muslims maintain Urdu and Gujarati to some extent with private instruction, but attrition is apparent.

Swahili is also taught in some Asian schools, but African teachers of Swahili are hard to find and schools have three alternatives: French, Swahili with Asian teachers, or 'provision for Swahili'. Asian teachers rarely know enough Swahili to teach it and the government maintains evening classes to fill the gap between the household Swahili of the teachers' homes and the Standard Swahili at school.

'Former Indian school languages' are also represented in the Kenya Asian population, and one cannot assume a lack of education in non-English-speaking Asians. Kenya-born Asians learned English as a primary or secondary language in their schools and many use 'educated' and 'un-educated' as synonyms for 'English-speaking' and 'non-English-speaking' but the reference is local. Some Asian children fail to make a distinction between 'English' and 'education' but immigrants with Indian school languages are also educated by adult standards.

Government control of Asian school languages is clearly extensive and a distinction is, therefore, made between the Asian domain of recreation and the public domain of education, but some autonomy remains; communities can still maintain unaided schools if they choose to do so, and Indian languages can still be taught as subjects in all schools.

(e) WORK LANGUAGES

Government control over Asian work languages has been reduced by the Kenyanization of Asian civil servants, but teachers in Asian schools have now become government servants and large numbers of Asians still use English as the work language of government service. Others also use it in offices of foreign companies (British, American, etc.), and often as a work language in their own offices (doctor, dentist, lawyer, etc.). Literacy in English is a requirement for all, but professional people also have a clientele of Africans and Asians and their overlap with traders with African and Asian customers is apparent. Both use Swahili with African clients and Indian languages with Asians and the primary difference between their work languages is in the language of record keeping: traders normally use Gujarati or Punjabi and professional people normally use English.

English is also used as a spoken language by traders and professional people with European clients (or English-speaking Africans) and their work languages often include 5 languages or more: non-English-speaking clients and customers are, however, a majority and non-English-speaking traders are common.

Asians who claim to use 5 languages or more at work are typically traders or professional people and the needs of both clearly exceed those of the government servant who often claims only English. One tends to think in these stereotypes, but it will be appreciated that the Asian population has a norm of 4 languages. Artisans and government servants often use other languages at work in secondary roles (e.g. Swahili with office messengers), and their self-reports of English or Swahili alone are an oversimplification.

CONCLUSIONS

My description of the language use of the Kenya Asian population has been characterized by a tendency to oversimplify, and readers will find many variations between the self-reports on the one hand and my summary on the other; Asian languages often change as they move from one domain to the next, and some tend to concentrate on the primary languages and overlook the others. Languages also change from one group to the next and observers tend to focus on the primary contrasts and overlook the rest. Diversity in language use has been reduced, for example, by focusing on three regional groups of Gujaratis, Punjabis, and Goans and classifying the rest as 'others'; Asians will recognize many other cases of oversimplification, but also recognize the reasons. Asian diversity is sometimes confusing to others, and my presentation has been given in the Kenya Asian fashion—with round numbers for statistics, and many generalizations. Census takers recognize a discrepancy between real ages, for example, and reported ages of Kenya Asians and I recognize the difference between an exact report on language use of Kenya Asians and my own, and apologize to the Asians for presenting them as stereotypes—sociolinguistic groups have been substituted for individuals—and much is lost.

311

Something has, I hope, been added by taking the well labelled Asian (e.g. the Sikh, the Ismaili) and showing how a number of variables affects his use of language in the different domains in which he finds himself daily in the company of co-religionists, workmates, family, employees, etc., some of whom are of his own language community, many of whom are not.

It is important to realize that current language use is partially determined not only by the post-independence situation in which Asians are obliged to adapt to government directives concerning school languages, but by the colonial situation before the 1960s, when social segregation allowed all communities a larger measure of autonomy. Thus, the language patterns of early immigrants differ from those of their children and grandchildren. The immigrants acquired languages as they needed them, while others grew up in a more varied linguistic environment. Again, the language patterns of recent immigrants from India will for obvious reasons differ from those of settled Kenya Asian families, and to explain their linguistic resources and the adaptations they make we must look at their language training.

The reader could gain a clearer understanding of the interaction of all these variables by following a Sikh, say, or a Goan, through the different situations of his daily life; informants do this in language diaries. It would be clear that the patterns of a Goan and a Sikh in similar situations would not exactly coincide. Part of the explanation of such differences is to be found in the varying opportunities which members of different communities have to learn a variety of languages; but we may be puzzled unless we look at the individual's various groups of identification in the past as well as in the present, in addition to his opportunities for learning. Linguists talk about the privilege of occurrence of a word in several different functions—e.g. noun, verb, adjective—but also realize that one word may have two functions (e.g. 'walk' as verb and noun) and another one (e.g. 'cat' as noun). We could say that an individual, similarly, has privileges of occurrence in a number of different groups; and we should note that his identifications now are partly determined by the privilege of occurrence of his community in the past, in its history; and that identification is signalled by the use of languages associated with specific groups. Thus, we are interested in the range of social repertoires of individuals and may get a distinction between overlap in function and difference in range, e.g. between the Sikh as Sikh and trader *v.* the Goan as Goan and non-trader. To take another example, Sikh children are now undergoing the same experience as Africans in using English as a medium of instruction in their schools, so their language repertoires are expanding. Goans, on the other hand, adopted English many years ago, so that the experience of transition of the two groups is different. The social repertoires of different Asian communities are expanding in the same way at the present time, but some groups are better equipped linguistically to handle wider and more varied contacts in the new society.

No generalizations are made about the language use of the Asian population as a whole in this report, and none are possible. Asians had a large measure of autonomy in the colonial period and diverse patterns of adaptation are reflected in their current language use.

NOTES

[1] *Statistical Abstract, 1967*, p. 151.

[2] Secondary sources for this chapter include unpublished papers for a New Delhi seminar on 'Indians Abroad: Asia and Africa'. Interested readers may contact the Indian Council for Africa, 5 Balvantray Mehta Lane, New Delhi, for further details.

[3] R. H. Desai, *Indian Immigrants in Britain*, Oxford University Press, London, 1963.

[4] See e.g. M. Marriott, *Caste Ranking and Community Structures in Five Regions of India and Pakistan*, Poona, 1965.

[5] Asian households have an average size of 5.9, with a total of 30,200 households for the 1962 Asian population of 176,000. Urban households are typically rented (69.3 per cent) or owned by occupant (19.2 per cent); constructed of brick or stone (91.4 per cent), with W.C. sanitation (88.3 per cent.) See J. G. C. Blacker, 'Population Growth and Urbanization in Kenya', *United Nations Mission to Kenya on Housing*, L. N. Bloomberg and C. Abrams (eds.), Nairobi, 1965. Comparable data on ownership, etc., of rural households is not given and projections for 1970 have been invalidated by Asian emigration.

[6] Leading Asian entrepreneurs are listed in *Who Controls Industry in Kenya?*, East African Publishing House, Nairobi, 1968. See esp. Africindo Industrial Development, p. 14; Industrial Promotion Services Ltd., p. 174; Kenya's Top Fifty Directors, 1968, p. 145; the Madhvani and Mehta Groups, pp. 7–8.

[7] See bibliography to Chapter 2 for publications in African languages. Other publications can be obtained from local Kenya Asians, and religious organizations abroad, e.g. the Sikh Students' Federation, Nairobi; The Ahmadiyya Muslim Foreign Missions Department, Rabwah, W. Pakistan.

[8] G. Wilson, 'Mombasa—a Modern Colonial Municipality' in A. Southall (ed.), *Social Change in Modern Africa*, Oxford University Press, London, 1961, p. 100.

[9] D. M. Halliman and W. T. W. Morgan, 'The City of Nairobi' in W. T. W. Morgan, (ed.), *Nairobi: City and Region*, Oxford University Press, Nairobi, 1967, pp. 98–120.

[10] See Desai's analysis in 'Leadership in an Asian Community', *Proceedings of the East African Institute of Social Research*, June 1963. My own is similar, but Desai uses 'linguistic affiliation' as a distinctive feature where I use region of origin in India, classifying Konkani- and English-speaking Goans, for example, as 'Goans', and Cutchi- and Gujarati-speaking Ismailis as 'Gujaratis'.

[11] See D. Steel, *No Entry*, Hurst, London, 1969, for a general review of Kenya Asian citizenship. Also Chanan Singh, 'The Problem of Citizenship', unpublished report to seminar on 'Indians Abroad: Asia and Africa', New Delhi, 1969.

[12] Government officials in Kenya cite the figure of 45,000 Asian citizens (e.g. Mr James Gichuru in *East African Standard*, January 1969; the late Mr Tom Mboya in *The Times*, London, 13 January 1969). Some 10,000 Asian applications for citizenship were pending in 1969 (Mr Mboya, op. cit.) which would reduce the number of British Asians to 100,000 when granted. Martin Ennals quotes a British High Commission estimate of 100,000 British Asians, and an Asian estimate of 52,000—placing his own at 67,000,

'Report on U.K. Citizens of Asian Origin in Kenya' in D. Steel, op. cit., pp. 248–51. My figure of 110,000 British Asians may therefore be too high: local Asian leaders accepted the British High Commission estimate of 100,000 (plus 10,000 pending applications) as valid in the Survey year of 1968–9 in order to account for the difference between the current population estimate of 174,000 (or more) and the citizenship figure of 45,000. Citizens were thought to be largely children and Ismailis.

[13] *Statistical Abstract, 1967.*

[14] *Statistical Abstract, 1967.* The *Abstract* for the following year has a more inclusive list of public services, e.g. E.A. Airways Corp.—Kenya only—and the figures for Asian public servants is accordingly raised to 10,600.

[15] I am grateful to the Ministry of Economic Planning and Development for this information.

[16] *Statistical Abstract, 1967,* p. 150. The 1968 *Abstract* cites 27,400 for 1966 and 31,000 for 1967.

[17] *Kenya Population Census (1962),* vol. IV. p. 7.

[18] ibid., table 1.5. Also cited in Appendix A to this chapter as Table 11. A2.

[19] No official statistics are available. Resident Asians supplied my figures for current population of Kitale, Eldoret, Kisii, Kericho, etc.

[20] Government expected 3,000 non-citizen Asians to be refused trade licences in 1969–70, involving some 30,000 Asians, i.e. 1.5 families in each shop with 4.5 people per family, thus affecting 7 people per family. 21,000 would be affected by trade licensing restrictions, and another 10,000 by notices to stop trading in specified goods (*East African Standard,* 6 January 1969). A leading Asian businessman estimated the number of non-citizen Asian businesses in Kenya at 9,000 (Mr Mulchand Khimasia, *The Reporter,* 10 January 1969).

Notices were subsequently served in all towns, but appeals were later granted in some areas where African traders were unavailable (e.g. Kitale with 79 quit notices and 15 successful appeals—*Daily Nation,* 19 April 1969). Citizens normally retained their licences, but Kiambu banned all Asian traders (*Daily Nation,* 8 January 1969), and county officials expected full refusals for Nyeri, Fort Hall, Saba Saba and Maragua (*Daily Nation,* 13 January 1969). Elsewhere quit notices involved one-quarter to one-half of the local traders, e.g. 120 refusals in Kiambu County, 49 in Machakos, 18 in Embu, 16 in Meru, 9 in Isiolo, 20 in Kitale, etc. Observers estimated a total of 730 refusals by late January, including 320 in Nairobi (*The Observer,* London, 19 January 1969). 2,670 Asian traders were eventually licensed for 1968–9, and 1,082 were given quit notices (*Daily Nation,* 23 May 1969). Britain was then prepared to issue 1,500 entry vouchers to East African Asian household heads, at the rate of 125 per month (*Daily Nation,* 25 April 1969). The Nairobi press now estimates another 1,000 trade licence refusals in 1970–71, with roughly 400 for Nairobi, and 250 for Mombasa (*East African Standard,* 13 January 1970). 9,000 East African Asians were said to be 'queueing' for vouchers with another 400 currently in Europe awaiting entry to Britain (*The Guardian,* 14 July 1970).

[21] Kenya had 594 medical men—doctors, dentists, etc.—in 1962, including 330 Asians; 1,745 male teachers, including 1,005 Asians; and 354 male jurists (including advocates) including 229 Asians. Others in all three categories were largely Europeans—*Population Census (1962),* vol. IV, p. 92. No official statistics are available for female teachers. My sample surveys of Nairobi Asians included 31 teachers in an adult population of 478; the Nairobi West sample of 76 adults had 4 women teachers and no men; the Ngara sample of 402 adults had 17 women teachers and 10 men.

APPENDIX

TABLE 11.A1   *Asian population of Kenya by religion, 1931, 1948 and 1962*

Religion	1931		1948		1962	
	Number	Percentage	Number	Percentage	Number	Percentage
Hindu	19,748	45.3	51,395	52.6	97,841	55.4
Muslim	15,006	34.4	27,585	28.2	40,057	22.7
Sikh	4,427	10.1	10,621	10.9	21,169	12.0
Christian	4,131	9.5	7,613	7.8	16,524	9.3
Other	311	0.7	473	0.5	1,022	0.6
Total	43,623	100.0	97,687	100.0	176,613	100.0

TABLE 11.A2   *Asian population of main towns 1948–62*

Town	Population 1948	Population 1962	Net increase	Percentage increase
Nairobi	41,810	86,453	44,643	106.8
Mombasa	25,580	43,713	18,133	70.9
Kisumu	4,973	8,355	3,382	68.0
Nakuru	3,247	6,203	2,956	91.0
Eldoret	1,845	3,758	1,913	103.7
Thika	1,383	2,336	953	68.9
Kitale	1,314	2,065	751	57.2
Kericho	758	1,462	704	92.9
Nyeri	604	1,147	543	89.9
Nanyuki	731	982	251	34.3
Machakos	422	719	297	70.4
Kisii	348	673	325	93.4
Meru	559	662	103	18.4
Kakamega	604	601	−3	−0.5
Gilgil	384	593	209	54.4
Fort Hall	698	556	−142	−20.3

TABLE 11.A3   *Local-born and foreign-born Asians in census years*

Census year	Local-born		Foreign-born	
	Number	Percentage	Number	Percentage
1931	13,987	32.1	29,636	67.9
1948	47,429	48.6	50,258	51.4
1962	108,978	61.7	67,635	38.3

TABLE 11.A4 *Percentage distribution of Kenya Asian population by education group*

Age group	Sex	Education group					Total
		0 or Not stated	1–4	5–8	9–12	13 and over	
10–19	Males	7.3	11.7	52.4	27.8	0.9	100
	Females	9.6	12.5	55.0	22.2	0.8	100
20–29	Males	8.1	5.1	27.8	53.1	5.9	100
	Females	17.1	11.0	38.7	30.2	3.0	100
30–39	Males	10.8	9.5	28.8	44.6	6.3	100
	Females	30.9	18.2	33.8	15.8	1.4	100
40–49	Males	17.7	15.1	30.2	31.5	5.5	100
	Females	49.8	18.8	23.1	7.7	0.8	100
50–59	Males	25.8	16.0	27.0	26.4	4.9	100
	Females	60.0	17.1	17.6	4.9	0.4	100
60–69	Males	33.5	17.4	26.4	19.3	3.3	100
	Females	72.9	14.1	9.3	3.4	0.3	100
70 and over	Males	46.5	15.3	23.2	12.1	2.9	100
	Females	83.3	8.4	6.5	1.4	0.3	100

TABLE 11.A5 *Size and number of Asian households*

	Total Asian population	No. of households	Household size
Nairobi	87,000	15,000	5.8
Mombasa	43,000	7,000	6.2
Other towns	35,000	6,000	6.0
Rural	10,100	2,200	4.6

TABLE 11.A6 *Economically active Asian males by major occupation group and occupational status*

Major occupation group	Employees		Employers & Own account workers		Unpaid family workers		Total	
	Number	Percentage	Number	Percentage	Number	Percentage	Number	Percentage
Professional and managerial	2,471	9.0	6,577	58.8	282	14.9	9,330	23.0
Technical and supervisory	1,438	5.2	211	1.9	25	1.3	1,674	4.1
Clerical and sales	14,452	52.4	1,547	13.8	1,088	57.6	17,087	42.1
Craftsmen and skilled manual workers	7,868	28.5	2,390	21.4	315	16.7	10,573	26.0
Semi-skilled and unskilled workers and all others not elsewhere classified	1,337	4.9	453	4.1	180	9.5	1,970	4.8
Total	27,566	100.0	11,178	100.0	1,890	100.0	40,634	100.0

Sources: Table 11.A5 figures from J. G. C. Blacker, 'Population Growth and Urbanization in Kenya', *United Nations Mission to Kenya on Housing, 1964.* Others from *Kenya Population Census (1962)* vol. IV.

12

Some Patterns of Language Use in the Rural Areas of Kenya

W. H. WHITELEY

INTRODUCTION

To achieve the degree of control and detail for the rural areas that has been presented for Nairobi, would have required intensive studies of selected communities over long periods. This was not possible; instead I have, in the main, had to rely on people's own views of how and when they use the languages in which they claim some competence. These were obtained through four pilot-type surveys:

1. The questionnaire and interviews discussed in Chapter 1. The discussion with the interviewees of their language behaviour during the preceding twenty-four hours in particular and more generally during the previous week, produced material of widely differing quantity and quality, varying from terse one-word answers to extended accounts—sometimes in minute detail—of day-to-day activities. In some cases the interviewees (and perhaps also the interviewers) became bored, in others they were suspicious or even hostile. One interviewer commented that members of one community were most reluctant to talk about their language behaviour lest it prejudice their claim with the Voice of Kenya for a programme in their local language.

    Despite these limitations, however, I am certain that the use of local people as interviewers, speaking the local language, has given to the material a reliability it would otherwise have been impossible to obtain, from which certain gross features of language use in the rural areas emerge rather clearly. We can now also see which geographical areas and which domains of language use would most repay further, more detailed study.

2. A questionnaire administered to civil servants when on a course at the Kenya Institute of Administration, and designed to elicit

information about language use at place of work, and attitudes towards languages.

3. Essays submitted for a competition sponsored by the Survey and advertised in Swahili and English through the *Nation* group of newspapers. The Swahili advertisement yielded only a handful of essays, but the English version elicited over 80 entries. Participants were asked to write an essay on two of the following quotations:

   (a) 'Most people like to use their mother tongue some time during the day—I certainly do'

   (b) 'I don't speak much Swahili, but it is often very useful'

   (c) 'Many Kenyans try to use English as much as possible, but I only use it when it is most appropriate'

   (d) 'Swahili is very important to me at the present time'

   (e) 'I am always finding myself in situations where one language is more appropriate than another'

   Nearly half the essays came from Luo and Kikuyu: virtually all were from men under thirty, and almost half were still at school. On the other hand, many describe in great detail the conflicts imposed on them by their formal language training when they return home, and the effect of that training on their own attitudes to languages. In this respect the essays are a useful adjunct to other sources of information.

4. A questionnaire modified from one originally prepared by the Mary Knoll Fathers, and sent out to Protestant and Catholic missions. This questionnaire suffered from some important deficiencies, which not only made quantification difficult but precluded access to certain kinds of information which would greatly have enhanced the value of the exercise. It is clear that a whole year could easily have been spent on investigating language use in this domain alone. The availability of the Catholic Directory[1] meant that questionnaires could easily be sent to all missions listed, and rather more than 80 per cent of the 211 addressees responded. The Protestants proved more difficult, since no comprehensive list of missions is available, but thanks to the help of the Christian Council of Kenya it was possible to draw up a substantial list for circulation, and about 70 per cent answered the questionnaire.[2]

This information was supplemented by material that I gathered myself during 1968/9 during the course of extensive travelling in six provinces. Previous field-work in Kisii and Kitui districts from 1954 onwards greatly facilitated my work in these areas.

TABLE 12.1 *Claimed frequency of use of Swahili in rural Kenya*

	Percentage of total sample claiming competence in Swahili at some level	Percentage of total sample claiming 3/5 frequency, i.e. several times a week or more often	Percentage of total sample claiming 1/2 frequency, i.e. once a week or less
Kikuyu (Kiambaa)	100	88	12
Pokomo (Salama)	99	81	18
Gusii (Manga)	90	68	22
Luyia (Bukusu)	100	66	34
Kamba (Kambai)	86	61	25
Embu	86	47	39
Luyia (Idakho)	84	47	37
Pokomo (Zubaki)	84	43	41
Taita	83	39	42
Luyia (L/Luy. border)	75	37.5	37.5
Kikuyu (Kirimukuyu)	96	35	58
Kuria	75	32	43
Luyia (Khayo)	91	31	60
Meru (Katheri)	53	27	26
Kipsigis (Lugumek)	61	19	43
Luo (L/Luy. border)	26	11	15
Luo (*Oyugis*)	33	11	22
Luo (L/G/K border)	58	10	48
Kipsigis (L/G/K border)	48	4	48
Gusii (L/G/K border)	40	nil	40

It should be stressed that the percentages in columns 2 and 3 relate to the total sample and not to the part of the sample who claim some competence in Swahili.

CLAIMED FREQUENCY AS OPPOSED TO CLAIMED COMPETENCE

It will be observed that in 13 samples more than 75 per cent claimed some competence in Swahili (see Table 12.1), while the Luo groups were at the bottom with 33 per cent or less. In only 2 samples, however, do more than 75 per cent claim a competence of 'quite a lot or more', these understandably being Pokomo (Salama) and Taita, with Kikuyu (Kiambaa), Pokomo (Zubaki) and Kamba (Kambai) close behind (see Table 1.18 in Chapter 1).

In the frequency table (12.1) only in two samples, Kikuyu (Kiambaa) and Pokomo (Salama), did 75 per cent or more of the sample claim to use the language 'several times a week' or more, and only in three more samples, Gusii, Luyia (Bukusu) and Kamba (Kambai), did 50 per cent or more claim this level of frequency, Luo again being very low down on the list with 11 per cent or less. No explanation is necessary for Pokomo but the other areas need some comment. While Kiambaa itself may be linguistically homogeneous, it is sufficiently close to Nairobi for people to commute, and, as will have become clear from the preceding chapters, a knowledge of Swahili is extremely valuable in the capital, which also provides many opportunities for using such skills. It must also be remarked that the average level of education in this sample is high, and that the average age is low (see Table 1.7 in Chapter 1). Finally, it may be worth pointing out that there does seem to be some evidence that Kikuyu 'go in' for trade to an extent not matched by other groups, and as will become clear in the discussion of trade below, Swahili is undoubtedly the language through which much trading is carried on. The Gusii situation is more difficult to account for (see also p. 328). An additional factor here may be that the sample was taken from an area quite near to the Gitutu divisional headquarters at Manga, where a District Officer is stationed. Many *barazas* in Swahili are held here, and this is also true of the many smaller meetings of the coffee, tea and pyrethrum growers which are held in different parts of the area, though it was my feeling that a great deal of simultaneous translation went on at those meetings I attended. Bukusu adjoins areas of relatively high heterogeneity with Teso, Päkot and other Luyia. All the language diaries report encounters with members of other ethnic groups.

The areas in which low-level frequencies are most noticeably higher than the high-level frequencies are Kikuyu (Kirimukuyu), Kipsigis, Luyia (Khayo), Luo and the L/K/G border area (see Table 12.1). In the case of the last mentioned it seems likely that the function of Swahili as a means of communication between differing ethnic groups is here taken over by other local languages, and especially Luo (see below 'Trade' and Tables 1.8–1.16 in Chapter 1). In the case of the Kikuyu sample which has a very high average education it may be that children who are taught it at school have rather little opportunity for using it in such a homogeneous area (cf. Kiambaa), and where, with such a level of education, English is more useful (cf. English competence/frequency figures in Table 12.2). On the other hand, if my remarks above are valid, that Kikuyu propensity for trade involves the necessity for using Swahili, some explanation for its not operating here must be sought. In the case of Kipsigis where there is a rather high overall percentage in the age group over 30, one might suggest that though many may have acquired some competence in the language while in the police, army, etc., this is of little relevance on their return home. Only a small proportion of the total Luo sample (33 per cent) claims any competence in Swahili, and the fact that more claim to use it less, rather than more, frequently, is entirely in keeping with other evidence about Luo and Swahili. Luyia (Khayo) remains a somewhat difficult case: it is the most heterogeneous sample, except for the border areas, with 37 per cent of the total sample claiming to speak L1+L2+Swahili. It is also unique in that nearly 90 per cent of the

322

total sample are over 30, and more than half are women. These are age groups with little education, and while this is likely to have included some Swahili, there would certainly be no English (see their position in the English competence/ frequency Table 12.2). Thus, while it is reasonable to assume that a large percentage will have some competence in Swahili (91 per cent), it seems evident that the existing pattern of heterogeneity involves fairly extensive use of Luyia by Teso and vice versa. This would seem to be one factor in the high incidence of low-level frequency.

TABLE 12.2 *Claimed frequency of use of English in rural Kenya*

	Percentage of total sample claiming competence in English at some level	Percentage of sample claiming 3/5 frequency, i.e. several times a week or more often	Percentage of sample claiming 1/2 frequency, i.e. once a week or less
Kikuyu (Kiambaa)	95	100	
Embu	92	67	25
Kikuyu (Kirimukuyu)	96	65	31
Luyia (Bukusu)	66	51	15
Kamba (Kambai)	57	48	9
Luo (L/Luy. border)	59	41	18
Taita	56	39	17
Meru (Katheri)	51	37	14
Luyia (L/Luy. border)	50	33	17
Pokomo (Salama)	38	31	7
Luyia (Idakho)	40	30	11
Kuria	40	29	11
Gusii (L/G/K border)	55	25	30
Luo (*Oyugis*)	36	22	14
Gusii	34	22	12
Kipsigis (L/G/K border)	23	15	7
Kipsigis	18	13	5
Luo (L/G/K border)	26	10	16
Luyia (Khayo)	31	9	22
Pokomo (Zubaki)	10	8	2

A final comment is provided by the diagram in Table 12.3 where an attempt is made to link claims about low-level competence with claims about low-level frequency. Clearly the five-point scales are not comparable, but some gross features may be picked out. It is, after all, reasonable to suppose that people who claim to have a high degree of competence in a language which is widely spoken in the area, should also make use of their skills fairly frequently, and vice versa. The table demonstrates that if low-level competence and frequency are compared, rather more than half the sample reveal a *lower* percentage of low-level (1/2) frequency, i.e. they use the language more often, while the remainder show a *higher* percentage of low-level frequency, i.e. they use the language less often. Generally speaking the former situation occurs where competence percentages are high, the latter where the percentages are lower. In other words, in those areas where a large proportion of the sample claim only a minimal knowledge of Swahili, there is nevertheless a tendency to use the language more often, i.e. several times a week or more. The occurrence of Luo in this group should be noted. On the other hand, and in contrast with the situation for English, a sizeable number of samples report lower frequencies than might have been expected from their competence.

As far as competence in English is concerned, three samples reported very high percentages claiming some competence in the language: the two Kikuyu samples, 95 and 96 per cent, and Embu 92 per cent. The remainder of the samples reported percentages of less than 70 per cent, with 11 groups reporting less than 50 per cent, and Kipsigis and Pokomo (Zubaki) reporting less than 20 per cent. The first three groups mentioned above also reported high-level frequencies of over 65 per cent, while 14 groups reported less than 40 per cent. The reasons for the predominance of these groups is not hard to find: all have a high average education and a majority of the two Kikuyu groups are under 30. It seems not improbable that the low figures reported from elsewhere can be attributed to variations in the availability and length of education. One interesting difference between frequency in use of Swahili and English may be observed by comparing Table 12.3 with Tables 12.4 and 12.5. While almost half the samples report an increase in low-level frequency in Swahili, i.e. an increase in infrequency, the corresponding area of the English diagrams is much smaller, with a large area of increase for the high-level frequency. It must be stressed again that the term 'increase' has no diachronic implications, the tables simply show the discrepancy between the two sets of responses. On the other hand it does rather look as if people are more anxious to use English more often at the present time.

What would, however, be extremely interesting would be to attempt to replicate these samples at fairly frequent intervals, to see whether the size of the segment indicating lower frequency increases or diminishes in relation to claimed competence, and indeed to see whether the levels of competence themselves changed. As the areas in which the samples were taken are known rather precisely this should not be too difficult a task.

DOMAINS OF LANGUAGE USE

In the rural areas language choice is exercised in a number of domains, with the constraints varying from domain to domain. The actual choices made vary not only from district to district but from location to location, and even within the location, depending upon a number of factors such as education, age, sex, the linguistic heterogeneity of the participants, and the long-term and short-term objectives of participation, etc. For example. one man may visit the 'dukas' twice a week, while his neighbour

TABLE 12.3 *Comparison between low-level frequency and low-level competence in Swahili*

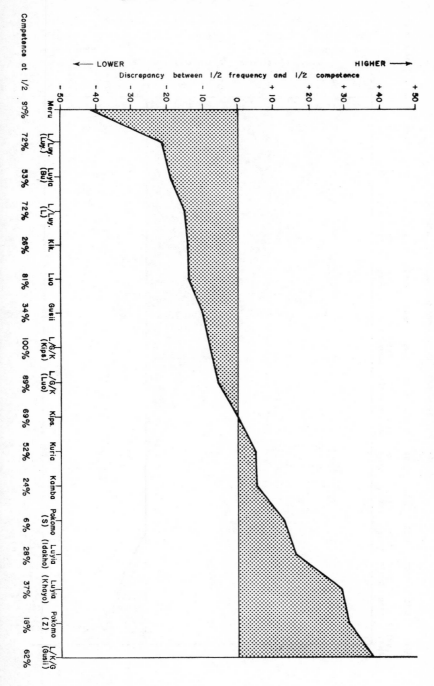

TABLE 12.4   *Comparison between low-level frequency and low-level competence in English*

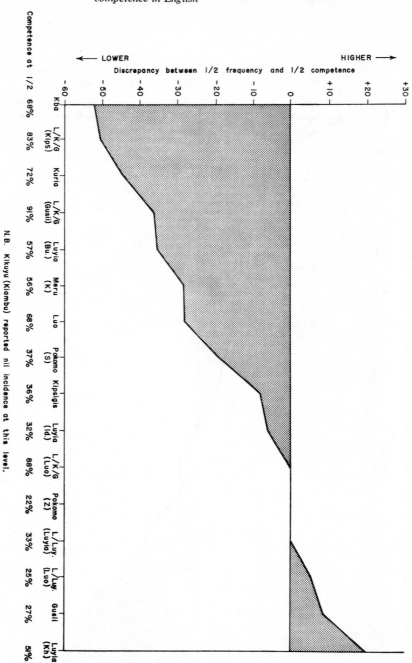

TABLE 12.5 *Comparison between high-level competence and high-level frequency in English*

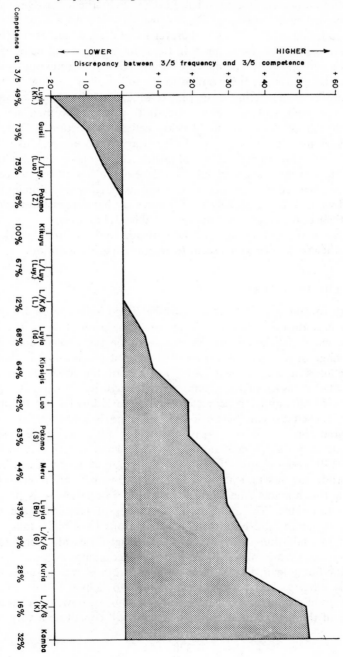

goes only once a month: it may pay the former to increase his competence in Swahili to an extent not considered necessary by the latter. One cannot talk of typical cases, but some of my Gusii friends have a pattern of life which I found widely replicated wherever I travelled. Much of the time is spent in or around the homestead, in the fields, visiting and being visited by friends and relatives. The men spend a good deal of time out drinking with friends or in bars; the women do a good deal of visiting. The men attend local council meetings from time to time, and other more specialized groups connected with cash crops, etc. Both men and women may also attend church services and mid-weekly religious functions. There will be sporadic need to visit the local dispensary, post office, 'dukas' and markets with wide variations in frequency. They may visit the district headquarters at intervals, perhaps even have a brush with the police and attend the local court—as spectator if not as participant. Finally, both men and women, but especially the former, may have spent time working outside their home areas (see Chapter 1, Tables 1.4 and 1.5).

Of these various domains, the homestead, trade, church, work and certain other social occasions seem to warrant special attention.

A. THE HOMESTEAD

There are several important factors which shape language choice in the home: it may turn out that it is, in the great majority of cases, the local language which is chosen, but the reasons for the choice show quite a wide range of diversity. A rather obvious, but crucial, fact is that the language used must, in most cases, be that of the least linguistically sophisticated member of the group. As a Kikuyu woman put it, 'When I visit my parents and old people, I like to use Kikuyu when talking to them or in their presence even if they have no business or interest in what is going on. One obvious reason why is that it is very rude to speak a language they don't understand . . . and I feel that I owe it to them to respect their inevitable "ignorance" and not to scorn it . . . '. She refers here to the fact that many older men and women are monolingual, and while this remains true of the rural areas no alternative is possible, let alone thinkable. Yet an increasing number of families share more than one language, and here other considerations have to be taken into account. The additional language may be English, Swahili or another local language. While all of these may have comparable 'utility' value around the homestead, English has a higher 'prestige' rating and is more frequently cited as being used in the home 'to help the children', 'to discuss current affairs' and so on. Such behaviour, is, however, character-istic only of the more educated families, who still constitute a very small minority of the rural population. A more common view is that expressed by a Luo student, aged 23, who comments, 'All my brothers and sisters, and my father too, understand and speak English quite well, but still we find that we speak our vernacular all the time . . . It is natural that back at home where nearly all our neighbours speak the vernacular, and for the purposes of social harmony, we should speak the language that furnishes us with a rich sense of humour . . . and in any case just for the mere pride that we attach to the use of vernacular . . . I would find it difficult to complain to any member of the family in English or Swahili. In fact, when quarrelling with my brothers and sisters, I always do it in vernacular, the same language that my father employs when issuing orders in the house.'

A husband and wife may share more than one local language, either because they come from different ethnic groups and each has acquired the language of the other, or because the community itself is heterogeneous and there is advantage to be gained in having a competence in two local languages, e.g. settlement areas, border areas, or because they are both immigrants into the community, e.g. Teso in Luyia (Khayo) or Waata in Pokomo and Giriama. In the case of these immigrant groups there is inadequate data at the present time, but a Teso in Khayo reported that he and his wife 'spoke Luyia simply because both live in Luyia and had been brought up in Luyia traditions'. From my own observations in southern Pokomo, at least some Waata families persist in using Waata, though virtually all appear to be bilingual in Waata/Pokomo.[3] Inter-ethnic marriages in my samples were extremely rare, only in Luyia (Khayo) did they constitute anything like a significant proportion of the sample, and even here the reports of behaviour are not adequate for any useful generalization. There are, however, numbers of reports like the following—and by no means restricted to this area—where the Luyia husband uses Teso for his Teso wife because ' . . . he likes to please her by talking her language.'

In some cases language choice may be determined less by what is common than by what is not. Thus, the man who finds that his wife cannot or will not learn his language, or vice versa, will be forced to learn hers or a third language. A Teso reported sorrowfully that ' . . . he spoke to his Luyia wife and children in Luyia since none has taken the trouble to learn Teso.' In this situation, however, Teso are in a minority, and, as will be recalled from Chapter 1, claim a greater competence in Luyia than do Luyia in Teso. No reports of the reverse situation were presented. Finally, the choice of the local language may be determined primarily by the respect and adherence to the set of values and institutions which the local language is held, in some way, to embody. Thus the Kikuyu woman, quoted above, comments, 'I feel that I have an important maternal obligation to give my children what my mother gave me—a priceless mother tongue—the most proper thing is to help my children to master Kikuyu and to know their African identity and their people . . . '

In brief, then, one can say that the homestead is the focus for the use of the local language, despite the use of English in certain circumstances, and also of Swahili, in activities like ploughing.[4] Yet this is simply a gross characterization: it ignores completely the subtle shifts that occur to signal micro-changes in the setting. I have been present in homesteads when they occur and all our interviewees reported their occurrence, but it is rather difficult to provide adequate documentation of their form, as also of their actual occurrence. Since the ability to make choices is a function, among other things, of education, the frequency of these shifts tends to be in inverse proportion to the age of the speaker, is more frequent among men than among women, and is largely restricted to Swahili and English. Their occurrence signals one or more of the following three strands in inter-personal relations:

    (a) exclusion;

    (b) status reinforcement;

    (c) shift in the level of formality;

with a fourth strand of somewhat less relevance to inter-personal relations:

    (d) shift in the topic of discourse.

(a) Many interviewees, especially among the younger generation, commented on their use of English when they wanted privacy, or wished to refer to something without the parents hearing, while one Pokomo woman said she and her husband used Swahili rather than Pokomo when they wished to be intimate. A Kikuyu primary school teacher said he used English to his wife ' . . . when discussing the maid's salary and work schedule. He did not agree that this is backbiting someone by using a language the third party does not understand. It is useful, he feels, to have a language in which you can discuss your servants. He also spoke a few English words to their two small children. He would like to see them learn both English and Gikuyu before they grow up.'

(b) I have myself been present in Gusii homesteads when a father has switched from Gusii to English in order to quieten his children, and then immediately justified this by reference to the classroom situation, commenting that nowadays children take much more notice of their teachers than they do of their parents. A number of interviewees reported the use of English to give added authority to the user, who in every case is cited as the father: the following Kikuyu comment is typical: ' . . . the father often spoke some English sentences in pompous tones.' Among Bukusu the use of Swahili is often cited as the language for reprimanding children.

(c) It does not seem possible to correlate the choice of any particular language with a shift along the scale of formality. Both English and Swahili are cited as being used with what might be termed formal and informal overtones, and much more needs to be known about the total social situation than can be gleaned from the language diaries. The following comment from a Pokomo is, however, rather typical in its sentiment. '. . . When he was involved in a quarrel with a neighbour on the ground that he raped his neighbour's wife, he lost his temper and for that matter he used the Swahili language partly because it was easier for him to express himself without any problems.' Equally common, however, are reports of shifts between husband and wife which appear to add or detract little from the existing level of formality.

(d) Many people report a shift in language following a change in the topic of conversation or on the radio; thus an Embu comments, 'Today since morning, conversations held in the mother tongue except for two or three English sentences at breakfast time. His eldest daughter had asked a question about her homework. Explanation given by him partly in English and partly in Kiembu.' Again, a Kikuyu woman comments that 'English is used in the house occasionally when they are discussing a rather serious subject—and when they are discussing their lessons.' Finally, several people commented that if they were listening to the Swahili service of the Voice of Kenya, and the announcer suddenly introduced a topic in which they were interested, it was quite likely that they would continue in Swahili until something provoked a shift back.

I have referred several times to different scales along which particular patterns of language use should be plotted. A particularly important scale is that relating to the length of the stretch of speech taken up by each of two or three languages. At one end of the scale it is usual to find the utterances in each language taking several minutes, and the change from one language to another I designate 'language alternance'; at the other end, the change is much more frequent and may occur within the clause or phrase; this has been widely discussed under the rubric of 'code-switching'.[5] Many respondents report behaviour somewhere in between, of a variety which is widespread in other domains (see Chapters 5–9) and which invests the encounters within which they occur with an apparent game or competition-like character. The gambits are usually played in one language, with the addressee replying in the same language as that used by the addresser to demonstrate comparable skill; the middle game is then carried on in a second or third language depending on the nature of the transaction; the terminal game reverts back to the language of the opening moves. I have recorded many examples of such encounters but the commonest variety in the home seems to take place between coevals and to utilize a local language and English. Thus a Kikuyu girl is wakened by her sister with the words, 'So you are still asleep, Rosemary!' and she retorts, 'It is none of your business!' and the conversation then proceeds in Kikuyu. Or a schoolboy visited by his friends greets them in English, to which they reply, 'This is a damned good place for study . . . ' and the conversation then continues in Kikuyu, but may revert to English if parents come in, or if there is any other reason for wishing to pursue a conversation to exclude others.

B. TRADE

I use the term 'trade' to cover a wide range of exchanges: from buying and selling in the market, through buying, selling and working in 'dukas', to buying stamps at the post office or ordering a dress from the local tailor. The term also covers the wide range of informal exchanges which are characteristic of daily life in the rural areas.

From all the diaries there was general agreement on the use of Swahili in this domain, and this was borne out from my own observations and also from the essays, thus:

'I have failed to get a needle in the local market here because not knowing how it is called in Swahili, I was unable to ask for it from the local traders.' (Kiga, 22, engineer.)

'In shops, even the very efficient ones, either you use Swahili for quick service or you use English and you are apt to meet with misunderstandings of the worst kind regarding colours, names etc. of articles.' (Luo, 23, clerk.)

'Because I knew very little of Swahili, I could not keep the bargain for long and get things with the price I need.' (Kamba, 15, student.)

'If you happen to be impeccably dressed and start bargaining with the poor Asian shopkeeper in English, he will take one look at you and instinctively raise the price of the article by a large percentage.' (Luo, 17, student.)

There is nothing particularly remarkable in this. Centres of exchange in the broadest sense are likely also to be areas of high heterogeneity: many shopkeepers are not local men, the post office staff are government servants and liable to be transferred to other parts, the markets attract not only local buyers and sellers but residents of differing ethnic groups, government servants, lorry drivers, workers, etc. In such settings, where a high level of education is not a prerequisite, Swahili is the obvious choice for communication.

The following table has been compiled from those samples where the diaries provide quantifiable material, and provide information on the percentage of the samples claiming to have used Swahili in some domains during the preceding week, and the percentage of those domains relating broadly to trade:

	Percentage of total sample claiming to have used Swahili in some domain during preceding week	Percentage of those domains relating to trade	Did any other domain receive a higher score, if so, which?
Luyia (Bukusu)	79	20	Talking to friend
Kikuyu (Kiambaa)	63	21	No
Kipsigis (Lugumek)	51	31	No
Luyia (L/Luy. border)	50	61	No
Meru (Katheri)	46	30	Talking to friend
Meru (Ntima)	43	31	No
Gusii (L/K/G border)	35	50	No
Luo (L/K/G border)	32	42	No
Kipsigis (L/K/G border)	30	82	No
Luo (*Oyugis*)	19	52	No
Luo (L/Luy. border)	15	60	No

The figures, of course, are culled only from what is specifically cited in the diaries, and for the border areas in particular, numbers are rather small, but the evidence, coupled with that from the other areas which have not proved susceptible to quantification, suggests a strong correlation between the use of Swahili and trading. English is also mentioned as being used in this domain, but in no case does the percentage exceed 10, and is usually less. In the border areas the position is complicated by the use of other local languages: for example, in the Luo/Luyia area 83 per cent of Luyia claim to have used Luo during the previous week: of the domains listed, 13 per cent related to trade, while a further 6 per cent related to working in bars or in one's own shop. Only 48 per cent of Luo claim to have used Luyia during the preceding week, but 23 per cent of the domains listed related to shopping in 'dukas' and 50 per cent to working in one's own shop. This ties in well with the fact that almost twice as many Luo as Luyia listed their occupations as 'traders'. In the Sondu border area the most striking feature is that 70 per cent of the Kipsigis claim to have used Luo at some time during the preceding week and 54 per cent of the domains listed related broadly to trading, with the market place being the most commonly mentioned.[6] By contrast only 15 per cent of Gusii claim to have used Luo—none at all claimed to have used Kipsigis—but of the small number of domains listed 50 per cent related to trading. Luo respondents did not specify use of any other local languages. The dominance of a Luo trading group in the Luo/Luyia border is repeated in Sondu but much less markedly—7 Luo to 6 Kipsigis—and this is perhaps one factor in the very small number of references to the use of Luo in 'dukas' by Kipsigis, despite the high overall figures. In this connection it is interesting to note that shopping in 'dukas' is listed by Luo as the domain, within the general category of trading, for which Swahili is most used, in contrast to the market-place which is mentioned only once. One might suppose from this that if Luo patronize non-Luo shops they prefer to use Swahili to Kipsigis, while in the market Luo was probably dominant, Sondu being after all in Luo country.[7] It must not be supposed, however, that the local language is only used for trading in the border areas; not everyone mentioned this specifically in the diaries but comments like the following are not uncommon: 'I spoke Swahili in the market when I was bargaining with a Kikuyu shopkeeper. This I did only once (notice that even Kikuyu in our market now speak Bukusu).' In those samples where specific mention was made of the fact we find that 40 per cent of Kikuyu spoke Kikuyu; 12 per cent of Bukusu spoke Bukusu, and 11 and 6 per cent respectively spoke Meru in Meru (Ntima) and (Katheri). Clearly the position varies according to the overall degrees of linguistic heterogeneity obtaining in each of the areas, and more detailed studies of the language of trade in selected rural communities would be most rewarding.

Concerning the use of Swahili as evidenced by the preceding table, the most striking fact is the difference between the frequency of use of Swahili claimed in the questionnaires and that evidenced by the diaries—leaving aside the possibility that for some unidentified reason the particular week in question was anomalous. Both Kikuyu and Bukusu samples appear to have used it less frequently than was claimed, Luo and Luyia (L/Luy. border) report equal frequencies, and all the rest greater frequencies. This is particularly marked in the case of Kipsigis and the Sondu area discussed above, and of interest, bearing in mind the proportion of the domains listed relating to trade. Such differences as these show up the weakness of this and similar questionnaires when used without supporting evidence of a 'diary' or 'observational' type.

C. CHURCH

Our information on this domain was derived entirely from the questionnaires circulated to missions, in which, as has already been pointed out, there were certain serious inadequacies (see p. 320). Nonetheless some useful information emerged. The material is presented basically in two columns, with that relating to the Protestants on the left, and that to the

Catholics on the right; thus, with reference to the type of area in which the mission is situated:

	Protestant	Catholic
Rural	22 (59.4 per cent)	130 (78.3 per cent)
Urban	4 (10.8 per cent)	11 (6.6 per cent)
Combination	11 (29.8 per cent)	25 (15.1 per cent)

1. Language use in mission or mission area

	Protestant	Catholic
No. of times Swahili mentioned	25 (67.5 per cent of cases)	89 (53 per cent of cases)
No. of times English mentioned	15 (40.5 per cent of cases)	57 (34.3 per cent of cases)
Indian languages	2 cases (Machakos, Nyeri)	3 cases (French, Italian, Konkani from Mombasa)
Arabic	1 case (Machakos)	1 case (Changamwe)

In some cases Swahili is not mentioned, although it is later said to be used in church services.

2. Number of local (tribal) vernaculars spoken in mission area

No. of vernaculars mentioned	No. of cases		No. of cases	
0	—		1 (M'sa)	0.6%
1	12	32.5%	82	49.4%
2	8	21.6%	26	15.7%
3	5	13.5%	25	15.1%
4	1	2.7%	12	7.2%
5	5	13.5%	11	6.6%
6	—		5	3.0%
7	—		—	—
8	1	2.7%	—	—
9	1	2.7%	—	—
10	—		—	—
11	1	2.7%	—	—
00	3	8.1%	4	2.4%

It should be noted that these are only the vernaculars *mentioned* by respondents and not necessarily the actual number spoken in the area. Some respondents may have named only the primary language in their area and omitted to mention languages spoken by minorities.

3. Does mission work include all the people mentioned in the area?

Protestant			Catholic		
Yes	29	78.4%	Yes	146	87.9%
No	8	21.6%	No	17	10.3%
			Not clear	3	1.8%

It is not always clear from the comments why certain ethnic groups are excluded from mission work. In some cases there is a frank admission

335

of problems of communication, but in other cases these are dealt with
by means of interpreters or third parties (African 'pastors'). In some cases
the reasons are not linguistic but religious—the Muslims in an area may
not be included in mission work, and in one case (Gatab, Marsabit)
the AIM respondent remarks that 'The El Molo are the preserve of a
Catholic Mission.' In other cases the area may be too large to cope with
all groups.

4. *Frequency of use of Swahili in mission area*

Frequency	*Protestant* No. of cases	*Catholic* No. of cases
Never	2	22
Some of the time	27	107
Most of the time	2	10
Usually	2	8
All of the time	1	3
Not clear	3	16

Of those who said Swahili was used very frequently, most were respondents answering from towns such as Nairobi, Mombasa, Nyeri or
Eldoret.

5. *Frequency of use of vernacular in mission area*

Frequency	No. of cases	No. of cases
Never	0	0
Some of the time	2	17
Most of the time	8	27
Usually	11	37
All of the time	12	76
Not clear	4	9

As might be expected, there is a distinct contrast between this table and
that preceding it. Neither table shows any difference between Catholic and
Protestant.

6. Language used in church work

(a) Language used

Protestant / No. of cases — Catholic / No. of cases

Language used	Protestant Liturgy	Protestant Baptism	Protestant Marriage	Catholic Liturgy	Catholic Baptism	Catholic Marriage
Vernacular only	17 45.9%	18 48.7%	17 45.9%	73 44.0%	91 54.9%	90 54.2%
Swahili only	1 2.7%	3 8.1%	4 10.8%	33 19.9%	33 19.9%	35 21.0%
Swahili and English	2 5.4%	2 5.4%	1 2.7%		6 3.6%	7 4.2%
Vernacular and Swahili	7 18.9%	7 18.9%	7 18.9%	12 7.2%	12 7.2%	10 6.1%
Vernacular and English	1 2.7%	1 2.7%	3 8.1%	5 3.0%	2 1.2%	5 3.0%
English only	2 5.4%	1 2.7%	1 2.7%	0 —	0 —	0 —
V. (inc. Sw.)+Latin	0 —	0 —	0 —	26 15.7%	13 7.8%	10 6.1%
Other combinations and possibilities	4 10.8%	4 10.8%	3 8.1%	9 5.4%	8 4.8%	8 4.8%
Not clear/No answer	3 8.1%	1 2.7%	1 2.7%	1 0.6%	1 0.6%	1 0.6%

(b) Language used

Language used	Protestant Preaching	Protestant Benediction/Bible	Protestant Safari	Catholic Preaching	Catholic Benediction/Bible	Catholic Safari
Vernacular only	13 35.3%	14 37.8%	13 35.3%	100 60.3%	77 46.5%	94 56.6%
Swahili only	2 5.4%	3 8.1%	2 5.4%	27 16.3%	30 18.0%	31 18.7%
Swahili and English	2 5.4%	1 2.7%	2 5.4%	8 4.8%	4 2.4%	2 1.2%
Vernacular and Swahili	10 27.1%	10 27.1%	12 32.5%	15 9.0%	5 3.0%	22 13.3%
Vernacular and English	1 2.7%	1 2.7%	1 2.7%	6 3.6%	1 0.6%	4 2.4%
English only	3 8.1%	2 5.4%	1 2.7%	0 —	0 —	0 —
V. (inc. Sw.)+Latin	0 —	0 —	0 —	0 —	21 12.6%	0 —
Other combinations and possibilities	6 16.2%	5 13.5%	5 13.5%	9 5.4%	18 10.8%	7 4.2%
Not clear/No answer	0 —	1 2.7%	1 2.7%	1 0.6%	10 6.1%	6 3.6%

Points arising from these two tables:

1. The Catholics use more vernacular than the Protestants, most particularly in preaching and on safari work. There is also a greater percentage who use Swahili only—possibly because of the greater proportion of Catholics who were working on the coast (respondents, that is); in other words there may be as many Protestant missions on the coast as Catholic missions, but fewer of the former answered questionnaires.

2. Only the Catholics use Latin, of course. Curiously, it was only amongst the Protestants that English alone was used in services.

3. The figures for 'preaching' are perhaps the most significant, since here are the results of two tendencies. First, it is most important that here the actual *meaning* of the words gets across to the congregation. This is the explanation, I think, for the high percentage of vernacular used by the Catholics in this sphere, and the lack of use of Latin. Preaching, however, is also a task which is probably done by the most senior official—in most cases the respondent. It probably cannot be easily delegated. Thus the respondents are thrown back on their own language abilities—and in the case of some of the Protestants may have to use English (the rate for the use of the vernacular is at its lowest here for Protestants, highest for Catholics).

4. Many Protestants also added that English was used in education, in colleges, in Sunday school training and wherever wider groups were dealt with.

337

7. Use of Swahili vernacular with age-categorized groups

(a) Swahili

Age categories	Protestant						Catholic					
	Never	Some of time	Most of time	Usually	Always	Not answered	Never	Some of time	Most of time	Usually	Always	Not answered
Pre-school children	21	6	0	0	0	10	68	8	5	4	15	66
School children	10	9	4	4	0	10	56	17	12	6	17	58
School leavers	9	12	3	3	0	10	49	31	4	5	11	66
Adults	8	13	5	1	0	10	43	27	10	12	11	63
Educated people	9	13	3	1	0	11	39	31	3	5	8	80
Old people	14	11	0	2	0	10	66	22	3	7	10	58

The trend is obvious here; Swahili is used occasionally with all groups, but rarely with those who have never attended school. It is used most with adults and educated people (though from the comments English would seem to be used more with the latter). There were many who did not answer this question (27.4 per cent of the Protestants, and 39.2 per cent of the Catholics). This may have been either because the respondent did not understand the question, or because he or she did not speak Swahili.

(b) Vernacular

Age categories	Protestant						Catholic					
	Never	Some of time	Most of time	Usually	Always	Not answered	Never	Some of time	Most of time	Usually	Always	Not answered
Pre-school children	0	1	2	3	21	10	10	6	4	14	107	25
School children	4	10	4	5	2	12	11	23	18	30	53	31
School leavers	7	8	6	5	1	10	11	40	15	25	35	41
Adults	1	4	10	4	8	10	6	21	4	38	68	29
Educated people	12	10	4	0	0	11	22	60	7	14	15	48
Old people	0	2	4	6	15	10	6	14	2	19	108	17

More Catholics answered this question than the other, 28.3 per cent of the Protestants did not answer the question and 19.1 per cent of the Catholics. This is probably because slightly more Catholics could speak the vernacular than the Protestant respondents. It is not at all clear, however, whether the respondents were answering in terms of their own actual usage, or in terms of what usage would be most logical. Thus some respondents who obviously did not speak the vernacular, nevertheless answered the question about their usage of vernacular with age-categorized groups.

It seemed reasonable then to attempt some estimate of the respondents' own language abilities. Although no specific question was asked on this point, many respondents thought it relevant to state their own language abilities, and in many other cases it was obvious from the answers.

8. Respondents' language abilities

Languages spoken	Protestant				Total	Catholic
	CMS	AIM	SDA	C of G		
Vernacular only	4	4	1	0	9 24.3%	40 24.0%
Swahili only	5	2	0	0	7 18.9%	22 13.3%
Vernacular & Swahili	3	6	1	1	11 29.8%	41 24.7%
Vernacular & some Swahili	0	0	0	0	—	25 15.1%
Swahili & some vernacular	1	0	1	1	—	15 9.0%
English only	1	0	1	1	4 10.8%	0 —
Not clear	3	3	1	0	6 16.2%	23 12.9%

There is not very much difference here between the claimed language abilities of Protestants and Catholics. Taking the totals together we can say that 54 per cent of the Protestants claimed a knowledge of the vernacular and 48.7 per cent a knowledge of Swahili. Excluding the figures for 'some vernacular' and 'some Swahili', 63.8 per cent of the Catholics claimed to know the local vernaculars, compared with 47 per cent who claimed to know Swahili. These are of course only 'claimed' language abilities—we have no evidence as to the language competence of the respondents. Only the Protestants had mission workers who were completely unequipped to deal with people who could speak no English.

Several respondents claimed to speak vernaculars that were not relevant in the areas in which they were now working—there were two cases like this amongst the Protestants and three amongst the Catholics. This suggests that there is some transfer of staff from areas in which they are linguistically competent to areas in which they are not.

9. *Attitudes to Swahili v. vernaculars*

Language attitudes were indicated to some extent by the answers to the following questions:

(a) Are there types of work in which Swahili cannot be used profitably?

Protestant: Yes 30   Catholic: Yes 108
          No   7   No   45
                                       Not clear   13

Old women were often said not to speak Swahili as well as young children. People who were uneducated or lived in isolated areas did not speak it. Swahili was said not to be popular with Luos, and Kikuyus were said to prefer their own language to Swahili.

(b) Are there types of work in which the vernacular cannot be used profitably?

Protestant: Yes 15   Catholic: Yes 50
          No 21   No 97
     Not clear   1   Not clear   19

Towns and ethnically mixed gatherings were mentioned as places where the vernacular could not be used and a lingua franca had to be resorted to. But on the whole the missionaries seemed well disposed towards the use of vernaculars and emphasized their importance in missionary work. Perhaps this is summed up by one man who said: 'When talking on spiritual matters one feels one might "get through" better in their own vernacular rather than English.'

10. *Use of language with 'educated Africans'*

The answers to this question probably suggest the percentage of respondents who felt secure enough in their use of vernacular or Swahili to use it even with those who were competent in English.

Protestant: 62.1% used only English
            37.8% used English together with Swahili or the local vernacular

Catholic: 51.7% used only English
            45.8% used English together with Swahili or the local vernacular
            2.4% did not answer properly

Again there is a slight difference here between the Protestants and the Catholics in that the latter have a greater percentage who are competent in local languages.

11. *General comments*

The majority of missionaries working in tribally homogeneous areas feel that their work must be carried out in the vernacular in order that they be fully understood. Because of the intimate nature of their work, they and their ideas are more readily accepted if the vernacular is used. In most areas Swahili is not sufficiently known—especially by women and children—for proper communication, let alone full understanding of religious teaching.

In Samburu, Taita and Mijikenda areas the missionaries, for some reason, appear not to know the vernaculars very much and all church services are in Swahili. Interpreters have to be used for safari and other work in most cases, and difficulties of communication with many people are expressed, especially in Samburu and Taita, and to a lesser extent in some Mijikenda areas with women. The CMS practice differs in the latter case as they have always used Giriama in their mission, though they say that Swahili is understood by more people these days.

Although the vernacular is used in all Kikuyu missions, most missionaries maintain that Swahili is not sufficiently known for their purposes, but others say it is.

Swahili is found useful for contact with minority groups in such areas—migrants, some officials, police, etc.—*if* the missionary knows it. Otherwise there is often a lack of communication. Most missionaries would find Swahili useful for travelling through Kenya and for listening to the radio, as well as communicating with people who speak neither English nor the vernacular they know. Swahili is also used for church services and all other work involving tribally mixed groups in the following: urban areas; townships where there is substantial ethnic heterogeneity; estates (e.g. Kericho, Nandi Hills, Kibwezi) and certain mixed settlement areas; in cases where the mission runs a leprosarium or is involved in teaching in a college; a few border areas.

In areas such as Rift Valley (Nakuru diocese especially) which are ethnically heterogeneous, missionaries find they are unable to communicate with many people whose vernaculars they do not know, because Swahili is not sufficiently known. One respondent is unable to communicate with two-thirds of the people in his parish, a border area in Trans Mara in Narok district. He uses Maasai and Swahili but finds that Kipsigis especially and also Gusii do not know enough Swahili.

Some missionaries feel that *if* Swahili were more widely known, it would be a useful unifying factor. There is also more literature available in Swahili. One or two would find it easier to teach liturgy, for example, in Swahili, as it has a wider vocabulary than, say, Kamba. Other missionaries feel that English is more useful, as people's knowledge of Swahili is not sufficient. English is being used increasingly with school children and those adults who know it, as well as where teaching is involved. Many educated people prefer to use English than Swahili, or even their own language.

D. WORKPLACE

By this I mean the place of work of those wage-earners other than the traders, previously mentioned. This would include teachers, mission employees, domestic staff, and a wide range of government employees.

A rather small minority of my rural samples were wage-earners at the time of the interview, and of these it was the teachers who provided the most unequivocal evidence of language use at school. A very large majority referred only to their use of English: where Swahili is reported as being used it is usually in connection with the use of the language in the syllabus.

It was the Kikuyu, in what is essentially the peri-urban area of Kiambaa, who mentioned language use at work most frequently. Twenty-five per cent of the sample claimed to have used Swahili during the previous week at work and on semi-official business (e.g. visiting a government office), and a similar percentage made a claim regarding English. It must be stressed, however, that such claims do not refer to the exclusive use of one or other language, since, as has been pointed out earlier (see above and previous chapters), people tend to manipulate their language skills to their own advantage. Thus, a man wishing to see a government officer to renew a licence, for example, may state his request in Swahili to the girl typist as a suitably neutral language if he does not know her. To start out in English would be unfortunate if she did not know it well, and on her good will depends his gaining access to authority reasonably quickly. She may reply in Swahili, if she knows it as well as he does and wishes to be co-operative; or in English if she is busy and not anxious to be disturbed; or in the local language if she recognizes him and wishes to reduce the level of formality. If he, in return, knows little English, he may be put off at her use of it and decide to come back later; or, if he knows it well, he may demonstrate his importance by insisting on an early interview and gain his objective at the loss of good will from the typist. The interview with the officer may well follow a similar pattern, being shaped by the total repertoire available to each on the one hand, and on the other by their respective positions in relation to the issue involved.

No information was available from the diaries on how usage in Swahili, English and the local language was distributed (but see below), and in the other samples no more than 5 per cent provided information on language use at work, and this is a quite inadequate basis from which to draw any conclusions.

On the other hand, from the questionnaires given to members of the civil service, the situation is clarified somewhat, as can be seen from Table 12.6.

TABLE 12.6 *Patterns of language use in the civil service*

	Friends & relatives	Colleagues & superiors	Sub. staff (esp. messengers, drivers)	The public	Unspecified
District magistrates (13)					
(Av. age 30)					
Settings when Swahili used	1	5	1	4	—
,, ,, English used	—	11	—	1	—
,, ,, loc. lang. used	—	—	—	3	3
Accountants (47)					
(Av. age 32)					
Settings when Swahili used	2	3	36	13	4
,, ,, English used	—	40	—	4	3
,, ,, loc. lang. used	4	—	1	3	—
Police officers (15)					
(Av. age 35)					
Settings when Swahili used	—	5	2	6	4
,, ,, English used	—	12	—	1	3
,, ,, loc. lang. used	—	—	—	—	—
Nursing sisters (12)					
(Av. age 28)					
Settings when Swahili used	—	—	9	9	—
,, ,, English used	—	12	—	4	—
,, ,, loc. lang. used	—	—	—	—	—

While the total number of settings in which Swahili is used may be equal to or often greater than the number in which English occurs, a fairly clear pattern of usage is discernible, in which Swahili is used for communicating with the general public or with subordinate staff, while English is used for communicating with fellow officers or superiors. The local language plays a very small part in this domain. The importance of language as a status-marker is here, I believe, clearly demonstrated, and receives some corroboration from my own observations of language use in a quite different setting, that of tea-picking. Here, in a number of different estates, I noticed that the pickers clustered in language groups, and I could distinguish Gusii, Luo, and Luyia; the overseer, however, who moved behind the pickers to see any bad picking, used Swahili. Not only was its use here essential as the only common language, but, along with his demeanour, dress and equipment served to distinguish the overseer as the man with authority. It would, of course, have been quite impossible for him to have used his own local language (Gusii, Luyia) since this would have served to split the workers into factions. The question of status is a difficult and delicate one to investigate, but the following comment by a senior administrator represents, I believe, a widely held view:

' . . . no one minds speaking English badly because it is a mark of hard work, initiative, etc., to have tried to learn it at all. A man who corrects one's Swahili may be no better than oneself, this cannot be true of someone who corrects one's English. So. . . those of us who speak Swahili badly are ashamed or shy of speaking it at all . . . '

E.   OTHER DOMAINS

Talking with friends/acquaintances/strangers

It has been necessary to put these three together because it is frequently not clear from the diaries just what degree of acquaintance is involved, even though the patterns of language use are likely to vary greatly. At least the following subdivision should be recognized:

(a) Friends of long standing, close friends.
(b) Casual acquaintances from work, bars or market.
(c) Strangers, whom one is meeting for the first time.

In each case the pattern of usage within the encounter is liable to involve some shifting and switching.

(a)   In a majority of cases among the samples close friends belong to the same ethnic group and in such cases the language of conversation is either the local language or English, the former stressing group solidarity, the latter education. The following comment is typical of many: 'When greeting friends around, English was mostly used. But this was only a sentence or so followed almost immediately by the mother tongue' (Embu). Such a pattern is similar to that discussed above from the homestead.

(b)   A great deal depends here on the nature of the relationship. Where the participants are from different language groups, the language used is commonly Swahili, at least until it is established that both parties are equally conversant with English. As Parkin has noted (see Chapters 6 and 7), Swahili is a good neutral language. Thus, ' . . . talked to a Kikuyu in Swahili at the Baraza' (Bukusu); ' . . . he used Swahili on at least four occasions when talking to some friends from K—' (Embu); 'I spoke with one of my friends in both English and Swahili when harvesting coffee, in Meru town when shopping to general friends' (Meru). The diaries are here quite inadequate for making any useful inferences: one does not know, for example, what the purpose of the conversation was, whether prestation was involved or contemplated, whether competition was involved. Encounters of this kind, marked by unstable social relations, are the focus of carefully manipulated choices of the kind described by Parkin in the preceding chapters. On the other hand, it is certainly true amongst the younger generation that language choice is also determined by the topic of conversation: many people report that they talk about work or education or politics in English, while others mention politics as a subject for Swahili—'When discussing academic or political issues we tend to use English . . . ' (Luo); 'One has to know Swahili to become a politician' (Luyia).

(c) Most respondents in the diaries report the use of Swahili for casual encounters with strangers, e.g. in buses, markets, meetings and on roads, paths, etc., at least until the initial exchanges have been made.

It is evident from the diaries and from other evidence that talking to friends in the widest sense is one of the most important activities in the daily life of rural Kenyans, and one which would well repay the kind of detailed study that has been done for Nairobi. Some indication of this is provided from those diaries where information is sufficiently detailed to be quantified, thus:

Percentage of domains listed relating to friends

	Talking to friends		Receiving/Visiting friends	
	Swahili	English	Swahili	English
Meru (Ntima)	22% (2nd largest domain)	27% (largest domain)	5%	6%
Meru (Katheri)	37% (largest domain)	27%	6%	12%
Kipsigis	21% (2nd largest domain)	27%		
Kikuyu	17%	not listed	9%	33%
Bukusu	38% (largest domain)	9%	6%	33%

Perhaps the most interesting feature of these figures is the high percentage of occasions on which the use of English is mentioned.

Meetings

I do not feel that I can make a generalization for the whole country, but from the various meetings I attended or observed or had described to me, a number of characteristics emerge which I will illustrate from Kisii, an area which I know well:

(a) Where members are expected to have a high level of education and/or the topics to be discussed are technical the language is English, e.g. finance committees, certain agricultural, veterinary, medical, committees, which may or may not have a simultaneous Swahili or Gusii translation.

(b) Where members are not expected to have a high level of education and/or there is ethnic heterogeneity, e.g. county council meetings; D.C.'s and D.O.'s barazas, and similar meetings held by government officers who are themselves non-Gusii; local KANU meetings, etc., the language is Swahili.

(c) Where membership is entirely homogeneous ethnically, e.g. area council meetings, chief's barazas, local church meetings, local co-operative meetings, etc., the language is Gusii.

(d) Where the membership of the meeting is liable to fluctuate then both Gusii and Swahili are used, e.g. KANU meetings, community development meetings—when the Community Development Officer, a Logoli, came in, co-operative meetings when local officers participated, etc.

(e) Where the emotional tone of a meeting is raised by a particular topic then Gusii is likely to be used in meetings under (b).

In all cases there may be differences between the language of the meeting and that of the correspondence relating to it, and the minutes. For example, the minutes of the Coffee and Pyrethrum Co-operative Unions are now written up in Swahili, though they were formerly written up in English and though some of the discussion at the meetings takes place in English. This is less a reflection of language preference than of the fact that formerly the membership of these unions included members of an educated élite who found the unions a good training ground for initiative but who have now gone into politics. Again, while the area council meetings are held in Gusii, the correspondence was in Swahili.

It is important to stress, however, that such patterns are likely to change rather quickly, not only in response to changes in the educational level of members, but as a result of such factors as the enunciation of a national language policy, the use of local rather than non-local government personnel, and local sentiment towards the local language.

NOTES

[1] *Catholic Directory of Eastern Africa (1968–9)*, T. M. P., Tabora, n.d.

[2] I should like to express my gratitude to a number of people for their help in collating and abstracting data from the questionnaires: to Mr P. Wilkinson, Mrs H. Johansen and Miss J. Roberts, students at the School of Oriental and African Studies; to Mrs Monica Parkin and Dr Janet Bujra for their work on the mission questionnaire; and to my father for working on the figures of Swahili frequency.

[3] This may well be the situation in Mukogodo, referred to in Chapter 1.

[4] A number of respondents from the Luyia areas comment that Swahili is traditionally the language of ploughing, since it was introduced first by Europeans who used it with their employees.

[5] The scale could be further extended: the material is rich in examples of speech where the following additional stages might be recognized:
1. The use of isolated phrases within an otherwise undifferentiated stretch.
2. The use of isolated words without any assimilation to the patterns of the 'host' language.
3. The use of partially assimilated words, e.g. with Bantu affixes.
4. The use of fully assimilated 'loans'.

[6] The interviewer, who was a Luo, reported that the Kipsigis interviewed expressed a marked desire that the interview should be conducted in Luo rather than Swahili.

[7] The position at Sondu is complicated by the fact that there are two markets, an upper and a lower. The former has a higher 'Gusii component' and the latter is undoubtedly 'more Luo'. While there is certainly a great deal of interaction between the two, it seems probable that there are quite marked differences in the language use patterns and this would be a most fascinating area in which to make a more detailed study.

APPENDIX A

Degrees of frequency claimed in Swahili and English

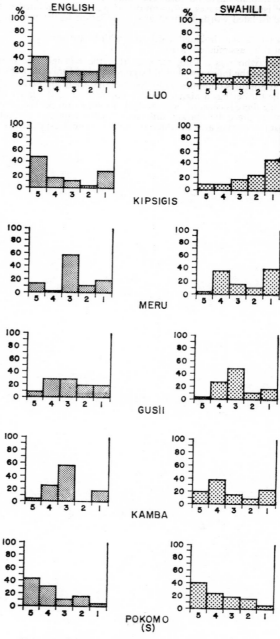

Note: Frequency decreases from left to right.

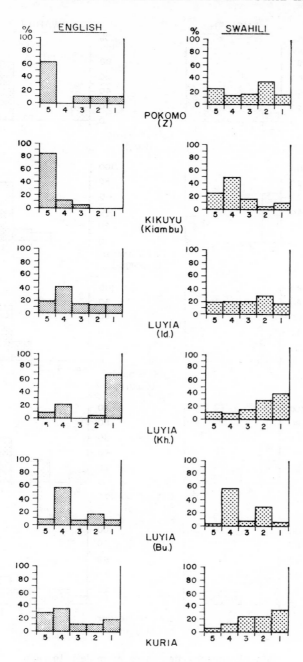

Note: Frequency decreases from left to right.

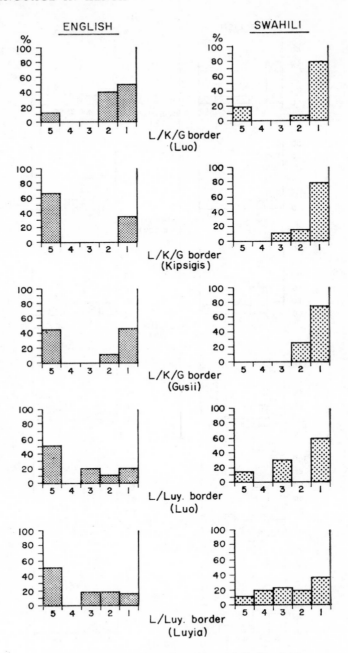

Note: Frequency decreases from left to right.

13

Patterns of Language Use among School Children and their Parents

T. P. GORMAN

The information given in this chapter was gathered in a series of investigations undertaken over a period of three years between April 1967 and June 1970.

The research project had two aims. Firstly, it was conceived of as an exercise preliminary to the investigation into levels of attainment of children in Swahili and English, which is discussed in Chapter 16. Many individuals in Kenya make use of three languages—their first language, Swahili and English—and it appears that in certain respects these languages have complementary functions. Before an attempt was made to construct attainment tests in any language therefore, I thought it relevant to obtain information about the functional ranges of the different languages in the usage of secondary school children and their parents in the eight major language groups.[1] Such an undertaking was also relevant to a consideration of aspects of language teaching in the schools as it is clearly desirable that course content should be related where feasible to the actual uses to which a language is put.

Secondly, I considered that the results of the inquiry might yield information about the complex processes associated with language shift and language maintenance in the usage of those involved in the inquiry.[2]

In retailing such facts as were reported and observed concerning the language use of school children, I have not attempted to interpret these systematically in relation to such processes of socio-cultural change as appear to be in progress, as I am aware that I have much to learn about the causes and direction of such developments. Indeed, because of the complexity of the factors involved, a sociolinguistic inquiry of this nature cannot be adequately undertaken by a person trained in a single discipline, and I was fortunate to have had the advice of two colleagues who had considerable experience of social research in Africa when I was preparing the initial research design; and of another colleague who had teaching experience at each level of the school system in Kenya.[3]

In this chapter I have detailed information relating to the claimed competence in different languages of students and in some cases of their parents and to the reported use of the languages in particular situations of interaction and reception. The information is intended to be interpreted in relation to that given in Chapter 16 and it has been selected primarily for its relevance to this.

THE SUBJECTS

The study was concerned primarily with the language use of pupils in each of eight major language groups in Kenya in their first year at government-maintained and -aided secondary schools. Over 80 per cent of the population of Kenya belong to one of these eight groups (Kikuyu, Luo, Luyia, Kamba, Meru, 'Mijikenda', Gusii, and 'Kalenjin').

The information was not available in 1968 to enable a purposive sample of a number of schools to be selected, and a form of cluster sampling was adopted in the rural districts in which the eight languages were known to preponderate; the school 'stream' rather than the individual child constituted the sampling unit.

In addition, two large urban samples were chosen in Nairobi and Mombasa on the assumption that the larger language groups would be sufficiently represented in the urban schools to allow us to draw conclusions about differences in the behaviour of children in urban and rural settings.[4]

Given the nature of this dual purpose sampling technique, it is clear that one would not be justified in applying to the data statistical calculations relating to population values. The study did, however, provide indications of fairly consistent trends and patterns of language behaviour among secondary school entrants which were subsequently investigated in greater detail.

INSTRUMENTS

To each pupil a questionnaire was administered together with a simple cloze test in English and Swahili.[5] The questionnaire was designed to obtain information relating to the following aspects of language use.
  A. Languages known by the child and by members of his family. The pupil was asked to indicate which languages various members of his family could speak, write, read or understand, and to rate their 'competence' in each mode of use along a four-point scale.
  B. Language use within the home. The pupil was asked to say which languages were spoken to him by various members of his family and which languages he spoke to them, and to rate the frequency with which this was done along a three-point scale.

C. Active and receptive language use of the child at home and in school (e.g. the pupils were asked to indicate the language(s) of the radio programmes they listened to, and of the newspapers they read, and which language(s) they used to write letters).

D. Languages used by the child in certain situations outside his home and school.

E. Other information considered to be relevant to the language use of children, such as details of their primary school background and of the language of instruction used in the primary schools attended; details of their age, sex and the length of their residence in an urban or rural setting; and such questions as I considered might be appropriately included in a questionnaire of this nature about the educational background and socio-economic status of their parents.

F. The teachers of English and Swahili in each school were asked to rate the children in what they considered to be the rank order of their level of attainment in the two languages. These ratings and the cloze tests were included to help us evaluate the accuracy of the child's self-ratings in the two languages.

The information collected in 1968 was analysed in two stages. Initially certain selected questions, primarily those relating to the educational experience of the child and to the language use of the pupil and members of his family at home, were analysed and the answers given by members of different language groups were tested for significance of difference. The answers given by pupils in Mombasa were excluded from this initial analysis. Certain of the results obtained at this stage have been described in an earlier paper.[6] Other results are set out below. They are differentiated by the heading 'Stage I'.

While the initial analysis was under way, the data were coded and transferred to cards. The resulting corpus consisted of 24,800 cards (the information for each child being stored on 10 cards). These were then part processed by computer. For convenience this stage of analysis has been termed 'Stage II'.[7]

To verify certain of the results obtained in 1968, a purposive sample of twenty-seven schools was selected at the beginning of the 1969 school year, and questionnaires were completed by the 803 children in the first forms in these schools. Seven schools in the Luyia- and three schools in the Meru-speaking areas were included in the sample, as the initial analysis had revealed certain significant contrasts between these groups which I wished to investigate further. The results of this supplementary inquiry, which completed the first stage of the survey, are described as 'Stage III'.

In the final and fourth stage of the inquiry, which was completed in 1970, children in four Form 1 classes in Nairobi and 14 classes in the rural areas completed a second questionnaire on language use, which was designed to provide more detailed information about their exposure to and use of Swahili and English and their own and other vernaculars in specific situations of interaction and reception.[8]

In many cases, the answers given were discussed with the pupils. At each stage also I spent as much time as possible observing pupils in the Nairobi schools in the classroom and outside it. During the fourth stage I administered to the children in these schools the tests of attainment discussed in Chapter 16.

I have described the stages in which the information was gathered in some detail as survey techniques involving self-report measures such as were used in the first three stages of the inquiry have certain inherent disadvantages which can best be offset by repeated sampling and personal observation where this is feasible.

The information given about each stage of inquiry and analysis must be related to the information about the geographical distribution of the schools that is given on the map at the end of this book, particularly as regards the situation of schools in towns, along main highways, or in 'border' areas and areas of recent settlement. The numbers of the schools that took part in the 1968 inquiry are preceded by 1, and those in the 1969 and 1970 inquiries by 2 and 3 respectively.

In most instances, details are only given of the results of the answers of children in the major language groups. However, when reference is made to the rural sample or to the Nairobi sample, without further specification, this should be understood as referring to all the children in the schools of the rural sample or of the Nairobi sample who answered the question and not only those who belonged to one of the eight largest language groups. Figures are not generally reported if less than 30 pupils in any language group in a sub-sample answered.

PARENTAL LANGUAGE USE

In this chapter I am concerned with parental patterns of language use only in so far as they demonstrably relate to those of the children. It is of some relevance, however, that the great majority of the children in all the samples reported that their fathers knew Swahili but there was very considerable variation in the different groups in the extent to which the mothers were reported to know the language. There were significant differences in both urban and rural samples between the reported knowledge of the language on the part of parents of different sexes and this was also the case as far as their knowledge of English was concerned. Figure 13.1 gives an indication of this variation. The figure is based on results obtained from the initial analysis, and combines data from the rural and urban samples.

FIGURE 13.1 (Stage I) *Knowledge of Swahili and English by parents*

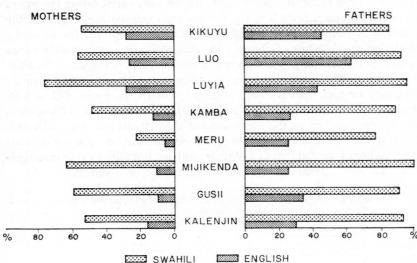

The children were asked to rate their own proficiency in Swahili and English and that of other members of their families on a four-point scale. In all but the Mijikenda group, the majority of the children rated their father's proficiency as being above their own. The reported proficiency

FIGURE 13.2 (Stage I) *Competence in Swahili—students and fathers*

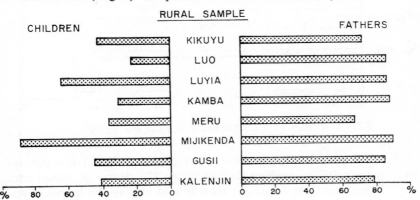

ratings in Swahili in the two highest categories (good or very good), of fathers and children in the rural samples are indicated in Figure 13.2.

Needless to say it is necessary to qualify any generalization about the characteristic language behaviour of a particular linguistic group. Within the linguistic areas[9] of the language groups with which this study has been primarily concerned there are wide variations in the extent to which competence in languages other than the mother tongue of the children is claimed. Figure 13.3 illustrates the variation, for example, in the reported claims of children in schools in the Luyia-speaking area as to the competence of themselves and their parents in the use of Swahili. The diagram shows the percentage of children in each school who claimed that they or their parents were able to speak the language with a high degree of proficiency (good or very good). As a matter of information, the dialects spoken in the areas around the schools are also indicated. There does appear to be a degree of correspondence between the claimed competence of the children and of their mothers, but until further investigation has been carried out a relationship cannot be assumed.[10]

FIGURE 13.3 (Stage III)   *Competence in Swahili of students and parents in Luyia-speaking areas*

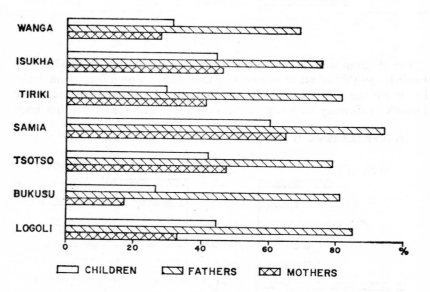

The diagram only illustrates the competence that the children claimed for their parents in *speaking* the language. The degree of competence they claimed for their fathers in reading and writing the language was

356

characteristically lower, as is shown in Figure 13.4, which illustrates the differences in the reported competence of the fathers of children in school.

FIGURE 13.4 (Stage III) *Fathers' knowledge of Swahili in different modes (school 2/25)*

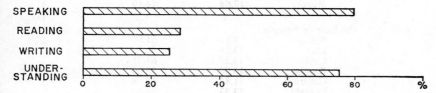

The results indicate that reports about competence that do not give an indication of the *degree* of competence are of very limited value. The 'knowledge' reported is in a number of cases of the kind that Diebold termed 'incipient bilingualism' and speakers with this degree of competence are not functionally bilingual for most purposes.[11]

THE ACQUISITION OF SECOND LANGUAGES

The extent to which children claim to have acquired a knowledge of English and/or Swahili before attending school varies according to a number of factors, the most important of which appears to relate to the linguistic area in which they were brought up and, again, whether this was an urban or a rural area.

In all the different linguistic groups and in the urban and rural samples more children claimed to have acquired a knowledge of Swahili than English before entering school. In 1968 55 per cent of the children in the Nairobi and Mombasa samples claimed to have had a pre-school knowledge of the language, as opposed to 31 per cent who claimed to have learned English at this stage. For the total rural samples the proportions were 44 per cent and 13 per cent respectively. Within the eight major groups in the rural sample pre-school knowledge of Swahili ranged from 73.23 per cent among the children in the Mijikenda group to 19.47 per cent of the children in the Meru group.

The numbers of children in these groups who claimed to have learned English before school was very much lower, as was the range of variation in this respect between the different groups.

Figures 13.5(a)–(d) and Tables 13.1(a)–(d) illustrate the extent to which the children claimed to have learned the two languages before school. The reported claims of children belonging to the two main Indian language groups in the urban samples, are also shown for the purpose of comparison.

TABLE 13.1 (a)–(d)   *English and Swahili learned before primary school*

	English %	Swahili %
(a) Total		
Nairobi	37.33	47.35
Mombasa	24.05	61.60
Rural	12.68	44.19
(b) Nairobi Sample		
Kikuyu	9.17	61.67
Luo	13.51	56.76
Luyia	14.29	65.71
Kamba	10.00	75.00
Gujarati	51.85	13.58
Punjabi	53.33	24.44
c) Mombasa Sample		
Mijikenda	3.70	85.19
Swahili	11.48	100.00
Gujarati	51.56	7.81
(d) Rural Sample		
Kikuyu	8.20	31.23
Luo	6.20	42.64
Luyia	6.98	67.44
Kamba	4.76	51.02
Meru	5.31	19.47
Mijikenda	1.57	73.23
Gusii	11.90	41.27
Kalenjin	8.40	36.97

The survey carried out in 1969 confirmed the trends indicated in the first inquiry though the claims made by the Luo- and Luyia-speaking children with regard to their pre-school knowledge of Swahili were lower relative to those of the children in the other groups, as is indicated in Figure 13.5(e). It is clear that most children acquire a knowledge of Swahili outside their homes from acquaintances who are not members of their families. In the 1970 inquiry the highest proportion of children in any one group who claimed to have learned the language from their brothers or sisters was 15.6 per cent. The highest percentage of those claiming to have learned the language from one or both parents was 6.4 per cent. In the rural areas taken as a whole more children claimed to have first learned Swahili at school than in any other locale though the degree of variation between groups varied from 17.4 per cent to 78 per cent.

The great majority of the children in both rural and urban areas claimed also to have first learned English at school. A relatively small number of children in these groups said that they learned English from acquaintances outside school, the highest proportion being 11.5 per cent. 4.1 per cent of the children in the rural groups claimed to have first learned the language from older brothers and sisters and less than 1 per cent from parents.

FIGURE 13.5 *Pre-school knowledge of Swahili and English*
(a) (Stage II)

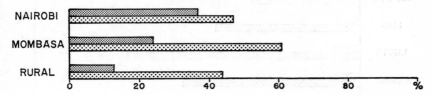

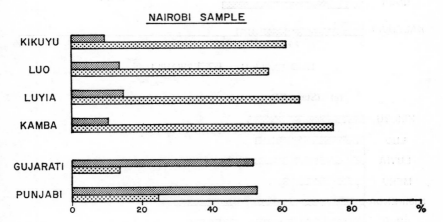

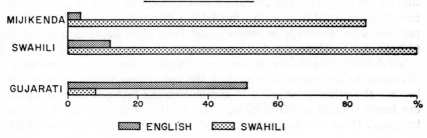

(d)

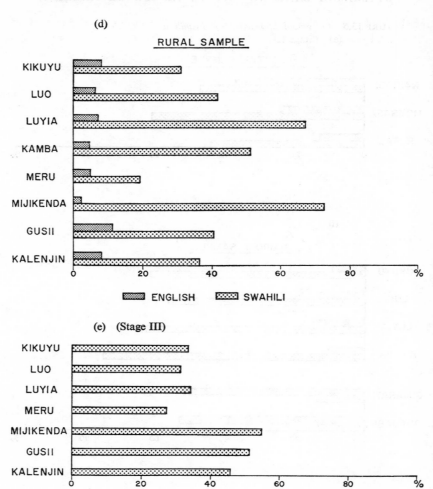

RURAL SAMPLE

ENGLISH   SWAHILI

(e)   (Stage III)

The children in the Nairobi sample showed similar patterns of acquisition in general, with the exception that a large proportion claimed to have learned Swahili outside school (46.1 per cent as opposed to 30.5 per cent who learned it in school); and from elder brothers and sisters (7.2 per cent) and parents (6.4 per cent).

In relatively few cases has the process of language substitution apparently advanced to the extent that one of the two major lingua francas has become the primary language of communication between parents within the home so that children claim one of these languages as their first language. However, there were examples of language shift of this nature in the urban areas; for example, of the 94 children in Nairobi who claimed that the language they first learned to speak was English, less than half had parents whose first language was English. 41.5 per cent had parents who spoke Indian languages (23 per cent Konkani, 15.5 per cent Gujarati and 2.2 per cent Punjabi). The process of language shift is clearly more advanced among certain groups in the Asian community in the towns, than in other communities. Of the other children who made the claim 14.5 per cent had parents or grandparents who spoke African languages. In this sub-group only three children reported, however, that English was the primary language used in conversations between their parents and it is clear from their reports that in each of these cases they acquired a knowledge of the language from older brothers and sisters.

In Nairobi 26 children claimed that Swahili was their first language. Of those, 50 per cent had parents or grandparents who spoke another language. In three cases, the parents of the children concerned spoke a language which would be understood by relatively few people in Nairobi and it is likely that the child was encouraged to learn a language of wider communication. In the majority of the other cases the parents belonged to different language groups, and in most of these cases the father was reported to speak Swahili very well. With two exceptions the children who claimed to have learned to speak Swahili first had lived in the city for most of their lives.

In Nairobi the shift in the majority of cases was in the direction of a greater use of English. But in Mombasa Swahili is the more dynamic element in the process of language shift. In both cases the process is uni-directional. The results of the survey indicated that the first language speakers of Swahili, for example, do not characteristically learn a second language other than English and vice versa.[12]

Out of the 19 children in Mombasa who claimed English as their first language, 4 were native speakers, 42 per cent had Gujarati-speaking parents and 9 per cent Konkani. In Mombasa only three children whose parents spoke African languages claimed to have learned English as a first language. Of the total of 77 children in the Mombasa sample who spoke Swahili as a first language 57 per cent were native speakers, and 26.5 per cent had parents who spoke one of the languages of the Mijikenda peoples, or Taita; 14.2 per cent had parents who spoke other African languages, including Luo (5.3 per cent), Luyia (2.6 per cent) and Kamba (2.6 per cent). In two cases the parents spoke different languages.

In this discussion I have restricted myself to a consideration of the pupils' use of, and exposure to, three languages. Naturally, in a number of linguistic groups both children and their parents—more particularly their fathers—use other languages. Figures 13.6(a) and (b) give an indication of the incidence of quadrilingualism reported by the children in the 1968 survey. The direction of predominant patterns of inter-lingual activity is shown in the diagram on the following page (Figure 13.7).

FIGURE 13.6 (Stage I)   *Quadrilingualism among students*
(a) Differentiated schools

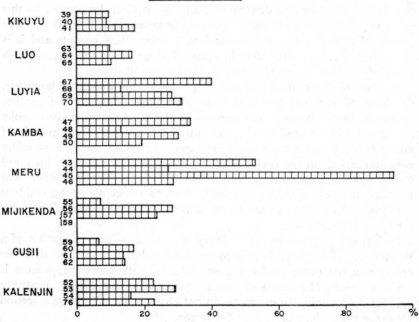

RURAL SAMPLE

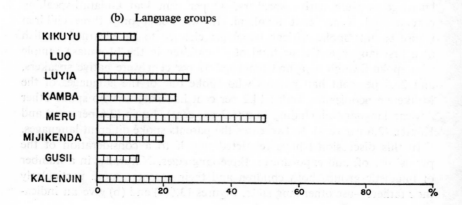

(b) Language groups

FIGURE 13.7 *Patterns of inter-lingual borrowing*

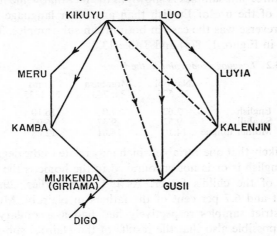

LANGUAGE USE IN THE HOME

At home and at school the behaviour of the students, linguistic and otherwise, is affected by a number of constraints which are in certain respects counter-productive. In only a minority of cases do grandparents, parents and teachers have precisely the same linguistic repertoire as the child and this naturally affects the degree of language choice the latter can exercise. In many cases, moreover, both in school and at home, the restrictions thus placed on the child's choice of languages in particular circumstances are made explicit.

In 80 per cent of the schools that co-operated in the 1968 inquiry, for example, I was informed by teachers that the use of languages other than English was discouraged in the school setting. Conversely, it appears from the answers of the children that the use of English is disapproved of in certain circumstances in the homes of many children in the rural areas, though it appears less so in the urban areas.

Pupils were asked to say whether their parents disapproved of their using any language or languages in the home.[13] The answers indicated that a minority of the parents did in fact impose such restrictions. In each sub-sample there were parents who evidently discouraged the use of the children's mother tongue in the home, the proportion varying from 13 per cent in the rural areas to 15 per cent in Mombasa. Swahili was also discouraged by a proportionately smaller number in each of the sub-samples and again the proportions in each group were rather similar. The only marked contrast betweeen the direction of parental discouragement in the three sub-samples is shown in the fact that while more parents disapproved of the use of English than any other language in the rural sample, the reverse was the case in both urban sub-samples. The contrast is illustrated in Figure 13.8(a) and Table 13.2.

TABLE 13.2 *Language constraint in the home*

	Nairobi N. 525	Mombasa N. 243	Rural N. 1435
English	3.62	7.0	16.10
Swahili	9.52	9.47	6.97
Mother tongue	14.10	14.81	12.68

I think it likely that one variable which may relate to the degree to which the use of English is or is not encouraged in the home is the educational background of the child's father. As indicated earlier, 29.9 per cent, 14.8 per cent and 6.7 per cent of the fathers in Nairobi, Mombasa and the rural district samples respectively had had a secondary education. I thought it possible also that the results of the Nairobi sub-sample may have been biased by the presence in the total sample of children speaking Indian languages but Figure 13.8(b) shows that this is not the case.

FIGURE 13.8 (Stage II) *Language constraint in the home*
(a)

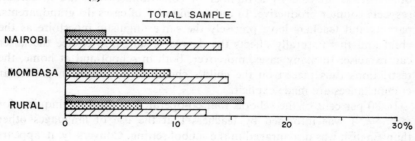

(b)

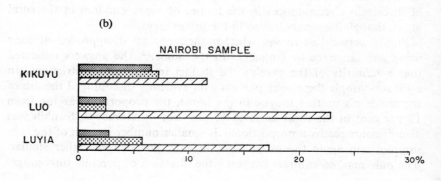

(c)

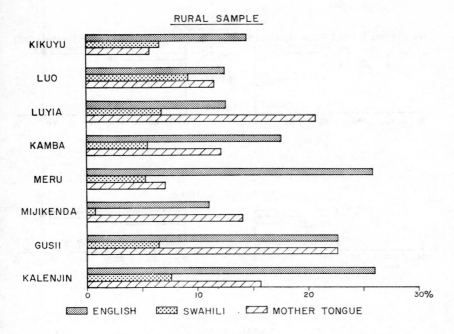

The fact that the mother tongue of the children and English are the two codes that parental sanctions appear to be related to most frequently indicates that it is these that are generally thought to be the languages 'in conflict', as it were, and this was subsequently borne out by other evidence given.

The children were asked to say what language or languages they spoke to various members of their families at home and alternatively what languages were spoken to them by different members of their families, and to indicate the relative frequency with which different languages were used on a three-point scale. The reports confirmed what one might expect, namely that the mother tongue was used as the only language of communication with decreasing frequency in conversations with grandparents, parents, younger brothers and sisters, and older brothers and sisters, in that order. The relative uniformity in this respect in the general configurations of language use within each group in both rural and urban samples was striking. This behaviour pattern is illustrated in Figures 13.9(a)–(c), which indicate the extent to which children in the different sub-samples claimed that their parents and their older and younger brothers spoke exclusively to them in their mother tongue in the home.

FIGURE 13.9 (Stage II)   *Monolingualism with parents and siblings*

(a)

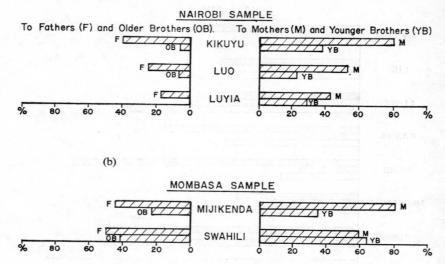

NAIROBI SAMPLE

(b)

MOMBASA SAMPLE

(c)

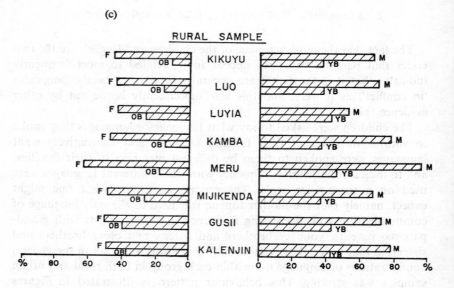

RURAL SAMPLE

The answers which the children gave to a question which required them to say what language or languages they spoke to younger brothers and sisters, and to older brothers and sisters, when talking at home *about school* indicated that, typically, as children grow older a marked degree of language substitution takes place involving an increased use of English and a decreasing use of the children's mother tongue. The substitution also characteristically involves a decrease in the frequency of use of Swahili. The process is illustrated in Figures 13.10(a)–(c) and Tables 13.3 (a)–(c), which record the nature of the answers given to a question in which the children reported what language or languages they used when talking to older and younger brothers and sisters at home about school. It cannot of course be assumed that the extent of the substitution would be as marked if the children were asked to say what language or languages they used in discussing another topic.

TABLE 13.3 (a)–(c) *When you are at home what language or languages do you like to speak to the following when talking about school?*
(1) younger brothers and sisters
(2) older brothers and sisters

	English		Swahili		Mother tongue	
	To younger siblings	To older siblings	To younger	To older	To younger	To older
(a) Nairobi						
Kikuyu	21.89	63.02	22.69	14.29	50.42	15.13
Luo	22.97	60.81	28.38	14.87	47.29	17.57
Luyia	20.00	74.29	22.86	11.43	48.57	5.71
Kamba	5.00	95.00	35.00	5.00	60.00	0.00
(b) Mombasa						
Mijikenda	11.11	51.85	59.26	18.52	18.52	22.22
Swahili	13.12	49.90	72.13	37.71	3.28	1.67
					(Mijikenda)	(Mijikenda)
(c) Rural						
Kikuyu	22.39	69.08	10.09	4.10	61.51	17.35
Luo	29.46	60.47	7.75	5.43	61.24	27.13
Luyia	26.74	62.79	8.14	5.81	62.79	18.61
Kamba	21.09	68.70	5.44	3.40	70.07	23.13
Meru	27.43	58.41	1.77	1.77	66.37	34.51
Mijikenda	17.32	39.37	29.13	18.89	46.46	23.62
Kipsigis	32.77	54.62	5.88	5.88	59.66	34.45
Gusii	26.40	49.60	3.20	3.20	65.60	39.20

The extent to which topic variation can affect the choice of different languages was indicated in the children's answers to a question which asked them to say which language(s) they would normally expect to use when talking about a traditional ceremony to a friend, or talking about a problem in mathematics. In the case of the latter English was the primary language, and in the case of the former the children's mother tongue, as is indicated in Figure 13.11. The variation is to be expected. The first topic is one associated with the home and the local community and the latter with the school. It is also the case that these topics would characteristically be discussed within these two distinct settings.

FIGURE 13.10 (Stage II) *Language use with older and younger siblings*

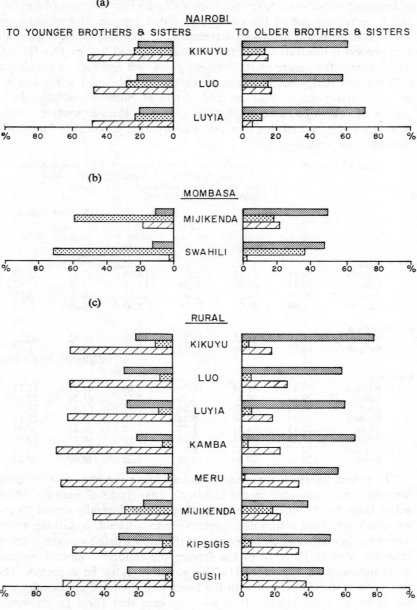

(a)

NAIROBI

TO YOUNGER BROTHERS & SISTERS   TO OLDER BROTHERS & SISTERS

KIKUYU
LUO
LUYIA

% 80 60 40 20 0   0 20 40 60 80 %

(b)

MOMBASA

MIJIKENDA
SWAHILI

% 80 60 40 20 0   0 20 40 60 80 %

(c)

RURAL

KIKUYU
LUO
LUYIA
KAMBA
MERU
MIJIKENDA
KIPSIGIS
GUSII

% 80 60 40 20 0   0 20 40 60 80 %

▓ ENGLISH   ▒ SWAHILI   ▨ MOTHER TONGUE

FIGURE 13.11 (Stage IV) *Language choice in relation to topic variance*

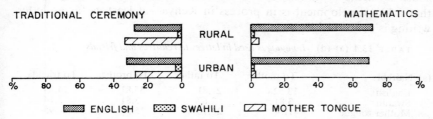

ENGLISH   SWAHILI   MOTHER TONGUE

LANGUAGE USE IN SPECIFIC SITUATIONS OF INTERACTION

In speaking to older brothers and sisters and to friends the choice of different languages by the pupils is naturally affected by conventions associated with the use of particular languages in particular settings, by the role-relations between the participants, by the topic which is being discussed and by the manifest and latent function of the conversation.[14] For instance, when the children were asked to indicate what language or languages they preferred to use when talking to older brothers and sisters and secondly to their closest school friends '*about school outside their homes*, for example, in a bus or shop', a large majority of the children in all the groups in the urban and rural samples that answered both parts of the question said that they preferred to use English in such circumstances. One reason for this might be that in such a setting the language could serve as an index of status rank.

Dr Parkin has indicated that the selection of different languages within a conversation can have the latent function of expressing degrees of social distance, respect or disrespect, 'flattery' or condescension. In most circumstances, however, speakers select languages in particular situations according to their experience as to which can be appropriately used without causing offence or impeding comprehension.

The pupils were also asked to say what language or languages they used when writing to various members of their families and to friends. Their answers indicated that in most groups English was used almost exclusively, in letters to friends and predominantly in letters to older brothers and sisters while the first language was used predominantly when writing to their parents (except among the Mijikenda group). The variation reported in 1968 is shown in Figures 13.12(a)–(d) and Tables 13.4(a)–(d). The preponderant use of English in letters to girlfriends and boyfriends was confirmed in the 1970 inquiry. N. Tanner noted in a study of language use among educated Indonesians that English had become 'the language of Romance' for some segments of Indonesia's youth and it is interesting to speculate that a like development is in process in Kenya—at least as far as letter writing is concerned.[15]

TABLE 13.4 (a)–(d) *Languages used in letters to relatives and friends*

(a) Nairobi	To mother	To father	To brother	To friends
English	13.52	27.81	55.81	74.29
Swahili	3.81	2.67	3.81	5.14
Mother tongue	41.74	28.76	5.90	4.95
Mombasa				
English	9.05	20.99	56.79	77.78
Swahili	19.34	18.52	7.40	6.99
Mother tongue	28.39	19.75	6.17	3.70
Rural				
English	4.95	16.72	70.59	83.69
Swahili	6.55	10.38	4.95	3.48
Mother tongue	61.81	51.43	10.80	5.57

(b) Nairobi		To mother	To father	To brother	To friends
Kikuyu	English	10.00	22.50	69.17	83.33
	Swahili	2.50	1.67	5.83	5.83
	Mother tongue	65.83	47.50	8.33	4.16
Luo	English	5.41	31.08	63.51	68.92
	Swahili	4.05	0.00	4.05	4.05
	Mother tongue	64.87	41.89	10.81	10.81
Luyia	English	14.29	31.43	62.86	74.29
	Swahili	0.00	2.86	0.00	8.57
	Mother tongue	51.43	40.00	8.57	2.86
Kamba	English	10.00	30.00	75.00	90.00
	Swahili	0.00	5.00	5.00	5.00
	Mother tongue	70.00	50.00	10.00	0.00

(c) Mombasa					
Swahili	English	6.56	19.67	52.46	70.49
	Swahili	45.90	37.70	18.03	16.39
	Mother tongue	9.84	8.19	3.28	4.92
Mijikenda	English	0.00	25.93	70.37	85.18
	Swahili	44.44	48.15	14.82	11.11
	Mother tongue	22.22	3.70	3.70	0.00

(d) Rural					
Kikuyu	English	4.73	17.98	74.13	83.91
	Swahili	0.63	2.84	1.89	2.84
	Mother tongue	67.51	53.63	7.57	3.47
Luo	English	5.43	23.26	73.64	86.05
	Swahili	2.33	2.33	1.55	2.33
	Mother tongue	79.85	57.36	12.40	4.65
Luyia	English	8.14	24.42	76.74	76.74
	Swahili	1.16	4.65	1.16	6.98
	Mother tongue	76.74	56.98	15.12	12.79
Kamba	English	1.36	6.80	71.43	89.79
	Swahili	2.04	2.04	2.04	1.36
	Mother tongue	82.31	74.83	17.69	4.08
Meru	English	0.00	7.97	72.57	84.96
	Swahili	0.00	7.08	4.43	1.77
	Mother tongue	62.83	60.18	14.16	8.85

Languages used in letters to relatives and friends

		To mother	To father	To brother	To friends
(d) **Rural** (Cont'd.)					
Mijikenda	English	0.79	8.66	68.50	76.38
	Swahili	37.79	51.18	17.32	10.24
	Mother tongue	29.92	22.84	4.72	3.15
Gusii	English	0.80	19.20	74.40	84.60
	Swahili	0.80	4.00	3.20	0.80
	Mother tongue	65.60	60.00	15.20	8.00
Kipsigis	English	2.52	10.92	79.83	87.39
	Swahili	3.36	5.88	3.36	4.20
	Mother tongue	76.47	71.43	14.29	8.40

FIGURE 13.12 (Stage II) *Language use in correspondence with relatives and friends*

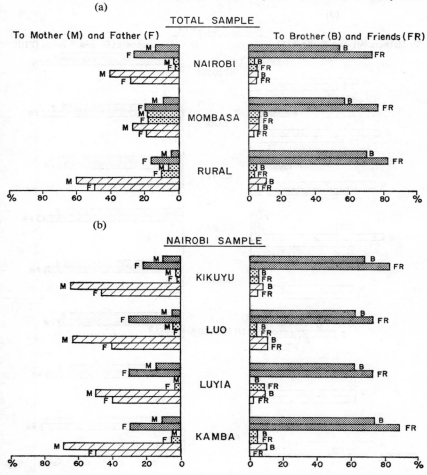

(a)

TOTAL SAMPLE

To Mother (M) and Father (F)   To Brother (B) and Friends (FR)

NAIROBI

MOMBASA

RURAL

(b)

NAIROBI SAMPLE

KIKUYU

LUO

LUYIA

KAMBA

ENGLISH   SWAHILI   MOTHER TONGUE

371

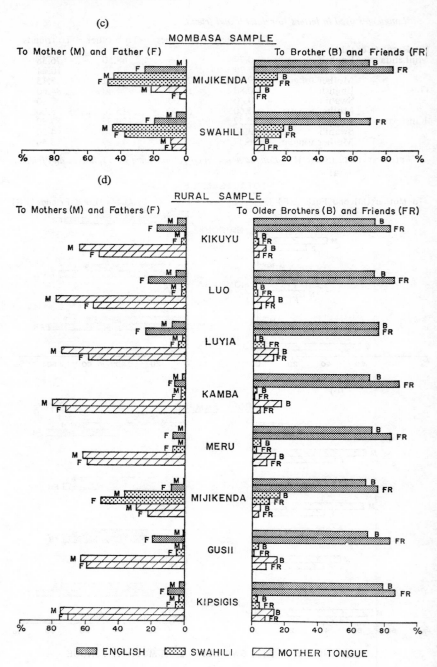

(c)

MOMBASA SAMPLE

To Mother (M) and Father (F)
To Brother (B) and Friends (FR)

(d)

RURAL SAMPLE

To Mothers (M) and Fathers (F)
To Older Brothers (B) and Friends (FR)

ENGLISH   SWAHILI   MOTHER TONGUE

372

The use of English as the primary language of written communication is not restricted to romantic missives, however. An instance of the virtually exclusive use of the language by school children in Kenya was remarked upon by Dr A. Molnos in a report of a research project in which 392 secondary school children and 560 primary school children were asked to complete a questionnaire which had equivalent forms in English and Swahili. Only 2.3 per cent of the Kenya sample answered the questionnaire in Swahili (22 out of 932), whereas in Tanzania 43.1 per cent (420 out of 975) had done so.[16] It is, however, of some relevance that half the sample was drawn from Nairobi and half from predominantly Luo-speaking areas. Some possible reasons for such behaviour will be considered in the following section.

The answers to other questions revealed that the two situations in which the language choices of the children appeared to be most variable were in conversations with their brothers and sisters at home and with their fellow students at school in the playground or compound. In such circumstances where their status as educated people is recognized, as it were, it seems that display of English is not required. I observed in schools also that in 'spontaneous' or 'casual' speech in such circumstances, the degree of language switching that took place was very marked.[17] It is clear that language switching is much less common in written communication between friends than in conversations between them.

To provide an indication of the choices exercised by children when speaking to others of different social 'standing' and of the same mother tongue in the one instance and a different mother tongue in the other, the children were asked to say what language they thought they would normally begin to speak to a variety of persons in particular settings. In such a circumstance, a 'neutral' code would normally be used, that is to say, a language which it could be anticipated would serve to establish a relationship without further implication.

While there were marked differences in certain instances between the answers given by children in the different language groups, the answers which are illustrated in Figure 13.13 showed a high degree of consistency. The use of the children's first language in some instances when they are speaking to people belonging to a different linguistic group might best be explained by the fact that the majority of the children in the rural areas where this incidence is most evident live in areas of relatively high linguistic homogeneity, and in consequence they might assume that a person living in the area who spoke another language could be expected to understand common greetings in their own language.

Clearly the degree to which the speaker's first language or English in the first case, and English and Swahili in the second, are used initially, varies according to assumptions made by the speaker about the educational background of the person addressed.

Naturally this statement needs qualification. There were certain significant differences in the answers of the boys and girls in the Nairobi sample (Stage IV). In two cases the contrasts in the extent to which the first language was used in the replies of the different sexes were marked, viz. in supposed conversation with a nurse, and with a police officer. The girls were evidently very much more likely to use English in addressing a nurse whether they assumed the person concerned spoke their own language (61.5 per cent) or not (88 per cent). The boys would characteristically use their mother tongue in the first case (72 per cent as opposed to the girls' 40 per cent) and Swahili in the second (86.5 per cent as opposed to 26 per cent). It can perhaps be inferred that in such a circumstance the boys would be less concerned to express deference or respect than the girls to the person involved. A significant but less marked contrast showing precisely the same patterns of language choice was evident in the answers of children of different sexes with regard to conversation with a police officer.

With one exception there was a relatively high degree of correspondence between the summed answers given by children in the rural sample and those of the children in the urban sample. The exception was that in all cases, children in the urban sample appear to be more likely to use Swahili and less likely to use their first language in conversations in the market place, even when speaking to a co-lingual (25.1 per cent as opposed to 14.8 per cent). As there was a degree of variation between the answers of the children in the rural sample to this question it might be of some relevance to detail the answers given. In the following table sex and language of the children are indicated, together with their answers to the question. The percentages for each language choice are not mutually exclusive.

TABLE 13.5   *What language(s) would you normally begin to speak to a woman selling potatoes (viazi) in the market near your home?*

Rural Sample		To a woman from the same language group			To a woman from a different language group		
	Sex	English	Swahili	Mother T.	English	Swahili	Mother T.
Kikuyu	F	20.0	13.3	86.5	58.7	35.0	12.5
	M	5.7	20.0	74.0	37.0	70.5	0.0
Luo	M	19.3	7.7	88.5	33.3	50.0	22.0
	F	0.0	11.4	77.0	19.0	66.5	19.0
Luyia	M	0.0	20.0	86.9	4.2	95.9	0.0
	M	0.0	12.5	100.0	13.1	63.4	6.6
Kamba	F	15.6	9.4	90.5	50.0	93.0	21.4
Meru	M	5.8	3.8	88.5	45.0	45.0	10.0
	M	3.1	6.4	100.0	31.8	63.5	9.1
Mijikenda	M	0.0	25.0	83.3	18.2	91.0	18.1
	M	0.0	29.0	78.4	7.1	96.4	10.4
Gusii	M	9.1	18.2	82.0	30.9	77.0	0.0
Kalenjin	M	8.0	28.0	72.0	23.1	88.4	3.8
	M	13.1	17.2	82.5	41.1	64.9	35.3

FIGURE 13.13 (Stage IV) *Language use in specific situations of interaction*

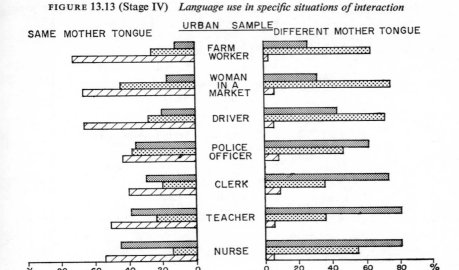

SAME MOTHER TONGUE   URBAN SAMPLE   DIFFERENT MOTHER TONGUE

FARM WORKER

WOMAN IN A MARKET

DRIVER

POLICE OFFICER

CLERK

TEACHER

NURSE

% 80 60 40 20 0   0 20 40 60 80 %

▨ ENGLISH   ▨ SWAHILI   ▨ MOTHER TONGUE

The extent to which children in certain areas claimed that they would use English in the circumstance specified was unexpected; but it becomes less surprising when it is understood that the use of the language in a conversation can be taken to reflect both on their own role and status and that of the person addressed.

In considering the process of language substitution in different areas of activity I obtained information about the frequency with which children listened to broadcasts and read newspapers in different languages. Naturally, the degree of choice that can be exercised in situations of reception such as listening to the radio is limited both by the fact that programmes are produced in a restricted number of languages and because the younger members of a household are not always in a position to decide what programmes are to be listened to or, in other circumstances, what papers are to be read.

Most children who read newspapers regularly claimed to read them in English. A much lower proportion said that they read newspapers in Swahili and a negligible proportion reported that they did so in their first languages. In contrast, the majority of the children in each language group, with the exception of the Luo-speaking children in the rural sample, claimed to listen to broadcasts in Swahili more frequently than to those in English or their mother tongues. Figures 13.14 (a)–(d) and

Tables 13.6 (a)–(d) show the percentage of children in each group who claimed to read newspapers regularly, in different languages.

TABLE 13.6 (a)–(d)   *Newspapers*

(a) Total	English	Swahili	
Nairobi	78.2	9.33	
Mombasa	79.0	14.80	
Rural	60.2	14.81	

(b) Nairobi	English	Swahili	Mother T.
Kikuyu	64.17	15.83	0.00
Luo	81.08	8.11	1.35
Luyia	80.00	8.57	0.00
Kamba	70.00	10.00	0.00
Swahili	75.00	25.00	—
English	88.16	1.32	—
Gujarati	88.89	0.00	1.23
Punjabi	84.44	2.22	0.00

(c) Mombasa			
Mijikenda	55.56	18.52	0.00
Swahili	68.85	19.67	—

(d) Rural			
Kikuyu	61.83	8.83	0.63
Luo	71.32	5.43	0.00
Luyia	58.14	15.12	0.00
Kamba	36.05	12.93	0.00
Meru	64.60	14.16	0.00
Mijikenda	52.76	19.69	0.00
Gusii	42.06	9.52	0.79
Kalenjin (Kipsigis)	65.55	5.04	0.00

Figures 13.15(a)–(c) and Tables 13.7(a)–(c) show those who said they listened 'always' or 'often' to broadcasts in English, Swahili or their first language.

TABLE 13.7 (a)–(c)   *Radio broadcasts*

(a) Nairobi	English	Swahili	Mother T.
Kikuyu	26.55	49.33	8.73
Luo	25.75	49.18	1.50
Luyia	15.33	72.00	0.03

(b) Mombasa			
Mijikenda	10.00	62.00	0.00
Swahili	9.48	72.20	—

(c) Rural			
Kikuyu	23.28	32.46	4.94
Luo	44.13	28.60	15.98
Luyia	31.28	60.27	8.08
Kamba	21.78	49.94	7.81
Meru	32.64	40.45	0.50
Mijikenda	7.27	69.9	0.00
Gusii	23.35	44.50	1.80
Kalenjin (Kipsigis)	30.55	30.51	34.13

376

FIGURE 13.14 (Stage II) *The language of newspapers read*

(a)

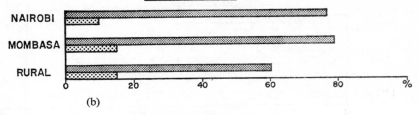

(b)

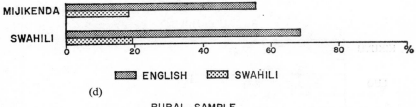

(c)

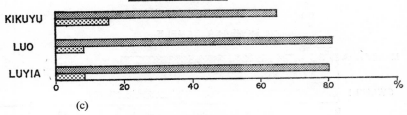

(d)

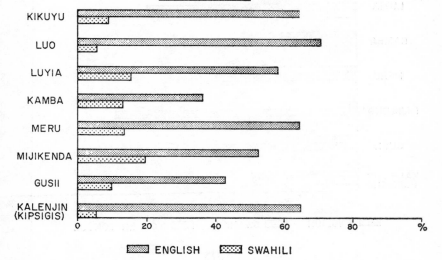

FIGURE 13.15 (Stage II)   *The language of broadcasts heard*

(a)

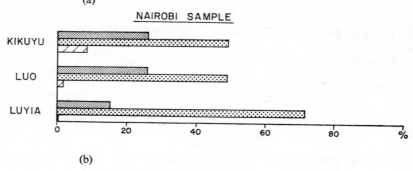

NAIROBI SAMPLE

(b)

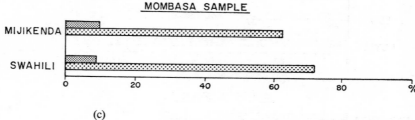

MOMBASA SAMPLE

(c)

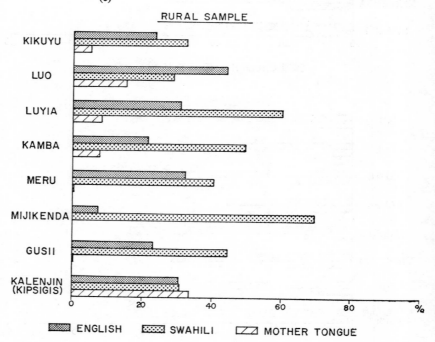

RURAL SAMPLE

▨ ENGLISH   ▧ SWAHILI   ⧄ MOTHER TONGUE

In answer to a question asking for precise details of which programmes were listened to, the majority of the children involved in the 1970 inquiry indicated that they listened to programmes in which popular records were played and to news broadcasts. While English is a predominant linguistic vehicle of popular 'Western' music it is not exclusively so, particularly in so far as popular songs and music are concerned.

In this connection it might be apposite to consider the relevance of J. Fishman's observation in relation to the processes of language maintenance and language change among immigrant communities in the United States that 'adolescence is the juncture at which the impact of mass culture and of ethnically based language maintenance is most clearly felt'.[18] 'Mass culture' as most pupils are exposed to it through the media of films, pictorial magazines, and to a lesser extent popular songs and dance tunes, is in most cases primarily transmitted in English, and Professor Fishman's observation holds true in Kenya as in other areas.

LANGUAGE USE IN THE SCHOOL

The use of different media of instruction in schools in Kenya is discussed in Chapter 16 and I will not elaborate upon the situation here. The majority of children in the rural areas in the 1968 sample had been educated initially through the medium of their mother tongue and subsequently through the medium of English.

The recommendation made by the Beecher Commission in 1949 that Swahili should remain the initial language of instruction in primary schools in urban areas was still officially in operation in 1960 when most of the children involved in the 1968 survey began their schooling, but 46 per cent of the children in the Nairobi sample claimed that English was in fact the language used to teach most subjects in Standard I at the time they entered school. The percentage was slightly higher in Mombasa (52 per cent). Thirteen per cent of the children in the rural sample made the same claim.

Sixteen per cent of the children in Nairobi and 33 per cent in Mombasa stated that they were first educated in Swahili; the percentage for the rural sample was 17 per cent although this figure is largely accounted for by the fact that 87 per cent of the children in the Mijikenda group were initially educated in this language.

The children in each of the sub-samples and in the different language groups, with the exception of the Meru-speaking children and the Mijikenda group, claimed that after the first two years of education English was the language used to teach most subjects at school. Among the Meru group the use of the children's first language was slightly greater than the use of English in Standard III, and among the Mijikenda group Swahili was still the most common medium of instruction at that stage. The details reported in the first survey are indicated in Figures 13.16(a)–(d) and Tables 13.8(a)–(d).

TABLE 13.8 (a)–(d) *Languages of instruction in primary schools (Stage I)*

(a) **Total**	N.	English	Standard I Swahili	Mother T.	English	Standard III Swahili	Mother T.
Nairobi	524	45.802	16.412	37.786	78.626	7.824	13.550
Mombasa	243	51.852	32.510	15.638	80.247	14.403	5.350
Rural	1,436	12.953	16.643	70.404	56.267	11.630	32.103
(b) Nairobi							
Kikuyu		15.000	30.833	54.167	64.167	13.333	22.500
Luo		20.270	24.324	55.405	68.919	12.162	18.919
Luyia		20.000	28.571	51.429	65.714	17.143	17.143
Kamba		5.000	15.000	80.000	70.000	5.000	25.000
(c) Mombasa							
Mijikenda		22.222	74.074	3.704	66.667	33.333	0.000
Swahili		49.180	42.620	8.190	75.410	21.310	3.280
(d) Rural							
Kikuyu		8.517	11.041	80.442	52.366	8.517	39.117
Luo		10.078	11.628	78.295	56.690	3.876	36.434
Luyia		5.814	9.302	84.884	48.837	6.977	44.186
Kamba		3.401	5.442	91.156	51.701	4.082	44.218
Meru		2.655	0.000	97.345	49.903	0.000	53.097
Mijikenda		3.150	87.402	9.449	36.220	62.205	1.575
Gusii		0.794	2.381	96.825	64.286	7.937	27.778
Kalenjin		6.723	9.244	84.034	61.345	6.723	31.933

Reports given by children in 1969 confirmed the accuracy of those given in 1968. There was, however, evidence of a trend toward an increasing use of English as a medium of instruction in Standard III. To take examples from the answers given by children in the three largest language groups (Kikuyu, Luo and Luyia) in the rural areas, 69 per cent, 72 per cent and 73.5 per cent respectively claimed that English was the primary medium at this level in the 1969 survey. In general there was little change in the position as regards the use of different languages in Standard I. It is apparent, however, that the use of English at an increasingly earlier stage as the medium of instruction predated the 'official' introduction of the English medium scheme (subsequently termed the New Primary Approach) in many areas.

FIGURE 13.16 (Stage II)   *Media of instruction in primary school: Standards I and III*

(a)

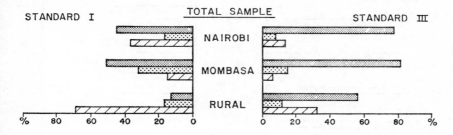

(b)

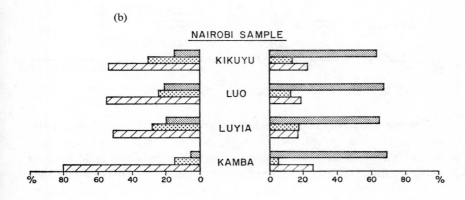

(c)

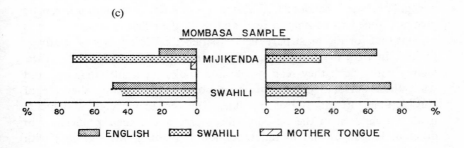

381

(d)

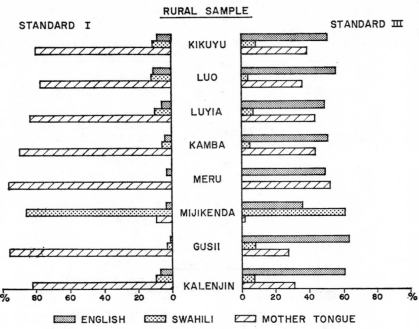

The great majority of the children in both the rural and urban samples claimed to have studied Swahili in primary school, but there were considerable differences in the average number of years which children from different linguistic areas claimed to have done so and it is evident that there was considerable variation in this respect in different districts (cf. Chapter 16).

The training given to children in the schools is one factor which naturally affects the facility with which they use different languages in various activities. With the exception of the children in the Mijikenda group and of 23 per cent of those in school 53, almost all the children in the major linguistic groups claimed to be able to read and write their first language but it is evident that for the most part their experience of doing so was relatively limited. In 1970 the subjects answered a number of questions about the facility with which they read, wrote and spoke different languages, and while these personal judgements have no objective validity they are of considerable interest. It was possible, however, to correlate statements made by children in the Nairobi sub-sample about their proficiency in different languages and in different modes (reading, writing, etc.) with their scores on a test of Swahili grammatical structure and the results confirmed the general accuracy of the pupils' personal assessments in this connection (cf. Chapter 16). Figure 13.17 gives an indication of the answers of the children in the rural and urban samples to these questions.

It is clear from the pupils' answers to other questions that in general they were seldom required to read or write their mother tongues. In 1970 76.8 per cent of the rural sample and 82.7 per cent of the urban sample said in answer to a question about their reading habits that they seldom had occasion to read books, papers or notices in their mother tongue (i.e. 'not at all' or 'less than once a month'). In answering questions about the frequency with which they wrote their mother tongues, English and Swahili, the total percentages of children in the rural sample who said that they did so frequently (i.e. 'several times a week', 'at least once a day' or 'several times a day') were 83.7 per cent for English, 23.9 per cent for Swahili, and 21.5 per cent for the mother tongues respectively. Table 13.9 gives an indication of the languages in which children in the 1968 inquiry claimed to have read books outside school in the six months previous to the inquiry.

TABLE 13.9 (Stage II) *Leisure reading: books read in given languages (percentages of books read by children in each language group)*

Nairobi	English	Swahili	Mother T.	Other languages
Kikuyu	59.47	3.10	0.31	0.40 (Meru)
Luo	85.86	8.08	6.06	0.00
Luyia	90.91	7.27	1.82	0.00
Kamba	95.83	4.17	0.00	0.00
Swahili	95.24	4.76	0.00	0.00
Mombasa				
Mijikenda	82.26	12.90	4.84	0.00
Swahili	80.24	10.00	0.00	0.00
Rural				
Kikuyu	93.08	5.38	0.77	0.38 (Kamba)
Luo	88.97	4.41	5.15	0.00
Luyia	81.48	16.05	2.47	0.00
Kamba	83.87	13.71	1.61	0.81 (Kikuyu)
Meru	87.80	9.76	1.63	0.81 (Kikuyu)
Mijikenda	86.27	11.76	0.98	0.00
Kalenjin (Kipsigis)	91.74	6.61	0.83	0.00

FIGURE 13.17 (Stage IV) *Competence of the students in mother tongues, Swahili and English in different modes*

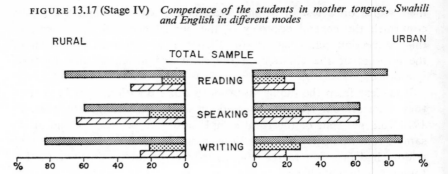

ATTITUDES TO LANGUAGE USE

While there was considerable similarity between the answers of children in the different language groups to the questions concerning the extent to which different languages were used in different modes, some significant differences did emerge: for instance, in 1970 in reply to questions concerning the language(s) they could read 'most easily and quickly', the frequency with which they wrote in their mother tongue and the language(s) they considered that they spoke 'best' at that particular time, the claims of the *boys* in the Luo-speaking group in the rural area who named their mother tongue in answer to the questions were proportionally more numerous than those of the children in any other group. Forty-eight per cent, 53.9 per cent and 80 per cent of the group named their first language in answer to these questions, as opposed to overall claims of 33.9 per cent, 21.5 per cent and 66.7 per cent respectively.

While such variation may in fact be indicative of use-rates, there is little doubt that it is indicative also of attitudes the children have towards the use of their mother tongue in this instance and I would also like to mention some findings related to this rather complex issue.

For the most part the motivation of children to acquire languages other than their mother tongue is instrumental.[19] To be socially mobile they need to acquire a knowledge of English and Swahili. At present, however, the potential economic advantages of knowing the former are greater than those of knowing the latter. This fact affects to a certain extent their attitudes towards the two languages, particularly as subjects of instruction.

E. Haugen has pointed out as regards language instruction that 'the most important thing is to make sure that those who are to do the learning are motivated by some genuine advantage which will accrue to them in return for their effort'.[20] As I indicate in Chapter 16, in certain areas a number of pupils appear to feel that the knowledge of Swahili they have on entering secondary school is adequate for their purposes, and the fact that in many instances they speak attenuated forms of non-standard dialects does not appear to concern them greatly. It seems, however, that most children accept the need for and the utility of having a good command of the language.

An indication of the children's recognition of the utilitarian value of different languages was given in their answers to a question which asked them to say which three languages they would like their own children to speak really well, and to rank these languages in order of choice. The majority of children in each sample ranked English as the first choice, Swahili as the second, and their mother tongue as the third. The details of the choices made by the children in the rural group are shown in Figures 13.18(a)–(c) and Tables 13.10(a)–(c).[21]

TABLE 13.10 (a)–(c)

(a) *Language Choice 1*

Rural	English	Swahili	Mother T.
Kikuyu	59.62	6.31	34.07
Luo	51.94	6.20	41.86
Luyia	54.65	17.44	27.91
Kamba	53.74	10.88	35.37
Meru	65.49	7.08	27.43
Mijikenda	43.31	10.24	46.46
Gusii	51.20	9.60	39.20
Kalenjin	49.58	14.28	36.13

(b) *Language Choice 2*

Rural	English	Swahili	Mother T.
Kikuyu	30.60	39.43	29.97
Luo	33.33	43.41	23.26
Luyia	25.58	55.81	18.60
Kamba	25.85	59.86	14.29
Meru	21.24	60.18	18.58
Mijikenda	18.90	57.48	23.62
Gusii	33.60	52.80	13.60
Kalenjin	34.45	47.06	18.49

(c) *Language Choice 3*

Rural	English	Swahili	Mother T.
Kikuyu	6.31	49.84	43.85
Luo	10.85	42.64	46.51
Luyia	15.12	22.09	62.79
Kamba	18.37	26.53	55.10
Meru	11.50	32.74	55.75
Mijikenda	27.56	23.62	48.82
Gusii	14.40	34.40	51.20
Kalenjin	10.92	32.77	56.30

FIGURE 13.18   *Ranking of language choice*
(a)   (Stage II)

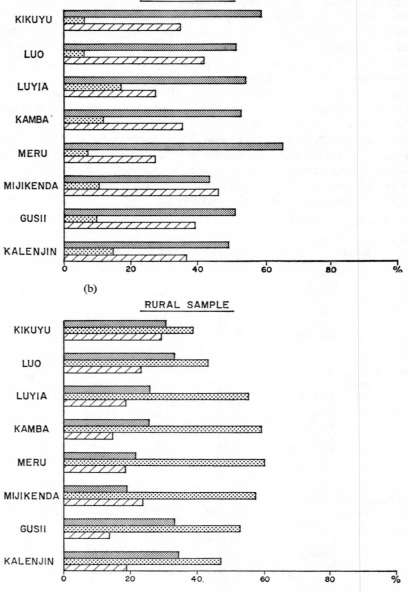

RURAL SAMPLE

KIKUYU
LUO
LUYIA
KAMBA
MERU
MIJIKENDA
GUSII
KALENJIN

0   20   40   60   80   %

(b)

RURAL SAMPLE

KIKUYU
LUO
LUYIA
KAMBA
MERU
MIJIKENDA
GUSII
KALENJIN

0   20   40.   60   80   %

▨ ENGLISH   ▨ SWAHILI   ⧄ MOTHER TONGUE

(c)

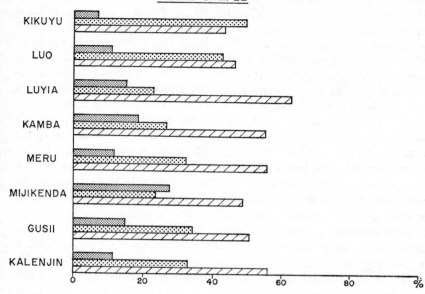

RURAL SAMPLE

(d) (Stage III)

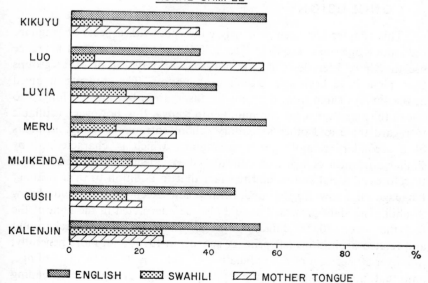

RURAL SAMPLE

ENGLISH   SWAHILI   MOTHER TONGUE

It is, however, of some interest that the pupils in the Mijikenda group alone, the majority of whom spoke Giriama, gave a higher rating to their first language than to any other languages. Similarly, in answer to a question about the desirability or otherwise of the teaching of the first languages of the pupils at secondary level, this was the only group in which a considerable number of children (43 per cent) showed marked interest in this possibility. Their comments in these respects may be indicative of a form of reaction against the relative disuse of their languages in educational practice and in activities such as broadcasting, etc.

In 1969 a similar set of responses was obtained from the schools sampled apart from the fact that there was a significant difference in the answers given by the Luo-speaking children in the direction of a higher rating for their first language and a consequent alteration in the pattern of choices in relation to other languages, cf. Figure 13.18(d). It has frequently been observed that manifestations of language loyalty generally occur in circumstances in which a particular speech community feels the need to draw attention to symbols of group identity. Such a situation appears to have occurred at this time among this group of pupils. I do not think it is justifiable to claim, however, that the answers given are a reflection of attitudes in the sense the term is normally understood by social scientists. At most one might claim that they provide an indication of opinions and judgements expressed under relatively unusual conditions.

CONCLUSION

This chapter has been primarily concerned with aspects of language use among one social group in Kenya. Naturally the patterns of language use that have been described are not necessarily typical of other groups that might have been selected for examination. The students involved in the surveys came from different linguistic areas but most belonged to one of the major language communities in Kenya. It is, however, justifiable to regard these and other secondary school entrants as being members of a secondary school speech community which is characterized by similar attributes of age and educational experience and in one respect therefore, of social status, and the fact that in addition to their primary language all know English and, with a few exceptions, claim to know Swahili. The data presented should also be interpreted in the light of the fact that over 120,000 children with a similar educational background and related aspirations left primary schools in 1970; and, more generally, that over 50 per cent of the population of Kenya is under 16 years of age, and that most children in the appropriate age groups are attending school. The behaviour reported, therefore, might serve in some respects as a pointer to directions of language shift and areas of language maintenance.[22]

It is clear, however, that it is difficult to generalize about these trends because forms of language shift or language substitution proceed at different rates, as it were, in relation to the diverse activities in which the individuals are involved and vary according to a complex of factors such as setting, topic, participants and mode of use. Moreover, it is sometimes misleading to consider the processes such as have been described as necessarily involving the *substitution* or *displacement* of one language by another. The languages concerned differ in their functional ranges, and the uses to which their specialized varieties can be put; and the increasing use of one language in particular modes is often a function of the *additional* roles that the speaker is called upon to assume. English has not for example *replaced* the first language as the appropriate language for discussing a problem in mathematics, as the first language has not been used at any stage for this particular purpose.

Such trends cannot normally be affected or arrested by decree or exhortation. Numerous social forces influence children born for the most part in a 'monocultural' and monolingual environment to develop bilingual and trilingual skills. All members of society are affected by these influences, even those most concerned to resist acculturation, as is indicated by the fact that the lexicons of the major languages spoken in Kenya are being rapidly extended by the infusion of loan words from Swahili and English.[23]

The extent to which such infusion varies according to topic and setting and to other variables that have been seen to affect language switching; the consideration of other aspects of 'superposed' variation in style in the speech of particular pupils and the use of linguistic features of non-standard dialects of Swahili and English are matters whose discussion is outside the scope of this chapter.[24]

To obtain more detailed profiles of language use it would be necessary to consider such variation and more generally to investigate in greater detail the proficiency with which the children use different languages for different purposes. A sociolinguistic perspective, however, requires the use of functional measures of proficiency just as it requires the utilization of a functional definition of bilingualism itself.[25] That is to say, the important question is whether a person's control of a language is sufficient to enable him to communicate effectively in a specific situation of interaction or to comprehend adequately what is spoken or written in situations of reception similar to those in which he is obliged to make use of a particular language. Attempts to measure language skills and language relationships *in vacuo* have limited applicability even though the results of such tests not infrequently correlate positively with other measures of performance.

For this reason I have not made use of some of the techniques that have been widely used to measure forms of 'linguistic dominance' and 'bilingual balance' such as tests of translation response, reaction time tests and other measures that require the subject to respond to uncontextualized verbal stimuli.[26]

Nor have I attempted to interpret the information obtained in terms of current hypotheses regarding the forms of mental activity that are thought to be characteristic of bilingual behaviour. In doing so it would be necessary to make use of rather more complex theoretical constructs than those commonly referred to in terms of the compound/co-ordinate hypothesis in which a distinction is recognized between speakers who can be said to operate a single 'fused' linguistic system and those who operate two or more co-ordinate systems—the kind of operation in each case resulting from the circumstances in which the languages were acquired.[27]

In a subsequent section I have considered some aspects of the proficiency of the children involved in the fourth stage of the inquiry in terms of their ability to perform tasks analogous to those that they are required to perform at school and in activities that involve the use of Swahili and English. The inquiry is thus advanced to a stage at which it is possible to consider not simply what languages are used in particular circumstances but how efficiently they are used in certain of the diverse but nonetheless determinate forms of activity in which the children make use of Swahili and English in their daily lives.

NOTES

The projects described in Chapters 13 and 16 were undertaken with the support of a grant from the Survey Council of the Survey of Language Use and Language Teaching in Eastern Africa.

[1] The term 'functional range' is used in the sense of 'the specialisation of particular languages or varieties to particular situations or functions', cf. D. Hymes, 'The Ethnography of Speaking', T. Gladwin and W. C. Sturtevant (eds.), *Anthropology and Human Behaviour*, Anthropological Society of Washington, Washington D.C., 1962.

[2] It would be rash to attempt to summarize these processes but it might be relevant to itemize certain factors which can be related to the study of communal and individual maintenance and change in language behaviour in Kenya. Language use in many speech communities in the country is obviously affected by historical events and geographical facts too complex to be facilely enumerated; and by economic forces such as the development of urbanization, industrialization and consequent social stratification, and of networks of transportation; and by social goals and values such as nationalism.

In the usage of any particular individual, patterns of language use may be related to the characteristics of age, sex, religion, education and occupation; language can assume significance as a symbol of self-identity. It may also become a symbol of group identity and integrity, which development might give rise to language loyalty or linguocentrism and conversely to language antipathy.

[3] I am grateful to Mr Mark Wheeler of the Institute of Development Studies, Nairobi, for his advice on the sample design of the initial survey; and to his wife Mrs Sally Wheeler, a psychologist who assisted in the administration of the tests and questionnaires and in the statistical interpretation of the data in the first stage of the inquiry; and to my colleague Mr Abud Bashir, former Deputy Head of the Language Section of the Kenya Institute of Education who scrutinized the contents of the questionnaires used and constructed the cloze test in Swahili used in the 1968 survey. The advice of Mr J. Watson, a systems analyst, was of great assistance to me in the first stage of preparation of the data for computer analysis. I am also grateful to Mr Bob Scott of the University Computing Centre, and to Mr D. Willis and Mr P. Lany for their assistance in preparing the computer programmes. While the responsibility for the design of the project was mine it could not have been successfully undertaken or concluded without their co-operation and that of ministry personnel and of many school principals and teachers. The extent of this support was indicated by the fact that of 70 secondary schools involved in the initial inquiry, 67 returned the questionnaires and tests used in time for processing.

[4] The sample and details of the stratified random technique are described in greater detail in T. P. Gorman, 'Sociolinguistic Implications of Choice of Media of Instruction' in W. H. Whiteley (ed.), *Language Use and Social Change*, Oxford University Press, London, 1971, pp. 198–220.

About two-thirds of the urban population live in Nairobi and Mombasa, and in the capital this population is drawn primarily from members of the four largest language groups, viz. Kikuyu, Luo, Luyia and Kamba.

[5] For a discussion of such tests, cf. E. F. Rankin, 'The Cloze Procedure—a Survey of Research' in L. T. Thurstone (ed.), *Yearbook*, National Reading Conference, 1965, pp. 50–93. The method seems to be an effective technique by which to test a pupil's ability to comprehend the total language context of a passage rather than his knowledge of discrete lexical or grammatical items.

[6] T. P. Gorman, op. cit., 1971.

[7] There was one significant difference in the method of analysis used at this stage. During the initial analysis, it had become evident that a very considerable proportion of the children in schools in the urban areas had received all their previous education in rural areas. To exclude children who had only recently entered the city from the urban samples, I decided to classify as 'urban' only those children who had spent at least four years in an urban environment. This factor primarily accounts for the numerical variation in the groups reported in the two stages of analysis.

[8] I have made a distinction between *situations of interaction* which are characterized by reciprocal language behaviour and *situations of reception* in which the subject is the receptor in a non-reciprocal exchange such as listening to a radio.

[9] I am using the term in the sense it was defined by J. J. Gumperz as a 'social group which may be either monolingual or multilingual, held together by frequency of social interaction patterns and set off from the surrounding areas by weaknesses in the line of communication.' cf. J. J. Gumperz, 'Types of Linguistic Communities', *Anthropological Linguistics*, vol. 4, no. 1, 1962, p. 31.

[10] It has been argued that in the formation of language habits, the attitude of the mother is of particular importance 'because of her role as the pivotal centre of the home', cf. J. Bossard, 'The Bilingual Individual', *American Social Review*, 10, 1945, pp. 699–709.

[11] A. R. Diebold Jr., 'Incipient Bilingualism', *Language*, vol. 37, no. 1, 1961, p. 111.

[12] 31.8 per cent of the fathers of the Swahili-speaking children in Mombasa were reported to know Arabic, but there are relatively few speakers of Arabic as a first language in the town.

[13] The question was (a) 'Do your parents allow you to use any language you want to in your house at any time? Yes......No......
(b) If there is a language or languages that your parents do *not* like you to use at home say which it is.

[14] I am using the terms 'manifest' and 'latent' in the sense they are used by S. Ervin-Tripp in 'An Analysis of the Interaction of Language, Topic and Listener' in J. J. Gumperz and D. Hymes (eds.), *The Ethnography of Communication*, American Anthropologist, 1964, vol. 66, no. 6, part 2.

[15] N. Tanner, 'Speech and Society among the Indonesian Elite', *Anthropological Linguistics*, vol. 9, no. 3.

[16] cf. A. Molnos, *Attitudes towards Family Planning in East Africa*, Weltforum Verlag, C. Hurst and Co., London, 1969.

[17] I am using the terms 'spontaneous' and 'casual' in the sense these are used by W. Labov, viz. 'excited emotionally charged speech when the constraints of a formal situation are discharged' and 'normal speech used in situations where no attention is directed to language'. cf. W. Labov, 'Phonological Indices to Social Stratification' in the *Ethnography of Communication*, op. cit., p. 167.

[18] J. Fishman, 'Language Maintenance in a Supra-Ethnic Age', in J. Fishman (ed.), *Language Loyalty in the United States*, Mouton and Co., The Hague, 1966, p. 409.

[19] W. Lambert uses the term 'instrumental' to apply to circumstances in which the purpose of language study 'reflects the more utilitarian value of linguistic achievement, such as getting ahead in one's occupation', cf. W. Lambert, 'Psychological Approaches to the Study of Language', part II, *Modern Language Journal*, 47, 1963.

[20] E. Haugen in 'Linguistics and Language Planning', in W. Bright (ed.), *Sociolinguistics*, Mouton and Co., The Hague, 1966, p. 65.

[21] In 1969, Mr J. Anderson of the Institute of Development Studies, University College, Nairobi carried out a survey of the judgements of 798 pupils in harambee schools in the Rift Valley, Central, Eastern, Western and Nyanza Provinces regarding the utility of various school subjects. Mathematics, English and agricultural science were the three subjects that the pupils considered would be of most utility to them after leaving school. J. Anderson, unpublished materials, 1969.

[22] It should be borne in mind that the general level of the education of the fathers of the children was higher than that of those in the same age group in the rest of the population. In 1968, for example, 6.7 per cent of the fathers of the children in the rural sample, 14.8 per cent of those in the Mombasa sample and 29.4 per cent of those in the Nairobi sample were reported to have had a secondary education. Conversely, 24.9 per cent, 32.5 per cent and 46.3 per cent of the fathers in the Nairobi, Mombasa and rural samples respectively, were reported to have received no formal education.

This fact is of some importance in considering the patterns of language use among the group. The pupils are drawn more than proportionately from the educated sector of the population.

[23] I am using the term 'loan words' in the sense it is used by E. Haugen in *Bilingualism in the Americas: a Bibliography and Research Guide*, University of Alabama Press, 1956, p. 60.

[24] For a definition of the term 'superposed' cf. J. J. Gumperz, 'On the Ethnology of Linguistic Change' in J. Bright, *Sociolinguistics*, p. 29. Many children operate a form of pidgin Swahili in addition to a form of the standard dialect. Under the prevailing social conditions the development and diffusion of non-standard forms of standard English and ultimately of a non-standard dialect or set of related dialects can be anticipated.

[25] The use of the terms is discussed by S. Ervin and C. Osgood in 'Second Language Learning and Bilingualism' in C. E. Osgood and F. Sebeok (eds.), *Psycholinguistics*, Indiana University Press, 1965, 139f.

[26] The terms are used by Professor W. Lambert with reference to circumstances in which 'a person shows essentially similar skills in both languages' (bilingual balance), and 'where he has a measurably greater facility in one language' (linguistic dominance), cf. W. Lambert, op. cit. p. 118. The attempt needs to be made to delineate degrees of 'linguistic dominance' with reference to variables such as the topic and setting of discourse which affect or determine whether one language or another is 'dominant' in a particular situation.

[27] In this respect E. Haugen's definition of the minimal skill in a second language necessary for bilingual status, i.e. the ability to produce 'complete meaningful utterances' in the other language, is not functional (cf. E. Haugen, *The Norwegian Language in America: a Study in Bilingual Behaviour*, 2v., University of Pennsylvania Press, 1953,

p. 7); whereas E. Malherbe employed a functional definition of bilingualism in the sense I am using the term when he stated with reference to the situation in South Africa 'that the lowest possible stage at which the term bilinguality can be applied' is the stage at which a man must be able 'to follow an ordinary conversation, speech or sermon in the second language both in its written and spoken form'. (E. Malherbe, *The Bilingual School*, Johannesburg, 1934, p. 19).

PART THREE

Language in Education

14

The Development of Language Policy in Kenya with Particular Reference to the Educational System

T. P. GORMAN

INTRODUCTION

It will be as well initially to indicate the nature and scope of this inquiry into the development of language policy in Kenya. The term 'language policy' itself is open to numerous interpretations. In this chapter I will use the term to refer to decisions taken by bodies with administrative and juridical responsibilities of such a nature that their decisions affected procedures and practice at the level of national organization and activity. I will be concerned primarily with explicit statements about language use in various domains, particularly in the educational domain.

In a sense, the consideration of such decisions or policies as categories of activity dissociated from the historical and social circumstances from which they are derived or towards which they were directed is a questionable undertaking. Decisions on language use in a particular society are almost invariably subordinate to, or a reflection of, underlying political and social values and goals. Even in the educational domain, pedagogical considerations, while relevant, are seldom primary in influencing decisions relating to the use of particular languages as media or subjects of instruction, and this is to be expected.

It is necessary also to remember in discussing language use in any community that factors affecting individual and, to a less evident extent, 'institutional', language use within a speech community are in normal circumstances the result of complex historical, social and economic forces in relation to which the decrees or exhortations of policy-making bodies can in many circumstances have relatively little effect.

Where it is thought to be relevant, therefore, certain aspects of the

397

historical and social developments affecting policy decisions in Kenya have been briefly indicated.

For the most part, the commentary in this chapter will be concerned with language policy decisions made after the proclamation of the East Africa Protectorate in July 1895. Naturally, however, the basic conditions affecting subsequent decisions on language policy are to be found in what might be termed the linguistic demography of the areas designated, and the contiguous regions.

There are over 30 distinct language and dialect clusters spoken in Kenya. Approximately 66 per cent of the population speak languages belonging to the Bantu branch of the Niger-Congo family, the largest language groups in this category being Kikuyu, Kamba and Luyia. Nearly 31 per cent of the population speak Nilotic and Para-Nilotic languages while 3 per cent speak Cushitic languages. Other languages spoken include the languages of the immigrants from the Indian sub-continent, the most important being Gujarati, Punjabi, Urdu and Hindi. According to initial figures derived from the *Kenya Population Census (1969)*, eight African languages were spoken as first languages by over 500,000 people, including four languages spoken by over 1,000,000 people, these being Kikuyu, Luo, Kamba and Luyia. Just over 88 per cent of the population belong to one or the other of eight major language groups, a fact that has significantly affected policies regarding the use of vernacular languages as media of instruction. It is perhaps worthwhile at this point, to remark upon the contrast between Kenya and the neighbouring Tanzania, where over 95 per cent of the inhabitants speak Bantu languages, as the linguistic heterogeneity in Kenya is a factor that must be taken into account in considering the different language policies in the two states, particularly as regards the use of Swahili, a Bantu language, as a medium of instruction.

The census does not provide data about the number of speakers of Swahili as a first language but I have given reasons elsewhere for estimating that Swahili is spoken as a first language in Kenya by not less than 60,000 persons.[1] The majority of first language speakers in Kenya speak the Kimvita dialect, but six other dialects (and three sub-dialects) are spoken in the coastal area of Kenya. Varieties of the Kiunguja dialect of Swahili are spoken extensively by Kenyans as a second or third language.

THE DIFFUSION OF SWAHILI INTO THE INTERIOR

As it is of considerable importance that the dialect associated with Zanzibar and not that of Mombasa is most widespread in Kenya I think it is relevant at this point to say something very briefly about the diffusion of Swahili as a language of intercommunal communication in the area in the period immediately preceding the establishment of colonial rule.

While not all authorities would agree with Dr G. S. P. Freeman-Grenville that Swahili was probably the ordinary tongue of Kilwa and the rest of the coast by the thirteenth century,[2] the relative antiquity of the coastal civilization is not open to question. Although a number of the more northern settlements in which the language was understood were abandoned in the sixteenth and seventeenth centuries as a result of the depredations of Galla, and later of Somali-speaking peoples, the language was used in settlements on the coast from Mogadishu to at least as far south as Cape Delgado.

It has, however, been frequently emphasized by historians concerned with the coastal culture that the Swahili-speaking societies that developed along the coast had little discernible contact with or influence on the peoples of the interior before the nineteenth century. Their way of life was essentially mercantile, their culture primarily Islamic. In N. Chittick's words, 'the impact of this civilisation on much of the mainland coast was slight, and inland non-existent'.[3] In this instance, his observations were concerned with the situation before the arrival of the Portuguese, but the generalization held true for the most part until the nineteenth century. This is not to ignore the evident fact that the development of the culture of the coast and of the Swahili language itself implies continuous contact over centuries between the immigrant races and Bantu-speaking peoples; of particular interest and relevance is that contact of which the oral traditions of the north-eastern Bantu-speaking groups give evidence, which took place in the 'Shungwaya' dispersion area, north of the Tana River; and more specifically in relatively modern times it is necessary to take note of the alliances for military and economic purposes that developed and endured particularly during the rule of the Mazrui liwalis in Mombasa between certain of the language groups that constituted the population of Mombasa and its environs and the societies in the immediate hinterland. One of the Thalatha Taifa (the three tribes) and five of the Tisa Taifa (the nine tribes) had such a relationship with members of the Mijikenda group of peoples.[4]

The first incursions of the coastal inhabitants into the interior for the purposes of trade, however, appear to have occurred about 1780.[5] It was not until Seyyid Said, the head of the Al-Busaidi dynasty, established his permanent residence in Zanzibar in 1832 that the exploitation of trade in the interior developed systematically; and with the expansion of trade the spread of Swahili as a lingua franca correspondingly increased.

There is much evidence to indicate that by the fourth decade of the nineteenth century, men who could serve as interpreters of Swahili could be found in many parts of the interior, but for a number of reasons the spread of the language as a trade language in what is now Kenya was not nearly as extensive as it was in the areas that constitute present day Tanzania. In the first half of the nineteenth century, the initiative for the exploitation of internal trade lay with the Mijikenda and the Kamba peoples in the areas with which we are concerned. The Kamba established settlements at the coast including a large settlement at Rabai, and at the open markets operating at these centres, groups from different linguistic communities met and exchanged goods. Digo and Duruma traders acted as middlemen between the groups from the interior and the Arab and Swahili merchants, although some important traders such as Kavoi had direct contact with merchants of Mombasa.[6] While the knowledge and use of Swahili as a trade language must have been fostered by such trade, it is relevant to note that, unlike the Yao and Nyamwezi who controlled much of the interior trade in Tanzania, the Kamba traders did not adopt or imitate to any degree the culture of their coastal contacts. Nor for the most part did the Mijikenda peoples.[7]

Other factors prevented the development of trade routes in the area and the consequent spread of Swahili in the first half of the century. While the threat of the Maasai to groups of traders moving across territory controlled by them has undoubtedly been exaggerated, financers of caravans from Mombasa would clearly have to consider this eventuality among others as a hindrance to commercial activity. More significantly, from the 1830s sporadic warfare between the Borana Galla and the remnants of the Iloikop, which took place in the interior of Mombasa, was a hindrance to penetration,[8] as was the inhospitable nature of this interior which involved a long trek across the waterless Taru desert. The long resistance of the Mazrui family to the claims of the Sultan of Zanzibar which did not finally end until 1895, may also have been a contributory factor discouraging trading initiatives from the town.

Perhaps the most important factor, however, which until the 1860s discouraged penetration into the interior lay in the fact that in addition to the Maasai, the powerful communities occupying areas between the coast and the Lake, and in particular the Kikuyu and the Nandi-speaking peoples, did not co-operate with the traders, who therefore found it difficult to establish bases where porters could be recruited and supplies replenished; whereas in the south among the Nyamwezi and Sukuma in particular, these were forthcoming.[9] Characteristically, therefore, caravans from Mombasa used to move south and take more frequented routes from the southern towns of the northern Mrima.

By the middle of the nineteenth century, however, traders from the coast had begun to penetrate the former trade routes of the Kamba.[10]

They were never able to establish settlements on this northern route of penetration of the same size as the settlements established at Tabora and Ujiji in the south or to take a similar active part in the social and political life of the northern communities as was the case in the southern areas. Relatively few leaders, such as Shiundu, king of the Wanga, and his son Mumia, actively entered into forms of political alliance with the traders from the coast in order to extend their political hegemony. Again, there was little active slave trading on the northern trade routes and this in turn meant that settlements inhabited by large numbers of members of different linguistic groups who used Swahili as a lingua franca, of the kind that grew up both on the coast and in the interior of present day Tanzania, were not established in the interior of present day Kenya.

By the 1860s traders, principally from Pangani, had penetrated the Lake regions from the south and by the 1870s they had reached Mt. Elgon. A route from Taveta to Ngong was also developed. In the last decades of the century, as trade increased, a number of centres of influence were established at Mumia's and at Kitoto's for example, but as has been stated, these were never comparable in size or in importance to the major settlements in the south.[11] Aspects of this influence are still in evidence today. There are many Muslims among the inhabitants of Mumias, for example, and in East Africa there is a certain degree of evidence to indicate that the adoption of Islam is in general positively associated with the acceptance of other traits of Swahili culture and language.[12] In general it is true to say, however, that in the area constituting present day Kenya, *Ustaarabu*— the coastal way of life and the language with which it is associated— never assumed the prestige with which it was associated in parts of Tanzania and the Congo, particularly in the early twentieth century.[13]

THE ESTABLISHMENT OF COLONIAL ADMINISTRATION

At the Berlin Conference of 1885, the colonial powers with interests in the area assumed 'the obligation to insure the establishment of authority in the region ...'. In 1886, a joint commission consisting of the representatives of Britain, Germany and France met to decide upon the limits of the Sultan's authority on the East African coast. The Sultan was not represented.[14] At the meeting, the British representative, Kitchener, argued that the authority of the Sultan extended throughout the coastal belt up to 40 miles inland and along the main caravan routes, and these arguments give an indication of the extent of the spread of the Sultan's influence in the interior since the arrival of Seyyid Said. Nevertheless, the commission reached a 'unanimous agreement' by which the Sultan's

401

authority over Zanzibar and the adjacent islands and a ten-mile strip along the mainland was confirmed. Subsequently in the Anglo-German Agreement of October 1886, Britain and Germany agreed upon their respective spheres of influence in the area. That part of the coastal area in which the agents of the Sultan had been most active was decreed to be within the German sphere of influence. Paradoxically, as will be seen later, the advent of German rule accentuated the processes by which the use of Swahili in the interior spread rapidly. In the 1890s the validity of Margery Perham's statement that Swahili was as yet very far from being a lingua franca and was even less widely known in Uganda and Kenya away from the coast, is clear.[15]

The British East Africa Association was founded in 1887, and a Provisional Concession Agreement was concluded with the Sultan by which the Association gained rights to exercise administrative authority on the mainland subject to his sovereign rights. In 1888 the Association was granted a Royal Charter and became the Imperial British East Africa Company. The concession by which the Company was empowered to administer districts and promulgate laws was renegotiated. In June 1895, the British government declared a protectorate over the territory administered by the Company which was named the East Africa Protectorate the following year.

Initially, the authorities of the Company employed the agents of the Sultan, the liwalis and their subordinates, as administrative and political agents in their activities along the coast, as did the officers of the German administration. By the beginning of the century, however, the administrative focus of the East Africa Protectorate had moved away from the coastal area, Nairobi replacing Mombasa as the headquarters of the Uganda Railway in July 1899. In 1907, the capital of the protectorate was moved from Mombasa to Nairobi and there is no doubt that this transfer diminished the influence on Kenya's development of the coastal Swahili culture that became so important in Tanzania's history.[16]

In 1905 the protectorate was transferred from the Foreign Office to the Colonial Office. The position of Governor was created in 1906; an Executive Council was formed and a Legislative Council to which European unofficials were admitted by appointment was also established.[17] Despite these local instruments of government, however, the Colonial Office remained the supreme legislature and executive. The Secretary of State acting for the Imperial Government could disallow any ordinance of the Council and could legislate directly for the protectorate if the occasion arose.

I have briefly mentioned these facts because it is necessary in considering the formulation of colonial policy in Kenya to have in mind the not infrequently conflicting objectives of politicians and civil servants in Britain, of the local colonial administrators, of the European settler organizations and of the people as a whole in so far as their demands and requirements were taken into account. While the ultimate policy on general matters was laid down by the authorities in London, in practice the local authorities were primarily responsible for the conduct of affairs as the diversity in administrative practices in the three adjacent countries in East Africa might be seen to indicate. The relative independence of these authorities and the influence that the small settler community had on the conduct of government in Kenya were frequently commented upon in London.[18]

Decisions on language policy were naturally affected by the fact that the members of the administration, the judiciary and the great majority of the settlers were of British origin. After the First World War, also, the territories on the south-west and north-west of Kenya were under British control and this also affected certain decisions, as many administrators realized the value of fostering similar patterns of language use over the adjacent territories.

The settlers established in the colony an economic structure based largely upon a system of migrant labour in both urban and rural sectors.[19] Certain patterns of internal migration established as a result of this economic structure are still operating today, as Professor Ominde has shown.[20] The former scheduled areas and the two major towns are the foci of population movements in the country and such movements naturally have far-reaching linguistic consequences, as has been indicated in earlier chapters.[21]

British policy in East Africa was based primarily on the need to make the protectorate economically self-sufficient as quickly as possible. At the same time, however, it recognized its moral obligation to provide for the welfare of the indigenous people.[22] It is in relation to this obligation that the provision of educational structures and the policies associated with these can appropriately be considered.

EDUCATIONAL LANGUAGE POLICY AND PRACTICE, 1909–45

MISSIONARY ENTERPRISE

In the first two decades of the present century and in the period preceding this, the obligation to provide educational facilities was assumed in Kenya almost entirely by the missionary orders.

It is of some relevance that several of the larger orders originally established stations along the coast and that among their members were a number of noted scholars of Swahili. The contributions that such missionaries as Bishop Steere, the Reverend Krapf and Father Sacleux made towards the systematic study of the language need no elaboration here. The enthusiasm with which a number of them advocated the use of Swahili for purposes of missionary activity is also well known.[23]

The enthusiasm of the early missionaries, however, was not shared by all their successors. The primary purposes of missionary activity, educational and otherwise, were, for the most part, religious.[24] Many of them conceived it as their primary duty to provide translations of parts of the Bible and to equip the children in their schools to read these in their own languages. In *The Missionary Factor in East Africa*, Professor Oliver noted the resolution of the Continental Missionary Conference at Bremen where the participants decided that subsidies for educational purposes, if offered by the German administration in the then German East Africa, should be refused unless the principle could be preserved that education should be given in the vernacular. He deduces that with a consistent policy, Swahili, which was already widely understood as a lingua franca, 'could easily have become the lingua franca of East African Christianity had the Livingstonian principle been less firmly established in the minds of the missionaries that Africa would only be converted by Africans'.[25]

There were factors apart from 'the Livingstonian principle', however, that affected the attitudes of missionaries and other educators towards the use of vernacular languages as the media of instruction in primary education·

In the first decades of the twentieth century, the principle that the language best known and understood by the child on his entry into school life was, from the educational point of view, the most effective medium of instruction in the preliminary stage of school education was generally accepted by educators in East Africa.[26] In contrast this principle was neither accepted nor implemented by most French authorities and missionaries in other parts of Africa, nor by the Portuguese. Furthermore, many missionaries would agree with the statement made in the Phelps-Stokes Commission report that the use of the language of the child in education was 'one of the chief means of preserving whatever is good in native customs, ideas and ideals, and therefore preserving . . . self respect.'[27] Others avoided the use of a lingua franca on principle, 'as being unfitted to reach the innermost thoughts of those undergoing the conversion to Christianity'.[28] Some also, as C. Hobley testified to the 1919 commission, associated Swahili with the 'spirit of Islamicisation', and avoided it for that reason.[29]

The attitudes of the missionaries were of significance because as Lord Hailey observed, 'it was in the mission schools in all parts of Africa that the problem was posed whether the first steps in education should be taken in the local vernacular and it was the missionaries who were responsible for the earliest efforts at reducing the vernacular languages to written form.'[30] Their responsibility was particularly heavy in areas controlled by Britain as in these areas the policy of leaving the control of the educational system to the missionary orders was more marked than was the case in French colonial territories for example, or more relevantly, in Tanganyika during the period of German occupation. Indeed, the relative success of the German government in establishing government schools at which future members of the administrative service were educated in Swahili, according to a consistent policy, facilitated the spread of Swahili in Tanganyika as the language of administration and as the lingua franca.

THE COMMISSION ON EDUCATION
IN THE EAST AFRICA PROTECTORATE, 1919

Questions relating to the use of Swahili and English and the vernacular languages as media of instruction were discussed at length at the United Missionary Conference in 1909 in Kenya. At this conference the Protestant mission representatives who attended adopted a common educational code. The elementary code for teaching in village schools provided for instruction in the vernacular for the first three classes. and in Swahili in classes four and five. The advanced code for central mission schools provided for the teaching of Swahili in Standard III, and for optional instruction in English between Standards IV and V.[31] The decisions of the missionary bodies regarding media of instruction were reiterated in evidence presented to the Education Commission which was established in 1919 to consider educational policy in the protectorate. As the evidence given to the commission is illustrative of the different viewpoints of those concerned with the development of educational policy it will be relevant to consider this in some detail.

The policy of the Representative Council of the Allied Missionary Societies, an associated body of Protestant missionary societies, was stated clearly in a memorandum submitted by the Reverend John Arthur and the Bishop of Mombasa. They showed themselves to be strongly in favour of the teaching of Swahili as opposed to English in the 'upper schools' and stated that 'the Alliance, while fully recognising the value of English in the higher training of natives and emphasising their readiness to develop the same, . . . solemnly deprecate any attempt to displace Swahili from its natural position as the lingua franca of the great mass of the natives of British East Africa.' Bishop Willis of Uganda also commented to the effect that 'in East Africa, Swahili should be the lingua franca. I should make it compulsory in upper schools. I would go from Swahili on to English'.[32]

Fr J. Bergmans, a Roman Catholic priest who gave evidence, similarly opposed the teaching of English in elementary schools and supported the use of Swahili at this level.

None of the missionaries who gave evidence to the commission demonstrated any of the 'hostility' to the use of the language that is sometimes thought to have characterized the attitudes of some members of their calling.

A number of the members of the administration also expressed their views on the issue and the majority of those who did so stated their support for the teaching of Swahili. C. Hobley, then a Provincial Commissioner, argued that 'the two languages should be English and Swahili'. He added, 'I am not in favour of the continuation of the teaching of up-country languages . . . (this) . . . impedes trade and courtwork etc. and retards advancement as a whole.'

It is evident therefore that missionaries and members of the administration in Kenya in so far as the views of those who spoke at the conference were representative, were in favour of the use of Swahili as one of the media of instruction in the elementary schools. The most telling arguments for the use of English that were presented to the commission came from a teacher—the headmaster of the Arab High School in Mombasa—who drew an unfavourable contrast between the situation in Kenya and that in West Africa as regards the extent to which Africans had taken administrative responsibilities, for which the use of English was requisite.

It is of some consequence, however, that in a paper tabled before the commission the Director of Education, Mr J. R. Orr, gave it as his opinion that 'the teaching of Swahili is a waste of time . . . I think teaching in the vernacular is absolutely necessary'.[33] His attitude towards the use of Swahili was reflected in the conclusions of the commission which stated that 'with regard to the language in which education is to be given . . . the Commission is of the opinion that the initial stages must be in the vernacular. The Commission is strongly of the opinion that after the necessary initial instruction in the vernacular English should be taught in all native schools, both on patriotic and practical grounds.' The commission went on to refer to Swahili as 'a language that is foreign both to the employer and the employee. As a rule it is equally badly spoken by both . . . The Commission thinks that if a foreign language is to be taught, it should be English'.

To this recommendation a minority report was appended, which was agreed to by four of the ten members of the commission, and which argued that the 'wholesale teaching of English . . . at present is impracticable. On the other hand, as a *Lingua Franca* the Swahili language is the most easily attained . . .'[34]

The educational requirements of Indian and Arab children were also stated at length before the commission by various spokesmen. In general, the comment of one participant to the effect that 'it is the sincere wish of all Indians that their children should first receive the necessary education in the vernacular before they learn a foreign language', generally reflected the views of members of the Indian community.[35]

A spokesman for the Arab community stated that they would be in favour of compulsory education provided that the Qur'an and Arabic were taught. The Assistant Liwali of Mombasa, however, made the point that 'there is no use for Arabic on the East Coast' and stated that English should be the medium of instruction.

In September 1919 the Director of Education issued instructions regarding the education to be given in schools assisted by the government, which stressed the need to teach English where this was possible. This emphasis was not welcomed by all missionary bodies and the response to the instruction was gradual.

THE REPORT OF THE PHELPS–STOKES COMMISSION

From 1911 to 1918 grants were paid by the government to missions to start 'industrial' education only, but after the First World War the British colonial authorities began to concern themselves more seriously with the nature of the educational facilities provided for the peoples in territories under their control.[36] The report of the first Phelps-Stokes Commission which examined the educational systems of areas under British rule in West Africa, in 1922, gave impetus to these concerns.

The first report of the commission had drawn attention to the fact that the major issue to be faced in the colonial territories was that of the relationship between the government and the missionary orders that provided virtually all the facilities for primary education. A memorandum drawn up by the Reverend J. Oldham at the request of the Colonial Office regarding such co-operation, was considered and approved in London in June 1923 at a meeting attended by the Governor of Kenya and other administrative and ecclesiastic dignitaries. It was also decided that a permanent Advisory Committee on Native Education in Tropical Africa should be established to advise the Colonial Office on issues relating to education.

Early in 1924, a second Phelps-Stokes Commission visited East Africa, accompanied by Major Vischer, a representative of the Colonial Office who was to become the first secretary of the Advisory Committee.

407

The report drew attention to what was termed 'the unfortunate divergence in the attitudes of missionaries, settlers and government officials towards native education' and to 'the present confusion in educational thought and practice and failure to define the aims of education'. In elaborating the nature of this confusion, the report stated that the attitude of the missionaries was determined by their desire to impart their religious ideas to the native people; that of the government officials by their concern for the running of the administration and the consequent need for clerical help and skilled workers; and that of settlers and traders by the various needs of their occupations.

As has been implied, each of these sets of attitudes has its relation to educational language policy in so far as this was affected by the demands of the different groups. One cannot help but note the omission of any reference to the demands or requirements of the people themselves.

With respect to the basic principles that they understood to underlie issues relating to the use of different languages in education, the commission, echoing the report of the Calcutta University Mission in 1919, stated that 'all peoples have an inherent right to their own language. It is the means of expression to their own personality . . . and no greater injustice can be committed against a people than to deprive them of their own language'. They remarked that 'in the past, practically all controlling nations forced their language on the native peoples and discouraged the use of their native tongue . . . Fortunately at the present time the only powers that still maintain this attitude in their possessions are the French and the Portuguese . . . whatever the motives . . . the policy is unwise and unjust.' While concluding that the appeal to the people 'cannot be effectively made without the adequate use of the native language . . . ' the commission accepted that 'it is equally important that advanced pupils should have some opportunity to learn in a European language as they themselves demand.'[37]

In attempting to apply the principles they had stated to the situation in Kenya, the commission recommended that the 'four major languages', Swahili, Kikuyu, Luo and Luyia, should invariably be recognized as first languages of instruction. They then drew attention to the question of 'the choice of a second language for more general exchange' which they attested had aroused difference of opinion and continued:

The Government Commission of 1919, the present Colonial Secretary . . . and most of the missionaries support the view of the Director of Education that in the course of time, Kiswahili should cease to be taught except in the Coastal area where it is the vernacular and English should be taught as a second language even in the village schools as soon as reading and writing in the vernacular have been mastered.

From the proceedings of the 1919 commission and from subsequent evidence that will be considered, it is not at all clear that the unanimity referred to as regards the discontinuation of the teaching of Swahili was as emphatic or widespread as the commission implied. However, in their sojourn in Kenya of less than a month it was perhaps inevitable that their views should have been influenced considerably by the Director of Education and his associates.

The most significant recommendations of the commission related, however, to the general inadequacy of the educational facilities provided in the areas they visited and in this connection they made a number of suggestions regarding co-operation between missionary orders and government authorities. They observed that 'hitherto Governments have not taken education seriously'. They noted the inadequate and, in some cases, almost negligible proportion of colonial revenue that was spent on education. They deplored the absence of any schools open to Africans in East Africa which could properly be described as secondary schools. While praising the missionary efforts to supply education they recognized the inadequacy of the teaching provided in many instances and the dangers inherent in the unsupervised extension of schools. The commission supported, however, what they termed the wise government policy in Kenya to work through mission schools. They made the point that 'the recognition of the better-organised African languages in their respective areas confirms the wisdom of the policy of using mission schools as the agencies of education, for the reason that missionaries remain more continuously in one section, reducing their language to writing and publishing books with great expense of time, energy and money'. However, while commending the missionaries for their work of translation and publication, and observing that 'Governments have not sufficiently encouraged this important service to the people of Africa', the members of the commission were agreed that 'in African Vernaculars with a few notable exceptions suitable books scarcely existed' for the attainment of the educational aims they identified.

In effect, the recommendation of the Phelps-Stokes Commission lent support to the general principles previously espoused by the Director of Education with regard to the use of the mother tongues and of English in education, but the principles they adumbrated regarding the use of the different languages could not help to solve the specific problems faced by the department in the teaching of children in Kenya. That a policy based on these principles was impracticable in certain respects and in consequence open to modification was implied in the Departmental Report in 1924 where it was stated that 'the extent to which various languages e.g. the Vernacular, Kiswahili and English are to be taught in schools has been the subject of frequent discussion but at the time of writing no decision has been reached'.[38] It would perhaps have been more accurate to say that decisions had been reached but that they could not be implemented.

The policy which the Education Department had adopted with regard to the teaching of Swahili was questioned in the memorandum on Certain Aspects of Arab and African Education which was submitted by Mr E. R. Hussey in 1924 at the request of the Governor, and which contains a useful summary of the situation at that time.[39] In describing the situation, he pointed out that there was no separate code of instructions or syllabus regulating the work of village schools but that the Education Code drawn up by the 'Missionary Alliance' in January 1919, had been adopted temporarily by the Education Department. He also observed with regard to teaching of English that 'there is a note to the effect that this subject should be taught only in Higher Grade Schools where the teachers are capable of teaching it'.

Mr Hussey considered that 'it would be feasible to drop the local vernaculars though in many cases they would be used by the teachers in explanations during the first and second standards'. He gave as his reason for making this recommendation the fact that 'Swahili is becoming more and more known, especially by those who travel and the local dialects have no value from a literary or educational point of view'; and concluded that 'if Swahili was the sole language taught in the elementary schools, it would be possible for pupils to learn it thoroughly in a four-year course'.

THE REPORT OF THE EAST AFRICA COMMISSION, 1925

In 1925, the report of the East Africa Commission drawn up under the chairmanship of Ormsby-Gore drew further attention to the lack of educational facilities in the area as a whole and made specific recommendations in relation to these. In addition to reiterating the need 'to secure good will and co-operation between Government and missionary educational activities' the report stated that government activities 'cannot be confined to the provision of schools of a technical or higher type but it must provide increasing educational facilities of an elementary kind in areas not served by the Christian missions, and particularly for Mohammedan tribes, who would be reluctant to send their children to missionary schools'.[40]

The commission also reiterated in relatively forthright terms a statement of educational language policy which bears close relation to recommendations made by the Phelps-Stokes Commission. The statement was as follows:

During the elementary and primary stages we regard it as essential that the medium of education should be a native language, and that English should be introduced only at a later stage. In the secondary and further stages English and English alone should be the medium of instruction . . . When English is taught at all, it must be taught thoroughly and completely and only to such pupils as are undergoing a period of school life long enough to enable English to be learnt properly.

THE MEMORANDUM ON EDUCATIONAL POLICY IN BRITISH TROPICAL AFRICA

In March 1925 the Advisory Committee on Native Education in Tropical Africa presented a memorandum providing guidance to educators in the colonies.[41] Not surprisingly, as the committee met under the chairmanship of Ormsby-Gore, the recommendations of the committee concerning language in education were not dissimilar to those made by the East Africa Commission. The committee emphasized that the educational use of the vernaculars and the provision of textbooks were of primary importance and that qualified personnel should devote their energies to this purpose. In 1926 the effect of the recommendations made by the various bodies concerned with education was reflected in the fact that four Inspectorships were established, the incumbents of which were to concern themselves primarily with the education of African pupils. Some thought had also been given to the implications of the acceptance by the Education Department of the recommendation that education must be 'based on literacy in the mother tongue'. The local Advisory Committee on African Education which had been established in 1924 had discussed the standardization of Swahili, Luo, Kikuyu, Luyia and Nandi and a survey of the literature suitable for use in elementary schools had been made. The paucity of this is indicated in the list of mission publications in the languages of Kenya that is appended to the annual Departmental Report.[42] This indicates that the missions had at that stage produced fifteen texts in Swahili suitable for use in schools, four in Kikuyu, one primer in Luo and one in Maasai, a primer and first reader in Kamba and very little else. In addition the Education Department had prepared certain textbooks in Swahili and revived the monthly issue of *Habari*.

It was apparent even to the Director of Education that the grand designs of the various advisory bodies regarding the use of the mother tongue in education could hardly be implemented on the basis of such literary resources. The recognition of this fact is implicit in his comments regarding the available materials. 'Can we preserve', he asked somewhat rhetorically, 'the folk-lore and the songs handed down from generation to generation? If so, in what language?' He made the suggestion that 'if all schools in one province will combine, a literature can be built up in the mother

411

tongues and the tribes will preserve their individuality. Otherwise, the literature of the African school must be standardised in Swahili. The choice lies with the schools'.

The statement of the Director of Education regarding the standardization of Swahili no doubt alluded to the proceedings of the Educational Conference in Tanganyika Territory held in 1925 and to the report on the standardization of Swahili which was issued with the report of the conference.[43] As this report was concerned with the use of Swahili in East Africa as a whole and as representatives from Kenya participated in the conference, its proceedings are of some relevance.

At the Dar es Salaam conference the Deputy Director of Education in Tanganyika, Mr A. Isherwood, presented a paper to the conference on 'The Problem of the Vernaculars in Native Education' in which he outlined some of the educational consequences of the multiplicity of languages in the region. In doing so he affirmed his support, as did the Governor, of the general policy recommended by the report of the East Africa Commission, which had recommended the use of the mother tongues in initial education and 'English and English alone in higher education'. He then proposed or rather outlined, somewhat in contradiction to this policy, a system of education involving first the use of the mother tongue in elementary education, then the acquisition of literacy in Swahili and finally the introduction of English. He also mentioned the fact that in government schools the three-year elementary course was conducted in Swahili.[44]

The decisions of the committee concerning the standardization of Swahili were, however, the most significant results of the conference. It was accepted that the Kiunguja dialect of Zanzibar should form the basis of the proposed standard form and the establishment of a permanent Publication Committee which would concern itself with the provision of school textbooks and which would have members from Tanganyika, Kenya and Zanzibar was proposed.[45]

The report of the committee on the standardization of Swahili contained a number of proposals relating to the spelling and word-division of Swahili together with a list of the new and forthcoming books which generally conformed to these proposals.

MEMORANDUM ON THE PLACE OF THE VERNACULAR
IN NATIVE EDUCATION

In May 1927 the Advisory Committee of the Colonial Office issued a memorandum on the Place of the Vernacular in Native Education[46] which was in effect a consideration and summary of views expressed by administrators in the different colonies in reply to a 'tentative' memorandum on the same question, that had been issued in July 1925.

Before adverting to the position in the different areas the committee drew attention to the resolution of the Imperial Education Conference and to statements of the Calcutta University Mission and Professor Westermann regarding the primary role that should be given to the use of children's mother tongues in education.[47]

The committee, however, recognized three main practical difficulties with which educators were confronted in giving effect to such a policy, viz:

(a) an enormous number of different languages and even dialects of the same language (b) the training of teachers in a multiplicity of languages and (c) . . . (perhaps) the greatest difficulty lies in the production of text books and literature . . . it is manifestly out of the question, if only for financial reasons, to secure the publication of a sufficient range of books in more than a limited number of native languages.

In their consideration of the policies of specific territories, they remarked of Swahili that 'its use as the first language of the people is spreading slowly, not only in Tanganyika Territory but also in Kenya and Zanzibar, but it is extending more rapidly as the second language of inter-communication between members of different tribes and between natives and Europeans'; but they concluded that 'in spite of the predominance of Ki-Swahili we are of the opinion that in Kenya at any rate it is desirable that the use of the indigenous vernaculars should not be altogether superseded in the schools'. In a subsequent paragraph, however, the committee remarked upon the 'tendency in some parts of Africa towards the spread of a dominant language displacing vernaculars spoken by a more limited number of people', and asserted that this tendency was likely to increase and should be encouraged.

In considering the duration of teaching in vernacular languages the memorandum stated that there was 'common agreement that vernaculars must be used in the first stages of elementary education'. In this connection they quote with approval the reply from one of the West African colonies where it was suggested that 'in all training colleges for teachers there should be a lectureship where practicable in every vernacular of importance. The object should be that all teachers leaving a training college would not merely have been well trained in English but would also have got a literary training in their own language . . . '

In dealing with the question of the stage at which English should be introduced into the curriculum, the committee remarked that

There can be no doubt that one of the main incentives if not *the* incentive of African parents in sending their sons to school is for them to acquire a knowledge of English. A knowledge of English is naturally regarded by them as the principal means whereby economic advance can be obtained by them in later life. Any attempt, therefore, to delay unduly the introduction of English into African schools would be regarded as the attempt of Government to hold back the African from legitimate advance in civilisation.

They expressed concern, however, that 'wherever and whenever English is introduced . . . it should be on the clear understanding that the teaching of English should be real and thorough and should be given in every case by a teacher competent to teach it.' The committee considered English to be 'a necessity in all intermediate, secondary and technical schools' and deduced that 'if it is a necessity in these its inculcation must start from the higher standards of the elementary schools'.

In conclusion, the committee acknowledged the inconsistency in certain respects of the 'transitional policy' that they had recommended. They recognized that it implied that 'ideas as to the more skilful class-teaching in the vernacular and the enshrining of local tradition in a vernacular . . . may in some cases have to be postponed, though never abandoned', but considered that at this stage it was necessary to be content with 'practical expedients'. Certain implications of this policy statement will be discussed later.

THE MOVEMENT TOWARDS CLOSER UNION IN EAST AFRICA

Political developments in the East African territories were, however, to have more significant effects on educational language policies in 1927 and subsequent years than policy directives from the metropolis. In 1926 the first Conference of Governors of East African Dependencies was held. At the conference matters concerning education were briefly discussed, and a resolution was adopted that called for the 'adoption of some such system as has been recommended in the report of the Phelps-Stokes Commission on education'.[48] It appears that this vague recommendation alluded in part to the general recommendations made in the first Report of the Phelps-Stokes Commission on West and Equatorial Africa, and which were repeated in their subsequent report, viz.,

1. The tribal language should be used in lower elementary standards or grades.
2. A *lingua franca* of African origin should be introduced in the middle classes of the school, if the area is occupied by large Native groups speaking diverse languages.
3. The language of the European nation in control should be taught in the upper standards.[49]

Increasingly, in London and in East Africa, questions relating to the possibility of closer union between the different states were being discussed, and when the Governors of Uganda, Tanganyika and Kenya decided in 1927 to promote Swahili as a common language throughout the whole of East Africa critics of the policy suspected that the decision was connected with the movement for closer union of the three areas.[50] While there is a certain amount of evidence to indicate that this was the case, the memorandum submitted to the Chief Secretary from the Governor of Uganda on the issue in November 1927, primarily concerned what he considered to be the *educational* advantages of the adoption of Swahili. He argued that 'Kiswahili was the only vernacular language in East Africa which can prove in the long run anything but an educational *cul-de-sac*, in Uganda as in Kenya and Tanganyika'[51] and that the 'vast majority of Africans who will be brought within the orbit of the educational system of East Africa for the next generation or two will never have the opportunity or the time, or the need to learn English thoroughly . . . . From the educational point of view the difficulty of making English the *medium* of instruction in elementary schools seems to me insuperable'. He therefore argued that 'for the areas I am at the moment dealing with, Kiswahili should be introduced as soon as possible as a medium of instruction in all elementary vernacular schools, and that this should be a condition precedent to the receipt of a grant in aid from Government funds'.

The decision of the Governors encouraged activities that were in progress in connection with the use of Swahili as an educational medium. In 1928 Professor Meinhof attended a conference in Mombasa at which there were further discussions about the standardization of Swahili, where outstanding issues were settled and where proposals for the establishment of an interterritorial language committee were put forward.[52] Subsequently the Acting Colonial Secretary of Kenya circulated a letter to the other governments on the question of setting up a body that would concern itself with the selection, revision and translation of educational texts, and the preparation of a new dictionary and grammar of Swahili.

THE 1929 EDUCATION CONFERENCE

In 1929 the Directors of Education in the East and Central African Dependencies met in conference in Dar es Salaam, and the recommendation to establish an Interterritorial Language Committee which was to 'concern itself with language research and the standardization of orthographies' was approved.[53] The development of this committee in effect and subsequently in name into an East African Swahili Committee which concerned itself solely with this language is a matter of some interest.

The conference adopted a number of resolutions. The resolution in regard to languages in schools read as follows: (1) In every case the first medium of instruction should be the local vernacular; (2) as soon as possible the local vernacular should give way to the dominant native

415

language (where there is a dominant native language), which should first be taught as a language and thereafter be used as the medium of instruction until the stage is reached at which English can be used; (3) in areas in which there is a dominant native language the teaching of English, which was provided for in Resolution No. VI, should be postponed until the pupil has reached an approved standard in that native language and then only if recognized teachers of English are available.[54]

In effect, therefore, this resolution strongly supported the use of Swahili as a medium of instruction in elementary schools and thus ran counter to the recommendations contained in a number of other reports that have been considered.

It is of some relevance that with the retirement of Mr J. R. Orr, the Director of Education in March 1928, the question of the relations to be established in the schools in Kenya between the local vernaculars, Swahili and English had again come under reconsideration. The Departmental Report for 1928 stated that 'everyone is agreed that the local vernacular should be used at the first stages of education and that the higher stages will have to be conducted through the medium of English. It remains for a final decision as to whether and, if so, where Swahili should be brought in, and what part it should play in schools'.[55]

In Kenya the conference proposals aroused a considerable amount of controversy and they were discussed at length in the Legislative Council which was asked on 18 Octobeı 1929, to approve the terms of the resolution.[56] When introducing the resolution to the Council the Director of Education, Mr Scott, referred to the controversy 'that had been raging for some years in Kenya in regard to the second stage of the child's education' and 'which had been holding back and is holding back the general development of education in this country', viz. whether English or a dominant African language should succeed the vernacular as the medium of instruction.

The Director also referred to an earlier statement of the Governor in the opening speech of the session to the effect that 'the aim of the Government must be to secure English as the lingua franca of East Africa' and agreed in Emerson's words that that was 'the star to which we must hitch our wagon'. He remarked upon the demand for the teaching of English from the people and asserted that progress towards this goal was limited primarily by the lack of adequately trained teachers.

Mr Scott then itemized with enthusiasm the advantages of the use of Swahili which he argued was the greatest of all the Bantu languages. He stated that 'it has an advantage over other native languages in that it is a flexible language, an admirable educational medium through its flexibility. It is a rich language, enriched where it is itself deficient by one of the

416

greatest of the oriental languages. It is a standardised language in a way that no other of the languages of East Africa is standardised. Lastly, it is a literary language and there is one final advantage; it is a common language already in common use in East Africa.'[57] Mr Scott remarked also that the majority of the missionary bodies in Kenya were in general agreement with the terms of the resolution.

Opinion in the Council was however divided on the issue. The majority of unofficial members wished to see the teaching of English extended and regretted the shortage of qualified teachers.[58] Canon A. Leakey, stating that he was 'representing the African point of view' proposed an amendment to Resolution No. VI to the effect that 'in Kenya Colony every effort should be put forth to increase the number of competent teachers of English at the earliest possible date, so that it may be taught at an early age in the scholar's career'. In moving the motion he drew a distinction between what he termed the 'beautiful language spoken up and down the coast' and the 'kitchen Swahili of up-country', and observed that 'it is the latter of these two that is the dominant language', not the 'real Swahili'. He also drew attention to the effect that would be created in England 'if any suspicion at all should reach there that the Europeans in this Colony—settlers, administrative officers, and everybody else, in any way desired to keep Swahili as the language of the Africans'. This comment may have been inspired by the fact that the Dar es Salaam resolution received the enthusiastic support of Major E. S. Grogan, former chairman of the settlers' Convention of Associations, who made little attempt to conceal his lack of concern for the welfare of the people and who stated at a later stage of debate that he could not 'imagine a more desperate happening than which we should introduce the language (English) to large numbers of people, . . . whose proper education is to work in the fields . . . '[59] These remarks were made in connection with the revised amendment submitted by Canon Leakey, after an adjournment, which added the following words to the end of the motion: 'but welcomes the Government's assurance that it is the policy of the Government to establish English as a lingua franca of this Colony as soon as possible'. The amendment was carried.

In relation to Canon Leakey's argument it is of significance that, as J. B. Ndung'u has demonstrated in some detail, the use of English as a medium of instruction at an earlier stage was one of the issues on which the organizers of the Independent School Movement stated their disagreement with government policy.[60]

I have recorded the statements of the members of the Legislative Council in some detail as they give an indication of the conflicting motives with regard to the use of English in education, of the men primarily responsible for guiding local educational policy at this time. One might infer that while politicians such as Major Grogan wished to discourage the spread of English among the people because they recognized that 'for educated East Africans English is a political need',[61] others such as the Hon. F. A. Bemister who cherished the idea of the growth of an English-speaking empire, wished to encourage the use of English. Both motives were clearly more inspired by political than educational considerations. Other members such as Canon Leakey, evidently wished to initiate a policy which they believed to be in the interests of the people and in accordance with their wishes.

As a result of the qualified adoption by the Legislative Council of the resolutions of the Dar es Salaam conference, the Department of Education issued a circular which laid down the following regulations:

(a) The vernacular will be used for the first four years of school life.
(b) Swahili will be introduced as a subject during this period.
(c) English may be taught in those classes where there are competent teachers.
(d) After the first four years Swahili will be the medium of instruction.
(e) In those schools in which English has been taught, English may be used as the medium.
(f) After the completion of six years' study it will be introduced as soon as possible.

Subsequently a revised primary school syllabus was drawn up in 1934 and came into force on 1 July 1935. The course covered Standards IV–VI and in the examination at the end of the course English and Swahili were both required subjects: the normal medium for the course and for the examination was Swahili but provision was made that if the managers of any school desired for any special reason to use English as a medium they might make application to the Director for permission to do so. In 1934 one such application had been received, and the number of schools using English as a medium did not increase between 1934 and 1938.

THE JOINT SELECT COMMITTEE ON CLOSER UNION IN EAST AFRICA

The question of the development of closer ties between governments in the region was examined in 1928 by the Commission on the Closer Union of the Dependencies in Eastern and Central Africa (the Hilton Young Commission). The report of the commission was submitted in January 1929. Subsequently Sir Samuel Wilson reported on local reactions to the proposals contained in the commission's report. Neither of the two reports mentioned referred to matters concerning language policy, but in the deliberations of the Joint Select Committee of both Houses of Parliament to which the proposals on closer union were referred, questions relating to language policy and language use were raised on numerous occasions.[62]

A considerable amount of evidence was given to and elicited by the committee regarding the advantages and disadvantages of the use of Swahili or English as official languages, and as a corollary to this as languages of education. The objection of the Baganda delegate, Mr Kulubya, to the introduction of Swahili, 'a foreign language altogether', and his indication of a strong preference for English 'which', he stated, 'is the key to everything' was one feature of this evidence. In making his statement however, Mr Kulubya was simply reiterating arguments presented earlier by the Kabaka and Government of Buganda.[63]

In the hearings of the commission, the earlier decision of the Governors to make Swahili the language of administration and of education came under review. The argument for what was termed 'the Government policy to bring all East Africa together under a common national language' (minute 5860) and in particular the need for the use of Swahili in the administrative and educational systems in Uganda was put most strongly by B. Aston Warner, Deputy Provincial Commissioner in Uganda, who stated that 'the introduction of Swahili as the common native official language has these advantages: (a) It is not the vernacular of any one tribe in the Protectorate and therefore its use in documents such as Court Records does not provoke the jealousy that would I think be provoked if one of the local vernaculars were used instead. (b) The use of one native official language makes it possible for officers to check Court Records themselves without recourse to an interpreter . . . . ' He added that 'Swahili is already the commercial and social lingua franca . . . in that part of Africa'; and concluded with the familiar argument that 'to make English the official language would involve teaching it well in all the local schools which besides being impossible at present would be of little practical advantage to the peasant or artisan' (minute 6066). The policy of encouraging the development of Swahili as the lingua franca in East Africa was also supported by Mr C. Dobbs, the former Chief Native Commissioner of Kenya.

The committee was, however, concerned with educational language policy primarily in its relation to political developments. It was concerned, for example, to ascertain which language would be able to be used in a common council for East Africa, if such were created (minute 6097), and with the possibility of translating laws into Swahili and other languages (minute 8800). The general opinion of the administrators who were asked for comments on the possibility of using English in such a council, was that this would not be practicable at that time, primarily on the grounds that relatively few African leaders could speak it sufficiently well for the purpose. As far as Kenya was concerned, it should be remembered in this context that the ability to speak English was a prerequisite of entry to the Legislative Council,[64] and the lack of suitably qualified speakers of the language was on several occasions given as one of the reasons for the maintenance of the system whereby the African people were represented in the Legislative Council by a European. That this was a pretext was pointed out just as frequently, for example, by Senior Chief Koinange in a memorandum written in 1929. (In discussion of this issue it was not mentioned that English-speaking leaders such as Mr Kenyatta and Mr P. G. Mockerie had been refused permission to present evidence to the committee.) In its recommendations the Joint Select Committee advised that the existing practice of representation should be terminated as soon as was feasible, but the first African member of the Legislative Council was not in fact appointed until thirteen years later.[65]

In their report the committee stated that

There can be no question that some official lingua franca must be adopted. Kiswahili has become the communal lingua franca . . . and for this reason among others, it is maintained by many competent witnesses that . . . it is at the moment the only suitable official language. The obvious difficulty in the way of adopting this latter course at the present time is the very small percentage of Africans who are sufficiently educated to speak it with any fluency and the still smaller number who are qualified to teach it. Nevertheless the Committee feel the desirability of encouraging a gradual change from Kiswahili to English.[66]

This viewpoint was subsequently supported by the Secretary of State for the Colonies,[67] and the move that had begun locally for the encouragement of the development of Swahili as an official language was in consequence discouraged.

In commenting on the recommendation the Governor of Kenya wrote that 'this Government holds the view that a gradual change from Kiswahili to English should be encouraged' and that 'the ultimate aim in Kenya is that English should become the one recognised lingua franca. It is necessary, however, to look forward to a prolonged intermediate period in which English will be the lingua franca for only a small educated class of Africans. During this period Kiswahili will be developed as a subordinate lingua franca'.[68]

The recommendations of the Joint Committee do not appear to have had any immediate effects on local educational practice. In 1935 Swahili was still the medium of instruction in all government schools, except

Kisii. In 1936, however, the syllabus for elementary schools was revised. The two chief innovations were the provision of a course in oral English for Standard III in schools where qualified teachers were available and the addition of a Standard IV finishing year in which a course in elementary business method and further English might be taken. The difficulty faced by the department in its attempt to reconcile the long-term aims of the government with the recommendations of the Dar es Salaam conference is manifest in these developments.

THE COMMISSION ON HIGHER EDUCATION IN EAST AFRICA

In 1937 the report of the Commission on Higher Education in East Africa which contained a number of observations on language use in the schools, was published. While the commission recognized 'that Swahili possesses many local and incidental advantages, and instruction in Swahili should be provided where it is desired', they considered that 'it would be a mistake to delay the teaching of English for the sake of Swahili'.[69] They pointed out what they considered to be the emphatic evidence that the people 'will increasingly demand earlier instruction in English'. With regard to the use of Swahili they agreed with the Director of Education in Uganda that as far as that country was concerned there were very few educational situations in which Swahili should be used as the medium or vehicle of instruction and in general with his statement that 'educational principles should be given more weight than administrative convenience'.[70] The commission suggested that those children who were selected by the Education Department for further education should be taught English not later than the end of the third year but recommended that 'for those in the primary schools who will not continue into secondary classes, English should not come into question even as a subject'.

The report, however, also reiterated the familiar argument that 'there may too be a danger of teaching with English a contempt for the vernacular and for all that it means in African life' and stated that education should guard against this possibility.

THE REPORT ON MASS EDUCATION IN AFRICAN SOCIETY

During the Second World War the most important initiatives affecting the educational system of Kenya were taken outside the country. As a result of the passing of the first Colonial Welfare and Development Act in July 1940, provision was made for financial support to be given to

Kenya both for economic development and for the development of social services including education.

In 1941, also, a sub-committee of the Advisory Committee was establish-ed in London which had among its terms of reference the requirement 'to consider the best approach to the problem of mass literacy and adult education'. The committee issued its findings on the matter in 1943 in a paper entitled 'Mass Education in African Society'.[71] The report re-emphasized the policy that 'a popular mass education movement must be based on literacy in the mother tongue'. But having said this, the committee qualified the statement on two grounds: '(a) the complexity of the vernacular situation (b) the differences of opinion among Europeans and Africans about the place of English in the educational system.'

In section 94 the committee elaborated upon this last statement with the observation that 'we are aware that almost everywhere, after the first stages of learning to read and write have passed, the interest of the African in education is centred to a great extent on their desire to learn and read English. This interest must be catered for in planning for mass education'.

MEMORANDUM ON LANGUAGE IN AFRICAN SCHOOL EDUCATION, 1943

In the same year the Advisory Committee on Education in the Colonies issued a memorandum on Language in African School Educa-tion.[72] The committee justified the issue on the ground that the great changes and developments which had taken place in the 16 years since the issue of the memorandum on the Place of the Vernacular in Native Education made it appropriate for a further examination of the problem of language. The 1927 memorandum was taken as a starting point by the committee in its considerations and it began by affirming two general propositions that were laid down in the earlier memorandum; the first being that education should begin in the vernacular of the child, and the second that the teaching of English is essential. The committee considered these general propositions to be acceptable both on educational and political grounds. In their argument that 'from a purely educational standpoint it is not open to question that the longer the vernacular is used the more effective is the instruction likely to be', and in their statement that it is 'surely unquestionable that in a school course of 6 years the instruction must be given entirely through the medium of the vernacular', they reiterated as strongly as the earlier commission this basic principle.[73]

The memorandum then stated that if it was the case that the mother tongue could not be used as a medium of instruction over the whole period of school life it would be necessary to introduce a second language and that 'it may be necessary to meet the difficulty either by the introduction of English at a stage earlier than is right on educational grounds or by the introduction of a second vernacular closely akin to the child's vernacular and more easily acquired by him than English'.

In relating the principles they had accepted to educational practice, they concluded that 'it seems inevitable that the vernacular should be the language of instruction throughout the whole of the elementary stage', but added the familiar provision that if the vernacular was to be the medium at this stage 'we must make one assumption of importance and that is that the vernacular is capable of use as the medium of instruction and that the provision of textbooks and simple material does not present insuperable difficulties'.[74]

In regard to the teaching of English the memorandum stated that the point at which such teaching was introduced must depend on the decision of the local education authorities but asserted that 'it should generally be begun only when sufficient progress has been made to give the children ability and a fair degree of facility in reading and writing their own vernacular'. In considering the question of the use of English as a medium the committee thought that 'there should be no objection in the last year of the elementary course to a slight departure from the principle laid down', and considered that 'it should be permissible to give one or two lessons occasionally through the medium of the English language and that, if the course covered six full years, it might be possible to use English as the medium of instruction in one or two subjects'. However, they advised that the use of English should be most sparingly permitted with the aim of 'enabling a pupil to take the bulk of his instruction through the medium of English in post-primary courses'.

The memorandum also made reference to the problem of areas where educators were faced with the use of three languages in the educational system, one being a 'dominant vernacular'. The committee had little positive to say about the matter, however, but simply asserted that the local educational authorities must in such circumstances 'either make special provision for the unduly early introduction of English or impose the handicap of the dominant vernacular. In either case', they remarked, 'the children concerned will suffer'.

A REVIEW OF THE RECOMMENDATIONS OF THE ADVISORY COMMITTEE ON LANGUAGE POLICY

It might be appropriate at this stage to make a number of comments regarding the recommendations of the Colonial Office on educational language policy in so far as these were reflected in the memoranda of 1927 and 1943.

It is evident that during the sixteen years between the issuing of the two reports on language use in education by the Advisory Committee, the basic principles that the members accepted as necessarily underlying educational practice had not changed or evolved to any discernible degree. Both reports were of some utility in that they drew attention to the difficulties that faced educators in Africa but their guidance as to the solutions that should be adopted in the face of these difficulties was of relatively little practical value in the very different circumstances that prevailed both in the East African territories and, more evidently, in Africa as a whole. The first report offered suggestions regarding a transitional policy, arguing 'we must be content with practical expedients'. The second offered 'a compromise in the face of the clash between the two basic principles'.

The first basic principle concerned the use of the mother tongues as media of instruction. Both Advisory Committee reports quoted with approval an extract from the report of the Calcutta University Mission (1919) to the effect that 'it is through our vernacular, through our folk speech that most of us attain to the characteristic expression of our nature and of what our nature allows us to be or to discern. A man's native speech is almost like his shadow, inseparable from his personality . . . hence in all education the primary place should be given to training in the exact and free use of the mother tongue'.[75] The recommendations of the committee were no doubt inspired by a well-intentioned desire to encourage the implementation of prevailing educational theory but it appears that insufficient thought was given to the practical implications of the policy they avowed or to the long-term consequences of this emphasis.

The provision of adequate teaching materials in all but a relatively small number of languages in East Africa was not possible at the time the reports of the Advisory Committee on language use in education were issued and it is not possible now. The 'dissipation of energy and resources involved in the translating and printing of school literature in many local languages' which had been remarked upon by Governor Gowers in his 1927 memorandum to the Secretary of State, continued for decades with the encouragement of the Advisory Committee without remarkable effect. The difficulty of obtaining suitable school materials was constantly commented upon by educationalists in East Africa in the period between the issue of the two memoranda. In 1929, for example, the Director of Education in Kenya stated that 'the grave difficulties in regard to the extended use of the vernacular', which derived from the multiplicity of vernaculars, 'made the provision of books for the use of schools beyond the very earliest stage impracticable'. The problems were more serious in Kenya than in Tanzania or Uganda but they had to be faced in each state.

Thus, despite the fact that the educational authorities in Uganda had simplified their difficulties in this regard by allowing the use of only five languages (and Swahili) as media of instruction, the report of the conference held at Makerere in 1944 to discuss the memorandum on Language in African School Education stated that 'it was to be deplored that after so many years of educational mission in this country the reading material available in the five main vernaculars was grossly inadequate'.[76]

In Kenya no clear policy was laid down until 1949 as to which vernacular languages were to be used at specific stages in the educational system and then the recommendations made regarding the use of twenty languages were patently unrealistic.

One major difficulty that had to be met before the provision of literature could be undertaken concerned the establishment of standardized orthographies in the different languages. The Education Department Annual Report for 1927, which was drawn up after the issue of the memorandum on the Place of the Vernacular in Native Education, had stated for instance that 'considerable difficulty is being experienced in the printing of literature in the vernacular owing to the different methods of spelling being used by the various authorities.' In 1928 renewed efforts were made to remedy the situation and conferences were held at which orthographic conventions to be adopted in teaching Kikuyu, Nandi, Kipsigis, Luo, Swahili and other languages were discussed and the Departmental Report for that year noted that the visits of Professors Westermann and Meinhof had stimulated interest in these matters.

Two decades later 'discussions' were still being held about the writing systems of most of the languages in question. The devising of a phonemic alphabet to provide the basis of the orthography for any particular language is a relatively simple matter. In the absence of guidance that was both informed *and* authoritative, however, few enterprises appeared to present officials with more difficulty than that of getting all concerned to agree on a standard orthography.

This can, perhaps, be illustrated by a brief reference to the development of an orthography for Kikuyu, the language of the largest speech community in Kenya. A United Kikuyu Translation Committee was established by the Protestant missions in 1908 and the United Kikuyu Language Committee on which missionary scholars such as Barlow, Leakey, Downing and Henderson served was established in 1913. It was not until 1933, however, that a uniform orthography was agreed upon for Kikuyu which was accepted by the government. The official ratification of this orthography, however, caused serious dissatisfaction among certain sections of the Kikuyu-speaking people, and government approval of the orthography was withdrawn in 1935. A form of orthography for Kikuyu was eventually agreed on in 1949.[77]

In 1944 at the Conference of East African Directors of Education a concerted if largely ineffectual attempt was made to deal with the question of the production of vernacular literature in accordance with recommendations in the report on Mass Education in African Society and in the 1943 memorandum. The Directors recommended the establishment of an interterritorial organization which could provide textbooks for the schools and literature of various kinds and suggested that this should absorb the existing interterritorial language committee.[78]

As a result of this recommendation and of a report by Mrs E. Huxley the East African Literature Bureau was founded in 1948. No single institution, however well it was managed or staffed, could meet the requirements of school children in the different language communities in the three countries and the textbook section of the Bureau made provision initially for the supply of textbooks in four languages only, viz. Swahili, Luganda, Luo and Kikuyu, although arrangements were made with writers outside the Bureau to provide literature in other languages.[79]

It is clear that in effect the stress laid by the Advisory Committee on the use of vernacular languages as media of instruction led in many cases to a situation whereby children were prevented from gaining access to education in *any* language after the initial stages. In terms of long-term policy, the committee showed itself to be aware of the possible adverse social effects of a policy that might lead to 'the creation of new classes of African society separated from the vast mass of their fellow countrymen by loss of contact and ready communication'; but they did not appear to recognize that in practice a policy which laid stress on the use of the mother tongues as media of initial education in circumstances in which the great majority of the children who were fortunate enough to go to school did not proceed beyond Standard III, served to perpetuate the linguistic barriers that separated them from the majority of their fellow countrymen. If one assumes that this end result was not deliberately fostered, it appears that in few areas of concern was the 'lack of constructive thinking where large issues are involved and . . . lack of consistent policy',[80] which Sir Donald Cameron, a former Governor of Tanganyika, identified as being the weakness of the Colonial Office, more evident than in the matter of language policy in Africa generally and in East Africa in particular.

The 'fragility' of the theoretical corpus on which the recommendations of the Advisory Committee on this issue were based is indicated by the alacrity with which the policy was abandoned when it seemed opportune for English to be used more generally as a medium of instruction.[81]

EDUCATIONAL LANGUAGE POLICY AND PRACTICE, 1945-63

GENERAL

As the end of the Second World War marked a new stage in educational development it might be of value to summarize some aspects of the educational situation at that time. Less than a third of the total children of school age attended school and of a total of some 5,000 teachers employed in the schools only half had any recognized qualification, the majority of those qualified having the elementary teaching certificate (six years' education and one year's training). Although there were about 80,000 children in the elementary classes at the end of 1946, less than 6,000 had passed beyond Standard III. The majority of children were therefore exposed to education in their mother tongue only. The majority of children who were educated in the schools were boys. At the time mentioned there were just over 46,000 girls in elementary classes but only 769 in primary classes and only one girl in a secondary school. Less than 400 children had entered a secondary school course. Until the beginning of 1946, the missions offered the only secondary school education open to African children, in four schools, only two of which took classes to Cambridge School Certificate level.[82]

After the war, the newly appointed local Advisory Council on African Education in Kenya discussed a report on the Teaching of Languages in African Schools which had been drawn up by a committee appointed in December 1942 under the chairmanship of the Venerable Archdeacon L. J. Beecher. The committee's main recommendations on educational principles were that more emphasis should be placed on the teaching of the vernacular languages, and that English should take the place of Swahili as the colony's lingua franca in as short a time as practicable. The council recommended the adoption of the report.

In March 1945, a committee was appointed to consider the needs and future organization of the training of teachers. The committee made a recommendation on measures to be taken over a five-year interim period, which included one for the establishment of twelve large government centres each capable of accommodating 300 students, and another for the establishment of new mission centres and the expansion of some already existing.

THE TEN YEAR PLAN FOR THE DEVELOPMENT OF EDUCATION

Specific plans for educational development were prepared for each district and summarized in the *Ten Year Plan for the Development of*

Education which was published in 1948. The first objective of the plan was that of providing within ten years a four-year primary course for approximately 50 per cent of the children of school age. Secondly, provision was made for the establishment of twenty-four elementary teacher training centres and sixteen lower primary teacher training centres and it was proposed to increase the number of junior secondary schools from two to sixteen.[83]

The expansion of educational provisions, at a time when it had been accepted that the use of Swahili within the educational system should not be encouraged, had significant consequences, and the acceptance of the first Beecher Report, if it may be termed such, signified in certain respects the end of the attempts that had been made towards the greater utilization of Swahili as a medium of instruction.

In summarizing the state of the existing school system the 1948 report observed that in the past the language of instruction in sub-elementary schools was the vernacular, 'but from standard 3 onwards Swahili is taught as the *lingua franca* of the Colony and has been the medium of instruction in junior secondary schools, although it is being rapidly replaced by English'. In the commentary on the junior secondary schools the statement was made that 'the language of instruction has generally been Swahili in the past with English taught as a subsidiary language. Recently, however, there has been such a demand for the use of English instead of Swahili that with the increase in the teachers capable of teaching English it has been possible in some of the schools to give intensified instruction in English in Standard 6 to enable it to be used as a medium of instruction for the remainder of the course'. The report thus drew attention to the progressive replacement of Swahili as the medium of instruction in the educational system.

A new syllabus for primary schools was introduced at the beginning of 1949, in which it was stated that 'the aim of the first three or four years of the six year primary course is to achieve literacy in the vernacular'. This statement regarding the aims of the primary school course continued to appear regularly in reports of the Education Department for the next thirteen years (until 1962).

The departmental report for the year, however, contained a remark regarding the primary school syllabus to the effect that 'Swahili, which is still the lingua franca of the Colony, is taught as a subject. At later stages, normally in the third and fourth years, Swahili becomes the medium of instruction and English is introduced as a subject'.[84] The writer added that 'although an effort has been made to introduce English at earlier stages in the primary course, it is doubtful whether it can be considered a sound educational policy until there are sufficient qualified teachers to teach the language successfully'. The report also drew attention to the pedagogical handicap of the use of three languages of instruction, to the lack of textbooks in many vernaculars, and to the consequent need to use Swahili textbooks in the upper classes of the primary course. One might infer from the report that members of the Education Department were not convinced of the viability of the proposals of the 1942 committee regarding the use of English as a lingua franca and as a medium of instruction.

Both the *Ten Year Plan for the Development of African Education* and the report of the Salaries Commission issued in 1948 envisaged a marked increase in educational expenditure. A committee was therefore established under Archdeacon Beecher to inquire into the scope, content and methods of African education, its administration and finance. The recommendations of the Beecher Committee were published in September 1949 and accepted by the government in 1950.[85]

THE BEECHER REPORT

Not unexpectedly, the committee's recommendations on language in the schools were similar to those put forward by the 1942 committee. It suggested a curriculum which 'would concentrate on literacy in the vernacular, simple arithmetic, elementary practical skills and fundamental discipline'. It also recommended the establishment of 340 intermediate schools in which the course of instruction would be 'based on English, elementary mathematics and a suitable combination of practical subjects'· Provision was made for 13 senior secondary schools to be in operation by 1958. The report made a number of recommendations on language policy. One was

. . . that Swahili be the language of literature and of instruction in primary schools in towns and settled areas, and that for rural areas provision be made for textbooks in Dabida, Kamba, Kikuyu, Masai, Meru, Nandi, Luyia, and Luo covering the whole four years, and in Giriama, Pokomo, Galla, Sagalla, Taveta, Suk, Kisii, Tende, Tesiot, Boran, Turkana, and Somali textbooks be translated for the initial stages only, after which, Swahili should be used for literature, while the vernacular continues as the medium for oral instruction.[86]

The committee looked to the East African Literature Bureau to produce material in a wide range of vernaculars for recreational as well as instructional use. Clearly the supply of such literature was crucial if the aims of the committee were to be realized, as they envisaged that 'three quarters of the Primary school population will receive only such instruction as will enable them with further practice after leaving school to read and write'.

429

The magnitude of the task being required of the Literature Bureau did not appear to be fully realized by the members of the committee.

As regards the teaching of English the committee called attention to the fact that 'at this stage we have not felt it possible to suggest the general introduction even of spoken English in the Primary school because many of the teachers will not be qualified to give this'. Nevertheless they considered that 'the transition from a vernacular or from Swahili to English at Standard V is something for which the syllabus must provide and which can, in any case, easily be accomplished'. It is perhaps relevant to mention that it had been recognized in the 1943 memorandum of the Advisory Committee that 'if the introduction of English as a medium is not to be a most serious handicap to educational progress . . . the introduction must be gradual and not involve a catastrophic changeover'.[87] It is difficult to appreciate why the members of the Beecher Committee did not recognize the seriousness of this problem. Nor does it appear that the committee had considered in depth the pedagogical implications of their recommendation that in twelve of the language groups mentioned, Swahili should be used for 'literature' while the vernacular language should continue as the medium of oral instruction.

One may infer from what is stated that the members of the committee considered that English should be or would be the medium of instruction after the initial stages of education in the rural areas but in this they were simply acknowledging an existing trend rather than initiating an original policy. In the *Proposals for the Implementation of the Recommendations of the Report on African Education in Kenya,* published as Sessional Paper No. 1 of 1950,[88] it was affirmed that the 'language policy in the schools is that English shall be adopted as soon as possible in the post-primary classes'. It was stated with regard to the other recommendations mentioned, that the government agreed with these in principle but that they might have to be modified from time to time on the advice of the members of the Education Department and the Advisory Council on African Education.

In the debate on the report which took place in August 1950 in the Legislative Council, Mr Ohanga strongly criticized certain of the proposals made regarding the stage at which English should be introduced. In his reply to Mr Ohanga's criticism the member for Health and Local Government stated that the government's ultimate aim was eight years of education for every African child and added 'this Government's ultimate aim for the people of this country is a population literate in English.'[89] Mr Ohanga subsequently stated in debate that, 'I should like to say that for a long time very many of us have pressed that the teaching of English should be at an early stage and the . . . general policy of the

430

country has not always been sympathetic to this view . . . If the suggestion that has been made that English be started at the earliest possible time is carried out generally, I am quite sure that we shall be satisfied completely.' Aspects of the report were subsequently discussed in the House of Commons in December. Mr J. Johnson, M.P., agreed with Mr Ohanga that the four-year primary course that was recommended was insufficient but the recommendations on questions of language use were not criticized.

In both 1950 and 1951, Departmental Reports again drew attention to what was considered to be the pedagogically unsatisfactory system of using three languages of instruction in the primary schools.[90] Both reports mentioned also the 'demand to start English even earlier and to eliminate Swahili,' but recognized that there were 'insufficient teachers competent to teach English in the primary schools, and at present the supply of vernacular literature is quite inadequate to take the place of the large amount of Swahili reading material now available'. It was, however, stated clearly for the first time that it was the policy of the Department 'to stop the use of Swahili as the language of instruction in those areas in which a vernacular is spoken by enough people to warrant the output of vernacular literature in sufficient quantity; enough Swahili will still be taught to give the pupils a working knowledge of it. In the weaker vernacular areas there will still have to be a stage when Swahili is used as the language of instruction'.

In 1950 mention was first made of arrangements that had been made to introduce English as the medium in the very first year in two or three classes in each of the large primary schools for Indian children in Nairobi and Mombasa. This was in accordance with a recommendation of the Select Committee on Indian Education in their commentary on the report of Mr A. A. Kazimi on the *Enquiry into Indian Education in East Africa*.[91]

In the early 1950s the trend for English to be used as a medium of instruction in the primary schools in urban and rural areas increased, although it was admitted in the Education Department Report for 1952 that 'possibly the transition was premature in the more backward areas'. The report also noted that a few schools had applied for permission to revert to the use of Swahili for examination purposes.[92]

The policy of replacing Swahili as a medium proved to be difficult to implement in many areas, primarily because of a lack of suitable school texts in many languages and the lack of qualified teachers to teach English. As I have mentioned earlier, an attempt to alleviate the shortage of reading materials had however been made with the establishment of the East African Literature Bureau. In 1950 the Bureau published 64 books, 21 of which were in Kenyan languages (Kikuyu, Luo, Luyia, Meru and Kamba) and 23 in Swahili. In 1950 also, after considerable debate, an orthography for the Nandi, Kipsigis, Elgeyo-Marakwet and Tugen dialects was agreed upon. 'Kalenjin' thus came into existence as a written language. In 1951 the supply of readers in the vernacular languages slowed down but certain vernacular readers were completed and translations continued to be made in the textbook section of the Bureau in Swahili, Kikuyu and Luo. The reduction in the number of books was apparently associated with the fact that as a consequence of the Beecher Report, new syllabuses for primary and intermediate schools were under consideration. These were approved in 1952. However, in publishing terms, Swahili remained 'the most popular language as far as the Bureau was concerned', and in this year the Bureau began to publish a weekly magazine, *Tazama*, in Swahili and English.[93]

In 1953 a tentative syllabus for African intermediate schools was issued by the Education Department in Kenya which was compiled on the basis of the recommendation that 'apart from Religious Instruction, English should be the main subject of the curriculum, both for its general educational value and for its use when pupils leave Form II for employment . . . ' and the main aim of the syllabus was stated as being to enable the child to read, write and speak simple idiomatic English suited to his environment.[94] Two periods a week were set aside in the curriculum for the teaching of Swahili.

The suggested syllabus for the teaching of vernacular languages was said to *presuppose* the existence of a series of graded class readers: which, it is apparent, were not available for most languages. The recommendation was therefore made that where there was not sufficient material for the teaching of the vernacular in the higher classes, the timetable should be modified to cater for the needs of other subjects. The same presupposition is made in the recommendations contained in the syllabus for primary schools also issued in 1953.[95] The curriculum was designed 'so as to concentrate on literacy in the vernacular, simple arithmetic and elementary practical skills' and thus implemented the recommendations of the Beecher Report, but Swahili remained 'the second language at the primary stage with the intention that it should be used as a medium of instruction for the first year or so in the intermediate course until it can be replaced by English'.[96] English was taught from Standard III or IV in most areas.

In 1953 English became the compulsory medium in the examination held at the end of the eighth year of primary education. This was of course a most significant development. The result was that Swahili, no longer an optional medium of examination, was used less widely as the medium of instruction in the lower classes in areas where it was not itself a vernacular. However, Swahili continued to be widely taught in the intermediate schools to allow it to continue as a second language in secondary schools.[97]

The conditions under which English was taught were ostensibly strictly controlled. Attention was drawn in the 1953 syllabus to the decisions of the Advisory Council on African Education in Kenya concerning the conditions that had to be observed before English was taught in primary schools. These were that (a) suitably qualified staff must be employed to teach English at the primary level, (b) syllabuses and schemes of work must be submitted to the Education Department for approval, and (c) children who had been taught the groundwork of English at the primary stage must be able to continue from that stage to the intermediate level. Attention was also drawn to the recommendation of the Board of Examiners to the effect that English should be taught in a primary school only with the express permission of the Education Department on the recommendation of the Provincial Educational Officer, and that authority should be given for the withdrawal of the grant-in-aid to primary schools where English was taught without permission. In drawing attention to these conditions and sanctions relating to the teaching of English, the syllabus was again serving to implement the recommendations of the Beecher Report.

A STUDY OF EDUCATIONAL POLICY AND PRACTICE IN EAST AND CENTRAL AFRICA

In 1951, A. L. Binns led a party of educationists to East and Central Africa, who produced a report on behalf of the Nuffield Foundation and the Colonial Office on educational development in the areas.[98] While it is something of an exaggeration to say as Professor L. Lewis did at the time, that the report represented 'for today what the Phelps-Stokes Reports were in 1925',[99] it did provide an indication of trends in the educational practice in 1950 in Kenya and the neighbouring states and served to influence general colonial policy.

Indirectly, the report drew attention to the divergence in educational practice in the three neighbouring states. In Tanganyika, all education in primary schools up to Standard VI was given in Swahili as soon as possible and English was begun in the fifth year (as compared with the second year in the then Northern Rhodesia and the third year in Nyasaland). In Uganda six vernacular languages were used as media of instruction in different areas and English was introduced in the fifth year or occasionally somewhat earlier. The situation in Kenya was more complex still, as has been indicated, with the vernacular languages being used as media of instruction, while Swahili was generally taught from the third year onwards.

While the study group had no specific recommendations to make regarding language use in Kenya, their statements concerning educational practice in Tanganyika and Zanzibar are of some relevance in that their general lack of support for the use of Swahili as an educational medium and proposals for 'the giving of a quite new emphasis both to the vernacular and to English studies' confirmed the current policy in Kenya. The significance of the report, however, and that of the report on the situation in West Africa, in which among other possibilities the use of English as the medium of instruction throughout the full course of primary education was considered, lay in the fact that these undoubtedly influenced the deliberations of the members attending the subsequent conference on African education held at Cambridge, many of whom held positions of authority in the educational systems in the different African countries. At the conference the question of the use of different languages was considered and while various possibilities were mooted, it was confirmed that 'a large majority of our group including all our African members feel strongly that the teaching of English should have priority'. In view of the evidence presented and interpreted by Mr Binns and his colleagues this is not an unexpected conclusion.

THE EAST AFRICAN ROYAL COMMISSION REPORT 1953–5[100]

In 1953 the commission appointed by the British government to make a general review of development in East Africa considered aspects of educational policy and their recommendations regarding language use in schools were brief and clear. They disregarded completely the basic principle that ten years earlier the Advisory Committee on Education had stated to be 'not open to question', viz. that the longer the vernacular was used in education the more effective was the instruction likely to be, and stated that 'we think that the teaching of English should begin in as low a class as possible, and should become the medium of instruction as early as it can be followed by the pupils'. The reason given was that the people of East Africa were 'very keen on learning English', which the commission termed the 'gate of entry into a new world'. The commission also stated curtly that 'we regard the teaching of Swahili as a second language to children whose early education has been in other vernaculars as a complete waste of time and effort'.[101]

In commenting on the report of the commission the Governor of Kenya accepted this last statement with qualification. He wrote that it was indeed the policy to teach English as soon as possible and that it was introduced into schools in Standard III but added that 'in areas where the pupils are of mixed tribes, Swahili is essential and is used as the vernacular'.[102]

The Governor added, seemingly rather apologetically, that 'in secondary schools it is taught as the second language for School Certificate; for this reason, and because of its usefulness in later life a few periods are still devoted to it in Intermediate schools'.

As a result of these reports and as a consequence of the educational trends that had been in evidence and in operation for a number of years, it appears that by 1958, Swahili was 'no longer taught extensively in . . . Primary schools'.[103]

THE USE OF ENGLISH AS A MEDIUM OF INSTRUCTION

The statement referred to above, regarding the relative curtailing of the teaching of Swahili, was made in 1958 in an article by Mr G. Perren which also referred to the 'considerable demand to begin English as a second language in the first year'. He noted also that at the time many schools did in fact begin the teaching of English in the second year though the majority began it in the subsequent year; and in most schools it became the medium of instruction in the sixth year. The major drawback in this system was thought to be 'the setback to all learning which took place when the language medium changed in the Intermediate school (the fourth to sixth year) from the vernacular to English, as this change took place at the time that the content of instruction was becoming more considerable'.[104]

In April 1957, a 'Special Centre' was established by the Ministry of Education to investigate this problem and to consider the methods of teaching used in primary schools generally. The immediate aim of those involved was to alleviate difficulties deriving from multilingualism in the schools attended by Asian children. As I have indicated earlier the Select Committee appointed in 1948 to discuss the recommendations made in the *Enquiry into Indian Education in East Africa* had advised that an experiment should be undertaken in schools in Nairobi and Mombasa in which English would be used fiom the first year. The Aga Khan Education Board had also taken a decision in 1953 to use English as the medium of instruction in schools sponsored by it, and approximately thirty Standard I classes under the Board's sponsorship were, in fact, being taught through the medium of English by 1957.

In the circumstances, it was decided that a pilot course using English as the medium of education should be introduced into a number of schools for Asian children in Nairobi and the project, which involved twenty-five teachers, was started in 1958. The innovation was described by one of the officers concerned as being of 'a revolutionary nature running counter to established linguistic opinion in particular that of the UNESCO authorities'.[105] In certain respects the development project as it was conceived and executed, did introduce new teaching practices into the schools, but it can also be seen as the culmination of a long process of development in which English had been introduced at an increasingly earlier stage, and there were in fact in Kenya and elsewhere in Africa a number of precedents for this development. Nevertheless, the decision to begin English medium teaching did run counter to educational theory of long standing and it might be of interest to detail some of the reasons for the change to English that were given in the *Report of the Work of the Special Centre* at the end of 1957.[106]

Whereas in most of the previous reports that have been considered, the early introduction of English was justified on the grounds of 'practical expedience' in the absence of suitable literature in the vernacular languages, it was argued in the 1957 report that 'on purely educational grounds there are strong arguments for using English as the medium as soon as possible', and that 'if English is the only medium, then the incentive to learn English becomes greater, the transition to the full use of English becomes quicker and general progress in the higher classes where English must be used, is likely to be faster'. The report continued:

By using English as medium at a low level it becomes possible to teach a great deal of English through its use in other subjects . . . it appears that the mental strain of learning a foreign language and using it with a limited vocabulary is less for young children (whose need to express abstract or generalised concepts in language is small) than it is for older children. It is easy to teach the vocabulary of use needed by a six-year-old for his classroom environment and then progressively expand it as required, but it is not easy in a similar period to teach that needed by a ten or eleven-year-old who wishes to generalise or express more sophisticated ideas . . . While the change from one language to another at 10 or 11 might handicap the educational progress of an intelligent child unfairly, it is less likely to do so if the change is made earlier. Moreover, the younger the child, the less conscious is the effort required in foreign language learning and the less the change demanded in his pattern of thought when he has to replace one language by another.

In the second report of the Special Centre, Mr Perren went further and argued that:

Assuming that it is required to teach English to young children so that it may become eventually an effective medium of instruction in higher classes, English stream teaching is probably the *only* effective method. Orthodox 'second language' teaching techniques —where the new language is restricted to formal periods on the timetable—are not likely to be successful. If a new language is thus divorced from reality and immediate application, it has little or no interest to young children. It appears doubtful whether orthodox second-language teaching can be very successful before about the age of ten, when children may become capable of some logical analysis.

While it is possible to question some of the arguments presented in favour of English-stream teaching, as it was then termed, it is evident that the experiment proved to be relatively successful for a variety of reasons: it solved the problem of giving instruction in several languages, and of the changeover to a new language of instruction; it provided more adequate teaching materials than had been available for the teaching of English, and as Mrs E. Gachukia has observed, 'not only did the use of the English medium course bring with it more adequate texts and materials both for the teacher and the pupils than had been provided before, but its introduction was also accompanied by the activities of a team of supervisors and advisers who provided close supervision, in continuous in-service courses for the teachers'.[107] Most significantly, the course introduced child-centred activity methods of instruction along with the change of medium.

In 1961, the course was adopted for general use in the schools and in the following year all first year classes in Nairobi made the changeover. In this year also, the various racial divisions of the Kenya Preliminary Examination which had previously existed were abolished and a single preliminary examination was taken by all children at the conclusion of their primary school course. Before this time, the fact that different languages were used as media of instruction in the educational system of the colony was one reason that had frequently been given for the fact that a common syllabus had not been adopted earlier.[108]

The use of English as a medium of instruction continued to spread and all training colleges were asked to prepare their teachers for this system of teaching English in 1962.[109] The number of English medium classes in African primary schools rose from 14 in 1962 to 290 in 1963.[110] The introduction of the scheme, often referred to from 1964 as the New Primary Approach, continued to gather momentum and it was remarked in the Triennial Survey issued in 1964 that the method of instruction was 'gaining rapidly in popularity with the pupils, teachers and parents' and that 'its entry into all primary schools is prevented only by a lack of teachers trained to provide this type of instruction'.

LANGUAGE POLICY IN KENYA
SINCE INDEPENDENCE

In this chapter commentary has been confined to the development of educational language policy as it was affected by metropolitan or local directives and as it was implemented in schools below secondary level.[111] I would like to reiterate, however, my earlier statement that decisions on language use in a particular society are almost invariably subordinate to or a reflection of underlying social values and goals. I have not attempted earlier in this chapter to consider in any detail the development of educational language policies in the context of such goals. A more adequate survey would, however, require that educational language policy be related to language policy, both implicit and explicit, in other domains.

As it is of some relevance to the information given subsequently about patterns of language use among children and their parents I will, in conclusion, outline certain policy decisions made or accepted by the Government of Kenya since the attainment of independence in December 1963 and indicate other legal prescriptions in force which affect language use in different sectors. This procedure may serve to place educational language policy in perspective and at the same time, to indicate certain of the social and political forces that affect the language use of members of the community in some degree.[112]

CONSTITUTIONAL PROVISIONS

The Constitution of Kenya, which was revised in 1969, lays down a number of provisions regarding language use in particular circumstances.[113] Perhaps the most significant of these is Article 7(e), which enjoins that certain categories of persons eligible to be *naturalized* as citizens must satisfy the minister concerned 'that they have an adequate knowledge of the Swahili language'. To be eligible for *registration* for citizenship, citizens of certain other states are required to have an adequate knowledge of the Swahili or the English language.[114] However, the Article in the Constitution that has attracted most commentary and which has been the subject of a number of parliamentary debates is clause 55, which states that 'the business of the National Assembly shall be conducted in English'. Clause 40(1) (b) relates to this and provides that a person shall not be qualified for election to the House of Representatives 'unless he is able to speak and, unless incapacitated by blindness or other physical cause, to read the English language well enough to be able to take an active part in the proceedings of the National Assembly.'

On more than one occasion in Parliament, President Kenyatta, speaking in Swahili, has referred to the desirability of using Swahili in the House of Representatives. On several occasions also, motions have been introduced containing resolutions to this effect. However, a dateline for the introduction has not yet been established primarily perhaps for reasons relating to what the Minister of State in the President's Office termed in 1966, ' . . . the unsurmountable practical difficulties in translating our laws and other legal and quasi legal documents into Swahili'.[115] Whether

438

this requirement would need to follow from the introduction of the language as one of the languages of debate is, it would seem, an open question.

THE COURTS

At present the laws of Kenya are written in English. This is the primary reason for the language requirement for those seeking election to the House of Representatives.[116]

The official language of the High Court is English, but in all lower courts other than Muslim courts, English, Swahili or a vernacular language may be used as is appropriate.[117] Written records must be kept of the proceedings as a judge of the High Court has periodically to inspect the records of the court and these are kept in English for this reason.[118]

THE CIVIL SERVICE

At present there are no regulations in force governing the use of different languages by civil servants in their various administrative activities. Since independence, a number of prescriptions relating to the languages to be learned by government officers in certain positions and the financial benefits that accrued to those who passed language examinations have been withdrawn, as their provisions were inappropriate in certain respects for Kenyan officers. Officers in the colonial service were required to take a preliminary oral examination and a written standard examination in Swahili. They were also given certain inducements to pass an examination in another language or languages.[119] Discussions are, however, underway for the introduction of regulations that will provide inducements for officers who learn languages other than their own.

LOCAL GOVERNMENT

As far as I am aware there are no regulations imposing restrictions on language use in the activities of local government bodies.[120] In September 1969, Mombasa Council agreed in principle that Swahili should become the official language of the council. The matter was, however, subsequently referred to the Ministry of Local Government for a ruling.

THE PRIVATE SECTOR

The law requires that the Memorandum of Association, the Articles of Association and the books of account of all companies are to be written in English[121] and also requires that the constitution or rules of any society must be written in English or that an English translation of the constitution or rules should be attached to the application for registration.[122]

MASS MEDIA

Radio and television are a responsibility of the government. On the assumption of independence, the broadcasting services were provided by an independent corporation which had a contractual obligation to transmit daily news broadcasts in English, Swahili and Hindustani. Other languages were broadcast but not legally prescribed. When the government nationalized the Kenya Broadcasting Corporation in June 1964, they took over this commitment.[123] Subsequently the Hindustani service was incorporated into the series of services provided in vernacular languages.[124]

The National Service in Swahili and the General Service in English are now broadcast throughout the day. In addition, daily broadcasts are given in fourteen other African languages, in the Kimvita dialect of Swahili and in Hindustani. Broadcasts are not given in a number of numerically important languages, such as the languages in the Mijikenda cluster as the speakers of these languages are assumed to be served by the National Service.

There are no government-owned daily newspapers and in this respect Kenya differs from Tanzania and Uganda where government-controlled daily newspapers are published in English. No newspapers are now published by the Ministry of Information in any of the indigenous languages. The *Daily Nation* and the *East African Standard* have an approximate daily circulation in Kenya of 40,500 and 38,000 respectively. *Taifa Leo*, a Swahili daily paper, has a circulation of approximately 17,500. Other weekly papers with an extensive circulation in Kenya are *Baraza* (c. 28,000) and *Taifa Weekly* (c. 35,000).[125]

THE EDUCATIONAL SYSTEM

After Kenya became an independent state, the Minister for Education appointed a commission under the chairmanship of Professor S. H. Ominde of University College, Nairobi, to survey the existing educational resources of Kenya and to advise the government in the formulation and implementation of national policies for education.

The first part of the Report of the Kenya Education Commission was submitted a year later in December 1964, and the recommendations of the report established the guidelines for the present system as regards language use in education.

In its membership and aims the commission differed from previous bodies in several respects, most significantly perhaps in that the inquiry constituted 'an attempt to ascertain as accurately as possible the views of the people of Kenya as a whole'.[126] Evidence was taken by the commission in both English and Swahili.

In outlining the terms of reference of the commission, the minister stated that among other matters the commission must weigh the influence of language on education and on the unity of Kenya.[127] In his background paper on 'Fundamental Assumptions of Education in Kenya', the Chairman considered proposals regarding the question of education for national unity, and practical difficulties that limited the application of a single policy throughout the country. In this connection he observed that 'the difficulty is largely linguistic though other factors are no doubt important'. The role of language in education was therefore a factor that the commission considered seriously in relation to national educational aims and priorities.

In its statement on language policy the commission reported that 'the great majority of witnesses wished to see the universal use of English language as the medium of instruction from Primary I'. They also stated their agreement with this view and gave the following reasons:[128]

First, the English medium makes possible a systematic development of language study and literacy which would be very difficult to achieve in the vernaculars. Secondly, as a result of the systematic development possible in the English medium, quicker progress is possible in all subjects. Thirdly, the foundation laid in the first three years is more scientifically conceived, and therefore provides a more solid basis for all subsequent studies, than was ever possible in the old vernacular teaching. Fourthly, the difficult transition from a vernacular to an English medium, which can take up much time in Primary V, is avoided. Fifthly, the resulting linguistic equipment is expected to be much more satisfactory, an advantage that cannot fail to expedite and improve the quality of post-primary education of all kinds. Lastly, advantage has been taken of the new medium to introduce modern infant techniques into the first three years, including activity and group work and a balanced development of muscular coordination. In short (the report concluded), we have no doubt about the advantages of English medium to the whole educational process.

As had numerous earlier bodies, the commission considered the possible effect of the use of English as a medium on the mother tongues of the children, and in this connection they stated that 'the vernacular languages are essential languages of verbal communication and we recognize no difficulty in including a daily period for story-telling in the vernacular, or similar activities, in the curriculum of Primary I, II and III'. They added, however, that they saw 'no case for assigning to them a role for which they are ill-adapted, namely the role of educational medium in the critical early years of schooling'.[129]

Finally the commission made a number of recommendations in regard to the use of Swahili. They stated that 'those giving evidence were virtually unanimous in recommending a general spread of this language, not only to provide an additional, and specifically African, vehicle for national co-ordination and unification, but also to encourage communication on an international basis, not only within East Africa, but also with the eastern parts of the Congo and parts of Central Africa. Kiswahili is, therefore, recognized both as a unifying national influence, and as a means of pan-African communication over a considerable part of the continent. In view of these important functions, we believe that Kiswahili should be a compulsory subject in the primary schools.' They added also that 'the proper and general cultivation of this African language is so important, that it warrants attention in our primary schools from the lowest practicable level'.[130]

The significance of this recommendation is clear, and in making it the commission recommended the reversal of a policy which had been sanctioned, as it were, by the Beecher Reports and by the recommendations of subsequent advisory bodies. It is however necessary to add that the Ministry of Education had already reversed this policy in practice and Swahili had been allocated three periods a week in the primary school syllabus.[131]

The most striking feature of the evidence presented to the commission was, as they themselves remarked, the virtual unanimity of the witnesses with regard to two basic features of educational practice, namely, that English should serve as the medium of instruction in primary schools and that Swahili should be a compulsory subject of instruction.

On the matter of the use of vernacular languages in education, evidence was divided. The members of the Primary Panel reported that 'there were those who said that they should not be taught because they do not serve a very useful purpose either as media of instruction or in the creation of unity in Kenya . . . ' Those who said that it should be taught 'were of the opinion that in order to preserve one's culture, it was necessary to learn the vernacular seriously at school'.[132] It is of some interest that it was in evidence presented by witnesses from Nairobi and Mombasa and from the Coast Province that statements were made to the effect that the teaching of vernacular languages promoted sectionalism and hindered progress towards national integration[133] and it is of interest also that for the first time, the use of the vernacular languages in education was called into question by an advisory body not only on educational grounds but also in relation to the issue of national unity and integration.

442

It says little for the foresightedness of numerous earlier commissions and in particular the Advisory Committee on Education in the Colonies that this issue had at no stage been seriously taken into account as a guiding principle in their recommendations on language policy in African states.

The problem remains, however, as was stated by several of those who gave evidence to the commission, of finding ways in which elements of diverse cultures which are language-related may be preserved and embodied in a common culture and a second language.

At the time the commission drew up its report, the introduction of the New Primary Approach was gathering momentum with practically every district planning to open more classes, and the report reflects the general enthusiasm that was initially felt for the scheme. The Ministry Report for 1964 stated that the problem of training teachers and the provision of supervisory staff 'to cope with the great expansion dictated by popular demand' were the chief problems facing the programme. Subsequently other problems became evident.

At the invitation of the ministry, Professor C. Prator and Mr M. Hutasoit undertook a study of the New Primary Approach in the schools of Kenya, which was issued in March 1965.[134] They concurred that the introduction of the NPA scheme brought with it a number of educational advantages but they also recommended that new NPA classes should not be authorized until the necessary funds were available for school buildings, supplies and equipment, trained teachers and adequate supervision.[135] They advised that teachers of NPA classes should have a minimum of two years of secondary education and two years in a teachers' college, as it was apparent that the effectiveness of the approach was heavily dependent on the language control of the teacher and on a system of close supervision.[136] However, the shortage of teachers so trained made it impossible to implement this recommendation and the introduction of the New Primary Approach continued rapidly after the issue of the two reports. The Triennial Report for 1964–66 reported that 'development was so rapid that by 1966 half the Standard I classes in the country were being taught in English using the New Primary Approach'.[137]

As development was so rapid the impression has sometimes been given that it was also uncontrolled. A study of the records shows that in fact expansion at this period was very carefully controlled by the ministry. A 'permissive policy' was maintained which allowed local authorities the initiative to open new classes but in controlling expansion the ministry insisted that regional expansion schemes must be dictated by the availability of the equipment that formed an intrinsic part of the course and of funds to permit adequate supervision of classes.

Since the report of the Kenya Education Commission, the use of English and Swahili has been given emphasis in the schools but provision for the teaching of mother tongues has not been ignored. For example, in June 1965, a ministry circular was sent out to schools which stated that 'in some schools we have come across neglect for teaching an African language and teachers in these schools use the period for revision of other subjects on the understanding that no vernacular or Swahili should be taught in the English-medium classes. This misunderstanding of the teachers should be corrected . . . whatever the position is about English medium teaching, the vernacular and/or Swahili will still be taught in the schools as a subject'.[138]

The report of the Upper Primary Workshop held in September 1964, drew attention to the fact that 'there is a strong feeling in the country that there must be a place on the primary school timetable for three languages'[139] and both the report of the Ominde Commission and the Prator-Hutasoit report emphasized that literacy in the children's mother tongue and in Swahili was compatible with the use of English as a medium and made suggestions as to how this could be achieved. As the effects of rapid expansion in rural areas became apparent, however, the education authorities began to lay increasing stress on the fact that the 'New Primary Approach' was not synonymous with English medium teaching but that the method could be applied in languages other than English. The Chief Education Officer, for example, stressed in an address in April 1967 that there were three discernible aspects to the Approach namely, (a) the creation of positive attitudes in the teacher which means that the teacher must respect the child and his ability to participate more; (b) the development of suitable material and equipment and (c) the use of a medium of communication *which can be any language* (my italics). Provincial Education Officers were also advised by the ministry that in planning school expansion in 1967 they should bear in mind that 'although no language policy has been issued so far it is generally considered that for sound education and taking into account the needs of the young child, education should begin as far as possible in the language that the child speaks before going to school, and for this reason greater effort should be directed towards improving the quality of teaching the normal classes, by employing modern teaching methods similar to those used for NPA classes. To facilitate this policy, plans for an amended Kenya Primary School Course were put forward by the Curriculum Development and Research Centre in December 1967, which involved the preparation of further reading materials for use in the vernacular periods and the writing of a new English-as-a-subject course for use in Standards I to III. Since then, supplementary reading materials have

444

been written at the Kenya Institute of Education in 14 languages including Swahili.[140] In 1967, an experiment was begun in eight classes that involved the use of the children's mother tongue in the first two years of education in conjunction with a modern lower primary curriculum. The aim of the course was to provide for literacy in the children's first language and to ensure that the discovery methods of a modern curriculum are unhampered by language problems.[141] Preparation of the course was, however, discontinued in 1970.

In accordance with the recommendations of the Ominde Commission report, emphasis has been placed on the preparation of materials for the teaching of Swahili, which is a compulsory subject in primary schools. It is normally taught from Standards IV to VII in schools in rural areas and from Standard I in urban areas. A course has been prepared for use in Standards IV to VII for speakers of Swahili as a second language and there are plans for the preparation of a course for use in Standards I to VII.[142]

Work has continued also on the preparation of English-teaching materials for use at primary level by children who have been taught through the New Primary Approach.

The preparation of texts for use in primary schools is now co-ordinated through the Kenya Institute of Education which incorporates the Curriculum Development and Research Centre established in 1965. This co-ordination has led to a greater degree of co-operation between those responsible for the preparation of subject teaching materials and language teaching texts than was previously possible.

Since the report of the Education Commission much has been done to remedy the serious shortage of qualified teachers of Swahili. The Ominde Commission had recommended a crash training programme for teachers, and also placed on record its opinion that the establishment of a department concerned with the study of the language at University College 'would greatly assist in the promotion of Kiswahili as a national language in Kenya'. Upgrading courses were subsequently organized at Kenyatta College to equip P1 teachers of Swahili and other subjects to teach in secondary schools, and a Department of Linguistics and African Languages, in which Swahili is the central subject of study, was established in the Faculty of Arts of University College, Nairobi in 1969.

In April 1967, the then Minister of Education, Mr J. Nyagah, stated that Swahili was to become a compulsory subject at all levels of the school system and in teacher training institutions in Kenya.[143] This has not yet been done, as qualified teachers are still in relatively short supply, but most maintained and aided schools now teach the subject.

THE NATIONAL LANGUAGE ISSUE

Since the attainment of independence the position of Swahili as the national language of Kenya has been affirmed though no constitutional provision has been made to this effect. Both on the occasion of the granting of independence in December 1963 and when Kenya became a republic a year later, President Kenyatta spoke in Swahili in Parliament to emphasize the importance of the language. The President's use of the language in such circumstances has frequently been cited as a demonstration that Swahili is *de facto* the national language of Kenya. Dr Waiyaki, speaking for the government in reply to a motion in April 1965 on the question of the use of Swahili in Parliament, remarked, for example, that 'there is no question now of deciding whether or not Swahili will become a national language. The President of the Republic decided for us and we are committed to accept Swahili as the National language'.[144] Similarly, in a debate in July 1969 Mr Mwai Kibaki stated that 'Swahili is, in fact, today a National language for Kenya. There is no point in the Hon. member asking to get it declared—what we should be asked for is a formal recognition'.[145]

In August 1969, formal recognition of Swahili as the national language was given by the National Governing Council of KANU and in April 1970 detailed plans relating to an increasing use of Swahili were announced by the Acting Secretary General of the party. These suggested that more emphasis should be given to a candidate's competence in Swahili in the appointment or promotion of officers in government and quasi-government bodies. He also stated that more emphasis should be given to Swahili in primary and secondary schools and that centres for the teaching, learning and promotion of Swahili should be established. At the same time he affirmed that 'KANU is in no way underestimating the usefulness of English as a world language. Kenyans must know as much English as possible . . .'[146]

Mr Matano reiterated the party's decision to make Swahili the national language by 1974 on two further occasions in April 1970. He emphasized on the first occasion the essentially *advisory* nature of the statement issued earlier and said that it was up to the government to decide whether legislation was necessary to back up KANU's plans for the encouragement and development of the Swahili language.[147] At the time of writing no further legislation has been introduced relating to language use.

The result of the reiteration of the position of Swahili as the national language has been to encourage those concerned to intensify their efforts to implement the major policy decisions already taken earlier as a consequence of the Ominde Report.[148]

CONCLUSION

At present therefore as the primary aim of internal policy is the fostering of forces conducive to national unity, the educational role of Swahili as a subject of instruction is being emphasized and that of English as a medium of instruction maintained, while less emphasis is being laid than was previously the case on the educational roles of the vernacular languages. I have discussed the implications of this circumstance elsewhere and do not intend to replicate here the comments made and the suggestions advanced.[149] It is clear that there are aspects of contemporary policy that require reconsideration and review; but it is also evident that present policy is based on a clearer assessment of the needs and wishes of the people of Kenya than was generally the case in the past. The major difficulties now relate not to the formulation of policy but to its effective implementation, and the following chapters deal, in part, with this concern.

NOTES

[1] T. P. Gorman, 'Language Policy in Kenya', a paper given at the second Eastern African Conference on Language and Linguistics, Nairobi, June 1970.

[2] G. S. P. Freeman-Grenville, *The Medieval History of the Coast of Tanganyika*, Oxford University Press, London, 1962, p. 204.

[3] N. Chittick in B. A. Ogot & J. A. Kieran (eds.), *Zamani*, East African Publishing House and Longman, Nairobi, 1968, p. 117.

[4] F. J. Berg in B. A. Ogot & J. A. Kieran, op. cit., p. 135. Also cf. J. S. Kirkman, *Men and Monuments of the East African Coast*, Lutterworth Press, London, 1964.

[5] G. S. P. Freeman-Grenville, 'The Coast, 1498–1840' in R. Oliver and G. Mathew (eds.), *History of East Africa, vol. I*, The Clarendon Press, Oxford, 1963, p. 168.

[6] cf. J. L. Krapf, *Travels, Researches and Missionary Labours in Eastern Africa*, London, 1860, p. 287.

[7] J. S. Trimingham, *Islam in East Africa*, The Clarendon Press, Oxford, 1964, p. 27.

[8] J. Lamphear, 'The Kamba and the Northern Mrima Coast' in R. Gray & D. Birmingham (eds.), *Pre-Colonial African Trade*, Oxford University Press, 1970, p. 97.

[9] O. F. Raum, 'German East Africa 1892–1914' in V. Harlow & E. Chilver (eds.), *History of East Africa, vol. II*, The Clarendon Press, Oxford, 1965, p. 168.

[10] D. A. Low, 'The Northern Interior 1840–84' in R. Oliver & G. Mathew, op. cit., p. 316.

[11] Marie de Kiewiet Hemphill, 'The British Sphere, 1884–94' in R. Oliver & G. Mathew, op. cit., p. 420.

[12] cf. A. Mazrui, 'Islam and the English Language in East and West Africa' in W. H. Whiteley (ed.), *Language Use and Social Change*, Oxford University Press, 1971, pp. 179–197.

[13] cf. T. Ranger, 'The Movement of Ideas, 1850–1939' in I. N. Kimambo and A. J. Temu (eds.), *A History of Tanzania*, East African Publishing House, Nairobi, 1969, p. 165.

[14] Y. P. Ghai & J. P. W. B. McAuslan, *Public Law and Political Change in Kenya*, Oxford University Press, Nairobi, 1970, p. 5.

[15] M. Perham, 'Introduction' in V. Harlow & E. Chilver, op. cit., p. xix.

[16] cf. B. A. Ogot, 'Kenya under the British, 1895 to 1963' in B. A. Ogot & J. A. Kieran, op. cit., p. 264 and C. Rosberg & J. Nottingham, *The Myth of 'Mau Mau'; Nationalism in Kenya*, Praeger, New York, 1966, p. 23.

[17] Thirteen years later the European settlers obtained a franchise to elect members to Legislative Council.

[18] The statement of Col. Joshua Wedgwood in the House of Commons in July 1922 is illustrative of such comments: 'It appears to me that the Government of Kenya is strangely independent of the Colonial Office itself.' He also said, 'The people who control the Government, the settlers in that country, administer the country in the interests of the settlers . . . ' (Quoted in M. R. Dilley, *British Policy in Kenya Colony* (2nd ed.), Cass, 1966, p. 33.

[19] Initially the groups that supplied labour were the Kikuyu, Luo, Luyia, Taita and Giriama and later the Nandi and Kipsigis.

[20] S. H. Ominde, *Land and Population Movements in Kenya*, Heinemann, London, 1968.

[21] In 1962, for example, 83.6 per cent of Nairobi's total African population were 'migrants'. The urban population of Kenya is drawn primarily from the four major linguistic groups, cf. S. H. Ominde, op. cit., pp. 124, 192.

[22] This conflict of interests was later reflected in the bitter debate on the issue of paramountcy and its interpretation.

[23] Bishop Steere wrote: 'Neither is there any way by which we can make ourselves so readily intelligible or by which the Gospel can be preached as soon or so well as by means of the language of Zanzibar'. E. Steere, Preface, *A Handbook of the Swahili Language as spoken at Zanzibar* (1st. ed.), Sheldon Press, 1870. Details of the missionary contribution to Swahili studies are given in W. H. Whiteley: *The Rise of a Swahili National Language*, Methuen, London, 1969, pp. 15–17, 53ff.

[24] Fr J. Bergmans in giving evidence to the 1919 Education Commission spoke for many of his colleagues when he stated that 'Our principal aim is religion. We give education in connection with religion'. *Evidence of the Education Commission of the East Africa Protectorate*, Swift Press, Nairobi, 1919, pp. 22–3.

[25] R. Oliver, *The Missionary Factor in East Africa*, pp. 22–3, Longmans, London, 2nd ed., 1965, p. 181.

[26] It was the second of six principles accepted at the Imperial Education Conference in 1923.

[27] T. J. Jones, *Education in East Africa*, London, undated. The assumptions reflected in this statement were re-echoed in the 'Binns Report' some thirty years later. cf. *African Education, A Study of Educational Policy and Practice in British Tropical Africa*, Crown Agents, 1953, p. 80.

[28] W. H. Whiteley, op. cit. (1969), p. 55.

[29] *Evidence of the Education Commission of the East Africa Protectorate*, op. cit., p. 42.

[30] Lord Hailey, *An African Survey*, Oxford University Press, London, rev. 1956.

[31] cf. *The Report of the United Missionary Conference*, Nairobi, June 1909. I am grateful to Dr B. G. McIntosh for allowing me to read his doctoral thesis, 'The Scottish Mission in Kenya, 1891–1923', University of Edinburgh, 1969, in which the background to the conference is described.

[32] *Evidence of the Education Commission of the East Africa Protectorate*, op. cit., p. 93.

[33] However, the curriculum he suggested in a memorandum to the commission on 'Proposed Policy for Native Education in the East African Protectorate' made provision for reading, writing and arithmetic, in Swahili, or the vernacular and Swahili in 'village schools', and for 'composition in Swahili and English in Central, District or mission schools.'

[34] *Evidence of the Education Commission of the East Africa Protectorate*, op. cit., pp. 8–9.

[35] As a consequence of linguistic diversity within the community, both government schools made provision for classes to be taught in both Gujarati and Hindustani by bilingual teachers. In Sikh schools, which were not supported by the government,

Punjabi was used as the medium of instruction along with the course adopted in the 'Urdu Section' of the government schools.

[36] Roland Oliver points out that at the time of the Phelps-Stokes Commission inquiry 'the Colonial Governments of Kenya, Uganda and Tanganyika were spending respectively 4 per cent, 2 per cent and 1 per cent of their revenue on education'. op. cit., p. 270. The proportion in Kenya was in fact 3.7 per cent and slightly less than half of this amount was spent on the education of African children—less indeed in 1924, than was spent on the upkeep of the prison system.

[37] T. J. Jones, 'Statement of Educational Objectives', op. cit., pp. 19–22.

[38] *Education Department Annual Report 1924*, Nairobi, 1925, p. 23.

[39] E. R. Hussey, *Memorandum on Certain Aspects of Arab and African Education*, Nairobi, 1924.

[40] *The Report of the East African Commission*, HMSO, 1925, p. 51. In Tanganyika the Muslim population at the coast had enjoyed certain educational advantages as a consequence of the establishment by the German administration of government schools on the coast. Similar facilities were not available in Kenya and the Muslim population quite naturally tended to avoid sending their children to the primary schools staffed by the missions.

[41] *Memorandum on Educational Policy in British Tropical Africa*, HMSO, 1925.

[42] *Education Department Annual Report 1926*, Nairobi, 1927.

[43] *Report of the Education Conference 1925*, Dar es Salaam, 1926.

[44] 'It had been the policy of both the German and British administrations in Tanganyika to make Kiswahili almost exclusively the common vernacular, both for administrative and educational purposes.' cf. the *Memorandum on the Place of the Vernacular in Native Education*, no. 1110, HMSO, 1927.

[45] In the memorandum to the Governor which was appended to the report of the conference on the issue, mention was made of the fact that 'it has been suggested that a permanent committee will in some sense answer to the French Academy in its relation to the Swahili tongue'.

[46] *The Place of the Vernacular in Native Education*, op. cit.

[47] Westermann's influence on educational thought was considerable. He advanced the thesis that 'mental life has evolved in each people in an individual shape and proper mode of expression; in this sense we speak of the soul of a people and the most immediate, the most adequate exponent of the soul of a people is its language. By taking away a people's language we cripple or destroy its soul and kill its mental individuality.' At the time his theories were widely accepted, as was his assumption that 'any educational work which does not take into consideration the inseparable unity between African language and African thinking is based on false principles and must lead to the alienation of the individual from his own self, his past, his traditions, and his people'. Uriel Weinreich has indicated how other German scholars who were preoccupied with questions of assimilation and racial admixture (Unvolkung) had concerned themselves with the psychology of bi- or multilinguals in relation to the problems of ethnic politics and ethnic and cultural biology. The relatively unscientific nature of much of the research associated with the question is evident. cf. U. Weinreich, *Languages in Contact*, Mouton, The Hague, 1966, pp. 117–18.

[48] *The Conference of Governors of the East African Dependencies*, Summary of Proceedings, London, p. 32.

[49] T. J. Jones, op. cit., p. 22.

[50] cf. R. C. Pratt, 'Administration and Politics in Uganda, 1919–45' in V. Harlow & E. Chilver, op. cit., p. 525.

[51] The annexure was included in the *Correspondence arising from the Joint Committee for Closer Union in East Africa*, Cmnd. 4141, HMSO, p. 20. Governor Gowers argued that 'for the area I am at the moment dealing with, Kiswahili should be introduced as soon as possible as a medium of instruction in all elementary vernacular schools, and that this should be a condition precedent to the receipt of a grant in aid from Government'. He excluded Buganda, Bunyoro, Toro, Ankole and Busoga from this recommendation.

[52] cf. W. H. Whiteley, op. cit. (1969), 80–81.

[53] *Annual Report of the Education Department*, Tanganyika Territory, 1929, Dar es Salaam, p. 11.

[54] cf. *Education Department Annual Report 1929*, Nairobi, 1930, p. 17. Resolution VI was 'The Conference recommends that English should not be taught in elementary schools except where there are teachers recognized for the purpose'.

[55] *Education Department Annual Report 1928*, Nairobi, 1929, p. 18.

[56] *Kenya Legislative Council Debates*, 18th October, 1929, p. 430.

[57] op. cit., p. 436.

[58] e.g. The Hon. E. Powys Cobb; 'For the last thirty years or so we have followed a policy which has led to the spread of Swahili and in consequence it has retarded the spread of English. The result of that thirty years policy is that we are now very short of persons qualified to teach English. I think the time has now come when they should, by every means within our financial powers, endeavour to increase the number of teachers who will be available in a few years time to take over the work of spreading the use of the English language. op. cit., p. 443.

[59] op. cit., p. 547.

[60] J. B. Ndung'u, 'Gituamba and Kikuyu Independency in Church and School' in B. G. McIntosh (ed.), *Ngano*, East African Publishing House, Nairobi, 1969, p. 136. In discussing the movement, J. Middleton has referred to 'the desire for the use of English as a medium of instruction in the higher forms. Swahili . . . was unwanted as being associated with settler domination'. J. Middleton, 'Kenya: Administration and Changes in African Life 1912–45' in V. Harlow & E. Chilver (eds.), op. cit., p. 369.

[61] *Higher Education in East Africa*, Col. no. 142, HMSO, 1937, p. 73. cf. also W. H. Whiteley, 'Language and Politics in East Africa', *Tanganyika Notes and Records*, 47/48, 1957.

[62] *Joint Select Committee on Closer Union in East Africa*, vol. 1, HMSO, 1931.

[63] The three delegates from Uganda were not, however, unanimous in their opinions. The representative from Busoga stated that 'in the Kingdom of Bunyore we have got no objection to this new language', and he thought that both English and Swahili should be taught in the schools and that preference should be given to English (minute 5652). He subsequently remarked, however, that 'people can pick up Swahili, and there was no need for it to be taught' (minute 5837).

[64] This fact was reiterated by the leader of the Kenya Settlers' Delegation to the committee (minute 6399).

[65] Mr E. Mathu was appointed in 1944.

[66] *Joint Committee on Closer Union in East Africa*, op. cit., p. 45.

[67] *Correspondence arising from the Report of the Joint Select Committee on Closer Union in East Africa*, Cmnd. 4141, 1932.

[68] op. cit., p. 69.

[69] *Higher Education in East Africa*, op. cit., p. 43.

[70] The statements referred to were made in a Provisional Memorandum on Language Policy which was submitted to the Makerere Commission. In this memorandum Mr Jowitt, then Director of Education in Uganda argued that the African pupil should receive 'mother tongue instruction, this gradually being replaced by the English medium, if he remains within the school system sufficiently long, and that Swahili, where its introduction is justified, should be treated as a subject.' cf. *A Provisional Memorandum on Language Policy*, Uganda, 1944, p. 10. The memorandum was published some years later as a supplement to the report on the conference held to discuss the *Memorandum on Language in African School Education*.

[71] *Mass Education in African Society*, Col. no. 186, HMSO, 1944, p. 30.

[72] *Memorandum on Language in African School Education*, African no. 1170, HMSO, 1943.

[73] op. cit., p. 3.

[74] op. cit., p. 6, section 26.

[75] The reference is to the *Report of the Calcutta University Mission, 1919*, vol. 1, part 1. pp. 244–5.

[76] *A Provisional Memorandum on Language Policy*, op. cit., p. 6.

[77] Shortage of materials in the vernaculars was due to at least three major causes. Firstly, the commitment of the vernacular to the lowest forms of the primary school meant that no one was likely to spend much time on, nor gain much prestige from, work at this level. Secondly, the vernaculars were—are—essentially spoken languages as far as adults are concerned; no place had been discovered for them as written languages. The recent discovery of oral literature was made by the élite, and will probably be made accessible to university students before anyone else. Finally, many languages were still caught up in orthographic toils in the 1950s (see the account of the standardization of Luluyia in Chapter 3). In Gusii, for example, spoken by around half a million people, the Catholics and the Seventh Day Adventists peddled their own orthographies and encouraged—perhaps only by implication—the view that they were right on these matters as on others more spiritual. Attempts to agree on a common orthography between 1954-8 were hampered by ignorance, bigotry, emotionalism, lack of interest and lack of funds to publicize what was being attempted. A new orthography, with long vowels being doubled, was ultimately agreed to, but a reader in this orthography prepared by Fr Mol met with little success and another ten years passed without production of 'literature', though the Swedish Mission continued work on translating the Scripture, using a modified version of the agreed orthography. When the TKK series of readers were produced in 1968/9 the orthography adopted seems to have been a new one devised on the spot. (Note supplied by W. H. Whiteley.)

[78] cf. *Annual Report of the Education Department* (for the year ending 31st December 1944), Uganda, 1945.

[79] cf. *The Report of the East African Literature Bureau*, Nairobi, 1950, p. 5.

[80] D. Cameron, *My Tanganyika Service and some Nigeria*, London, 1939, pp. 255–6.

[81] cf. Subsequent comments on the reports of the 'Binns Committee' and of the Royal Commission in East Africa.

[82] cf. *Education Department Annual Report 1946*, Nairobi, 1947, pp. 7–8.

[83] *A Ten Year Plan for the Development of African Education*, Nairobi, 1948, pp. 4–5.

[84] *Education Department Annual Report 1949*, Nairobi, 1951, p. 33.

[85] *Report on African Education in Kenya*, Nairobi, 1949.

[86] op. cit., recommendation 54.

[87] op. cit., section 30, p. 7.

[88] *Proposals for the Implementation of the Recommendations of the Report on African Education in Kenya*, Sessional Paper No. 1 of 1950, Nairobi, 1950.

[89] *Legislative Council Debates*, 25 August 1950, Cols. 263, 264.

[90] *Education Department Annual Report 1950*, Nairobi, 1951, p. 11. *Education Department Annual Report 1951*, Nairobi, 1953, p. 12.

[91] A. A. Kazimi, *An Enquiry into Indian Education in East Africa*, Nairobi, 1948.

[92] *Education Department Annual Report 1952*, Nairobi, 1953, pp. 10, 11.

[93] cf. *Report of the East African Literature Bureau*, Nairobi, 1952.

[94] *Tentative Syllabus for African Intermediate Schools*, Section 1, Nairobi, 1953.

[95] *Syllabus for African Primary Schools*, Eagle Press, Nairobi, 1953.

[96] *Education Department Annual Report 1952*, Nairobi, 1953, p. 10.

[97] *Education Department Annual Report 1954*, Nairobi, 1955, p. 27.

[98] *African Education, a Study of Educational Policy and Practice in British Tropical Africa*, Crown Agents, 1953, p. 5. This contains the reports of the Binns and Jeffreys missions to East and West Africa in 1951, and the proceedings of the conference on African education held at Cambridge in December 1952.

[99] L. J. Lewis, *Educational Policy and Practice in British Tropical Africa*, Nelson, London, 1954, p. 15.

[100] *The East African Royal Commission Report*, 1953–5, Cmnd. 9475, HMSO, 1955.

[101] op. cit., para 36, p. 184.

[102] *Despatches commenting on the East African Royal Commission 1953–55 Report*, Cmnd. 9801, HMSO, 1956.

[103] cf. G. Perren, 'Bilingualism or Replacement', *English Language Teaching*, XIII, 1, 1958.

[104] cf. H. A. Curtis, 'The New Primary Approach', *Kenya Education Journal*, October 1965, p. 31.

[105] C. O'Hagan, 'English Medium Teaching in Kenya,' *Oversea Education*, 34, no. 3, October 1962. The reference is perhaps to the report of the meeting of experts organized by UNESCO at Jos in Nigeria in 1952 where 'the ideal . . . that the medium of education for a child living in its own language environment should be the mother tongue' was reiterated.

[106] G. Perren, *Report on the Work of the Special Centre to 1st December 1957*, Appendix I, p. 1, Nairobi (mimeographed).

[107] E. Gachukia, 'The Teaching of Vernacular Languages in Kenya Primary Schools' in T. P. Gorman (ed.), *Language in Education in Eastern Africa*, Oxford University Press, Nairobi, 1970, p. 21.

[108] cf. *Ministry of Education Annual Summary 1961*, Nairobi, 1962, p. 2.

[109] *Ministry of Education Annual Summary 1962*, Nairobi, 1963, p. 6.

[110] *Ministry of Education Triennial Survey 1961–63*, Nairobi, 1964, p. 11.

[111] The limitation was imposed primarily because at secondary level there has never been any controversy in Kenya as to the medium of instruction. Nor has there been at any stage a strong demand for the introduction into the secondary syllabus of an African language other than Swahili.

[112] I have discussed the subject at greater length in T. P. Gorman, 'Language Policy in Kenya', op. cit.

[113] The Kenya Independence Order in Council, 1963, schedule 2 of the Order, Constitution of Kenya, *Kenya Gazette Supplement*, No. 105, Nairobi, December 1963; and Constitution of Kenya, *Kenya Gazette Supplement*, No. 27 (Act No. 3), Nairobi, 18 April 1969.

[114] *The Kenya Citizenship Bill*, 1963, Cap. Part II, 3(i) (b) and 5 (1) (d).

[115] *House of Representatives Official Report*, Nairobi, 2 September 1966, Col. 98.

[116] cf. *Daily Nation*, 19 January 1970. It was reported that in speaking to a group of elders in Mombasa Mr Kenyatta said that the laws and books governing Kenya were written in English . . . 'it was only appropriate at this period for every member of Parliament to be able to speak English'.

[117] *The Criminal Procedure Code*, Cap. 75 (rev. 1962), 198(4).

[118] *The Courts Act*, Cap. 10, 8(1) and (2).

[119] cf. *Code of Regulations for Officers of the Government Service*, Second Edition Nairobi, 1922; Third Edition, 1931; Fourth Edition, 1948; Fifth Edition, 1951; Sixth Edition, 1956.

[120] Local Government Regulations, 1963, *Kenya Gazette Supplement*, No. 33, Nairobi, April 1963.

[121] *The Companies Act*, Cap. 486, Article 5(1); Article 12 (a), Article 147 (1).

[122] *The Societies Act*, Cap. 108, Article 2.

[123] *The Kenya Broadcasting Corporation (Nationalisation) Bill*, Cap. 1964, Article 5 (a).

[124] In commenting upon the change of policy the Hon. Mr Muliro expressed what appeared to be a common sentiment in the House when he said: 'I feel that the two languages, English and Kiswahili, should be the effective media and the chief languages for K.B.C.'. cf. *House of Representatives Official Report*, Nairobi, 24 June 1964, Col. 545.

[125] The figures were obtained from the Circulation Managers of the papers concerned, and they relate to Kenya only.

[126] cf. The letter from the Chairman of the Kenya Education Commission to the Minister for Education, 22 October 1964, *Kenya Education Commission Report*, *Part 1*, Nairobi, 1964, p. 5.

[127] Minutes of the First Meeting of the Commission, KEC. (64) Minutes 1, 20 February, 1964 (mimeographed).

[128] *Kenya Education Commission Report, Part 1*, Nairobi, 1964, p. 60, Section 170.

[129] op. cit., p. 60, Section 171.

[130] op. cit., pp. 60–61, Section 172.

[131] cf. The report by the Chief Inspector of Schools on 'The Languages taught and used in Kenya', KEC. (64), 9, 27 February 1964 (mimeographed).

[132] Appendix 1, Summary of Discussion on Primary Education, Minutes of the Fifth Meeting of the Commission, KEC (64), Minutes 5, 15 July 1964, p. 3 (mimeographed).

[133] cf. KEC. (64) Primary 47, 6 July 1964 and KEC. (64) Primary 45 and KEC. (64) Primary 27, 2 June 1964 (mimeographed).

[134] M. Hutasoit and C. Prator, *A Study of the 'New Primary Approach' in the Schools of Kenya*, February-March, 1965 (mimeographed), Nairobi, 1965.

[135] op. cit., p. 56.

[136] It appears that the practical problems associated with these factors have not always been taken fully into account by advocates of the NPA. cf. For example, G. Bowman, in 'English in Africa', *Oversea Education*, vol. 32, no. 3, October 1960, where it is stated of the teacher that 'no remarkable skill is required or desirable. All that is required of him linguistically is that he should be able to pronounce correctly the contents of the course and understand the meaning.' At the same time, it was envisaged that the first two years of instruction in English 'would be entirely oral, concerned with teaching the items of communication commonly used by young children. From that point the children would be looked upon as English speakers and their English studies would follow the normal course of Primary English study in Great Britain, with such modifications as expediency and experience would suggest'.

[137] *Education Department Triennial Report 1964–66*, Nairobi, 1967, p. 5.

[138] Inspectorate Circular, IMS/C/10/5/40 5 June 1965. The reasons for the issue of the circular are discussed in E. Gachukia, op. cit., p. 21.

[139] The interesting suggestion was made that 'in order, first English should be taught, then Swahili, and later the Vernacular (mother tongue), cf. *Final Report of the Upper Primary Workshop*, September 1964, p. 6, 1964 (mimeographed).

[140] The TKK Series consists of a basic pre-reading course, common for all languages, which is followed by an additional pre-reading book, TKK 1b, for the different languages. These are followed by the basic readers and supplementary readers for Primary I and II. The series was first introduced into schools in January 1968 and is available in Swahili, Luo, Kikuyu, Meru, Kamba, Gusii, Luyia, Lugoli, Masai, Dabida, Kalenjin, Giriama and Ateso. With the exception of the pre-reader it is published by Longman Kenya Ltd.

[141] The background to the course and its nature are described by R. P. Fawcett, in 'The Medium of Education in the Lower Primary School in Africa with Special Reference to Kenya' in T. P. Gorman (ed.), *Language in Education in Eastern Africa*, op. cit., pp. 51–69.

[142] *Masomo ya Kiswahili*, Jomo Kenyatta Foundation, Nairobi, 1966–70.

[143] In a speech at Kenyatta Teachers' College, cf. *Daily Nation*, 8 May 1967. The minister had stated on another occasion speaking at Kenya High School that he believed Swahili would become a compulsory subject in secondary schools 'because if we are to build one people together as one nation, and in as short a time as possible, communication in this language is an essential link, for vernaculars are too numerous and English is spoken and understood by too few'.

[144] *House of Representatives Official Report*, Nairobi, 23 April 1965, Col. 1477.

[145] *House of Representatives Official Report*, Nairobi, 1 August 1969, Col. 6771.

[146] *East African Standard*, 7 April 1970.

[147] *East African Standard*, 9 April 1970. Of themselves decisions of the Party have no legal force.

[148] For example the City Education Officer in Nairobi announced that from 1971 Swahili would be taught in all primary schools in Nairobi.

[149] cf. T. P. Gorman, op. cit., pp. 1–12.

15

Language Use and Language Teaching in the Primary Schools of Kenya

R. J. HEMPHILL

INTRODUCTION

This survey was carried out during the period from September 1968 to September 1969, using three different methods of gathering information. Information was collected by one or more of these methods for 39 of Kenya's 41 districts, and a general picture of the situation in the other two districts was obtained by interviewing an education officer who had served there.

The three methods were:

1. Questionnaires sent out from the Kenya Institute of Education and returned from 522 schools in 39 districts. (Appendix A)

2. Visits to 68 schools in 6 districts by university students who were native to the respective districts.

3. Visits to 157 schools in 20 districts by the author.

In considering the whole picture of language use and language teaching in the primary schools it is convenient to define four broad areas: the teaching of the mother tongues, the teaching of Swahili, the teaching of English and the use of these three languages by children and teachers, both in the classroom and at school outside of the classroom.

Observations which are relevant for all of these four areas can be listed under the following headings:

Organization of the teaching staff
Ordering and delivery of school supplies
Utilization of teaching materials
Schools' physical plant and equipment

Headings under which appropriate remarks can be made for the teaching of the mother tongues are:

455

Qualifications of teachers
Teaching materials available
Attitudes towards the mother tongue

Headings for the teaching of Swahili are:
Qualifications of teachers
Attitudes towards Swahili
Teaching materials available

Headings for the teaching of English are:
Qualifications of teachers
Teaching materials available
Achievement of pupils in English
Attitudes towards English

Headings for language use in the school are:
Language backgrounds of children and teachers
Attitudes towards all three languages—mother tongue, Swahili and English

This report is presented in terms of the four areas and the headings listed above.

OBSERVATIONS ON ALL FOUR AREAS

ORGANIZATION OF THE TEACHING STAFF

One of the most striking aspects of many schools is that the ratio of teachers to children is not high enough to permit consistently good teaching, quite apart from other factors which limit the effectiveness of the teaching being done. In many districts visited the number of teachers authorized for a school was determined by the total number of children in the school without consideration for the way in which they were distributed over the separate classes. In some districts, for example, the requirement is one teacher for every forty children. If a school in such an area has 280 or more children and seven classes there is a teacher for each class. If, however, a school has an enrolment of fewer than 280 and seven or more classes (by no means an unusual situation in rural schools) it is allowed only six, or five or even fewer teachers—not enough to provide each class with a teacher. In such cases one of several arrangements is made, none of them conducive to adequate instruction of the children. In some schools visited two classes on different levels were combined under one teacher, in others the classes were held following each other on the same day, giving the teacher a teaching day twice as long as

456

usual, and in three schools the teacher oscillated between two classrooms keeping the children busy with 'seatwork' when he was in the other class. Such an arrangement, of course, not only deprives the children of an adequate amount of contact with the teacher, but also reduces the teacher's efficiency in a situation where more than normal demands are being made on him.

In the schools visited where this situation obtained the headmaster was considered a full-time teacher in determining the teacher-pupil ratio, and so was not available to help an over-burdened teacher. In most districts visited, especially in rural schools, this policy was followed, leaving the headmaster little time or energy to attend to the administrative aspects of the school's operation. There were exceptions, usually in schools located within the municipal boundaries. In some such areas the headmaster was not expected to teach or took only one or two classes. One large township school was provided with a class teacher for each class, a headmaster and a supernumerary teacher.

Closely related to the organization of the teaching staff is the supervision available to teachers and headmasters. As it affects language teaching this has until recently been the responsibility of Assistant Education Officers whose duties included administrative supervision of schools as well as assistance to teachers and headmasters in improving their teaching methods. In practice it has been left pretty much to individual officers to decide how they will divide their time and energy between the two in the very large number of schools for which they are responsible. Some fifteen or twenty such officers in the country have for five or six years addressed themselves particularly to the problems of language teaching and have done a most creditable job. The areas where there are such people are fortunate in this respect—many others are far less so.

In 1969 the appointment was made of seventeen Primary School Supervisors with responsibility for the supervision of teaching methods. From the way they have begun their work it looks as though this highly qualified and dedicated group of people will do a good deal to improve the teaching of languages in the primary schools of Kenya.

ORDERING AND DELIVERY OF SCHOOL SUPPLIES

As head of the Language Section of the Kenya Institute of Education one of the author's concerns in carrying out this survey was to determine the effectiveness of the materials recently produced by the Institute for the teaching of languages in primary schools. That this part of the investigation was far less complete than had been hoped was due to the ineffective system of distribution of school supplies being used at the time the survey was being made. Since good teaching of languages, or of any subject, depends largely on the availability of suitable textbooks and teacher's guides some of the problems in the present distribution system will be described in the hope that such a description by an impartial observer will contribute to the improvement of the system.

Almost without exception, headmasters and teachers interviewed called attention to the fact that the supplies they had ordered had arrived late, had arrived in incomplete lots, had not arrived at all or that materials that they had not ordered had arrived in place of those they had ordered. Following regulations set up under the new central distribution system headmasters ordered materials for use during the school year beginning in January 1969, in April 1968. As late as September 1969 most orders had not been properly filled. On the basis of interviews with 225 headmasters in all provinces except North Eastern Province this investigator estimates that an average for the whole country of between 30 per cent and 50 per cent of the supplies ordered had arrived by the end of September 1969. Headmasters, observing that this undesirable state of affairs had only come about in 1969, attributed it to the change from the old system where distribution was the responsibility of individual counties, to the present one where all distribution of school supplies is made from a central point in Nairobi. They were of the opinion that the staff in Nairobi was inadequate to cope with the volume of orders received, that the actual transportation of the materials was not well handled and that the personnel in the central distribution office, not being familiar with the numbers and locations of the schools throughout the country, were not able to fill the orders properly. They also said that when the wrong materials were received it was not possible, as it had been in the past, to return them to the county education offices for replacement.

Having failed to receive large parts of their orders by April 1969, headmasters were in many cases at a loss to know what to order for 1970, since they had no way of knowing whether or not what they had ordered the year before would arrive. One headmaster probably expressed a general feeling when he said, 'With a poor supply system we cannot have a steady learning.'

UTILIZATION OF TEACHING MATERIALS

The rapid strides made in methods of teaching languages in recent years have led to the production of up-to-date course materials which when properly used are far more effective than the materials previously available. The Kenya Institute of Education has produced modern materials for the teaching of English, Swahili and a number of the country's local languages for use in the primary schools. A general observation resulting from the present survey is that many teachers, unfamiliar with the features of the new courses, are not using them to the best advantage. One of these features is a teacher's book designed to accompany the children's book and giving detailed instructions on how to use the children's book as well as on how to conduct oral lessons which do not require the children to use their books. Being familiar with an older type of course consisting only of a children's book, many teachers fail to understand the importance of the teacher's book and often tend to minimize its importance or to fail to use it altogether. Although the teacher's books were intended to be self-explanatory, the survey has made it apparent that in many cases the teacher needs additional help in order to use it and the children's book effectively.

One common misunderstanding on the part of teachers is that since the teacher's book is, in effect, a lesson plan, something the teacher was formerly responsible for writing himself, there isn't the necessity to prepare the lesson in advance that there was with the older courses. This, of course, is not the case, and although the introduction to the teacher's book points this out, the teacher usually needs help in the form of individual supervision or in-service courses in order to learn how best to use the new materials. With some forty thousand teachers in the primary schools this will not be easily effected, though the appointment of the Primary School Supervisors holds out hope for the future in this respect.

In a situation where for too long, teachers have not had adequate or sufficient teaching materials there has grown up a tendency for them to improvise and to wander off from the main teaching points in a lesson, even when they have a carefully graded and sequenced course to follow.

It is doubtful whether the teacher is to blame for this when he is presented with a set of new and unfamiliar materials without being given some amount of instruction in their use. Much less is he to blame when furnished with children's books and no teacher's books, or the other way round, something that has happened all too frequently.

In many of the schools where teachers were asked about the use and effectiveness of the language-teaching programmes broadcast by the Voice of Kenya's Schools Broadcasting Division, the comment was that the school could not afford a radio, that one had been ordered but not yet received, or that reception was not good enough to make listening to them worthwhile. In the schools where there were radios and good receiving conditions reports on the efficacy of the broadcasts were generally favourable.

SCHOOLS' PHYSICAL PLANT AND EQUIPMENT

In visiting schools throughout Kenya observers are impressed by the variation from one school to another in the construction of the buildings and the equipment with which they are furnished. School buildings range from those of permanent and modern construction to those with thatched roofs, mud walls and bare earth floors. Furnishings and e quipment also vary greatly in different schools. Generally speaking the schools in or near urban centres are better off in these respects than those in rural areas. In many such areas where funds are not available for the construction and maintenance of adequate school buildings, parents of the children donate their labour in building new classrooms and improving existing ones.

In many schools the walls between classrooms do not go up to the roof of the building, there being a large, empty triangle between the top of the wall and the roof. Such an arrangement does little or nothing to prevent the sounds from one classroom from interfering with the work going on in the adjoining rooms. This is especially annoying in the case of language lessons when pupils' progress in a language depends on their being able to hear the teacher clearly. The relatively small expense of continuing the walls of the classroom up to the roof has proved well worthwhile in a number of the schools visited.

A problem in the matter of classroom equipment that is apparent in many schools is an inadequate number of books to provide each child with his own. The general rule in most parts of the country seems to be one book for two children, but it is not uncommon to find three or four or more children sharing a book. (See Appendix E.) Even with an improved system of distributing supplies this situation is not likely to get better as long as the present allotment of fifteen shillings per child per year for supplies is maintained. In ordering books most headmasters do it on a basis of twenty books for a class, most classes having forty or more children in them.

A comment made by a perceptive school official in this connection was, 'Perhaps it's time we stopped looking forward for a while and began looking backward at some of the areas where schools have been unable to keep up with the nation's progress.'

THE TEACHING OF THE MOTHER TONGUES

QUALIFICATIONS OF TEACHERS

For a good many years it has been the policy in most of Kenya's primary schools for children to be taught in their own language for at least the first three years, English becoming the medium of instruction in the fourth, fifth or even sixth year. Teachers were considered qualified to teach the mother tongue by reason of being native speakers, although the teaching involved almost exclusively (in the mother tongue period) was the teaching of reading, for which many teachers had had no special training. In 1957 an all-English medium course, the New Peak Course, was introduced in a group of Nairobi schools and is now used in over 60 per cent of the country's schools. Provision was made in this course for one period a day for the first three years to be devoted to teaching the child's mother tongue, but no detailed directions on how to do it were given to the teacher, as was done for the teaching of other subjects. The teacher, having neither the training nor the materials for the teaching of reading and writing in the mother tongue, generally neglected this activity in favour of the other subjects for which he was given adequate materials and direction.

TEACHING MATERIALS AVAILABLE

In 1967 the Ministry of Education, concerned by this situation in which the teaching of the children's own languages was being virtually ignored, gave the Kenya Institute of Education the task of producing materials for the teaching of reading in the country's major languages. The result was the TKK materials, consisting of a teacher's manual, three class books and two supplementary readers for the first year of the primary school. These materials were produced in thirteen languages.

The TKK course proved effective in the schools where it was tried out by the writers from the KIE. There was, however, little opportunity for the investigators in the present survey to assess its effectiveness since only a very small number of the schools visited had received the books. Even in the schools where the materials were being used, few schools had complete sets. This resulted, in some cases, in using a book for the whole year which was designed to be used for only the first term. In other schools the first term book was being used in Standard I, the second term book in Standard II and so on. This was being done in spite of the fact that on the order form used by headmasters to order new books there was a footnote to the TKK listings which explained how many books there were in the course and at what stage each book was to be used.

From this and other observations made in schools it is apparent that there are difficulties involved in getting into the schools courses which consist of more than one book for use during a school year. Until the distribution system is better organized, there is little likelihood that complete sets will get to schools, even if properly ordered. Many headmasters, however, are unfamiliar with this kind of course, having worked in the past with one book for a class for a year, and they often fail to realize that one of a series of children's books is of little use without the others in the series. Some headmasters, having a limited amount of money to spend, deliberately choose one or two books out of a series of several. The concept of a course consisting of a teacher's book and accompanying children's books is not understood in some schools. There is a tendency to order only the children's book, regarding the teacher's book as something extra rather than an integral part of the course without which the children's book cannot be used with anything like full effectiveness. Since all of the modern language-teaching courses being produced by the KIE in English, Swahili and the mother tongues are designed in this way, the matter is a serious one. In this situation it is the responsibility of the KIE to see to it that headmasters and supervisors clearly understand the textbook requirements of these courses.

ATTITUDES TOWARDS THE MOTHER TONGUE

School personnel interviewed in the course of the survey generally agreed that the children's own language should be a part of primary education, especially in the first three years. This reflects the fact that it is used as the medium of instruction on this level in almost half of the country's schools, and that even in the English medium schools it is frequently used when the children's command of English is inadequate for the subject matter being studied. Perhaps as a legacy from the suggestions in the New Peak Course, where teachers are told to use the mother tongue period for telling stories, having children describe their homes, etc., teachers sometimes fail to realize that the purpose of a first-language class on the lower primary level is not to teach the children to speak their language, but to teach them to read and write it. This investigator's impression was that the teachers tend to take work in the mother tongue less seriously than they do that of giving the children competence in English and, to a lesser extent, in Swahili. This tendency is enhanced in many areas by the fact that there are no books available for many of the local languages.

THE TEACHING OF SWAHILI

QUALIFICATIONS OF TEACHERS

On the questionnaires returned from schools the great majority listed as the qualification of their teacher of Swahili a special interest in the language, as opposed to being a native speaker or having had specific training in Swahili teaching, either in a teacher training college or in in-service courses. Many headmasters interviewed said that there was no one on the staff really qualified to teach the language, and that therefore it was impossible to teach it well. In some schools the headmaster took the Swahili class in addition to his other duties in order to leave other teachers to handle classes they were well qualified to teach. In other schools Swahili was taught by a considerably older man who had been teaching it for a long time and whose methods had changed little over the years. In a few schools the headmaster admitted that a teacher had been assigned to teach Swahili because he could not teach anything else.

This state of affairs reflects several aspects of the position of Swahili in the primary schools. One is that there is not much interest in teaching the language in many areas. Another is that until very recently materials available and methods of teaching have lagged far behind the advances made in the teaching of other languages. A third is that there is a great difference between the 'lingua franca' kind of Swahili that is spoken in and around many schools, and the near-native, more or less literary variety that is found in the textbooks.

ATTITUDES TOWARDS SWAHILI

In the primary schools 'Swahili' seems to mean two quite different things. On one hand it has been a rather arcane subject in the curriculum, taught very largely from the point of view of reading and writing and bearing little relation to the other school subjects in terms of practical value to the children. On the other hand it is a more or less effective means of oral communication used in situations where no other language will work, the frequency of these situations varying greatly, depending on the location of the school, the language backgrounds of the children and the tribal homogeneity or lack of it among children and teachers.

Given this situation, attitudes towards the language means attitudes towards what is taught in schools during the period allotted to Swahili. The children, it appears, generally dislike it for reasons already mentioned. Teachers and headmasters are divided in their opinions, one group feeling that it is pretty much a waste of time, and also being a little afraid of it in the form in which it is supposed to be taught, the other feeling that it is important as a potentially more effective unifying factor for the people of the nation than a thoroughly foreign language like English. A change in the more negative of these attitudes may well come about if the new Swahili-teaching materials produced by the KIE come into general use.

463

The *Masomo ya Kiswahili* course for the teaching of Swahili as a second language in Standards IV through VII has recently been completed, the Standard IV materials having been available since 1968. It is a graded and sequenced series of teacher's and children's books based on modern language-teaching principles and designed to give children a practical command of oral and written Swahili. At the time of the survey the supply to schools of the course was affected by the shortcomings of the new central distribution system. Even so, it was being used in a considerable number of the schools included in the investigation. (See Appendix E.) From the point of view of proper use in schools it presents many of the same problems as the TKK materials do. For Standard IV there are two children's books, leading in some cases to the placing of the first book in Standard IV and the second in Standard V. As in the case of the TKK courses the concept of an essential teacher's book is often not well understood, especially in schools where no teacher's book arrived in response to the headmaster's order.

Teachers interviewed showed considerable enthusiasm for the course, though it was apparent that it will be some time before they are familiar enough with it to use it with maximum effectiveness. This is an area where Primary School Supervisors can play a most valuable role in the schools they are able to visit.

THE TEACHING OF ENGLISH

QUALIFICATIONS OF TEACHERS

While some teachers in Kenya's primary schools have had secondary school experience, the great majority are qualified by having had eight years of primary school and two years of teacher training college work. They were taught English as a subject starting anywhere from Standard I to Standard IV, and had English as the medium of instruction beginning in Standard IV or V. The two-year course of teacher training was divided in content between adding to what had been learned in the primary school in the various subjects, and introducing the prospective teacher to methods of teaching. As there are teachers with more than this typical background, so there are some who have finished primary school, but have not had any teacher training, and even some who have not finished primary school or who have not passed the school leaving examination.

As is to be expected under these circumstances, the level of control of

English of these teachers is often not very much higher than the level of control they are expected to impart to their pupils by the time they finish Standard VII. In the rural areas teachers have little, if any, opportunity for improving their command of English or, indeed, for maintaining it at the level they attained by the time they finished their training. Most of them do speak English with their fellow teachers during school hours, at least part of the time, but since they are all pretty much on the same level of competence this is not likely to lead to improvement. On the contrary there is, in this situation, the usual tendency for mistakes they make in the language to be accepted by their co-workers, and even for these mistakes to be reinforced and perpetuated within the group of teachers. Reading materials in English are not easily available in these areas, and even if they were it is not likely that teachers would have the time, energy or inclination to do much reading in the evening after a full day at school and often several hours' work in the family garden as well.

In urban areas the situation is usually much better. Here teachers often have contact with English speakers other than those on the school staff, reading materials are easier to obtain and there are more occasions when English is the only common language between them and the people they are speaking to than is the case in the rural areas. Schools in towns and cities are often better off financially than those in the country, have a higher proportion of teachers with more than the minimum amount of training and, being more easily accessible, have benefits of supervision and in-service training courses often denied to their counterparts in more remote areas.

TEACHING MATERIALS AVAILABLE

Since English, beside being taught as a subject in the primary schools, at some point becomes the medium of instruction and the means whereby the children learn in all the other subjects in the curriculum, the importance of good English teaching can hardly be overemphasized. The Ministry of Education is well aware of this and for many years has done what it could to provide primary teachers with course books in English which, it was hoped, would help to make up for the inadequate training in English and English teaching given to most teachers. There is a wide variety of these books in use in Kenya's schools today, ranging from outdated and inappropriate children's readers to an up-to-date course written especially for Kenyan children and teachers.

In the course of this survey it became apparent that any set of books for the teaching of English must include as a basic component, a teacher's guide, not only to help the teacher in applying effective methods of teaching the language, but also to supply some of the background knowledge of English that the teacher never had the opportunity to acquire and which, for most of the forty thousand teachers in the country's primary schools, cannot be provided for by supervision or by in-service courses.

To this end a number of English courses have been introduced into the schools, some of them incorporating teacher's notes or a teacher's manual, but few of them are more than minimally effective in the local situation. The same shortcomings are common to all of them. They assume a familiarity with the culture of English-speaking countries which Kenyan children do not have; the level of English and the rate at which it is introduced are both too high and, perhaps most important, they assume a command of English and a knowledge of English-teaching methodology on the part of the teacher which he does not possess. Four years' work with the teachers of Kenya have convinced this investigator that it is not enough, for example, to give a teacher one or two sample sentences to be used with pupils in a given lesson and then to tell the teacher to go on making up similar sentences for the rest of the lesson.

Two courses written expressly for Kenyan schools and now being used in many parts of the country are the New Peak Course for Standards I through III and the Safari English Course for the upper primary level. At the time of the survey only the Standard IV Safari materials were in use in schools, the Standard V books having just recently been produced, and the Standards VI and VII materials still being written.

When the New Peak Course was written it was introduced into a number of Nairobi schools and the teachers of the classes where it was being used were brought in to the Special Centre, a section of the Ministry of Education, to be given daily briefings on how to use the teacher's notes to present the next day's lesson. The course proved to be far more effective than any previously used and its use was extended in the following years until, by the time of this survey, it was being used in more than half of Kenya's primary schools. (See Appendix F.) Teachers interviewed said the course was better than any other they had used, but many felt that the teacher's notes were too brief and too general and did not give them enough help, especially in the third year. Apparently the kind of notes which were effective when accompanied by briefing of the teachers on their use were not sufficiently detailed for use by teachers who were not given the benefit of such explanations.

With this in mind the writers of the Safari English Course, which was designed to follow the New Peak Course in Standard IV, attempted to remedy the defect by including a great deal of detail in the teacher's notes, telling him what to do throughout each period and providing him with the actual language he was expected to teach, lesson by lesson. They felt that since the New Peak Course worked better when teachers had frequent briefings on the use of the notes, this approach would make the course more or less self-explanatory and would thereby cater for the teachers who would not have the chance to attend in-service courses on the new material.

Conversations with teachers and observation of classes where the Safari Course was being used indicated that this hope was being only partly realized. Teachers, while they agreed that the course was superior to others they had used, found that the notes still did not give them the help they felt they needed. In the opinion of this observer this was at least partly due to the teachers' misinterpretation of the notes, and to their being unfamiliar with this kind of detailed guidance. It was also certainly caused in some cases by failure of teachers to read the notes carefully or, indeed, to read them at all. This is, however, part of the problem and no easy solution seems possible.

One frequently offered suggestion from teachers and headmasters was to give more help to teachers from supervisors than they are now getting. Another was to provide in-service courses to more teachers than now have access to them. The team of Primary School Supervisors may well be able to help significantly in the first connection, but it is doubtful whether an appreciable proportion of the country's teachers can be given in-service courses on the scale that seems necessary. The answer would seem to be in raising the minimum level of training of primary school teachers—something that the Ministry of Education realizes and has plans for doing as soon as it is possible.

This observer feels that now that suitable English-teaching materials are available, teacher training colleges could do much more than most of them are doing at present to prepare student teachers to make the best use of these materials.

ACHIEVEMENT OF PUPILS IN ENGLISH

While systematic testing of pupils' proficiency in English was beyond the scope of this survey, conversations were held with children in most schools visited. This usually took place in one of the upper primary classes, Standards IV through VII, and consisted of the investigator's first asking questions of the class and then getting them to ask him questions. Most children spoken to were able to understand reasonably well. The observer's questions were of the order of, 'Who lives nearest to the school?', 'Who lives farthest away?', 'How do you come to school?', 'How long does it take to get to school from your house?'

467

The children's questions were usually personal: 'Where do you come from?', 'How old are you?', and sometimes quite unexpected: 'What is your mother's name?' Many children were shy, especially in the presence of an obvious foreigner, but those who did talk seemed animated and at ease. The student investigators reported that children were tense and unresponsive when spoken to in English, but responded well when spoken to in their own language.

In trying out materials over a period of four years in Kenya's primary schools, the staff of the Language Section of the KIE observed that there was a serious problem of children who had not learned to read in English by the time they had got to Standard IV. In many classes visited such children constituted as much as a quarter of the class. Teachers questioned about this during the survey said that the situation existed in many of their classes. A number of teachers attributed it to the oral emphasis of the New Peak Course, saying that their Standard IV pupils handled spoken English better than those who had used other courses, but that their ability to read and write was not as good as that of the children who had preceded them.

ATTITUDES TOWARDS ENGLISH

There was general agreement among teachers that English was an important and valuable part of the primary school curriculum, though opinions varied on the merits of its use as medium of instruction. They all thought it should be the medium in the upper primary classes, but many objected to the practice of requiring children to use a foreign language from the beginning of their school experience, pointing out that they had a hard enough time adjusting to school life without having to struggle with a new language in addition.

There is a strong tradition in most schools of emphasizing the learning of English in preparation for the school-leaving examination. Since this examination, besides being in English, is wholly written, this emphasis often takes the form of concentration on vocabulary building and on a form of rather literary language, to the neglect of control of the spoken form of English.

It is an almost universal practice in schools for the headmaster to assign his better trained and more capable teachers to the beginning standards and to Standards VI and VII, leaving the middle of the school, Standards III through V, to the less able ones. They feel that it takes a good teacher to handle the English medium course in the lower standards, and an equally good one to prepare children for the all-important school-leaving examination.

468

LANGUAGE USE IN SCHOOLS

LANGUAGE BACKGROUNDS OF CHILDREN AND TEACHERS

In the three-language situation existing in primary schools the way they are used outside of the classroom depends very much on the first languages of the children and their teachers. In schools where there is one first language common to everyone it is the language most often heard in the schoolyard among children, and is used extensively by teachers. In this sort of environment teachers speak to lower primary children in their own language, even in schools where English is the medium of instruction from Standard I. In an effort to improve the English of children in the upper standards, teachers usually speak to them in that language, expecting, though often not getting, responses in English. Among themselves teachers speak both their own language and English, depending partly on what they are talking about. School matters are usually discussed in English, but if teachers are talking about almost anything else, they tend to use their own language. This is probably because their knowledge of schools and school activities was acquired in English in the teacher training colleges and because English is regarded as the official language of the school. This was given by headmasters as the reason why staff meetings are conducted in English, as they invariably seem to be. Minutes of these meetings are always written in English as are most posted notices in the schools and written communications among members of the staff.

Swahili in such schools is very seldom spoken, although most teachers have a reasonably good command of it, and the older pupils can at least understand it on a fairly elementary level. The reason is a practical one. With a local language and a second language in which teachers feel pretty much at home, there is little point in using a far less effective means of communication. Teachers in this sort of situation said that the only occasion they have to speak Swahili is in shops run by Asians or by Africans from another linguistic area who have not learned the local language. The same thing applies to those pupils who have learned enough Swahili, often in places other than the Swahili classroom where the emphasis is usually on reading a rather literary variety of the language or on exercises like changing nouns from the singular to the plural.

The linguistically homogeneous schools just described are usually located in rural areas some distance from the nearest town. Township and city schools and those located near an urban centre usually have pupils with different language backgrounds. Teachers in these schools also often come from different parts of the country and do not share the same first language, or the language of some of their pupils.

469

In these schools Swahili is an important and viable means of communication, more so in most cases than English, certainly among the children. Practical competence in Swahili was observed in such schools among lower primary children who had never studied Swahili formally. Apparently children going to school in a language area other than the one they were born in have learned Swahili in travelling around the country with their parents as they are assigned to different linguistic areas. An interesting case was observed in Isiolo where a Standard I Kikuyu child, the son of a police officer, was found to speak fluent Swahili at the age of seven.

In several areas visited there was a community of native speakers of Swahili whose children attended some of the township schools. As might be expected there was a wide and effective use of Swahili in these schools, having little to do with what went on in the Swahili classroom.

While Swahili and to a lesser extent English serve as lingua francas in these linguistically mixed schools, local languages are also very much used in the area of the school. In one school located in a large town the following was observed in the school playground. 1. A group of African boys representing different language backgrounds, playing football and speaking in Swahili. 2. A group of Asian girls sitting on the grass and speaking Gujarati. 3. A group of African girls speaking Kiembu. (See Appendix D.)

ATTITUDES TOWARDS LANGUAGES

In all schools visited there was a policy, in theory at least, of encouraging the use of English in the school grounds. In most schools this took the form of a system of monitoring the language of children and of imposing penalties for speaking a language other than English. When a child is heard speaking his own language during school hours he is given an object, usually a coin, which he must carry around until he hears some other child committing the same 'offence' when he gives the object to him. The child in possession of it at the end of the day has to perform some task before going home. Schools varied considerably as to whether children were penalized for speaking any language other than English, or whether Swahili was permitted in areas where it is not the local language. Some headmasters said that the system was effective, others that it was not, and some were against the whole idea, saying that it tended to discourage the social development of children who were not permitted to express themselves naturally.

Before Kenya became independent there were primary schools, usually located in big towns and cities, whose pupils were all European, or European and Asian. In these schools with their large proportion of native speakers of English, the language was the medium of instruction throughout the school and the only language spoken outside the classroom. Although the majority of pupils in these schools are now Africans with a smaller number of Asians and, in most cases, no children whose first language is English, the standard of English in the school is generally high and it is the only language used, except in the Swahili and mother tongue classes. That this is true even though everyone in the school is usually competent in Swahili, seems to be due to a definite policy on the part of the school's administrators who in turn are under pressure from parents to equip the children with the best possible command of English.

APPENDIX A

Questionnaire for Headmasters—Language Teaching in Primary Schools

Kenya Institute of Education,
P.O. Box 30231,
Nairobi.
29th October, 1968.

Name of school...

Address:..

How far is your school from
the nearest Post Office?...

How many miles is it to the
next primary school to yours?...

1. How many standards are there in your school?   ....

   How many streams in each standard?   Std 1: ....

   Std 2: ....

   Std 3: ....

   Std 4: ....

   Std 5: ....

   Std 6: ....

   Std 7: ....

2. How many children are there in each stream of: Std 1: ....

   Std 2: ....

   Std 3: ....

   Std 4: ....

   Std 5: ....

   Std 6: ....

   Std 7: ....

472

3. Please list the qualifications for the teacher(s)
in each standard (Unqualified;P–4; P–3; P–2;
P–1; S–1; Graduate)

Std 1: ....

Std 2: ....

Std 3: ....

Std 4: ....

Std 5: ....

Std 6: ....

Std 7: ....

4. Have any of your teachers been on in-service
courses this year?

....

If so, how many and from what standards?

....

5. If your school had a Standard 7 last year, how
many children took K.P.E.?

....

How many passed?

....

6. Please check below the statement that most
accurately describes the language background
of your Std. 1 and Std. 5 classes (or Std. 1
and Std. 4 if you haven't got Std. 5)

(a) Teachers and children all speak the same
mother-tongue

....

If so, what language is it?

....

(b) The children all speak the same mother-
tongue, and the teacher speaks another

....

What is the teacher's language?

....

What is the children's language?

....

(c) The teacher speaks the same mother-tongue
as some of the children, but other children
speak some other mother-tongue

....

What is the teacher's language?

....

What are the children's languages?

....

473

7. In your school, what languages are used:

   (a) As the medium of instruction in

Std 1: ....

Std 2: ....

Std 3: ....

Std 4: ....

Std 5: ....

Std 6: ....

Std 7: ....

   (b) Between you and the teachers: ....

   (c) Outside of class between you and the children   ....

   (d) Outside of classes among the children   ....

8. In what standards are the following languages taught as subjects?

   (a) Mother-tongue
   (b) Swahili
   (c) English

Std 1: ....

Std 2: ....

Std 3: ....

Std 4: ....

Std 5: ....

(List more than one language per standard
if more than one is taught.)   Std 6: ....

Std 7: ....

9. (i) How many of your teachers of Swahili
     are qualified by:

   (a) Being a native speaker of Swahili   ....

   (b) Specific training in a T.T.C.   ....

   (c) In-service training   ....

   (d) Special interest in teaching Swahili   ....

474

9. (*cont.*)

    (ii) How many of your teachers are not
qualified to teach Swahili? . . . .

    (iii) How many of your teachers have received
special training in teaching their mother-
tongue? . . . .

10. About what proportion of books to children do
you have in your school?

    (a) One book for each child (1 to 1)
    (b) One book for every two children (1 to 2)
    (c) One book for every three children (1 to 3)
    (d) One book for every four children or more (1 to 4)
        Please indicate: for Swahili . . . .

                   for English . . . .

11. How many of your children can read in
their mother-tongue?   In: Std 1: . . . .

                                    Std 2: . . . .

                                    Std 3: . . . .

How many can read in Swahili?   In: Std 1: . . . .

                                    Std 2: . . . .

                                    Std 3: . . . .

                                    Std 4: . . . .

                                    Std 5: . . . .

How many can read in English?   In: Std 1: . . . .

                                    Std 2: . . . .

                                    Std 3: . . . .

                                    Std 4: . . . .

                                    Std 5: . . . .

12. Are your classes using the New
Peak Course?   In: Std 1: . . . .

                                    Std 2: . . . .

                                    Std 3: . . . .

13. If you answered "no" to question 12, what books are your classes using for teaching English in

Std 1: ....

Std 2: ....

Std 3: ....

14. Are you using Masomo ya Kiswahili?

....

If so, in what standard?

....

15. Is Standard 4 using the Safari English Course?

....

16. If you answered "no" to question 15, what English course are you using?

....

APPENDIX B

Kenya Preliminary Examination—1967

Province	Coast	Eastern	Rift Valley	Central	Nairobi Area	Western	Nyanza
Number of schools	99	102	145	98	8	20	50
Number of pupils who took exam.	2,316	2,377	3,706	4,079	426	633	1,426
Number of pupils who passed	716	1,335	2,551	2,938	309	478	950
% of pupils who passed	30.5	56.5	67	72.5	71	74.5	64

APPENDIX C

Language Backgrounds in Standards I and V

Province	Coast	Eastern	Rift Valley	Central	Nairobi Area	Western	Nyanza
Total number of schools	99	102	145	98	8	20	50
Number of schools where the children and teachers all speak same mother tongue	62	83	75	86	7	20	42
Number of schools where children all speak same mother tongue and teacher speaks another	15	6	14	0	1	0	3
Number of schools where teachers speak same mother tongue as some children, but other children speak a different mother tongue	22	13	56	12	0	0	5

APPENDIX D

Languages Used in Schools Outside the Classroom

Province	Coast	Eastern	Rift Valley	Central	Nairobi Area	Western	Nyanza
Number of schools	99	102	145	98	8	20	50
Between headmaster and teachers							
Mother tongue	3	37	28	28	4	7	26
Swahili	42	13	23	7	0	0	3
English	98	93	140	81	7	17	36
Between headmaster and children							
Mother tongue	9	57	59	56	3	11	24
Swahili	53	14	43	11	1	3	3
English	85	70	117	68	5	20	48
Among the children							
Mother tongue	41	80	68	67	6	15	38
Swahili	53	46	53	13	1	0	5
English	59	15	97	55	3	15	29

APPENDIX E

Approximate Ratio of School Books to Children

Province	Coast	Eastern	Rift Valley	Central	Nairobi Area	Western	Nyanza
Number of schools	99	102	145	98	8	20	50
Number of schools with one book for a child:							
English	20	28	16	17	1	3	8
Swahili	17	16	13	9	0	0	6
Number of schools with one book for 2 children:							
English	51	43	39	50	3	6	16
Swahili	33	33	42	38	5	3	5
Number of schools with one book for 3 children:							
English	15	20	49	15	2	8	6
Swahili	22	27	34	29	1	8	4
Number of schools with one book for 4 or more children:							
English	10	10	11	15	2	3	17
Swahili	23	25	24	19	2	9	13

APPENDIX F

Language Courses in Use in Schools

Province	Coast	Eastern	Rift Valley	Central	Nairobi Area	Western	Nyanza
Number of schools	99	102	145	98	8	20	50
Number of schools using the New Peak Course (NPA) in:							
Standard I	82	84	90	84	6	16	37
Standard II	78	79	79	84	6	16	34
Standard III	67	71	68	84	5	16	32
Number of schools using the *Masomo ya Kiswahili* Course	44	61	87	58	5	17	26
Number of schools using the Safari English Course	43	46	74	74	3	10	21

16

The Teaching of Languages at Secondary Level: Some Significant Problems

T. P. GORMAN

INTRODUCTION

I would like initially to indicate the scope of this chapter and to specify more clearly the implications of the general title.

After consideration, I came to the conclusion that while many experienced and informed educationists in Kenya were concerned with, and well qualified to expound, the various problems that were encountered by teachers and learners of English and Swahili at secondary level and to prescribe, in part, 'remedies' for these diverse problems, there were two areas of inquiry where further elucidation of the difficulties encountered would be of some value. These concerned the nature of the problems encountered by students and teachers at the transitional stages of the educational system, i.e. from primary to secondary level and from secondary to university level.

I have written elsewhere that 'there is an element of discontinuity between the three stages of education in the formal educational system, in the sense that those making the transition are at each stage confronted by radical changes in teaching methods, and asked to perform different learning tasks, which in turn require the exercise of new language and study skills', and that 'the discontinuity is accentuated in countries in which the secondary and tertiary level are staffed by teachers who have not themselves passed through the system and who are not normally acquainted with curricula at other levels'.[1]

One of the consequences of the unprecedented expansion of the educational system in Kenya since independence has been that far greater numbers of children are being given the opportunity to gain secondary education than was previously the case. Similarly, larger numbers of

481

students after completing their secondary schooling are able to gain access to a university education.

One consequence of these developments to which attention was drawn in a ministry circular in 1965 is that 'present and future secondary expansion means that teachers have to cope with a considerable and increasing amount of low language ability' in the pupils entering secondary schools.[2]

In the instructions issued by the relevant authorities in the Ministry of Education, teachers are naturally exhorted and instructed to use such methods and materials as are appropriate to the levels of attainment of the pupils entering secondary schools. The circular quoted above, for example, makes the point that for 'extensive' reading in English, 'texts will be graded in Forms 1 and 2 and normal English thereafter . . . In Forms 1 and 2 the aim is one book a week each book ideally just beneath the pupils' language attainment at that time . . . '. Similarly in a circular on the teaching of Swahili in secondary schools, the point was made that 'when drawing up a scheme of work teachers will have to take into consideration the standard of Swahili reached by the pupils admitted to Form 1'.[3]

In the circumstances it seemed to me that it would be both feasible and practical to gather information about what might be loosely termed the levels of attainment of pupils entering secondary schools in both English and Swahili in different modes, and a research project was organized to this end.

The information was gathered in two stages. In the first place, to provide background information for the inquiry, and because the judgements and attitudes of the teachers in a school system provide more valuable information about the problems to be faced than any other source of information however expert, teachers of English and Swahili in the schools involved in the survey completed a schedule in 1968 and 1970, in which they gave their personal assessment of their pupils' approximate levels of attainment in the two languages.[4] In addition, they provided information about the course books used in teaching, about any restrictions that were placed on language use in schools and about specific problems they were faced with in teaching particular classes. In 1970, teachers were additionally asked to say whether they were acquainted with the language courses given in primary schools.[5] Over the same period relevant information about the situation in the primary school was assembled.

Secondly, a considerable number of tests of different kinds were constructed to measure aspects of the language attainment of a sample of the children who entered school in 1970. Some of the results of these tests will be indicated in the second part of this chapter.

In reporting the teachers' responses it has been thought relevant in some cases to indicate generally the source of a particular observation by indicating whether the school is in an urban or rural area, the language group predominant in the school concerned in the rural schools, and the sex of the pupils. No other details of the schools are given. The following codes are used to signify these factors:

Geographical setting		Sex of pupils		Language groups			
Nairobi	N	Male	M	Kikuyu	1	Meru	5
Mombasa	M	Female	F	Luo	2	Mijikenda	6
Rural	R			Luyia	3	Gusii	7
				Kamba	4	Kalenjin	8
				Mixed language group 0			

The symbols (R.M.4) therefore indicate that the school concerned is in the rural sample, that the pupils are boys, and that they are predominantly speakers of Kamba.

THE TEACHERS' RESPONSES: A. TEACHERS OF SWAHILI

The Pupils

The primary problem and the one mentioned most frequently by the teachers, concerned the range in the levels of attainment in Swahili of pupils in the same class. The observation was made by numerous teachers both in schools in which the majority of the children spoke Bantu languages, and in schools where speakers of non-Bantu languages predominated; it was made also by teachers in the major towns. For example, teachers in five schools in or near Mombasa, the focal point of the Swahili-speaking area in Kenya, drew attention to it; one teacher, for instance, reported that 'six know the language well, ten a little, and the rest none' (M.F.0). The problem of variation in language attainment is not, therefore, one that is restricted to any particular geographical area or linguistic group.

Several teachers attempted to categorize the levels of proficiency they noted. One made a triple distinction between the proficiency of the children from the coast, from the towns and from the rural areas (N.F.0); a second teacher added a further category, viz. that between Bantu and non-Bantu language speakers (N.M.0). A summary of the situation was given by a teacher at a boys' school in Mombasa to the effect that 'some boys have no background at all. Others are conversant with "pidgin" Swahili of their own tribal or racial background and others speak Swahili as their mother tongue. Some have had no teaching in Primary Schools, others have had some Swahili taught' (M.M.0).

The teachers attempted in a number of cases to itemize the reasons for the variation in attainment of the pupils and these explanations indicated in some cases a second set of difficulties which they faced.

A relatively small number of teachers gave as a reason the fact that the children did not use the language outside school, e.g. 'My major problem in the Northern Division of Meru is teaching a language that is not spoken by the people around' (R.F.5), or again, a teacher in a Kamba-speaking area wrote: 'I have great problems with the teaching of Swahili in this area as it is quite foreign to most of the people and pupils' (R.F.4).

A comment from a teacher in Kitui to the effect that 'almost all the pupils in Form 1 are just beginning to learn Swahili' (R.F.4.) is a further indication that from the point of view of certain teachers the previous exposure to Swahili which the majority of the children claim is not adequate to provide a suitable basis for intermediate level instruction.[6]

In attributing causes for the differences in proficiency, however, most teachers who mentioned the issue stated that the children were not trained effectively at primary school level. It might be relevant to mention at this stage that in 1970 only three teachers were able to reply in the affirmative to a question in which they were asked to indicate whether they had had the opportunity to look at the *Masomo ya Kiswahili* course, which is the recommended course for pupils in the higher standards in the primary schools; and one who so replied was using the second book of the course as the class text.

Other problems that a number of teachers drew attention to concerned what might be termed the negative attitudes of certain of the students to the subject: 'Some of them do not love Swahili at all' (M.F.0). 'A lack of interest' was mentioned by teachers in a number of different region (e.g. R.F.2; R.M.8; N.F.0). One teacher who remarked upon the facts that 'the subject was not taken seriously' in the schools (N.M.0), implied that this 'lack of seriousness' was not simply confined to the pupils. Three teachers drew attention to the fact that outside class the students were discouraged from using any language other than English, and implied that this was a reflection upon the status of Swahili. (As will be indicated later the majority of schools in the sample imposed some form of control on the language use of the students in school hours.)

Several teachers attempted to give reasons for the different attitudes of pupils to the subject and a number of the related factors were summed up by one teacher as follows: 'Their former primary schools' standard in the subject, their own environment, and the language used at home play a great part in making them approach the subject with interest and enthusiasm' (M.M.0).

One reason given by teachers in two schools (R.M.3; R.M.2), however, regarding the attitudes of the pupils, indicated a third problem area. In the first school mentioned, the teacher explained that the pupils argued that 'even old women when they go to town learn Swahili, though the grammar may be bad . . . '

It is of course the case that in most parts of the country a form of Swahili can be acquired outside the educational system and clearly some students feel that the knowledge of the language so acquired is sufficient for their purposes. This argument is one that is encountered frequently, but needless to say it does not commend itself to educators for a number of reasons, some of which will be considered later.

From the point of view of most of the teachers who mentioned the issue, however, the problem related to usage acquired outside the classroom was not that such attainment lessened the pupils' desire to learn 'Standard' Swahili, but that it *interfered* with their performance in the standard dialect. Three main areas of interference were commented upon. The first I have already mentioned, viz. interference from dialects acquired outside school. More teachers remarked upon a second source of interference, however, which derived from the influence of a related Bantu language on Swahili (e.g. R.M.1, R.F.4, R.M.5). In schools in the coastal areas teachers referred to the interference from dialects of Swahili spoken as first languages. According to the teachers such interference manifested itself most evidently in the written mode. Two teachers in schools in Coast Province remarked that in consequence the children could speak the language well but could not write it with proficiency. Relative lack of proficiency in writing was also remarked upon by teachers in two schools in Nairobi.

The Syllabus or Scheme of Work

The majority of teachers who referred to this matter mentioned the 'lack of suitable syllabus or scheme of work' (e.g. M.F.0; N.F.0; R.M.8). A number asserted that there was no syllabus. However, two of the teachers who appeared to have taken part in the Swahili teachers' workshop held at the Kenya Institute of Education in 1968 considered that the scheme of work elaborated at that meeting provided an adequate guide for capable teachers. Others felt, however, that the selection and grading of items of the scheme of work were not appropriate for their purposes (R.M.1; N.F.0). It was suggested that what was required was a syllabus covering four years' work to School Certificate level, and two years' work to the Kenya Junior Secondary Examination (R.M.3; R.F.1). The fact that there was little uniformity in the courses given in different schools was also remarked upon (M.M.0).

Course Books

The demand for a suitable course book 'with grammar and comprehension exercises, like the course books for English', together with 'a teacher's book which explains vocabulary and idioms' was widely recognized.

Teachers remarked upon the lack of wide variety of books from which to choose and upon the unavailability of graded texts (R.F.1; M.M.0; N.M.0). A number of teachers made it clear that they were aware that the materials available did not lend themselves to the use of modern methods of language teaching. 'Neither the content nor the style of the books available reflect modern approaches to language study' (R.M.8).[7]

Teachers in different areas saw the problems in a different light. While several teachers pointed out that 'suitable books were not available for up country children' (R.M.8; R.M.2), one teacher from Mombasa wrote that 'the problem of the supply of appropriate books does not arise at this level' and that 'the book list given in the outline of the scheme of work is comprehensive and suitable'. These statements are not necessarily contradictory. Texts that would be appropriate for use with children who use Swahili habitually, as would be the case with many of the children in schools in Mombasa, would be wholly inappropriate for the use of children in a number of other areas.

An indication of this is given in the comments of two teachers regarding one of the texts recommended in the scheme of work for Form 1. While making the point that simpler course books are required for children who have not done Swahili in primary school, a teacher in a school in Nyanza Province pointed out that the book in question, *Hekaya za Abunuwas* was 'too difficult for *Form 3*' and wholly inappropriate for Form 1 (R.F.2). The same book was referred to by a teacher from Coast Province who commented to precisely the opposite effect, in saying that the book was too simple for Form 1 (R.M.6).

It became clear that it was not only the variation in proficiency but also the difference in the pre-school experience of the students that made it occasionally difficult to select texts appropriate to all students. In connection with the content of the School Certificate examination, a teacher from a school in which the pupils were Kalenjin speakers pointed out that the comprehension and essay questions were frequently too difficult for his students and often concerned the history of the coast and included 'strange ideas puzzling to most up country students' (R.M.8).

All the texts listed as being in common use were among those recommended for Form 1 teachers and pupils in the experimental scheme of work, issued by the members of the Kenya Institute of Education after the Swahili workshop that was held in 1968.[8]

It is perhaps relevant to observe that the majority of the readers mentioned are, however, also recommended for use in the primary syllabus as group readers or class library books for speakers of Swahili as a mother tongue, as is the *Tusome Kiswahili* series (in Primary IV–VII).[9] In two cases, also, the readers (B2, B6) are recommended for use as readers in the primary syllabus designed for children learning Swahili as a second language, who would also have been using in Primary VI and VII the *Tusome Kiswahili* series Books 1 and 2, which is the text prescribed until the *Masomo ya Kiswahili* series is available for the four-year course.[10]

There is a likelihood therefore that in 1968 many pupils who had studied Swahili at primary school level would have already studied the texts and readers used in the first year of secondary schooling. This could lead in some cases to a relative disinterest on their part in the subject.

The teachers were asked to say in what respect if any their teaching in Form 1 was affected by the nature of the school examinations that were set. The majority of those who answered remarked upon the undesirability of the emphasis on translation in the examinations and particularly of the questions that required the student to translate from Swahili into English.[11] It was pointed out that this emphasis does not encourage direct method teaching (R.F.5). Some teachers felt that it would be preferable if the examination was based upon the comprehension of a series of set texts, as this would make preparation for the examination easier (R.M.3).

Teachers

Three teachers noted that one aspect of the problem concerned the lack of suitably trained teachers of the subject. This was also the reason given most frequently by headteachers of schools who did not teach Swahili as a subject but who replied to inquiries.

Teachers' Suggestions

It might be relevant finally to itemize certain of the suggestions made by the teachers in the form of proposals for the solution of certain of the problems considered.

Some were in favour of making Swahili a compulsory subject in the Certificate of Primary Education (R.F.2; N.M.0; N.F.0), and two felt that it should be a compulsory subject at secondary school level (R.F.2; R.M.3). Several teachers remarked that students would take more interest in the subject if a knowledge of the language afforded employment prospects in addition to those offered by the press and radio services. As has been stated, many teachers thought that their major problems could be solved by an improvement in the level of teaching in primary schools, but a number of teachers considered that the problem had to be faced within the secondary school system, and that improved methods of language teaching should be employed (R.F.1) together with suitable textbooks (R.F.4).

Certain of the implications of the teachers' commentaries will be considered subsequently.

Pupils

As was the case with Swahili, the primary problem that faced the teachers, if the assessment of the majority who replied to the inquiry can be taken as an accurate indication of the situation, is the fact that on entry to secondary school, the students' level of attainment in the language varies considerably. One teacher contrasted the proficiency of the children who had been in primary schools in a large town with that of the pupils from the county council schools 'who can neither understand spoken English properly nor read nor write with any sense of the language'[12] (M.F.0). Another teacher, also from a Mombasa school, remarked that the level of the proficiency 'differs to such an extent that it is difficult to set common work'.

As was the case with the teachers of Swahili, those teachers who attempted to assign causes for what they considered to be the variation in proficiency, tended to assign responsibility to the effectiveness or otherwise of teaching in the primary schools. However, various reasons were advanced. The nature of the examinations taken at the end of primary school, which, it was considered, affected the form of training given to primary school pupils was a matter on which a number of teachers remarked, e.g. 'It is my observation that primary pupils are trained to do tick-tests only. They cannot write a sentence, use capital letters or punctuation, or write any kind of connected composition' (R.F.7). Several teachers remarked that some pupils who passed the CPE were not all of 'CPE standard', whatever that might be taken to imply.

As has been mentioned, in 1968 the teachers were asked to ascertain whether teachers of specified subjects other than English considered that the proficiency of the students in different modes (speaking, reading, writing and understanding speech) was generally adequate for study of the subject they taught. The majority of the teachers approached, confirmed that the level of proficiency of the students was adequate for an understanding of the subjects they taught, although this affirmation was qualified in many cases. The majority of the teachers who stated that comprehension was limited or inadequate were teachers of 'science' subjects and in particular of physics, biology, and mathematics. A number of teachers referred to the difficulty students had in understanding the textbooks in these subjects, and their 'technical terms' (N.F.0) and the 'concepts that cannot be explained in simple English' (R.M.8) that were associated with these areas of study.

Proficiency in Different Modes

As I have indicated a considerable number of teachers made a distinction between the children's proficiency in different modes. Of those who made such a distinction by far the most frequent complaint or observation concerned the fact that the main difficulties of the children arose in connection with their written work and somewhat less frequently in their 'reading'. This fairly prevalent attitude was summarized by a teacher as follows: 'In general, proficiency at understanding of oral lessons is adequate but the ability to write their own work is quite inadequate' (M.F.0).

Four teachers made comments to the effect that 'many pupils were unable to write simple sentences when they first came into secondary school' (N.M.0). Relatively few teachers felt that they themselves were not adequately understood, but, as has been stated, a considerable number considered that the children's ability to write, read and to speak was inadequate for their instructional purposes, in that order of inadequacy.

Pupils' Attitudes

There were no generalized complaints about the attitudes of the children towards the subject. It is perhaps worth repeating at this stage that teachers in almost 80 per cent of the schools in the 1968 sample indicated that students were required to use English in a school setting. Two schools in the sample required the pupils to use Swahili (R.M.2; R.F.4), and one allowed them to use English or Swahili (R.F.1). The extent of this prescription is very considerable but its general effect was summed up by one teacher as follows: 'We have tried unsuccessfully to make the use of English compulsory during schooltime. I know of no instance where the compulsion has succeeded' (R.M.8). Only six schools admitted to using a language other than English in extra-curricular activities.

Syllabus

Very few teachers had any remarks to make about the syllabus, though some thought that more guidance might be given. In general, however, teachers seemed to consider the content appropriate and the guidance given adequate.

Course Books

Despite the relatively large number of course books available there was general agreement that no single course book was wholly suitable for use in Form 1.[13]

The most widely used course book was criticized by teachers on a number of grounds, the most frequent one being that the prose passages were not selected from contemporary writers. The second most frequently used was criticized sometimes rather vehemently for a relative lack of organization and because of what was termed its 'arid' section on grammatical structure. A number of general complaints about the available materials were summed up by one teacher as follows: 'We need simple books with an African setting. Simplified English classics are not satisfactory. Readers should be mature in content and easy to read. All of the "Grammar Usage" books are poor; either too mechanical and dull, or too complicated.' (The situation as regards the use of course books seemed to be relatively unchanged in 1970, with the exception that A.5 appeared to have become somewhat more widely used.)

Teachers

A number of teachers gave a clear indication of their lack of sympathy to what was termed the 'structural approach' to teaching. Several felt also that the necessary emphasis on what they considered to be the more 'mechanical' aspects of language use was a regrettable exigency. 'Lack of poetry', wrote one respondent, 'is disadvantageous since any language is best appreciated and understood from its poetry' (N.M.0). Seventy-six per cent of those teachers who completed the schedule indicated that they expected the children eventually to take the literature examination at School Certificate level, although one teacher remarked that the children would not take the subject 'since they do not do literature in the real sense, but learn five set books' (R.M.5). It is evident from the comments of a number of teachers that they found the task of teaching language to first year pupils exacting and less interesting than that of teaching 'literature' to more advanced forms. This is perhaps to be expected, but it is indicative also of the fact that relatively few teachers of English have been trained in techniques of second language teaching.

ASPECTS OF LANGUAGE USE AND LANGUAGE TEACHING IN PRIMARY SCHOOLS

Introduction

Certain of the patterns of language use that appeared to be characteristic of students entering secondary schools were clearly established during their attendance at primary school. Similarly, their levels of attainment in English and Swahili were determined in some degree by the teaching

490

they had undergone at primary level. It therefore seemed necessary to gather such information as could be obtained about the teaching of languages in primary schools in Kenya as an undertaking ancillary to the main inquiry. Access to such information was facilitated by colleagues at the Kenya Institute of Education who readily made much primary data available for analysis and this was supplemented by such investigation as I could carry out in the time available.

An indication of the extent to which English, Swahili and the mother tongue were used as media of instruction either singly or in combination in different parts of the country in 1968/9 is given on the map showing the school samples, at the end of the book, and in Tables 13.1 and 13.2. The information given is based on a re-analysis of the questionnaires drawn up by Mr Hemphill which were returned from 44 districts and municipalities in 1968-9; and of 474 questionnaires drawn up by Mr Cahill returned from schools in 39 districts in 1967. The information was supplemented by visits I made to schools in 1969 and 1970 and by information gathered by Mr Hemphill and six university students in 1969, which Mr Hemphill kindly made available to me for analysis.

I have found it convenient to distinguish between what I have termed Eastern Province A and B and Rift Valley Province A and B. Schools in Eastern Province B (Isiolo and Marsabit) and Rift Valley A (Elgeyo-Marakwet/West Pokot, Laikipia, Trans-Nzoia, Uasin Gishu and Nakuru) tend to be taught by teachers and attended by children drawn from different language groups. In the majority of schools in the other areas the children have a language in common.

The survey did not provide information about Samburu and Turkana districts in Rift Valley Province and Garissa, Wajir and Mandera districts but I obtained information about the situation in these areas with the co-operation of officers in the provincial headquarters. There are relatively few schools in these areas. (In 1968 there were less than 30 free primary schools in the five districts.) In the majority of schools teachers from outside the particular linguistic area are to be found and in many cases such teachers made use of both Swahili and English in instruction, the former generally predominating at lower primary level and the latter at upper primary level.

In considering the use of various media of instruction it is possible to distinguish seven permutations, as it were. The reported patterns of combination for the country as a whole can be itemized as follows (the percentage of schools said to use the media is given in brackets). 1. English (56); 2. Mother tongue (14); 3. English and the mother tongue (9); 4. English and Swahili (7); 5. English, the mother tongue and Swahili (6); 6. Swahili (4); 7. Swahili and the mother tongue (1).

The following tables give an indication of the media of instruction that were reported to be introduced in the *first* year of primary school in the different provinces. In interpreting the figures it is essential to bear in mind that in many instances headmasters reported that two or even three languages were used as media of instruction, and that each of these has been taken into account. The second table indicates the extent to which the three media were used whether in combination or otherwise. Statistics obtained by the Ministry of Education regarding the number of NPA classes operating in these provinces in 1968 indicated that the percentage of such classes of the total was 54 per cent, which seems to confirm the relative accuracy of the data obtained by questionnaire.

Mother Tongues

In every district except Kakamega and Nandi districts and Kwale district, English was stated to be the predominant single medium of instruction. Other districts in which between 20 per cent and 40 per cent of the schools were reported to use vernacular medium only were Central Nyanza (Luo), Kisii (Gusii), Bungoma and Busia (Luyia), Narok and Kajiado (Maasai), Machakos (Kamba), Baringo (Kalenjin), and Meru (Meru). Visits to schools in Kericho district (Kipsigis) also showed that the mother tongue appeared to be used as a medium more extensively than was indicated in the survey by questionnaire (4 out of 9 schools visited used English and the mother tongue as joint media of instruction).

In Kitui (Kamba), Embu (Embu), Kirinyaga, Murang'a and Kiambu (Kikuyu), Busia (Luyia), and Baringo between 17–25 per cent of the schools used the mother tongue *and* English as predominant media. Each of the districts mentioned are inhabited predominantly by members of one of the major language groups. Other factors which appear to be related to the extent to which the first language of the pupils was used as the initial medium of instruction will be considered later.

At the time the survey was carried out the TKK readers, prepared in various mother tongues at the Institute of Education, were beginning to be used quite extensively in the schools. However, it was not infrequently remarked that there was not sufficient guidance given to teachers for the use of these books (though these courses are relatively simple in comparison to other courses prepared by the Institute). Very few teachers indeed claimed to have had initial training in the teaching of their first language and many found the texts, simple though they are, difficult to make use of. The fact is that even in the major vernacular languages there are no courses available which draw upon modern methods of first language instruction. Most teachers simply did not know what to do in

492

TEACHING OF LANGUAGES AT SECONDARY LEVEL

	English	Swahili	M.T.	E/M.T.	E/Sw.	E/Sw./M.T.	Sw./M.T.
CENTRAL PROVINCE							
Kiambu	56.6	3.6	13.3	23.3	3.6	—	—
Murang'a	75	—	—	25	—	—	—
Nyeri	75	—	5	10	—	10	—
Kirinyaga	70	—	10	20	—	—	—
Nyandarua	81	7.7	3.85	—	7.7	7	—
NYANZA PROVINCE							
Central Nyanza (Kisumu/Siaya)	55.5	—	27.7	5.5	—	11	—
South Nyanza (Homa Bay)	60	—	10	10	—	20	—
Kisii	54.5	—	18.2	13.6	—	13.6	—
WESTERN PROVINCE							
Kakamega	23.5	5.8	41	5.8	2.9	20.5	—
Bungoma	43	—	39	13	—	4	—
Busia	60	—	20	20	—	—	—
EASTERN PROVINCE (A)							
Embu	62	—	4.7	19	—	14	—
Meru	70	—	17.6	5.9	5.9	—	—
Machakos	65	—	21.8	8.7	—	4.4	—
Kitui	64	—	10	21	—	3.5	—
EASTERN PROVINCE (B)							
Isiolo	42.8	28.6	—	—	28.6	—	—
Marsabit	44.5	22	—	—	22	11	—
RIFT VALLEY PROVINCE (A)							
Elgeyo-Marakwet/ Pokot	50	25	—	—	25	—	—
Laikipia	60	6.1	—	13	20	—	—
Trans-Nzoia	17	52	—	—	31	—	—
Uasin Gishu	30	20	10	—	30	10	—
Nakuru	50	12	—	12	12	—	6
RIFT VALLEY PROVINCE (B)							
Baringo	40	—	40	20	—	—	—
Nandi	14	—	43	14	28	—	—
Kericho	83.5	4	8	—	4	—	—
Narok	35	5.9	35	11.8	5.9	5.9	—
Kajiado	57	—	14	14	14	—	—
COAST PROVINCE							
Lamu/Tana River	76	—	—	—	23	—	—
Kilifi	70	23	—	—	6.7	—	6.7
Kwale	37	12.5	—	—	50	—	—
Taita	76	—	—	8	8	8	—

Media of instruction in Standard I

	English	Swahili	Mother Tongue
Central Province	89	7	23
Nyanza Province	80	14	44
Western Province	57	14	58
Eastern Province (A)	86	7	33
Eastern Province (B)	75	56	6
Rift Valley Province (A)	72	48	12
Rift Valley Province (B)	69	14	41
Coast Province	88	30	7

the vernacular period other than to tell stories and, regrettably, many teachers and pupils clearly thought this activity to be largely a waste of time.

A prevalent attitude towards the educational use of the mother tongues was reflected in the fact that in every province many schools were found in which the children's use of their first language at school was discouraged, particularly at upper primary level. There were also many schools at which headmasters had imposed and subsequently abandoned this practice. The headmaster of Oreru Primary School for example said he had done so (a) because it was difficult to administer, (b) it encouraged dishonesty, (c) it encouraged bullying and (d) it discouraged children with little confidence in themselves or their proficiency in English from communicating at all. In a number of schools the use of a language other than English at upper primary level in the classroom was severely discouraged in theory if not in practice, and after Standard III most children very seldom have occasion to read or write in their first languages although most can do so if required.

Swahili

Swahili was the predominant single medium of instruction only in Trans-Nzoia district in the Rift Valley. In combination with English it was used as an initial medium in between 20–30 per cent of the schools in Nandi, Laikipia, Trans-Nzoia, Nakuru and Uasin Gishu, Pokot and Elgeyo-Marakwet districts in the Rift Valley. These are areas to which for many years members of different language communities have migrated to work formerly on the European farms and since independence to settle in areas set aside for settlement by the government.

It was also reported to be used in a number of schools and in approximately the same proportion in Marsabit and Isiolo districts in Eastern Province and in Tana River and Lamu districts in Coast Province. In Kwale district where it is the primary language of the majority of the children, approximately half of the schools claimed to use both English *and* Swahili as initial media of instruction. It is perhaps worth remarking that a higher proportion of school children now have their initial education through the medium of English in Coast Province, in which the majority of the speakers who learn Swahili as both a first and a primary language live, than in any other part of the country. This is a relatively recent development in an area in which Swahili has been the primary medium of instruction for decades. This issue will be considered briefly later.

In areas of linguistic heterogeneity the use of a particular vernacular as a medium of instruction is normally excluded. A choice has therefore to be made between the adoption of Swahili or English for this purpose. Some of the factors that determine this choice can perhaps be inferred from the description of the situation in Trans-Nzoia district, where at the time of the inquiry a greater proportion of the schools used Swahili as the initial medium of instruction than in any other part of the country.

Of the 18 schools in Trans-Nzoia district that returned questionnaires, 52 per cent were reported to use Swahili as a medium, 31 per cent used English *and* Swahili as the initial media, and 17 per cent English only. Every school in Trans-Nzoia was reported to have children speaking different languages, these varying in number from eight to two (including Luyia, Bukusu, Luo, Kikuyu, Kalenjin (several dialects), Teso, Maasai and in town, Punjabi and Gujarati).

In such circumstances either Swahili or English must be adopted as the medium of instruction. One factor that appears to influence the choice of a medium is the proximity of a school to a town or centre of commercial and administrative activity and its position of relation to a communication network. A general indication of this variable was obtained by asking the headmaster to indicate how far the school was from the nearest post office. I related the schools' choice of medium to the variable and found that the average distance of the schools using English as an initial medium from an administrative focal point in Trans-Nzoia was 2.9 miles; that of schools using English *and* Swahili 6.5 miles; and that of the schools using Swahili 11.7 miles.

It would of course be very surprising if any single factor could be held to account for the reason for which those responsible for the organization of primary schools in particular districts choose whether or not to retain vernacular medium instruction. The influence of local education officers, missionary bodies, tutors in teachers' colleges and influential teachers and members of the local community can affect such decisions, as can the availability of funds for the purchase of books and equipment, the possession of secure and weather-proof amenities, and, most significantly, the presence of trained teachers and supervisors.

While most schools in the Coast and Rift Valley Provinces introduce Swahili as a subject in Standard I the majority of schools in Central, Nyanza, Western and Eastern Provinces introduce the language as a subject in the third or fourth year. Most of these schools are now beginning to use the *Masomo ya Kiswahili* course. However, it is also used quite commonly in areas where Swahili is spoken as a first language. For example, three out of nine schools sampled in Kinango in Kwale district use it in Standards I to III.

A number of criticisms were made of the course and particularly of the first book (which has been revised). Most of the criticism, however, was to the effect that the course was either too hard or too simple for the classes for which it was intended. In three out of eight schools observed by one of the students in South Nyanza, the former point was made. The student remarked on the 'characteristic fear of Swahili' among the pupils. In other schools such as Nyanchwa Full Primary School in Kisii, which has a linguistically mixed population (Luo, Gusii, Luyia, Kikuyu), precisely the opposite statement was made and it was repeated in other areas in which the children knew the language on entry to school, e.g. in Nakuru West and Golini Primary School in Kwale district and in Matinyani County School. Such criticism parallels the comments made by secondary school teachers regarding various texts and reflects again the fact that the same course books have to be used to meet the requirements of students with very different levels of achievement.

In the majority of schools in which Swahili is now used as the initial medium of instruction it is spoken as a second language by the pupils and teachers. Work has not begun on the preparation of a modern course for use in such circumstances; and in the absence of such a course it seems probable that an increasing number of schools in the areas where Swahili as a medium is now used will gradually adopt English as the primary medium of instruction. The process has already taken place in the towns designated as major growth centres in addition to Nairobi and Mombasa, viz. Kisumu, Kakamega, Nakuru, Eldoret, Nyeri, Thika and Embu and in the majority of the planned Urban Centres.

Students' Levels of Attainment and Motivation

Swahili

Some pupils speak Swahili well on entry into primary school, others know very little or none, and most have a rudimentary knowledge of some features of the language. While there is great variation in different parts of the country in this respect, within particular schools the levels of attainment of the children tend to be relatively similar. In the majority of schools in Coast Province and most of the schools in what I have termed Eastern Province B and Rift Valley Province A and in the municipalities children come to school with a certain knowledge of the language and in each province one finds schools where it is in fact the primary language of communication among the children themselves. This appears to be the case, for instance, in Embu County School, in Kitui Central Primary School, Isiolo County Township Primary School, Meru County School, in Busia township, etc. In many cases, however, only a few miles away from the townships, one encounters schools in which the children do not use Swahili at all amongst themselves. The contrast for example between Meru County School and CCM Township School, in Kinoru Division of Meru, was an interesting illustration of this. In many of the rural areas where there is relative linguistic homogeneity the children hardly speak the language. At Sira R.C. School and Kisoko Boys' School for example, in Bukhayo Location, a former headmaster in the area assisting in the survey reported that the children in Standard IV could 'hardly utter a correct sentence in Swahili'. He reported of the students at another school in the same area, that 'Swahili is but Greek to them'. However, a few miles away in Otimong R.C. Primary, attended by pupils who spoke Bukusu and Teso, the children were reported to be very fluent in the language.

In situations where a large number of the children can speak Swahili the teacher's task is largely remedial, as at secondary school level. As at secondary level also many pupils speak non-standard variants. At Karanda Full Primary School, for example, the teacher reported that the class could get along in 'broken Swahili' but added—'it isn't the one we teach them here—we teach them grammar'. Indeed, the extent to which the Swahili taught in school affected usage was not always apparent. The teacher at Kisulusuli Primary School in Nakuru, for example, did not think that the teaching had any effect in this regard.

In relatively few schools was much interest expressed in the course in Swahili either by teachers or pupils. The attitudes of the latter are of course influenced by those of the former, and repeatedly teachers stated that as the subject was not examinable there was not a great deal of interest in it.

English

Approximately 77 per cent of the teachers who returned questionnaires in 1968/9 indicated that English was used as a medium of instruction in Standard I, in a minority of cases in combination with another language or languages. Most of the schools made use of the New Peak Course prepared at the Institute of Education. A considerable number of teachers made the point that the course resulted in a class becoming relatively proficient in speaking English but that their proficiency in reading and writing was not comparable. In certain areas quite a proportion of the teachers also expressed concern that the use of English as the primary medium of instruction was affecting the students' facility in their own language. Many other teachers in Western Province and Nyanza argued that more attention should be paid to the teaching of the mother tongues in the English medium scheme.

The two main systems involving English medium and non-English medium instruction initially, have already been discussed in detail.

It is assumed by members of the Kenya Institute of Education in their recommendations regarding books for the different classes that by the end of Standard IV classes that have been instructed in English can be considered to be about a year in advance of other classes with regard to the reading materials that can be recommended for them. However, it is also recognized that at the end of Standard IV the majority of the children generally do not know all the structures covered by the course and the Safari Course which is intended to succeed the lower primary course book incorporates extensive revision of this material.

It was the intention of those who prepared the New Peak Course that the language relating to the 'content' subjects taught in English should be introduced in the course. With the introduction of new courses in mathematics, New Science, and Movement, however, the course no longer serves this purpose and it is due for extensive revision— a development that is anticipated in the development plan of the Kenya Institute of Education.

A matter that has caused much concern is the apparent disadvantage in terms of the learning of English encountered by children who are educated initially through the medium of their first language. This concern arises primarily from the fact that the most modern texts used for teaching other subjects even in the early stages are written in English, as is the leaving examination which governs entrance into secondary schools. The English-as-a-subject course used extensively in non-English medium schools does not serve effectively to prepare the children to deal with these materials, such as the mathematics textbook used in Standard IV, for example.

It has already been pointed out, however, that the distinction between the two systems of education is not always evident in practice. A considerable majority of the primary schools who returned information said that they used some English in initial instruction in the first year and a minority of schools in areas of linguistic homogeneity vigorously exclude the use of other languages in instruction at lower primary level.

Patterns of Language Use

Headteachers were asked to give information about languages used in certain circumstances by teachers and students. The observations of the teachers are of interest in so far as they indicated certain general contrasts between the different areas. For example, the reports indicated that Swahili was used as the *single* primary medium of communication outside school by children in what I have designated the Rift Valley A area (27.4 per cent) and Coast Province (21 per cent) and was also used extensively in Eastern B (13 per cent). No other area recorded over

3.6 per cent under this category. The observations confirm other indications that the language is used extensively as a lingua franca in these areas. In the other areas the children's mother tongue was stated to be the predominant medium of conversation outside class followed closely by a combination of English and the mother tongue as joint media. Again in the areas Rift Valley A, the Coast and Eastern B, a combination of English and Swahili was more prevalent than English and the mother tongue. The combination also appeared to be relatively prevalent in Rift Valley B (17 per cent) but in the other areas the highest recorded percentage was 4 per cent (in Nyanza).

In considering the responses it was necessary to bear in mind that, as has been mentioned, the practice of using 'monitors' of some kind to encourage or enforce the use of English and in some cases Swahili is widespread. Such enforcement cannot be justified on pedagogical grounds. There are also strong objections, which need not be elaborated, to the practice, which I think should be discouraged wherever possible.

The attitudes towards English which are demonstrated in the use of monitors is also reflected in the fact that in every province over 79 per cent of the teachers reported that they used English in speaking to other teachers and less than 12 per cent said that they used Swahili. The extent to which vernacular languages were stated to be used varied from 2 per cent in the Rift Valley to 20.4 per cent in Central Province. At teachers' meetings English was invariably reported to be the language in which minutes were taken or official records made. It is unnecessary to draw attention again to the fact that there is generally a considerable difference between what speakers do and what they say (and usually think) they do, but the figures may serve to give an indication of attitudes regarding language choice in particular situations.

LEVELS OF ATTAINMENT IN SWAHILI AND ENGLISH

In the second stage of the secondary school survey, we were concerned to obtain more detailed 'profiles' of language use for a smaller group of children in more varied situations of interaction and reception, and to devise methods of measuring certain of the language skills involved in the production and reception of Swahili and English, in tasks analogous to those faced by children entering secondary schools. I have described aspects of the former in Chapter 13.

In this section I will detail some of the results obtained in the process of investigating the language attainment of the children. For each child in the sample information relevant to language use and attainment was recorded. This included details of language group membership, urban/ rural residence, age, sex, age of entry into primary school, and initial medium of education, father's education and what I considered to be relevant details of the children's socio-economic background. These variables were taken into account in interpreting the test scores.

The Subjects

The research was carried out intensively with the co-operation of four Form 1 classes of children in two schools in Nairobi, but children in schools in the rural areas were asked to complete certain of the tests and exercises for purposes of comparison and control. Sixteen schools in the rural areas were selected to participate.[14] The schools were selected from among those that had co-operated in the 1968/9 surveys, i.e. schools attended by children belonging to the major language groups. They were chosen primarily because on the basis of past results the classes could be expected to be linguistically homogeneous and because the majority of the children in each school had been educated in a 'rural' environment, in the sense that they would have spent less than two years in a town or city.

The Urban Sample

The selected schools in Nairobi were both day schools, although a small number of the girls in the sample boarded at their school. Half the sample were boys and half girls and 138 children participated in the project in Nairobi. The choice of schools was made after careful consideration. The girls' school is situated on an estate in which a relatively large proportion of the residents have a comparatively high socio-economic rating; and this fact is reflected in the figures indicating the proportion of girls' fathers who received secondary education. The boys' school, in contrast, is situated more centrally, in an area of comparatively low socio-economic rating. In each case, however, the majority of the children in each school travel to school from other areas of the city.

Linguistically, the group showed a heterogeneity characteristic of the schools in the city, although the boys' school is more representative of the population of Nairobi in the proportion of children belonging to the four language communities that constitute the majority of the city's African population.[15] The linguistic 'breakdown' for the urban and rural samples is indicated in Figures 16.1(a) and (b).

Forty-seven per cent of the children had lived for five or more years in a town or city, 28 per cent had been educated through the medium of English from their first year of primary education, and 16 per cent through the medium of Swahili. Forty-six per cent of the fathers of the children had received 4–8 years of education and 15 per cent had received additional education at secondary level. The average age of the girls in the sample was 13 years 11 months and that of the boys 15 years 6 months.

The proportion of the children in each school who had spent five or more years in the city was virtually the same, i.e. 46 per cent and 47.5 per cent respectively. These proportions are relatively high, but meant that a sufficient number of children in the sample were educated in Nairobi, initially through the medium of English or Swahili, for meaningful statistical analysis of their scores as sub-groups to be made on various exercises.

Instruments

Various exercises were used to measure aspects of the attainment of the children in the samples in English and Swahili. The purposes and objectives of a number of these exercises will be specified in detail, but the following list will provide an indication of their range.

Exercise 1   Swahili Grammatical Structure
Exercise 2   Swahili Vocabulary (receptive)
Exercise 3   Swahili Vocabulary (productive)
Exercise 4a/b   Reading Comprehension (Swahili and English)
Exercise 5a/b   Reading Comprehension (Swahili and English)
Exercise 6a/b   Listening Comprehension B (Swahili and English)
Exercise 7   Written Exercise (Swahili)
Exercise 8   Written Exercise (English)
Exercise 9   Reading Comprehension A (English)
Exercise 10   Reading Comprehension B (English)
Exercise 11   Listening Comprehension A (English)
Exercise 12   Verbal Meaning sub-test
Exercise 13   Verbal Meaning, Verbal Fluency and Reasoning
                sub-tests
Exercise 14   Productive Vocabulary (Swahili, English, mother tongue)

All the tests were given to children in the Nairobi sample. Children in the rural sample took five of the tests constructed to measure aspects of attainment in Swahili, as earlier research had indicated that we could expect variations in levels of attainment in the language among the children belonging to the major language groups.[16]

Exercises in Swahili

Exercises 1 and 2 in Swahili are survey tests indicating the general level of the achievement of the children in different language and residential groups. At the time of preparation there were no objectively defined criteria in relation to which attainment or diagnostic tests in Swahili for children entering secondary schools could be constructed or in relation to which precise test specifications in terms of the items to be tested, the relative importance of particular objectives, and the kinds of learning to be tested could be drawn up. Detailed syllabuses specifying the language skills to be learned at each stage are not available. The situation as regards English was not dissimilar, particularly with respect to the primary school curriculum.[17] However, the fact that English is used as the medium of instruction at secondary level in all subjects provided guidelines for the construction of proficiency tests related to the learning tasks for which the language is used.

These comments should not be interpreted as being in the nature of a criticism of what is being done in the schools. In certain circumstances, the lack of precisely specified objectives and detailed syllabuses at different levels may be justified. The observations are simply made to indicate one aspect of the problems that had to be tackled in the process of test construction.

Exercises in English

The primary purpose of the tests in English with the exception of 4b, 5b and 6b was to ascertain the extent to which the children as a group were equipped to deal with a number of specific learning tasks with which they are faced at the moment of transition from primary to secondary education. They are therefore tests of student proficiency in performing particular tasks within the classroom.

Tests 4b, 5b and 6b were constructed as 'equivalent' forms of Swahili tests so that we might gain an indication of the relative proficiency of the children in performing similar or closely related tasks in the two languages, though, as will be indicated, the purposes of the tests were not solely comparative.

Exercises 2 and 14 were not proficiency tests. Exercise 3 (productive vocabulary in Swahili) was constructed so that I might obtain an indication of the ability of the students to recall lexical items in association with specific locales (classroom, home and street) just as Exercise 2 measured their ability to recognize items in association with specific topics. Exercise 14 was a form of 'semantic richness' test which was added primarily to reflect variation in the pupils' ability to produce in writing in the classroom 'synonyms' in English, Swahili and their first language for words of high frequency in these languages that were judged to be semantically equivalent for the purpose of the exercise; earlier inquiry having underscored the fact that the former was the language habitually used in this locale and in this mode.

The scores for certain sub-groups within the urban sample will be given for particular tests; more specifically, mention will be made of the performance of children belonging to the three major language groups in the sample, to children who have been educated through the medium of English or Swahili from their first year of schooling; to children who have spent five or more years in the city; to boys and girls, and to children of different ages.

1970 was the first year in which appreciable numbers of children who had been educated in Nairobi wholly through the medium of English entered secondary schools, and separate consideration has been given to their performance and to that of children educated through the medium of Swahili.

The number of children who took each test of which the results have been processed, and the mean scores and standard deviations, are in most cases indicated in the text. Correlation coefficients between certain of the test scores have been given; and tests of significance have been used to indicate significant differences between the scores of children belonging to the different language groups, on certain of the tests. For the most part, however, in accordance with the purposes of this volume, an attempt has been made to present statistical data simply, in the form of line charts. More detailed statistical analysis of the results will be undertaken in a subsequent publication.[18]

Exercise 1: Swahili Grammatical Structure

The test contained 76 questions, testing 108 items, and a passage of continuous prose testing 12 items of Swahili morphology and syntax. The test was in seven sections, the first six of which made use of multiple choice techniques of increasing complexity.

The selection of items was based upon a list of graded grammatical structures drawn up by Dr Joan Maw of the School of Oriental and African Studies, and supplemented by Mr Claessen on the basis of his experience of the students in schools in Kenya.[19] As far as the content validity of the test is concerned, I have already pointed out that it was not possible to construct a test covering a representative sample of the curriculum content. The face validity of the test was checked in pre-tests. The test gave an indication of the child's knowledge of the grammatical structure of Standard Swahili and yielded a composite score. It was untimed.

Figure 16.3 and Table 16.1 give an indication of the mean scores and standard deviations of the children in the major language groups in the rural areas and of the three largest language groups in Nairobi. Other information about the test results is given after the discussion of Exercise 2.

TABLE 16.1   *Exercise 1: Swahili grammatical structure*

| | Rural | | | Urban | | |
	N	X̄	S.D.	N	X̄	S.D.
Kikuyu	69	49.54	13.43	72	78.75	13.49
Luo	67	42.49	15.36	33	73.94	18.92
Luyia	62	57.9	15.26	13	78.33	11.95
Kamba	35	57.80	14.42			
Meru	66	66.86	14.07			
Mijikenda	66	97.68	8.14			
Gusii	27	63.67	13.60			
Kalenjin	64	57.36	15.18			

There were no significant differences in the urban sample between the scores of the children belonging to the three language groups.

However, in each case the differences between the scores of the children in the three groups and the children speaking the same languages in the rural areas were significant.

Within the rural sample, the scores of the Luo-speaking children were significantly lower than those of the sample as a whole. In this respect the results paralleled results obtained in an earlier investigation. In 1968, cloze tests in English and Swahili, consisting of passages of simple prose from which every fifth word had been deleted, were administered to the children involved in the survey. It was found that there was a significant difference at the 0.05 level between the scores of the Luo-speaking children in the rural sample, and those of children in the other language groups.[20]

Exercise 2: Swahili Vocabulary

The test contained 140 items of Swahili vocabulary. The child was required to write an equivalent term for each item in English *or in his mother tongue*. The items were divided into 14 groups, each containing 10 words. Each set of 10 items was drawn from a particular area of experience or lexical field, viz. (1) The schoolroom; (2) Illness and treatment; (3) The body; (4) Political activity; (5) Building materials and construction; (6) Common emotions; (7) Crops and cultivation; (8) Natural physical phenomena; (9) Commerce; (10) Social life and custom; (11) Religious activity; (12) 'Shopping'; (13) 'Abstract' qualities, e.g. pride, hypocrisy; (14) Common actions, e.g. 'to throw', 'to carry', etc.

The division into sub-tests was made for two reasons. First, undifferentiated tests of vocabulary are of little value in circumstances in which the language concerned is characteristically used for restricted functions. Secondly, I considered that a test of this nature might serve to indicate, very generally, specific areas of activity for which the language was used by the children in different groups and anticipated that the results could be related to other information obtained about the language use of the children. The test was untimed.

Both the total score and the scores for each sub-test were computed. The 'total' mean scores and standard deviations for the children in the different language groups in both the urban and rural samples are given in Figure 16.4 and Table 16.2.

TABLE 16.2 *Exercise 2: Swahili vocabulary*

		Rural			Urban	
	N.	X̄	S.D.	N.	X̄	S.D.
Kikuyu	69	44.6	12.04	72	62.22	17.77
Luo	67	39.80	16.85	31	58.48	24.12
Luyia	63	41.23	13.15	12	70.50	16.46
Kamba	35	50.40	11.91			
Meru	66	51.26	12.77			
Mijikenda	55	75.56	13.82			
Gusii	27	45.51	16.70			
Kalenjin	64	57.77	13.85			

Again the scores of the children in the three main language groups in the rural sample were significantly lower than those of the children in Nairobi. In the rural sample the scores of the children in the Mijikenda group were significantly higher than those of the children in the other groups. A breakdown of the scores by language group and topic is given in Figure 16.5 and Table 16.3. In relation to the test scores it is evident that linguistic affiliation is clearly not as important a variable as locale of residence, which is of course associated with numerous other factors fostering the use of the lingua franca.

The mean scores of the children in the urban and rural areas in ten of the sub-tests are shown in Figure 16.6 and Table 16.4(a). The range of scores of children in both samples on the different sub-tests is very similar though the scores of the 'urban' children on sub-tests of terms associated with 'common emotions' and 'illness and treatment' are markedly higher than those of the children in the rural areas.

TABLE 16.4 (a)

	1	2	3	4	5	6	7	8	9	10
Rural	7.48	4.46	4.85	4.70	4.06	3.81	2.26	2.95	2.91	2.11
Urban	7.95	5.46	5.26	4.85	4.41	4.22	3.51	3.33	3.09	2.74

TABLE 16.3 *Exercise 2: Swahili vocabulary*

	Shopping	Common emotions	Crops & cultivation	School-room	Social life and custom	Political activity	Illness & treatment	Religion	The body	Natural phenomena	Mean scores by language group (Rural)
Kikuyu	7.36	4.04	4.03	4.59	3.59	2.97	1.77	2.27	2.49	1.84	3.44
Luo	6.91	3.04	3.94	2.64	2.66	3.24	1.49	1.49	2.07	1.07	2.80
Luyia	7.37	3.55	4.08	3.41	2.97	3.20	1.86	2.43	2.22	1.28	3.19
Kamba	6.14	4.54	4.37	5.20	4.26	3.63	2.26	3.17	2.44	2.23	3.78
Meru	7.75	5.10	5.13	4.87	3.86	3.33	1.64	2.42	3.54	2.20	3.82
Mijikenda	8.73	6.46	6.12	7.31	5.31	5.00	4.65	6.85	5.69	4.42	5.90
Gusii	6.46	3.57	4.66	3.74	2.74	3.60	1.60	2.29	2.76	1.66	3.35
Nandi	8.63	5.46	6.23	6.03	4.43	5.57	3.23	3.91	3.39	2.94	4.94
Kipsigis	7.97	4.46	5.14	4.51	3.74	4.51	1.83	1.80	1.60	1.43	3.89
Mean scores by topic	7.97	4.46	4.85	4.70	4.06	3.81	2.26	2.95	2.91	2.11	

It will be appreciated that if the scores of the Mijikenda group were abstracted from the scores of the rural sample, the contrasts between the relative performance of children in the urban and rural samples would be accentuated.

The breakdown of scores in Table 16.4(b) will serve to indicate some contrasts between the two samples in terms of scaled scores.

TABLE 16.4 (b)

Scores	Urban	Rural
7+	Shopping	Shopping
6+		
5+	Common emotions	
	Crops & cultivation	
4+	Schoolroom	Crops & cultivation
	Political activity	Schoolroom
	Social life & custom	Common emotions
		Social life and custom
		Political activity
3+	Illness & treatment	
	Religion	
	The body	
2+	Natural phenomena	Religion
		The body
		Illness & treatment
		Natural phenomena
1+		

A number of tentative conclusions can be drawn from the scores on the sub-tests of the vocabulary test. It is clear that the majority of the children in all the groups have sufficient control over the lexical system of the language to be able to buy provisions in a market or at a shop, and this one would expect. They could also talk about aspects of cultivation or farming and about the animals associated with small scale animal husbandry. These two areas of experience are clearly related. Some of the children could understand a speech on a political theme, although the scores on this sub-test were lower than had been anticipated. Most of them were able to name a number of objects found in the classroom, and experiences undergone there.[21]

In general, one might tentatively infer that the children would not be able to describe natural scenery in Swahili with any subtlety, and one would assume that the language used for such a purpose would in most cases be their mother tongue; nor would they be able to describe in any detail the physical appearance of a person, or, more seriously, to explain to a medical assistant or a doctor symptoms of illness in themselves or others.

Sub-Group Scores (Exercises 1 and 2)

As one would expect, children who had spent five or more years in the city obtained higher scores than the others: $\bar{X} = 82.92$ on Exercise 1

(N. 63) and 70.7 on Exercise 2 (N. 64), but these differences are not significant.

In the urban sample, also, the scores of the children who had studied Swahili as a subject at school were not significantly different from those who had not. The mean score of such children on Exercise 1 was 79.81 (S.D. 14.86; N. 115) and on Exercise 2 63.83 (S.D. 18.35; N. 115).

However, as one would expect, the scores of the small number of Nairobi children who were educated initially through the medium of Swahili were higher than those who were not so educated. The mean scores and standard deviations of this sub-group are shown in Table 16.5.

TABLE 16.5

| | Exercise 1: Grammatical structure | | | Exercise 2: Vocabulary | |
	N.	$\bar{X}$	S.D.	$\bar{X}$	S.D.
Boys	13	90.00	10.19	78.85	14.98
Girls	8	88.75	8.77	67.25	11.61

The correlation coefficient of the scores of the children in the urban group on Exercises 1 and 2 was highly significant.[22]

Sex Differences

The scores of the children of different sexes in the urban sample are shown below.

TABLE 16.6

| | Exercise 1: Grammatical structure | | | Exercise 2: Vocabulary | |
	N.	$\bar{X}$	S.D.	$\bar{X}$	S.D.
Boys	68	78.35	17.80	67.07	19.98
Girls	68	75.99	14.98	56.96	18.24

A pattern of some interest, and one which recurs in each group in which the scores of children of different sexes were analysed separately, is indicated in the fact that the scores of the girls on Exercise 2 are in each case lower than those of the boys. This pattern does not occur in the tests of grammatical structure.[23] In the case of the children in the urban areas the difference is significant at the 0.01 level. The mean scores of the children of different sexes in the three major groups in the urban and rural areas are given in Table 16.7 and illustrated in Figure 16.7. One might draw a number of inferences from these results but at this stage it suffices to say that they indicate that the girls in the sample characteristically tend to use and to be exposed to, the 'informal' use of Swahili outside school less than the boys.

TABLE 16.7 *Mean scores of boys and girls on Exercise 2 in the largest language groups in the urban and rural samples*

		Urban	Rural
Kikuyu	Boys	67.43	46.68
	Girls	58.49	42.00
Luo	Boys	60.47	45.39
	Girls	56.07	34.55
Luyia	Boys	73.20	44.28
	Girls	57.00	38.55

In connection with the difference in performance of the boys and the girls it is perhaps of some relevance to note that there was an interesting difference in the nature of the claims made by the boys and girls with regard to their proficiency in Swahili. As has been stated earlier, each child was asked to rate his or her proficiency on a four-point scale as regards his or her ability in speaking, reading, writing and understanding the language. Naturally these ratings cannot be interpreted as giving evidence of proficiency but they provide an indication of the children's own assessment of their relative abilities in different languages and in different modes of the same language.

Thirty per cent of the boys rated their proficiency in speaking Swahili as very good and 38 per cent as good, as opposed to 19 per cent and 35 per cent of the girls. In contrast, the ratings of the two groups of their proficiency in English were virtually identical. Twenty-one per cent of the boys and 22 per cent of the girls rated their proficiency as very good, and 69.5 per cent as opposed to 68 per cent said that their proficiency was good (urban sample).

To obtain an indication of the validity of such personal ratings, the scores of the children in the Nairobi sample on Exercise 1 (Grammatical structure) were correlated with their personal proficiency ratings as regards their ability to *speak* Swahili. Figure 16.8 illustrates the relationship.

It is clear that the proficiency ratings have a degree of validity and they can be shown to correlate positively with performance on the tests of grammatical structure and vocabulary in Swahili.

Variation of Performance within a Language Group

An interesting indication of the fact that linguistic affiliation of itself is not necessarily a factor determining proficiency in Swahili is indicated by the highly significant differences between the scores on both tests of the children in the Kalenjin group.

The children of the schools involved spoke different dialects of the language. Those in school A were predominantly speakers of Nandi and in school B of Kipsigis. School B is situated approximately eight miles south of the town of Kericho in the direction of Kisumu, the main town in the Luo-speaking area, and was approximately three miles off the main road on a murram road. School A is situated approximately half way along the main road from Eldoret to Kakamega.

The scores of the children in the two dialect groups are shown in Table 16.8.

TABLE 16.8

	Exercise 1: Grammatical structure		Exercise 2: Vocabulary	
	X̄	S.D.	X̄	S.D.
Nandi	73.57	16.79	64.57	15.09
Kipsigis	41.15	13.56	50.97	11.45

Exercise 3: Productive Vocabulary Test in Swahili

The children in both samples were asked to write down in a specified time as many words as they could in Swahili that they saw or found in different places. Certain locales were specified: (A) In the classroom; (B) In your house; (C) In the main street of the nearest town or village.

They were given three minutes to complete each section. The relative number of words produced in each column was calculated. Words which could not feasibly be located in the relevant locale were omitted by the assessors from the final score.

The mean scores of the children in the *urban sample* on the three parts of the exercises are given below, as are the scores of children who studied Swahili in primary school, who were educated through the medium of Swahili, or through that of English. No significant differences between the groups were evident.

TABLE 16.9

	N.	A X̄	B X̄	C X̄
Urban sample	134	14.17	20.02	13.26
Swahili medium	19	14.45	23.44	12.34
English medium	24	14.65	23.19	15.27
Swahili in primary school	82	14.78	21.63	13.96

Among the children who were educated through the medium of Swahili there was little difference between the scores of the girls and the boys as is indicated in the following table, although it is of some interest that the mean scores of the girls were slightly higher on section A (school) and B (home), and lower on C (the street), than those of the boys.

TABLE 16.10

	A		B		C	
	X̄	S.D.	X̄	S.D.	X̄	S.D.
Boys	13.91	3.31	21.64	8.12	13.18	3.46
Girls	15.00	4.89	25.25	7.28	11.50	3.60

Nor were there any significant differences between the scores of children in the major urban language groups.

TABLE 16.11

	N.	A X̄	B X̄	C X̄
Kikuyu	55	14.11	21.02	12.89
Luo	22	13.09	20.82	14.41
Luyia	9	13.33	18.00	13.44

An interesting fact, which was not anticipated, was the fact that the locale of the home elicited more associations in each case than did the other locales. There was, however, relatively little variety in the range of associations. Members of their family, domestic utensils and furniture, characteristically provided the majority of such associations. Clearly the exercise did not serve to indicate whether the language was associated more specifically with one locale more than another, and for this purpose, more rigidly controlled stimuli would need to be provided. It did, however, indicate, as did the preceding tests, the similarity in performance of children in the urban sample of different linguistic and educational backgrounds.

Exercises 4 and 5: Exercises in Reading Comprehension using Equivalent Passages in Swahili and English

The children in both urban and rural groups were asked to complete tests of reading comprehension in Swahili and English so that an indication could be gained of their ability to read simple statements or instructions in continuous prose.

Exercises 4a and b (Forms A and B) consisted of a set of instructions issued by the Post Office authorities in Swahili and English regarding the operation of a Post Office savings account. Five open-ended questions were set on the passage.

Exercises 5a and b (Forms A and B) were constructed in the form of a letter written by a young schoolboy in Nairobi to his father. Ten open-ended questions were set on the test.

The children in each class were assigned numbers in sequence at random. Half the class were then given Test 4, Form A (Swahili), and half given Form B (English). After the completion of the tests Forms 5A (Swahili) and 5B (English) were administered. The children who had taken Forms

511

4A and 4B were required to complete Forms 5A and 5B respectively. Both tests were untimed.

The mean scores of children in the *rural* group on each test are indicated in Figures 16.9 and 16.10. One can infer from the results of these tests that the children in most groups would be able to read and understand simple reading materials in Swahili with accuracy, though they would have greater difficulty in following more complex instructions such as those issued for the information of the public by the Post Office. This is particularly the case with children in the Luo-speaking group. The majority of the children in the rural sample would find it somewhat easier to read the more complex instructions in English, though this is not the case with children in the urban sample.

The numerical breakdown of the scores for the rural samples is given in Table 16.12 and the mean scores for the total urban and rural samples are given in Table 16.13. The mean scores of the urban and rural samples are related in Figure 16.11. The fact that the scores of the urban group are higher on tests in Swahili than those of the rural group (and marginally lower in English), is the main point of interest.

TABLE 16.12   *Reading comprehension in Swahili and English (rural sample)*

	4A Swahili %	4B English %	5A Swahili %	5B English %
Kikuyu	76.0	71.4	75.0	86.5
Luo	41.8	73.0	70.3	82.5
Luyia	56.0	61.0	65.8	85.0
Kamba	74.4	66.0	78.9	78.9
Meru	65.2	86.0	79.4	85.0
Mijikenda	66.6	75.4	78.3	81.1
Gusii	51.8	81.2	79.4	87.6
Kalenjin	57.4	81.2	85.9	82.1

TABLE 16.13

	4A $\overline{X}$	4B $\overline{X}$	5A $\overline{X}$	5B $\overline{X}$
Urban	75.4	74.4	75.37	83.6
Rural	61.27	74.4	87.5	79.4

Exercise 6: Listening Comprehension Test B (Swahili and English)

A listening comprehension test was constructed, consisting of a recording of a five-minute extract from a news broadcast in Swahili (Test 6A) and an English version of the same broadcast (Test 6B). A set of multiple choice questions was prepared on the broadcast in English and Swahili. Half the children in five of the school samples answered the questions in Swahili on the broadcast in that language and half answered the equivalent test in English. As in other tests in which this procedure was used, the children were assigned to each group at random. The test was untimed.

The first set of questions required the children to recognize the factual accuracy of certain items stated in the broadcast. The second asked them to select terms of equivalent meaning to five terms of relative significance in the bulletin.

The exercise proved to be too difficult for the pupils generally and negative scores on the tests in both languages were recorded in many cases, although a control group of Swahili speakers to whom the Swahili exercise was administered gained relatively high scores ($\bar{X} = 4.2$) on the first part of the test. It would be premature to deduce that a majority of the pupils do not in fact comprehend with accuracy details of news broadcasts in either English or Swahili, and if time permits the test will be redesigned and administered to a different sample at a later date.

Exercises 7 and 8: Written Exercise in Swahili and English

The children in the girls' schools were asked to write a short essay in Swahili on a specified theme. They later wrote an essay on the same theme in English. Each essay was graded by two different markers to eliminate, as far as was possible, examiner bias, and the score out of twenty was expressed as a percentage. In each case, also, the type-token index is being calculated to yield what Carroll has termed an index of Vocabulary Diversity (or Range).[24] If time permits, errors made in the use of selected features of syntax and morphology will be subsequently categorized.

Exercise 9: Reading Comprehension in English (A)

Seven passages of between 300 and 600 words in length were selected from textbooks in common use in 1968 in the first forms in secondary schools in Kenya. The approximate difficulty level of each book was estimated using the Farr-Jenkins-Patterson adaptation of the Flesch Reading Ease Formula.[25] Representative passages (i.e. in difficulty level) were then selected from the tests and ten multiple choice questions were set on each passage. Five questions tested knowledge of significant lexical items, and five tested the children's understanding of the general import of the passage. The results on the seven texts were combined to give a single raw score of Reading Comprehension for each child in the urban sample. Tests were untimed.

The mean score of the children on the test was 37.0 (S.D.12.81), i.e. 53 per cent (out of a possible total of 70). An analysis of the results of the boys' scores showed no significant differences between children belonging to the major language groups nor between those who had spent five or more years in Nairobi and others.

As with the testing of vocabulary, however, it was found essential to consider the results of the sub-tests separately, as the variation between the scores on the sub-tests was considerable. Such variation was to be expected as the passages had been selected from different areas of study, and the range in the difficulty levels of the passages was large.

The difficulty levels of each sub-test, the topics dealt with in each passage and the mean scores of the children on each passage are indicated in Figure 16.12 and Table 16.14. The passages are arranged in order of their difficulty level.

TABLE 16.14

Topic	NIRE	$\bar{X}$
1. Shrubs	92.9	67
2. Fish	89.3	63
3. Heat. Water in plants	72.22	66
4. The Sahara	67.38	53
5. The Nile	66.28	61
6. Numbers and numerals	58.49	51
7. Air. Water supplies	52.30	42

A number of conclusions can be drawn from the results of this test. In general, as one would expect, the comprehension rate of the students decreases as the difficulty level of the reading material increases. But on the passages with an NIRE rating below 60, the children's comprehension score dropped sharply.

The reading achievement of school children is commonly evaluated in terms of independent, instructional and frustration levels. 75–90 per cent is a common standard of comprehension for instructional level and 50 per cent and below for frustration.[26]

It is, however, important to note that the texts selected for this test were among the simplest available to the children, and in two instances passages were taken from textbooks specifically prepared for use in East Africa. We have seen earlier that in their responses the teachers indicated that pupils had difficulty in comprehending materials relating to science subjects and mathematics. I therefore tested the difficulty level of the textbooks used in one of the urban schools in Form 1, for the teaching of chemistry, physics, biology, mathematics, and geography. In each case the textbooks used are texts in widespread use in Kenya. The ratings were as follows:[27]

Geography 58.04
Chemistry 59.20

514

Mathematics 62.71
Physics   68.23
Biology   70.61

If the NIRE index can be taken to give an accurate indication of the difficulty level of the books, it is clear that the children would have as much if not more difficulty understanding a number of these books than any of the materials tested in the experiment. Additionally it is apparent that as they will not have studied the physical sciences at primary level, the terms used in the teaching of these subjects and the language varieties used in the texts will be relatively unfamiliar to them.

As a follow-up to this investigation, the pupils of one of the Nairobi schools were asked to read and subsequently discuss the following passage taken from the chemistry textbook in use for the first form of one of the schools in the Nairobi sample.

The properties of a mixture are intermediate between those of its components, but a compound has properties which are different from those of its components. A mixture of iron and sulphur still behaved like both of those elements, but the compound, ferrous sulphide, does not resemble either iron or sulphur in its reactions. Sodium is a soft metal that takes fire on water; chlorine is a green poisonous gas: the compound made from them, sodium chloride or common salt, certainly has none of these properties.

Compounds are always made by some chemical change. This is often accompanied by the evolution of light and heat as in the case of the preparation of iron sulphide .

In the discussion, which was concerned with the meaning of the terms used in the passage, it emerged that it would be possible to group the words which the children had difficulty in understanding into three categories, which gave rise to increasing difficulty in comprehension. These were: 1. the names of chemical substances such as ferrous sulphide and sodium chloride. As such terms have a single and unvarying denotation, however, they are easily taught in context. 2. Unfamiliar but non-technical terms such as 'components' (and earlier on the same page 'specimens') that are characteristic of one of the varieties of language used in the book. 3. Terms such as 'intermediate', 'compound', 'reaction' and 'evolution'. Most of the pupils were familiar with these words but did not wholly understand the specialized meanings they had in this particular context. It is evident that similar difficulties are faced by the children in their attempts to comprehend passages in texts dealing with other subject areas, particularly the sciences.[28]

Exercise 10: Reading Comprehension in English (B)

The test comprised 10 passages written in a variety of written and spoken 'styles' and registers of contemporary English. The passages

515

were adapted from material published in the local newspapers (such as advertisements for jobs and correspondence courses, etc. or notices of public interest) or were written to replicate verbal experiences that the children would be likely to encounter, e.g. a dialogue between a teacher and a schoolboy, a speech by a headmaster, etc.

Each passage was followed by four sentences, not all of which were stylistically appropriate. The children had to select one sentence to complete the passage. The test gave an indication of the ability of the children to recognize grammatical and lexical features associated with particular varieties of English. One mark was given for each correct answer, to yield a total of 10 marks.

The mean score on the test was 3.85, with a standard deviation of 1.34. The scores on this test which yield a mean percentage of 38.5 per cent indicate that, as would be expected, the majority of the children are not able to discern with any marked discrimination, differences between spoken and written styles or registers of English appropriate to particular contexts.

This is to be expected in view of the fact that for the majority of children the use of English would be associated primarily with the diverse but nonetheless restricted language activity related to the locale of the school and the experience of formal education; and such activities would normally have been mediated by teachers who themselves used the language with a restricted verbal repertoire.

Exercise 11: Listening Comprehension Test A (English)

The children in the girls' school were asked to write down a passage comprising two paragraphs of 67 words in length with a difficulty level of 92.9 (NIRE), which I read to them at a speed of approximately 90 words a minute.[29] The passage was taken from a textbook in common use in the first forms of secondary schools in Kenya, and it had been read in the previous term by the children to whom the Listening Comprehension test was given, as one of the passages in the Reading Comprehension Test A. The intention of the exercise was to simulate a situation in which a schoolteacher would dictate notes to the children on one of their subjects of study.

In marking the exercise, no marks were deducted for misspelling or for errors in punctuation except when these indicated that a significant juncture phoneme had been misunderstood.

The mean score of the children in the sample who took the test was 39.24 with a standard deviation of 20.97 This is in fact a relatively low score given the brevity and simplicity of the passage and the familiarity of the subject matter; and it indicates that out of every utterance ten words in length, approximately two words were misunderstood or not understood by the average child who took the test.

Teachers' Assessments

The teachers of English and Swahili in the girls' school were asked to provide an assessment of the pupils' proficiency in these languages based on their experience and on any school tests administered. The assessment served as an indication of the concurrent validity of certain of the tests.[30]

Exercise 12

The raw scores obtained in Exercise 9 were related to the scores of the children on the sub-test of Verbal Meaning (VW) in the *Primary Mental Abilities Test* (*Form AH for Ages 7–12*). The correlation was highly significant.[31] This test yields information in the form of regression equations for the estimation of a child's Current Estimated Reading Age at the time the test was administered, according to norms provided by speakers of English as a first language.[32] The norms are of course only relevant in so far as the children taking the test are expected to read materials in school that have been prepared for speakers of English as a first language. At present, as far as children entering secondary schools in Kenya are concerned, this is the case in most instances (except in the 'extensive reading' periods provided for in the English syllabus, when the use of simplified texts is recommended).

The results on the sub-test indicate that the mean reading age of the children is generally lower than their chronological age, as measured by norms obtained on the results of native speakers of English; and as bilingual children characteristically obtain lower scores on tests of verbal meaning in a second language than native speakers, this is to be expected.[33]

The average chronological age of the boys was 15 years 6 months and of the girls 13 years 11 months.[34]

TABLE 16.15

	N.	$\bar{X}$	Current estimated reading age (Years and months)
Total	131	26.53	11.7
Boys	64	27.11	11.6
Girls	67	25.97	11.6

The lack of congruence between chronological age and attainment in tests of Verbal Meaning was also indicated by the scores of the children on the Verbal Meaning sub-test of the PMA Test Form AH Ages 11–17 which was also administered to the children.[35]

The mean scores of the children on this sub-test and on the sub-test of Reasoning are indicated below and tabulated according to the age of the children in the sample. The mean score percentile equivalents according to norms derived from native speakers are also given.

TABLE 16.16

	Verbal Meaning				Reasoning		
Age	N.	$\bar{X}$	P.R.	Age	N.	$\bar{X}$	P.R.
12	6	9.67	21	12	5	13.20	68
13	24	9.90	12	13	24	10.20	42
14	47	9.63	9	14	47	9.04	22
15	41	9.60	7	15	41	9.56	18
16	5	11.20	6	16	5	8.80	11

On the Verbal Meaning test the scores in the different age groups are not significantly different (F=0.408). The mean scores of the girls and boys were 8.85 and 10.65 respectively. It is again apparent that an increase in age does not correspond with an increase in general performance on the test (as is shown by the fact that the equivalent percentile ranks decrease as the age grading increases).

It would be possible to draw a number of inferences from this result and one might deduce that the scores may simply reflect the exposure of the children in the different groups to the use of English as a school subject, and, as all the children in the sample have had seven or perhaps eight years of schooling, age might be less significant a variable than primary school experience.

There is, however, another hypothesis that might be advanced to account for the performance of the children, which requires further careful investigation. The age at which children enter secondary school is in most cases related to their age of entry into primary school. There is evidence to indicate that in the case of most children, verbal learning such as is required in language learning is accomplished with greater facility earlier in the child's life than otherwise. The acquisition of the grammatical system of a language is a very complex intellectual achievement but it is generally accepted that by the age of four most children have learned the basic structural features of their language and many of the details, after which a long period of linguistic consolidation follows.[36]

The evidence may point to the fact that in certain circumstances children who begin schooling at a relatively late age have more difficulty acquiring the linguistic medium through which instruction is given; and the relative handicap may be accentuated when this learning of necessity involves the mastery of a second set of linguistic systems. The extent of a child's verbal aptitude as manifested in tests of verbal meaning has been shown in numerous experiments to relate significantly to 'scholastic aptitude'; and this correlation may be even more marked in situations where instruction is given and examinations taken in a second or foreign language.[37] The hypotheses that in certain circumstances the age at which a child enters primary school and begins to learn a second language is a significant factor in determining aspects of his subsequent attainment in the language—and that the effects of a late start in learning may be irremediable, are areas of investigation indicated by this inquiry that need to be further investigated. The hypothesis that there is a 'critical age' for language acquisition is not a new one, but it is one for which relatively little cross-cultural data has been obtained. One must also take into account, at this stage, the likelihood that further analysis will indicate the effect of 'hidden' correlations on the scores of the children on this test.[38]

At this point I wish to refer to a study by H.C.A. Somerset of the secondary school achievement of children in Uganda, which constitutes the most carefully controlled investigation of this nature that has been undertaken in the region.[39] He came to the conclusion that the results of his investigation 'suggest strongly that the effects of inferior education at the primary and junior secondary levels are largely irreversible'; and 'the quality of the instruction pupils have received in their first eight years of schooling sets the limit upon the level they will reach in the School Certificate Examination'. Mr Somerset also gave evidence to indicate that older children benefit less from improved educational circumstances than younger children.[40]

The results of the test given to the Nairobi sample indicate that the hypothesis needs to be further investigated that the effectiveness or otherwise of the teaching of the language of instruction in a school is the primary determinant of what Mr Somerset termed without further specification the 'quality of instruction'.

The sub-tests of Verbal Meaning and Reasoning in the PMA Test yield a 'scholastic aptitude score'[41] and the mean scores of the children in each age group on the two tests were combined according to the formula $2V+R$ and converted into quotients. The results are given in Table 16.17.

TABLE 16.17

Age	Score	Scholastic Aptitude quotient
12	34	91
13	29	80
14	29	78
15	28	72
16	31	68

It must be emphasized again that the scores are only of interest in so far as they reflect the relative aptitude of the children *within* the sample in terms of the abilities measured by the test.[42]

The 'English Medium' Sub-Group

One reason for the inclusion of the S.R.A. tests was that it was anticipated that the results might serve to indicate whether the performance of the children who had been educated through the medium of English differed significantly from that of other children. It has been stated on numerous occasions that the level of attainment in English of children who have been taught through the New Primary Approach exceeds that of the children who have not been so educated.[43] There was no significant difference between the mean scores of the children who had been educated through the medium of English and others in the tests of Verbal Meaning and Reasoning and their derived Scholastic Aptitude scores and quotients.

The relative performance of the children who had been exposed to the New Primary Approach in English and those who had not on Exercises 7, 8, 11, and 12 was compared and no significant differences were found. While the pupils in this sub-group were rated slightly higher on the teacher's assessment of proficiency ($\overline{X} = 5.69$ as opposed to 4.75) again the difference was not significant.

The possibility needs to be investigated that gains in attainment in the first three years of education through the New Primary Approach are not maintained at upper primary level.[44] It is fortunate that one of the stated research priorities identified by the Kenya Institute of Education is the need to investigate the consequences of multilingualism and in particular the effect of the use of different languages in the initial education of school children.[45]

Finally, it is perhaps of some relevance to note that in no instance were the scores of the children who had studied through the English medium scheme lower than those of the total sample on any of the tests involving the reception or production of Swahili. I have mentioned earlier, however, that continuous urban residence is likely to be a significant variable in the case of scores on these tests.[46]

Exercise 14

The children in Nairobi were finally asked to complete a short form of a test of a kind that Macnamara has termed a 'Richness of Vocabulary Test'. In this exercise they were asked to write down in English, Swahili, and in their first language in the case of children who spoke Kikuyu (i.e. the majority of the children in the Nairobi sample) as many words as they could recall that had 'the same meaning' as eight words in a list presented in each of these languages. The words were selected from among those which had proved to be productive in the pre-tests of the exercise.

I considered that the results might serve to provide an indication of a child's relative 'verbal fluency' in each of the three languages, in the written mode and in the classroom setting where English is the primary language. The scores in the case of each language were based on the total number of the equivalents given. The children were given five minutes to complete each of the three sections. Table 16.18 indicates the relative mean scores and the standard deviations of the students in the three languages.

TABLE 16.18

	English	S.D.	Swahili	S.D.	Mother tongue	S.D.
M	7.19	2.82	3.76	2.23	4.45	2.00
F	6.82	3.07	2.87	2.25	5.18	2.56

When the scores of children in the different language groups were considered the same pattern emerged as regards the English and Swahili scores.

TABLE 16.19

	No.	English	No.	Swahili	No.	Mother tongue	(Kikuyu)
Kikuyu	61	7.13	57	3.23	51	4.67	(4.44)
Luo	24	8.17	21	3.86			
Luyia	9	6.56	8	3.63			

It cannot be assumed that the difference between the mean scores on the English and mother tongue exercises represents a difference in verbal fluency in the two languages in the sense the term is usually defined. Several of the children showed a degree of embarrassment or reluctance when asked to complete the third section, which required the use of their mother tongue. In subsequent discussion a number of them stated that they were not accustomed to writing their mother tongue and others said that they did not consider it really appropriate to do so in the classroom and in the company of their friends who spoke other languages. Inhibiting influences of several kinds, therefore, might have served to affect the scores on this test.

As regards the Swahili mean score it has already been shown that the passive vocabulary of the children in the language varies according to the contexts in which the language is used and the topics that are discussed. It is likely that although the terms used in the basic list were of relatively high frequency in each language, the children would not characteristically use Swahili in describing the personal qualities (physical or intellectual) to which the majority of the terms referred.

One might conclude that a 'richness of vocabulary test' of this kind is of limited validity, in cases other than in the relatively rare instances when the subjects are balanced bilinguals in the sense that they use two languages with equal facility in similar contexts and when discussing similar topics. The children in our sample are not 'balanced bilinguals' in this sense; the three codes are as I have stated elsewhere characteristically used for complementary functions in restricted contexts. Any attempt to estimate relative 'fluency' in the three languages would need to take account of this factor. In general, however, the exercise did serve to corroborate statements made by the students regarding the relative facility with which they wrote different languages.

PRACTICAL IMPLICATIONS
OF THE PROJECT

It is possible to draw a number of conclusions based on information gathered and presented in part in the previous sections. Some issues relating to the teaching of Swahili in secondary schools will be further considered by Mr Claessen in his appendix to this chapter.

Although the situation has been described in some detail by Mr Hemphill in Chapter 15, it might be relevant again to draw attention to some features relating to the teaching of language in primary schools, in so far as these relate to the levels of attainment of children entering secondary schools. The quality of the language teaching given in primary schools is the determining influence in the majority of cases of the children's attainment in English in all areas in Kenya, and of Swahili in certain areas. Numerous factors, some of them financial or administrative, affect the quality of this teaching in various respects. However, confining oneself to a consideration of the directly pedagogical issues, one might say that in most areas of Kenya, the quality of the language teaching in both languages at this level is determined primarily by the standard of the teachers' own language attainment, by the training given to the teacher in language teaching, and by the effectiveness of the teaching materials available. Of these, the first is perhaps the most important.

The majority of primary school teachers have received seven or eight years of education plus two years of teacher training and a considerable number of teachers are untrained. Inevitably, therefore, the level of attainment of many teachers in the two languages is limited.

THE TEACHING OF SWAHILI

An indication of the difficulties faced by some of the teachers who are responsible for teaching Swahili was given in the inquiry referred to earlier by a member of the former Curriculum Development and Research Centre in connection with the use of the primary Swahili course that was in preparation. A questionnaire was circulated among primary school teachers of Swahili in each province and comments of the teachers on the course book were requested. They were also asked to give comments upon difficulties they encountered in teaching Swahili. Fifty-three per cent of the teachers of Swahili in the total sample reported that they had difficulty in teaching the language and the report of the inquiry states that 'a relatively large number of teachers felt the need for instruction in Swahili grammar. This suggests that part of the difficulty these teachers experienced was due to their having an inadequate command of the language themselves'.[47]

It is likely that many teachers have similar difficulty in teaching English and in using it as a medium of instruction. However, the difficulties they have in teaching English would have been alleviated by the fact that, if they had attended a teacher training college, considerable attention would have been given to a course of instruction in methods of teaching English and of using the course books prepared for use in primary schools. For various reasons, such extensive training would not have been given in most cases in methods of teaching Swahili.[48]

I should perhaps mention here that in 1968 proposals for the reorganization of certain aspects of the curriculum in the teachers' colleges were set out in a report on *New Directions in Teacher Education* in Kenya. One recommendation concerned the establishment in the colleges of departments dealing with *communication skills* in which language teachers would take common courses when appropriate. Implementation of the proposals of the report could markedly alter the quality of the training given to teachers of language.

The lack of suitable course materials to which the instruction given to teachers could be related has been a problem that has affected both the quality of the training given to teachers and that of the teaching given to the pupils.[49]

With the introduction into the primary schools of a four-year course of instruction in Swahili prepared at the Institute of Education for speakers of Swahili as a second language, it is to be expected that both the prescribed course of training for teachers and the general level of teaching in the primary schools will be improved.[50] However, it would be unrealistic to anticipate that the wide variation in the levels of attainment of children entering the schools will be radically affected by the prescribed use of the course. There are numerous factors apart from the standard of instruction that gave rise to such variation; and it can be anticipated that in general the range in the levels of attainment in Swahili of the children entering secondary school will continue to be far greater than their range of attainment in English, variable though this may be, unless of course there was a change of policy regarding the stage at which the language is introduced in the primary curriculum.

The observation of the ministry officials concerned, the comments of teachers referred to in the first section of this chapter and the results of the tests show that in many instances the aims of the second language course in Swahili that is given in primary schools are not attained at the present time.[51]

However, even if the situation improves in the future, secondary school teachers will still be faced with a number of major teaching problems. As practically all the children entering secondary schools know some Swahili, the teacher's work, which in many cases involves an attempt to teach the children to use a second dialect of the language, must initially be primarily remedial; and in certain respects remedial teaching of the kind required is very much more difficult and naturally requires different techniques, than are required, for example, in the teaching of French in secondary schools in Kenya in which the teacher does not have to take into account previous exposure of the children to the language, nor the effect of interference from cognate languages.

Until recently, moreover, many of the teachers who were required to undertake this most difficult task were not trained to cope with it.[52] This situation is, however, being rapidly remedied, primarily through a special programme for the training of non-graduate teachers of Swahili that has been mounted at Kenyatta College Teacher Training Division.

In contrast to teachers of most other subjects, furthermore, teachers of Swahili do not have access to appropriate course books for use at secondary level, nor in the absence of an Inspector of Swahili, is the guidance available to them from the ministry that is available to teachers of most other subjects at secondary level.[53] In the absence of such guidance, and of the lack of a detailed syllabus, the teachers themselves and members of the Kenya Institute of Education drew up a scheme of work for the teaching of Swahili at secondary level in April 1968.[54]

The scheme provided information to teachers concerning the selection of extracts from readers and guidance about specific grammatical items to be dealt with sequentially, during the first two years of secondary schooling. In addition to a period of 'Reading' and one of 'Grammar', a period of 'Comprehension' exercise was recommended. It is evident from the comments of a number of teachers that the scheme of work has served a useful purpose but naturally in the light of the difficulties faced by teachers of Swahili, its utility is limited.

To go some way towards meeting these difficulties, a course, remedial in intent and constructed so as to be appropriate for use by pupils of different levels of attainment, is required. Initially the oral component of such a course would need to be considerable. The pedagogical justification for this emphasis need not be elaborated upon here but it is also necessary to bear in mind that the majority of children are required to speak and understand spoken Swahili far more frequently and in more varied situations than they are required to read or write it.

At present the differences of attainment of children in the same class are frequently so considerable that teachers are obliged to divide the class into groups for certain teaching purposes or else to direct their teaching primarily towards students who are of a relatively similar level of attainment and to assist the others with supplementary exercises as far as this is possible.[55] The fact that the revised alternative scheme of work makes provision for a year's separate instruction for pupils of lower attainment is indicative of the increasing recognition that different courses are required to meet the needs of the pupils. Mr Claessen's subsequent observations on the need for separate syllabuses and examinations appear to suggest a logical extension or consequence of this development.

THE TEACHING OF ENGLISH

The suggestion in the report on *New Directions in Teacher Education* that courses for teachers of different languages should be related where possible stemmed from a recognition of the fact that certain principles of language teaching, and the procedures derived from these, have application to the teaching of any language. The attention of teachers of Swahili in secondary schools was drawn to this fact in the circular on the teaching of Swahili referred to earlier, where it was stated that suitable secondary school methodology is expounded in detail in the battery of inspectorate circulars on the teaching of English.

While it is the case that much could be learned from these circulars, the guidance given concerning the content of the English course in secondary schools and the teaching methods that are suggested in relation to this, are naturally of limited application to the teaching of Swahili. One reason that this is so is the fact that as is stated in a ministry circular, 'in the secondary school, reading is the basis of the English course'.[56]

In a relatively recent statement of time allocation for various elements in the English course it was stated that 'fundamental are four or five or more periods a week devoted to reading of various types of which one period may be given to a course book, mainly for diverse sorts of intensive reading. Then come three periods of expression, written and oral. Finally there is the equivalent of one period a week especially in junior forms, for formal drills such as sentence drills and pattern drills . . .'.[57]

As the emphasis on the reading component of the English course given to children entering secondary school is so marked, it will not, I think, be inappropriate to consider certain implications of this. Before doing so, it is necessary to reiterate that the emphasis appears to have the support of the majority of the teachers of English in so far as their attitudes are reflected in the answers given to the first schedules and that the very real assistance that the detailed Inspectorate circulars on the teaching of English gave to teachers in implementing the recommendations was commented on several times. As a practical expedient therefore the emphasis can be justified.

It seems, however, that 'the insistence on reading of all kinds'[58] as the basis of the course has led considerable numbers of teachers in Form 1 to overlook the principle (which underlies the sequencing of the course materials constructed for use in the primary schools) that 'oral language is primary and pre-requisite to reading'.[59] Recent research has confirmed the importance of developing skill in the spoken language before extensive work in reading[60] and there is indeed increasing evidence that 'children have to learn to understand and to operate language before they can read it well or intelligently'.[61] More particularly, scholars such as C. A. Lefevre, P. Tyler, D. Lloyd and R. MacDavid have argued that it is particularly important for children to understand what have been termed the 'meaning bearing patterns'[62] that are signalled by intonation if they are effectively to relate in reading what MacDavid calls the linguistic phrase and the typographical phrase. It is, however, not very helpful to adumbrate general principles without attempting to indicate how these might be implemented and it might therefore be appropriate to make a number of tentative proposals towards this end.

At present Form 1 teachers have before them the somewhat amorphous ideal that students should be able to use 'normal' English by the end of Standard II. It would be possible and it might be helpful to set out the objectives of the first two years of instruction in more detail. As is the case at primary level, teachers need to have some conception of the sequence of grammatical and to a less significant extent lexical elements which are to be taught or revised in the time available and of the general objective in terms of language performance which it is intended to attain within this time. Even if a good course book is available teachers need such information to assist them to select and elaborate upon the sections of the text which are most relevant to their purposes. The information could also be presented in such a way as to help teachers deal in sequence with elements of the grammatical structure and related phonological features of the language, during the periods set aside for 'intensive reading'. The corpus of material that will form the basis of the Safari English Course that is to be used at upper primary level in Kenya is known. As very few teachers in secondary school appear to know what is taught at primary level the scheme might appropriately begin with an outline of this corpus and might then indicate how particular elements could best be revised and how more complex forms in written and spoken registers could be introduced.

Such a scheme of work might well be distributed in a form which would allow for constant revision and supplementation, and should be accompanied by a handbook to assist teachers to implement suggestions made in the scheme. In preparing such handbooks it has proved useful in Tanzania, for example, to draw upon the expertise of members of the language panel associated with the Institute of Education, which has members drawn from the university, teachers' colleges, secondary schools and officials of the Ministry of Education. There would seem to be no reason why such expertise could not be similarly exploited in Kenya to this end and I think it is to be regretted that since 1969 the secondary English panel in Kenya has been required to devote its attention primarily to questions relating to the selection of set texts for school examinations in literature.

In relation to what has been said about the emphasis on reading it is relevant to mention again that the results of Exercise 9 indicated that a considerable number of the children tested were deficient in skills associated with listening comprehension. As methods of teaching at secondary level necessitate the constant exercise of such skills, it would seem that it might be of some assistance to pupils if considerable stress were laid initially in the English course for secondary school entrants on exercises in listening comprehension, which could appropriately be followed by related reading comprehension exercises. S. Duker and others have shown that the two sets of skills have numerous factors in common,[63] and training in one set of skills can improve proficiency in the other.[64] Training in auditory discrimination can serve to improve the child's skill in word recognition and to remedy forms of spelling errors which derive from the effect of interference from the sound system of the child's first language.[65]

Such exercises could also be prepared in the form of school broadcasts without undue difficulty. There are certain other areas of activity that an initial course might appropriately deal with that are referred to in subsequent paragraphs.

The comments above concerning what may be termed the centrality of speech in the structure of any language course at this level are equally relevant to the teaching of Swahili; indeed they are perhaps more relevant as the materials available for the teaching of the language at secondary level are markedly inadequate and experiments such as those carried out by R. Golden, have clearly indicated the pedagogical superiority of speech exercises over reading materials in circumstances in which a standard form of language has to be taught to children who use a non-standard dialect.[66] At the same time it is necessary to recognize the interrelatedness of the different skills involved in speaking, listening, reading, and writing. The emphasis given here to the first is a reflection of what I consider to be the overt concentration on the third set of skills in the syllabus.

However, the purpose of these comments is not to provide in any degree a form of prescription for difficulties facing teachers but simply to make the obvious point that it is necessary or at least useful to keep under review accepted policy and practice in rapidly changing conditions. When the policy that 'the insistence on reading of all kinds' was clearly reiterated as the main feature of the recommendations for the teaching of English, there were less than 10,000 students entering secondary schools, many of which had libraries. It was feasible to recommend in such circumstances that 'about three dozen books a year should be read by pupils in Forms 1 and 2'. The number of schools has since increased by over six hundred per cent, and that of entrants accordingly, and relatively few of the newer schools have the materials to facilitate the main goal of the syllabus. The activities of those responsible for the implementation of decisions on educational language policy in Kenya during the past decade have been characterized by a willingness to experiment and innovate and the effectiveness in the past of the programmes at primary and secondary level is borne out in the results of the School Certificate examinations. Without wishing to exaggerate the seriousness of the situation, therefore, I wish to record my opinion that a reconsideration of the objectives of the present syllabus relating to English teaching in Forms 1 and 2 and of the methods used to attain these would be of some utility.

THE TEACHING OF OTHER SUBJECTS

There are other principles apart from that reiterated above which might appropriately be taken into account in the preparation of teaching materials for children entering secondary schools. Two such principles were summarized in the proposals made in the final report of the Upper Primary Workshop in Kenya in 1964, which drew attention to 'the need for effective co-ordination of all the activities connected with the development of the programme' in the schools and 'the need for the language of instruction to be maintained at the level of the pupils' attainment in that language in all subjects and spheres of educational activity'.[67] The report dealt with the application of these principles in the upper primary course but the conclusions have direct relevance,also, to secondary level language teaching.

It is an evident feature of the organization of syllabuses that the extent of integration or co-ordination between the teaching of different subjects and the extent to which the language course constitutes the basis of such integration, as it were, in that it provides pupils with the specific language skills required for the learning of other subjects, does lessen considerably in the higher level of the educational system, and indeed is little in evidence at the secondary level. To a certain extent, as the necessity for the acquisition by the children of factual data associated with content subjects increases, this process of divergence is inevitable, but, as has been stated, neither the first nor the second principles are wholly inapplicable at secondary level. The language content of the planned series of secondary English courses in Ethiopia has, for example, been partly selected on the basis of an analysis of other subject textbooks,[68] and ideally one would wish to see such integration between courses increasingly taken account of in all schools in which the medium of instruction for all subjects is a second language.

While the wider recognition of the fact that at secondary level 'English is a service course'[69] radically affects the content of the initial course for pupils entering secondary schools, it is becoming increasingly recognized that the specific reading and study skills associated with particular content areas are best taught by the teachers responsible for these subjects; indeed it appears that the kind of co-ordination that can best be realized at the secondary level is one which, rather than obliging the teacher of English to attempt to teach the language skills required in other subjects, involves a development of the awareness in teachers of other subjects of their responsibilities in extending the children's knowledge of the medium of instruction as it relates to their content field. Most teachers of subjects other than English who co-operated in the survey did recognize that proficiency in the medium of instruction affected the performance of the children in these subjects. They recognized also that the children's ability in forms of listening and reading comprehension, in outlining, note-taking, and summarizing, their ability to write assignments using the verbal conventions associated with their particular subject area, and their methods of revision, critically affected their academic achievement; primarily in non-science subjects but also in subjects such as geography, biology, health, science and chemistry. Relatively few teachers, however, considered that they were either responsible for instructing, or equipped to instruct, the children in the skills mentioned.

It is of some relevance in this connection that in Tanzania and more recently in Zambia an interesting teaching development has been undertaken which involved the participation of all teachers responsible for content areas in Form 1 and which is primarily directed towards familiarizing students entering secondary school with certain of the language and study skills they are required to exercise. The classwork as originally planned consisted of an intensive six-week course taken before the students began their normal secondary school work.[70]

While it has been found that there were ways in which the course might be improved, primarily in the direction of increasing the number of remedial oral exercises involving the active participation of the pupils, and in increasing the complexity of the listening comprehension exercises, the utility of the experiment is generally acknowledged, and in Zambia the use of the 'remedial course in the medium of instruction', as it is termed, has now been recommended in all schools.

As first conceived the intention of the course was not only to assist the students but also to guide the teachers in methods of stimulating and controlling group activity and discussion and in ensuring that they understood the importance of the need for the language of instruction to be maintained at the level of the pupils' attainment in so far as this was possible. In this respect the experiment might be seen as an attempt to introduce into an area of secondary school instruction some of the principles and procedures generally accepted and used in primary schools.

While the value of a transitional course of this nature is unquestionable, it is apparent that the skills itemized cannot be imparted by any short-term measures. Ideally, their inculcation should begin at the primary level and continue in the secondary school. At secondary level the realization of the principles underlying the transitional course described would involve the participation of teachers of all subjects and this involvement should ideally extend throughout the school course. It is somewhat paradoxical that at the present time the course in English is the only one in which teachers are asked to give careful attention to the use of texts in which the language has been simplified so that 'the correct degree of difficulty can be presented to stretch the child without causing frustration and a sense of futility'.[71] It would perhaps be unrealistic to expect that texts adapted to the language attainment of students entering secondary schools in Kenya will be forthcoming but one would expect that in selecting textbooks, teachers who were aware of their students' problems would consider readability to be one of the criteria of acceptability.

In most subject areas, even when texts which have been written with the needs of East African students in mind are available, teachers are necessarily responsible for familiarizing their pupils with the terminology and linguistic content of their discipline. The pupils' difficulties could be alleviated if the teachers concerned accepted that the effective teaching of their subject involved an element of language instruction and if the courses of instruction given to teachers and the induction courses which might appropriately be provided for expatriates, were organized to this end.

NOTES

[1] 'The Educational Implications of Multilingualism in Eastern Africa' in T. P. Gorman (ed.), *Language in Education in Eastern Africa*, Oxford University Press, Nairobi, 1970, p. 10.

[2] In 1968 there were 387 maintained, 51 assisted and 561 unaided classes in schools in Kenya at Form 1 level. 1,356 students from Kenya were studying at the University of East Africa in the same year. cf. Ministry of Education Annual Report, Government Printer, 1968.

[3] Inspectorate circular INS/C/4/3114, November 1965.

[4] Details of the sample design are given in Chapter 13.

[5] The schedules issued in 1968 and 1969 were not identical in every respect. In 1968 the teachers were asked to ascertain whether their colleagues teaching certain specified subjects to the pupils involved in the survey considered that the children's academic performance in the subject taught was affected by their proficiency in the medium of instruction.

[6] Tests that were given indicated that most of the children in the school concerned had a knowledge that was above average taking the sample as a whole. The teacher was clearly judging their ability to use the 'standard' written dialect of the language whereas they spoke a non-standard dialect.

[7] The most common teacher's books, course books and readers in use in the schools in question were as follows (in order of frequency of use):

A. *Course books/Teacher's books*
  1. *Swahili Grammar*, E. O. Ashton (Longmans)
  2. *Sarufi ya Kiswahili*, G. W. Broomfield (Sheldon)
  3. *Swahili Exercises*, E. Steere (SPCK, Sheldon)
  4. *Teach Yourself Swahili*, D. V. Perrott (EUP)
  5. *Tusome Kiswahili*, I–IV, A. E. Bull (OUP)

B. *Readers*
  1. *Alfu Lela Ulela* Bk. 1 (Longmans)
  2. *Hekaya za Abunuwas na Hadithi nyingine* (Macmillan)
  3. *Kisiwa chenye Hazina* (Longmans)
  4. *Hadithi za Esopo* (Sheldon)
  5. *Uhuru wa Watumwa* (Nelson)
  6. *Nakupenda lakini* (OUP)

[8] cf. Swahili Scheme of Work for Secondary Schools, 1968. (Mimeographed.)

[9] cf. Primary School Syllabus, Ministry of Education, Kenya, 1967, p. 84 ff.

[10] op. cit., p. 92.

[11] The senior examiners for East Africa made the same objection in their report to the East African Examinations Council and the Cambridge Examinations Syndicate in 1969.

[12] Again, it is necessary to interpret the teacher's comments in the light of the common assumption that children who do not use a form of the standard dialect do not know the language.

[13] The five most common textbooks in use in 1968 were:

A. 1. *A Course of English Study*, R. Mackin (OUP)
  2. *English Course for Secondary Schools*, D. Grieve (Nelson)

3. *Patterns and Skills in English*, J. Bright (Longmans)
4. *Junior English Composition*, J. Bright (Longmans)
5. *Practical English*, P. Ogundipe and P. Tregidgo (Longmans)

[14] Fourteen of the schools in the rural areas were boarding schools; eleven were boys' schools and five were girls' schools. All but two had a Ministry of Education Certificate A rating.

[15] It is perhaps relevant to note that Professor S. Ominde's analysis of the results of the 1962 census revealed that 83.60 per cent of the city's total African population were 'migrants'. Of those, 44.90 per cent came from areas that are predominantly Kikuyu-speaking, 35.28 per cent from Nyanza (15.8 per cent from predominantly Luo-speaking areas, and 14.8 per cent from predominantly Luyia-speaking districts), and 16.7 per cent from Kamba-speaking areas. cf. *Land and Population Movements in Kenya*, Heinemann, 1968, p. 124 ff.

[16] The tests were administered over a period of three months, so that in some cases the number of children who took each test in the Nairobi schools varied slightly. Tests 7, 8 and 11 were completed by the girls in the Nairobi sample only. Exercises 1 and 6 were constructed by Mr A. Claessen, tutor in Swahili at the Kenyatta Senior Teachers' College. The other tests were constructed by the writer, with the exception of the two tests published by the Science Research Associates.

[17] The Safari English Course, and the *Masomo ya Kiswahili* course now being introduced into schools at upper primary level will provide a basis for certain kinds of test construction at the level with which the survey was concerned.

[18] Occasionally I have made use of symbols commonly accepted as abbreviations for statistical concepts. The most commonly used are:

X   raw score   X̄   mean score   Md median score
P.R. percentile rank   S.D. the standard deviation of a sample
σ   the standard deviation of a population   N   number of subjects
r   correlation coefficient

In non-technical terms, the mean score is the 'average' score of a group; the median score is the score above and below which half of the scores fall. The standard deviation might be said to represent an average of all the deviations (differences in score) from the main score. A correlation coefficient expresses the degree of relation or correspondence between two sets of scores.

[19] Report of the Swahili Workshop held at Dar es Salaam Teachers' College, July/August 1965, in *Swahili*, 36, 1, 1966.

[20] Mean scores (out of a total of 20) and standard deviations of the children in the major language groups are indicated below:

	X̄	S.D.
Kikuyu	10.77	3.79
Luo	7.75	4.38
Luyia	9.52	4.03
Kamba	9.31	3.86
Meru	8.97	3.11
Gusii	10.84	4.04
Kipsigis	11.76	3.03

[21] As stated in Chapter 13, the majority of children in both rural and urban samples claimed to have studied Swahili in primary school but there were considerable differences in the average number of years which children in the different language groups claimed to have done so. Clearly a great deal of reliance cannot be placed on the precise estimates of their educational exposure to the language that were given by the children, but that there is considerable variation in this respect in different districts is also clear. Similarly and relatedly, there was marked variation in the percentages of children in each group in the rural sample who claimed to have studied the language at *any* stage in the primary system; and who claimed to have been educated initially through the medium of Swahili. The percentage of each group in the rural sample in this last category is indicated below:

Swahili medium	%		%
Kikuyu	1.4	Meru	0.0
Luo	10.0	Mijikenda	78.0
Luyia	13.0	Nandi	31.5
Kamba*	—	Kipsigis	5.6

*Information was not supplied to enable us to calculate the percentage for the Kamba-speaking group.

The relatively high rating for the Luyia and Luo children is not unexpected in view of the fact that one of the schools attended by the children in each language group, was situated in a 'border' area. The high rating for the Nandi speakers within the Kalenjin group as opposed to that of the Kipsigis-speaking children is patent.

[22] A Pearson-Product-Moment Correlation Coefficient was used to calculate the degree of relationship. $r = 0.77$. In the girls' group the correlation coefficient was 0.72, and in the boys' group 0.78.

[23] The mean scores of the children in the three language groups on Exercise 1 (Grammatical Structure) are indicated below.

		Rural $\bar{X}$	Urban $\bar{X}$
Kikuyu	Boys	42.15	80.18
	Girls	56.94	77.72
Luo	Boys	37.06	74.41
	Girls	48.09	73.36
Luyia	Boys	61.10	78.80
	Girls	55.21	76.00

[24] An index of Vocabulary Diversity is obtained by dividing the number of different words by the square root of twice the number in the sample. cf. J. B. Carroll, *Language and Thought*, p. 54.

[25] The Farr-Jenkins-Patterson 'New Index of Reading Ease' measures difficulty on a scale from 1–100 approximately: higher values representing *easier* material. cf. N. Farr, S. Jenkins & D. Patterson, 'Simplification of Flesch Reading Ease Formula', *Journal of Applied Psychology*, 35, October 1951, pp. 333–7. Like all measures of difficulty level based on average word and sentence length this measure is in certain respects inadequate. However, I decided to use it in this case as it is as effective a measure as is the Flesch Reading Ease Index on which it is based, and it is easier to apply. It has one deficiency which it shares with the Flesch index, which is that it has not given a very accurate indication of the difficulty levels of passages taken from scientific materials. For a consideration of the problems involved in such assessment, cf. J. Marshall, 'Comprehension and Alleged Readability of High School Physics Textbooks', *Science Education*, 46, 1962, pp. 335–46.

[26] cf. L. T. Barrett (ed.), *The Evaluation of Children's Reading Achievement*, International Reading Association, Newark, 1967, pp. 82–5.

[27] The difficulty ratings represent the average of the ratings of five or more extracts from each book.

[28] According to the readability formula used the difficulty of the passage was 73.4. This does seem to indicate the validity of J. Marshall's contention that formulae developed in relation to non-technical, non-scientific materials were not necessarily helpful in indicating the readability level of scientific texts.

[29] i.e. A somewhat slower rate than a normal rate of speaking, which is between 130 and 165 words a minute.

[30] The correlation between the English teachers' assessment and the children's performance on the listening comprehension test was highly significant ($r = 0.73$). A number of tests were also inter-correlated. The relationship between Exercise 11 and Exercise 9 (Reading Comprehension) was highly significant ($r = 0.46$) as was that between Exercise 11 and Exercise 8 (Written Exercise in English) ($r = 1.23$).

[31] $r = 0.64$. This was to be expected, as there is evidence that a factor of verbal ability or knowledge of word meaning accounts for most of what is measured in tests of reading comprehension. cf. J. W. Schneyer, 'Significant Reading Research at the Secondary School' in R. Karlin et. al. (eds.), *Reading Instruction in Secondary Schools*, IRA, 1967, pp. 131–49.

[32] Current reading age is calculated with reference to the Gates Reading Test. Correlations between PMA 7–11 sub-test of Verbal Meaning (VW) and scores on the tests = 0.75. 'The VW score particularly is a useful predictor of reading ability as measured by the Gates test. For this reason, it is recommended that the VW score alone

may be used as an index of "reading aptitude".' *SRA Primary Mental Abilities 7–11, Technical Supplement*, 1st. edition, 1954, p. 4.

[33] I am aware of the problems involved in the use of the tests that have been standardized on populations other than the population in question, and I would like to indicate the reasons for the choice of the sub-tests that were judged to be appropriate for use among the children in the urban sample.

The reasons I made use of the sub-test of Verbal Meaning in the PMA, were, (a) as has been mentioned, the score can be used to predict reading ability according to the Gates tests, and an estimate of a child's Current Reading Age. (As is indicated in the title of the test it is intended for use with children who are slightly younger than the majority of the children in the sample but provides for the estimation of reading ages between 6 and 14 years. It was anticipated and demonstrated that the scores of the children in the sample would fall within this range.) (b) While in the 7–11 battery all the tests are speeded, Professor Anastasi has shown that the Verbal Meaning sub-test is primarily a power test, that is, the results are not dependent on speed of reading. (cf. A. Anastasi, *Psychological Testing*, 3rd. ed., Macmillan, London, 1968, p. 91.) This is an important consideration in testing children in a second language. (c) Scores for the batteries at the levels used can be expressed as percentiles and stanines and are therefore useful in plotting individual profiles. (d) The sub-tests selected had a high face validity in the judgement of a number of experienced secondary school teachers in Kenya. Possible objections to the use of the PMA 7–11, which I did not consider significant enough to warrant its exclusion, are that reliability coefficients are not reported fully, nor is information regarding standard error computations for each sub-test available. It has also been objected that the validity figures provided for the test are correlations with other tests. Given the nature of the sub-test, I do not, however, consider this last objection to be a serious one.

[34] Chronological age and reading age are generally closely related among children who speak English as a first language.

[35] Again, to state the reasons for the choice of this test. (a) In the 1958 Manual, several hundred correlations between the PMA sub-tests and other test scores are given. The tests of Verbal Meaning and Reasoning, the most reliable sub-tests, show the highest correlations with other tests (cf. O. Buros (ed.), *The Fifth Mental Measurements Yearbook*, Gryphon Press, New Brunswick, 1959, p. 116.) Multiple corrections with tests of general intelligence or scholastic aptitude are high. (b) The profiles are plotted on a sliding percentile scale in which the units are adjusted to conform to the normal distribution. The same profiles form provides for the calculation of a scholastic aptitude score. (c) The tests of Verbal Meaning and Reasoning have a high face validity.

Recent research has indicated that Thurstone's conception of Primary Mental Abilities as illustrated in the test needs considerable elaboration, but it is still accepted that the factor of Verbal Comprehension or Verbal Meaning is best measured by vocabulary tests of the type used in the PMA tests, although Verbal Ability can of course be tested by a variety of items.

[36] A summary of relevant research is given in S. F. Irwin & W. Miller, 'Language Development', *62nd Year Book of the National Society for the Study of Education*, p. 125.

[37] In his report to the Kenya Education Commission about experiments carried out in Uganda, Mr J. Silvey indicated that the scores of children on the Examination of English Usage and Comprehension correlated more closely with school performance ($R = 0.473$) than their scores on any other test. 'A verbal intelligence test correlated 0.410 and a non-verbal test bore virtually no relation.' cf. J. Silvey, Memorandum on Selection for Secondary Schools in Kenya (KEC, 64, Primary), April 1964, p. 3.

[38] The Reasoning sub-test involves the manipulation of letters in relation to conventional alphabetical sequence. It is possible that if a child had not learned the alphabet by repeating the letters in sequence, his score on the test would be affected by this fact.

[39] H. C. A. Somerset, *Predicting Success in the School Certificate*, East African Publishing House, Nairobi, 1969, p. 74.

[40] Mr Somerset refers to an experiment by E. Lee which shows that children from rural areas who entered Philadelphia schools in the first grade showed a marked spurt in intellectual growth in their first three years; by the time they reach the fourth

grade their mean IQ was more than 5 points higher than it had been in the first grade. By contrast children who migrated when they were older showed more modest gains. Those who entered Philadelphia schools in the third and fourth grades, for instance, gained only 3 IQ points in the five years between Grades 4 and 9. cf. Somerset, op. cit., p. 79.

[41] The score corresponds to normalized standard scores with a mean of a hundred and a standard deviation of 16.

[42] The scores are heavily influenced by the children's performances on the tests of Verbal Meaning and it is necessary to reiterate that on such tests the performances of children such as those in the sample are characteristically lower than the scores of first language speakers. Such experiments as have indicated that bilingual children have performed as well on tests of Verbal Meaning as monolingual children have involved children drawn from groups characterized by relatively high socio-economic status, who were literate in their first language and who were taught the medium of instruction by native speakers of the language.

[43] cf. The Report of the English Medium Survey carried out by B. J. Carroll and Mrs S. Wolofsky and appended to the Memorandum on English Medium Teaching submitted to the 1964 Education Commission (KEC, 64, Primary), 16 May 1964. In this report it was stated that initial results confirmed 'what is known by all teachers and observers: that the children's growth in both language and general aspects of development is achieving in two years what formerly took at least four years . . . By contrast the children in non-English medium streams seem poorly educated in linguistic skills . . . ' (p. 3). cf. also Mr R. Fawcett's statement that '. . . the children in the present non-English medium class would appear to be at a disadvantage, especially in learning English'. He concludes that ' . . . if this prognosis is correct, consideration might be given to weighting the marks in the Certificate of Primary Education in such a way as to compensate for the disadvantage under which the latter group is working . . .' R. Fawcett, 'The Medium of Education in the Lower Primary Schools in Africa, with Special Reference to Kenya' in T. P. Gorman (ed.), op. cit., p. 56.

[44] As Mr Fawcett points out, the gradual introduction of the continuation course for students who have been instructed through the New Primary Approach may materially alter this situation. This cannot be assumed, however, and the success or otherwise of particular programmes cannot be ascertained without continuing controlled research.

[45] It should be remembered, also, that the distinction between the procedures used in 'English medium' and 'non-English medium' schools is not always as great as one might anticipate. In non-NPA classes teachers are instructed that 'there should be an increasing use of English as soon as it is clear that the pupils are ready for the beginning of the change over. Some use of English as a medium should be encouraged at as early a stage as Primary I.' (*Primary School Syllabus*, Ministry of Education, 1967, p. 39) and in NPA teachers are advised to use the children's mother tongue for the teaching of Religious Education and naturally of the mother tongue itself and for the teaching of history in Primary III, in schools where it is taught. With the introduction of NPA methods in schools where the mother tongue is the initial medium of instruction, the distinction will become even less evident in a number of schools in the future. The introduction of an experimental course in which the initial medium of instruction is the mother tongue of the children and in which English is used as the medium for most subjects from Primary II is in some respects a logical extension of current developments.

[46] The contrast noted earlier between the scores of the boys and girls in the Nairobi sample on Exercise 2 (Vocabulary) was evident also in the scores of the children in this sub-group. On Exercise 1 the boys had a mean score of 79.75 (S.D. 15.93) as opposed to the girls' score of 79.00 (S.D. 13.56); and of 75.94 (S.D. 15.06) as opposed to the girls' score of 60.68 (S.D. 19.59) on Exercise 2.

[47] W. F. Cahill, 'General Features of the Standard of the Swahili Class in Kenya', Curriculum Development and Research Centre, Ministry of Education, Nairobi, November 1968.

[48] In this connection the Head of the African Language Unit of the Institute of Education has written that 'Kiswahili is among the neglected subjects in many colleges', and he added that 'this negligence is not always intentional. Many colleges, in the absence

of qualified Swahili tutors, leave Kiswahili in the hands of the English tutor' and this has the result that 'students end their training equipped with the general methods of language teaching but with very little reference to the Swahili syllabus or Swahili course books'. D. Michuki, 'Problems of Teaching Kiswahili in Primary Schools', Conference on the Study and Teaching of Languages in Kenya, December 1969.

[49] In this regard, also, Mr Michuki stated bluntly that 'in the absence of suitable Swahili teaching material and the lack of supervision, much of the teaching of Kiswahili in primary schools has resulted in a mere waste of time'. op. cit., p. 1.

[50] *Masomo ya Kiswahili*, Jomo Kenyatta Foundation, Nairobi, 1967–70.

[51] Two of the aims are (a) to develop ability to understand and converse in Swahili to the point where the pupil can use the language competently in future contacts with people in cases where there is no common linguistic medium, and (b) to teach the art of writing good clear Swahili, to enable the pupil to communicate effectively in writing through this medium. cf. *Primary School Syllabus*, Ministry of Education, Kenya, p. 89.

[52] 'The teaching of Kiswahili in secondary schools is largely left in the hands of non-graduate teachers, some of whom have not had any specific training in the teaching of Kiswahili or in second language methodology.' A. Bashir, 'The Teaching of African Languages in Secondary Schools', a paper given at the Second Regional Eastern African Conference on Language and Linguistics, Nairobi, 1970, p. 6.

[53] The development plan of the Institute of Education makes provision for the work on the preparation of a secondary school course in Swahili to begin in 1972. Provision has also been made by the ministry for the appointment of an Inspector of Swahili.

[54] The first scheme was issued as a result of a conference of teachers of Swahili held at the Kenya Institute of Education. The Inspector of Swahili from Tanzania and Professor Lyndon Harries attended the workshop as a result of a grant from the Survey Council of the Survey of Language Use and Language Teaching in Eastern Africa.

[55] The scheme of work outlined in 1968 made provision for students of a lower level of attainment to be given separate lessons based on Book 1B of the *Masomo ya Kiswahili* primary course for a period of one term, after which it was suggested that they could be integrated, as it were, into the class. The inadequacy of this provision for students who in some areas constituted a majority of the class was soon recognized and this alternative scheme of work, as it was termed, was subsequently extensively revised. The revised course provides for a year's instruction for pupils of lower attainment. Greater emphasis is laid on oral activity and practice and a number of revision periods are incorporated into the course as integral units.

[56] INS/C/4/3/114, 1 November 1965.

[57] G. Bowman (Inspector of English), 'The Teaching of English in Secondary Schools in Kenya', a paper read to the First Regional Conference on Language and Linguistics, Dar es Salaam, 1968, p. 5. In pursuance of the aims of the course a great deal of guidance has been given to teachers in connection with the selection of class and library readers. They are advised that simplified readers should be used in the first two forms of secondary school for extension reading; and that in Form 1 graded readers with a word level of 1,500–3,000 should be selected and in Form 2 readers of a word level of 3,000 and above should be used. Form 2 is said to be a 'transition form reaching up to normal English, at which level all pupils should be confidently established by the beginning of Form 3', cf. INS/C/4/3/116, p. 9.

[58] INS/C/4/3/56.

[59] C. Fries, *Teaching and Learning English as a Foreign Language*, Michigan University Press, 1945, p. 6.

[60] cf. Report of the National Council of Teachers of English, 'Language Programmes for the Disadvantaged', NCTE, Illinois, 1965.

[61] This statement is by A. Davis, 'Teaching Language and Reading to Disadvantaged Negro Children', *Elementary English*, November 1963, p. 995.

[62] cf. C. A. Lefevre, *Linguistics in the Teaching of Reading*, Chicago, 1962; P. Tyler, 'Sound Patterns and Sense', *Education*, May 1963; D. Lloyd, 'Intonation and Reading', *Education*, May 1967.

[63] S. Duker, 'Listening', *Review of Educational Research*, 34, 1964, pp. 156–62.

[64] R. Strang briefly reviewed a number of experiments in which a significant coefficient of correlation between these two sets of skills was indicated in *Reading Diagnosis and Remediation*, IRA, 1968, p. 14.

[65] Such interference accounted for over 30 per cent of the deviant spellings produced in the essays written by the girls in the Nairobi sample who spoke Kikuyu as a first language.

[66] R. Golden, 'Changing Dialects by Using Tapes' in R. Shuy (ed.), *Social Dialects and Language Learning*, 1964, pp. 63–6.

[67] Final Report of the Upper Primary Workshop, Ministry of Education, 1964, 1–2, (mimeographed). In their statement about co-ordination those attending the workshop were referring to the fact that whereas in the first three standards of primary school, learning in all subject areas has 'been inter-related and developed by means of the English medium materials', in subsequent years the emphasis has been upon the teaching of separate subjects.

[68] cf. S. C. Murison-Bowie, 'The Role of the Textbook in Transferring Media at the Junior Secondary School', a paper given at the Language Association of Eastern Africa Conference, Nairobi, 1970.

[69] cf. Inspectorate circular ME/101/7/40, May 1970.

[70] The course was constructed to give pupils practice in the following skills: aural comprehension and reading comprehension, followed by group discussion and summary; reading comprehension followed by questions, discussion and composition; extensive reading, intended to foster increased reading speed; training in reference skills involving the rapid extraction of specific information from reference books and a number of grammatical exercises involving sentence expansion.

The course content is described in some detail in R. Isaacs, 'Learning through Language' in T. P. Gorman (ed.), op. cit.

[71] INS/C/4/3/56, p. 51.

FIGURE 16.1   *Linguistic composition of the samples*
(a)   Urban

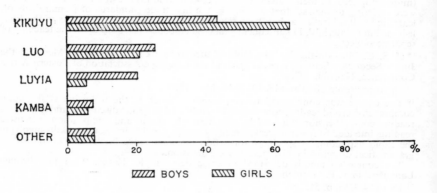

(b)   Rural

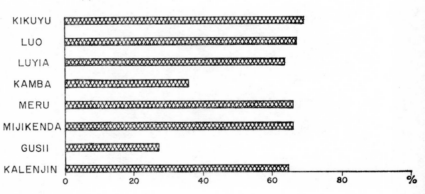

FIGURE 16.2 *Details of the urban sample by sex*

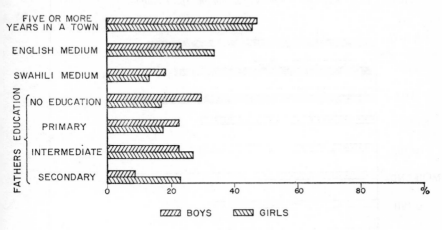

FIGURE 16.3 *Exercise 1: scores of urban and rural samples*

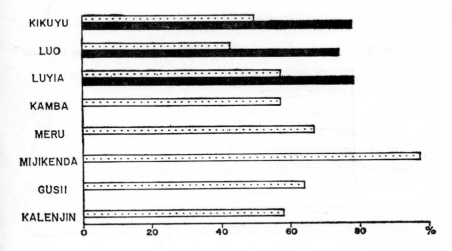

FIGURE 16.4   *Exercise 2: scores of urban and rural samples*

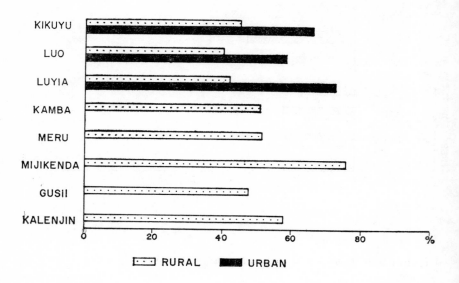

FIGURE 16.5   *Exercise 2: mean scores of rural language groups (ten sub-tests)*

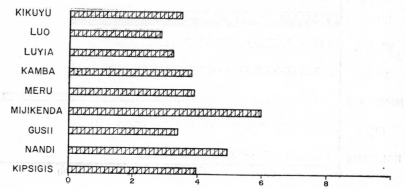

FIGURE 16.6 *Exercise 2: scores of urban and rural samples on sub-tests (different topics)*

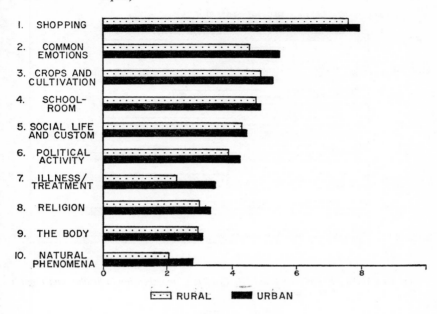

1. SHOPPING
2. COMMON EMOTIONS
3. CROPS AND CULTIVATION
4. SCHOOL-ROOM
5. SOCIAL LIFE AND CUSTOM
6. POLITICAL ACTIVITY
7. ILLNESS/TREATMENT
8. RELIGION
9. THE BODY
10. NATURAL PHENOMENA

⋯ RURAL ■ URBAN

FIGURE 16.7 *Exercise 2: mean scores of different sexes in the urban and rural samples (major language groups)*

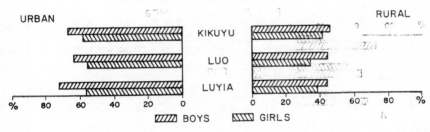

URBAN RURAL

KIKUYU
LUO
LUYIA

% 80 60 40 20 0   0 20 40 60 80 %

▨ BOYS ▧ GIRLS

FIGURE 16.8 *Scores on Exercise 1 related to proficiency rating*

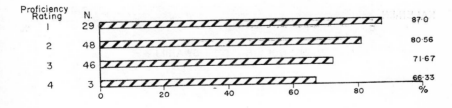

Proficiency Rating   N.
1   29   87·0
2   48   80·56
3   46   71·67
4   3   66·33

0 20 40 60 80 %

541

FIGURE 16.9   *Exercises 4A and 4B: Reading Comprehension in Swahili and English* (*rural sample*)

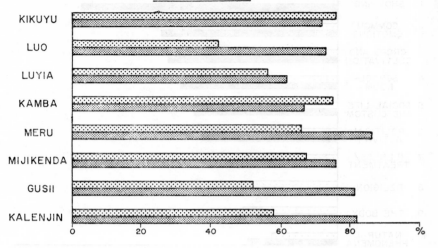

FIGURE 16.10   *Exercises 5A and 5B: Reading Comprehension in Swahili and English* (*rural sample*)

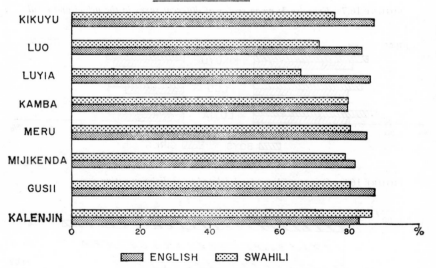

FIGURE 16.11 *Exercises 4A, 4B, 5A and 5B: mean scores (urban and rural samples)*

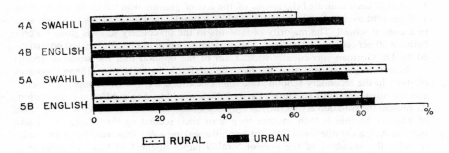

FIGURE 16.12 *Exercise 9: Reading Comprehension in English. Mean scores related to difficulty level of passages*

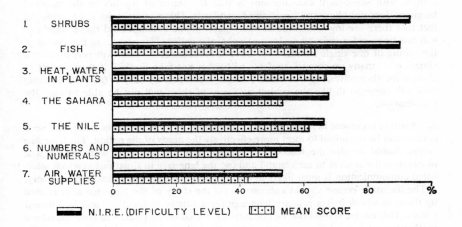

APPENDIX A

The Examining of Swahili at Secondary Level
A. CLAESSEN

1.   As has been indicated the results of the test of grammatical structure ranged from a 35 per cent average in a school attended by Kipsigis-speaking students to 85 per cent in a coastal school. The majority of students in the up-country schools gained scores between 50 per cent and 60 per cent. The range of scores in the vocabulary test constructed by Dr Gorman was equally wide. I am of the opinion that the students' results in these exercises suggest that it might be advisable to start two different courses of study in the secondary schools; one might be called the 'Swahili Language Course' and the other 'Swahili Literature'. Each of them would lead to a different examination. At present the situation is that there is only one examination for all students, irrespective of whether Swahili is their mother tongue or their second or third language. There is, moreover, a definite trend from the Swahili-speaking areas, especially from Tanzania, to raise the standard of the present Swahili paper in the EACE/SC examinations. I consider it unreasonable to expect people whose knowledge of the structure of the language is almost nil, to compete with others who, at the start of the same course with an equal number of allocated periods, have already mastered the essential features of that language.

  The argument that is generally advanced against the introduction of two different courses with subsequent examinations is that the status of Swahili as the national language does not allow any lowering of standards. This argument does not refute the fact that there *are* low standards in many parts of the country. And those standards will not be raised merely by declaring Swahili the national language. On the contrary, the setting of one single standard for Swahili speakers and others will perpetuate the situation, as many up-country students will either not take Swahili, if they are left to choose for themselves, or if Swahili is made a compulsory subject (as I would urge) they will come to dislike the subject as many of them will not be able to pass the examination.

2.   Another argument in favour of the introduction of two different courses is that such courses can be organized to meet more effectively the needs of the nation. The language course should involve the teaching of graded structure and lexis with the purpose of enabling the student to understand and use the language in situations in which inter-tribal communication is most likely to occur. This course should be made compulsory.

  The literature course should concentrate on the study of the language as it is used by those to whom it is a primary language for a variety of functions and in different genres. This course should not be compulsory but could be offered to students whose mother tongue is Swahili and to others who have already mastered the subject matter of the language course, because the results of the test did often show a great variety of ability among the students of one group. This procedure would help teachers to establish classes which would be more homogeneous in linguistic ability. At present teachers are often obliged to direct their teaching towards students with greater proficiency in the language in order to get at least some of the students through their final examinations.

544

3.   The suggested two courses could also make the training of teachers more effective, especially when, as at present, short courses are still needed to cater for the huge demand for Swahili teachers. The misconception is still widespread that anybody who can speak Swahili, can also teach it, whether he has or has not received any training in teaching the language or in language teaching in general. Many teachers also think that the teaching of Swahili means, in essence, the teaching of 'difficult' words, such as are used in works of literary expression, and 'rules' which govern the morphological changes of the language. Such teachers would certainly profit from intensive training courses directly related to the teaching of the language course. Longer training courses, such as are given in Kenyatta College, could in addition offer to train teachers to teach the substance of the literature paper.

4.   Finally, as the respective objectives of the two courses can be more easily specified, it will be easier to prepare an integrated course of study for both. Such definition will at the same time establish the basic criteria for the grading and writing of textbooks, class readers and teachers' guides.*

* At present the scheme of work described earlier is being used in many schools. This syllabus is unsatisfactory in several aspects. It divides the subject matter into periods for 'Reading', Comprehension', 'Grammar' and at a later stage 'Composition'. Why 'Reading' and 'Comprehension' are divorced from each other is difficult to understand. No system of grading or sequencing underlies the suggested work on grammatical structure. For composition no guidelines are given apart from a recommendation of the book *Kielezo cha Insha*, which expounds a relatively formal and outdated approach to composition work. Nowhere is the relationship mentioned between all these language activities. Students are expected to read books which use almost the entire range of grammatical structure while in the 'Grammar' period the teacher is supposed to teach the Ki-Vi agreement.

BIBLIOGRAPHIES

LIST OF PERIODICALS AND ABBREVIATIONS USED

AA	American Anthropologist, Wisconsin, U.S.A. 1899–
AEO	Archives d'études Orientales, Uppsala, 1910–
AFRICA	Journal of the International Institute of African Languages and Cultures, London, 1928–
AHKI	Abhandlungen des Hamburgischen Kolonialinstituts, Hamburg, 1910–20.
ALS	African Language Studies, London, 1960–
ANTHROPOS	Internationale Zeitschrift für Völker- und Sprachenkunde, Modling-Wien, and later, Posieux (Freiburg), 1906–
A St.	African Studies, Johannesburg, 1942–. Previously Bantu Studies.
BAfr.	Bibliotheca Africana, Innsbruck, 1924–34.
BSGI	Bollettino della Società geografica italiana, Rome, 1868–
BSO(A)S	Bulletin of the School of Oriental (and African) Studies, London, 1917–
EAAJ	East African Agricultural Journal, Nairobi, Kenya, 1935–
ETHNOGRAPHIA	Budapest, 1890–
JAL	Journal of African Languages, London, 1961–
JAS	Journal of the African (later Royal African) Society, London, 1901–43. (African Affairs as from 1944–)
JEASC	Journal of the East African Swahili Committee, Kampala, 1953–
JRAI	Journal of the Royal Anthropological Institute of Great Britain and Ireland, London, 1871–
JRGS	Journal of the Royal Geographical Society, London, 1830–
J. Sem. St.	Journal of Semitic Studies, Manchester University Press, 1956–
MAKERERE	Makerere College, Kampala, Uganda, 1964–49, 1953.
MAN	The Royal Anthropological Institute, London, 1901–
MOr.	Monde Oriental, Uppsala and Leipzig, 1905–
MSOS	Mitteilungen des Seminars für Orientalische Sprachen, Berlin, 1898–
PRGS	Proceedings of the Royal Geographical Society, London, 1855–78. New Series, 1879–
RSt.O	Rivista degli Studi Orientali, Rome, 1921–
WORD	Linguistic Circle of New York, Columbia University, 1945–
WZKM	Wiener Zeitschrift für die Kunde des Morgenlandes, Wien, 1893– (OR 1915–)
ZAOS (ZfAOS)	Zeitschrift für Afrikanische und Ozeanische Sprachen, Berlin, 1895–1901.
ZAS (ZfAS)	Zeitschrift für Afrikanische Sprachen, Berlin, Berlin, 1887–90.
ZDMG	Zeitscrift der Deutschen Morgenländischen Gesellschaft, Leipzig/Berlin, 1847–
ZES (ZfES) (ZKS, ZfKS)	Zeitschrift für Eingeborenen Sprachen, Hamburg/Berlin, 1910– (Currently, Afrika und Übersee.)

| ZFE | Zeitschrift für Ethnologie, Berlin, 1869 |
| ZFK | Zeitschrift für Kolonialsprachen, Hamburg/Berlin, 1910–20 |

OTHER ABBREVIATIONS

AIM	Africa Inland Mission
EALB	East African Literature Bureau
EAPH	East African Publishing House
FAM	Friends' African Mission
IAI	International African Institute
OUP	Oxford University Press
SOAS	School of Oriental and African Studies
SPCK	Society for the Propagation of Christian Knowledge

1. KENYA LANGUAGES

W. H. WHITELEY

INTRODUCTION

The aim of this Bibliography is to provide an exhaustive documentation of grammatical and lexical studies of Kenya languages, whether published or unpublished. There are two conscious exceptions to this, Somali and Swahili, which have both received detailed bibliographical treatment in recent years, as follows:

JOHNSON, J. W. *A Bibliography of Somali Language Materials*, Hargeisa, 1967. 'A Bibliography of the Somali Language and Oral Literature', *African Language Review*, 8, 1969.

VAN SPAANDONCK, M. *Practical and Systematical Swahili Bibliography, Linguistics 1850–1963*, Leiden, 1965, supplemented by A. Mioni in *Cahiers d'Etudes Africaines*, 27, 1967, 485–532. Further material is listed in my *Swahili: the Rise of a National Language*, Methuen, 1969.

The bibliography for Somali is, therefore, selective, and in the case of Swahili restricted to materials relating to the Kenya dialects. Galla, also, is more fully documented in Bryan (1947), q.v. under Galla.

More general bibliographies are also available for Luo and Maasai:

DUPRE, C. E. *The Luo of Kenya: an Annotated Bibliography*, Institute for Cross-cultural Research, Washington, 1968.

JACOBS, A. H. 'Bibliography of the Masai', *African Studies Bulletin*, VII, 3, 1965.

Mention must also be made of linguistic work that is in progress or recently completed though it cannot be claimed that this list is complete:

DE WOLF, J. Linguistic sketch and word-list of Bukusu, 1968/9

DONOHEW, G. Study of the verbal system of Shisa (Luhya), 1970

ELDERKIN, D. Study of the Waata/Dahalo languages, 1969–71

SHARMAN, J. C. Comparative Bantu, 1969–72

SLAVIKOVA, M.   Comparative study of the Dabida/Sagala group, 1969/70
TUCKER, A. N.   A linguistic description of Luo. Completion 1970.
In the bibliography each language is followed by a reference to the classification
adopted in Chapter 1, thus: C—Cushitic; B—Bantu; PN—Para-Nilotic; N—Nilotic.
Bantu languages are followed by their numeration according to Guthrie (1948).

SELECT GENERAL REFERENCES

ANONYMOUS   'A Veterinary Glossary for Kikuyu, Nandi and Masai Veterinary
Services, Kenya', EAAJ, January 1968.
ATKINS, G.   'Notes on the Concords and Classes of Bantu Numerals', *ALS*, II, 1961.
BECK, H.   'Problems of Orthography and Word-Division in East African Vernacular
Bantu Languages', *Bible Translator* (London), 11, 4, October 1960.
BENDER, M. L.   'The Languages of Ethiopia', *Anthropological Linguistics*, 13, 5, 1971.
(Vocabularies of Galla, Mogogodo, Rendille, Somali.)
BRYAN, M. A.   *The Bantu Languages of Africa*, Handbook of African Languages, 4,
OUP, London, 1959.
COLDHAM, G. E.   *A Bibliography of Scriptures in African Languages* (2 vols.), British
and Foreign Bible Society, London, 1966.
DER-HOUSSIKIAN, H.   'Linguistic Assimilation in an Urban Center of the Kenya Coast',
JAL, 7, **2**, 1968, pp. 83–7.
DOKE, C. M.   *Bantu: Modern Grammatical, Phonetical and Lexigraphical Studies since
1860*, IAI, London, 1945.
GARDNER, H. M.   *Trees and Shrubs of Kenya Colony* (Being a revision and enlargement
of 'A Descriptive Catalogue of some of the common trees and woody plants of Kenya
Colony'—E. Battiscombe, 1926), Government Printer, Nairobi, 1936. Contains
names for the following languages: Swahili, Duruma, Digo, Giriama, Nyika, Boni,
Sanye, Pokomo, Bajun, Kikuyu (Kiambu, Fort Hall, Nyeri, Embu, Chuka, Mwimbe
districts), Meru, Lumbwa, Nandi, Dorobo, Elgoni, Kamba, Masai, Kavirondo, Luo,
Kakamega, Tiriki, Kabras, Kitosh, Bugishu, Kamasia, Elgeyo, Marakwet, Cherenga-
ni, Suk, Somali, Galla, Boran, Samburu, Taita, Taveta.
GUTHRIE, M.   *The Classification of the Bantu Languages*, OUP, London, 1948.
KNAPPERT, J.   'Compound Nouns in Bantu Languages', *JAL*, 4/4, 1965.
KOHLER, O.   *Geschichte der Erforschung der Nilotischen Sprachen* (Afrika und Übersee,
Beiheft 28), Berlin, 1955.
TUCKER, A. N. AND BRYAN, M. A.   *The non-Bantu Languages of North-Eastern Africa*,
Handbook of African Languages, 3, IAI, OUP, London, 1956.
——*Linguistic Survey of the Northern Bantu Borderland*, IV, OUP, London, 1957.
——*Linguistic Analyses: the non-Bantu Languages of North-Eastern Africa*, OUP,
London, 1966.

ARIANGULU—see **Waata** and **Dahalo**

BONI—C. Some groups refer to themselves as **Aweera**

TUCKER, A. N.   'Sanye and Boni', in GRESCHAT, H. J. AND JUNGRAITHMAYR, H. (eds.),
Wort und Religion—Kalima na Dini, Stuttgart, 1969.

BORAN—C

ANDRZEJEWSKI, B. W.   'Some Preliminary Observations on the Borana Dialect of Galla', *BSO(A)S*, XIX, 2, 1957.
——'The Categories of Number in Noun Forms in the Boran Dialect of Galla', *Africa*, 30, 1, 1960.
——'The Role of Tone in the Borana Dialect of Galla', *Proceedings of the Third International Conference of Ethiopian Studies*, Addis Ababa, in the press.
FISCHER, G. A.   'Die Sprachen im Südlichen Galla-Lande', *ZFE*, X, 1876.
WEBB, G. H.   *Boran Vocabulary*, The Literacy Centre of Kenya, Nairobi, 1969. (For limited distribution only.)
WEBSTER, E. J.   *Boran Grammar*, MS. (Deposited with The Literacy Centre of Kenya, Box 12511, Nairobi.)
——*Boran Dictionary*, MS. (Deposited with The Literacy Centre of Kenya, Box 12511, Nairobi.)
——'The Particle in Boran', *African Studies*, 19, 1, 1960.

DAHALO—C

TUCKER, A. N. 'Sanye and Boni' in Greschat, H. J. and Jungraithmayr, H. (eds.), *Wort und Religion—Kalima na Dini*, Stuttgart, 1969.
DAMMANN, E.   'Einige Notizen über die Sprache der Sanye', *ZES*, XXXV, 1950.

DOROBO—PN. Several distinct groups may be involved here: note various names by which they refer to themselves, e.g. Okiek, Elmolo, Kipkurerek, etc. A further group, Omotik, has recently (1970) been reported.

HUNTINGFORD, G. W. B.   'Modern Hunters' (Includes grammatical notes and vocabulary), *JRAI*, LIX, 1929.
——'Dialects of Dorobo', *Man*, XXXI, 1931.
MAGUIRE, R. A. J.   'Il-Torobo' (Includes a comparison of 2 dialects of Dorobo with Nandi and Maasai), *Tanganyika Notes and Records*, 25, June 1948. (Originally published in *Royal African Society Journal*, 1928.)
MEINHOF, C.   'Linguistische Studien in Ostafrika, XIII, Ndorobo', *MSOS*, X, 1907.

EMBU—B (E.52)

BENNETT, P. R.   'Dahl's Law in Thagicũ', *ALS*, VIII, 1967.
——'An Eighth Vowel in Thagicũ', *JAL*, 7, 2, 1968, pp. 140–55.
——'A Comparative Study of Four Thagicũ Verbal Systems: the Inflectional Systems of Kikuyu, Kamba, Embu and Mwimbi.' (Ph.D. thesis, University of London, 1969.)

ENDO—PN. Dialect of Päkot (Suk), q.v.

BEECH, M. W. H.   'Endo Vocabulary', *Man*, XIII, 1913.

GALLA—C

ANDRZEJEWSKI, B. W. 'Some Preliminary Observations on the Borana Dialect of Galla', *BSO(A)S*, XIX, 2, 1957.

——'My Recent Researches into the Dialects of Galla', *Atti del Convegno Internazionale di Studi Etiopici, Accademia dei Lincei*, Rome, 1960.

——'The Categories of Number in Noun Forms in the Borana Dialect of Galla', *Africa*, XXX, 1, 1960.

——'The Position of Galla in the Cushitic Language Group', *J. Sem. St.*, 9, 1964.

BORELLO, M. *Grammatica di Lingua Galla (Oromo) 1. Fonetica e Morfologia*, Turin, 1939.

BRYAN, M. A. *The Distribution of the Semitic and Cushitic Languages of Africa*, IAI, OUP, London, 1947.

CECCHI, A. *Da Zeila alle Frontiere del Caffa* (Vol. III contains 'Grammatica a Dizionario della lingua Oromonica' by E. Viterbo), Rome, 1885–7.

DA THIENE, G. *Dizionario della lingua galla*, Harar, 1939.

DUCATI, B. *Corso di lingua Galla in dodici lezioni* (a gramophone course), Soc. An. Naz. del Gramonofono, Milan, 1936.

——*Dizionario galla-italiano e italiano-galla*, Rome, 1937.

FISCHER, G. A. 'Die Sprachen im Südlichen Galla-lande', *ZFE*, X, 1878.

FOOT, E. C. *A Galla-English, English-Galla Dictionary*, Cambridge, 1913.

HODSON, A. W. AND WALKER, C. H. *An Elementary and Practical Grammar of the Galla or Oromo Language*, London, 1922.

KLINGENHEBEN, A. 'Zur Nominalbildung im Galla', *ZES*, XXXV, 1949.

KRAPF, J. L. *An Imperfect Outline of the Elements of the Galla Language*, London, 1840.

——*Vocabulary of the Galla Language; together with an English-Galla Vocabulary, prepared from a MS Galla-German Vocabulary* (translated by C. W. Isenberg), London, 1842.

MORENO, M. M. *Grammatica teorico-practica della lingua Galla esercizi*, Milan, 1939.

NORDFELDT, M. *A Galla Grammar* (Galla words written in Amharic syllabary), Lund, Sweden, 1947.

PRAETORIUS, F. *Zur Grammatik der Gallasprache*, Berlin, 1893.

ROBECCHI-BRICCHETTI, LUIGI 'Lingue parlate somali, galla e harari. Note e studi raccolti ed ordinati nell' Harar', *BSGI* (Rome), 3, 3, 1890.

TUTSCHEK, C. *Dictionary of the Galla Language* (Galla-English-German), Munich, 1844.

——*A Grammar of the Galla Language* (translated in Munich, 1845), Munich, 1845.

VITERBO, E. *Grammatica e dizionario della lingua oromonica*, 2 vols. (See also entry under Cecchi, A.), Milan, 1892.

GUSII—B (E.42)

BEAVON, E. A. *A Gusii-English, English-Gusii Dictionary* (typed only). SDA Mission, Nyanchwa (?), 1921–30.

——*A Gusii Grammar* (typed only). SDA Mission, Nyanchwa, 1921–30.

MOL, FR. F. *Kisii-English Vocabulary*, MS.

WHITELEY, W. H. *A Practical Introduction to Gusii*, EALB, Nairobi, 1956.

——'Kinship Terminology and the Initial Vowel', *Africa*, XXIX, 1959.

——*The Tense System of Gusii*, East African Linguistic Studies, 4, Kampala, 1960.

——*A Gusii-English Word List* (some 3,000 entries), MS.

HANGA—B (E. 32). See **LUYIA**

KADAM—PN. Dialect of **PĂKOT (Suk)** q.v. Virtually extinct—see Bryan & Tucker (1956), p. 116.

KAMBA—B (E. 55)

ANONYMOUS *Kikamba-English Dictionary* (roneo edition), AIM, Ukamba, 1939.

BENNETT, P. R. 'An Eighth Vowel in Thagicŭ', *JAL*, 7, 2, 1968, pp. 140–55.

—'A Comparative Study of Four Thagicŭ Verbal Systems: the Inflectional Systems of Kikuyu, Kamba, Embu and Mwimbi.' (Ph.D. thesis, University of London, 1969.)

BRUTZER, ERNST 'Handbuch der Kambasprache', *MSOS*, IX, 1906.

BUTTNER, C. G. 'Deutsch-Kikamba Wörterbuch', *ZAS*, 1888.

EWALD, H. V. 'Über die Völker und Sprachen südlich von Aethiopien', *ZDMG*, 1, 1846. (Available in the University Library, Dar es Salaam.)

FARNSWORTH, E. M. *A Kamba Grammar* (cyclostyled), AIM, 1954.

FULLER, P. *Notes on the Kamba Verb*, Mangu Catholic Mission, 1949.

HINDE, H. *Vocabularies of the Kamba and Kikuyu Languages of East Africa*, Cambridge, 1904. (Available in Makerere University Library.)

HOFMANN, J. *Wörterbuch der Kambasprache, Kamba-Deutsch*, Leipziger Mission, 1901.

HORBEN, FR. *Kamba-French Vocabulary* (typescript), Kilungu Catholic Mission, n.d.

KRAPF, J. L. *Vocabularies of Six East African Languages*, 1850.

LAST, J. T. *Grammar of the Kamba Language*, 1885.

——*Polyglotta Africana Orientalis*, London, 1885.

LECONTE, FR. *Kamba-French Vocabulary* (typescript), Kabaa Catholic Mission, *c.* 1913–20.

LINDBLOM, G. 'Notes on Kamba Grammar', *AEO*, X, 1926.

LYDEN, FR. P. *English-Kamba Vocabulary*, n.d.

MBITI, JOHN S. *English-Kamba Vocabulary*, EALB, 1959.

NDUMBU, J. M. G. AND WHITELEY, W. H. 'Some Problems of Stability and Emphasis in Kamba One-word Tenses', *JAL*, 1, 2, 1962.

SHAW, A. *A Pocket Vocabulary of the Ki-Swahili, Ki-Nyika, Ki-Taita and Ki-Kamba Languages*, London, 1885. (In the possession of C. G. Richards.)

TATE, H. R. 'Notes on the Kikuyu and Kamba Tribes of British East Africa' (a short vocabulary), *JRAI*, XXXIV, 1904.

WAKEFIELD, T. 'Routes of Native Caravans' (Kamba, Daiso Vocabularies), *JRGS*, XL, 1870.

WATT, S. *Vocabulary of the Ki-Kamba Language*, Kelker, Pennsylvania, 1900.

WHITELEY, W. H. AND MULI, M. G. *A Practical Introduction to Kamba*, OUP, London, 1962.

WHITELEY, W.H. 'Loan-words in Kamba: a Preliminary Survey', *ALS*, IV, 1963.

KIKUYU—B(E.51)

ANONYMOUS *Gekoio-Kiswahili na Kiswahili-Gekoio Dictionary*, Nyeri, n.d.

ANONYMOUS *Italian-Kikuyu and Kikuyu-Italian Dictionary*, Italian Mission, BEA, n.d. (Consolata Mission?)

ANONYMOUS   *Vocabularie Kikuyu*, Catholic Mission, Nyeri, 1910.

ANONYMOUS   *Lexicon Latinum-Kikuyense and a Lexicon Kikuyense-Latinum*, Catholic Mission, Nyeri, 1931.

ARMSTRONG, L.   *Phonetic and Tonal Structure of Kikuyu*, Oxford, 1940.

BARLOW, A. R.   *Studies in Kikuyu Grammar and Idiom* (revised), W. Blackwood, Edinburgh, 1957.

BARRA, G.   *1,000 Kikuyu Proverbs with Translations and English Equivalents*, Macmillan, London, 1960.

BEECHER, L. AND BEECHER, S.   *A Kikuyu-English Dictionary* (3 vols.), Kahuhia, Fort Hall, 1935.

BENNETT, P. R.   'Dahl's Law in Thagicŭ', *ALS*, VIII, 1967.

——'An Eighth Vowel in Thagicŭ', *JAL*, 7, 2, 1968, pp. 140–55.

——'A Comparative Study of Four Thagicŭ Verbal Systems; the Inflectional Systems of Kikuyu, Kamba, Embu and Mwimbi'. (Ph.D. thesis, University of London, 1969.)

——'The Problems of Class in Kikuyu', *ALS*, XI, 1970.

BENSON, T. G.   *Kikuyu-English Dictionary*, Clarendon Press, Oxford, 1964.

BENSON, T. G. AND KAHAHU, P. S.   *A Kikuyu Course*, SOAS, University of London, 1970.

GORMAN, T. P.   *A Glossary in English, Kiswahili, Kikuyu and Dholuo*, Cassell, London, 1972.

HARRIES, L.   'Some Tonal Principles of the Kikuyu Language', *Word*, VIII, 2, 1952.

——*Grammatical Studies in Kikuyu*, MS. n.d.

HEMERY, A.   *English-Kikuyu Handbook; Grammar, Vocabulary and Phrase-Book*, London, 1903.

HENDERSON, J. E.   *Easy Gikuyu Lessons*, n.d.

HINDE, H.   *Vocabularies of the Kamba and Kikuyu Languages of East Africa*, Cambridge, 1904. (Available in the Makerere University Library.)

KAGO, F. K.   *The Teaching of Vernacular; a Handbook for Kikuyu Teachers*, Nelson, Edinburgh, 1963.

KIRKALDY-WILLIS, W. H. AND GECAGA, B.M.   *A Kikuyu-English, English-Kikuyu Vocabulary*, EALB, Nairobi, 1952.

KIRKALDY-WILLIS, W. H. AND GECAGA, B. M.   *A Short Kikuyu Grammar*, EALB, Nairobi, 1953.

LEAKEY, L. S. B.   *First Lessons in Kikuyu*, EALB, Nairobi, 1959.

LE BERNHARD, P.   *Grammaire Gikouyou* (cyclostyled), Mission Catholique, Nairobi, 1908.

MACGREGOR, A. W.   *English-Kikuyu Vocabulary*, SPCK, London, 1904.

——*Grammar of the Kikuyu Language*, SPCK, London, 1905.

PICK, V. M.   *Elementi di Grammatica Gekoyo*, Nyeri, 1938.

SHARP, A. E.   'Vowel-length and Syllabicity in Kikuyu', *ALS*, I, 1960.

TATE, H. R.   'Notes on the Kikuyu and Kamba Tribes of British East Africa' (a short vocabulary), JRAI, XXXIV, 1904.

KIPSIGIS—PN. With NANDI this is frequently referred to as 'Kalenjin'

ANONYMOUS   *Tentative Grammar of the Kipsigis Language*, n.d.

ANDERSON, E. J.   *A Kipsigis Grammar*, 1948. (The estate of W. H. Whiteley.)

GLOVER, P. E.   *A Botanical Kipsigis Glossary*, E. A. Ag. and For. Res. Organization, 1967.

NG'ELECHEI, C. A.   *Sirutik che ilititotin* (Kalenjin orthography), EALB, Nairobi, 1966.

——*Kitaput ap Grama Ne Bo Kalenjin*, EALB, Nairobi, 1966.

——*Kalenjin-English and English-Kalenjin Dictionary*, MS.

ORCHARDSON, I. Q.   *A Grammar of Kipsigis*, MS. n.d.

TOWETT, T. A.   *A Kipsigis Grammar*, MS. n.d.

TUCKER, A. N.   'Kalenjin Phonetics', *In Honour of Daniel Jones*, Longmans, London, 1964.

TUCKER, A. N. AND BRYAN, M. A.   'Noun Classification in Kalenjin: Nandi-Kipsigis', *ALS*, V, VI, 1964 and 1965.

WORLD GOSPEL MISSION   *Introduction to Kipsigis Grammar*, WGM, Kericho, 1968.

KURIA—B (E.43). Known in Kenya as **Tende**. All the works listed relate to Kuria as spoken in Tanzania.

DEMPWOLFF, O.   'Beiträge zur Kenntnis der Sprachen in Deutsch-Ostafrika', No. 5 Kulia, *ZFK*, V, 1914–15. (Available in the Dar es Salaam Museum.)

REINHARDT, J.   *A Grammar of Kuria*, MS. 1945–50 (?). (In the possession of the author, Catholic Mission, Rosana, Tarime.)

SILLERY, A.   'Notes for a Grammar of the Kuria Language', *B.St.* vol. X, 1936.

WERNER, A.   'Specimens of East African Bantu Dialects', *B.St.*, vol. III, 1927.

WHITELEY, W. H.   'The Structure of the Kuria Verbal and its Position in the Sentence.' (Ph.D. thesis, University of London, 1955).

——'Kinship Terminology and the Initial Vowel', *Africa*, XXIX, 1959.

LUYIA—B. This is the spelling accepted by the Luyia Language Committee but the form **Luhya** is possibly in more common use.

The following sub-groups are included here: Khayo, Idakho, Isukha, Kabras, Shisa (Kisa), Marach, Logoli, Marama, Nyala, Nyore, Samia, Tachoni, Tiriki, Tsotso, Bukusu (Kitosh), Wanga.

ANONYMOUS   *A Luragoli-English Vocabulary*, FAM Press, 1940.

ANONYMOUS   *Outline of Luragoli Grammar* (cyclostyled), FAM, n.d.

APPLEBY, L. L.   *Luluhya-English Vocabulary* (stencilled), Maseno, 1943.

——*A Luyia Grammar*, new edition, 1952.

DONOHEW, N. G.   *A First Course in Luyia*, MS. 1957. (In the possession of the author and the estate of W. H. Whiteley, SOAS, University of London.)

GODIA, STANLEY   *Rules for Logoli Orthography*, EALB, Nairobi, n.d. (1959?)

HUNTINGFORD, G. W. B.   *Grammar of Lubukusu*, MS. 1924. (In the possession of the author.)

——*Grammar and Vocabulary of Luisuxa*, MS. 1924. (In the possession of the author.)

——*Comparative Grammar of the Luhya Languages*, MS. 1925. (In the possession of the author.) Contains material on Isuxa, Nyala, Tsotso and Bukusu.

——*The Eastern Tribes of the Bantu Kavirondo*, 'Peoples of Kenya Series', No. 14, Nairobi, 1944. Contains material on the distribution of the groups.

QUICKLEY, FR.   *English-Idakho Vocabulary*, MS. n.d. (In the possession of J. J. Dames, Nairobi.)

——*English-Isuxa Vocabulary*, MS. n.d. (In the possession of J. J. Dames, Nairobi.)

REES, E. J.   *Grammar of Luragoli* (exact title), Kaimosi, *c*. 1915. This may be the same or an earlier version of item two above.

LUO—N

ANONYMOUS *Elementary Grammar of the Nilotic Kavirondo Language* (Dho Luo), London, 1910. (See Mill Hill Fathers below.)

ANONYMOUS *Vocabulary Nilotic-English*, Nyeri Catholic Mission Press, 1922.

BAUMANN, D. *Durch Masailand zur Nilquelle*, Berlin, 1894.

CLARKE, G. *Luo-English Dictionary*, EAPH.

GORMAN, T. P. *A Glossary in English, Kiswahili, Kikuyu and Dholuo*, Cassell, London, 1972.

GREGERSEN, E. 'Luo: a Grammar.' (Ph.D. thesis, Yale University, 1961.)

HUNTINGFORD, G. W. B. *Elementary Lessons in Dho-Luo*, SOAS, University of London, 1959.

MALER, S. *DhoLuo Without Tears* (roneoed locally), Kisumu, n.d.

MILL HILL FATHERS *An Elementary Luo Grammar*. 2nd ed. enlarged 1920. 3rd ed. 1955. (For variant title see ICCR Bibliography, pp.118, 152.)

OWEN, W. E. Miscellaneous manuscripts (in the possession of the Rev. R. L. Stafford, P.O. Ng'iya, Kisumu.)

RAVENSTEIN,—'Vocabularies from Kavirondo, British East Africa' (collected by C. W. Hobley), *JRAI*, XXVIII, 1899.

CONTI-ROSSINI, C. 'Lingue Nilotiche', *R.St.O.*, 11, 1926.

SPCK *Dholuo Primer* (Nilotic Kavirondo). (For use in schools of the Native Anglican Church, Mombasa Diocese), Nairobi, 1928.

STAFFORD, R. *An Elementary Luo Grammar* (with vocabularies), OUP, Nairobi, 1967.

TUCKER, A. N. 'My Recent Linguistic Tour in East Africa', *Makerere*, 1947.

——*A Luo Grammar* (in preparation).

WAKEFIELD, T. 'Native Routes through the Masai Country', *PRGS*, 4, 1882.

MARAKWET—PN. Dialect of PÄKOT, q.v.

MAASAI—PN

BAUMANN, D. *Durch Masailand zur Nilquelle*, Berlin, 1894.

DREXEL, A. 'Gleiderung Afrikanischer Sprachen', *Anthropos*, XVI–XVII, XVIII–XIX, 1921–2, 1923–4 and 1925.

ERHARDT, J. *Vocabulary of the Enguduk Iloigob, as spoken by the Masai tribes in East Africa*, ed. J. L. Krapf, Wurtenberg, 1857. (In the possession of C. G. Richards, and A. H. Jacobs, University of Nairobi.)

FIELD, H. *Contributions to the Anthropology of the Faiyum, Sinai, Sudan and Kenya*, Berkeley, Calif., 1952. (Short vocabulary and phrase list of Kenya Maasai.)

FOKKEN, H. A. 'Einiges über die Sprache und Horkunst der Arusaleute', *Evangelisch-lutherisches Missionsblatt*, 1905.

——'Einige Bemerkungen über das Verbum im Masai', *MSOS*, X, 1907.

——*Die Spruchweisheit der Masai*, Verlag, d. Evang. Mission, Leipzig, 1914.

——'Erzählungen und Märchen der Larusa', *ZFK*, VII, 1916.

FOSBROOKE, H. A. *English-Masai Vocabulary*, MS, n.d. (In the possession of the author, Box 900, Lusaka.)

FOSBROOKE, J. 'Masai Place Names', *East African Annual*, 1945.

GREENBERG, J. H. 'The Origin of the Masai Passive', *Africa*, 29, 1959.

HAMILTON, SIR? *An English-Masai Vocabulary*, MS. *c.* 1920? (In the possession of A. N. Tucker, SOAS, University of London.)

HINDE, H. *The Masai Language*, Cambridge, 1901. (Available in the Makerere University Library.)

HINDE, H. & S. L. 'Notes on the Masai Section of Lieut.-Colonel McDonald's Vocabulary', *JRAI*, XXIX, 1899.

HOLLIS, A. C. *The Masai, their Language and Folklore*, Clarendon Press, Oxford, 1905.

HOHENBERGER J. 'Comparative Masai Word-List' (Nilotic, Nilo-Hamitic, Masai, Hamitic-Semitic), *Africa*, XXVI, 1956.

——*Semitisches und Hamitisches Sprachgut im Masai* (mit Vergleichendem Wörterbuch), Sachsenmuhle, 1958.

HOMBURGER, L. 'Le genre sexuel dans le sous-groupe Choli-Shillouk des langues nilotiques', *XVIe Congr. Int. d'Anthrop.*, Brussels, 1935.

——'Le Peul et les Langues Nilotique', Société de Linguistiques de Paris, *Bulletin*, XXXVII, 1936. (Maasai and Teso vocabulary.)

JACOBS, A. H. *Maasai-English, English-Maasai Dictionary*, MS, n.d. (In the possession of the author on 3″ × 5″ cards, Box 30197, Nairobi.)

JOHNSTON, H. H. *The Kilimanjaro Expedition*, London, 1886.

KRAPE, J. L. *Vocabulary of the Engutuk Eloikob*, Tubingen, 1854.

——'Kurze Beschreibung der Masai-und-Wakuafi Stamme in Süd-ostlichen Afrika', *Ausland*, 19–20, 1857.

LAST, J. T. 'A Visit to the Masai living beyond the Borders of the Nguru Country' (a vocabulary and phrases), *PRGS*, 1883.

——*Polyglotta Africana Orientalis*, London, 1885. (Maasai vocabulary pp. 190–93, 219–20, 234–9.)

MACDONALD, J. R. L. 'Notes on the Ethnology of Tribes met with during Progress of the Juba Expedition of 1897–98', *JRAI*, XXIX, 1899.

MAGUIRE, R. A. J. 'Il-Torobo', *JAS*, XXVII, 1927–8.

MEINHOF, C. 'Die Sprachen der Hamiten', *AHKI*, IX, 1912.

MPAAYEI, J. TOMPO OLE *Engolon Eng'eno* (A First Maasai Reader), Nairobi, 1960.

MULLER, F. 'Die Sprache der Il-Oigob', *Grundriss der Sprach-Wissenschaft*, III, Vienna, 1884, 1877–8 (?).

NJAO, G. 'English-Masai Vocabulary', MS. See H. Field. University of California Expedition, II, Sudan and Kenya, *AA*, LI, 1949.

RICHMOND, C. *Grammar of Masai*, MS. n.d.

CONTI-ROSSINI, C. 'Lingue Nilotische', *R.St.O.*, II, 1926.

SABBADINI, E. 'Considerazioni sulle lingue Maasai', *Africa* (Milan), XIII, 1958.

SCHMIDT, W. 'Sind die Masai Semiten?', *Mitteilungen der Anthropologischen Gesellschaft in Wien*, LX, 1930.

SCHUCHARDT, H. 'Zu den Verben mit i—im Masai', *WZKM*, XXIV, 1917 (?).

SHAFFER, R. T. *Twelve Lessons in Masai* (cyclostyled), EALB, Nairobi, 1955.

SIMPSON, MISS? *Notes on Masai* (*with English-Masai Vocabulary*), *c.*1898. (In the possession of C. G. Richards.)

TUCKER, A. N. AND MPAAYEI, J. TOMPO OLE *A Maasai Grammar* (*with Vocabulary*), Longmans, London, 1955.

WOLFE, H. 'Review Article' on *Semitisches und hamitisches Sprachgut im Masai*. *African Studies*, XVIII, 1959.

MERU—B (E.53)

BELLANI, A. *Kimeru-Italian Dictionary*, MS. 1922.

BENNETT, P. R. 'An Eighth Vowel in Thagicũ', *JAL*, 7, 2, 1968, pp. 140–55.

——'A Comparative Study of Four Thagicũ Verbal Systems; the Inflectional Systems of Kikuyu, Kamba, Embu and Mwimbi'. (Ph.D. thesis, University of London, 1969.)

BENSON, T. G. AND MBUREA, E. *An Introductory Course*, MS. 1966.

FARANO, B. AND CASOLATI, G. *Kimeru-Italian Dictionary*, 1942.

GIORGIS, B. *A Meru Grammar*, Meru Catholic Bookshop, 1964.

——*A Tentative Kimeru Dictionary*, Meru Catholic Bookshop, 1964.

LAUGHTON, W. H. *Language Study in Meru*, Meru Catholic Bookshop, n.d.

MIJIKENDA—B. Comprising the following languages: **Chonyi, Digo, Duruma, Giriama, Jibana, Kambe, Kauma, Rabai, Ribe.** (The Mijikenda were in the past referred to as Nyika.)

DEED, F. I. *Dictionary, Giryama-English*, MS. n.d.

——*Giryama Exercises* (cyclostyled), n.d.

——*Outline English-Giryama Dictionary*, n.d.

——*Giryama-English Dictionary* (*revised*), EALB, Nairobi, 1964.

KRAPF, J. L. *Outline of the Elements of the Kiswahili Language*, 1850.

——*Vocabulary of Six East African Languages*, 1850.

KRAPF, J. L. AND REBMANN, I. *A Nika-English Dictionary*, 1887. Edited by T. H. Sparshott.

MEINHOF, C. 'Linguistische Studien in Ostafrika—No. IV. Digo', *MSOS*, VIII, 1905.

——'Linguistische Studien in Ostafrika—No. VI, Nika', *MSOS*, VIII, 1905.

NEW, E. *Nika Vocabulary*, 1873.

SHAW, A. *A Pocket Vocabulary of the Ki-Swahili, Ki-Nyika, Ki-Taita and Ki-Kamba Languages*, London, 1885. (In the possession of C. G. Richards.)

TAYLOR, W. E. *Giryama Vocabulary*, 1887.

——*Giryama Vocabulary and Collections*, SPCK, London, 1891.

WERNER, A. 'Giryama-Texte', *ZFK*, V, 1914–15.

ZANI, Z. M. S. 'A Comparative Note on the Possessive in ChiDigo', *JEASC*, 24, 1954.

MUKOGODO—C. Also referred to as **Mogogodo, Yaku.**

GREENBERG, J. H. 'The Mogogodo, a Forgotten Cushitic People', *JAL*, 2, 1, 1963.

LAMBERT, H. E. *The Systems of Land Tenure in the Kikuyu Land Unit*, Communications from the School of African Studies, University of Cape Town, 1950. (There is no linguistic data in this study, but there is an interesting comment on p.63 about their possible affiliation.)

NANDI—PN. With **KIPSIGIS** commonly referred to as '**Kalenjin**'.

BRYSON, S. M. *Nandi Grammar*, AIM, 1940.

——*English-Nandi Dictionary* (cyclostyled), AIM, 2nd ed. 1951.

HOLLIS, A. C.   *The Nandi: their Language and Folklore*, Oxford, 1909.
HUNTINGFORD, G. W. B.   *Nandi-English Dictionary*, MS. 1926. (In the possession of the author.)
——'Miscellaneous Records relating to the Nandi and Kony Tribes', *JRAI*, LVII, 1927.
——'Studies in Nandi Etymology', *B.Afr.*, 1929.
——*Manual of the Nandi Language*, MS. 1931, later revision 1958, cyclostyled. (In the possession of the author.)
——A Comparative Study of the Nandi Dialects, MS. (Including Suk, Kony, Sapei, Dorobo, Nandi, Keyo and Terik), 1950. (In the possession of the author.)
——*Outline Grammar of Nandi* (mimeographed), SOAS, University of London, 1954.
——*Nandi-English Vocabulary* (mimeographed), SOAS, University of London, 1955.
——'Nandi Place-names', *ALS*, 2, 1961.
LINDBLOM, G.   'Some Words of the Language spoken by the Elgoni People' (Kony dialect), *M.Or.*, 1924.
MAGUIRE, R. A. J.   'A Short Vocabulary of Nandi', *JAS*, XXVII, 1927–8.
MUMFORD, F. J.   *Nandi Studies*, Kapsabet, 1959.
NG'ELECHEI, C. A.   *Sirutik che ilititotin* (Kalenjin orthography), EALB, Nairobi, 1966.
——*Kitaput ap Grama Ne Bo Kalenjin*, EALB, Nairobi, 1966.
——*Kalenjin-English and English-Kalenjin Dictionary*, MS.
TUCKER, A. N. AND BRYAN, M.A.   'Noun Classification in Kalenjin: Nandi-Kipsigis', *ALS*, V and VI, 1964 and 1965.
TUCKER, A. N.   'Kalenjin Phonetics', *In Honour of Daniel Jones*, Longmans, London, 1964.

POKOMO—B (E.71) The two most northerly dialects, Malankote and Korokoro, are said to be varieties of Galla.

ANONYMOUS   *Ki-Pokomo Grammar and Dictionary*, Neukirchener Missionsanstalt, n.d.
KRAFFT, H.   *Grammatik der Pokomo-sprache*, Neukirchen, 1904.
KRAPF, J. L.   *Vocabulary of Six East African Languages*, 1850.
MEINHOF, C.   'Linguistische Studien in Ostafrika. No. VII', *MSOS*, VIII, 1905.
WHITELEY, W. H.   *Grammatical Notes and Word-lists for Salama, Gwano and Zubaki dialects*, MS. (Collected 1968/9)
WURTZ, F.   'Lieder der Pokomo', *ZAS*, I, 1889.
——'Kipokomo-Wörterverzeichnis', *ZAS*, II, 1889–90.
——'Zur Grammatik des Ki-Pokomo', *ZAS*, II, 1889–90.
——*Vokabularium in Deutsch-Kiunguya, Kiamu, Kitikuu und Kipokomo*. (Available in the Johannesburg Public Library, Strange Collection of Africana.)
——'Wörterbuch des Ki-Tikuu und des Ki-Pokomo', *ZAOS*, I, 1895.
——'Grammatik des Pokomo', *ZAOS*, II, 1896.

PÄKOT (Suk)—PN

BAUMANN, O.   *Durch Masailand zur Nilquelle*, Berlin, 1894.
BEECH, M. W. H.   *The Suk: their Language and Folklore*, Clarendon Press, Oxford, 1911.

COLLINS, T. *A Suk-English Dictionary*, MS. n.d. (In the possession of the author.)
CRAZZOLARA, FR. J. P. *A New Pokot Grammar* (in the press).
TOTTY, L. A. *Suk Grammar*, MS. n.d.
TUCKER, A. N. AND BRYAN, M.A. 'Noun Classification in Kalenjin, Päkot', *ALS*, 3, 1962.

RENDILLE—C

FLEMING, H. C. 'Baiso and Rendille: Somali Outliers', *Rassegna di Studi Etiopici*, XX, 1964.

SAMBURU—PN

SOMALI—EC. See Introduction

ANONYMOUS *Wan baranaya akriska Somalida: J'apprends à lire le Somali*, Imprimerie Administrative, Djibouti, 1951.
ABDULLAHI, HHAJI MAHHAMUD & BRUNO, PANZA *Afkayaga Hoyo*, Edizioni Arte e Cultura, Mogadiscio, 1960.
ABRAHAM, R. C. *A Somali-English Dictionary*. (Contains an outline grammar of Somali as an appendix to the dictionary). University of London Press, 1964.
ANDRZEJEWSKI, B. W. 'Pronominal and Prepositional Particles in Northern Somali', *ALS*, 1, 1960.
——'Notes on the Substantive Pronoun in Somali', *ALS*, 2, 1961.
——'Speech and Writing Dichotomy as a Pattern of Multilingualism in the Somali Republic', Report of the CCTA/CSA Symposium on Multilingualism in Africa, Brazzaville, 1962; pub. 1964.
——*The Declensions of Somali Nouns*, SOAS, University of London, 1964.
——'Inflectional Characteristics of the so-called "Weak Verbs" in Somali', *ALS*, IX, 1968.
——'Some Observations on Hybrid Verbs in Somali, *ALS*, X, 1969.
——'The Role of Broadcasting in the Adaptation of the Somali Language to Modern Needs' in W. H. Whiteley (ed.), *Language Use and Social Change*, OUP, London, 1971.
ANDRZEJEWSKI, B. W., TUBIANA, J., AND STRELCYN, S. 'Somalia: the Writing of Somali', *Somaliya—Antologia storico-culturale*, Ministry of Education, Cultural Department, Mogadishu, No. 7-8, 1969. (Reprint of UNESCO Report under the same title, Paris, 1966.)
ARMSTRONG, L. E. 'The Phonetic Structure of Somali', *MSOS*, XXXVII, 3, 1934.
BELL, C. R. V. *The Somali Language*, Longmans, London, 1953.
CERULLI, E. *Somali-Scritti vari editi ed inediti* (3 vols), Instituto Poligrafico dello Stato, Rome, 1957-64.
DA PALERMO, GIOVANNI M. *Dizionario Somalo-Italiano e Italiano-Somalo*, Tipografia Francescana Missione, Asmara, 1915.
DE LARAJASSE, F. E. *Somali-English and English-Somali Dictionary*, London, 1897.
GALAAL, M. H. I. 'Arabic Script for Somali', *The Islamic Quarterly*, 1, 2, Islamic Cultural Centre, London, July 1954.

KIRK, J. W. C. *A Grammar of the Somali Language with Examples in Prose and Verse and an Account of the Yibir and Midgan Dialects*, Cambridge, 1905.

KLINGENHEBEN, M. VON TILING 'Die Vokale des bestimmten Artikels in Somali', *ZFK*, IX, 1918–19.

——'Adjektiv-Endungen im Somali', *ZES*, X, 1919–20.

LEWIS, I. M. 'The Gadbuursi Somali Script', *BSO(A)S*, XXI, 1, 1958.

MAINO, M. *La Lingua Somala: Strumento d'insegnamento professionale*, Alessandria (Italy), 1953.

——*Terminologia Medica e sue voci nella Lingua Somala*, Alessandria (Italy), 1953.

MORENO, M. M. *Il somalo della Somalia, grammatica e testi del Benadir, Darod e Dighil*, Instituto Poligrafico dello Stato, Rome, 1955.

——'Brevi Notazioni di Giddu', *Rassegna di Studi Etiopici*, X, Genn. Dic., Rome, 1951.

——Il dialetto degli Asraf di Mogadiscio', *Rassegna di Studi Etiopici*, XII, Genn. Dic. Rome, 1953.

PIRONE, M. 'La lingua somala e i suoi problemi', *Africa*, 22, 2, Rome, 1967.

REINISCH, L. *Die Somali Sprache, 1 Texte*, Vienna, 1900.

——*Die Somali Sprache, II, Wörterbuch Somali-Deutsch, Deutsch-Somali*, Vienna, 1902.

——*Die Somali Sprache, III, Grammatik*, Vienna, 1903.

STEPANCHENKO, D. I. AND MOKHAMED KHADZHI OSMAN *Kratky somali-russky i russko-somali slovar'* (a short Somali-Russian and Russian-Somali dictionary), Moscow, 1969.

SWAHILI—B (G.42). See Introduction.

HOLLIS, J. C. 'Vocabulary of English Words and Sentences', *JAS*, X, 1910.

LAMBERT, H. E. *Ki-Vumba* (a Dialect of the Southern Kenya Coast), Studies in Swahili Dialect, II, Kampala, 1957.

——*Chi-Jomvu and Ki-Ngare* (Sub-dialects of the Mombasa Area), Studies in Swahili Dialects, III, Kampala, 1958.

——*Chi-Chifundi* (a Dialect of the Southern Kenya Coast), Studies in Swahili Dialects, V, Kampala, 1958.

SACLEUX, C. *Grammaire des Dialectes Swahilis*, Paris, 1909.

STIGAND, G. M. *A Grammar of Dialectic Changes in the Kiswahili Language*, 1915.

WHITELEY, W. H. 'Kimvita', *JEASC*, 25, 1955.

WURTZ, F. *Vokabularium in Deutsch-Kiunguya, Kiamu, Kitikuu und Kipokomo*, 1892. (Available in the Johannesburg Public Library, Strange Collection of Africana.)

——'Wörterbuch des Ki-Tikuu und des Ki-Pokomo', *ZAOS*, 1, 1895.

TAITA—B (E.74). A group comprising at least **Dabida, Sagala, Teri and Kasigau.**

HEMERY, A. *Vocabulaire Français-Swahili-Taita*, Catholic Mission, Zanzibar, 1901.

JOHNSTON, H. H. *The Kilimanjaro Expedition*, 1886.

MAYNARD, A. J. *Kidabida grammar* (vols. I and II), MS. n.d.

——*Dictionary of English-Kidabida*, MS. n.d.

SHAW, A. D. *A Pocket Vocabulary of the Ki-Swahili, Ki-Nyika, Ki-Taita and Ki-Kamba Languages*, London, 1885. (In the possession of C. G. Richards.)

TATE, H. R. 'Notes on the Kikuyu and Kamba Tribes of British East Africa' (Includes a short vocabulary of Taita), *JRAI*, XXXIV, 1904.

WILLIAMSON, J. 'Dabida Numerals', *A.St.*, II, 4, 1943. (Available in the University Library, Dar es Salaam.)

WOODWARD, H. W. 'Kitaita or Kisighau', *ZFK*, IV, 2, 1923.

WRAY, J. A. *An Elementary Introduction to the Taita Language*, SPCK, London, 1894.

TAVETA—B (G.21)

ANONYMOUS *Vocabulary in English, Ki-Chaga, Ki-Taveta*, Meshi, 1891–5. (In the possession of C. G. Richards.)

TESO—PN. Since the majority of Teso live in Uganda, virtually all the work in this language has been carried out from there.

ANONYMOUS *Ekitabo Loisisyanakin Aswarin* (Teso sentences translated into Swahili, together with vocabularies), Sheldon Press, London, 1933.

HALL, C. R. *An English-Teso Vocabulary*, Portsmouth, n.d.

HENDRIKSEN, FR. *Grammar of Teso*, MS. n.d.

HENDRIKSEN, FR. A. W. *Notes on the Teso Verb* (cyclostyled), 1958.

HILDERS, J. H. AND LAWRANCE, J. C. D. *An Introduction to the Ateso Language*, EALB, Nairobi, 1956.

——*English-Ateso and Ateso-English Vocabulary*, EALB, Nairobi, 1958.

KIGGEN, J. *Grammar of Teso*, Mill Hill Mission, Ngora, n.d

——*Grammar Nak'Ateso*. (Perhaps the same as the preceding entry.) Ngora, 1928. (?) (Available in the Uganda Bookshop Files.)

——*English-Ateso and Ateso-English Dictionary* (2 vols.), Tanganyika Mission Press, 1953.

KITCHING, A. L. *Handbook of the Ateso Language*, London, 1915.

MCGOUGH, FR. *Grammar of Teso*, MS. n.d.

WILD, J. V. *Vocabulary of a Few Words and Sentences of Orom*, MS. n.d.

WILSON, W. A. *Teso-Karamojong-English Dictionary*, MS. n.d. (The estate of W. H. Whiteley.)

THARAKA—B (E.54)

LINDBLOM, G. 'Outline of a Tharaka Grammar', *AEO*, 1914.

TURKANA—PN

BARTON, J. 'Turkana Grammatical Notes', *BSO(A)S*, II, 1921. (Available in the University Library, Dar es Salaam.)

GULLIVER, PAMELA *Turkana-English Dictionary*, MS. (In the possession of the author.)

HULLEY, D. M. *Vocabulary and Grammar for use in Turkana, Karamoja and Tapossa*, Kampala, 1923.

RAGLAN, LORD 'Some Roots Common to the Turkana, Kotuko and Bari Languages', *BSO(A)S*, IV, 1926.

WAATA—C. Also known as **Ariangulo, Ariangulu** (among Giriama), **Langulo** (among Duruma). May also have been included under earlier references to **Sanye.**

DAMMANN, E. 'Einige Notizen über die Sprache der Sanye', *ZES*, XXXV, 1950.

HOBLEY, C. W. 'Notes on the Wa Langulu or Arangulu of the Taru Desert', *Man*, 12, 1912.

TUCKER, A. N. 'Sanye and Boni' in GRESCHAT, H. J. AND JUNGRAITHMAYR, H. (eds.), *Wort und Religion—Kalima na Dini*, Stuttgart, 1969.

2. WORKS RELATING TO THE ASIAN COMMUNITIES

BARBARA NEALE

APPANYA, S. W. P. 'British Indians in East Africa', *Fortnightly Review*, 8, 1907, pp. 595–8.

AWORI, W. W. W. 'African and Indian Co-operation in East Africa', *African World*, October 1946, pp. 16–17.

BENEDICT, B. *Indians in a Plural Society*, HMSO, London, 1961.

——'Family Firms and Economic Development', *Southwestern Journal of Anthropology*, 24, 1, 1968, pp, 1–19.

BHARATI, A. 'A First Appraisal of the Indian Minority in East Africa', *Sunday Post* (Nairobi), 22 March 1964.

——'Problems of the Asian Minority in East Africa', *Pakistan Horizon*, 17, 4, 1964.

——'The Indians in East Africa: a Survey of Problems of Transition and Adaptation (Preliminary Report)', *Sociologus* (Berlin), 14, 2, 1964, pp. 169–77.

——'The Asian Entrepreneur in East Africa', paper presented at the African Studies Association Annual Meeting (Philadelphia), 1965.

——'Indo-African Cultural Ties', *India News* (Nairobi), 15, 4, March 1965.

——'Patterns of Identification among the Indians in East Africa', *Sociologus* (Berlin), 15, 2, Fall 1965, pp 128–42.

——'Political Pressures and Reactions in the Asian Minority in East Africa', *Program of Eastern African Studies, Syracuse University, Occasional Paper No. 12*, 1965.

——'Possession and Divination among the Lohana Hindus in East Africa', paper presented at the American Anthropological Association 65th Annual Convention.

——'A Social Survey' in D. P. Ghai (ed.), *Portrait of a Minority: the Asians in East Africa*, Oxford University Press, Nairobi, 1965, pp 13–61.

——'The Unwanted Elite in East Africa', *Trans-Actions* (St. Louis, Missouri), July-August 1966.

BLOOMBERG, L. N. AND ABRAMS, C. *United Nations Mission to Kenya on Housing*, Nairobi, 1964.

CUMPSTON, I. M. *Indians Overseas in British Territory, 1834-1954*, Oxford University Press, London, 1953.

DAS, N. 'Indians in Kenya', *Indian Review*, 28, 1927, pp 246–48.

DE SOUZA, F. R. S. 'Indian Political Organizations in East Africa,' Ph. D. thesis, London, 1958–9.

DELF, GEORGE *Asians in East Africa*, Oxford University Press, London, 1962.

DERRETT, J. D. M. 'East Africa: Recent Legislation for Hindus', *American Journal of Comparative Law*, II, Summer, pp. 23–5.

DESAI, D. B. 'Indians in East Africa', *Indian Review*, 21, 1920, pp. 260–63.

——'Indians in Kenya', *Indian Review*, 24, 1923, pp. 354–8.

DESAI, R. *Indian Immigrants in Britain*, Oxford University Press, London, 1963.

DESAI, R. H. 'Leadership in an Asian Community', *East African Institute of Social Research, Conference Proceedings*, June 1963.

——'The Family and Business Enterprise among the Asians in East Africa', *East African Institute of Social Research Conference Papers*, Makerere University College, 1964.

DIGGS, IRENE 'The Indian in East Africa', *The Crisis*, 63, April 1956, pp. 215–17.

DOTSON, F. AND DOTSON, L. O. *The Indian Minority of Zambia, Rhodesia and Malawi*, Yale University Press, New Haven, 1968.

EHRENFELS, U. R. 'Cultural Needs of Indians in East Africa', *Indo-Asian Culture*, 8, 2, 1959, 169–78.

FORAN, ROBERT 'Indian Trading Practices in East Africa', *The Crown Colonist* (London), 19, 210, May 1949, pp 322–69.

GHAI, D. (ed.) *Portrait of a Minority: Asians in East Africa*, Oxford University Press, Nairobi, 1965; revised edition 1970.

GHAI, Y. P. 'The Asian Dilemma in East Africa', *East Africa Journal*, 1, 10, March 1965, pp. 6–21.

HEYER, SARJIT S. 'The Asian in Kenya', *Africa South in Exile*, 5, January-March 1961, pp. 77–84.

HOLLINGSWORTH, L. W. *The Asians of East Africa*, Macmillan, London, 1960.

JAMES, L. 'The Indian Problem in Eastern and Southern Africa', M. A. thesis, Liverpool, 1940.

——'Indians in East Africa', *United Empire*, 29, 9, pp. 412–14.

JOHNSTON, HARRY HAMILTON 'Asiatic Colonisation of East Africa', *Journal of the Royal Society of Arts*, 37, 1889, pp. 161–72.

JONES, H. 'Asian Communities in British East and Central Africa', *New Commonwealth* (London), 26, 5, 31 August 1953, pp. 219–20; 6, 14 September, pp. 277–8.

KAZIMI, A. A. *An Enquiry into Indian Education in East Africa*, Nairobi, 1948.

KIANO, J. G. 'Kenya Minister of Commerce on Asian-African Relations', *East African Trade and Industry*, 7, 75, May 1960, p. 69.

KIRK, W. 'Indian Community', *Scottish Geographical Magazine*, 67, 3 and 4, December 1951, pp. 161–77.

KLASS, M. *East Indians in Trinidad*, Columbia University Press, New York, 1961.

KONDAPI, C. *Indians Overseas, 1838–1949*, Indian Council of World Affairs, New Delhi, 1951.

KUPER, H. *Indian People in Natal*, Natal University Press, 1960.

LAGDEN, G. Y. 'Our Protectorates and Asiatic Immigration', *19th Century*, September 1908, pp. 386–99.

LEYS, N. M. 'Indian in Africa', *Church Mission Review*, 72, 1921, pp. 199–214.

MANGAT, J. S. *A History of the Asians in East Africa c.1886 to 1945*, The Clarendon Press, Oxford, 1969.

MAINI, P. L. 'The Indian Problem in Kenya', M.Sc. (Econ.) thesis, London, 1944.

MALIK, M. H. 'Indians in East Africa', *Hindu Review*, 44, 1921, pp. 32–7.

MARRIOTT, M. *Caste Ranking and Community Structure in Five Regions of India and Pakistan*, Poona, 1965.

MARTIN, C. J. 'A Demographic Study of an Immigrant Community, the Indian Population of British East Africa', *Population Studies*, 6, 3, March 1953, pp. 233–41.

MAYER, A. C. *Peasants in the Pacific*, Routledge & Kegan Paul, London, 1961.

——*Indians in Fiji*, Oxford University Press, London, 1963.

MORAES, FRANK   'Asians in Africa', *Atlas*, 6, July 1963, pp. 37–8.

MORGAN, W. T. W. (ed.) *Nairobi: City and Region*, Oxford University Press, Nairobi, 1967.

MORRIS, H. STEPHEN   'Indians in East Africa: a Study in a Plural Society', *British Journal of Sociology*, 7, 3, September 1956, pp. 194–211.

——'Communal Rivalry among Indians in Uganda', *British Journal of Sociology*, 8, 4, 1957.

——'The Plural Society', *Man*, 57, 1957, pp. 124-5.

——'The Divine Kingship of the Aga Khan: a Study of Theocracy in East Africa', *Southwestern Journal of Anthropology*, 14, 4, Winter 1958, pp. 454–72.

——'The Indian Family in Uganda', *American Anthropologist*, 61, 5, part 1, 1959.

——'Immigrant Indian Communities in Uganda', Ph.D. thesis, London, 1963.

——'Some Aspects of the Concept of Plural Society', *Man*, New Series, 2, 2, 1967.

——*The Indians in Uganda*, University of Chicago Press, 1968.

MUKHERJEE, MUKUL   'European Jingoism in Kenya (the Program of the Kenya Electors' Union to Prevent Indian Immigration)', *Indian Affairs*, 2, December 1949, pp. 214–17.

MULER, A. L.   'The Economic Position of the Asians in Africa', *South African Journal of Economics*, 33, 2, June 1965, pp. 114–30.

NATIONAL CHRISTIAN COUNCIL OF KENYA *Who Controls Industry in Kenya?* East African Publishing House, Nairobi, 1968.

PANDIT, S. *Asians in East and Central Africa*, Nairobi, 1963.

PICKLAY, A. S. *History of the Ismailis*, Bombay, 1940.

POCOCK, D. F.   'Indians in East Africa, with Particular Reference to their School and Economic Situation and Relationships', D. Phil. Dissertation, Oxford, 1954–5.

——'Movement of Castes', *Man*, 79, 1955, pp. 71–2.

——'Difference in East Africa: a Study of Caste and Religion in Modern Indian Society', *Southwestern Journal of Anthropology*, 13, 1957, 289–300.

——'The Ismaili Khojas of East Africa', *Middle Eastern Studies*, 11, 4, October 1964, pp. 21–39.

POLAK, H. S. L.   'East Africa Indian Problem', *East India Association*, 12, 1922, pp. 174–201.

Racial and Communal Tensions in East Africa, East African Institute of Social and Cultural Affairs, Nairobi, 1966.

RAO, G. RAGHAVA   'Indian Immigrants in Kenya—a Survey', *Indian Economics Journal*, 4, July 1956, pp, 33–42.

RAYNER, W. R.   'The Settlement of Indians on the Margins of the Indian Ocean', M.A. thesis, London, 1933–4.

RICE, STANLEY   'The Indian Question in Kenya', *Foreign Affairs*, 2,2, 1923, pp. 258–69.

RODGERS, W. C.   'The Role of the Immigrant Communities in the New Kenya', *The Kenya We Want*, Report of the Convention on Social and Economic Development in the Emerging Kenya Nation—held in Nairobi, August 1962.

ROSS, W. M.   *Kenya from Within*, 1937. 2nd Ed., Allen & Unwin, London, 1968.

SCHWARTZ, B. (ed.)   *Caste in Overseas Indian Communities*, Chandler Publishing Co., San Francisco, 1967.

SINGH, D.   'Indians in East Africa', *Africa Quarterly*, 1, 4, 1962, pp. 43–5.

SINGH, M.   *History of Kenya's Trade Union Movement to 1952*, East African Publishing House, Nairobi, 1969.

SINGH, N. (ed.)   'The Asian as Farmer', *Kenya Independence Day Souvenir*, Kenya Indian Congress, Nairobi, 1963.

SMALLWOOD, R. 'East Indians in Kenya; Indian Settlement an Obstruction to African Progress', *National Review* (London), 124, April 1945, pp. 301–5.

SOFER, C. 'Some Aspects of Race Relations in an East African Town'. Ph.D. thesis, London, 1953.

SOFER, C. AND SOFER, R. V. *Jinja Transformed*, Kampala, 1955.

SRINIVAS, M. N. AND BETEILLE, A. 'Networks in Indian Social Structure', *Man*, 67, 1964, pp. 165–8.

STEEL, ROBERT W. 'The Non-African Populations of British Central and East Africa', *Advancement of Science*, 19, 78, July 1962, pp. 113–120.

UDANI, R. J. 'Our Countrymen in Kenya', *Indian Review*, 29, 1928, pp. 841–6.

WATKINS, D. 'Indian Question in Kenya', *Fortnightly Review*, July 1923, pp. 95–103.

WILSON, G. 'Mombasa—a Modern Colonial Municipality' in A. Southall (ed.), *Social Change in Modern Africa*, Oxford University Press, London, 1961.

Official Sources:

Kenya Population Census (1962), Vol. IV. Non-African Population.
Statistical Abstract, 1967.
Statistical Abstract, 1968.

Bibliographies:

BRUWER, J. P. *Indians in South and East Africa : Preliminary Bibliography*, Suid-Afrikaanse Buro vir Rasse-Aangeleenthede, sewerde jaarvergadering, 1956. Die Asiaaten Afrika: referate. 114–20, Stellenbosch.

Index

Prepared for the press, designed and published by Oxford University Press, Eastern Africa Branch,
Electricity House, Harambee Avenue, P.O. Box 72532, Nairobi, Kenya and printed by English Press,
Accra Road, P.O. Box 30127, Nairobi, Kenya.